The Architecture of the Renaissance

The Architecture of the Renaissance

Leonardo Benevolo

Volume I

Westview Press · Boulder, Colorado

Published 1978 in the United States of America by
Westview Press, Inc.
5500 Central Avenue
Boulder, Colorado 80301
Frederick A. Praeger, Publisher and Editorial Director
First published in Italy in 1968 as
Storia dell' Architettura del Rinascimento
© Giuseppe Laterza & Figli, 1968
Translated from the second revised Italian edition, 1973,
by Judith Landry.
This English translation first published in Great Britain 1978 by
Routledge & Kegan Paul Ltd.
39 Store Street, London WC1E 7DD and
Broadway House, Newtown Road,
Henley-on-Thames, Oxon RG9 1EN

Library of Congress Cataloging in Publication Data

Benevolo, Leonardo.

The architecture of the Renaissance.

Bibliography: v. 1, p. 592; v. 2, p. 500
Includes index.
1. Architecture, Renaissance. I. Title.
NA510.B4713   724'.1   76-54186

ISBN 0-89158-720-9 (Set, 2 vols)

Filmset and printed in Great Britain by
BAS Printers Limited, Over Wallop, Hampshire

Contents

Acknowledgments

Various parts of the text were read in advance by Professor George Kubler of Yale, Professor Arnaldo Bruschi of Rome, Professor Gaetano Cozzi of Padua, the architects Stefano Chieffi and Giulio Mezzetti of Florence and Professor Eugenio Garin of Florence. The author would like to thank them all for their comments and advice.

The architect Paolo Pavin of Rome was of great assistance in the preparation of the first edition, the proof correction, the choice and arrangement of the illustrations and in numerous other ways. Miss Cristiana Coraggio was of great assistance in the preparation of the second edition.

A large number of the photographs were specially produced for the author to fit the needs of the text; the rest were supplied by the following: Alinari, Florence; Anderson, Florence; Bazzecchi, Florence; Fotocielo, Rome; Oscar Savio, Rome; Giovetti, Mantua; Archivio Fotografico Nazionale, Rome; Uffizi Gallery, Florence; Library of the Istituto di Archeologia e Storia dell'Arte, Rome; Vatican Library, Rome; Ferruzzi, Venice; Viollet, Paris; Photothèque Française, Paris; Bibliothèque Nationale, Paris; Caisse Nationale des Monuments Historiques, Paris; René Basset, Lyon; Keystone, London; Aerofilms Ltd, London; Stadsarchiv, Munich; Schnell & Steiner, Munich; Gundermann, Würzburg; Cabinet des Estampes, Antwerp; Il Polfilo, Milan; J. T'Felt, Antwerp; Gemeente Archiefdienst, Amsterdam; KLM, Amsterdam; USIS, Rome; British Embassy, Rome; Mexican Aerophoto Co., Mexico; Istituto Nacional de Antropologia e Historia (photographic archives), Mexico; Museo de la Ciudad de Mexico, Mexico.

Many friends have kindly allowed me to use photographs which they have taken or collected: Italo Insolera, Rome; Giulio Mezzetti, Florence; Paolo Portoghesi, Rome; Manfredo Tafuri, Rome; Graziano Gasparini, Caracas; Luciano Grossi Bianchi, Genoa; Alberto Vigevani, Milan; Massimo Montelli, Rome; Adalberto Tiburzi, Rome; Enzo Crea, Rome.

The photographs and topographical material on Lyon were collected by Messrs Mingotti, Tramontini, Amato, Carretta, Cacciaguerra, Lunazzi, Koechlin, Montanari and Di Leo, students of architecture at the University of Venice.

The plan of London at the end of the seventeenth century was conceived by Messrs Bonadonna, Biron, Canella, Carnieri, Cremonini, Franchini, Girelli, Mattioli, Parsafar, Presotto and Zambon, students of architecture at the University of Venice.

The photographs of Turin and of the *borgo*

teresiano of Trieste and the plan of Vienna in 1832 were produced by other groups of architectural students at the University of Venice of whom it is impossible to include a complete list.

The description of the Jesuits' *reducciones* in Paraguay derives in part from a study by Marco Fano.

The author and publishers would like to thank all these people for their help.

The city plans were produced by Umberto Fucci and Roberto Faini; plans of buildings were largely derived from the volumes of the Pelican History of Art, so as to obtain a consistent presentation. Otherwise they have been specially redrawn. Notable groups of illustrations were taken from: J. McAndrew, *The Open Air Churches of Sixteenth-Century Mexico* (Oxford University Press, 1965) and J. W. Reps, *The Making of Urban America* (Princeton University Press, 1965) for architecture in the New World; the volumes of E. A. Gutkind's *International History of City Development* (Collier-Macmillan, London and Free Press, New York, 1964 onwards) for the cities of Germany, Scandinavia and Spain; M. L. Gothein, *A History of Garden Art* (Hacker, New York, 1966) for baroque gardens; the enlarged edition of N. Pevsner, *An Outline of European Architecture* (Penguin, Harmondsworth, 1960) and M. Morini, *Atlante di storia dell'urbanistica* (Milan, 1963).

The author and publishers are grateful to the following for permission to reproduce copyright material: Academy Editions, London, for extracts from *Alberti: Ten Books on Architecture*, ed. J. Rykwert; Cambridge University Press for extracts from Descartes' *Philosophical Works*, ed. Haldane and Ross; Penguin Books Ltd for extracts from Rousseau, *The Confessions*, trans. J. M. Cohen, La Bruyère, *Characters*, trans. Jean Stewart, and Pascal, *Pensées*, trans. A. J. Krailsheimer; Pennsylvania State University Press for extracts from *The Life of Brunelleschi* by Antonio Manetti, translated into English by Catherine Enggass. Copyright © 1970 by The Pennsylvania State University. Reprinted by permission of The Pennsylvania State University Press.

Introduction

By 'architecture of the Renaissance' we mean the cycle of experiments which ran from the fifteenth to eighteenth centuries, and which made use of the stock of standard forms drawn from classical antiquity. This retrospective choice, taken by the artists of the early fifteenth century, gives a precise technical justification to the word 'Renaissance', so uncertain and controversial if used as a general historiographic category.

The meaning of this choice may be interpreted in different ways; the fact remains that throughout a certain period of history, over four centuries long, Italian, European and world-wide architectural culture (when the European system of life happened to dominate in the rest of the world) adopted a system of forms consciously drawn from the past and considered as virtually constant; this fact needs an explanation, and it constitutes the starting-point for our enquiry.

While this repertoire prevailed, architecture was included in a certain classification of human activities, which distinguished the differing attributes of the techniques considered as belonging to a common activity: art, which covered architecture, sculpture and the other denominations derived from the institutional groupings which emerged during the course of this period.

The combination of these two facts – the choice of the classical repertoire and the inclusion of architecture in the new cultural system – came about in the first half of the fifteenth century, and the information available to us still gives credit to the traditional hypothesis, that the responsibility for this transition lies with a single individual, Filippo Brunelleschi. Naturally our present-day conviction coincides only partially with that of the inventor of the new architecture. The two facts we have mentioned each have a history antedating Brunelleschi: his merit – if it is permissible to define it with a brief and necessarily imprecise formula – was to have put them into relationship with one another, i.e. to have discovered a new deployment for these two existing tendencies, which was to produce overwhelming effects.

Brunelleschi's operation – we may call it that even if we cannot be exact in evaluating his personal responsibility – was crucial for the whole of the following cycle. It implied the end of architecture as a common framework for the various techniques of production, and its assumption, in so far as its conceptual aspects were concerned, into the sphere of a mental activity preceding any technical specialization. To do this it was necessary to assign to architecture a specific formal repertoire, one which would define its representational nature independently of the various technical processes, and which was drawn from the buildings of classical antiquity.

Whatever the meaning, in antiquity, of this repertoire of forms, the fact remains that now they were chosen only as spatial shapes, and conceived of in a space where the conformation of the objects had a value that was independent of any further specification, i.e. in perspective space. Hence the extremely fruitful relationship between classical forms and perspective space, and the standardization of the elementary forms, utilized as an instrument that would reveal proportional values.

This scheme functioned on the basis of the new distribution of human activities which emerged at this period, and it entered into a critical phase when this distribution could no longer be maintained. More precisely it should be said that the architecture of the Renaissance was conceivable only within the framework of the broader cultural change that took place between the fourteenth and fifteenth centuries, which implied just this recognition of the unity and autonomy of art; and that furthermore the distribution of human activities in which art found a place as an autonomous and unfragmented operation could be maintained only as long as the above-mentioned pattern was functioning: i.e. for as long as the perspective conception of the space within which architecture worked was accepted, and for as long as this same standardized character was accorded to the classical forms or to any other group of forms, past or present.

The second part of the discussion is the more interesting as far as contemporary debate is concerned.

The Renaissance marks the beginning of the modern era, and discussion of the interpretation of the Renaissance corresponds to discussion of the nature of the whole subsequent era, which is called modern because,

at the other extreme, it involves our present situation. The problem of Renaissance architecture is interesting for the same reasons, and indeed it becomes extremely relevant again in crucial moments of transition in contemporary architectural affairs; one need think only of the books of Geoffrey Scott[1] and Wittkower.[2]

Attempts have also been made to simplify this relationship and to institute a direct comparison between the Renaissance and the present day; but a correct historical assessment should take into consideration the whole series of intermediate transitions, and in our field it forces us to conclude that the architecture of the Renaissance is a completed cycle, which is why we can finally describe its birth, its course and its end. This cycle is not characterized by a continuity of aims and operative instruments (on the contrary it includes many experiments that were heterogeneous in this sense, particularly if one considers the whole span of time defined at the beginning) but by a continuity of the institutional framework within which these experiments were set; using the language of art criticism, one might say that neither form nor content remained constant; what did remain constant was the idea that architecture was part of a representational activity, where content to be expressed and expressive forms were to be distinguished one from the other.

But today in fact this continuity is disappearing, and modern architecture emerges not as a new cycle of experiments that can be set within the same framework, but as a new hypothesis about the distribution of human energies, from which a new definition of the word 'architecture' is derived: as Morris put it in 1881,[3] the 'moulding and altering to human needs of the very face of the earth itself, except in the outermost desert'.

This definition now includes all the aspects of the man-made scene, material and formal, and reverses the traditional relationship between art and architecture; architecture was no longer considered as a part of art, but art – i.e. the aggregate of the qualitative aspects of the urban scene – was considered as part of architecture, as one of the components of the cycle of production upon which our living environment depends. The representational values which were considered as the specific aim of architecture had their place, as relaxation and contemplative pause, in the course of everyday experience, without being set aside in a specialized area of this experience and without giving rise to a separate cycle of production and utilization.

The novelty of modern architecture, as we have written elsewhere, lies in the noun 'architecture' and not in the adjective 'modern'. Awareness of this novelty enables us to assess more accurately the organizational implications of past experiences. In the early twentieth century modern architecture rejected continuity with the events of past architecture, while today, directly or indirectly, it inspires a new interest in historical studies; these studies are the direct consequence of that rejection, in as far as modern architecture has enabled us to judge the relativity of the institutional combinations that characterized the various periods of past history, to the point of casting doubt on the very framework of the 'history of art' within which these studies were provisionally placed.

The reason for the marked and growing interest in the architecture of the Renaissance is that we can consider it as the most recent cycle of experiment that can be judged historically as a concluded whole.

The coherence of the cycle, as we have said, depends upon the development of an institutional formula, all of whose ramifications we can follow, from its birth as an instrument of liberation, when it set in motion a vast process of renewal, to its decline as an instrument of conservation. Within the limits of this cycle the methods of art history coincide with the structure of the experiments to be studied, which is why they appear so clear and persuasive.

But it is precisely if one recognizes the historically conditioned character of this formula, that it becomes impossible today to write the history of these experiments *iuxta propria principia*, that is, to accept the selection of facts arrived at by the history of art, and to describe them while discounting the classification of human activities current at the time.

If one proceeded in this way one would not be able to explain objectively either the beginning or the end of the cycle, i.e. it would become impossible to characterize this series of experiments as a particular historical cycle which began and ended in time; they would form only a section of a single, infinite cycle, formed of the stream of constantly new experiments within a fixed classification outside the sphere of history.

We, on the other hand, shall start from the modern concept of architecture ('the moulding and altering to human needs of the very face of the earth itself') and we shall see how far the activities included in the sphere of art modified the spatial setting of life and of human enterprises in this period.

We shall discover a series of tensions between the cultural patterns and their effects upon the environment, and we shall have to extend our enquiry to other activities not included in the sphere of art, but necessary to explain the changes in the environment. Since our definition of architecture is strictly empirical in character, we shall not be bound by any criterion of prior exclusion or discrimination, and we shall examine all the data necessary to define our object, whatever their place in the old or new cultural system.

Our work will also bear the mark of the theoretical and operational interests typical of modern architecture; whatever the object of research – modern architecture or that of the past – we believe that this point of reference is inevitable, and cannot be done away with by a mere effort at abstraction. Provided it is correctly used, it is not inconsistent with objectivity of judgment; indeed it affords the only real criterion of objectivity in relation to the experiments of the past.

In our case, in fact, it makes it possible to emphasize the structural change that implies the beginning of the Renaissance, and the other change that implies the end of this cycle and the birth of the modern movement; furthermore, by examining the Renaissance cycle it enables us to detect the fluctuations of the institutional framework wherever relevant – i.e. the distribution of the human energies applied to the subjects and opportunities offered by historical development – even when these fluctuations are disguised by the continuity of the theoretical systems. In fact on this level it is possible in many cases to trace the deeper motivations for tendencies which reveal themselves in the various single activities classified as artistic.

Our account is thus valid only within the limits of historical contingency; it provides no guideline for anyone wishing to define the perennial and constitutional activities of the human mind, but describes a series of experiments included within the two moments nearest to us in which the classification of these activities has been radically changed. We do not mean to suggest any coincidence between the historical value and the philosophical value attributed to some of these activities. Notions such as 'art', 'science' and so on will appear as complicated historical constructions rather than as immediate projections of the human faculties which have received the same name.

It now remains to justify the chronological and geographical limits, and the themes of the chapters into which the work is subdivided.

The term 'architecture of the Renaissance' is used to define a movement, not a historical period; this movement began at the beginning of the fifteenth century, and continued for about four centuries, but coexisted with experiments of other kinds; in the fifteenth century it affected Italy almost exclusively, in the following centuries it involved the other countries of Europe and their colonial possessions, though without entirely supplanting the late Gothic tradition, which survived in some places until the seventeenth and eighteenth centuries and was strengthened by the later medievalist revivals.

Therefore the chronological limits indicated do not serve to circumscribe a period of the universal history of architecture; within these limits we propose to write the biography of a movement, not the systematic review of all the events that occurred.

We now have to relate the chronological interval selected for our account to the subdivisions discussed from a more general historical point of view, i.e. the suggested divisions into periods where the term 'Renaissance' is also used.

Our period coincides approximately with that of Toynbee's Italistic Age (1475–1875) or with the chronological limits of the Renaissance suggested by Denys Hay (1350–1700), regarded as basically correct by Cantimori[4] and Garin.[5]

As far as the starting date is concerned, clearly one could include in the period the developments in the cultural patterns which took place in Italy from the middle of the fourteenth century onwards or one could cover the diffusion of these patterns throughout Europe, from the last decades of the fifteenth century. We shall take the first alternative, and the date we have chosen is around 1420, when the new architectural culture was born of the meeting between the conception of perspective and reference to the exemplary forms of antiquity; we have preferred to skip the preparatory experiments, in both fields, and to emphasize the crucial value of the synthesis achieved at that moment.

Uncertainty about the concluding date is greater; the period indicated by Hay excludes the Enlightenment and the revolutions of the end of the eighteenth century, while Toynbee includes almost all the nineteenth century, when the cultural models produced by the Renaissance continued to operate as instruments of control and as brakes on the changes in industrial society. In our case neither date is suitable. The intellectual crisis which virtually put an end to the course of modern classicism was already felt by the last decades of the seventeenth century and the first of the eighteenth, as Hazard[6] has shown, but it influenced architecture only marginally and produced its effects, in our field, only after a considerable delay. The outward forms of classicism continued to be recognized as conventional norms, and largely conditioned building design at least until the end of the nineteenth century, and town-planning, to some degree, to the present day; but this survival – already largely described in my *History of Modern Architecture* – covered a series of technical and organizational changes that were in fact completely foreign to the spirit of classicism, and can be described only by giving the parallel history of the two classes of events.

We have preferred to end our exposition at a date midway between those mentioned: roughly, the middle of the eighteenth century, when an acceleration of actual experiments and a rapid change in theoretical tendencies produced a more noticeable break in the regressive process under way. The continuity of forms and institutions was not interrupted, but faith in the permanent value of the traditional rules largely disappeared, and this meant the end of the intellectual adventure that had begun in the first decades of the fifteenth century.

The two extremes of our account, for those who like precision, may be fixed as follows: 1418 (the competition for the dome of Florence cathedral) and 1750 (the success of Rousseau's dissertation in the Dijon academy competition).

It is important to emphasize that the authors mentioned above likewise consider the Renaissance period as absolutely concluded and worked out; this indeed is why we may consider it retrospectively as a completed cycle.

There would be a complete correspondence between our choice of dates for the period and the others mentioned, which are meaningful in a more general field, if we were to consider only the results of artistic culture, in that they were part of the cultural heritage which was transmitted by Italy to the rest of the world and is considered sufficient, according to the historians mentioned, to characterize the entire period.

But, by examining all the technical and cultural circumstances which went into the making of the built-up environment, our account tries to provide an image of the civil life of the time, including, however, a certain number of other aspects of life; it therefore confirms the unity of our chosen period, albeit in a specified field.

The wording we have used, 'architecture of the Renaissance', is not entirely satisfactory, because of the ambiguity inherent in the term 'Renaissance', which is used to designate both the initial phase of the new cultural outlook and the whole cycle throughout which its effects were felt. An expression such as 'classical architecture' would have been preferable – Hautecoeur, for instance, uses it in his *Histoire de l'architecture classique en France* (which does in fact cover the period from 1495 to 1900) – in so far as it makes a reference to one of the permanent features, i.e. the use of formal models derived from classical antiquity. But this expression, used in Italian and without the geographical limits which characterize Hautecoeur's work, would have been ambiguous: for this reason we have accepted the wording 'architecture of the Renaissance', attributing to it the second of the two meanings mentioned.

The geographical boundaries of the Renaissance movement coincide, from the sixteenth century onwards, with the boundaries of European political expansion, and include all parts of the world. In some cases European architecture replaced native systems of building and of moulding the landscape (as in America and tropical Africa); in other cases it existed along with the cultural systems which were already present and were no less stable and sophisticated than those brought by the Europeans (as in the Middle and Far East).

By considering Renaissance culture as a completed historical structure, and by recognizing the nature of its organizations – not including the ideas of professional grouping, i.e. the distinction between art and techniques of production – we shall be able objectively to assess its relationship to other cultures, the development of which was either interrupted by colonizers or continued during colonization. These cultures not only elaborated a completely different world of forms, but they were based on a different distribution of energies and were grouped together according to widely differing notions; none of them possessed either the concepts or the words suited to expressing the separation of artistic values from functional and representational ones which characterized the European movement.

It is important to draw attention both to the clashes between the various systems, and to their mutual influences, and in particular the importance of the local contributions absorbed by European settlers, which surface again in the new cultural system with results that are sometimes decisive; this clash of disparate elements had its repercussions in the Old World and hastened the crisis of values on which the cultural system established in the colonies was based. The examination of these contributions will help to establish the relative value of European artistic culture, which is not simply 'culture', but one of the cultures prevailing between the fifteenth and nineteenth centuries, and cannot take comparison with other cultural traditions without revealing its own accidental character.

In this way it becomes clear that it would be pointless to include the results of other cultures in the conceptual outlines of the European tradition, i.e. to write a 'universal history of art'; an objective comparison between the various traditions – which is becoming ever more essential – can be made only by going through the modern movement, within the framework of an empirical definition of architecture such as Morris's; the variety of methodologies, which is an essential feature of modern architectural culture, is also the key for a correct understanding of the various historical legacies which come together in modern architecture today and which have thus laid themselves open to comparison.

The subjects dealt with in these seven chapters do not provide a systematic covering of the cycle of experiments referred to; they single out a certain number of the more significant ones, which form a discontinuous but logically connected series.

The first chapter – 'The inventors of the new architecture' – discusses the experiments which brought about the transition from the old to the new cultural cycle: the work of Brunelleschi, the work of the painters and sculptors belonging to his generation and the following, who revived the practice of the figurative arts, and the work of Alberti, who supplied the new architecture and figurative arts with suitable theoretical foundations; these contributions firmly established and entrenched the autonomy, the scientific character and social function of the new artistic culture.

In organizing this approach, we have noted the uncertainty of the studies and documents available, despite the fact that these artists are among the most important and the most studied. Information and judgments are satisfactory only in the context of stable institutions whose continuity, at this precise moment, it is our business to question; the documentation and technical flexibility needed to stress the change in intellectual and organizational premises are lacking. For this reason, at least for Brunelleschi, we have had to carry out a series of detailed investigations (contrary to the rules, according to which general books on a subject draw upon the information amassed in specialist studies); mere soundings, by no means a systematic exploration but sufficient to demonstrate the need to proceed along these lines.

In the second chapter – 'Towards the ideal city' – we have tried to assess the effect of the new artistic culture on the changes in Italian cities in the fifteenth century; the applications of the new culture in town-planning were hampered by two different combinations of circumstances, at the beginning and end of the century, and they had the leeway to emerge in part only in the middle of the century. This initial separation between culture and implementation was to remain vital for the future, too, and gave rise to the myth of the ideal city, which was the ideological counterpart to the faults and imperfections of the real city.

In the third chapter – 'The beginning and end of the "third style"' – the object of discussion is not a period or a definite area, but the intellectual adventure embarked upon by the great artists active between the end of the fifteenth and beginning of the sixteenth centuries – Leonardo da Vinci, Bramante, Giorgione, Raphael, Michelangelo – and ended, during their own lifetimes, by a dramatic conflict of circumstances. It is an episode which takes place in the sphere of high culture, and is not directly concerned with the changes in the urban scene, so that the events described in the preceding chapter are linked coherently with those of the one following. Despite this, the works of these masters do continue the line of earlier endeavours as their ideal goal and culmination, and remained as a past image in the series of later experiments; indeed from then onwards they acted as a constant point of reference not only in the history of art, but in that of culture and manners.

The fourth chapter – 'Urban changes in the sixteenth century' – concerns the world-wide expansion of European civilization, and the town-planning activities connected with this expansion, both in Europe and in the other continents: the changes in the cities where political and economic power became concentrated, the new cities founded in Europe and above all in Latin America by the Spanish colonizers. We have given special emphasis to the cities of the New World, built according to specific legal, technical and architectural rules; they form a coherent and permanent system, and represent the only concrete model of a new city produced by the culture of the Renaissance. Despite the poverty of this model in comparison with its cultural premises, it should not be considered as secondary: on the contrary it reveals the disastrous distribution of cultural energies in relation to effective opportunities, which lies at the basis of the imbalance of the artistic experiments of the sixteenth century, and affords a glimpse of the deeper reasons behind the phenomena described under the label 'mannerism'.

The change of tone in the more advanced artistic activities at the beginning of the seventeenth century, linked to the economic depression, political struggles and dispersal of the ruling classes formed during the two previous centuries, coincided with the birth of modern science. Taking as a starting point an observation made by Lionello Venturi,[7] we have pointed out in the fifth chapter – 'The crisis of sensibility' – that the beginnings of experimental science made the scientific hypothesis of prevailing artistic culture untenable. Artistic culture found its own particular field in the sphere of sensibility, and took shape as the system of operations capable of affecting the emotions. The origin of the modern theatre and the buildings connected with it stems from this point too.

The sixth chapter – 'The *grand siècle*' – gives an account of the formation and climax of French court culture, which from the end of the seventeenth century onwards prevailed as the universal model throughout the area of European influence. The seventh chapter – 'Court classicism and bourgeois classicism in the formation of the modern city' – attempts to enumerate and classify the enormous range of urban changes encouraged by the new ruling classes from the beginning of the seventeenth century onwards, both in Europe and in the colonial territories; we have tried to explain the causes of the imbalance between the new economic and administrative apparatus and its effects on town organisms, and we have given the necessary emphasis to the cities of Holland, which were the happy exception in the economic-political picture as in that of town-planning.

This account could continue throughout the eighteenth century and much of the nineteenth; but it breaks off, as we have explained, in the middle of the eighteenth, when the overlapping between court and bourgeois classicism and the formation of the neo-classical ideology threatened the unity of the traditional artistic heritage. Later applications of classicism have already been de-scribed in the *History of Modern Architecture*, and could be treated with the same breadth in this book, from a different visual angle. But the two points of view are not equally instructive; we prefer to underline the fact that the cultural cycle which opened in the fifteenth century in Italy was already concluded by the late eighteenth, although its legacy of institutions and organizations still functioned for over another century.

One of the requirements of modern architectural culture is that it should confirm the conclusion of this cycle; the Renaissance city, after being poised precariously between reality and Utopia, ceased to exist as a vital hypothesis, and its models were reduced to covering instruments for many disparate interests, economic, social and political.

Attempts to create the modern city, i.e. the architectural hypothesis typical of our time, can be successful only by changing the terms of the debate once and for all.

The inventors of the new architecture

The Florentine scene at the beginning of the fifteenth century

On 19 August 1418 the Arte della Lana launched a competition for the model of the dome of Florence cathedral. Filippo Brunelleschi – with his collaborators Donatello and Nanni di Banco – and Lorenzo Ghiberti were initially selected; the two artists were invited to take part in a second competition, and in 1420 were appointed supervisors of the building of the dome, together with Battista d'Antonio; in 1423 Brunelleschi was recognized as the 'inventor and governor' of the main dome, and from then onwards he became the undisputed arbiter of all Florentine building problems. He was originally trained as a goldsmith, and took part in the 1402 competition for the new doors of the baptistery of S. Giovanni, won by Ghiberti; he worked as a military engineer, and possibly before 1418 he established the canons of perspective experimentally with the two famous panels. Donatello – Brunelleschi's companion in his journeys to Rome after 1402 and apprenticed to Ghiberti until 1407 – emerged the following year as an independent sculptor with the *David* intended for one of the buttresses of the transept of the cathedral (Nanni di Banco sculpted the other statue, *Isaiah*, to be placed beside it) and in 1415 he

was commissioned to carve the statues of the prophets for the campanile. Nanni, who did the sculptures for the Porta della Mandorla to a programme by Coluccio Salutati, was certainly influenced by Brunelleschi in the *Four Crowned Saints* and the *St Philip* in Orsanmichele, before reverting to Gothic models, between 1418 and his early death in 1421.

Between 1418 and 1421 Brunelleschi received commissions for the main Florentine buildings of those years: the new S. Lorenzo, the adjoining sacristy, the Ospedale degli Innocenti, the enlargement of the Palazzo di Parte Guelfa. From 1421 onwards he designed the machinery for the building of the dome, and in 1424 patented a self-propelled river-going ship; meanwhile he continued work on the sacristy, completed in 1428, and from 1424 onwards on the Ospedale degli Innocenti. Donatello and Michelozzo, from their joint workshop opened in 1423, sent their sculptures to Montepulciano, Siena, Rome and Naples; in 1425 Michelozzo designed the niche in Orsanmichele for Donatello's *St Louis*, using the classical forms proposed by Brunelleschi. In 1422 the young Masaccio was admitted to the Arte dei Medici as a painter, and perhaps in 1425 Brunelleschi collaborated with him on the

1 *Panel presented by Ghiberti for the competition for the baptistery doors in 1402. Museo Nazionale, Florence*

2 *Panel presented by Brunelleschi in the same competition. Museo Nazionale, Florence*

perspective background, constructed with scientific exactitude, of the fresco in S. Maria Novella. At this time the technique of linear perspective was spreading rapidly; it was applied by Masaccio in the lost works mentioned by Vasari: the 'history of little figures' in the house of Ridolfo Ghirlandaio, the *Annunciation* in S. Niccolò Oltrarno; by Paolo Uccello in the other *Annunciation* in S. Maria Maggiore; by Donatello – who in the relief of 1416 for the base of the *St George* had intuitively tackled the same problem – in the background to the *Feast of Herod* in Siena, completed in 1427, in the tondi for Brunelleschi's sacristy (if they were executed around 1428, as Sanpaolesi supposes) and in many later works; by Ghiberti in the Siena reliefs and panels of the third baptistery door, commissioned in 1425. Possibly the first theoretical formulation of perspective dates from this time; Paolo Toscanelli returned from Padua to Florence in 1424, was in close contact with Brunelleschi, as his biographers show, and might be the author of the anonymous treatise attributed by Bonucci to Alberti.

Between 1427 and 1428 Masaccio was working on the frescoes in the Carmine, an undertaking interrupted by his early death. In 1428 Brunelleschi was commissioned to rebuild S. Spirito, and in 1429 began the building of the Pazzi chapel in S. Croce. At the same time Fra Angelico was beginning his career, painting the first perspective landscape on the predella of the *Annunciation* in Cortona. During those crucial years, from 1425 to 1430, Paolo Uccello was in Venice, but soon afterwards he was painting the fresco of the *Nativity* in S. Martino, whose complex perspective construction is revealed by the *sinopia*.

In 1428, his ban suspended, Leon Battista Alberti was able to return to his native town, and in 1431 he went to Rome, where he met Donatello between 1432 and 1433. In 1433 Michelozzo followed Cosimo de' Medici to Venice and in 1432, after the return of his

patron, began work with Donatello on the Prato pulpit.

In 1434 Brunelleschi, at the height of his fame, was invited to Ferrara and Mantua, finished roofing the dome and was commissioned to work on the Rotonda degli Angeli; in 1436 he made the models for the lantern and for S. Spirito.

Also in 1436 Alberti published the vernacular translation of his *Trattato della pittura*, with its dedication to Filippo Brunelleschi, and Paolo Uccello painted the fresco of an equestrian monument to Hawkwood in the cathedral. Meanwhile the new generation of Florentine artists was making its début: in 1431 Luca della Robbia, in 1432 Filippo Lippi, about 1435 Bernardo Rossellino; and it may have been about this time that Domenico Veneziano came to Florence. Among his assistants, in 1439, we first hear mention of Piero della Francesca.

Thus in a period of less than twenty years – beginning ideally with the execution of Brunelleschi's dome – a limited group of artists, gathered together in a single city, brought about one of the greatest revolutions in cultural history, and set off a chain of incalculable consequences.

The present state of documentation does not enable us to reconstruct clearly the thread of mutual relationships and stimuli. It is easy to see that the interchanges of experience, within so restricted a period of time and place, must have been far denser than those actually ascertained so far, and it is not likely that future research, in a field so long explored, will come up with many further pieces of evidence directly concerning the activities of the artists. The effort of going beyond documents and using stylistic analysis to enlarge on biographies, attributions and dates, proves largely unwarranted, as the divergence between the theses so far upheld makes clear.

However, recent attempts to broaden the sectorial area of enquiry (by considering, within the chronological and geographical field defined by artistic events, the developments in civic, political, religious, scientific and technological history which acts as a setting for these events) have shown that it is possible to increase the documentation of this period crucially, in so far as the zone of interest where the art historians' research has been concentrated does not necessarily coincide with the areas most thoroughly explored by historians of science, engineering and economics. As a result of this type of approach, doubt has been cast upon the distinction between artistic events and the events in which they are set. In fact collation between compartmentalized historical discussions has gradually become more frequent as the firm belief in the absolute value of the distinction between sectors has weakened, and in its turn it helps to demonstrate the relative character of these distinctions.

The clarification of this problem would appear to be a necessary preliminary to any discussion of the period. The historical result of the choices made at that time is in fact the foundation of a clearly defined sector of activity – by isolating an intellectual operation within the generic ambit of the medieval *ars*, an operation to which from now on, in a more precise sense, the word 'art' was to be applied – separate from technical processes and independent of other spiritual requirements, scientific, religious and moral. As long as this framework served to regulate the distribution of human energies applied to the organization of the urban scene, the formation of this framework was made to coincide with the acknowledgment of a permanent theoretical concept, i.e. the autonomy of art, and it has seemed more interesting to trace the preparation for this transition in past history than to analyse precisely its scope and meaning.

But the experience of modern architecture, which entails a different framework of operation in laying out the modern city, enables us to recognize the fortuitous character of the synthesis reached at the beginning of the fifteenth century, and to study the events of this period in a new way, by trying to grasp the moment of transition in which the cultural specifications typical of the previous tradition interacted and merged, subsequently to be distributed in another way.

We must now list all the circumstances – apparently of many different kinds – which may throw light on the time and place of the events considered, bearing in mind the importance of Florence, one of the main political, economic and cultural centres of the time. Only against this background can we see objectively the actions of Brunelleschi and the other protagonists, without imprisoning them in the traditional patterns which they helped to break or in those which were the institutional outcome of the movement begun by them.

1 The artistic movement we have referred to did not coincide with any particular event in other areas of history, and occurred at a time which may be considered, in all other respects, as one of transition, a lull between the great upheavals which mark the end of the Middle Ages and beginning of the modern age.

The twenty years we have considered (1418–36) come towards the end of the great economic crisis which extends from the first third of the fourteenth century to the middle of the fifteenth. The demographic expansion typical of the previous centuries stopped or was reversed, particularly after the plague of 1347–8, which eliminated a large part of the population in various places.

Florence lost perhaps three-quarters of her 90,000 inhabitants in the first decades of the fourteenth century, and did not top the 70,000 mark again until the following century. The built-up area of the city stopped expanding and did not even fill the circle of the third walls and, within the confines established at the end of the thirteenth century, retained a

3 *View of fourteenth-century Florence, detail from the* Madonna della Misericordia. *Loggia del Bigallo, Florence*

mixed urban and rural character, like Siena, Ghent, Cologne and many of the main European cities.

The fall in population dominated the economic life of the time, which was characterized by the fall in prices for basic agricultural products, by a rise in prices for other goods and wages, particularly during the periods when labour was short. In many cases circumstances stimulated a spread of industrial activity, an increase in trade, an improvement in means of communication and hence an extension of the monetary economy over ever vaster areas. From the fourteenth century onwards the needs of a growing monetary circulation conflicted with a shortage in the production of precious metals,

particularly of silver; this was alleviated only after 1450, when the rational exploitation of German and Hungarian mines began.

The Italian cities were losing their exclusive importance in the fields of trade and industry.

In Florence the wool industry, which in 1339 according to Villani produced 70,000–80,000 lengths of wool and employed 30,000 people, entered a period of crisis in the middle of the century, and in the time of the *ciompi* (wool-carders) was to produce less than the 24,000 lengths laid down by the masters of the Arte as annual minimum. In the following century production did not rise above 30,000 lengths, and specialized in luxury fabrics; there was a similar tendency

4 *Model of the seventeenth-century centre of Ypres. Musée des plans reliefs, Paris*

in the silk industry, though this was in a state of expansion throughout the fifteenth century. Throughout the following two centuries this tendency, together with events in artistic culture, guaranteed Italy an almost undisputed monopoly in the production of the luxury goods necessary to the life of the new ruling classes.

Communications by land and sea between the cities of the north and Italy were increasing; in 1338 the first carriage road over the Alps was opened, from Chur to Chiavenna; the Arte di Calimala sent a messenger every day from Florence to the fairs of Champagne, and we know that at the end of the fourteenth century there was a regular service of carriers between Venice and Bruges.

In the first decades of the fifteenth century the economic situation seemed generally improved, even if over a large area of Europe civil activities were still severely hampered by the Hundred Years' War. The broadening of the trading area offered new opportunities to a group of capitalist merchants, mainly Italian, who acquired increasing influence in the international field from the beginning of the fifteenth century. The great development of European capitalism was to come later, in the second half of the fifteenth and the first half of the sixteenth centuries, and the merchants of this period – some of the most important of whom were the Florentine families of the Albizzi, Strozzi, Medici and Pazzi – were certainly the pioneers of later development, the propensities and psychological mood of which they anticipated. The volume of business of the Medici in the early fifteenth century was already three times that of the Bardi and Peruzzi, the main Florentine bankers of the fourteenth century.

It was now that business techniques developed an organization of their own, a development made possible by the progress in applied mathematics and particularly by the widespread use of Arabic numerals. The practice of double-entry book-keeping spread – it had already been used by the Genoese in the previous century – and so did long-distance economic transactions; this was the time of the Bank of Deposit in Barcelona (1401), the Taule de Cambis in Valencia (1407) and the Casa di S. Giorgio in Genoa (1408).

The new aristocracy of money obeyed an economic logic different from the traditional one, and made a decisive contribution to the crisis of the city's corporative institutions; the size of its business in fact put it on a level with the new national political organisms which were being formed outside Italy, with which it was to deal as an equal, like Jacob Fugger with Charles V.

This new class was linked to the world of artists both by the similarity of their cultural backgrounds – which put the emphasis on individual ability as against the traditional rules of collective action – and because the wealthier families began to replace public bodies in commissioning buildings and works of art; Brunelleschi's activity was largely determined by the commissions of the Medici and Pazzi. Later, when this same class gained political control, relations with the artists became even closer, as we shall see.

For Florence, the long period of internal stability which ran from the end of social struggle, in the penultimate decade of the fourteenth century, to the hegemony of Cosimo the Elder, was also a period of relative economic calm, only partially disturbed by the reverberations of the almost continual external wars. Three of these are important for their effects on building activity in the city: the first saw the Florentine troops defeated in 1424 at Zagonara and led in 1427 to the setting up of the land register; the second, between 1432 and 1433, cost Cosimo his exile; and the third ended with the Florentine victory at Anghiari and the peace of 1441.

The execution of Brunelleschi's works was repeatedly hampered by these wars and by the economic difficulties resulting from them; only after 1440 – i.e. in the few years before his death in 1446 – could work on his sites proceed unhindered.

Apart from these events the general economic and demographic stagnation ruled out large-scale town-planning undertakings throughout our period and meant that artists were asked to work upon the city created during the previous centuries, rather than to produce works of transformation or invention on an urban scale.

This circumstance favoured work of methodological reconsideration like that of Brunelleschi, or at least it provided the pause necessary to its gradual development; but meanwhile it rendered the extension of Brunelleschi's method to a town-planning scale purely hypothetical, and imposed a handicap on the new artistic culture which was never to be entirely overcome.

2 The technical and cultural activities of this period were still regulated by the model theories produced by medieval speculation in the twelfth and thirteenth centuries, crystallized in the schools, the literary heritage and the guild statutes.

While these theories came into ever greater conflict with the changed material and spiritual requirements, recent developments in theoretical thought gradually introduced a new scale of values, which was still not in a position to influence institutions and the organization of labour.

The nominalism of Occam and his Paris

followers, Buridan, Oresme and Albert of Saxony, stimulated not only the renewal of theological and philosophical thought, but also the development of science and experimental research; the new logical method found its application in mathematics and geometry and, combined with a concern for experiment, encouraged the study of mechanics, physics and the experimental sciences. Particularly important for later artistic culture were the studies on optics, based on the classical texts (Euclid, Ptolemy, Damian and Proclus), the Arabic ones (Alhazen, translated in the twelfth century by Gerard of Cremona) and the thirteenth-century ones (Roger Bacon, Peckham and Witelo) and continued in the fourteenth century by the pupils of Buridan, Domenico da Chivasso, Oresme and Henry of Langestein. These writings were circulating in Florence at the beginning of the fifteenth century; the library of Filippo di ser Ugolino, a notary who lived from 1401 to 1444, included a collection of the fourteenth-century texts mentioned, together with an anonymous treatise on perspective attributed by Bonucci to Alberti and by Parronchi to Paolo Toscanelli, and a copy of Peckham's *Perspectiva*, originally the property of Salutati, then passed on to Niccoli and Cosimo the Elder; in the catalogue of the library of Palla Strozzi of 1431 a *Perspectiva generalis* is mentioned, possibly the one by Alhazen with Witelo's commentary, together with two treatises by Albert of Saxony. The presence in Florence of Biagio Pelacani, author of the *Quaestiones perspectivae* written around 1390, is documented in 1389, 1394 and possibly as early as 1381, as Sanpaolesi suggests; on this occasion he seems to have been consulted about the foundations of the cathedral dome.

Studies on optics entailed the reduction of a class of physical phenomena to exclusively geometrical terms, and they therefore gained a general prominence in the scientific system of the time; light was considered as being on the border line between corporeal and in-corporeal, and as a preliminary condition for all the manifestations of the perceptible universe.

These arguments were linked to the progressive detachment from the Aristotelian concept of space as a place, i.e. as one of the accidents of corporeal matter. Aristotelian theory was discussed persistently in the fourteenth century by Henry of Ghent, Richard of Middleton, Walter Burleigh, Thomas Bradwardine and Nicholas of Autrecourt; about 1400 Hasdai Crescas – who belonged to the generation before Brunelleschi – put forward a complete alternative theory to the classical one for the first time, and anticipated with surprising clarity the concept of absolute space, developed by philosophers and scientists of the sixteenth and seventeenth centuries.[1]

But Crescas was working in isolation in the Jewish community in Catalonia, prematurely dispersed by the Spanish political upheavals of the fifteenth century. From a scientific point of view emancipation from the Aristotelian theory of space took place only in the late sixteenth century, through the work of Telesio, Patrizi and Campanella, and opened the way to the new physics of Galileo and Newton.

The new criteria of spatial representation introduced by the artists of the early fifteenth century were not the illustration of a new scientific argument, but the first answers to a group of commonly experienced difficulties; in fact, by modifying the habits of representation and practice at this stage, they perhaps contributed to the later theoretical turning-point.

The scientific studies of the fourteenth century, though important for the future development of experimental science, only marginally influenced the technology of productive activities. After the great inventions which made the economic developments of the eleventh to thirteenth centuries possible – the water mill, the stern rudder, the new system of harness for horses and oxen –

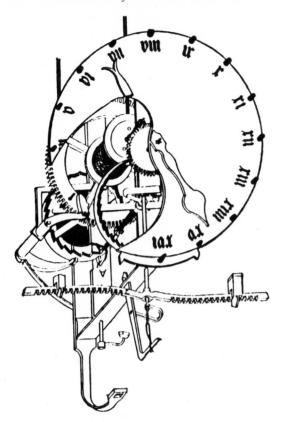

6   *Sketches for mills worked by the tide, by Mariano di Jacopo, 1438*

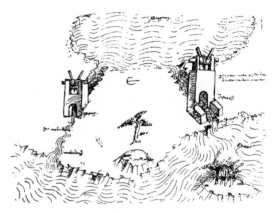

agriculture and the most important industries of the late Middle Ages (the textile, metallurgical and mechanical industries) remained linked to the systems of traditional manufacture, strengthened by the statutes of the guilds. What we call engineering was considered a science; in the *Didascalion* by Hugh of St Victor and the *Speculum doctrinae* of Victor of Beauvais, *mechanica* is placed on the same speculative level as logic and theology, but it dealt with the knowledge of a technical universe which was considered stable and complete, not the construction of a constantly changing universe. It was this technological bottleneck of the fourteenth century, among other things, that prevented the economic and demographic expansion of the previous centuries from continuing. But after 1450, when a new phase of economic expansion started, technical changes began in the field of metallurgy that were such as to set the basic industries into motion once again.

Fourteenth-century speculative research did have some influence on certain limited sectors of technology. The new mentality connected with nominalism demanded, in practical life as well, a more precise expression of the notions of time, place and number, and brought about progress in the fields of clock-making, geography and book-keeping.

The first mechanical clocks appeared in the thirteenth century; the first striking mechanism was made in 1386, and the spring was probably invented in the fifteenth. In the middle of the fourteenth century Giovanni de' Dondi built his astronomical clock, the prototype of the great clock buildings erected subsequently in the main European cities. Brunelleschi, too, as a young man worked on the building of clocks and striking mechanisms.[2]

Nicolas d'Oresme and Pierre d'Ailly were the first theoreticians of geography, which depended on the successive improvements of astronomical and topographical instruments, in the course of the fifteenth century. Genoa, Valencia and Palma di Majorca were the first centres of the cartographic techniques necessary to the development of navigation in the Atlantic.

Ptolemy's *Geography* was translated from Greek into Latin about 1406 by Jacobus Angelus, a pupil of Chrystoloras; in 1410 Pierre d'Ailly completed his *Imago mundi* and in 1413 the *Compendium cosmographiae*, a summary of Ptolemy's opinions widely read during the years that followed.

Fibonacci's *Liber abbaci*, written at the beginning of the thirteenth century, was the starting-point for a series of popular works, which spread the notions of computation to all the wealthy classes, and were mainly important for the new techniques of trade and business. In Florence there was an important school of applied mathematics, which took the name 'abacus'; among its masters were Paolo Ficozzi (d. 1372), the author of a collection of *Regoluzze* widely read during the following years, Antonio Mazzinghi and Giovanni dell'Abbaco, a little older than Brunelleschi. The latter, 'following the general custom for men of standing in Florence, . . . learned to read and write at an early age, and to use the abacus'[3] and Giovanni dell'Abbaco was frequently at work on the cathedral, in 1417, 1420 and 1425, as well as providing designs for it.

In the first decade of the fifteenth century interest in technology seems to have been particularly marked. At this time the most important innovations of the late Middle Ages were introduced: locks and dredgers for the navigable canals, hydraulic bellows for the working of metals, the crank and slider, from which a whole series of machines were derived, for instance the lathe, pump and spinning-machine. In 1405 Konrad Kyeser dedicated to the Emperor his treatise *Belli-fortis*, which contains a complete review of the mechanical repertoire of the age; the similar manuscripts of the anonymous writer of the Hussite wars, of Giacomo Fontana and Mariano di Jacopo, almost Brunelleschi's contemporaries, date from a little later. Civil and military engines remained associated with architecture in the treatises of Alberti (completed in 1452), of Francesco di Giorgio (written between 1470 and 1480) and in the experience of the main Italian artists throughout the sixteenth century.

The technical activities known, after the fifteenth century, as the 'fine arts' were not seen, in the late Middle Ages, as a single group, but appeared as scattered throughout the broader grouping of the 'mechanical arts'. The Florentine guild organization distinguished the Arti in relation to their economic importance, and did not originally recognize an independent position for either painters or sculptors, while it did not distinguish the architect from workers of the building guilds, subdivided in their turn into several groups.[4]

Workers in wood and stone formed one of the five Arti Mediane, which joined with the Arti Maggiori after the laws of 1293; at the beginning of the fifteenth century the group was in a state of crisis, exposed to the competition of the Lombard workers, and had to resort to the protective measures contained in the 1415 statute. Quarry-workers formed three autonomous guilds according to the provenance of the stone.

Workers who carried out supplementary work found themselves in a subordinate position. Ironware for building was not the concern of the ordinary smiths (Arte Mediana) but of the locksmiths, one of the Arti Minori; the less important work in wood and the furniture were the business of the carpenters, another of the Arti Minori, which included the important group of the coffer-makers, recognized as an autonomous body from 1315. Glass-makers formed a voluntary association in 1316, not recognized as a guild, and the use of panes of glass for windows is

7, 8   Building *and* Sculpture, *attributed to Giotto. Campanile of the cathedral, Florence*

documented as early as the first years of the fourteenth century (for instance in the convent of S. Croce and the Badia, 'so that those wishing to devote themselves to their studies might do so') but was still considered a luxury in the first half of the fifteenth century.[5]

Painters – who in 1295 had an associative organization of their own – were joined to doctors and apothecaries from 1316 because they depended upon these for their supply of raw materials; in 1339 painters founded their own religious guild, the Company of St Luke, to which glass-makers, furniture-makers and sculptors in wax were also admitted.

Sculptors, too, were distinguished according to the materials they used: those who worked in stone and wood belonged to the guild of masons and carpenters, those who used metal were associated with the goldsmiths, and belonged to the Arte della Seta, which grouped together the production of various luxuries.

In so far as they were incorporated into the Arte dei Medici and the Arte della Seta, painters and sculptors were part of the Arti Maggiori, i.e. the dominant groups of the Florentine corporative state. But from Cimabue onwards the most important painters and sculptors acquired an individual prestige which placed them above collective organisms, and they were considered experts of a higher level in the whole field of what was later to be called *le belle arti*, and therefore also in architecture, like Arnolfo, Giotto and Orcagna.

These artists, like poets and men of letters, were now moving outside the professional classifications of the Middle Ages, and had already entered the sphere of humanistic culture, which set individual talent against all collective traditions; Filippo Villani, in his *De origine Florentiae et de ejusdem famosis civibus*[6] listed and described painters and sculptors among them. The renown of artists

9 Painting. *Campanile of the cathedral, Florence*

throughout the fifteenth century found no echo, however, in their economic remuneration and did not alter their condition in law, which was one of subordination to their patrons. In the contracts quoted by Antal,[7] recompense for the artist is often left to the discrimination of the patron and there was no mutuality of rights between the two parties.

The Florentine municipality intervened in building in many ways, and in this way partly controlled the activities of painters and sculptors, at least as far as the great commissions for the churches and public buildings were concerned.

The office of the 'masters and surveyors of the commune', which was concerned with building and property controversies, had existed since the twelfth century; this office included two *misuratori* or *abbachisti*, two notaries and a carpenter and mason, elected every six months.

The municipality appointed special com-

missions for the laying of roads, was responsible for the building and upkeep of bridges, saw that property-owners paved the streets outside their respective buildings and gave an increasing amount of financial assistance to the building of churches. In 1322 a special office was set up to protect the property rights of the commune over its own creations (roads, squares, sites, walls, bridges, buildings).

Florentine humanist literature, as it emerged at the end of the fourteenth century and the beginning of the fifteenth, was undoubtedly the main preliminary to the artistic movement which began between 1410 and 1420. There were two features common to the two movements: faith in autonomous rational research into human values, and the reference to classical antiquity, where these values had already received exemplary definition; hence the break with recent tradition, against which a remote one, critically reconstructed, was set.

The work of the artists presupposed that of the writers, and the Brunelleschian programme may be described as the attempt to bring a part of the techniques of production on to the level of intellectual deliberation typical of humanistic enquiry in the moral field. In this sense the work of the artists was part of a wider movement, in which men of letters, politicians, entrepreneurs, scholars and jurists took part; this movement could not be fitted into the traditional institutional patterns, but it certainly produced a 'rupture of balance and patterns'[8] from which a new distribution of human activities was subsequently to emerge. Men of letters kept the leadership of this movement in many ways, they gave it expression and awareness, and artists constantly used them to mediate for them, particularly in their relations with the ruling classes.

In another sense the artistic programme – at least as formulated by Brunelleschi – cannot be understood wholly in terms of the literary programme, indeed it emerges as its technical antithesis. Men of letters tended to translate all the programmes of civil life into verbal terms, and they attributed to eloquence the dignity of a universal instrument of mediation ('*eodem, quasi in unum corpus scientiae omnes*'[9]); artists, for their part, tended to resolve all values into visible form, and attributed to *disegno* a similar value as a universal instrument; Brunelleschi did not leave a single line of writing, except possibly an enigmatic sonnet where he expressed the disdain of the practical man for the man who criticizes without due qualification, and Ghiberti contrasts the figurative arts with rhetoric, which cannot be described, as they can, as 'brief and open', i.e. capable of communicating its meaning, instantaneously, to everyone.[10]

Only at a second stage, through the work of Alberti, was a precarious balance established between the two contrasting programmes, which depended largely upon the way in which he, a humanist and architect, managed to yoke these two experiences harmoniously together in his own way of life. But the antithesis remained, and re-emerged at the end of the century in the case of Leonardo, '*omo sanza lettere*'. It is true that from Alberti onwards all important artists felt the need to explain themselves in writing too; but verbal explanations proved to be much more uncertain than stylistic choices, which were essentially fixed by Brunelleschi and remained stable throughout the following four centuries.

Brunelleschi was not a humanist, but he did conclude an analogous operation, within his own field, with no less certainty. He may have frequented the Florentine men of letters of his generation, Bruni, Bracciolini and Giannozzo Manetti, as Argan supposed;[11] but he had a different outlook, and could be compared rather to Valla, who belonged to the following generation; he had the same specialist education, the same polemical temperament, the same dogged attention to detail.

The architectural forms standardized by Brunelleschi, based on classical antiquity, have a meaning comparable to the Latin *elegantiae* theorized about by Valla, and they are the fruit of a very similar operation, but their function is only partly analogous, and their historical destiny completely different. Latin remained a language reserved for a learned minority, which fell into disuse as early as the sixteenth century, and in the following century became the Latin of Don Abbondio; but the classical repertoire of architecture, though utilized as a mark of classicism, remained recognizable and comprehensible to all, and soon made the 'vernacular' repertoire elaborated in the Middle Ages irrelevant. It determined the vocabulary of European architecture until the nineteenth century, even when the cultural contents were in fact completely changed.

It is interesting to compare the position of men of letters and artists *vis-à-vis* the natural sciences. Marsilius, Salutati and Bruni, continuing the polemic begun by Petrarch, tended to disparage the natural sciences, as opposed to the *studia humanitatis*, and they upheld the superiority of moral laws over physical ones; on the other hand Brunelleschi, Paolo Uccello and Piero della Francesca did not hesitate to make use of the contributions of contemporary science – indeed they liked to compare their work to that of the scientists. Of the liberal arts included in the traditional canon, they preferred to relate themselves to those of the Quadrivium (arithmetic, geometry, music and astronomy) rather than those of the Trivium (grammar, rhetoric and dialectic). Hence the importance attributed to mathematical matters and the occasional declarations of distrust in rhetoric, like the one quoted from Ghiberti.

The artistic operation took on the value of an experimental examination of physical truth, and concerned both man and nature, ignoring or by-passing the contrast of which men of letters spoke. This attitude revealed a new faith in the rationality of nature, based

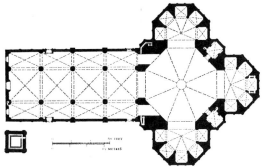

10 *Detail of fresco with the elevation of S. Maria del Fiore according to the fourteenth-century plan. S. Maria Novella, Florence*
11, 12 *Ground plan and interior of S. Maria del Fiore, Florence*

on the knowledge of the common laws inherent in nature and the human mind.

At the end of the fifteenth century, when the Platonic theme of the antithesis between man and the cosmos reappeared, the intuitive knowledge typical of art was once again opposed to the deductive knowledge typical of science: 'the artist knows scientific truth with means of his own, which may well be opposed to the traditional means of science, based on authority',[12] while the ways of art were founded on observation and experiment. In this way artistic research appeared linked to the basic themes of *studia humanitatis*, and anticipated the need for a completely humanized 'new science'. At this point Lionello Venturi's observation on the relationship between art and magic seems appropriate;[13] Garin recalls that in the Renaissance discussion of true and false magic was still very much alive, 'because people felt that this was the new path that would provide man with dominion over nature'.[14]

Drawn into this debate, artists developed to its limits the consequences of the intellectualist choice made by their predecessors, and thus made a necessary, if indirect, contribution to the birth of modern science.

3 In Florence, when Brunelleschi and Ghiberti were starting their careers, the rule of patrician oligarchy which had emerged victorious from the social struggles of the late fourteenth century had already lasted for twenty years.

This fact of Florentine life was part of a general European situation, connected with the acute stage of the fourteenth-century economic crisis, after the great plague of 1347–8. The famine of 1365–74, followed by a new epidemic in 1373–5, gave rise to, or exacerbated, the rebellion of the poorer classes in many places: the *ciompi* in Florence in 1378, the Flemish weavers in 1379, the *tuchins* of Languedoc in 1380, the English peasants of Mile End in 1381, the people of Paris in 1382. The repression of these uprisings, in the economically most advanced cities such as Florence and Ghent, had an absolutely analogous meaning; the claims of the town workers were put forward within the guild system, itself already threatened by the new developments of the mercantile economy, and they conflicted not only with the interests of privileged local guilds but with those of national and international capitalism, which were out of their range. The year 1382, when the dominant group in Florence brought about the dissolution of the popular guilds, with the help of Hawkwood's troops, was also the year of the battle of Roosebeke, won by the king of France against the Flemish rebels.

In 1379 the death of Charles IV of Bohemia and the election of Urban VI sparked off simultaneous crises for empire and papacy. The contest for the imperial crown ended in 1411 with the election of Sigismund of Luxemburg, but the empire had lost its universal significance and was becoming a definite territorial domain where the Hapsburgs reigned uninterruptedly from 1447 onwards. The unity of the universal church was compromised by the western schism and the heretical movements of Wycliff – who died in 1384 – and Huss, excommunicated in 1412; the Council of Constance, summoned in 1414 to end the schism, sent Huss to the stake in 1415 and re-established the unity of the hierarchy in 1417, but did not put an end to the innovating tendencies which emerged again later in Basle and produced the sixteenth-century movements of reform. The Hundred Years' War between France and England was temporarily suspended between 1377 and 1414, and when it started up again, the dynastic struggle had become a national conflict.

The political situation was no longer dominated by universal and feudal institutions, but by a multitude of national and city powers, which were confronting one another for the moment in a temporary state of balance.

13 *Back of the tabernacle by A. Orcagna. Orsanmichele, Florence*

In Florence the rule of the Arti Maggiori, dominated by the Albizzi and the Uzzano families, continued for another fifty years, becoming identified with the fortunes of the city; it was involved in the defending of the autonomy of the republic against the deadly threat of the dominion of Gian Galeazzo Visconti, from 1390 to 1402 – and participation in this episode was possibly a key factor for the generation of intellectuals who were young at the end of the century, such as Brunelleschi and Bruni, according to Baron's thesis;[15] it encouraged the formation of a territorial state extending from the Appennines to the sea, with the acquisition of Arezzo (1384), Pisa (1406), Cortona (1410) and Livorno (1421); it attempted to remedy the decline of the wool industry – on which the wealth of the city was based – with protective tariffs in 1393 and 1426, and from 1421 to facilitate trade by organizing its own merchant fleet in the Tyrrhenian ports. In accordance with this political line, it cultivated every manifestation of city cultural life and tended to organize current experiments into definitive and exemplary forms, such as would strengthen the prestige of the state. In this way it committed itself, within the circle of Arnolfo's walls, to completing the image of the city outlined in the previous century, and first of all to complete the unfinished public works.

The Arte della Lana (guild of cloth manufacturers) – responsible for the work on the cathedral site from 1331 – completed roofing the nave and aisles in 1380, and began the building of the tribune, completed as far as the impost just before the 1418 competition; from 1380 to 1404 the Arte di Por S. Maria had the loggia of Orsanmichele closed in and built the storehouse above it; between 1381 and 1389 the decoration of the loggia della Signoria was completed; in 1401 the Arte di Calimala (cloth-finishers) advertised the competition for the second baptistery doors, and in 1412 the cathedral, though incomplete, was solemnly dedicated to S. Maria del Fiore.

The aristocratic government deliberately encouraged the cult of city memories. Florence was regarded as the new Rome, heir to the cultural and civic virtues of ancient Rome – as in the polemic of Salutati against Loschi, at the time of the Visconti threat against Florence – or as the stronghold of the Hellenic tradition, older and more genuine than the Roman;[16] Byzantine scholars were encouraged to settle in Florence, and Emanuel Chrysoloras began the first public course in Greek in 1397.

One of the components of this municipal cult was the traditional veneration and exegesis of Dante, kept alive by men of letters, from Boccaccio onwards, and partly also by artists, who repeatedly illustrated scenes from the poem, and the figure of the poet himself; Brunelleschi, according to Vasari, studied the 'sites and measurements' of the *Commedia*, possibly to prepare a graphic scheme of Dante's universe.[17]

The eulogy of Florence written by Leonardo Bruni summarizes the themes of the municipal patriotism so widespread in the first years of the century in the most eloquent way. This ideal image of the city, in which memories of the past are mingled with present achievements, explains the confidence of Ghiberti, Brunelleschi and Donatello in their modification of the medieval scene and buildings, and also explains, in part, the lack of a definite plan for urban renewal, proportionate to the size of the methodological leap that had been made. This mythical Florence, where past and present came together, was already the first of the ideal cities towards which Renaissance town-planning interest was consistently directed.

The twenty years during which the new artistic movement was formed – from 1418 to 1436 – coincided with the transition from the oligarchic régime to the personal power of Cosimo de' Medici, exiled in 1433 and victorious in 1434. The family rivalry between the Albizzi and the Medici obscured the opposition between the old entrepre-

14 Portrait of Cosimo de' Medici *(Cosimo the Elder) by Bronzino. Palazzo Medici, Florence*

neurial aristocracy, still partially linked to the guild system, and the new capitalistic élite which, through credit, controlled many productive activities and therefore tended to break away from traditional rules and acted in a new economic dimension, where only rational calculation and success counted.

Imposing itself as a ruling class, this élite tended to exercise this same dominating mentality in the political field, and its success fitted into the vast movement of the restoration of authoritarianism which affected both secular governments and the Church in those years (in 1417 the election of Martin V re-established papal authority *vis-à-vis* the Council, and in 1419 Sigismund of Luxemburg once again united the imperial crown with that of Bohemia).

The new ruling class expected much more of artistic and literary culture than the old one had done.

This class, as we have said, was identified spontaneously with the lot of society in general, and expected artists and writers to celebrate the civic values whose management it was gaining. For this reason the first flowering of Florentine humanism – and primarily the work of Salutati, chancellor of the republic from 1375 to 1406 – appeared as both linked to the interests of the ruling oligarchy (indeed it outstripped and threatened the more humble literary phenomena inspired by the needs of the lower classes, of which the *Cronaca dello Squittinatore* (1378–87) is one of the last examples[18]) and rich in a genuine civic sense, which is not to be found later.

The theme of the need for social *rapport* was consistently present in all the literature of the time, and was found even in the religious devotion of S. Bernardino: 'True nobility does not lie in idleness, but in the activities carried out by you yourself, and your family, and your city.'[19]

But the new class, released from the bonds of collective solidarity, required culture to justify the individual values on which its success depended, and which were all the more indispensable because of the lack of general traditional security. For this reason, while it adopted some original themes of the humanist movement for its own, it ended by requiring that intellectuals should renounce all political activity or by demanding strict obedience from those who did remain involved in it, like Bruni, chancellor from 1427 to 1444, the last decade of his life, and his successors Marsuppini (1444–53) and Bracciolini (1453–8); if they refused this, they were forced into opposition, like Filelfo and Rinuccini.

Brunelleschi was of the same generation as Bruni and Bracciolini, and during his last years he enjoyed comparable prestige; his activities shielded him in part from the open polemics of the men of letters, but his position was similar to theirs, still sufficiently linked to the civic ideal of the previous generation – that of Salutati – to remain a part of the traditional community (Brunelleschi was also *priore* for the district of S. Giovanni in 1425), but already sufficiently confident in their autonomy to accept a direct and personal relationship with the new ruling class. From the start Alberti and the artists of the following generation were dependent on the approbation of those in power, upon whom all opportunities for work now depended.

The events of this period show the ambivalent and unpredictable character of the culture-power relationship; generally speaking, the stock of forms and symbols elaborated by humanist culture was partly brought into being by the demands of the new ruling class, but in its turn it had a crucial influence on the fortunes of this class, giving its undertakings the prestige of the classical tradition and the clarity which derived from a system of predetermined, eloquent and recognizable forms. In this way the contribution of writers and artists transcended particular political circumstances, though it was partly linked to them, and was projected into the future beyond the ups and downs of the Renaissance ruling class.

Brunelleschi's work: the machines and the dome

Brunelleschi's contemporaries and immediate successors have given us two different definitions of the work of Brunelleschi (1377–1446), echoed in the two epitaphs quoted by Vasari: the first, by Marsuppini and still there to be seen, celebrates Filippo for his superb art, whose evidence is the dome, '*huius celeberrimi templi mira testudo*' and the '*plures machinae divino ingenio ab eo adinventatae*'; the second defines him as '*antiquae architecturae instaurator*'. We may still accept these two definitions and, by considering the cultural world of Brunelleschi from the outside, attempt a critical analysis of their content.

According to the first definition, Brunelleschi was a brilliant, infallible technician, who succeeded where others blundered; he was not a scientist, but he had recourse to the mediation of scientists, such as Paolo Toscanelli, and was the first to introduce into building a rigorously scientific attitude, though one that lacked any theoretical approval ('he was not a lettered man', wrote Vasari, but he had an 'excellent memory' and was able to argue well 'from his own practices and experience'[20]). He may be considered as the first great specialist capable of distinguishing clearly between theory and practice and, because of this attitude, we must seriously consider the claim of his fifteenth-century biographer, who attributed to him, among other things, the invention of linear perspective. The principles of the perspective method were contained implicitly in medieval optical theory, but superfluous theoretical references (which encumbered Ghiberti's discussion in the third book of the *Commentari*) had to be eliminated; all that needed to be retained were the notions needed for the

exact formulation of the problem of three-dimensional representation on a flat surface.

Brunelleschi concerned himself with mechanics on at least four occasions: as a young man when he built clocks, when he made the machines to lift building materials for the work on the dome, when he patented the transport ship and when he organized the machinery for the representation of paradise in the church of S. Felice in Piazza.

The machines for S. Maria del Fiore were based on the use of cylinders with varying diameters to roll up ropes, and the worm screw, which functioned as a speed-reducer and braking device. These mechanisms had long been known, and Brunelleschi's merit lay in the technological formulation he chose to resolve his particular problems; the machinery for S. Felice belonged to the tradition of the medieval automata, and Vasari informs us that in his time 'they had completely fallen out of use'.[21]

The judgment of the old writers, who associated this mechanical activity with the building of the dome of S. Maria del Fiore, must be regarded as critically well founded even today. In fact not only had the constructional organism already been determined by the work of Francesco Talenti, who settled the definitive plan in 1360, enlarging that of Arnolfo, and of Giovanni di Lapo Ghini who, towards the end of the fourteenth century, decided to raise the impost of the dome about 13 metres above the roofing of the nave and aisles, building the octagonal drum with the circular windows; but the diameter of $41\frac{1}{2}$ metres was near the maximum limit possible for masonry domes of any type, and the outline of the vault was therefore almost entirely dictated by static requirements (the biggest masonry domes have a diameter of 41–3 metres, and even for the dome of St Peter's, which has almost the same diameter, the steep outline was seen to be inevitable at the moment of construction; the problem is comparable to that of a present-day bridge spanning over 1,000

15   *Bust of Filippo Brunelleschi. S. Maria del Fiore, Florence*

metres, whose static solution is, broadly speaking, unique and inevitable).

Brunelleschi's particular achievement lay, in fact, in roofing the dome, not in having chosen its shape; to succeed, and to avoid complete centering in timber which would have been too costly, or perhaps indeed impossible, the roof had to be self-supporting not only when the building was completed, but throughout every intermediate phase. All the features of the construction were subordinated to this primary requirement; the dome was outlined 'in five-part form in the corners',[22] i.e. at the intersections of the faces, and for the initial tracing provision was made for eight wooden centerings almost 40 metres long; the proposed thickness was 7 feet at the impost and 5 feet at the top; this vault was strengthened by twenty-four ribs, so as to break down the extensive surfaces of the side into three parts, and on these ribs a second outer skin was laid, less thick ($2\frac{1}{2}$ feet to $1\frac{1}{4}$) 'to protect it from the damp, and to give it greater magnificence and a swelling form'.[23] This phrase, which has led to the supposition that Brunelleschi wished to differentiate the outer surface from the inner,[24] must be interpreted bearing in mind that the two layers were always parallel, the protrusion of the ribs being uniform from impost to keystone. The outline of the outer layer is modelled on that of the inner, and increases it by a constant measurement; this device, like the original decision to raise the impost of the dome on the drum, stresses the importance of the dome in relation to the church; the two decisions tend towards the same end, and are linked by an obvious continuity; the width of the drum, too, initially determined the gap between the two layers, and perhaps, by the last decades of the fourteenth century, already suggested the idea of the double dome (although the inner layer was to be in stone, and the outer one possibly of wood and lead, as Sanpaolesi has recently suggested).[25]

For the actual positioning of the materials Brunelleschi thought of the 'herring-bone' pattern, possibly taking Roman ruins or medieval practice as his starting-point, and proposing it with full knowledge of the facts; he had tried out this method in the second model for the dome and in the small chapel for Schiatta Ridolfi in S. Jacopo Soprarno and then he adapted it to the much thicker roof of the real dome. We know that the overseers of the works had envisaged a stone vault supported by a series of tie-beams in masonry and timber; in the early phases Brunelleschi requested that stone should be replaced by brick and prepared a wooden tie-beam, but proved its pointlessness, so that no more were made. The herring-bone

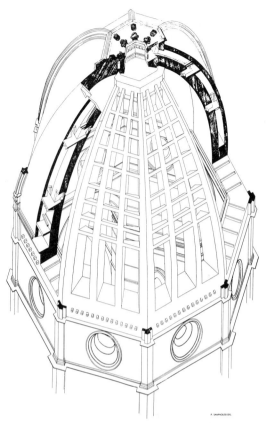

16 *Axonometric projection of the structure of the dome of S. Maria del Fiore (from Sanpaolesi)*
17 *Antonio da Sangallo the Younger: 'Rounded vaulting of medium-sized bricks as it is made without centering in Florence'. Uffizi, drawing no. 900A*

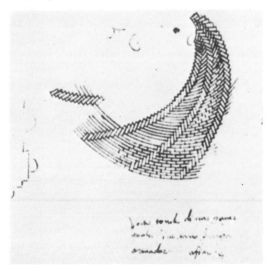

pattern was used systematically for the roofs of the other works by Brunelleschi, and was to become common in Tuscany at the beginning of the sixteenth century.

According to Sanpaolesi, Brunelleschi had originally suggested a ribbed dome – like the later domes of the sacristy of S. Lorenzo, the Pazzi chapel and S. Spirito – covered with a domical vault; later he decided that the domical vault was inevitable both for the ceiling and for its covering, and that it was necessary to change from the hemispherical form to the pointed form.[26]

Therefore the rationality of Brunelleschi's contribution lies in his recognition of the necessary and constant features of the solution, already contained in the given circumstances, while setting aside illogical features dependent on the persistence of habits now outdated.

This constructional undertaking – the most important one promoted by the aristocratic government to crown a vast programme of public works – symbolized the spirit of continuity typical of the whole programme, and was inspired by the desire to interpret, or rather to revive the character of the old unfinished buildings. But the traditional collective organization was no longer able to guarantee this continuity; what was needed was that a single designer should take up the traditional themes, one capable personally of guaranteeing the rationality of the process, even if it meant conflict with the collective bodies.

In this sense Brunelleschi's contribution was new and revolutionary; successive biographers, dwelling on Brunelleschi's devices to convince the overseers of works, then to free himself from collaboration with Ghiberti and to refuse the demands of the foremen, show that they had understood the novelty of his behaviour, even if their accounts were constructed in a rhetorical and conventional way. The care Brunelleschi took in hiding his secrets is certainly not an invention; one need only imagine the difficulty of his position, as

he fought alone against a whole set of traditional prejudices, habits and rules, and was obliged to use cold facts to gain himself a reputation previously unrecognized in institutions and in usage. His haughty and polemical temperament, like that of Le Corbusier, was the result of the constant strain of keeping to his chosen policy.

The famous episode of the strike is told as follows by Vasari:[27]

'At length the chains around the eight sides were completed, and the builders worked with spirit and a will; but as Filippo required more of them than before, and found fault daily with the building or some particular, they became discontented. The leaders then took counsel together, saying that the work was difficult and dangerous, and they would not go on with it except at high wages, although their pay had been higher than the usual rate. In this way they hoped to be revenged on Filippo, and to benefit themselves. This dispute was equally displeasing to the wardens and to Filippo, and the latter, after thinking over the matter, took the step one Saturday morning of dismissing all his workmen. Finding themselves thus dismissed, and not knowing what the outcome would be, these men waited results, full of ill-will. But the following Monday Filippo set ten Lombards on the work and stood over them himself, saying, do this and that, and in one day he succeeded in teaching them so much that they continued to work there for many weeks. On the other hand, the builders who saw themselves dismissed and deprived of employment as well as put to shame, since they had no other work which was equally desirable, sent representatives to Filippo, that they were willing to return, pressing him to take them. But he kept them in suspense for many days, pretending that he did not want them, and at length engaged them at less wages than they had received before. Thus instead of gaining advantage for themselves, and being revenged on Filippo, they suffered loss and contumely.'

This episode, however it took place in reality, certainly indicates the break in the class solidarity between designer and workers, in as far as the former aimed to identify himself with the new ruling class, and recognized only a subordinate position for the others. In 1434 Brunelleschi also refused to pay the tribute to the carpenters' and masons' guild and was supported in this dispute by the works department of the cathedral. This rift – which was to be the historical result of the revolution started by Brunelleschi – emerges from now on as an organizational necessity, given the novelty of his mode of procedure, which meant that he could not count on the traditional executive apparatus.

In fact Brunelleschi, contrary to what was to happen later on, personally took upon himself all the responsibilities of planning and execution, down to the smallest details. The biography attributed to Manetti insists with technical precision on this list of professional duties and also on the difficulties of communication between him and the executors:

'During his life not a small stone or brick was placed which he did not wish to examine to see whether it was correct and if it was well-fired and cleaned: something which no care was expended upon afterward, since today attention is paid only to what appears to be economical, and stones from the river and rough bricks and all sorts of crudity are employed. The care he gave to the mortar was wonderful. He personally went to the brickyard regarding the stones and the baking, the sand and lime mixture, and whatever was required.'[28]

When he discussed these things with the stonemasons they could not understand him at all. . . . For that purpose he also went to the ironmongers for various and diverse objects in iron which even the craftsmen understood with difficulty. He then was with the joiners with new methods and new conceptions and provisions for various kinds of object that it was believed no one else had even conceived of: e.g. lights for use in areas for climbing up and down and avoiding bumps, falls in the dark and dangers to those who had to go up to those places. These were useful not only for avoiding danger, but also for freeing those who used them from fear and apprehension.'[29]

To make himself understood by the workmen, Brunelleschi used to make models 'in soft clay and then in wax and wood. Actually those large turnips, called goblets, which come on the market in Winter were useful for making the small models and for explaining things to them. . . .'[30] Hence the need for his continual presence on the site, and the impossibility of his absenting himself from his work, or of supervising it from a distance.

Since the shape of the dome was rationally determined, the margin of inventive freedom allowed to the designer lay rather in the decorative details.

In their choice Brunelleschi amply demonstrated his capacity for invention of forms, and fixed the visual image of the great building with incomparable assurance. Inside, the dome is a great empty space, a sort of courtyard on to which the body of the nave and aisles and the three apses opened, along the orthogonal axis; in this way he avoided stressing the corners of the octagonal vault with intrusive ribs or other elements, and created a smooth surface, which was to be decorated with mosaics like the similar dome of the baptistery (subsequently it was covered with the frescoes (Fig. 18) by Vasari and Federico Zuccaro, between 1572 and 1579, using the anchorage already arranged by Brunelleschi as scaffolding).

Even today, entering by the doors of the façade and going down the church as far as the tribune, one is struck by the difference

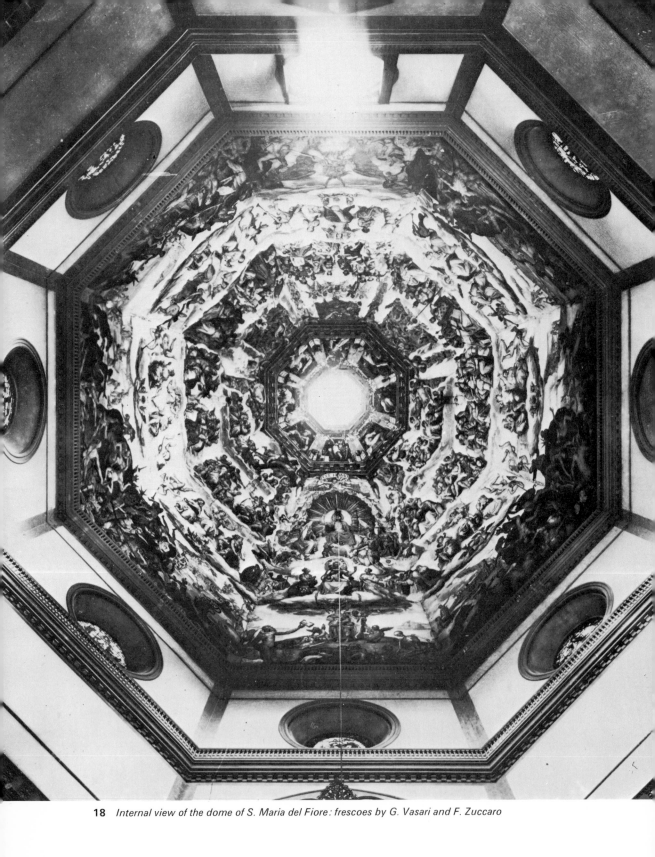

18 *Internal view of the dome of S. Maria del Fiore: frescoes by G. Vasari and F. Zuccaro*

between the initial impression and the final one; for someone standing in the nave the empty space of the dome appears as a distant background, definitely set back from the architecture of the fourteenth-century pillars and ceilings; but standing under the dome, it is the body of the nave and aisles that seems thrust into the distance, and takes on a subordinate value, not unlike that of the apses, so that the central symmetry of the enormous octagonal void is strengthened.

Much more difficult was the problem of the external detail, from the moment when the dome – rising over Giovanni di Lapo Ghini's drum – could no longer simply act as the final nexus of the apsidal structures, but overwhelmed them with its simple and grandiose volume.

Brunelleschi abandoned any attempt at echoing the minute design of the structures below, and from the outset concentrated only on the chromatic effect of the eight gleaming 'marble crests' which divide the vast expanses of red tiles and converge on the lantern.

The 'crests' correspond to the position of the eight corner ribs, but are not placed intentionally in relation to them (which would have implied needlessly underlining their function *vis-à-vis* the other sixteen in the intermediate fields); rather they mark the intersections of the overall surfaces, and give form to the main curves of the dome. The dome was traced from the corners, and the corners describe arcs of a circle, while the intermediate webs, sectioned according to the principal line, are elliptical in shape. The crests act as it were as stone replicas of the eight centerings used for the tracing, which we talked about earlier.

In fact the tracing, not the building, was uppermost in Brunelleschi's mind in conceiving his dome; by virtue of this choice the great structure, crowning the fourteenth-century cathedral, became comparable with the new organisms which Brunelleschi was designing during those years, and summed up the aspirations of all the Florentine artistic *avant-garde*.

In 1432 the form of the closing ring was discussed, a complete model was prepared and an octagon was decided upon; in 1436 Brunelleschi made the model for the lantern and in 1438 work began on the marble pieces required; assembly began only in 1446, the year of Brunelleschi's death, and was completed in 1471.

The choice of the octagonal form for the closing ring anticipated the fundamental character of the lantern, which gathers together the circle of ribs and concludes the general design of the dome. When they reach the ring, the ribs run round it so as to frame the fields of red brick at the top as well, and prepare a broad platform from which the octagonal prism of the lantern rises, considerably set back. Seen from below, this gives an impression of a sudden burst which underlines the eccentric and fantastical character of the forms used; but the graphic tallying between the pilasters at the angles of the lantern and the ribs is emphasized by the buttresses with the upturned consoles, which span the platform and turn the basic octagonal symmetry into a delightful spatial fan.

This strange complex at the top of the dome performs the function of nexus which was now lacking at the impost, and thus emphasizes the independence of the great dome from the church. The solid elements of the lantern intentionally outweigh the voids so as to stand out from a distance; the alternation of solid elements and openings is concluded above by the solemn progression which includes the cornice (higher than usual), the crown of niches and pinnacles, and the pyramid, still so concise in outline, that supports the ball (Fig. 22).

Brunelleschi's details give the dome an exceptional importance as part of the landscape; the octagonal dome – outlined by the white ribs on the red bricks – can be seen clearly from many miles away, while the complex mass of the cathedral merges with the surrounding buildings; in this way the

19 *The dome of S. Maria del Fiore*

20 *The dome amid the surrounding townscape*

22 *The lantern of the dome*

23   *Detail of the lantern*

24, 25 *Views of the dome from via dei Servi and from via dell'Oriuolo*

dome remains suspended over the city and detached from its expanse, entering into relation with the whole scene of the valley and surrounding hills. 'The mountains about Florence look like its fellows', observed Vasari;[31] indeed its scale, midway between the works of man and those of nature, makes it an inevitable landmark in every view, for as far as the presence of the city makes itself felt over the surrounding countryside (Figs 24–28).

No building can hold its own against the great roof, whose curved faces look on to the whole arc of the sky, right to the sweep of the horizon; thus the dome stands above the streets and squares of the town, with their varying lights, and reflects only the unchanging course of the sun throughout the days and seasons. But the fairly pronounced angle between the various faces and the clarity of

26   *The dome amid surrounding buildings*

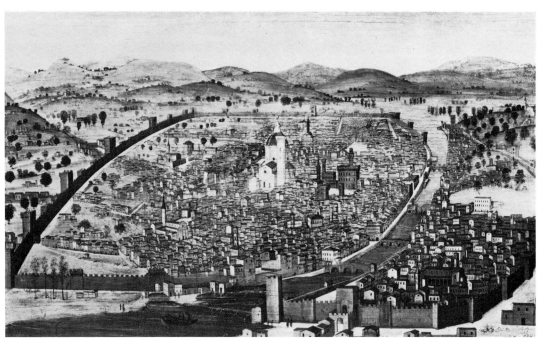

27 *A fifteenth-century view of Florence. H. Bier collection, London*

28 *View of Florence from S. Miniato al Monte*

the ribs, due equally to their actual prominence and to their colour, prevents its ever being seen as a bodiless silhouette or as a coloured mass floating in the sky; the geometrical device with its radial symmetry – made firm and bright by the enormous volume of air in which it stands – always gives the great mass a three-dimensional solidity and precise orientation in relation to the circle of the panorama. The arched ribs firmly separate the diametral planes of the building, and project them into the landscape like an ideal compass-card. The centripetal structure of the city, evoked as a literary image in the *Laudatio* of Leonardo Bruni, thirty years earlier, was summarized in an elementary and precise architectural form, which emerged as the distinctive element of the urban landscape in no uncertain terms.

But the simple and grandiose treatment of the dome, so effective from a distance, does definitely compromise the relationship between the dome and the church beneath it, considered from close to. In 1438 Brunelleschi built the closed tribunes above the four free façades of the drum, which complete a rough octagonal symmetry, and possibly designed the marble covering of the drum at the level of the round windows, slightly lightening the motifs of the lower inlay work; but the contrast in scale between dome and support was still very pronounced from close to, and the crucial problem of the decorative link at the impost of the roof, where the 1420 report foresaw a 'gallery . . . with consoles and openwork parapets' or 'two galleries, one above the other, above a much-decorated cornice'[32] was never to be approached with conviction, leaving the present-day unfaced strip from which the ribs spring unexpectedly.

Brunelleschi's contemporaries, and Leon Battista Alberti first of all, immediately celebrated the civic meaning of the immense construction, 'ample to cover with its shadow all the Tuscan people'. It was the visible result of the new interest in engineering which Alberti found when he returned from exile, and it was placed between past and future, as a symbol of the *patria*, 'adorned above all others';[33] it concluded the traditional image of the city, and hinted at the heights of future possibilities. Even today Brunelleschi's dome appears as unique, suspended between two eras. Basically it is a Gothic work, not because of its pointed shape but because of its organic links with Arnolfo's building and because of the importance of its structural commitment; as in the great thirteenth- and fourteenth-century cathedrals the intention was to reach the limits of the possibilities inherent in a given building system. At the same time it had a new formal deliberateness largely detached from the surrounding buildings and based on the extravagance of the geometrical outline – and it was the first important work where the architect was not only the high-level adviser to a collective body of executors, but the only one responsible for the form, decoration, structure and organization of the work; it therefore marks the transition towards a new architectural experience, whose methodological foundations Brunelleschi himself was working out.

Brunelleschi's work: perspective and the return to classical forms

The second epitaph recorded by Vasari praises Brunelleschi as the restorer of classical architecture.

The fifteenth-century biographer, too, attributes above all to Brunelleschi the glory of having brought back 'that manner of building, called *alla romana* or *alla antica*';[34] he is the first to tell of Brunelleschi's journeys to Rome with Donatello, and of his many-sided interests in matters of antiquity:

'He observed the method and the symmetry of the ancients' way of building . . . since this appeared very different from the method in use at that time, it impressed him greatly. And he decided that while he looked at the sculpture of the ancients to give no less time to that order and method . . . which is in the abutments and thrusts of buildings, [their] masses, lines and *invenzioni* according to and in relation with their function, and to do the same for the decorations. . . . He decided to rediscover the fine and highly skilled method of building and the harmonious proportions of the ancients and how they might, without defects, be employed with convenience and economy. . . . Noting the great and complex elements . . . did not make him change his mind about understanding the methods and means they used.'

(Here the author recalls Brunelleschi's mechanical competence and links his observations to the constructional problems of the roofing of the dome.)

There follows the account of how Brunelleschi and Donatello[35]

'together made rough drawings of almost all the buildings in Rome and in many places beyond the walls, with measurements of the widths and heights as far as they were able to ascertain [the latter] by estimation, and also the lengths etc. In many places they had excavations made in order to see the junctures of the membering of the buildings and their types – whether square, polygonal, completely round, oval, or whatever. When possible they estimated the heights from base to base for the height and similarly the entablatures and roofs from the foundations. They then drew the elevations on strips of parchment graphs with numbers and symbols which Filippo alone understood. . . .

Filippo spent many years at this work. He found a number of differences in . . . the masonry as well as in the types of columns, bases, capitals, architraves, friezes, cornices and pediments, and differences between the masses of the temples and the diameters of the columns; by means of close observation he clearly recognized the

characteristics of each type: Ionic, Doric, Tuscan, Corinthian and Attic. As may still be seen in his buildings today, he used most of them at the time and place he considered best.'

This account cannot be taken literally, because its author was certainly influenced by what was happening in his own time, i.e. the last years of the fifteenth century, when the habit of visiting and drawing plans of Roman monuments was widespread. The insistence on showing that Brunelleschi concerned himself with every aspect is connected with the general tone of apologia; the fifteenth-century biographer and Vasari insisted upon Brunelleschi's concurrent interest in building technique and architectural forms, with the aim of reinforcing both the technical and formal innovations he introduced with the authority of the ancients.

As far as structural technique was concerned, reference to ancient models is largely a fiction; the procedures used by Brunelleschi for the dome and other work, quite apart from the mechanical solutions used for his machines, are basically independent of ancient technology, and almost always find an exact equivalent in medieval experience, as scrutinized by a sharp and independent intellect.

But the range of forms used in the works after the dome of S. Maria del Fiore was undeniably derived from Roman models. As far as this was concerned the claim of the Renaissance biographers is literally true, and needs merely to be restricted.

In fact the types of ground plan and volumes typical of Brunelleschi's buildings, except perhaps for the centrally planned Rotonda degli Angeli, are quite different from those of antiquity. Surveys of the buildings drawn in Rome, 'whether square, completely round, or oval',[36] of which the fifteenth-century biographer speaks, and the fuller one reported by Vasari ('round and square and octagonal churches, basilicas, aqueducts, baths, arches, coliseums, amphi-theatres'[37]) are probably literary additions dependent upon the demands of post-Albertian culture, and are in fact foreign to Brunelleschi's architecture.

On the other hand the forms of the individual building elements – columns, pillars, cornices, arches, balustrades, tympana, corbels, etc. – are scrupulous reproductions of classical models, and repeated without important variations in works after 1418 (the loggia of the Innocenti, the church and sacristy of S. Lorenzo, the Pazzi chapel, the sala dei capitani in the Palazzo di Parte Guelfa, S. Spirito, the Rotonda degli Angeli).

The sixteenth-century writer Vasari was particularly well-qualified to assess the importance of this choice:[38]

'his only concern being architecture, which had been corrupted, studying the good ancient orders and not the barbarous Gothic style. . . . He then studied the Doric, Ionic and Corinthian orders, one after the other, and to such purpose that he was able to reconstruct in his mind's eye the aspect of Rome as it stood before it fell.'

Modern criticism, reacting to this judgment, has emphasized the constant classical inspiration in the Tuscan architecture of the Middle Ages, and hence the continuity between Brunelleschi and local tradition; precedents of Brunelleschi's style have been pointed to in the façade of S. Miniato, in the exterior of the baptistery and in SS. Apostoli.

As in literature, 'intense activity to re-discover the specific contents of the most solemnly hallowed Renaissance attitudes in the medieval past had a number of facile successes'.[39] But this type of claim – which is technically vague when applied to architecture – merely emphasizes the original attitude of the new culture, in relation to already known subject-matter as well. Medieval writers and architects communicated with the classical world through a tradition which was regarded as unbroken. Brunelleschi knew

this tradition, but ended it and broke it off, precisely by seeking a direct relationship with the classical models – in Rome and elsewhere – and using them with new criteria of selection and precision. He, like the humanists of his time, looked to the antique 'as something apart from ourselves, lovingly reconstructed but for this very reason no longer an intimate part of us'.[40]

The essence of this new relationship in architecture was precisely this distinction between the elements and the buildings themselves.

The distributive and constructional types of Roman buildings, linked to the demands of their time, were possibly studied by Brunelleschi – as later by many generations of artists – but with no attempt to reproduce them. On the other hand, the conventional forms of the architectural orders and their complements, which the Romans had taken from the Hellenic tradition, were once again recognized as ideal models, suited to transforming the infinitely variable repertoire of the Gothic tradition into a finite and standardized one.

It is essential to analyse the consequences of this choice which, starting with the details, completely altered the nature of architectural organisms and the process of planning:

1   The forms of the architectural elements were not planned *a posteriori*, building by building, but defined *a priori*, in their proportions and most of the decorative detail, that is, as we say today, they were standardized. The margin of variation which remained was gradually restricted within precise limits, and was not to compromise the recognizability of the forms. This pull towards standardization was so strong, for Brunelleschi, that it led him to restrict further the field of classical models, utilizing in practice only the Corinthian order, to which he might have been drawn by familiarity with medieval Florentine examples; but, whatever the source from which he drew his documentation, it is

certain that his choice was a deliberate one.

In fourteenth-century experience, in Florence, a special importance was already accorded to the creation of details, and people had become accustomed to considering them as independent matters: one need think only of the competition for the pillar of S. Maria del Fiore. But the idea of standardization was unknown before Brunelleschi; every decision, down to the last detail, was always taken occasion by occasion, and this habit – together with the need for a high standard of execution – had by now produced an impossible dispersal of energies. By abstracting recurrent building elements in single plans, and defining them conclusively by reference to the ancient orders, a new distribution of energies was obtained, the very one that had made possible the attainment of the exemplary perfection of Greek and Roman models. The process of planning was thus staggered over various phases: a certain number of elements entered into the planning equation as known terms, and were adjusted with small corrections: in this way an ideal form of collaboration with the ancients was established, on a pre-arranged and limited terrain, which could be repeated on other occasions and carried out by other planners, whose contribution would be commensurable with the previous ones. By using a series of known terms, the designer could concentrate every time on the particular unknowns of his case: since the elements were defined, he had to concern himself with their assembly, and this operation – which could be defined as leaving the form of the elements on one side – became the nub of the new method of planning.

2 The standardized elements based on ancient models were not independent pieces, but were linked among themselves by similarly standardized proportional relationships, and formed certain combinations which were called architectural orders.

The column or pilaster – composed of three parts, base, shaft and capital – was always associated with an entablature, composed in its turn of three superimposed layers, architrave, frieze and cornice. The presence of the entablature defined the two possible positions of the arch, which might be placed above the cornice or might meet the architrave at a tangent; the arch would be finished off by a fascia similar to that of the architrave, and in the second case the fascia might also be repeated on the impost blocks.

Having thus limited the range of possible associations, the composition of the building could be analysed and reduced to a geometrical schema – which defined the respective position of the typical elements – simple enough to be grasped clearly through the distribution of the elements.

Even in the Gothic period buildings, pictured in three-dimensional space, were frequently represented by linear geometrical figures: the sketches in the notebook of Villard de Honnecourt (Fig. 29) are examples of this. But the figure always served as an abbreviated representation of a structural cage, from which it was not detached

29 *Ground plan of a Cistercian church from the notebook of Villard de Honnecourt*

mentally. In fact constructional and decorative elements formed an open system where no measurement and no outer limit appear favoured in relation to the others; every geometrical layout – even if precise in itself, in so far as it was made up of a combination of regular figures, like that put forward by Stornaloco in 1391 for the cathedral of Milan (Fig. 30) – worked only as an approximate indication and could be met with in the completed building only with a certain degree of inexactitude. (As is well known, Stornaloco's diagram defined the cross-section of the building, and therefore the width and height of equilateral triangles; in this case it seems obvious that the width of nave and aisles would have been measured on the axes of the pillars, but the measurement of the heights is more problematical. They might have been taken from the lowest point of the keystone, from the intersection of the masonry fields which fill in the triangles between the ribs, or from a higher level, as far from the crossing of the ribs as the axis of the pillars from the impost of the ribs themselves.)

But the parts of an architectural order formed a closed system, linked by certain internal relations, and the whole order was connected to the other elements of the building by certain main measurements, which came into play only for the purposes of the general scheme.

In this way the scheme could refer unambiguously to the actual building, because it became possible to fix its points of application exactly as regards the building structures: if the scheme were to be subordinated to abstract calculations of proportion, these would lose their mysterious and cabbalistic character, because they served to link a limited number of measurements to one another: those which, in the assembling of the architectural orders, functioned as independent variables.

Therefore the standardization of the elements of building brought up the problem of a general representation of geometric space,

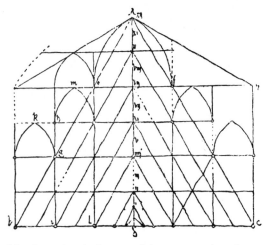

30   *Stornaloco's diagram of the cross-section of Milan cathedral*

to be made concrete by replacing linear elements with the thickness and densities of the standardized elements.

The conformation of the elements depended on the position they occupied in the scheme, and the elements which occupied equivalent positions had to be identical. This requirement – inevitable in Brunelleschi's methodology – was in complete contrast with the medieval habit of considering every form as perpetually variable until the moment of execution, and the building as an ever open site, where the stratification of successive activities could be read quite clearly; this habit could not be changed immediately, and it operated, to some degree, even in the buildings begun by Brunelleschi and continued some time later, where not only were distributional and constructional modifications introduced, but also some typical details like capitals were slightly varied; these variations, indeed, have been used to reconstruct the different phases of execution.[41]

Furthermore, the new mode of composition demanded a kind of abbreviated perception of the single elements, in fact just sufficient to establish their typical conformation. All the qualities beyond this level of perception could be evaluated in later examination, but they lost their old relationship

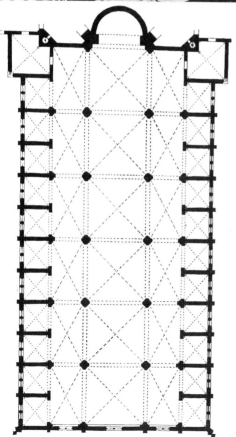

31–33 *View, ground plan and interior of S. Petronio, Bologna*

34   *The campanile of S. Maria del Fiore and baptistery, Florence*

with the architectural organism. In this way the exhausting late Gothic passion for total perfection in the execution of details disappeared, and naturally their quality was already declining, as Brandi has observed, as early as S. Lorenzo and S. Spirito.[42]

It is reasonable to conclude that Brunelleschi's researches into linear perspective preceded or at least were contemporaneous with the designs that document the methodological turning-point discussed so far (the Innocenti, the S. Lorenzo sacristy) and that the studies of the reproduction of space in painting had led Brunelleschi to approach the more general problem of architectural representation.

The text of the fifteenth-century biographer is clear: the two panels by Brunelleschi, representing the two Florentine squares of the baptistery and the Signoria, are illustrative applications of a rule for 'setting down properly and rationally the reductions and enlargements of near and distant objects as perceived by the eye of man'[43] and are presented so that the representation could be compared with the truth. This rule 'that is essential to whatever has been accomplished since his time in that area'[44] was common knowledge from 1425 onwards, and we shall have more to say about it later on.

As far as architecture is concerned, it is relevant to consider not the mechanism of the 'legitimate construction' – and even less to look for imaginary formal analogies with architectural planning – but the premises of this construction, which were common to painting and architecture.

Linear perspective differed from conventional methods used previously in that it made possible, with the method of projection and fixed units of measurement, a precise evaluation of distances as regards the picture plane; in fact pictorial representation was required to show clearly and truthfully the shape and position of the objects represented, so that one could pass from the representation

to the real model through the reverse process, i.e. the reconstruction of perspective.

Perspective made known the spatial relationships between objects, not their absolute measurements; it was held that the perception of relationships was sufficient without the knowledge of the measurements. In painting this state of affairs was concealed by the presence of human figures (or other objects whose dimensions were familiar), whose stature introduced an approximate reference to measurement and it became possible to establish, by comparison, the position of a hypothetical observer, whose eye would coincide with the viewpoint; but this case apart, perspective presupposes an awareness of space – understood as a system of relationships – independent of the objects that are placed in it, and also makes possible an abstract representation of this space, by means of the elements of reference – principal point and distance circle – which precede every representation of places or concrete things.

Perspective representation can be called objective in that, among the features of the things represented, the geometrical ones are regarded as essential, and of these the proportional and projective features rather than those of measurement; the word 'form' thus implicitly loses its complex metaphysical meaning – *forma vel essentia* – to assume a simpler and more tangible one – *forma vel figura*. This change preceded the future distinction between primary and secondary qualities and possibly prepared the way for it, acting on habits of perception, and produced the purely quantitative interpretation of sensible reality – *res extensa* – which was to help to revolutionize the knowledge of the world through the application of the mathematical methods of the natural sciences.

Applied to architecture, the concept of perspective space selected a homogeneous group from among the features of the products of building – the geometrical and proportional ones – to be defined separately from and prior to the others; it insisted that choices should follow a certain order, and in particular it separated the definition of the forms from that of their relation with the human scale (and made possible a series of new and exciting effects of dimension, although, ultimately, it heralded a progressive detachment of planning from the physical measurements of man); in this way it made it possible, in a precise and general way, to pose the problems of the relationships between the elements of the urban scene, and to resolve, ultimately, the whole of the built-up environment into a system of interlinked relationships.

The links between architecture and painting do not lie in a similarity between methods of operation, but in the adaptation of the two methods to the common objective, which was the most precise possible assessment of spatial structures; the preferable relationships, in architecture, were those which when put into perspective made possible an easier measuring of the three dimensions, that is to say, simple relationships and in particular the rhythmic succession of identical elements; both in the theoretical instructions of Alberti,[45] of Piero della Francesca[46] and Leonardo,[47] and in the practice of fifteenth-century painting the recurrent problem, which exemplifies the perspective method, was the representation of a squared field, where the various squares appeared reduced in proportion to their distance; the equivalent of this preference, in architecture, was not the use of diminishing elements, but the use of identical ones, or ones linked by easily recognizable relationships, expressed in whole numbers.

As we have already said, the application of the standardized elements derived from antiquity and recognizable for their intrinsic proportions was essential to this end, eliminating as it did the habitual links between form and dimension. The standard elements, by their repetition, drew attention to the recurring structures of the new architectural

organisms. The placing of these elements in perspective space, in its turn, substantially altered their original meaning, and gave them a completely new conceptual character.

The form and proportions of the architectural orders – which in Greek architecture formed the substance of an autonomous constructional language – were used in Roman architecture to translate the articulations of vaulted organisms, irreducible to traditional visual conditions, into plastic terms, as walls. This gave rise to an immense range of possibilities for associations between the orders and masonry structures, though never one that was complete and general, because the single solutions were linked to the peculiarities of the organisms in question, and the types of organisms in their turn were less numerous than those made possible by masonry technique, because of the reluctance to experiment with associations different from those already successfully tried out.

But Florentine artists started from the experience of late Gothic space, which was continuous and isotropic and which was to be made measurable and rationally ordered; in Roman buildings they looked for the principles of a lost method, not for a repertoire of ready solutions, and they tended to make this method general, not being bound to the same conceptual obstacles. One need think only of the simplest example of associations, that of the arch set between two columns and the entablature, as in the outer wall of the Colosseum and so many other ancient buildings; the support of the arch ends with a small version of a cornice, and is not comparable, for its part, to an architectural order, in that the arch is conceived as cut out of a continuous wall, and there remains only the problem of providing its front, where it stands out from the masonry mass, with a frame which defines its proportions (hence the rule, later enunciated by Alberti, that arches should be supported by piers and entablatures by columns). But in S. Lorenzo and S. Spirito Brunelleschi supported the arches and roofs of the aisles on a low order and circumscribed them with a high one, which acted as a support for the covering arches of the nave, i.e. he arranged a framework, formed of two different orders, which was placed in space in its own right and defined the distribution of all the masonry elements.

The architectural result has a systematic spirit completely different from the ancient models; its positive results, lucid and cogent, may be compared to those of fifteenth-century Latin, purified by the humanists on Ciceronian examples, but animated by a new life and new need for communication; 'a new Latin – as it has been said – in which the old complexity gave way to modern fluency'.[48]

The mental distinction between the plastic treatment of the details and the perspective structure of the building was always clear. The standardized elements, which helped to emphasize this structure, were also instrumental in the crisis that befell the building types with which they were associated, together with the traditional details, and in the invention of a series of new and virtually infinite types. Brunelleschi 'used to say that if he were to have to make one hundred models of churches or other buildings, he would make them all varied and different'.[49] The following generation selected a certain number of canonic types from this potential variety, and codified their use, but did not exhaust the impetus of Brunelleschi's method, which continued to have its effect throughout the centuries that followed and started a surge of activity so vast as almost to translate into reality the theoretical infinity of the possible combinations.

We must now consider more closely the articulations used by Brunelleschi in some of his works: the Ospedale degli Innocenti, the churches of S. Lorenzo and S. Spirito and the Pazzi chapel.

About 1419 Brunelleschi designed the Ospedale degli Innocenti for the Arte della Seta, the sacristy of S. Lorenzo for Giovanni de' Medici, who was buried there in 1428, and perhaps began to work on the plan for the renovation of the church of S. Lorenzo.

The hospital was positioned so as to create a regular square in front of the church of the Annunziata (completed by Antonio da Sangallo the Elder, who built a second building symmetrical to Brunelleschi's in the early sixteenth century); as far as we know, Brunelleschi fixed the general distribution (with the external loggia and two cloisters round which are grouped the dormitories and service buildings; this was the uniform scheme of the earlier hospitals by Bonifacio Lupi and Memmo Balducci) and he provided a design for the loggia; work began in 1421 and Brunelleschi supervised it until 1424. His successors then altered the original plan, but we have not enough evidence to distinguish their contribution from the original one by Brunelleschi (Figs 35–7).

The entrance loggia is formed of nine bays on a square plan, as is evident from the shape of the sail-vaulting which Brunelleschi regularly substituted from now on for the usual cross-vaulting. In the round arches the ratio between span and rise is fixed at the start, so that all the elevation measurements depend upon a single factor – the height of the support of the arches – as the ground plan measurements depend upon the side of the bay, i.e. the interaxis between the columns.

This was the opposite procedure to that of Gothic architecture, where the pointed arch was needed to make the rise independent of the span, and to allow the number of combinations between the vaulted elements to be unlimited. The use of the rounded arch – here as in classical antiquity – limited the number of possible combinations from the start, and imposed a type of planning where every partial element was complete in itself; the associable elements would have to be identical (as in this case) or subordinated among themselves according to a pre-established hierarchy.

It is unclear whether the two basic measure-

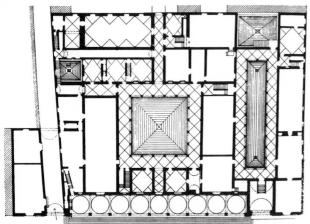

35, 36 *Loggia and ground plan of the Ospedale degli Innocenti, Florence*

37 *Detail of the loggia of the Ospedale degli Innocenti*

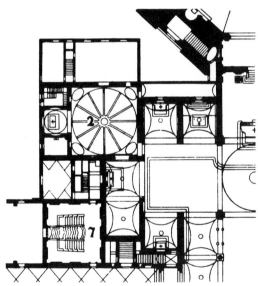

38, 39 *Interior and ground plan of the S. Lorenzo sacristy, Florence*

ments, for ground plan and elevation, were themselves linked by a geometrical ratio. The architectural device does not necessarily demand it, and admits the presence of two independent variables, while it does require the dependence of each of the two series of dimensions upon the basic measurement. But here and in later works the basic measurements, expressed in Florentine *braccia*, correspond to whole numbers and often to round figures,[50] i.e. they are therefore commensurable as multiples of the units of measurement used in operations on the site. In the Innocenti the interaxis of the columns is equivalent to 10 *braccia*, and the height of the column is just that much lower so that the height of the whole arcade, including the thickness of the archivolt, is 15 *braccia*, as is emphasized by the pilasters at the two ends.

The relationship between plastic elements and overall composition remains uncertain; the columns of the loggia are considered as free elements, as in the Middle Ages, and have no entablature, but a cyma recta moulding; on the inside, they are echoed by corbels isolated on the smooth back walls. An order with pilasters and complete entablature intervenes to frame the sequence of arches on the wall of the façade, and creates a frontal framing for the whole recess, as in many ancient examples.

The sacristy of S. Lorenzo (Figs 38–42) – begun in the interval between the first and second competitions for the cathedral dome – is clearly linked to Brunelleschi's researches on domed spaces carried out at that time, for instance the destroyed Ridolfi chapel in S. Jacopo Soprarno.

The dome-type roof determines the square plan of the main space; off this opens a secondary space or *scarsella*, also square and roofed in the same way. The imposts of the two ceilings are at the same height, and are emphasized by an order of pilasters, which are used in both spaces and outline their plan. The pilasters mark the corners of the two square spaces and are treated in two

40 *S. Lorenzo sacristy*

ways: those belonging to the large square are bent round at a right angle, in such a way as to turn the corners, so that four independent moulded extradoses for the large arches which support the dome, half the width of the pilaster, can spring from above the entablature; those leading to the small square run round the masonry linkage between the two spaces, traverse the thickness of the wall between and are arranged in such a way that the outward corners correspond to the vertex of the square; for this reason only small corners of the two end pilasters protrude from the wall, their size depending on the depth of the pilaster against the wall. In this case the extradoses of the arches which support the dome, though only of limited width, are completely interpenetrated at the impost.

The two domes rise at a tangent to the supporting arches, so that their volume is determined exactly by the structures beneath. The larger one is built '*a creste e vele*', to contain the circle of round windows in the lunettes and the generous hemispherical surface is graphically divided by the twelve ribs; the smaller dome is windowless, with no projections and is painted in a dark colour.

The framework made up of the pilasters, entablature and extradoses of the arches, emphasized by the chromatic contrast between the *pietra serena* and the white plaster, completely defines the articulations of the room; all the secondary elements – windows, decorative medallions, cornices framing the strange flattened niches on the walls of the smaller space – are tangential to the main ones, so that their position is clearly determined.

Where the entablature runs between two very widely spaced pilasters, it is supported by punctuating corbels which divide the empty space between the shafts into equal parts. The corbels, as in antiquity, replace the missing supports, and here they also have an extremely delicate function: they prevent the secondary walls being completely empty of

architectural features, but at the same time avoid the presence of elements not essential to the articulation of the space.

The whole composition depends upon three measurements: the basic side of the large square, the basic side of the small one and the height of the architectural order which enters the two spaces, fixing the height of the impost of the ceilings.

The side of the large square, considering the space from wall to wall, measures approximately 20 Florentine *braccia*; this is the dimension we read of in the Renaissance plans of the chapel, like that of Sallustio Peruzzi (Uffizi no. 672 A). But it must be deduced from the interaxis of the pilasters, which is almost exactly equivalent to $19\frac{1}{2}$ *braccia*.

The side of the small square is deduced in its turn from the interaxis of the pilasters which frame its opening, taken on the wall of the large space, and which is equivalent to exactly 8 *braccia*.

If the calculation made on the axes of the pilasters is the right one – and undoubtedly it is the one where the measurements taken come closest to the theoretical dimensions in *braccia* – this would confirm that the architectural orders were not thought of as finishing touches for spaces defined beforehand, but as primary elements, from which the positions of the masonry planes against which they rested, were deduced. The wall of the main space on to which the arch leading into the smaller one opens must be considered as the compositional key to the whole organism; the interaxes of the four pilasters which figure there (equivalent to $5\frac{3}{4}$, 8 and $5\frac{3}{4}$ *braccia*) define all the measurements of the ground plan of the chapel.

All the ceilings start from one single height, i.e. above the cornice of the order that runs around the two spaces. To take into account the variation in level of the two steps between the two floors, Brunelleschi raised the dado under the base of the pilasters so that it corresponded to the whole difference in

41 *Ceiling of S. Lorenzo sacristy*

level; thus the pilasters which frame the arch between the small and large space are arranged so that the curved moulding of the bases stands directly on the floor of the small space (but the bases of the other two pilasters which stand out at the back of the small space are again provided with the prescribed dado, even though in this way the shafts are proportionately shortened; this confirms the improvised character of the solution here adopted to take into account the difference in level between the two floors).

In this way a characteristic ambiguity is generated in measuring the height of the order; starting from the floor of the main space the order is $12\frac{1}{2}$ *braccia* high, $1\frac{1}{3}$ of which belongs to the entablature (with a ratio of $1:7\frac{1}{2}$); starting from the floor of the smaller space, i.e. not counting the dado, the order measures $11\frac{11}{12}$ *braccia*, i.e. eleven times the width of the pilaster which is $1\frac{1}{12}$ *braccia*.

All the dimensions of height above the cornice are deduced from those of the ground plan, in that the arches are exactly semi-circular. (Brunelleschi did not adopt the expedient, which was to be common later, of slightly augmenting the rise, to compensate for the portion of the arch hidden by the projection of the impost cornice.)

The three series of dimensions therefore

42　*Ceiling of the* scarsella *of S. Lorenzo sacristy*

seem to originate from three basic measurements, which, expressed in Florentine *braccia*, correspond to whole numbers and must be regarded as the object of deliberate choices.

The reasoning behind the planning, expressed in verbal directions or in drawings, was probably still similar to that contained in the famous *prescrizioni* of 1420 for the dome; except that here the designer did not have to list a whole series of measurements – still insufficient completely to define the work to be built – but had to fix only the measurements corresponding to the particular unknowns of the organism (the loggia of the Innocenti is an equation with two unknowns, the sacristy of S. Lorenzo one with three).

In reality the supreme balance of this architecture does not require the support of a hidden geometrical theorem, but coincides with the obviousness of an immediately legible design. But what is essential is that all the spatial ratios should be identifiable in the framework of the standardized plastic elements, placed at the articulations of the organism. The fixed conformation of the elements (bases, shafts, capitals, architraves, friezes and cornices, archivolts, corbels) and the constancy of the elementary associations (base, shaft and capital in the pilaster; architrave, frieze and cornice in the entablature; pilaster and entablature; archivolt springing from the entablature or at a tangent above it; corbel and entablature) help to make consideration of the partial incidents implicit in the act of recognition, and immediately make possible a precise representation of the whole.

Brunelleschi was concerned with the selection and standardizing of the elements and association of the elements, but not the overall solutions; indeed, the correlative of the standardization of the elements was an unlimited freedom in the choice of their combinations. This special balance between order and fantasy, a systematic spirit and an empirical one (almost exactly the contrary to that of the Gothic tradition, where it was possible to vary the choice of details *ad infinitum*, within a small number of canonic building types) vindicated the compactness and persuasive power of Brunelleschi's new architecture, which interrupted the course of a highly developed tradition, and emerged from then onwards as a comprehensive alternative to this tradition.

In the third decade of the fifteenth century this balance was not a result attained, but a battle in the process of being waged; the enormous tension needed to achieve this step can be felt in the dense organism of the sacristy of S. Lorenzo, and today, five centuries later, we can measure the sum of the consequences.

While it was being built, the sacristy 'aroused the marvel, for its new and beautiful style, of everyone in the city and the strangers who chanced to see it. The many people constantly assembling there caused great annoyance to those working'.[51] This episode reported by the unknown biographer, and alive in the memory of the Florentines of the late fifteenth century, may perhaps afford a sense of the great ideological impact that Brunelleschi's architecture must have produced from the moment it first appeared.

The sources allow only a hypothetical reconstruction of the technical modes of procedure of Brunelleschi's planning. In the biography attributed to Manetti we read that:[52]

'his tendency concerning the models he made for the buildings that were required and which he built was to indicate little about the symmetrical elements. He took care to have only the principal walls built and to show the relationships of certain members without the ornaments (e.g. capital types, architraves, friezes and so on). Thus his own provisions later caused him much annoyance and sorrow, since many did not understand the overall complex and made quite a hodge podge of his things.'

According to tradition, models acted as

rough reproductions of the finished building and laid down the basic lines of the organism; the executors proceeded from the model by fixing the exact forms of the details by a series of successive decisions.

But this stringing out of decisions was no longer admissible in the new architecture; perhaps Brunelleschi utilized the models only in his dealings with his clients, and insisted that execution should proceed from plans, which made it possible to fix the dimensions of the unfaced masonry in advance in relation to the system of details, and then to propose to the executors, in an inverse order, the results of the planning discussion.

In this way the plan not only implied the definition of the executive measures from the start, but emerged basically as a dimensional device which helped to translate into a unitary system all the processes necessary to the execution of the work, processes which originally had their traditional units of measurement, their own degree of approximation and allowances.

The translating of these different scales of measurement into a single scale was in fact the technological achievement of the perspective ideal, and had as its historical consequence the breakdown of the compartments in which the various processes were placed; this transformation could be studied analogously by comparing the systems of measurements existing in the medieval guilds, and their successive evolution into a single system of measurement.

Naturally the new planning procedure affected only a portion of the details of building, i.e. those which had to be made uniform for the ends of perspective regularity. All that remained variable – and could be assigned to individual specialists – were certain limited additions clearly circumscribed by the architectural framework: in the case of the sacristy, the reliefs in the eight great medallions and the two doors flanking the arch of the *scarsella*, with their surrounds which invade the two 'walls between the corner pilasters',[53] and the altar in the *scarsella* itself.

The balance between these additions and the architecture of the space as a whole was still committed as always to the specialists' subjective capacity to grasp the character of the setting, but required that they should give up treating their portions as homogeneous parts of the architecture, therefore as centres of maximum plastic and chromatic density in relation to a continuous range.

Here in the sacristy of S. Lorenzo the specialist was Donatello: but in fact it was his long acquaintance with Gothic buildings which led him to overemphasize the plastic prominence of the medallions (lessened, in the four stucco ones, by their uniform colour) and particularly of the secondary doors, inscribed in two arches with splayed jambs which reproduce and weaken the motif of the niches on the adjoining walls of the *scarsella* (Fig. 40).

The bronze doors (which are, for the sculptor, the focus of the composition) loom out from the areas of shadow cast by the strongly protruding columns and tympana; Donatello's two niches, with their unbecomingly harsh profiles, thus become a cumbersome antithesis to the pure and relaxed elements of the main architectural mood. The fifteenth-century biographer recalls that Donatello wanted to act on his own, 'without consulting Filippo, presuming on his authority as the sculptor of the bronze doors'; hence the dispute, recounted with the usual lively frankness.[54]

Of all Brunelleschi's works, the church of S. Lorenzo was perhaps the most dogged by complex vicissitudes of execution. It could be that the prior Dolfini, who died in 1420, had prepared a plan for the rebuilding of the old Romanesque church before Brunelleschi's intervention, and that the shape of the site (acquired in 1418) remained linked to the previous plan. Work on the church began in the summer of 1421, but went ahead slowly

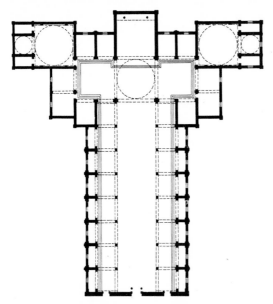

43   *Ground plan of S. Lorenzo*

because of economic difficulties (while the sacristy, financed by Giovanni de' Medici, was completed by 1428) and was practically suspended in 1425; only in 1442, thanks to the subsidy given by Cosimo de' Medici, did work continue under the direction of Brunelleschi, but it was still very much behindhand at the time of Brunelleschi's death, and was completed subsequently by Antonio Manetti and his successors. Both in the first and second phases the new structures were subordinated to the need to retain a part of the old Romanesque church, so as not to interrupt the continuity of worship; the old church was demolished only after 1465.

In the first phase the longitudinal body was planned without chapels, while after 1442 Brunelleschi or his successors planned the two rows of shallow chapels which flank the aisles. From the beginning the architectural organism was restricted by the related needs of its double purpose, public and conventual; the plan (Fig. 43) was therefore similar to that of the other Florentine convent churches, S. Maria Novella and S. Croce, as indeed the fifteenth-century biographer remarks.[55]

Because of the circumstances in which it

was planned, S. Lorenzo remained a sort of experimental work-site at every stage, where Brunelleschi himself, no less than his successors, proceeded tentatively, testing the possibilities of his methodology in relation to the restrictions and opportunities which gradually emerged.

The ground plan of the church, as we see it today, reproduces a well-known medieval monastic model: a body with a nave and two aisles which run into a transept with five chapels along the end, of which the largest is as wide as the nave and the four smaller ones as wide as the aisles. In this case six more smaller chapels open off the transept: two on the axis of each extremity, leaving space for the doors leading to the sacristies; two on the inner side, opposite the pair of outermost chapels on the end side; and two adjacent to the axial chapels and communicating with them. The central cross formed by the nave, transept and main chapel, has a flat roof, except for the central point of juncture with the dome; the aisles and ten smaller chapels of the transept have sail-vaults. Along the aisles, where the wall space is not taken up with the walls of these chapels or side doors, there are twelve smaller, lower chapels, roofed with barrel-vaulting.

In this way the organism is made up of three series of spaces, characterized by the different level of their roofing; the central cross, aisles with the transept chapels and the chapels on the longitudinal body.

The problem of rationally articulating the different ceiling levels had clearly concerned Florentine builders from the thirteenth century onwards: in S. Maria del Fiore the levels of the two systems of roofing were indicated not only by the traditional capitals, placed at the impost, but were subordinated to the heavy cornice-gallery from which the main roofs spring and against which the vertices of the lesser ones end.

In our case the two architectural orders form the articulations of the three systems of arches on which the roofing depends; the

44 *Interior of S. Lorenzo*

45 *An aisle in S. Lorenzo*

46 *The transept of S. Lorenzo*

entablature of the lower order establishes the keystone height of the arches of the smaller chapels, and marks the impost of the arches surrounding the sail-vaults which roof the aisles and chapels of the transept; in its turn the entablature of the higher order, which runs tangential to the tops of the arches, establishes the impost of the main arches on which the central dome and ceilings of the middle sections rest.

The conformation of the whole church thus depends on four basic measurements, except for the depth of the side chapels, which has no influence on the rest of the organism: the interaxis of the minor order, which determines the side of all the square spaces with sail-vaults; the distance between the pilasters of the major order, which determines the width of the nave and transept, slightly different one from the other; lastly, the heights of the two orders upon which, as we have seen, the height of all the ceilings depend (the second is, however, linked to the first, with the addition of the arched lintel,

the arch and the thickness of the entablature).

The low order, with pilasters or columns, is responsible for the articulation of all the spaces surrounding the central cross, and is sufficient to resolve all points of juncture, with the exception of the four pillars around the dome.

Only here does the high order intervene to determine the form of the support, in so far as the presence of the two main pilasters produces a separation of the two minor ones, reducing the arch which leads from the aisles into the transept *vis-à-vis* the other parallel arches which separate the bays of the aisles themselves; and since this arch is part of the same system as those which frame the chapels of the transept, it indirectly influences their measurements (their spans are halfway between those of the arches leading from the transept into the aisles and those of the arches surrounding the bays of the aisles, so that the differences are not easily noticeable, except in the last bay of the aisles, where the difference is revealed by a joining of the sail-vault to the corner pillar, resolved with a small embrasure).

The cornice of the major order, which runs unbroken along the four arms of the cross, is supported on a series of corbels, which mark the axes of the underlying elements; at some points, however, certain peculiar heads of pilasters appear from the surface of the wall, which sometimes (at the joins of the corner pillars) are placed directly above the minor pilasters, giving an impression of their continuation upwards to the higher entablature, and sometimes (at the end corners of the transept) do not correspond with the elements of the first order, i.e. they suggest the image of non-existent corner pilasters, which definitely affect the real conformation of the support.

In many places the designer retained the freedom to alter measurements of height independently of those of the ground plan. Of four corner pillars the first two which stand on the floor are taller than the others which stand on the steps of the presbytery. In the aisles, too, the columns are longer than the pilasters which frame the small chapels (this is the drawback of which Vasari speaks, and which 'gives the whole work a stunted appearance'[56]), but even more significant is the fact that the pilasters of the high order have the same width as those of the lower order though they are much higher, so that the corner pillars where the nave crosses the transept, formed of two high pilasters and two low ones, have a regular cruciform plan.

This solution, which still adheres to Gothic tradition – the same thing happens, for instance, in S. Maria· Novella, where the supports from which the ceilings of nave and aisles spring have the same semi-circular section, and determine a compound pillar of symmetrical shape – decidedly weakens the solidity of the major order, whose pilasters appear too slight, and reduces it almost to a decorative surround, circumscribing the elements of the minor order. The ratio between pilasters and entablature is as much as 9:1.

It is as though the pilasters are there only to vindicate the meaning of the cornice, which establishes the maximum height of all secondary spaces, and in fact they could all be removed at every point, except in the pillars of the transept (indeed this is precisely what the designers of the internal façade did); but their presence, even where it is decoratively unpleasing, as at the corners of the transept, is more convincingly attributable to Brunelleschi himself than to his successors, precisely because of its theoretical and doctrinaire significance. Brunelleschi was concerned with studying the consequences of a rigorous method, even if it meant leaving the formal dissonances that resulted from it in evidence, rather than composing the single details in an enforced harmony.

If this was the spirit of his research, it is not possible to discriminate between his work and that of his successors by imputing all the 'mistakes' to them, as the fifteenth-century biographer and Vasari have done, in the name of a style which, after two or three generations, had already selected the 'correct' and 'incorrect' solutions, and as many contemporary critics continue to do, judging Brunelleschi according to a criterion of formal perfection which in fact he deliberately sacrificed, committed as he was to an inflexible, uneven methodological research, consisting of attempts and rethinkings, but all the more revolutionary and forward-looking for that.

The Pazzi chapel (Figs 47–51) is the logical continuation of the research started in the sacristy of S. Lorenzo, and was begun probably after work on the sacristy had been finished, between 1429 and 1430.

This, too, like most of Brunelleschi's works, went ahead slowly because of the economic difficulties of those years, and got under way only after a new allocation of funds by Andrea de' Pazzi in 1442, i.e. in the year work was resumed in S. Lorenzo, financed by Cosimo de' Medici.

Andrea de' Pazzi's will, in 1445, destined other funds for the chapel, which was left

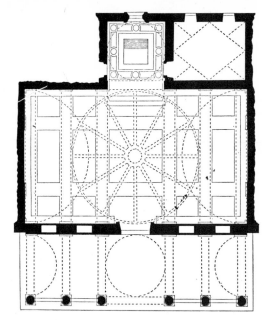

47–49 *Interior views and ground plan of the Pazzi chapel, Florence*

unfinished by Brunelleschi at his death in the following year. The date found in 1962 on the drum of the main dome shows that it was roofed only in 1459; and it is known that the details were still not completed in 1469 and 1473.

The organism, like that of the sacristy, is based on two domed and intercommunicating spaces, one large and one small; but the lesser interaxis of the pilasters at the side of the opening which leads into the smaller space is repeated on the outside, so that the main space becomes rectangular and the two side arches which support the dome are supported by two barrel-vaults; in this way the organism still depends on three measurements (two for the plan and one for the elevation), independent and expressible in whole numbers, but proportioned in a rather different way, as we shall see.

This space – intended as a chapterhouse and ancestral chapel – was built on a site bounded definitely to the left by the outer wall of S. Croce, and probably also to the right by monastic buildings which must also have been built before Brunelleschi's intervention, in that an early fifteenth-century fresco has been found on the outer face of the right side-wall. Perhaps there already existed on this site an earlier chapterhouse which was completely demolished to make way for Brunelleschi's.

In the first case (if the chapel was to adjoin only the wall of the church) the short side of the large rectangular space (i.e. the interaxis of the pilasters placed at the corners of the main dome) would be thus determined as would the short stretch of end wall up to the opening of the smaller square space (i.e. double the minor interaxis we have mentioned) and the plan of the chapel can be deduced entirely from these limiting conditions, as Laschi, Roselli and Rossi have shown in the study they made in 1962;[57] in the second case, the long side of the rectangle would also have been fixed, i.e. there would have been numerous restrictions making the site suited to this architectural solution and this one alone (Fig. 49).

This observation becomes all the more paradoxical, if one considers closely the modular relationships between the elements of the ground plan.

The interaxis between the pilasters at the corner of the main dome is almost identical to that of the pilasters in a similar position in the sacristy of S. Lorenzo, and is equivalent to $19\frac{1}{2}$ *braccia*; the diameter of the cupola is, however, less, because the four supporting arches are completely interpenetrated at the impost; in other words, if the domed space were square the four pilasters would protrude only for a stretch corresponding to their thickness, as happens in the small squares of the sacristy and Pazzi chapel; this solution is imposed by the fact that the main space is rectangular, and the pilasters extend along the main side of the rectangle.

The proportion between the two domed spaces, too, is different, because the interaxis of the pilasters which support the communicating arch is $9\frac{1}{2}$ *braccia* instead of 8; as a result the two lateral interaxes – which are repeated on the outside corresponding to the barrel-vaulting – are 5 *braccia* rather than $5\frac{3}{4}$, and contain no door, but only the windows

open towards the façade whose outlines are repeated, as a decorative theme, on all sides of the room. The interaxes can be seen on the floor, in the form of slender strips of stone which divide up the brick paving.

In this way not only does the organism obey a rigorous geometrical construction, but the basic measurements correspond to whole numbers, and one of these is identical in the similar organization of the sacristy of S. Lorenzo; yet the chapel was built on an area of predetermined shape.

To make sense of this set of observations we must consider that Brunelleschi's method, in liberating himself from traditional building schemes, was not linked in any way to new models, which were to be selected and fixed only subsequently. For this reason it is not likely that he conceived the scheme of the chapel, and then decided to adapt it to the site; but it is probable that he should mentally have examined a large number of schemes (the 'hundred models . . . all . varied and different' that he boasted of being able to invent) and chose the one that suited the limitations of the site, playing on the small margin of freedom allowed by different solutions of detail (for example the position of the pilasters in the corners) so as to obtain an exact symmetry. Another margin for minor adjustments derived from the need to thicken the walls of the church to eliminate the protrusion of the Gothic pilasters; though the measured drawings have shown that these thickenings were everywhere reduced to the barest minimum.

We must now take a closer look at the details of Brunelleschi's structure. The main innovation, in relation to the sacristy, lay in the aim to repeat, on all four walls, the architectural decision deriving from the incorporation of the smaller domed space into the larger, by giving them all the same decorative appearance.

To this end the pilaster at the corner of the main space ran along the long side for its whole width ($1\frac{1}{4}$ *braccia*) and around the short

50 *Pazzi chapel*

51 *Façade of the Pazzi chapel*

side for quarter of a *braccio*; this continuation affected not the adjacent small interaxes (which had to incorporate the repeated window frames) but the central interaxis of the short side, which is therefore shorter by half a *braccio*. As a result the arch above it is lower than the one on the long side; but the extrados too of the higher arch turns a quarter of a *braccio* on to the short side, like the pilaster from which it springs, and lowers the two concentric arches, so that it is still tangential to the two extradoses.

To resolve the problem of the difference in level between the two spaces, Brunelleschi here utilized the low bench which runs all around the large space, level with the floor of the small one. This bench, a *braccio* high and

equally deep, is used when the chapel is functioning as chapterhouse, and provides a uniform plane of support for the pilasters of the architectural order. The order here is somewhat higher than in the sacristy, and measures *in toto* 15 *braccia*, including the dado; 13 *braccia* are taken up by the pilasters, 2 by the entablature. The ratio between the minor interaxis – recurring on all sides – and the height is therefore 1:3, and determines the positions of the secondary elements, windows and medallions. The arches of the roofing are always exactly semi-circular, so that the form of the vaulting is completely determined, from the height of the impost upwards.

In the Pazzi chapel the balance between

architectural detail and sculpture is more satisfying than in the sacristy; Sanpaolesi has put forward the hypothesis that the four evangelists in polychrome terracotta in the medallions of the pendentives are by Brunelleschi himself.

The researches of 1962 have shown that the outer porch was completed in 1461, and must be considered as a variant on the original plan. At first a smooth façade was planned, traces of which were found on the front wall, and the two barrel-vaults (which still support a tiled extrados roof) were to remain visible, stating the arrangement of interior volumes on the outside.

The porch was built soon after the completion of the main dome, possibly by Brunelleschi's successors but possibly also along the lines of a design by Brunelleschi (a possible 'change of idea by Brunelleschi'[58] is far from unlikely, indeed it is in perfect agreement with the experimental idea of his research).

The interaxes of the porch are the same as those of the inner wall, in that the columns have to frame the same windows, which open on to the exterior; but it is clear that an attempt was made to contain their heights as far as possible so as not to hide the dome. The dry, stiff forms of the attic above the entablature do indeed imply the hand of other designers, possibly Giuliano da Maiano, as has been suggested.

Brunelleschi prepared a first plan for the church of S. Spirito (Figs 52–6) in 1428. The fifteenth-century biographer recounts at great length the circumstances surrounding this commission: the notables of the district decided to rebuild the church and chose five overseers, who called upon Filippo Brunelleschi as the most famous architect in the city; Brunelleschi designed an initial plan and gave a verbal description of the shape of the elevation, after which he was asked to make a 'most beautiful model' in wood.

He and the overseers apparently wanted to reverse the direction of the church, so that it looked towards the river, but without success. After this disagreement (but we do not know exactly when) work began, starting from the tribune, and went ahead slowly 'because of the adversities of the city'; from 1439 the work was financed by funds drawn from the tax on salt, and work went ahead at a normal rate, but was concluded only in 1487, many years after Brunelleschi's death.

The biographer records that 'when Filippo had made the model and founded a part of [the church] he said at some point that, in so far as the composition of the church was concerned, it seemed to him that he had begun a church in accordance with his intentions'.[59]

This satisfaction certainly derived from the geometrical arrangement, much more compact and unified than in S. Lorenzo since it was based on a small square bay which was repeated along the whole of the outside of the church, forming a continuous ambulatory and also determining the width of the nave and transept; the perimeter wall had a series of niches, whose depth was regulated by the need for the windows of the two niches near the re-entrant corners to meet up, on the outside, along the axis of the building; for this reason this depth is equivalent to half the side of the bay. All the ground plan measurements of S. Spirito were therefore derived from one single one: the side of the smaller bay, which measures exactly 11 *braccia*.

The measurements of the elevation are determined, as in S. Lorenzo, by the two architectural orders, which mark the impost of the ambulatory and of the central cross.

Only the first order was realized according to Brunelleschi's designs; the second was executed later, possibly varying the ground plan ratios with the first, and almost certainly increasing the height – i.e. detaching the entablature from the crown of the underlying arches, or by increasing the three areas of the entablature itself – to absorb, at least in part, the considerable difference in level between the arches and the windows in the walls of the

52–54 *Exterior, ground plan and interior of S. Spirito, Florence*

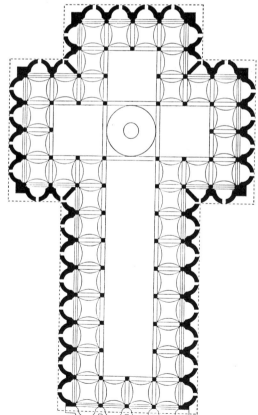

nave, above the bulk of the roofs of the aisles.[60]

The small order is $16\frac{1}{2}$ *braccia* high, i.e. eleven times the diameter of the base of the columns (which is $1\frac{1}{2}$ *braccia*) and one and a half times the interaxis. The ratio between column and entablature is $6:1$, even less than that found in previous works; it seems clear that Brunelleschi tried out various formulations of the ratios which later were to be codified by the treatise-writers.

The arches above the small order are circular, and the decoration of the archivolt is equivalent to half the thickness of the entablature; in this way the total height of the system formed of the order and the arches, measured above the archivolt, is 22 *braccia*, i.e. twice the interaxis.

If the entablature of the major order were tangential to the archivolt, as in S. Lorenzo, the same measurement would determine the height of the pilasters of the main order; but we see that on the outside of the moulded archivolt there is a second smooth surround, and the entablature is further raised, so that the height of the pilaster is 23 *braccia*. The end entablature has the unusual height of 5 *braccia*. These measurements may have been increased at the moment of execution, as we have said, and they cast doubt on the original ratios established in the plan.

Apart from this anomaly, the ground plan and elevation measurements of S. Spirito form a homogeneous system, determined by a single dimension, i.e. the interaxis of 11 *braccia*. This result is simply a development of the method of planning with whole numbers, tried out in the previous works; in this case the submultiple is not the *braccio*, but a larger measurement: the interaxis of 11 *braccia* or, if one prefers, half the interaxis ($5\frac{1}{2}$ *braccia*). All the main dimensions of the building are deduced from this last measurement, multiplying it by arithmetical progression:

1   depth of niches
2   interaxis of small order
3   height of small order, and height of impost of roofs of aisles
4   keystone height of the arches of the aisles, and interaxes of the main order
5   original height of impost of arches and roof of nave.

The two arms of the Latin cross formed by the nave are obtained from the same measurement, multiplying it by twelve and twenty-four, and the two axes of the church (imagining that the series of the minor bays of the niches would also continue along the façade, as according to Folnesics' hypothesis)[61] multiplying it by eighteen and thirty.

These overall measurements are related by a constant figure ($2:3:4:5$) and could be imagined as having been obtained by multiplying a larger module, which was equivalent to the sum of the widths of the two naves. S. Spirito thus remained the prototype of the composition based on simple ratios – i.e. on the aggregation of equal elements of measurement – which Wittkower considers typical of Renaissance culture.[62]

If, as we have said, Brunelleschi's planning involved mediation between different scales of measurement, corresponding to different processes, it is here possible to pick out at least three of these scales: one is that of overall measurements, concerning the whole organism and its relations to its surroundings, determined by the module of $5\frac{1}{2}$ *braccia*; another is that of detailed building measurements, determined by the *braccio* and its submultiples up to the twelfth; yet another is that of the stone trimmings (moulding, capitals, recurrent decorations) which certainly utilize a further series of sub-multiples. The largest module ($5\frac{1}{2}$ *braccia*) and the smallest (half a *braccio*) are the measurements which make possible movement between the three scales, and ensure the continuity of the whole system of measurement.

This coherence extending from the whole to the detail must have greatly struck his contemporaries, though they were not in a position fully to accept the master's lesson:

hence the great fame of the building which Vasari considers 'the most perfect church in Christendom'.[63] But it was just this building, because of its rigour and novelty, that caused the greatest perplexity to Brunelleschi's successors, who had to execute it and who were persuaded seriously to alter the original arrangement.

The conformation of the outer wall, broken up by the series of niches, is linked to the idea of a vaulted roof for the nave. The niches could have supported the basis for a series of buttresses, as in other buildings of the fifteenth century quoted by Sanpaolesi.[64]

By giving up this idea, the executors irredeemably altered this motif, as seen from the outside; furthermore during the actual building they displaced the correspondence between the diametral plane of the niches and the surface of the outer wall, making it very difficult to trace the roofs of the niches; signs of attempts made to resolve this problem, all faulty, have been found, and this led to the decision to close the niches behind a straight wall.

Other uncertainties sprang from the conformation of the corner elements, which form the hinges, as it were, of the Latin cross.

The corner pillar, which supports the dome at the crossing of the arms, is fitted in axially in the place of the missing column; consequently the adjacent arches are narrower, and spring at a higher level; we know that around 1479[65] there was some talk about the shape of the pillar, and Antonio da Sangallo the Younger in a drawing in the Uffizi (no. 900 A) quotes a variant which would have left all the arches identical, because in the place of the two half-columns there is a single column in the correct position, three quarters emerging from a pillar whose position was here altered so as to look towards the dome. We do not know if Brunelleschi's original solution was the present one, the one indicated by Sangallo or indeed another different one.

The half-columns at the sides of the niches

55 *Diagonal view of two niches level with the point of juncture, S. Spirito*

become quarter-columns where the ambulatory turns an acute angle, and three-quarter-columns where it turns an obtuse angle; here the two niches adjacent to the corner, if they were the same shape as the others, would interpenetrate, and their shape has therefore been altered, i.e. made asymmetrical and shallower, so as to guarantee a minimum thickness of the masonry where the two curves come closest to one another (Fig. 55).

This distortion is more noticeable than one might expect, and is concealed by a skilful correction of the surround of the end window, which makes one think of the late fifteenth century rather than of Brunelleschi; it may therefore be that the problem arose from an alteration of the shape of the normal niches, introduced by the executors and possibly connected with the problem of the outer wall surfaces that we have mentioned.

On the basis of this data various hypotheses could be made, and it may never be possible to ascertain exactly how things actually

56   *External view of S. Spirito*

happened. But at all events they attest Brunelleschi's cultural conflict with his generation, and with the following one too; the executors were betrayed by their habit of considering architectural details as variables independent of the general scheme, coming upon an organism where the form of the details was closely linked to the whole.

The damage done by the executors was deplored, at the end of the century, by the most advanced section of Florentine intellectuals, and their polemic may possibly have produced the biography of Brunelleschi attributed to Manetti; but more than the incompetence and high-handedness of those who did the damage, one should consider the changed conditions of architectural thought and practice in the late fifteenth century. This culture, which started from Brunelleschi's revolution, was dominated by new needs, and above all by the aim to sort through previous experience in order to determine a range of typical solutions and organisms. Building technique, interrupted as an independent pursuit by Brunelleschi's cultural system, had definitely declined and, in another way, hindered the invention of new organic types.

Thus the executors of Brunelleschi's unfinished works could not help eliminating the characteristics incompatible with the selective tendency of the time: the last of these incidents was the debate over the façade of S. Spirito, designed by Brunelleschi with four doors – on the axes of the bays of the ambulatory which was to run round the façade as well – and implemented instead with three doors in accordance with the usual custom. In this debate, which ran from 1482 to 1486, Brunelleschi's original solution was defended by the son of Paolo Toscanelli, by Vittorio Ghiberti and Giuliano da Sangallo.[66] But the great architect who had died forty years before was already forgotten, and was presented now as a sage in the Ficinian style, encyclopedic, jealous of his learning and always sure of himself. The greatness of his intellect, which struck his contemporaries so strongly, continued to exercise immense power over subsequent generations, but his real physiognomy had already been obscured by a mythical image, answering the needs and ideals of a culture moving along other lines.

Let us consider again the specific novelty of his approach, inevitable yet promptly subjected to the hesitations of later debate: reference to the classical models.

This innovation raised the problem of the social purpose of the new architecture, i.e. the relations between production of monumental buildings and production of more humble ones.

For both Brunelleschi and his successors, the orders lost their original constructional meaning, which had been retained, to some degree or other, during classical times. They could not therefore function as prototypes for general architecture which used completely different building systems, and were valid precisely as instruments of formal qualification for more important buildings, in which their use was economically admissible. In this way monumental architecture grew away from ordinary architecture, in that it utilized a special morphology, that could not be made general.

This historical result is a product of the combination between Brunelleschi's approach and the needs of the ruling class with which Brunelleschi was involved. None the less, it is just possible to glimpse in Brunelleschi's experience possibilities other than the one historically developed.

Unfortunately the works of civil architecture, which could have shed light on this problem, are much less well documented than the religious ones we have discussed so far. The most important plan, for the new Palazzo Medici, was rejected by Cosimo as being too demanding; the palace for Luca Pitti (Figs 57, 58) though almost certainly designed by Brunelleschi, was built after his death. The work carried out on the Palazzo di Parte Guelfa (Fig. 59) is recognizable only in part, and that on the Palazzo della Signoria has been erased by later rebuilding. We know that he also worked on more modest buildings such as the house of Apollonio Lapi, the Barbadori house, the Villa Pitti at Rusciano, and the Palazzetto Busini, committing his designs to second-rate workers and taking numerous limitations into account.

Had it not been for these ups and downs, according to Manetti, 'private houses by him would have been marvels to see';[67] in the completed works which have come down to us we note a constant attempt to regularize and simplify the geometrical layout of space, in so far as this was allowed by the basic conditions, without necessarily having recourse to any reference to the architectural orders.

It has been already noted that, for the exteriors of his main works, Brunelleschi accepted a considerable simplification of the internal decorative apparatus, and used widely spaced plastic elements on masonry fields; in fact he preferred to gain an architectural effect from the play of the roofing, which was then almost always moderated or eliminated during the course of construction.

In secular buildings, where the overall composition is legible only in the dividing up of the façade, Brunelleschi seemed to look for a method of anchoring the perspective scheme to plastic elements other than the orders, even in important buildings like the Palazzo Pitti or the extension of the Palazzo di Parte Guelfa (Figs 57–9).

To do this he utilized single fragments drawn from the repertoire of the orders, like the moulded string course and fan-shaped voussoirs round the windows – which although isolated still retain a reference to the usual circumscribed order – or more daringly the design of the masonry facing itself, aptly standardized into clear and recognizable

57 *Palazzo Pitti, Florence. The photo shows the part built in accordance with Brunelleschi's plan*

geometrical lines. This motif, developed with splendid confidence on the façade of the Palazzo Pitti, was taken up again by Michel-ozzo (1396–1472) and by the artists of the following generation, and very soon it in its turn became a conventional decorative model, with its definitely noble connotations and indeed its quiet allusion to the medieval.[68]

But Brunelleschian experiments of this kind could have, indeed partly have, brought about a real link between monumental and ordinary building. Subsequent circumstances have prevented any sufficient development of this line of research, particularly outside the region of Florence, and the reconciliation between the aristocratic and the traditional repertoires took place on the basis of the Albertian thesis, i.e. of the distinction between 'walling' and 'ornament'.

Alberti considered perspective regularity as an intellectual requirement definable *a priori* in mathematical terms, and applicable to masonry surfaces without using this or that system of plastic supports; the architectural orders became a complement and an optional emphasis, and thus acquired a precise hier-archical significance, as tokens of power and prestige.

As we shall see, Alberti's opinion had a much wider and more immediate success; for almost a century the demanding freedom of Brunelleschi's works remained a stimulating but inaccessible example.

However, Brunelleschi's methodology continued to operate after the decline of the typologies elaborated from the late fifteenth century to the first half of the sixteenth, remained routine for all the successive come-backs of architectural classicism, and also laid down the terms of the neoclassical crisis,

58 *Detail of Palazzo Pitti*

which put an end to the cycle of classicism after four centuries. The normative value of the forms derived from antiquity lasted as long as they retained the ideal prestige which was accumulated before Brunelleschi's time, and which Brunelleschi in some way stabilized, removing them from the oscillations of taste and taking them up as fixed terms of subsequent exploration.

A conclusive judgment of Brunelleschi must put him in his own time, though without forgetting the immense consequences of his work, which had a crucial effect on four centuries of architectural history. There is nothing to prevent us from continuing to admire his genius as an artist, confident at 'the play of forms in light', in Le Corbusier's words, as few have been. The culture which takes its impetus from him has in fact attributed to the architect – together with the painter and sculptor – a special responsibility in the realm of formal values, to which we still refer when we talk of 'art' and 'artists'.

But Brunelleschi's work came at a moment of transition between the old system of values and this one, which characterized a new cycle of experiment. After some time his personal answer to the problems of the society in which he lived actually supplanted the building tradition of all Europe, and brought about a methodological leap everywhere, made inevitable in fact by subsequent events. The historical truth of his proposition completely justifies the admiration of his own and later generations; but it must not prevent us from recognizing the patient, empirical and troubled development of his research.

He did not work towards a style of his own, and he never managed fully to demonstrate his individual abilities by working on a

59   *Detail of Palazzo di Parte Guelfa, Florence*

60 *Brunelleschi's buildings in the organism of the city of Florence. From the left: S. Lorenzo, the Ospedale degli Innocenti, the Rotonda degli Angeli, dome of the cathedral, Palazzo di Parte Guelfa and the Pazzi chapel; on the other side of the river: S. Spirito and Palazzo Pitti*

subject that he knew in advance would suit his purposes. He inherited the technical experience of the medieval builders, adjusting it in the light of the new intellectual climate, and created the premises for a precise distinction between the sphere of the technician and that of the artist. He conceived of a system of planning that was basically incompatible with the customs of the building sites of his time, and had to adapt the character and order of planning procedures – designs, models, written instructions – to the particular difficulties of the groups of specialized workers with whom he had to deal.

The methodological leap destined to influence the future so widely cannot be reduced to a technical formula, and was not achieved at one go, but was developed and perfected in a series of attempts, experimentally, and in practical contact with the specific difficulties of the building practice of his time; he encountered 'ceaseless opposition' as Vasari puts it.[69]

Considering the timeliness and historical repercussions of this process, it is hard for us to attribute it to the initiative of a single person, and we have preferred to place Brunelleschi in a group, trying hard to catch glimpses of such uniformity as there might be between his work and that of other artists who were in contact with him.

Recent criticism has considered the joint responsibility of Ghiberti and Brunelleschi for the building of the dome;[70] the close relationship of Brunelleschi with Nanni di Banco at the time of the *Four Crowned Saints*[71] and with Masaccio in the frescoes of S. Maria Novella;[72] the possible influence of Masaccio on Brunelleschi after the frescoes of the Carmine;[73] the many instances of collaboration and mutual influence between Brunelleschi and Donatello. But ultimately, one cannot talk of group work, at least in the present state of our knowledge. Brunelleschi and Ghiberti were divided by a basic disagreement in assessing recent tradition, Nanni di Banco and Masaccio died young,

Donatello was drawn onwards by an overpowering personal vocation, which soon led to disagreement with his older friend.

But Brunelleschi did find himself at the centre of a close web of influences and relationships – not only with artists, but with scientists, writers, economic operators and administrators of his time – which has only partly been studied and collated in the relevant documents; but it still seems that he alone was responsible for the organic nature of these relationships. The polemical and jealous nature of which successive biographers write, attributing it to the reserve of misunderstood genius may perhaps hide bitter loneliness, which was the human result of his professional position.

As in other decisive moments in the history of architecture, we must recognize in Brunelleschi's work a dramatic combination of the historic with personal risk.

The decision to bring back the designing of buildings, and in general all the techniques of visual representation, into the rational sphere, subordinating them to the representation of a continuous and infinite geometric space, had long been prepared for by the work of late medieval theoreticians and artists of the fourteenth century, and itself heralded not only the recognition of art as an operation independent of technical processes, but also the birth of the new experimental science, when its methods were finally distinguished from those of art. Brunelleschi's contribution thus appears closely conditioned by a historical process already under way, whose extent and coherence we can now fully assess.

But the choice of the method of operating this transition, i.e. the decision to anchor the representation of perspective space to the use of the standardized elements derived from antiquity, must be considered – as far as we know – as an individual decision, among the most crucial and influential in all cultural history. With this choice Brunelleschi fixed the repertoire of architecture in relation to the other arts, i.e. he defined and circumscribed its specific figurative nature, which made it possible to place it, together with painting and sculpture, in the new system of the visual arts. Both the timeliness and the suddenness of Brunelleschi's approach helped to set off an irresistible process, which radically changed the theory and practice of architecture in the next two centuries in every country in Europe.

The renewal of the figurative arts

Brunelleschi, like many Florentine architects of the fourteenth century, began his career as a sculptor, and made a vital if fortuitous contribution in the field of painting by establishing the rules of linear perspective; he worked in contact with painters and sculptors, with Donatello, Nanni di Banco and Masaccio, and the artistic revolution in which he was involved concerns painting and sculpture as well as architecture.

The notion of architecture which was to remain unchanged in the cultural patrimony of the centuries to come emerged when Brunelleschi's research assigned a method and a precise content to the activity of building supervision exercised in the previous century by certain famous painters and sculptors: Giotto, Arnolfo, Talenti, Orcagna; it was therefore born unhampered by the manual character typical of the system of the medieval trade guilds.

Painting and sculpture, on the other hand, had a solidly founded tradition, connected with the exercise of certain manual activities; but while until the thirteenth century they were aligned with the other mechanical arts, in the course of the fourteenth century and more definitely in the fifteenth, they gained themselves an undisputed cultural superiority, as liberal arts.

The manual element inherent in their exercise was in fact considered secondary in comparison with other intellectual aspects, which formed the specific dignity of these

arts and put them on a par with architecture in the new cultural system.

Painting, sculpture and architecture finally emerged as different versions of a single creative activity, whose autonomy was recognized and which, later, was to be given the name 'art', previously used to designate the whole range of technical operations.

As long as this classification of human activities was regarded as stable – though justified by a variety of theoretical arguments – the cultural revolution brought about in the first decades of the fifteenth century was regarded, primarily, as the achievement of a permanent value, the autonomy of art, and it did not seem necessary to discuss the transition from the old to the new experiences in conceptual terms, in so far as the notion of art was considered as present in every age, whether or not it was backed up by conscious appreciation.

But if this notion was called into question, the problem would have to be differently posed; we must in fact examine both the ups and downs of theoretical opinion, which recognized the intellectual character of the work of certain artists and prepared the instruments for its speculative justification, and the changes in the specific content of this work, which at a certain point gained it a cultural and social prestige so marked as to entrench it in a stable and institutional form for four or five centuries, while writers theorized about this entrenchment, attributing to it a perennial philosophical value.

The dispute about the mechanical or liberal character of some of these operations already existed in medieval thought; Albertus Magnus[74] conceded an intellectual character to architecture, with regard to the exact procedures in Gothic building technique.

As far as the figurative arts were concerned, St Thomas Aquinas and St Bonaventura upheld the superiority of rational beauty (representation of truth and sobriety of representational means) over sensuous beauty (richness and preciosity of images); this

61 *Michelozzo's tabernacle with Verrocchio's* St Thomas and Christ. *Orsanmichele, Florence*

distinction was used in the literary apologias dedicated to the Florentine painters by Boccaccio,[75] Filippo Villani,[76] Cennino Cennini[77] and later by Cristoforo Landino.[78]

Villani, who was writing about 1390, says explicitly that painters must not be considered inferior to masters of the liberal arts, because their ability to reproduce nature is a matter of intellect, rather than of hand. Pier Paolo Vergerio in *De ingenuis moribus* – written between 1401 and 1402 – treats the teaching of drawing with that of the liberal arts, and writes:[79]

'The disciplines that the Greeks used to teach their children were four: letters, gymnastics, music and drawing, also called by them figurative art. In a moment we shall talk of the second and third. The fourth, or drawing, is today not usually taught as a liberal art, except as regards calligraphy (basically, writing being none other than drawing); as to the rest, it is all the affair of the painters. Despite this, as Aristotle observes, the knowledge of drawing for them was not merely an ornament, but also useful. For in the acquisition (in which these people so delighted) of vases and painted panels and sculptures, the knowledge of this art was extremely useful to them, both so as not to be misled about the price, and because with that aid they were able easily to distinguish the beautiful and graceful, which is born of nature as of art; matters which eminent men often find themselves having to discuss, and to judge.'

Painting had therefore already taken its place among the liberal arts which 'make men free'[80] in the theory and opinion of writers, before the innovations introduced by the masters of the early fifteenth century.[81] But these very innovations transformed a literary judgment into an institutional reality, more stable than the various theoretical justifications which it was to receive from then onwards, and convincingly incorporated into the new social and cultural system then emerging.

As has been observed,[82] the criteria of excellence assigned to artistic representation were two, which seem to us independent: truthfulness in reproducing nature, and internal coherence of the image, which the artist would not find in the single natural objects, but had to use his own particular talent to synthesize from many different objects.

Truthfulness of reproduction was guaranteed after about 1430 by an exact and scientific method: perspective (Figs 62–3). We have already said that perspective entails a selection of the elements to be represented, assigning a priority to geometrical features over chromatic ones and, among geometrical ones, a priority to features of proportion over those of measurement, i.e. it traces a conventional structure of the image, characterized according to the demands of the historical moment.

It is this very important feature that makes it possible to link together the two criteria we have just mentioned. The hierarchy among the features, which we regard as historically caused, was seen as consonant with the innermost structure of reality, and the coherence of the image which the artist had to extract from nature was itself considered as an objective element, to be drawn from external reality: the *concinnitas universarum partium*[83] was found in nature itself as a first principle recognizable by the human intellect, or in classical examples, in that the ancient artists themselves had already perfected this operation of identification and synthesis.

Here, too, one must distinguish the theoretical explanations, numerous and often contradictory, from the historical substance of this tendency. While writers tried to formulate a coherent system of intellectual references, artists were engaged in the building up of a method to explore and synthesize the whole world of visible appearances: the human figure, the natural land-

62, 63 *The* sinopia *of Masaccio's* Trinity. *S. Maria Novella, Florence*

scape and the artificial landscape conceived of by man.

The building up of this method made use of a large number of heterogeneous contributions, drawn from medieval tradition, works of antiquity, theoretical speculation and studio practice. The theme that brought together the various contributions, in the last analysis, was of a practical order: as men of letters eagerly explored the intellectual and moral aspects of the human condition,

recognized in its autonomy and freedom, so artists set themselves to exhaust the world of visual forms in which man's life took place, and offered the synthesis of this study as a model for the new society that was being formed.

The specific structure of perspective vision, by assigning priority to geometrical and perspective features, placed painting in a privileged position, as the depository of the universal instrument for the shaping of

64 *One of Donatello's* tondi *on the ceiling of the S. Lorenzo sacristy, Florence*

visible forms, i.e. drawing. And since the defining of forms was appreciated for its intellectual value, independently of a physical and dimensional realization, architecture – whose distinction was precisely that it realized a complex of created works which formed the physical scene of human life – for the first time lost its character as an all-embracing procedure, support and synthesis of the other arts, and became a specific application of a more general creative activity, more directly recognizable in the figurative arts and in particular in painting.

This is the sense in which the praise of painting, with which the second book of Alberti's treatise begins, should be understood:[84]

'Who can doubt that painting is the master art or at least not a small ornament of things? The architect, if I am not mistaken, takes from the painter architraves, bases, capitals, columns, façades and other similar things. All the smiths, sculptors, shops and guilds are governed by the rules and art of the painter. It is scarcely possible to find any superior art which is not concerned with painting, so that whatever beauty is found can be said to be born of painting.'

For architecture, the contribution of painting therefore concerned the conformation of the elements, specified and made stable by Brunelleschi's research. But the very distinction introduced by Brunelleschi, between standardized elements and the structures which resulted from their association, established the margin of professional independence between architects and painters, and guaranteed the new architecture the ability to modify the townscape. But in painting and the figurative arts a rigorous operation like Brunelleschi's was inconceivable, drastically limiting the morphological repertoire as it did, to reveal the coherence and freedom of perspective construction. The figurative arts had to remain infinitely free to manipulate all the forms of existing or imagined objects,

then to distribute the exemplary forms among the applied arts concerned with the various sectors. For this reason painting and sculpture long remained faithful to the traditional structural patterns, and even the technique of linear perspective was accepted, for many decades, only partially, as one of the available spatial hypotheses alternating and combined with other techniques such as that of axonometry. The most frequent models of presentation of the image were drawn from medieval practice – for instance the room with one or more walls missing, where an 'interior' scene is taking place, as in the miracles of St Peter painted in the Brancacci chapel – and possibly depended upon the theatrical technique in use in the late Middle Ages and the fifteenth century.[85]

Only by degrees, and over a fairly long period of time, did perspective technique succeed in co-ordinating and fusing these disparate contributions; the absolute freedom of Brunelleschi's architectural space became contracted and limited when it passed into the field of painting, and the theoretical continuity of spatial representation (extended from the foreground backwards *ad infinitum*) was almost always sectioned or interrupted by partial discontinuities. Painters were willing to give up coherence of composition in order to bring on the scene the whole world of appearances of the reality of their time, with its weight of symbolic, popular and esoteric associations.

In this way painting remained associated more closely than architecture with contemporary affairs, and its prestige was justified by its capacity to comment on all the circumstances of individual and collective life, while ideally going beyond immediate situations, and providing an advance representation of the background of future human experiments: the boundless and measurable world which was to be travelled by the sixteenth-century explorers and investigated by the scientists of the seventeenth century.

In fact the image of life reflected in the

65–67 *Predella of the* Annunciation *by Fra Angelico. Diocesan Museum, Cortona*

68, 69   *Two altar panels by Donatello. S. Antonio, Padua*

70   *The 'mazzocchio' used by Uccello to explain perspective constructions*

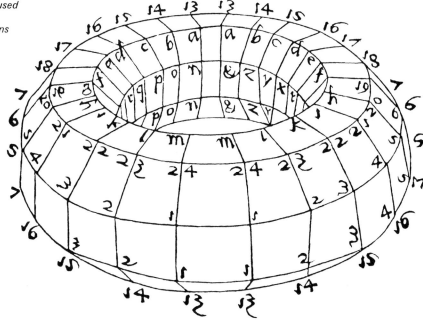

71   *The* Flood *by Uccello. Cloister of S. Maria Novella, Florence*

72 *Detail from Masaccio's frescoes in the Brancacci chapel. S. Maria del Carmine, Florence*

painting of the fifteenth century was strongly reductive – in the sense explained by Lévi-Strauss[86] – in proportion to the rigour of the new figurative methods and it, in its turn, influenced life; it established a model of formal coherence which remained valid for a time even while social conditions changed.

Vasari drew the collective character of the Florentine artistic movement at the beginning of the century;[87] but he wanted to show a trio of founding fathers for all the three arts, like Brunelleschi had been for architecture, and for sculpture he chose Donatello (1386–1466) and for painting Masaccio (1401–28), though they were only slightly younger than Lorenzo Ghiberti (1378–1455) and Paolo Uccello (1397–1475).

What was the basis of his choice? Donatello and Masaccio were friends of Brunelleschi's, they participated in his hazardous experimentation and were among the first to use the technique of linear perspective which he had studied. Still, their professional interest was always applied to things they could represent in statues and in pictures, and they used the new methods of representation as means of grasping more directly the reality of the visible universe. In taste they were both very far indeed from the ideal of perfection and refinement of their elders Ghiberti and Brunelleschi, as is quite evident even in the sculpture of the latter. Although they were among the first to use the technique of linear perspective, the two artists lived through the very moment of transition between the old and the new method of representation of plastic forms, and during this interim period they could look at the spectacle of nature with new eyes: hence the 'realism' which has been mentioned in connection with both of them. At the same time, their technical vocation was definitely specialized and exclusive, remote from the usual eclecticism common before and after their time.

The solemn figures of the frescoes in the Carmine devour the features of the represented space with their bulk; the painter seems much more concerned with the density and gravity of his characters than with the models of overall composition, which in many cases still adhere to traditional usage (Fig. 72).

The figures sculpted by Donatello stand proudly in natural space or at salient points of architectural space with the same powerful autonomy (Fig. 73). In the course of a long and stormy career he made it his business to broaden the field of sculptural experience so as to include the greatest possible number of aspects of reality, using various techniques (from *tutto tondo* to the shallowest bas-relief), various materials (metal, stone, plaster, clay) and accepting a large number of divergent influences, from classical examples to the Gothic tradition and the new theories of vision. Donatello's attempt to make sculpture rival painting as the universal instrument capable of exhausting the world of visible forms was sustained only by his dogged experimental commitment, and had no outcome in the changed mood of the late fifteenth century. But the painters' research acquired an increasingly marked hegemonic character, as it proceeded with the elaboration and differentiation of its methods of representation.

The postulate of the subordination of colour to drawing, at least in the form outlined so far, was proved untenable as early as the second half of the fifteenth century with the work of the new generation of painters who were active in a broader field: Piero della Francesca, born about 1420, Alessio Baldovinetti, born in 1427, Giovanni Bellini, born in 1428 and Antonello da Messina, born about 1430. The discovery of the laws of colour relationships was, technically speaking, as important as that of the perspective reproduction of volume, and made the function of painting convincing, from then onwards, as an activity that would reveal and regulate the world of visible forms.

In practice, there was a real conflict between developments in painting and archi-

73 *Monument to Gattamelata in Padua by Donatello*

74   *The Strozzi chapel with frescoes by Filippino Lippi. S. Maria Novella, Florence*

tecture; the new architecture, from Brunelleschi onwards, excluded the presence of wall-paintings, and the great new cycles of painting – the frescoes by Masaccio in the Brancacci chapel in the Carmine, by Piero della Francesca in Arezzo (Figs 80, 81), Filippo Lippi in the apse of the cathedral at Prato, Mantegna at the Eremitani in Padua, Ghirlandaio in the Sassetti chapel in S. Trinità and the Tornabuoni chapel in S. Maria Novella, Filippino Lippi in the Carafa chapel in S. Maria sopra Minerva in Rome and the Strozzi chapel in S. Maria Novella (Fig. 74) – are almost always in medieval buildings, as has been noted.[88] This is not a matter of chance; the spaces of the new architecture were framed by the architectural orders, and the walls acquired a virtually three-dimensional organization which excluded their simultaneous use as supports for the fiction of an autonomous pictorial space; if paintings had to appear in these spaces, they would be framed as independent objects, altarpieces or polyptychs; indeed Alberti's treatise specifically so prescribes. Pius II requested that no painting should disfigure the white of the walls in the church of Pienza (Fig. 75) and Bernardino Baldi, in the description of the palace at Urbino, noted that fresco decoration had been excluded 'because the eye should be concerned with nothing other than eternity and the essential beauty of the architecture'.[89]

In medieval buildings, on the other hand, the architectural elements formed an open system which did not exclude, indeed encouraged, the various spatial interpretations introduced by painters, and the great smooth walls of the churches or halls were actually intended for fresco decoration; these might be executed in the modern style without clashing with the building that held them. It was the painters, if anyone, who sometimes felt the need to protect their representations with a suitable architectural setting, as was the case with Filippino Lippi in S. Maria Novella.

75 *One of the paintings placed
in Pienza cathedral by Pius II*

76 *Detail from the* Legend of St
Ursula *by Carpaccio. Accademia,
Venice (from Chastel)*

77   *Intarsia by Pierantonio da Modena. Padua cathedral*

The relationship between architecture and sculpture was conditioned by the fact that the execution of the standard elements necessary to define the architectural spaces – bases, capitals, cornices, cornices, corbels, etc. – was the sculptor's responsibility. A methodological distinction similar to that in the sphere of painting grew up between this functional decoration and other possible plastic ornaments introduced into the architecture; but the borderline between the two types of decoration was frequently forgotten when architectural decoration proliferated, invading the entire wall space – as usually happened in Lombard architecture in the second half of the fifteenth century – or else when some plastic elements became so important that they actually conditioned the architecture, as for instance in the chapel of the Cardinal of Portugal in S. Miniato in Florence.

In this connection a positive rivalry grew up between sculpture and architecture in the second half of the century, which was interrupted only when the great masters of the early sixteenth century once again specified the autonomy of the two activities, and each could aspire to its own exclusive greatness.

Throughout the fifteenth century the close connection between the activities of sculptors and architects tended to limit the prestige of sculpture *vis-à-vis* painting, which was untouched by these controversies and could gather into its own ambit all the forms elaborated by the other arts. In this phase painting (both panel-paintings and frescoes) not only immortalized the fascinating scenery of a world of forms unified by light, but appropriated architectural design and anticipated the range of buildings realized around the end of the fifteenth century and the beginning of the sixteenth. The architecture of Giuliano da Sangallo, Francesco di Giorgio and Mauro Coducci was all painted before being built (Figs 78–80).

This situation is vividly described by Chastel:[90]

'A consequence of the modern reform of architecture was the elimination of frescoes. In the old style buildings, where it still had its *raison d'être*, and to which it was relegated, painting took its revenge by depicting ideal places (and particularly those buildings, such as basilicas or circular temples, in which there was no longer any place for painting, but which it could still depict).'

In the second half of the fifteenth century, there was a long series of innovations which gave new vigour both to the practice of painting and to the use made of its results. Oil colours and canvas directly transformed the technique of painting, and large canvases made it possible to prepare whole cycles of mural decoration actually in the workshops.

Preparatory designs laid down the aspects of the pictorial image which were considered the most important; better quality paper was available for them and a series of new drawing materials – red crayon, pastel – which were added to the traditional ones – pen, paintbrush, silverpoint and *pietra nera*. For fresco, too, the preparatory outlines were executed separately on cartoons, and then transported to the wall by means of the *spolvero*. This procedure, which came into use towards the middle of the century, replaced the *sinopie* drawn straight on to the plaster and, in painting, underlined the pre-eminence of the graphic construction.

Drawing had an extremely broad function at this time; being the science and technique mainly linked to the geometrical description of objects, it acted as the main instrument for the transmission of knowledge, and at a certain moment – towards the end of the century – seemed even more important than the written word. Hence the urgent need to reproduce drawings; the technique of wood engraving was joined, about the middle of the fifteenth century, by that of engraving on metal; Vasari attributed the invention to the Florentine Maso Finiguerra[91] but probably

78   *Painting by Gentile Bellini. Accademia, Venice*
79   *Painting by G. Mansueti. Accademia, Venice*
80   *Fresco by Piero della Francesca. S. Francesco, Arezzo*

81 *Fresco by Piero della Francesca. S. Francesco, Arezzo*

82 Battle of the Naked Men, *engraving by Pollaiuolo*

the same technique was perfected separately in Italy and Germany.

Eminent artists such as Antonio Pollaiuolo (Fig. 82) and Andrea Mantegna brought copper engraving to a high degree of perfection; the same procedure could be used to reproduce works of painting, with documentary intent, as is done today with photographs; in 1491 Mantegna explained, in a letter to Francesco Gonzaga, that he could easily repaint a work sold by the prince, because he had kept the engraved reproduction of it;[92] a few years later Giulio Campagnola was able to produce a line engraving of a painting by Giorgione.

The dawning art of printing used engraving, particularly in wood, for book illustration: in 1465 the first illustrated book was printed at Subiaco, and in 1472 the *De re militari* by Valturio with the illustrations by Matteo de' Pasti was printed at Verona.

Thus at the end of the fifteenth century painting became the dominant activity in a vast group of figurative techniques, indispensable to the life of the new society. The studies carried out by painters on panels and canvas, hierarchically influenced the work of numerous specialists.

Alberti and the theoretical ordering of the new artistic experience

Leon Battista Alberti (1404–72) occupies a dominant position in the history of literature as well as in that of architecture and the theory of art. His experiments, unique and unrepeatable if examined on their own account, left an extremely lasting mark on each of these fields and established some links between the one and the other which were to remain an inherent part of subsequent development.

Born in Genoa of an exiled Florentine family, he studied at Padua and Bologna, and only after 1428 – when the ban on his family was lifted – was he allowed to return to his family's native city.

Meanwhile he worked as secretary to important prelates, and frequently had to move around with them; from 1431 onwards he was in Rome, as abbreviator for the Apostolic Chancery, and after 1434 – when he was thirty – he was able to remain in Florence for a fairly long period. These were the first years of Medici power; Brunelleschi was about to complete the dome, Ghiberti was working on the third baptistery door, Paolo Uccello had been in the city since 1430. Donatello came back with Cosimo, and the new generation of Florentine artists – Michelozzo, Fra Angelico, Lippi, Rossellino and Luca della Robbia – was now entering the scene, given impetus by the discoveries of the previous fifty years.

Alberti entered this milieu with enthusiasm, became friends with Brunelleschi and the other artists, and himself experimented with painting and sculpture. Fired by these encounters, he wrote the treatises *De statua* and *De pictura*,[93] in which he attempted a first theoretical analysis of the ideas and experiments that had so far been produced by the Florentine workshops.

The two treatises are based on a precise technical exposition which demonstrates Alberti's liking for concrete processes; on to this he grafts an extremely lucid intellectual discussion, completely new in tone, and indeed it was the tone, rather than the specific theses, that caused the treatises to have so permanent an effect.

The *De statua* is a very short text, with no systematic character, but with an extraordinary polemical force, because it replaced the traditional technical description of artistic work with a completely new conceptual description.

We have mentioned the medieval classification of artists according to the materials they used, on which the trade guilds were based. Alberti devotes not a word to this subject, and puts forward a new classification of artists according to the logical form of their operations:

1   Those who work 'by adding to or taking from' (workers in stucco).
2   Those who work 'by taking away and carving out of the material that which is superfluous, whereby . . . they produce out of whatever mass of marble the shape . . . which was there hiddenly before . . .' (sculptors); engravers of seals should perhaps be classified here too, as they carve out the negative of forms to be reproduced in relief.
3   Those who work 'by only adding' (silversmiths). These are the nearest to painters, who apply the colours to the painting, but reproduce reality with a different 'artifice'.[94]

Among the objects to be represented, Alberti considers the human figure; sculpture can set out to achieve either a generic reproduction of the typical features of man or else a specific reproduction of individual ones.

But every representation is merely the transferring of a spatial form from one material to another, and may be described entirely in geometrical terms; Alberti wished to provide the rules of this representation, which are two:

1   *Measure*, which is 'a constant and certain observation, by examining the just number and measures, what habitude, symmetrie and correspondence (all the parts of the body have one towards another)'.[95] The necessary instrument is a ruler divided into six feet, where each foot is divided into ten inches and each inch into ten minutes; these are not absolute quantities, but relative to human stature and variable according to the scale of reproduction, and therefore measurable only with a conventional, independent system of current units of measurement. Alberti also gives a

table of the 'main measurements which are to be found in man', partly taken from Vitruvius, but much more detailed; this was the starting-point for subsequent study of the proportions of the human body (Leonardo, Dürer).

2 *Limitation*, i.e. 'the determining or fixing of a certain period in the drawing of all our lines, so as to direct to what point they are to be continued, whether to be extended out in length, or reversed; how angles are to be fixed, how parts are to be raised, or depressed'.[96] In this context, too, Alberti describes an instrument, consisting of a circular 'horizon' to be placed above the drawing, and of a plumb line, which makes it possible to plot the surface of the figure point by point.

The *De statua* lays the foundations for the idea of sculpture as a science of the three dimensional representation of objects, and more specifically of projective representation, i.e. of the passage from one scale to another keeping proportional features fixed. This led to both the intellectual dignity of sculpture and the primacy of working 'by taking away' – repeated, with fascinating Neoplatonic emphasis, by successive theorists, and also by Michelangelo in the well-known sonnet[97] – in that it stresses the power of the intellectual operation over the material.

Unlike *De statua*, the *De pictura* is a real systematic treatise. The scheme of exposition, as has been noted,[98] derives from that of the humanist treatises on rhetoric – which in their turn were based on the Latin texts of Cicero and Quintilian – and those on poetry, which were based on Horace; the original sources are Aristotle's *Poetics* and *Rhetoric*, translated into Latin only at the end of the century. Horace distinguished *ars* (which included the *inventio-argumentum* and the *dispositio-elocutio*) and *artifex*. The three books of the treatise on painting in the Latin edition bear the titles *rudimenta* (which contained the new treatment of perspective), *pictura* and *pictor*; it should however be noted that the first two books contain the precepts

on the form of representation, corresponding to the *dispositio* and *elocutio*, and the third the precepts on content, corresponding to *inventio*. Interest in form became preponderant over interest in content.

This bold transfer, far from mechanical but free and problematical, was made possible by Alberti's keen sense of the doubtfulness of the cultural compartments received through tradition, and it did not in the least compromise the autonomy of art *vis-à-vis* literature; indeed it underlined it, although later (when cultural compartments again became more rigid) it worked in the opposite direction.

Alberti soon put himself in an intermediate position between that of pure theorist and that of practitioner; at the beginning he warned that[99]

'I will take first from the mathematicians those things with which my subject is concerned. . . . In all this discussion I beg you not to consider me as a mathematician but as a painter of these things. Mathematicians measure with their minds alone the form of things separated from all matter. Since we wish the object to be seen, we will use a more sensate wisdom. We will consider our aim accomplished if the reader can understand in any way this admittedly difficult subject – and, so far as I know, a subject never before treated.'

In this famous passage there is certainly an echo of the constant Albertian polemic against abstract and scholastic thought;[100] but he devoted the whole of the first book of the treatise to questions of geometry, which are presented implicitly as the foundation of painting.

All visible things are simply surfaces; surfaces have some 'permanent' qualities[101] ('outline and surface', i.e. the edges and form of their volume) and some variable ones because of 'the changing of place and light'.[102] Painting must take these variations into account, but must refine its mechanism in such a way as to establish an exact relation between image and model.[103]

'Let us investigate the reasons for this, beginning with the maxims of philosophers who affirm that the plane is measured by rays that serve the sight – called by them visual rays – which carry the form of the thing seen to the sense. We can imagine these rays to be like the finest hairs of the head, or like linen paper, tightly bound within the eye where the sense of sight has its seat. The rays, gathered together within the eye, are like a stalk; the eye is like a bud which extends its shoot rapidly and in a straight line to the plane opposite. Among these rays there are differences in strength and function. . . . Some of these rays strike the outline of the plane and measure its quantity. Since they touch the ultimate and extreme parts of the plane, we can call them extreme or . . . extrinsic. Other rays which depart from the surface of the plane for the eye fill the pyramid with the colours and brilliant lights with which the plane gleams; these are called median rays. Among these visual rays there is one which is called the centric. When this one touches the plane, it makes equal and right angles all around it.'

The whole of the 'extrinsic rays', which start from the outline of the surface and converge upon the eye, form the 'visual pyramid'; the 'median rays' fill the pyramid and transmit to the eye the luminous and chromatic qualities, while the centric ray, together with distance, defines the position of the observer in relation to the surface;[104] in this way the traditional operation of the painter, who imitates objects on his panel or canvas, is interpreted as the result of an optical construction which involves the space between the eye of the painter and the things he paints, and guarantees the agreement between image and reality.

Alberti imagines the resistance that will be put up by common opinion: 'But, some will say, what use is so much investigation to the

painter?' Turning to 'studious painters', he observes:[105]

'They should know that they circumscribe the plane with their line. When they fill the circumscribed places with colours, they should only seek to present the forms of things seen on this plane as if it were transparent glass. Thus the visual pyramid could pass through it, placed at a definite distance with definite lights and a definite position of centre in space and in a definite place in respect to the observer. . . .

Where this is a single plane, either a wall or a panel on which the painter attempts to depict several planes comprised in the visual pyramid, it would be useful to cut through this pyramid in some definite place, so the painter would be able to express in painting similar outlines and colours with his lines. He who looks at a picture, done as I have described, will see a certain cross section of a visual pyramid, artificially represented with lines and colours on a certain plane according to a given distance, centre and lights.'

This construction leads to a purely projective representation of reality, where every variation is brought back to the optical relations between the elements, revealed by the intersection of the pyramid with the plane of the painting, and every value is known 'by comparison'.[106]

Hence the possibility of envisaging the formal conception not as embodied in the single technical operations, but as a unitary and intellectual operation, independent of the specifications of weight and measure that fit it into the fabric of material experiment. Thus the notion and the dignity of 'art' remained unassailed, together with the primacy of painting, which defined and administered the fundamental values of the new cultural universe and 'contains divine force', as we read in the eulogy already quoted, at the beginning of the second book.[107]

The principles laid out in the three books

of the treatise on painting are in a sense the account of a first exploration, carried out with feverish enthusiasm in an unknown world: the famous description of the perspective framework to be introduced into the painting 'which is considered to be an open window through which I see what I want to paint';[108] the breaking down of the process of painting into three phases, 'circumscription, composition and reception of light'[109] (which correspond to the three elements of Aristotelian and Ciceronian rhetoric, *inventio*, *dispositio* and *elocutio*, but which transfer these distinctions to the field of formal appearance; it should be noted that the role of *inventio* is attributed to drawing, i.e. to the definition of the geometrical features of what is to be depicted); and the rules on the content of the representation, referred to briefly in the third book.

When he wrote the treatise on painting, Alberti was already well versed and well known in the literary field: he had written the *Philodoxus*, the *De commodis litterarum atque incommodis*, some of the *Intercoenales* and possibly a part of *Della famiglia*. His eulogy of painting was not only the literary illustration of a specialized commitment – as in the professional writing of the artists, from Cennini to Ghiberti, or in the apologias that literary men addressed to artists – but served authoritatively to define the place of painting in the new cultural system, and to evaluate the relations between painting and literature objectively for the first time. The humanist could not bring himself to weaken the primacy of literature, but he wanted to procure a similar cultural prestige for painting by means of a long series of classical examples and to associate it closely with literature: 'Since all the other arts were recommended in letters by our great men, and since painting was not neglected by our Latin writers, I believe that our ancient Tuscan [ancestors] were already most excellent masters in painting.'[110] This judgment was connected with his own personal experience, as he himself recognized: 'Allow me to speak of myself here. Whenever I turn to painting for my recreation, which I frequently do when I am tired of more pressing affairs, I apply myself to it with so much pleasure that I am surprised that three or four hours have passed.'[111]

Alberti's acquaintance with architecture took place later, and amid more serious difficulties.

He had begun his exploration of the ancient monuments possibly as early as his first stay in Rome (1431–4), measuring them with instruments he had constructed himself. About 1443 he was in Ferrara, where he may have advised Lionello d'Este on the pedestal for the monument to Niccolò III and on the campanile for the cathedral.

Only when he returned to Rome to work for Nicholas V, and while he was again engrossed in his mathematical studies,[112] did he seriously tackle the study of architecture; it was during these years that he probably completed the *Descriptio urbis Romae*, collaborated on the building programme with numerous technical contributions, and possibly outlined the general town-planning framework for the works of Nicholas V, as we shall see later. In the same period he composed the *De re aedificatoria* (dedicated to the Pope in 1452)[113] and received his first professional commission: the rebuilding of S. Francesco in Rimini for Sigismondo Malatesta (from 1450 onwards), then the group of Florentine works commissioned by the Rucellai family: the Palazzo Rucellai in via della Vigna Nuova (possibly 1447–50), the open space with the three-arched loggia in front of the palazzo, the chapel of the Holy Sepulchre in the nearby church of S. Pancrazio (begun about 1457) and the completion of the façade of S. Maria Novella (probably begun about 1456).

These works – including the palazzo which was fitted in among the other houses fronting on to the street – in a sense amounted to exercises in the decoration of wall surfaces.

They show that Alberti underestimated both the contrast between old and new architecture, and the particular restricting character of the standard classical forms. The new architecture was conceived as a noble backdrop of interrelated elements, to be contemplated almost like a painting, and capable of ennobling the elements of the traditional city without contradicting its character.

These works record the features of the historical moment in which they were conceived with surprising immediacy: the confident and optimistic mood of the sixth decade of the century, in which long-standing disputes were ended (in 1449 the Council of Basle was concluded; in 1452 Frederick III had himself crowned emperor in Rome; in 1454 the Italian league was formed at Lodi); the mentality of the generation educated in the humanistic climate of the early fifteenth century, inclined to conciliation between old and new, which was rising to positions of power at that time and which included, as well as Alberti, his patrons Nicholas V, Sigismondo Malatesta, Lionello d'Este, Giovanni Rucellai; the oriental allusions were connected with the presence of members of the orthodox church at the Council of Florence in 1439 and with plans for the crusade, after the fall of Constantinople in 1453.

Alberti came to architecture through experience of literature and the figurative arts; this intellectual sequence inevitably influenced the character of his buildings, laden with didactic intentions and subtle formal expedients; but, as always, Alberti tackled the new field of problems with absolute commitment and faced the difficulties with an admirable effort at coherence and clarity.

The rebuilding of the church of S. Francesco in Rimini was begun in 1447 by Matteo de' Pasti, who laid out the first chapel on the right dedicated to St Sigismund and subsequently extended the same motif along both walls of the nave; in 1450 Alberti was commissioned to design the external architecture of the church, and attempted to break free as far as possible from the inner organism ('those widths and heights of the chapels trouble me', he wrote from Rome to the local builder[114] whom he used to execute his plans).

He decided to surround the building with a masonry casing, detached from the original masonry along the sides, in order to free the rhythm of the arches from that of the windows behind them (Figs 84, 85). On the front the motif of the arches continues and is transformed: the side arches – which were to hold the sarcophagi of Sigismondo and Isotta, and were later filled in to become almost level with the wall – are reminiscent of those along the sides in form and function; but the central arch is broader, deeper, and cuts away the continuous base to allow for the entrance. The motif of the three arches is framed by an order of half-columns, on which is raised a second, incomplete, order of pilasters. The whole block was to serve as a vestibule to a tribune roofed by a hemispherical dome, like that of the Pantheon; here Alberti would have obtained the coincidence between internal and external form, reducing the importance of the pre-existing organism which would have been incorporated in the new as a mere incidental episode. Work was interrupted in 1466, on the death of the duke, and the tribune was never even begun; it is significant, in any case, that the work of encasing the medieval structure should have taken precedence.

The organism conceived by Alberti is a synthesis of numerous ancient models: the idea of the 'temple' raised on a base, Roman structures with continuous rows of arches, either simple or framed by an order with entablature, the domed rotundas. In making use of these references, Alberti's method was virtually the opposite of Brunelleschi's; in fact he tended to reproduce the features of the overall composition exactly, but allowed himself to manipulate the details freely; an example of this is the architectural order of the façade, the capitals of which combine the

83 *Arch of Augustus, Rimini*

distinctive features of all four classical orders: first a crown of acanthus leaves derived from the Corinthian, then the echinus decorated with ovoli derived from the Doric, then the scrolls of the Ionic which, in connection with the other elements, are reminiscent of the organization typical of the composite.

Naturally the reference to ancient models, for the general composition, could not be absolutely rigorous, since pre-existing structures and modern distributive needs had to be taken into account; in its turn the margin of oscillation introduced into the details prevented a coherent distinction between standard forms and other plastic ornaments, and introduced the possibility of treating the whole plastic apparatus of a building in a single way, contrasting it with the perspective

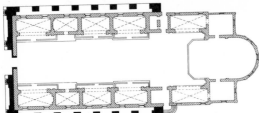

84–86   *Side view, plan and façade of the Tempio*
Malatestiano, Rimini
87, 88   *Details from the Tempio Malatestiano*

89 *The zodiacal sign of the Pisces: detail of the interior décor of the Tempio Malatestiano*

layout and referring both to two different levels of perception: the layout becomes a framework which regulates the distribution of the plastic elements, and they, as a whole, may thus be widely spaced, revealing the underlying system with maximum clarity – as happens here – or so massed as positively to compromise the recognizability of the structure, as happens in the internal décor designed by Matteo de' Pasti and Agostino di Duccio, possibly with the advice of Alberti himself (Fig. 89).

This possibility – which, in relation to Brunelleschi's method is something of a retreat to the methods of the late Gothic tradition – was to be exploited to the full in the second half of the fifteenth century, particularly in northern Italy; it allowed the use of a distribution of skills already approved by tradition, and conditioned the spread of the new architectural repertoire in Italy for almost a century.

The Florentine works were based on an intelligent reconciliation of the ancient repertoire and that of local tradition.

In S. Maria Novella (Fig. 90) Alberti's façade incorporates the medieval motifs of the base and frames it in a classical order, skilfully graduating the transition from the small scale of the medieval ornaments to the large scale of the modern ones; between the lower order of half-columns, set between the corner pillars, and the upper order of pilasters, supported by great scrolls, there is a band which separates the two motifs. The façade is decorated with marble inlay which unifies the various parts chromatically; the medieval rose-window is incorporated into this and is therefore reduced to a secondary position.

The Palazzo Rucellai is characterized by the three classical orders – Doric, Ionic and Corinthian – which frame the traditional rusticated covering and distinguish the three storeys of the building; here, too, motifs of differing origins – the facing with its varied recurrent ornaments, the two-lighted win-

dows and the classical apparatus of the pilasters, cornices and doorways – are fused into a skilful and sophisticated design (Fig. 92).

The loggia – the history of whose execution has still not been clarified – repeats the archaic pattern of the loggia of the Innocenti which Brunelleschi himself had already gone beyond in the naves of S. Lorenzo and S. Spirito; the columns have no entablature, but a simple moulding from which the arches spring; the order simply surrounds the arches and introduces them to their surroundings (Fig. 93).

In the last of the Florentine works – the Rucellai chapel in S. Pancrazio with the shrine of the Holy Sepulchre (Figs 94, 95) – the wall decoration is used to qualify an enclosed space; recent research[115] has shown that the space was already fixed, as far as the measurements of the ground plan were concerned; Alberti was able to decide only about the dividing-up of the walls and roof, like Brunelleschi in the Pazzi chapel.

The architecture of the chapel was entirely determined by the interplay of the standard elements – pilasters, cornices, arches – as in Brunelleschi's work, but the spacing of the pilasters was not linked to the spatial articulation of the room. The chapel originally opened on to the church along one of the main walls, where the pilasters were replaced by columns; thus the chapel was conceived in terms of this prospect, and its division was projected in depth to frame the space; the columns and pilasters placed on the two long sides are linked above by the soffits placed in the barrel-vaulting, i.e. they form a composition that runs around the room but is to a certain degree independent of it. The little shrine built in the middle of the chapel consists of an assembly of square panels, repeated both on the flat sides and on the curve of the apse; the architectural order is used to separate the panels and the pilasters are replaced, on the curved side, by simple white strips (Figs 94, 95).

90 *Façade of S. Maria Novella, Florence*

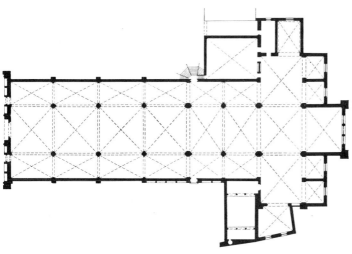

91 *Plan of S. Maria Novella with Alberti's façade*

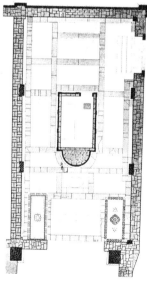

92 *Palazzo Rucellai, Florence*
93 *Loggia Rucellai, Florence*
94, 95 *Rucellai chapel in S. Pancrazio, Florence*

All these works, from the Tempio Malatestiano to the Holy Sepulchre, presented problems of general outline, traceable beneath the architectural composition.

The declarations contained in the treatise and the very character of these compositions, rigorous for their own part but always to some degree disconnected from the building organisms on which they were based, justify the search for a strictly geometrical internal rule of organization. Since it was basically a question of two-dimensional compositions, from the start this rule had a meaning different from Brunelleschi's modular restrictions: it did not involve spatial organization, it is not to be found in the ground plans but in the elevations, and it can be compared to the systems of lines introduced by painters into their frontal representations.

In some cases the nature of the rule is obvious, as with the façade of S. Maria Novella which is based on the assembly of so many squares, made obvious by the inlay whose panels are cut according to squares, and double squares; the same procedure, as we have seen, determined the measurements of the shrine of the Holy Sepulchre.

However, the deduction of the overall measurements from the rule of the square is not easy; until the time when an exact measured plan makes it possible to clarify the problem completely, one circumstance in particular seems significant: Alberti's geometrical rule serves to take net measurements of certain empty spaces. For instance, in the decorative panels of S. Maria Novella the proportion of the double square is valid for the white fields, excluding the green cornice; in other words all the strips, and the architectural elements comparable to the strips such as columns, pilasters and cornices, function as separating intervals, not as a primary framework of the composition; the significant measurements are not to be taken from the axes of the elements, but from the edges of the fields framed by them.

In other cases – the Tempio Malatestiano,

Palazzo Rucellai, the shrine of the Holy Sepulchre – the use of more complex ratios has been inferred, i.e. $\dfrac{1}{\sqrt{2}}$ and the golden section; the first of these ratios is indeed considered in *De re aedificatoria* for certain spaces, i.e. for those of doors,[116] while the second is not mentioned. Bruschi[117] has noted that in the long walls of the chapel in S. Pancrazio the fields included between the pilasters are golden rectangles, and this proportion has been confirmed by the measured drawings of Dezzi Bardeschi.[118] Zoubov, who systematically collated the proportions of Alberti's buildings with those prescribed in the treatise,[119] believes that Alberti used a rational ratio $(5:8)$ approximated downwards to the golden section.

The interpretation of these choices of proportion remains controversial, not only because of the lack of measured drawings but also because of uncertainty about the points of juncture of the geometrical layouts, when reference to the axes of the standard elements is absent. It is, however, certain that these works of Alberti mark the partial return in the direction of an esoteric tradition, temporarily interrupted by the rational researches of the previous generation, and they coincide with the beginning of the Neoplatonist turning-point: at this time the young Ficino was starting his career at the court of the Medici.

In the works of Brunelleschi the geometrical limitations were strictly structural; here, on the other hand, there existed additional intellectual restrictions, which indicated the desire to go beyond the physical appearance of the organism, and alluded to a truth hidden behind appearances. From now on this component remained engrained in the European artistic repertoire, and reappeared, more or less obviously, in subsequent developments.

The great influence of these works derives from the possibility of confronting them with an organized theoretical argument, i.e. with the treatise *De re aedificatoria*, completed at the same period. The written argument, in its terms, was persuasive because it presupposed the concrete experiments of the author, but extended them over a far broader cultural field which exercised a deep influence over both architects and contemporary and later writers.

The approach in the treatise on architecture is not as simple and immediate as in that on painting. Here Alberti was not fired by the enthusiasm of a recent discovery; instead he was trying to summarize a long series of experiments, and had to bear in mind Vitruvius' treatise (previously known through encyclopedic compilations, and rediscovered in the original text by Poggio Bracciolini in 1414), though he remains absolutely lucid and open-minded towards the ancient writer.

The definition of architecture, with which the treatise opens, is quite different in character from that of painting:[120]

'Him I call an architect who, by sure and wonderful art and method, is able, both with thought and invention, to devise, and with execution, to compleat all those works, which, by means of the movement of great weights, and the conjunction and amassment of bodies, can, with the greatest beauty, be adapted to the uses of mankind.'

The task of the architect is twofold: to invent and to execute; execution is no longer, as for the painter, a subsidiary technique of the intellectual representation incorporated in the latter, but becomes a distinct operation, which gains the building its completion as far as human needs are concerned; the aim of painting is to gain praise and fame for its author, the aim of architecture is also to satisfy some of the material needs of men.

While a painting can be considered only as an image,[121]

'an edifice is a kind of body consisting, like all other bodies, of design and of matter; the first is produced by the thought, the other by nature; so that the one is to be provided by the application and contrivance of the mind, and the other by due

preparation and choice. And we further reflected, that neither the one nor the other was sufficient, without the hand of an experienced artificer, that knew how to form his materials after a just design.'

The dignity of architecture depends upon the invention, and Alberti is committed to vindicating just this aspect, in opposition to medieval tradition; none the less it is the task of the architect to 'devise and complete' his works, making use of the 'manual operator' as 'instrument'.[122]

The two aspects of the architectural process are translated into two different operations: 'design and walling'. 'The whole force and rule of the design, consists in a right and exact adapting and joining together the lines and angles which compose and form the face of the building.'[123]

By this stressing of the geometrical aspect at the beginning of the discussion, architecture was drawn into the same intellectual field as painting and the figurative arts; but architectural design (to which the first book is devoted) is born of an extremely significant series of successive specifications, which include all the theoretical and practical requirements to be synthesized in planning:

1 The region, i.e. the place chosen to build upon, taking into account climate, security, pleasantness, the whole natural and artificial setting.
2 The site, i.e. the terrain on which the perimeter of the building is to stand, from which an initial range of circular, polygonal and square, etc. forms derives.
3 Compartition, which 'sub-divides the whole platform [site] of the house into smaller platforms'[124] and lays down the distributive pattern of the building.
4, 5 and 6 Walling, covering and apertures, i.e. the conformation of the vertical and horizontal structures and the apertures opened in these.

In the second book Alberti describes the

instruments of planning: drawings and models, concerning himself mainly with the exact correspondence between plan and execution, which was the crucial problem of the new architecture in this initial phase.

Models were not to be of account for their perfection, as independent works, but in terms of their functionality in establishing the form of the finished building, which is the aim of architecture. The author warns against any confusion between plan and execution; he advises repeated discussion of the plan through drawings and models, and even suggests that a little time should be allowed to pass, after the completion of the plan, before proceeding to its execution; in fact all technical and economic needs should be calculated in advance, to avoid interruptions and changes during the course of the work.

There follows an examination of building materials and component parts – foundations, masonry, carpentry, roofing and flooring – which occupies the end of the second and the third book. The description of the actual positioning again poses the question of geometry expounded in the first book; Alberti's advice is to trace two axes of symmetry, from which the position of all the other elements may be deduced.

Books 4–9 contain a classified description – the first to be attempted in modern times – of the various types of building (fortresses, palaces, churches, monasteries, other public buildings, private houses and villas) and of the city that contains them.

The terminology used is that of classical origin; temples are described, not churches, and his passion for completeness caused Alberti to describe some ancient buildings which had no equivalent in modern times: baths, theatres, amphitheatres and triumphal arches. But an experience of the modern city can be recognized in Vitruvius' terminology, and a first and thought-provoking ordering of it is attempted here; the image of the ancient city is superimposed as an ideal model upon the current one, without obscur-

ing the specific needs which were emerging just at this time.

The exposition is repeated twice: for buildings and for their 'ornaments'; the connecting-point is provided by the sixth book which defines 'beauty' and 'ornament' as related notions, though not identical, and which contains a brief historical excursus on the origin of architecture in the classical world.

This is the most problematical point of Alberti's argument.

His reasoning starts from the Vitruvian distinction between *commoditas*, *firmitas* and *venustas*, repeated word for word at the beginning of the sixth book.[125] Immediately afterwards Alberti launches into a eulogy of *venustas*, where 'beauty' and 'ornament' are used as synonyms, and excellence of form is considered as a quality contrasting with functionality and stability, or indeed almost as an extra layer that could be removed ('one would almost imagine that they had a mind to have it thought, that all those things (so absolutely necessary to the life of mankind) if stripped of their pomp and ornament, would be somewhat stupid and insipid').[126] But the beauty of which Alberti talks is the specific beauty of the new architecture, regenerated on classical examples and hence connected with perspective regularity and inseparable from the form of the building; for this reason Alberti distinguishes between beauty and ornament, though with some hesitation:[127]

'But what beauty and ornament are in themselves, and what difference there is between them may perhaps be easier for the reader to conceive in his brain, than for me to explain by words. In order therefore to be as brief as possible, I shall define beauty to be a harmony of all the parts, in whatsoever subject it appears, fitted together with such proportion and connection, that nothing could be added, diminished or altered, but for the worse. A quality so noble and divine,

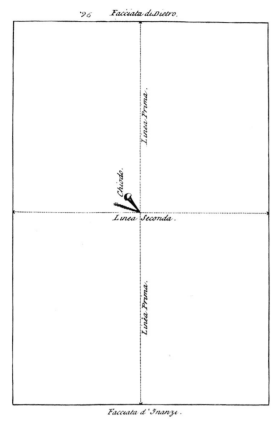

'96   Facciata di Dietro.

Linea Prima.

Chiusto.

Linea Seconda.

Linea Prima.

Facciata d'Inanzi.

96 *Sketch showing the two axes of symmetry in a building. Illustration from Leoni's third edition of Alberti's treatise, 1755*

that the whole force of wit and art has been spent to procure it; and it is very rarely granted to anyone, or even to nature herself, to produce anything every way perfect and compleat. . . . Ornament [is] a kind of auxiliary brightness and improvement to beauty. So that then beauty is somewhat lovely which is proper and innate, and diffused over the whole body, and ornament somewhat added or fastened on, rather than proper and innate.'

This argument starts from the rhetorical distinction between *dispositio* and *elocutio*, but develops it according to the specific nature of architectural experience.

Columns, i.e. the architectural order, are considered the 'main ornaments' of buildings. Thus Alberti failed to note the structural relationship between perspective composition and the recurrent forms of the orders, which was the essence of the new architecture from Brunelleschi onwards. The harmony of the proportions appears as an attribute of the bare masonry shell, and the purpose of ornament was to comment upon and accentuate it.

Alberti's architecture up to the sixth decade of the fifteenth century – i.e. the Rimini temple and the Florentine buildings designed for the Rucellai – is an experimental demonstration of this theoretical argument, providing an empirical justification which made good the margins of doubt left by demonstrations by logic.

But Alberti leaves the argument basically open; in the subsequent discussion (from the sixth to the ninth book) he talks of the 'ornaments' of the various buildings, but uses the word in its broadest sense, and simply runs over the discussion of the fifth book again with greater breadth; the tenth book discusses restorations and the control of waters.

At the end of the ninth book the author returns to the general problem: he lists the conditions of beauty – 'the number, figure and collocation of the several members'[128] – establishes a parallel between the proportions of architecture and the musical intervals,[129] and gives a series of pieces of advice for architects, including the famous and much debated ones on professional conduct:[130]

'You should not immediately run and offer your services to every man that gives out he is going to build; a fault which the inconsiderate and vainglorious are too apt to be guilty of. I know not whether you ought not to wait till you are more than once importuned to be concerned. Certainly they ought to repose a free and voluntary confidence in you, that want to make use of your labours and advice. . . .

For this reason a prudent man should take care to maintain his reputation; and certainly it is enough if you give honest advice, and correct draughts, to such as apply themselves to you. If afterwards you undertake to supervise and compleat the work, you will find it very difficult to avoid being made answerable for all the faults and mistakes committed either by the ignorance or negligence of other men. Upon which account you must take care to have the assistance of honest, diligent and severe overseers to look after the workmen under you.

I would also have you, if possible, concern yourself with none but persons of the highest rank and quality, and those too such as are truly lovers of these arts, because your work loses its dignity by being done for mean persons. Do you not see what weight the authority of great men is to advance the reputation of those who are employed by them? And, indeed, I insist the more upon this piece of advice, not only because the world has generally a higher opinion of the taste and judgement of great men, but also because I would have the architect always ready and plentifully supplied with everything that is necessary for compleating his edifice, which those of lower degree are commonly not so able, and therefore not so willing to do. To which add . . . that where the design and judgement has been perfectly equalled in two different works, one has been much more esteemed than the other for the sake of the superiority of the materials.'

This advice – which from a theoretical point of view adds nothing to the precise distinctions between 'design' and 'walling' contained in the opening remarks – must be seen in relation to Alberti's pessimism as a moralist, when he discusses the relations between *virtù* and fortune, and to the historical conditions of the architectural profession towards the middle of the fifteenth century: the cultural conflict between designers and builders was still strong enough to make distortions and errors inevitable; the separation of responsibilities was therefore an important prerequisite, indeed it was vital in order to maintain the clarity of the polemic of ideals. A closer relationship with the ruling class seemed necessary to maintain a position of strength, and to enable artists to emerge from the state of legal and economic subjection to which they were still confined, as we have said.[131]

The *De re aedificatoria* is the result of a noble effort to collect and co-ordinate a vast mass of material, only partly uniform and suited to theoretical exposition. At the beginning of the same book Alberti – always frank with the reader – gives a particularly vivid account of his literary activity, executed with much difficulty: 'The labour indeed was much more than I could have foreseen at the beginning.'[132]

'Continual difficulties every moment arose either in explaining the matter, or inventing names, or methodizing the subject, which perfectly confounded me, and disheartened me from my undertaking. On the other hand, the same reasons which induced me to begin this work pressed and encouraged me to proceed. It grieved me that so many great and noble instructions of ancient authors should be lost by the injury of time, so that scarce any bit Vitruvius has escaped this general wreck. A writer indeed of universal knowledge, but so maimed by age, that in many places there are great chasms, and many things imperfect in others . . . and he might almost as well have never have written at all, at least with regards to us, since we cannot understand him. There remained many examples of the ancient works, temples and theatres, from whence, as from the most skilful masters, a great deal was to be learned. But these I saw, and with tears I saw it, mouldering away every day. I observed too that those who in these days happen to undertake any new structure, generally ran after the whims of the moderns, instead of being delighted and directed by the justness of more noble works. By this means it was plain, that this part of knowledge, and in a manner of life itself, was likely in a short time to be wholly lost. In this unhappy state of things, I could not help having it long, and often, in my thoughts to write upon this subject myself . . . and I thought it the duty of an honest and studious mind to endeavour to free this science . . . from its present ruin and oppression. Thus I stood doubtful, and knew not how to resolve, whether I should drop my design, or go on. At length my love and inclination for these studies prevailed. There was not the least remain of any ancient structure, that had any merit in it, but what I went and examined, to see if anything was to be learned from it. Thus I was continually searching, considering, measuring and making draughts of everything I could hear of, till such time as I had made myself perfect master of every contrivance or invention that had been used in those Roman remains; and thus I alleviated the fatigue of writing by the thirst and pleasure of gaining information.'

His calm assessment of the need for this effort – though he referred rhetorically to ancient examples only – appears fully justified at the historical moment in which Alberti's treatise appeared.

The economic and political balance reached in the previous decade set off a further burst of building activity in the Italian cities (it should be remembered that work started again on Brunelleschi's sites after 1442; but he died soon afterwards, and his lessons were temporarily forgotten in the circle of his immediate successors); in Florence there followed the generation of artists born about the beginning of the fifteenth century (Michelozzo, Filippo Lippi and Rossellino) who scanned antiquity for examples of classical

elegance rather than constructional rigour.

This was the milieu that received Alberti's teaching, its vital importance hidden by the very extent of its immediate and remote consequences.

His commitment to instruction – like that of Gropius in the years between the two world wars – influenced a large number of otherwise disparate experiments, making comparison between them possible. His human as well as scientific involvement in architecture as 'part of life' enriched professional culture with many implications. It weakened the barriers deriving from individual choices and town and regional traditions, it hastened the spread of the Florentine movement throughout Italy, and a little later outside it as well.

Alberti was always primarily a man of letters, and his literary commitment was to cast a shadow over his architecture even when letters had their sphere of interest restricted, becoming a progressively serious impediment; on his own account, the author of *De re aedificatoria* was confident of being able to comprehend and order all the aspects of material reality on the printed page; the anonymous biographer presents him to us 'in the workshops of industrious artisans' to learn from 'smiths, builders, shipwrights and shoemakers'.[133] Technical application and theory were momentarily at one, though later they were to tend towards separation.

Alberti's Mantuan works, and his work on the tribune in the Annunziata, form a group different to the previous ones and demonstrate an extremely conscientious effort to overcome some of the contradictions previously illustrated.

Clearly his release from the post of apostolic abbreviator, in 1464, left Alberti more time to devote himself to the works commissioned by Ludovico Gonzaga; in 1470 he designed S. Andrea, and modified the plan of S. Sebastiano begun in 1460; S. Sebastiano was completed and subsequently altered, while S. Andrea was begun by

Fancelli only after Alberti's death. Alberti supplied advice and drawings for the choir of the Annunziata about 1470, and the great dome was built by Michelozzo in 1477. All three buildings were altered and redecorated in the seventeenth and eighteenth centuries, so that Alberti's conception is to be seen only by looking beyond the double mask of posthumous execution and baroque refurbishing.

The three organisms exemplify the main ground plan variants of the 'temples' discussed in the seventh book of the treatise on architecture: the 'round', the 'square' and the 'quadrangular temples, twice as long as broad'.[134]

S. Sebastiano (Figs 97–9) is a large square church, with four chapels 'twice as wide as they are from front to back'; the proportion of the chapels, too, in relation to the main space, seems to be that prescribed in the treatise ('divide the breadth of the temple into four parts, and give two of these parts to the breadth of the chapel'[135]). The state of the décor, inside and out, does not allow one to be able to say much more; but it seems certain that the ratios between the central space and the arms of the cross would have been emphasized by a single order, which would have stressed the common height of the impost of all the ceilings.

In S. Andrea (Figs 100–6) the organism is more complex. The rectangular nave has three chapels on each side ('it will be better to make an odd number on each side than an even one'[136]) and is ended by a domed tribune; the builders repeated the motif of the nave with side chapels on the arms of the transept too, but we do not know how far they respected Alberti's plan.

The most important innovation was the use of two complete orders, which form the upright elements of the chapels and those of the central cross respectively; Alberti was here applying to an organism of solid masonry, without columns or isolated supports, the Brunelleschian rule of two connected orders, where the arches supported by the minor order are framed beneath the entablature of the major one. This arrangement was coherently repeated in the interior – in the nave and three arms of the cross – and on the exterior, on the main façade, which was to be repeated at the two ends of the transept. The rigour of the organism is reminiscent of that of S. Spirito, which was born of a similar geometrical principle, and Alberti certainly wished to give this building a similar value as a prototype, all the more suitable for repetition in that it was not linked to any difficult or sophisticated building technique, like S. Spirito in Florence.

The two orders of the façade correspond roughly to the two inside; bearing in mind possible distortions in execution modern critics feel in a position to affirm that the façade reproduces the interior motif exactly and, more precisely, a typical bay of the walls of the nave, with the alternation of a broad interaxis between two narrow ones ('*rhythmische Travée*'[137]).

The tribune of the Annunziata is a broad circular space, surrounded by ten chapels; the axial chapel, towards the nave, is replaced by a wide arch, leading from the tribune to the church. We do not know the exact nature of Alberti's contribution for these works (an opinion or a plan), or how much the actual building owes to his intervention. From the very beginning this work was criticized because the arches of the chapels were cut out of the cylindrical wall, and were there distorted, giving an effect unusual for this period; the memory of this controversy was still alive when Vasari was writing the life of Alberti.[138]

The actual décor of these three buildings has been altered so frequently that an exact assessment of the relations between architectural orders and apertures is impossible; Alberti's discussion of proportion, as far as we can judge, directly concerned the masonry shell, on to which the columns, pilasters and cornices were applied.[139]

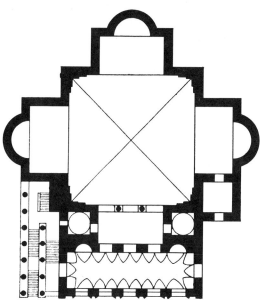

97–99 *Interior, plan and façade of S. Sebastiano, Mantua*

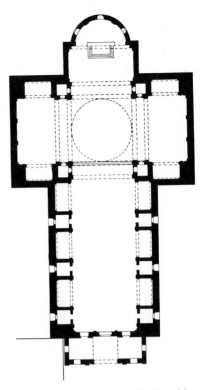

100, 101 *Interior and plan of S. Andrea, Mantua*

102, 103 *Façade and cupola of S. Andrea*

104, 105 *Side façade of S. Andrea and the church among the surrounding buildings of Mantua, 1628*

106 *Oblique view of the façade of S. Andrea*

107 *A detail of the campanile of Ferrara cathedral*

Restorations – like the one attempted in S. Sebastiano – finally laid bare the geometrical surfaces of the walls, and revealed an abstract and solemn architecture, which if it does not correspond to Alberti's intentions, certainly does reproduce a real phase of the Albertian method of planning.

The tendency to abstraction and the use of harmonic ratios as an intellectual guideline, concealed beyond the play of visible appearances, indicated a new outlook, definitely Neoplatonic;[140] the décor of the classical elements served to cover not the traditional components of the city, as at Rimini and S. Maria Novella, but the pure forms of an ideal and mathematical world. In the façades of the two Mantuan churches as well – analysed exhaustively by Wittkower[141] – Alberti used pilasters (not columns any longer) to divide up a compact and to some degree autonomous volume of masonry in the ancient style.

In these conditions, the relation between Alberti and the overseers, to whom the execution of the building was committed, may perhaps be conceived as a real example of planning collaboration, because the details did emerge in effect as independent – to some degree – of the masonry organisms, and variable according to time and place.

We do not know if this collaboration was ever regarded as admissible by Alberti; in reality that is how things happened, and not without reason. By having Matteo de' Pasti working in Rimini, Giovanni di Bertino at S.

108   *A detail of the main doorway of S. Andrea, Mantua*

Maria Novella and Luca Fancelli at Mantua, Alberti was doing much more than profiting from their technical experience as executors of his plans; he was setting up an inevitable dialogue with them, because his designs enabled him to lay down certain features of the general composition, but not most of the details. In this way a demonstration that the new architecture could be realized in many different ways was obtained, and that its meaning did not depend upon the form of the details, but rather upon the 'compartition' and rational placing of the single parts. In the field of plastic detail, too, various groups of skilled workers, bearers of independent traditions, were led to reproduce the canonic elements derived from the classical repertoire, and to maintain their recognizability, while using decorative variants far more numerous than those used in the restricted Tuscan circles.

The distributive solutions of Alberti's last works, which in one sense belong to the platonizing passion for ideal harmonic models, were received into the current repertoire as canonic examples, and helped to form that range of typical solutions which was one of the most characteristic requirements of the artistic culture of the late fifteenth century.

Here, too, Alberti's influence was enormous; for a whole century his solutions were regarded as absolutely authoritative, and only Palladio's generation succeeded in putting forward a new repertoire, selected with other criteria.

two

Towards the ideal city

About the middle of the fifteenth century we can list a series of military, diplomatic and religious events which concluded some long-standing controversies, typical of the preceding period, and which stabilized the European political scene on new foundations, making economic revival possible in the second half of the century.

The Hundred Years' War between France and England ended with the truce of 1444 and, after its resumption in 1449, was concluded definitively in 1453. In 1456 an ecclesiastical court rehabilitated Joan of Arc, and in 1461 Louis XI began his reconstruction of the French monarchic state.

The year 1438, after the death of Sigismund, saw the beginning of the series of Hapsburgs on the German imperial throne; Frederick III was the last emperor to go down into Italy, in 1452, to be crowned by the Pope. Dynastic stabilization favoured the detachment of the German regional states from the fortunes of the empire.

In 1449 the Council of Basle ended, and Nicholas V was recognized as sole Pope; the conciliar doctrine, vigorously upheld eighteen years before and accepted by Eugene IV in 1433, was in fact rejected, and condemned in 1460 by the Bull *Execrabilis* of Pius II.

The fall of Constantinople to the Turks in 1453 and the rapid expansion of the Ottoman empire persuaded the Italian states to conclude the Peace of Lodi in 1454; a league was formed between the five main states – Milan, Venice, Florence, Rome and Naples – which managed to avoid or contain Italian regional disagreements for forty years.

In 1450 Francesco Sforza seized power in Milan; Italian politics appeared dominated by the agreement of a few important figures: Francesco Foscari Doge of Venice, Cosimo de' Medici in Florence, Alfonso of Aragon in Naples and Federigo da Montefeltro, supreme *condottiere* of the league. The first four disappeared from the scene in the following decade – Foscari in 1457, Alfonso of Aragon in 1458, Cosimo de' Medici in 1464, Sforza in 1466 – leaving a power vacuum only partly filled by their successors; the balance established in 1454 was seen to be precarious and was to be suddenly upset, at the end of the century, by the clash between the great nation states.

The political truce and move towards authoritarianism encouraged a *rapprochement* between bourgeoisie and aristocracy, which also corresponded to the common interest of the new national monarchies. The class of entrepreneurs and bankers sought charters of nobility and aspired to mingle with the nobles

109 *Detail of the predella of the* Annunciation *by Fra Angelico. See also Figs 65–7*

and imitate their style of life; hence the resurgence of heraldic and late medieval elements in the literary and figurative arts from the middle of the century (Pisanello, Tura, Crivelli, Agostino di Duccio).

In the second half of the fifteenth century an increase in population, in agricultural and industrial production and in settlement generally began again everywhere; the exploitation of the silver and copper mines of central Europe, from 1460 onwards, eased the previous monetary crisis; the discovery of alum mines at Tolfa procured a new, consistent source of wealth for the papal state.

As in antiquity, the mining industry encouraged the formation of large-scale capitalism, which was to develop fully in the first half of the sixteenth century, outside the limits of the town economy.

The protagonists of the new political balance, as they consolidated their personal power at the expense of the old civic organization, willingly took upon themselves the task of patrons and organizers of culture. Some of them were learned humanists, like Nicholas V and Pius II, or connoisseurs of art and letters like Alfonso of Aragon, Cosimo de' Medici, Lionello d'Este and

Federigo da Montefeltro. One of the most important results of the new patronage was the formation of the great public libraries, which largely absorbed the private ones of the first half of the century and were often sufficient to establish the importance of cities as centres of culture.

Cosimo the Elder collected manuscripts, particularly during his stay in Venice, acquired the library of Niccolò Niccoli (who died in 1437) and founded the Medici library, enlarged by his successors. In 1450 Nicholas V founded the Vatican library which was later opened to the public by Sixtus IV. Cardinal Bessarion in 1468 left the Venetian republic his private library, which became the first nucleus of the Marciana. Federigo da Montefeltro founded one of the most splendid Renaissance libraries in Urbino and commissioned the Florentine bookseller Vespasiano da Bisticci to have copies made of the most important works of classical and modern literature.

About 1450 the printing press of Schöffer, Gutenberg and Fust was functioning in Mainz (Fig. 110). The new process of printing with movable characters spread rapidly: it appeared in Subiaco in 1464, in Paris and Rome in 1470, then in Florence and Venice.

The new organization of culture had its repercussions on the organization of the universities; Bessarion's reforms in Bologna dated from 1450, Cardinal d'Estouteville's in Paris from 1452. Meanwhile many new cultural organisms were developing: from 1463 to 1464 the Roman academy and Platonic academy were formed, almost simultaneously; so that the literary and artistic movement begun in the first half of the fifteenth century achieved a firm basis in new institutions, which became increasingly numerous and important towards the end of the century but broke off previous contacts with city life and concerns, and encouraged the formation of a general synthesis, autonomous and detached from concrete interests.

An examination of these changes is essential in order to assess the new culture's opportunities for action in the field of town-planning.

Brunelleschi's architecture, thought of as a total alternative to the Gothic tradition, contained the criteria for new town-planning praxis, and in at least two cases his building plans modified the distribution of the surrounding urban spaces: one example was when he fixed the position of the Ospedale degli Innocenti in relation to the church of the Annunziata and the via dei Servi, determining the organization of the future symmetrical piazza, and another was when he suggested to the monks of S. Spirito that he should reverse the direction of their church, turning the façade towards the Arno.

But the main object of the Florentine undertakings in the early fifteenth century was not the creation of a new city, but the completing of the urban design traced at the end of the thirteenth century and still unfinished; neither economic resources nor cultural ideals allowed for the planning of anything other than detailed and minor interventions in the shape of the city. There seemed to be no discrepancy between the ideal image of the city and the one accepted by tradition; hence the continuity of the municipality's building policy and the confidence of artists in completing the monuments of the past, but also the difficulty of gaining credence for the new methods of planning, beyond a certain scale. For this reason Brunelleschi's works of architecture remained isolated incidents, in fact, within the city scene, and were restricted to a condition of interior spaces, unresolved and improperly finished in relation to their immediate surroundings; even the dome and lantern stand in the space of the atmosphere, and exist in a general relation to the landscape, above the outline of the walled city.

The first ideal city of the Renaissance was therefore Florence itself; the great masters, who began the renewal of architecture and the figurative arts, saw their work as enriching

𝕬𝕯 𝕮𝕺𝕽𝕴𝕹

bro · Et quosdã quidẽ posuit de-
us in ecclia · primũ aplos · secũ-
do pphetas · tercio doctores : de-
inde virtutes · exinde gratias curationũ : opitulationes guber-
nationes · genera linguaꝝ : inf-
pretationes sermonũ · Nunqd
oẽs apli : Nunqd omnes pphe-
re : Nũquid oẽs doctores : Nũqd oẽs virtutes : Nũqd oẽs
gratiã habẽt curationũ : Nũqd
oẽs linguis loquũtur : Nun-
quid oẽs interptãt : Emula-
mini autẽ carismata meliora ·
Et adhuc excellẽtioꝛẽ viã vobis
demonstro · XIII

Si linguis hoĩm loquar et
angeloꝛ : caritatẽ aũt nõ
habrã : factus sum velut es so-
nãs aut cimbalũ tinniẽs · Et si
habuero ppheriam · ⁊ nouerim
misteria omnia ⁊ omnẽ scientiã
⁊ habuero omnẽ fidẽ ita ut mõ-
tes trãsferam · caritatẽ aũt non
habueo : nichil sum · Et si distri-
buero in cibos pauperũ oẽs
facultates meas · et si tradidero
corpꝰ meũ ita ut ardeã : carita-
tem aũt nõ habuero : nichil mi-
chi pdest · Caritas patiẽs est : be-
nigna est · Caritas nõ emulat-
nõ agit perperã : nõ inflat · nõ
est ambiciosa : nõ querit ꝗ sua
sũt · Nõ irritat : nõ cogitat ma-
lũ : nõ gaudet sup iniqtate : con-
gaudet aũt veritati · oĩa suffert-

oĩa credit · oĩa sperat : oĩ-
a sustinet · Caritas nũꝗ excidit ·
Siue pphetie euatuabũt : siue
lingue cessabũt : siue sciẽtia de-
struet · Ex parte eñ cognoscim⁹ :
⁊ ex parte pphetam⁹ · Cũ aũt ve-
neit qd pfectũ ẽ : euacuabit qd
ex parte est · Cum essem paruulus loquebar ut paruulus : sa-
piebã ut paruul⁹ : cogitabã ut
paruulus · Quando aũt factus
sum vir : euacuaui ꝗ erant par-
uuli · Videm⁹ nũc p speculũ in
enigmate : tunc aũt facie ad fa-
ciem · Nunc cognosco ex parte :
tunc aũt cognoscã : sicut ⁊ cog-
nitus sum · Nũc autẽ manet fi-
des spes caritas tria hec · Maioꝛ
aũt hoꝛ est caritas · XIIII

Sectamini caritatẽ : emula-
mini spũalia : magis aũt
ut pphetis · Qui eñ loquit̃ lig-
ua : non hoĩbus loquit̃ · sed
deo · Nemo eñ audit · Spiritus
aũt loquit̃ misteria · Nã qui p-
phetat : hoĩbꝫ loquit̃ ad edifi-
rationẽ et exhortationem et cõ-
solationem · Qui loquit̃ lĩgua-
semetĩpm edificat : ꝗ aũt pphe-
tat ecclesiã dei edificat · Volo aũt
oẽs vos loqui lĩguis : magis
aũt pphetare · Nam maior ẽ ꝗ
prophetat ꝗ̃ qui loquit̃ lĩguis
nisi forte inpretet̃ : ut ecclesia e-
dificationem accipiat · Nũc autem fres · si venero ad vos ling-

the time-honoured design of the city, and they made their mark on the features of this privileged image for ever with the rigour of their experiments.

When he wrote the introduction to the treatise *De pictura*, Alberti realized that the primacy of the city depended above all on the 'noble and marvellous intellects' of the new generation:[1]

'Since then, I have been brought back from here – from the long exile in which we Albertis have grown old – into this city, adorned above all others. I have come to understand that in many men, but especially in you, Filippo, and in our close friend Donato the sculptor and in others, like Nencio, Luca and Masaccio, there is a genius for [accomplishing] every praiseworthy thing. For this they should not be slighted in favour of anyone famous or of long-standing in these arts. Therefore I believe the power of acquiring wide fame in any art or science lies in our industry and diligence more than in the times or in the gifts of nature.'

The universal range of their activities concealed the contradictions of city reality, and fed the myth of Florence as heir of Rome, guardian of the ancient and also the Christian virtues, which appears in eulogies of the city, from the *Laudatio florentiae urbis* by Leonardo Bruni to Landino's proem to the *Divine Comedy*. Chastel has published the illuminated initial of a manuscript of *De civitate dei*, where the holy city contemplated by Augustine was in fact Florence, with its towers and campanili dominated by Brunelleschi's dome.[2]

In the course of the fifteenth century this situation changed; economic resources increased and, because of the accumulation of the results of the new artistic culture, so did psychological detachment from the traditional image of the city; but meanwhile the solidarity between the ruling class and the town community was diminishing, as was the civic commitment of the artists themselves, who were now definitely operating on the same level as their clients, i.e. they were no longer bound by local horizons. Thus at the end of the fifteenth century the possibility of regenerating town-planning activities was limited both by the precariousness of political leadership and by the detachment of professional practice from collective problems and responsibilities.

For a short time – after the middle of the century and particularly in the 1460s – the coincidence of two sets of circumstances produced propitious conditions for some significant experiments in urban change and invention; this was when economic resources and confidence in the innovatory powers of the new culture had grown sufficiently, and while the links between rulers, artists and the city community had not yet become too weak. At that point princes and popes seemed to be in a position to create new cities and to change the already existing ones coherently, at least in cases where circumstances made possible the implementation of a unified programme over a reasonably long period of time.

At this time architecture and the figurative arts came nearest to the realization of a new environmental balance, and gave a glimpse of a world of organized forms, corresponding to the intellectual order established by the humanists. For a moment the ideal city was partially translated into reality.

The momentary tallying between programme and implementation ceased soon afterwards, because of the divergent movement of circumstances already described; the aspirations of the planners were diverted into the field of theory, or drastically reduced by the clash of incidental obstacles.

The ideal city became a literary myth once more, or was set beyond the sea, in the island of Utopia.

110 *A page from Gutenberg's 36-line Bible*

Alberti's theory of the city

The methodology established by Alberti, and theorized about in *De re aedificatoria* in the middle of the fifteenth century, was at the root of the most important town-planning experiments of the second half of that century. Even before considering the norms concerning the city, we must look at the fundamental concept of buildings as *muramenti* ('walling'). Alberti was committed to stressing not the originality of the new process of planning, but its value as a solution in relation to experiments already under way, and his treatise contains scarcely any polemical judgments adverse to medieval works, as became customary half a century later. He intended to define the eternal, basic conditions of building, already laid down by the ancients and made explicit by the new architectural culture:[3]

'The whole art of building consists in six things, which are these: the region, the seat or platform, the compartition, the walling, the covering and the apertures. The region . . . shall be the whole large open space in which we are to build, and of which the seat or platform shall be only a part; but the platform shall be a determined spot of the region, circumscribed by walls for use and service. But under the title of platform, we shall likewise include all those spaces of the buildings which in walking we tread upon with our feet. The compartition is that which sub-divides the whole platform of the house into smaller platforms, so that the whole edifice thus formed and constituted of these its members seems to be full of lesser edifices. By walling we shall understand all that structure, which is carried up from the ground to the top to support the weight of the roof, and such also as is raised on the inside of the building, to separate the apartments; covering we shall call not only that part, which is laid over the top of the edifice to receive the rain, but any part too which is extended in length and breadth over the heads of those within; which includes all ceilings, half-arched roofs, vaults and the like. Apertures are those outlets, which are in any part of the building, for the convenience of egress and regress, or the passage of things necessary for the inmates.'

This famous passage, specifying all building processes in terms of space, expresses the new mental approach to the problems of architecture in the most significant way. At the same time, by describing spatial operations in terms of the Aristotelian categories of place and site, he implicitly accepted the current operative tradition according to which space was a property of objects, and the form of each thing must register all the ties and properties of its environment.

This terminology virtually contradicts the notion of perspective space developed elsewhere by Alberti; but it was precisely this theoretical contradiction – which emerged much later, at the end of the sixteenth century – which made reconciliation between present and past possible. In fact Alberti's analysis remained applicable to the modern urban scene; it made it possible to represent it critically and to rationalize it, without compromising the continuity of the new experiments with the old.

The architectural orders – i.e. the heterogeneous part of the new repertoire – were theoretically compared to the 'walling' ('they are none other than a wall open and discontinued in several places'[4]) but could not be reduced to the terms of the previous constructional pattern and were classified among ornaments, i.e. accessory parts, though connected with the general harmony of the building organism.

In its turn this argument – which is the weak point of Alberti's methodology, as we explained in the previous chapter – affords a possibility of mediation between the new buildings and the traditional cities, and therefore becomes the precarious but extremely fruitful basis of the town-planning experiments of court origin which began after the middle of the century.

The two passages of the treatise which discuss cities – in the fourth and seventh books – are less significant than one might expect.

The fourth book of *De re aedificatoria* is devoted to the city as a common framework for the various types of building. The examples quoted in connection with the various aspects of the city are both ancient and modern: Rome, Athens, Sparta, Babylon, but also Perugia and Volterra; the author sees no real difference between the cities of the classical world and those built during the Middle Ages, nor does he contrast the new rational criteria of planning with traditional habits, as he does for single buildings.

Dominated by the permanent factors of the climate, the city is considered as a complex object, not comparable with the single works of architecture; regularity and irregularity come together in it as in nature, and the work of man must adapt itself docilely to the terrain and general environment. The building of a city is not compared to that of a single building, in that the city is not thought of as an object of planning, but as the framework for many successive processes of planning.

The perimeter of the walls must be varied 'according to the variety of places'.[5] Roads are divided into three categories: main roads, minor roads and roads 'which may not improperly be called high streets, as are such which are designed for some certain purpose, especially any public one; as for instance those which lead to some temple, or to the course for races, or to a place of justice'.[6]

This terminology is valid both for town and country. The main roads in the country should be broad, straight and as direct as may be compatible with convenience and safety. In the town, if this 'is noble and powerful, the streets should be straight and broad, which carries an air of greatness';[7] but in a small town, the roads should become winding

before arriving at the main gate, and should be winding inside the town as well. Alberti enumerates the advantages of this arrangement (Figs 111, 112):[8]

'For thus, besides that by appearing so much the longer, they will add to the idea of the greatness of the town, they will likewise conduce very much to beauty and convenience, and be a greater security against all accidents and emergencies. Moreover this winding of the streets will make the passenger at every step discover a new structure, and the front door of every house will directly face the middle of the street; and whereas in larger towns even too much breadth is unwholesome and unhealthy, in a small one it will be both healthy and pleasant, to have such an open view for every house by means of the turn of the street.

Cornelius Tacitus writes, that Nero having widened the streets of Rome, thereby made the city hotter, and therefore less healthy; but in other places, where the streets are narrow, the air is crude and raw, and there is a continued shade even in summer. But further, in our winding streets there will be no house but what, in some part of the day, will enjoy some sun; nor will they ever be without gentle breezes, which whatever corner they come from, will never want a free or clear passage; and yet they will not be molested by stormy blasts, because such will be broken by the turning of the streets. Add to all these advantages, that if the enemy gets into the town, he will be in danger on every side, in front, in flank, and in rear, from assaults from the houses.'

Secondary roads should preferably be winding even in large towns, and should converge upon the main ones, but with staggered entrances:[9]

'The private ones [secondary ones] should be like the public ones unless there be this

111   *Detail of the* Adoration of the Magi *by Gentile da Fabriano. Uffizi, Florence*

difference, that they be built exactly in straight lines, which shall answer better to the corners of the building, and the divisions and parts of the houses. The ancients in all towns were for having some intricate ways and turn-again streets, without any passage through them, that if an enemy comes into them, he may be at a loss, and be in confusion and suspence; or if he pushes on daringly, may be easily destroyed. It is also proper to have smaller short streets, running cross from one great street and another; not to be as a direct publick way, but only as a passage to some house that fronts it; which will give both light to the houses and make it more difficult for an enemy to overrun all parts of the town.'

These specifications, though illustrated with examples from antiquity, in fact simply codify medieval town-planning experience, which Alberti is here not in the least concerned to attack.

In the eighth book Alberti returns to the subject and provides a much more precise description of the main elements of a town:[10]

'The streets within the city, besides being handsomely paved and cleanly swept, will be rendered much more noble, if the doors are built all after the same model, and the houses on each side stand in an even line, and none higher than the other.'

Similarly bridges, the 'meeting-points of several roads' (i.e. squares of all sizes) and 'spectacles', i.e. terraced squares used as meeting-places, are described as single architectural organisms, surrounded by porticoes and loggias.[11]

112 *The longitudinal street at Pienza, curved in accordance with Alberti's theories*

A few pages earlier, in the chapter devoted to towers, we have a specific example of disapproval of medieval building practice:[12]

'Not that I commend the age about two hundred years ago, when people seemed to be seized with a kind of general infection of building high watch-towers, even in the meanest villages, in so much that scarce a common house-keeper thought that he could not be without his turret. By which means there arose a perfect grove of spires.'

(This was in fact a view already common in the Middle Ages, taken from the municipal authorities' attacks on the nobles and their private quarrels.)

This second discussion is often regarded as contradicting the first and it has even been suggested that it was written some time later. But the difference in context sufficiently clarifies the divergence of the two arguments. In the eighth book Alberti is talking of ornaments, i.e. of public works and spaces, and considers them as single works of architecture. But in the fourth book, talking of cities, a similar planning problem does not arise, and he does not suggest any particular planning procedure or mode of composition. The founding of new cities and the radical modification of existing ones were operations that had now become rare and whose methodological aspects were forgotten. For this reason the city was presented as a mythical object, unchanging in time; its origin was lost in the mists of legend. In fact in chapter III of the fourth book Alberti fully describes the religious formalities observed by the ancients 'in beginning their towns' and the criteria used by soothsayers to know their destiny in advance:[13] as usual, this description is tinged with irony, and reveals the author's reluctance to commit himself to a technical discussion, since the operation is not regarded as the province of any clear-cut current field of responsibility: from chapters IV to XI in fact there follows a precise list of norms for the building of the single urban works which are considered as susceptible of planning: walls, roads, bridges, sewers and harbour installations.

Alberti's technical discussion is important for the understanding of the nature of the town-planning experiments begun after the middle of the fifteenth century, almost all of which were in fact linked to this great humanist.

His restricting concept of architectural composition introduced a really methodological leap between the planning of single works and that of whole cities, i.e. it confirmed the deficiency of the new planning method in the field of town-planning, which had been only potential in Brunelleschi and his immediate successors.

On the other hand, Alberti's taste for the systematic mediation between old and new reinforced the conviction that the methods handed down from medieval experience were still of value to regulate the development of the city. The new architecture bore the same relation to the city as the architectural 'ornaments' bore to the actual construction of the buildings, and might be considered as the ornaments that were suited to the scale of town-planning.

The conflict between the two traditions was thus psychologically eased, but none the less made itself felt by limiting the scope of the new town-planning enterprises; mediation of the Albertian type proved possible, and produced good results only in small towns (such as Pienza and Urbino) but failed in medium-sized ones (such as Mantua and Ferrara) and above all in large ones (such as Milan and Rome) where the Renaissance enterprises broke up the coherence of the earlier city without producing a new point of

balance, but opening the way to new, more radical transformations.

The reorganization of papal Rome

While he was writing the treatise on architecture, Alberti was in Rome working on the programme of building and town-planning reorganization initiated by Nicholas V.

It is known that he was consulted over the restoration and completion of the tottering basilica of St Peter's, begun in 1452 by Bernardo Rossellino; he carried out the restoration of S. Stefano Rotondo, S. Teodoro, S. Prassede, S. Maria Maggiore; he directed the works for the city's new fortifications and for the repairing of the Vergine aqueduct; he designed a roof for the ponte S. Angelo; he worked on possible ways to recover the Roman ships sunk in lake Nemi, and in this connection he wrote the treatise *Navia*, about 1448. It has therefore been suggested, quite reasonably, that Alberti was at least partly responsible for the programmes more particularly concerned with general town-planning, and particularly for that of the Borghi, with the three parallel roads which converge towards St Peter's, and link the city with the papal residence.

In the person of Nicholas V there was a combination of the experience of the humanist, the clear vision of the politician and the pastoral zeal of the prelate who set out with profound conviction to re-establish the autonomy and authority of the church. The brevity of his period of office (from 1447 to 1455) allowed for the completion of only a small part of the works planned, but the general lines of the programme and the reasons behind them – documented in the life by Giannozzo Manetti – were vitally important, because they fixed not only the broad lines of papal building policy for the following four centuries, but also the cultural and political attitude of the new ruling class with regard to a large city which was con-

113 View of Rome *by Masolino. Baptistery, Castiglione d'Olona*

sidered from the beginning as the city *par excellence*.

This programme referred not so much to medieval Rome, then inhabited by about 40,000 people and contained within the flattened loop of the Tiber (the only place where there was an adequate water supply), as to Imperial and Constantinian Rome, still present with its monuments and its uninterrupted prestige which had been recently heightened by the developments in humanistic culture.

Platina recounts that in 1420 Martin V found Rome 'a town so full of destruction that it no longer had the look of a city'.[14] The Roman monuments that dominated the

landscape of the city were measured and studied by Alberti in his *Descriptio urbis Romae* (written in 1432–4, or after 1443) and described by Flavius Blondus in *Roma instaurata* of 1446; the image of the old city was superimposed upon the present one, relegating it to a second place.

Nicholas V's programme foresaw the restoration of ancient buildings utilizable – as we would say today – as infrastructures of the papal city: the Aurelian walls, the bridges, Hadrian's mausoleum turned into a castle, certain aqueducts; the rebuilding or repairing of the forty basilicas of the Holy Stations according to uniform criteria and the creation of a citadel on the Vatican hill, including the

114 *View of Rome from Münster's* Cosmographia, *1550*

church of St Peter's (which was to be enlarged to make it clearly distinguishable from the other churches, so as to proclaim the primacy of the Pope as successor to St Peter), the papal palace and services necessary for the new protocol of the Holy See: a series of offices, a theatre, a chamber for meetings and conclaves, a hall for benedictions, a library, living quarters, a park, botanical gardens; attached to the palace was to be the *maxima quaedam Cappella*, which was to be built by Sixtus IV and which bears his name (Figs 116, 117).[15]

The Vatican citadel was conceived as a sort of holy city, distinct from the profane one, beyond the Tiber, communicating with it only by the link of Castel S. Angelo. Three straight roads were to run between the castle and the piazza in front of St Peter's, where the Neronian obelisk was to be erected, to mark the axis of the basilica as far forward as possible. Around the three roads rose the residential quarters of the papal troops, integrated into the Vatican complex and known, as it still is, by the German name of Borgo.

It was not therefore to be the creation of a new urban organism, but an adaptation of the existing one and an evocation of the structure of ancient Rome, subordinated to the presence of the papal See in its dual aspect, functional and symbolic.

The programme of Nicholas V was laden with symbolic references which are mentioned in Manetti's account[16] and have been studied, in all their complex stratifications, by more recent scholars.[17]

The new St Peter's, according to Manetti, was similar to a human body, with the transept representing the open arms and the tribune representing the head; the human body, furthermore, was similar to the cosmos, and for this reason the basilica symbolized the universe. The tribune designed by Rossellino was to have been illuminated by round windows to 'give a certain idea of divine glory'.[18] But, at the will of Nicholas V, St Peter's was also to be similar to Noah's Ark, at least in its layout, if not its dimensions. The two symbols aimed at the exaltation of the Roman Church, ark of humanity's salvation and extending over the whole earth.

The Vatican palace – which Manetti calls a 'labyrinth' and 'paradise' – was the visible representation of the city of God, in contrast to the city of men that faced it across the river. The contrast of the two cities made use of the double symbolic association of Rome with Babylon and with the heavenly Jerusalem. Lastly, the Sistine chapel – as Battisti has recently shown – represented the temple of Solomon, whose division into three parts and whose overall measurements it reproduces (Figs 116, 117).[19]

This grandiose programme, which was only partly realized by Nicholas V but was resumed by Sixtus IV and remained an ideal model for papal building activities during the centuries to come, was justified by a combination of religious, political and cultural reasons, expressed in a speech that Manetti has the Pope pronounce on his death bed:[20]

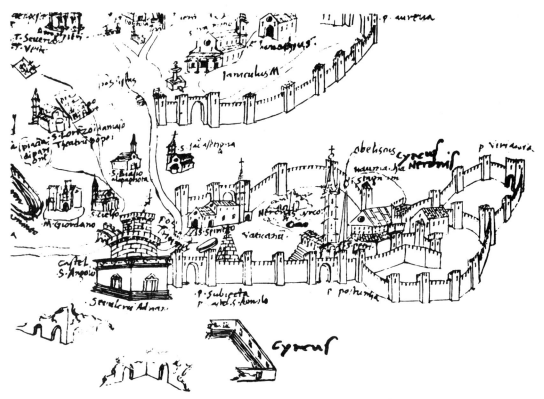

115 *View of Rome by A. Strozzi, 1474 (detail of the Leonine city). Laurentian Library, Florence*

'Hear now, o venerable brothers, the reasons, and consider the motives which have led us to build with such conviction. . . .

The great, the supreme authority of the Roman church, above all, can be understood only by those who are acquainted with its origins and its developments through the study of letters. But the mass of the people is ignorant of literary matters and devoid of culture; and though it often hears it proclaimed by the learned and erudite that the authority of the church is extremely great, and although it believes this assertion, yet it still needs to be impressed by grandiose spectacles; because otherwise, founded as it is on weak and unstable bases, its conviction would gradually fade away with the passing of time. But with the grandiosity of buildings and of monuments that are to some extent eternal . . . this same popular conviction which has its basis in the statements of the learned can be reinforced and confirmed. . . .

In the second place there is a need, as evidence of the devotion of the Christian peoples towards the Church and Apostolic See, for fortifications . . . which can be made more solid with the building of new works of defence, designed to resist the attacks of external enemies and internal subversives, always animated by desire of destruction.

For this reason we have built a large number of edifices at Gualdo . . . Fabriano, Assisi, Città Castellana, Narni, Orvieto, Spoleto and Viterbo and many other places, with the double aim that they should act as defences and inspire devotion. And impelled, possibly even more strongly, by the same motives, we have completed many extraordinary buildings here in Rome, and began work on others, even more excellent yet.

In so far as this city is considered as greater and more illustrious than any other . . . so we have thought it right that it

should be better adorned and fortified than others; we know in fact how it was designated by God Almighty as seat of the Supreme Pontiff. . . .

For this reason we have wished to repair the walls of the eternal city . . . we have restored forty basilicas of the Holy Stations, which were built in his time by our predecessor Gregory the Great . . . lastly we have initiated the works of transformation and restoration of this palace, worthy abode of the Supreme Pontiffs, and of the adjacent holy church of Peter, the Leader of the Apostles, as well as the great new adjoining district, to ensure worthy and safe accommodation for the head, the members and all the Curia. Works which we should certainly have completed . . . had unexpected death not crept up behind. Had these been completed, as was our desire, all Christian peoples would have felt greater veneration for our successors, who would have been able to reside in the eternal city with complete peace of mind and safety, easily avoiding the heinous persecutions that we have suffered in the past from enemies inside and out; a safety which it will however be possible to attain if these same works are actually implemented in the future.'

As we see, reasons of prestige and reasons of military security coexist in Nicholas V's speech; they are, as it were, the ideological aspect and the instrumental aspect of a single political and religious programme.

From now on the desire to arrogate the prestige of classical memories to the apostolic See remained constant in papal building and town-planning policy, though religious inspiration yielded its primacy, gradually, to profane motives. Sixtus IV rebuilt S. Pietro in Vincoli, S. Pietro in Montorio, the SS. Apostoli, put the ponte Sisto back into use and restored the Campidoglio, placing the bronze she-wolf on the façade of the Palazzo dei Conservatori, with Romulus and Remus

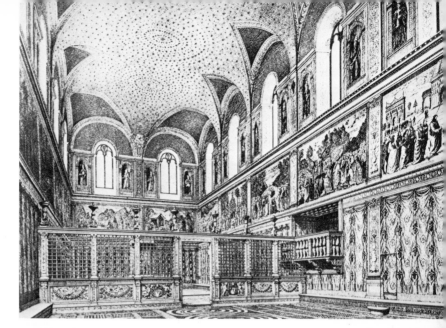

116, 117 *The Sistine chapel, Rome, at the end of the fifteenth century and today*

added by a sculptor of the time; but he also set out to attract the best artists and writers of the time to Rome, and to make it the capital of the new humanistic culture. The tomb of Sixtus IV by Pollaiuolo was the virtual translation into bronze of this broader cultural programme; the sleeping Pope was surrounded by the arts and sciences, among which appears perspective, the muse of the new figurative culture.

The concern for defence, which occupied so large a part in Nicholas V's speech, did not diminish during the decades to come, but was gradually transferred from Rome to the outlying cities and fortified towns of the papal states. The concern of the Pope does not seem excessive, if one bears in mind the recent revolts of 1435, 1443 and the anti-papal coalition of 1460, defeated the following year after bitter struggles. These dangers in fact became rarer later, and the papacy was able to shift its military operations progressively further from the capital. Furthermore the spread of artillery made works of fortification increasingly necessary, and this was not the only case when they acquired a decisive importance in determining the physiognomy of a city. (Town-planning and military engineering were closely linked, and theoretical discussions on the city – from Alberti's treatise to that of Francesco di Giorgio – were largely taken up with directions for defence, still mainly empirical.)

Alberti, a collaborator of Nicholas V and his successors until 1464, established the position of the artists employed in this ambitious and demanding programme for his own and future generations. It does not seem that he had any part in laying down the general lines and co-ordination of the various works, which was not so much an architectural matter as a political and symbolic one, and was the direct concern of the ecclesiastical authorities. He seems rather to have played the part of technical executor, sufficiently versatile to deal with fortifications, water mains and building works, and sufficiently close to his clients to interpret with awareness their complex functional and symbolic directions, though he received these from without and did not elaborate them on his own account.

Just after 1450 Alberti began his career as architect and actually confronted the difficult balance between 'walling' and 'ornaments', which was to be the recurrent theme of his successive experiments, for the first time. Alberti's repertoire – precisely because of its flexibility and the tenuousness of its syntactical links – was well-suited to bearing so huge a weight of conditions and meanings imposed from outside (unlike Brunelleschi's repertoire, anchored to the rigorous mechanism of the orders and much more intractable to every type of exterior pressure). From the very first the planners employed by Nicholas V and his successors, and those working in other Italian courts, drew upon this repertoire to realize similar town-planning and building programmes.

But there was much more to it than this: the typical procedure adopted from Sixtus IV onwards to reorganize the various zones of Rome – i.e. the opening of one or more straight roads, traced not so much to link up with a unified plan as to allow the erection of new monumental buildings along both sides; the trident of ponte S. Angelo under Sixtus IV, via Giulia and via della Lungara under Julius II; the trident of piazza del Popolo under Leo X and Clement VII – reproduced the Albertian description of 'high streets' as architectural settings isolated amid the complex framework of the city. This procedure worked for as long as the single streets were considered one at a time as isolated episodes, but was threatened when an attempt was made to link them into a general plan, as Sixtus V was to do at the end of the sixteenth century.[21]

At this point the religious and architectural ideal of resuscitating ancient Rome as the natural seat of the papacy had already lost many of its original implications; the humble and obscure city of Nicholas V had turned, fifty years later, into the important city of Julius II; as Chastel observes, 'In 1472 Fonzio, visiting Rome, sadly enumerated the moving vestiges of the past, but in 1506 Canon Albertini was counting up the magnificent edifices of the new Rome.'[22]

The first of these was the palace of Cardinal Pietro Barbo (Fig. 118), built from 1455 onwards next to the church of S. Marco, and characterized by the colonnaded courtyard of the *viridarium*, the first example of a link-up between palace and garden, repeated some years later by Pius II in his palace at Pienza. When Paul II succeeded him in 1464 he made plans for the extension of the building, adding an enormous square courtyard only partly completed after his death in 1471.

The new Pope Sixtus IV (1471–84) erected a large number of monumental buildings, and later – when the new papal Rome was a completely formed organism – he was regarded as the real instigator of the rebuilding of the city.[23] He employed some Tuscan artists such as Baccio Pontelli (1450–after 1494), Meo del Caprina (1430–1501), Giacomo da Pietrasanta, and Lombards like Andrea Bregno (1421–1506); side by side with the early-Christian and medieval churches there now stood the modern churches of S. Agostino, S. Maria del Popolo (Fig. 120), S. Maria della Pace and the Sistine chapel; the summoning of Umbrian and Tuscan painters to Rome in 1481 to paint the frescoes for this chapel – Botticelli, Perugino, Ghirlandaio, Pinturicchio, Signorelli, Rosselli, Bartolomeo della Gatta – was the most sensational undertaking of that time, after the cycle of works organized by Federigo da Montefeltro at Urbino, already nearing conclusion. From 1480 onwards the Pope's nephew Raffaele Riario had been building the Cancelleria (Fig. 119) with the great porticoed courtyard, repeating and extending the motif of that of Montefeltro.

The most important work of his successor Innocent VIII (1484–92) was the Villa

118–120 *Palazzo Venezia, Palazzo della Cancelleria and S. Maria del Popolo, Rome*

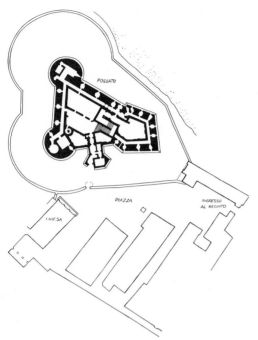

121   *Ground plan of the fortress and town of Ostia (from De Fiore)*

Belvedere, on a hill to the north of the Vatican palace; its position and the modernity of its construction formed the premises for later works by Bramante.

In the last decades of the century Francesco di Giorgio and Baccio Pontelli were engaged as military architects for the construction and remaking of the fortresses on papal territory. These works, in some cases, led to the building of real urban complexes, like that of Ostia (Fig. 121), where the two planners are mentioned together in 1483. Beside the castle, extremely modern in conception, there were three rows of terraced houses and a church, surrounded by a wall: a miniature city, overshadowed by the more important and physically dominating works of fortification.

Until this moment Rome and the papal court had attracted a large number of artists and intellectuals from the other Italian cities, but had failed to acquire a dominant position in the cultural developments of the period. It has been observed that the advisers of

Nicholas V, with the exception of Alberti, were not of the first order;[24] Sixtus IV employed second-rate architects, often summoning them from the court of Urbino which at this time was closely linked to the Holy See, and managed to get first-class painters to work for him but could not persuade them to settle in Rome.

Only the political upheavals which interrupted the life of the northern courts, and particularly the combination of interests which unified Rome and Florence from the beginning of the sixteenth century, were to make possible the formation of the Roman cultural domination which marked the decisive turning-point in the history of Renaissance culture.

Milan in the time of the Sforzas

There had long existed, in literature and in common opinion, a contrast in characteristics between Milan and Florence, which was elaborated with extensive cultural argument by Salutati and Loschi in a famous polemic, at the time of the wars of Gian Galeazzo Sforza.

This contrast derived from political, economic and organizational circumstances which manifested themselves in various fields, including that of building. Lombardy was the birthplace of skilled workers and businesses active in all parts of Italy, using a traditional ability to work stone and brick; in Florence, on the other hand, an idea and organization of building work developed that was to some extent antithetical, based on design and on visual authority, and technically on the importance attributed to the details – to marble facing, then to Brunelleschi's orders – which replaced the load-bearing structures in determining architectural effects.

In Florentine worksites, even in Brunelleschi's time, skilled Lombard workers competed with local labour, though without affecting the new methodology of planning, which from Brunelleschi onwards took place

Das Erst buch Vitruuij

Eygentliche Contrafactur des gewaltigen Schloß Meyland/
mit etlicher deßelbigen wehren verzeichung.

122 *Aerial view of Milan cathedral*
123, 124 *View of the castle of the*
Sforza family, Milan, today and from
Rivius' edition of Vitruvius, 1548

125 *Plan of the city of Milan, 1573*

on another plane, outside the scope of the executors. In Milan on the other hand, the old collective and hierarchical organization of the medieval site, where planning and execution were closely intermingled, survived tenaciously; and there was no room in this organization for intellectual stringency of a Florentine type, which in fact penetrated into Lombardy only later and only in part.

This organizational contrast was echoed and exacerbated by the propaganda of the two rival cities: Florence considered herself as the vessel of the ancient Mediterranean tradition, Milan cultivated her traditional ties with the European world. Milan cathedral was begun in 1386, in open competition with the resumption of the work on the cathedral in Florence, and was to be a monument of the most orthodox Gothic style; French masters were summoned to this end – Nicolas Bonaventure, Jean Mignot – and German ones – John of Freiburg, Henry of Gmünd,

Ulric of Ensingen. Until about 1460 the building remained in the hands of foreign artists and craftsmen, Germans and Burgundians; the Lombard artists active in the first half of the fifteenth century profited from these contacts, and learned some of the methods of planning widespread in the German world.[25]

The meeting between the Lombard tradition and the new Florentine culture took place during the reign of Francesco Sforza (1450–66).

The new lord of Milan, who came to power after the bloody war for the succession to Filippo Maria Visconti, inaugurated a period of peace and economic development. He initiated a large number of public works, and it was his ambition to raise the cultural life of the city to the level of the other more important Italian capitals; the Sforza court, from now on, became the meeting-place for many famous specialists from other regions of Italy, and especially from Florence, which was joined to Milan by close political links at this time.

The enterprises of Francesco Sforza were motivated by particular political or economic factors; in 1458 he summoned the Bolognese engineer Aristotele Fioravanti to complete the network of canals in the Lombard plain; on two occasions he employed the sculptor and architect Antonio Averlino, known as Filarete (c. 1400–69), recommended by Piero de' Medici: in 1451 to design the façade of the castle erected on the ruins of the Visconti fort of Milan, symbol of the prince's definitive settlement in the city (Figs 123, 124) and again in 1460–5, to build the main hospital, which was to be the most up-to-date one of its time.

In 1461 he sent Filarete to Venice to build him a modern palazzo on the Grand Canal which was to have demonstrated his prestige in the heart of the Serene Republic but was never built.[26]

The castle and hospital, and later the Lazzaretto designed by Lazzaro Palazzi in

1473, are impressive quadrilateral buildings, rigidly symmetrical. At Pienza or Urbino mediation between the new monumental buildings and the fabric of the city had been achieved by an unusual cultural involvement, but the setting of the great city made this impossible in Milan; here an involvement of this kind was totally lacking, and the gigantic scale of the two enterprises was deliberately contrasted with the minute pattern of the streets and ordinary houses. The ambitious attempt to translate the hierarchy of power and riches between prince and subjects into intellectual terms was not even hinted at; the architecture had a decidedly inferior function, in so far as the acceptance of modern forms answered a precise piece of political calculation; the prestige of the new culture had to legitimate a power by now uncontested, but devoid of traditional justifications and still legally disputable.

Political, too, was the journey made by Michelozzo to Milan between 1462 and 1468, when he was commissioned by the Medici to rebuild the palazzo of the Medici bank, presented by Francesco Sforza to Cosimo, and the ancestral chapel of the Portinari (the Milanese agents of the Florentine banker) in the church of S. Eustorgio. Michelozzo used a decidedly modern scheme, the Brunelleschian one of the two intercommunicating spaces covered by a dome, but the decoration carried out by Lombard masters – accustomed to translating all the articulations of an organism into decorative reliefs – did away with the distinction between the main standardized elements, bearers of the perspective pattern, and the secondary ones, variable at the decision of the sculptors and painters. Giovanni Antonio Amadeo (1447–1522) moved from this starting point, and built the Colleoni chapel in Bergamo (Fig. 126); a few years later in the last decades of the century this stylistic combination – based on simple, enclosed volumes, enlivened by compact plastic decoration, whose very continuity allowed the integrity of the masonry blocks to subsist intact – had a vast success all over Lombardy; for instance in the church of the Incoronata at Lodi, S. Maria dei Miracoli in Brescia, the pilgrimage church at Saronno, S. Maria presso S. Celso in Milan, the ornaments of the Certosa at Pavia, and also the Milanese works of Bramante such as S. Maria presso S. Satiro, and S. Maria delle Grazie.

Filarete may be regarded as the theoretician of this tendency, towards which he was attracted by his training as a sculptor and by the ease with which it could be adapted to the traditions of the place where he was working. During his second stay in Milan he wrote a treatise on architecture, dedicated to Francesco Sforza and later to Piero de' Medici, when he returned to Florence after 1465. The copy dedicated to Piero – still preserved in Florence – is decorated with splendid drawings of imaginary buildings, like those which figure in the paintings of the time. The fantastic distortions and disjointedness of perspective links between the elements of the classical repertoire may possibly be accentuated by the graphic presentation, and do not necessarily define Filarete's intentions as an architect (his works built in Milan, furthermore, retain their original layout only in part, and were completed by local builders; they are therefore the end product of the innovating activity of the Florentine architect, and of the reaction of an environment orientated and organized in quite another way).

But since the conditions to realize them were lacking, Filarete's plans were in fact diffused and had their effect in the form of graphic visions. The similarity between these visions and the imaginary buildings drawn by professional painters show that the relationship between painted architecture and actual architecture must be assessed bearing in mind the difficulties of town-planning which rendered many of the plans of the time unfeasible.

The demands of perspective completeness and of simultaneous definition of the parts, typical of the new architectural methodology, were in many cases incompatible with the uncertainty of the building programmes and with the lack of suitable spaces in the setting of the traditional cities. Pictorial space, on the other hand, allowed a coherent – if purely illustrative – development of the new architectural models (and painters attributed a precise representational function to the architectural repertoire, i.e. that of evoking an unreal or unrealistic landscape).

Similar considerations must be made for the extravagant tone of the treatise, and for its most striking novelty: the description of an ideal city which forms the unifying framework for the different buildings.

In the dedication to Francesco Sforza, in the Palatine manuscript in Florence,[27] the author lists the works undertaken by the Duke of Milan – the castle, canal, the hospital designed by himself – and he presents his treatise to him as a collection of practical rules: 'not that it is a work of eloquence; it simply presents the modes of measures that anyone wanting to build, should know'.

In the first book, however, he tells how he was at a banquet where one of the guests said that the art of building did not require the knowledge of theoretical rules. Filarete rejects this opinion, offers to 'describe the modes and measures of building' and divides his exposition into three parts:[28]

'The first will recount the origin of measure; the building, its sources, how it ought to be maintained, and the things necessary to construct the building; what one should know about building to be a good architect; and what should be noted about him. The second will narrate the means and the construction for anyone who wants to build a city, its site, and how the buildings, squares and streets ought to be located so that it will be fine, beautiful, and perpetual according to the laws of nature. The third and last part will tell how to make various forms of buildings according

126   *Colleoni chapel, Bergamo, by G. A. Amadeo*

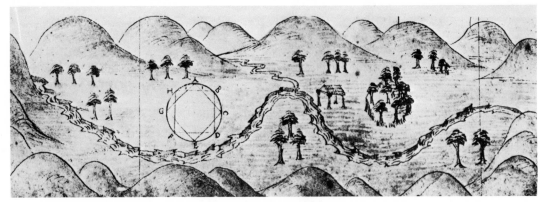

127   *The city of Sforzinda, in Filarete's treatise (Magliabechia MS.)*

to ancient practice, together with things I have discovered or learned from the ancients that are almost lost and forgotten today. From this it will be understood that the ancients built more nobly than we do today.'

There follows the famous comparison of the building with the human body. The measurements of the building derive from the measurements of man; the building has 'entrances and exits' and similarly it 'lives and dies', i.e. it needs upkeep, but it 'finally dies in its own time'.[29]

The architect is as it were the mother of the building, and the person commissioning it is like the father; in this passage – as in the Albertian rules in *De re aedificatoria* – one senses the preoccupation with the crisis in patronage, which was the difficulty characteristic of this moment in history.

There follows a classification of buildings into three categories: sacred, public and private; at this point Filarete introduced his idea of building a city:[30]

'Perhaps to some it would seem better to begin with small buildings in order to show the mode and order of building and then to continue in order to the largest. I have had an idea about undertaking to construct a city in which we shall erect all the buildings that belong there, each with its own suitable orders and measures. But because I cannot build it by myself, I want to talk first with the person who will bear the expense. If he is satisfied with the cost, I will build it.'

First of all he lays out the plan of the city, which is the result of the intersection of two squares: 'I shall call the drawing Averliano and the city I will call Sforzinda. We shall build it in this form';[31] he describes the chosen spot, i.e. the Inda valley crossed by a river and sheltered from the winds (Fig. 127); he considers the necessary building materials, the labour (12,000 master builders, 84,000 workers and 60,000 fillers-in), the timing of the building and the organization of the site. The starting date was fixed by an astrologer and miracles occurred during the work.

The sixteen-sided figure produced by the intersection of the two squares determined the perimeter of the walls, while the outer moat followed the course of the circumscribed circle. The protruding vertices of the walls were orientated according to the points of the compass and the intermediate points, and were occupied by eight towers, which bore the names of the eight winds; while the re-entrant corners were occupied by eight gates. Sixteen main roads, 40 *braccia* wide, started from the towers and gates and converged upon the centre; halfway along they were interrupted by sixteen secondary piaz-zas, of 80 by 160 *braccia*, occupied alternately by parish churches and markets. In the centre there was to be a main square which afforded direct access to the palace and the cathedral with the archbishop's residence, and two smaller piazzas, around which the other public buildings were to be distributed – the town-hall, the mayor's mansion, the prison, customs house, mint, slaughterhouse, public baths, brothel. All these spaces formed a rectangular system, but the treatise does not indicate how it is to be linked up to the radial roads. In reality the diagram contained in the sixth book is the result of two plans, the realistic one of the city centre and the sym-bolic one of the city as a whole, with the circle of roads running out to all corners of the territory and celestial horizon (Fig. 128).

The treatise continues with the description of other public and private buildings, includ-ing the cathedral, the hospital – which corresponds to the Milanese one designed by Filarete – a circus, basin for naval jousts, zoological garden and hunting lodge.

During the excavations for the building of the port a book is discovered, all of gold, containing the story of an ancient city that formerly stood on this spot, built by king Zogalia. The new port is built according to the model of this city, and the tale gives Filarete an opportunity to describe other ideal buildings: a temple, a garden and two educational institutions for boys and girls. There are also theoretical treatises on the orders, materials and perspective.

Sforzinda, as we have mentioned, is simply the unifying frame for the various buildings, where these can be placed without the problems and hindrances typical of concrete reality. The unrealistic tone of the treatise indicates both the urgency of an aspiration which was being experimented with in reality in Pienza and Urbino during these very years (with completely different instruments, as we shall see) and the awareness of the outdated-ness of an undertaking of this kind. The book

had a considerable success, and was even translated into Latin by Matthias Corvinus; from this moment the ideal city took on the form of a geometrical ideogram, which appears regularly in successive treatises; towards the end of the century the star-like shape, which was probably suggested here by a geographical and cosmic symbolism, was reinforced by the theory of bastioned peri-meters that arose to adapt masonry defences to the new power of artillery. The meeting of these two motifs produced the numerous graphic variations in the designs of the sixteenth century, and finally the achieve-ments of the later sixteenth century, which we shall discuss later on.

Filarete's text does perhaps reflect the point at which geographical reference ceases to be concrete and becomes abstract. In Alberti's treatise, written about ten years earlier, harmony between cities and settings entailed a close adherence to concrete situa-tions, so that no circumference and no form were actually favoured above any other; here the same reasoning became symbolic, and the harmony with astronomical factors – hence the use of the compass-card as a guideline to

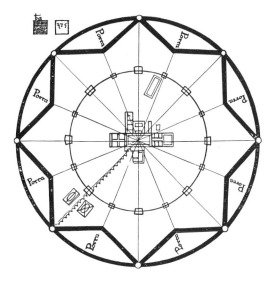

128 *Plan of the city of Sforzinda*

129–131 *Buildings in Sforzinda, from the illustrations in the Magliabechia MS.*

132 *Ducal square, Vigevano*

establish the form of the city – excludes harmony with topographical facts. This starting-point, thus weakened, could now act as a basis for the requirements of military technique, as happened from Francesco di Giorgio onwards. But we shall return to this later.

Even after the death of Francesco Sforza, in 1466, the importance of Milan as a cultural centre remained based on the economic and commercial prosperity of the city and was increased, from 1480 to 1492, by the prestige-seeking policies of Lodovico il Moro. In 1481 Lorenzo the Magnificent sent Leonardo to Milan from Florence, and sent Giuliano da Sangallo in 1493; specialists trained at the court of Federigo da Montefeltro – Bramante, Francesco di Giorgio, Luca Pacioli – came from Urbino. Later on we shall see the importance of these comings and goings for the development of the 'third style'.

However, court undertakings were increasingly restricted to the celebrative sphere: in Milan Leonardo was engaged mainly on the equestrian monument of Francesco Sforza and on staging festivities on which vast sums

were lavished; thus the exceptional concentration of talent at the end of the century only marginally influenced the development of the city, and simply contributed to the synthesis that was being formed, detached from now onwards from the individual centres.

But the most important transformations were taking place in the smaller cities; in Pavia, which remained the second capital of the Sforza court, the Certosa founded by Gian Galeazzo Sforza was still being built; in 1490 Amadeo began to assemble the façade, using a group of decorative specialists acquainted with the technical and figurative experiments carried out at Urbino. Meanwhile in 1488 the foundations were laid for the new duomo, the first modern church to emulate the great fourteenth-century cathedrals.

At Vigevano the Sforzas' plans entailed the reorganization of the whole city centre. The Gothic castle, already renovated by Galeazzo Maria Sforza on the occasion of his marriage, in 1468, was enlarged by Lodovico and linked to the main square, which was regularized by a continuous arcade (Figs 132–4). The

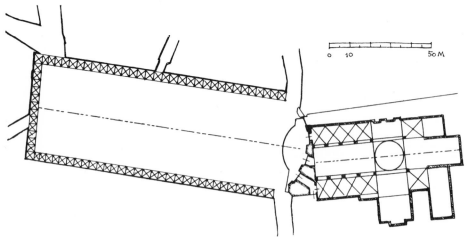

133, 134 *Aerial view and plan of the ducal square, Vigevano*

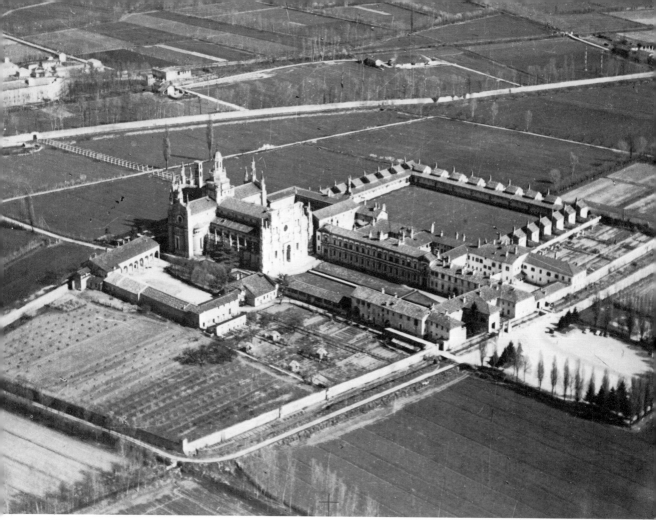

135 *The Certosa, Pavia*

laying out of the square at Vigevano, possibly to a design by Bramante about 1490, became the model for many others implemented by Lombard artists along the route leading south from Milan: the squares of Faenza, Imola, Carpi and Ascoli Piceno, where the medieval base was likewise regularized by superimposing a uniform arcaded motif upon the various buildings.

Pienza

On 21 and 22 February 1459 Pius II visited his native town of Corsignano, during his journey to Mantua, and decided to rebuild it as his ideal abode. In May of the same year

the general council of the city of Siena gave permission to the architect sent by the Pope to quarry stone, cut trees and set up brickyards free of charge.

The architect chosen by Pius II was Bernardo Rossellino (1409–64) assisted by his nephew Puccio di Paolo; on his journey to Mantua Pius II was accompanied by Alberti and certainly made use of his advice, both for the choice of planner and for the arrangement of the building programme. At this time Rossellino was regarded as one of the most illustrious of Florentine artists; in 1456 he executed the tomb of Orlando de' Medici in the Annunziata, in 1461 he was appointed master builder at S. Maria del Fiore (the

136, 137 *View and ground plan of Pienza. The monumental buildings round the square are shown in black*

greatest mark of professional recognition of the time) and in the same year he signed the contract for the tomb of the Cardinal of Portugal in S. Miniato.

Pius II's programme was described in the bull of 13 August 1462: 'To build, from its foundations, a church of magnificent structure, and to ornament that place with an illustrious palace, on the site of the family house, with several other buildings'.[32] In fact the Pope and architect respected the structure of the medieval village, aligned along a road on the crest of a hill, but where crest and road form a loop in the direction of the valle dell'Orcia they left available a considerable area where a group of monumental buildings could be built: the cathedral, the Palazzo Piccolomini, the Palazzo Borgia (later the bishop's palace) and town hall which surround a vast quadrangular square; behind the town hall a second square was built for the local market.

The cathedral occupies the most striking position, at the top of the loop, and has its apse facing the valley, extending considerably beyond the ridge, like Siena cathedral; here, too, its position makes it possible to create a second space beneath the apse for the baptistery, but it was utilized to obtain a series of absolutely novel architectural effects, required by their exceptional commissioner, and made possible by the new visual culture.

Seen from the valley, the volume of the cathedral is a feature which stands out from the alignment of the other buildings, and appears as the dominant element without actually being higher than the surrounding buildings (Fig. 136). To anyone arriving in the square, the façade is seen sharply against the light, and is framed between the diverging walls of the two palaces which visually reduce the space in front of the church and increase the monumental scale of the religious building; at the sides of the façade are two broad openings, which afford glimpses of the surrounding expanse of emptiness and allow the enclosed space of the square to communicate with the great open space of the

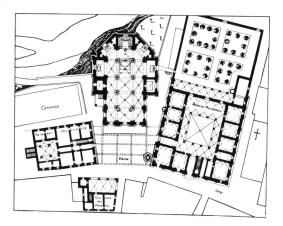

138, 139 *Plan and aerial view of the square at Pienza*

valley. The inner space of the church is divided into three sections, 'the middle one broader, but all of equal height; thus Pius ordained, having seen this model among the Germans in Austria, in that it makes the church more beautiful and luminous'. In fact the pointed windows, closed in by slabs of white glass, 'which they call crystal', open on to a free space to the south, and 'when the sun shines they let in so much light that the people in the church at the time feel as if they are in a house of glass, not a building of stone'.[33]

This organism, derived from the German *Hallenkirchen*, has nothing in common with the fifteenth-century Umbrian churches with three identical divisions, like Perugia cathedral and S. Fortunato at Todi,[34] and is developed in a way reminiscent of the description of the ideal church in *De re aedificatoria*.[35] The compound pillars are more or less shaped in the classical fashion and the ceilings are painted; but the walls 'shine with a marvellous candour' and have as their sole decoration the paintings which Pius II commissioned from the most famous Sienese painters of the time, Sano di Pietro, Giovanni di Paolo and Matteo di Giovanni ('within the temple I think detached pictures do much better than painting upon the wall itself').[36]

But what is particularly interesting is the conviction that the church, once built and decorated, must remain untouched by any subsequent alteration. In the seventh book of his treatise Alberti writes: 'Ornaments are in a manner infinite, and even in small temples there is always something which we imagine might or ought to be added. I would have the temple as large as the bigness of the city requires';[37] in the church 'everything which you behold should conduce to duration'.[38] Pius II radically resolved this problem with the Bull of 16 September 1462:[39]

'In this temple . . . no dead person shall be buried, with the exception of tombs for the bishops and priests; no-one shall violate the

140   *The campanile of Pienza cathedral*

141, 142 *Façade and interior of Pienza cathedral*

candour of the walls and columns; no-one shall add paintings; no-one shall hang pictures; no-one shall add other columns and other altars; no-one shall modify the form of the temple, either in the upper or the lower part. If anyone transgresses these regulations, he shall be excommunicated and shall be absolved only by the authority of the Roman Pontiff, except in case of death.'

The Palazzo Piccolomini is a three-storey quadrangular block with an inner courtyard, like the Florentine palazzi of the same period; this, with the bishop's palace which occupies the other side of the square, is always seen cornerways on by anyone going along the main street, coming from the eastern gate (Fig. 143), in so far as the two arms of the road arrive obliquely at the square; it is one of the advantages enumerated by Alberti, when he advises having winding streets in small towns.[40] The façade is decorated with a motif of superimposed orders, similar to the Albertian one on

Palazzo Rucellai. In making the comparison one must consider that here the palace is an isolated volume, and the rhythm of the windows is slower in relation to the size of the rooms within; but the most important innovation is the panoramic loggia which occupies the whole of the southern façade, linking the palace to the garden; a great hall (now known as *sala delle armi*) faces on to both courtyard and loggia, from which there is a view of the valley and Amiata, 'a mountain of extremely pleasant appearance'.[41] For the first time a monumental complex of this sort was linked organically to a green space and a view of the landscape.

Of his palace Pius II wrote:[42]

'If the first quality of a dwelling be light, certainly none could be preferable to this, which looks freely out to the four cardinal points and draws its light not only from outside windows, but also copiously from the inner ones through the courtyard, so that it pours right in, even down to the lower parts.'

143   *Corner view of Palazzo Piccolomini, Pienza*

144   *A window of the Palazzo Piccolomini*

145   *The pavement of the square at Pienza with the well in front of the Palazzo Piccolomini. To the left: the façade of the cathedral; to the right: the Palazzo Pubblico*

Church and palace were built at the same time, and were finished in 1462; then work was begun on the town hall and the other palazzi for the Cardinals Ammannati, Rodrigo Borgia and Francesco Gonzaga. In March 1462 the town officially took the name Pienza and housed the papal court for short periods. But work ceased even before the death of Pius II in 1464, and the town reverted to its former quiet life.

The medieval village and group of monuments placed in its centre coexist in a unique balance, produced by calculated relations of volume, despite the numerous and often disconcerting stylistic mixtures. For the first time a single planner had been able to supervise all the buildings looking on to a square and to define their proportions in terms of the intervening space, which thus

became the pivot of the whole layout of the town. The trapezoid form of the square made the curve of the crest on which the town was built evident and measurable; the divergence of the two lateral blocks splits open the compact fabric of the town at the two sides of the cathedral, and makes the presence of the great expanse of luminous air opening up behind the buildings felt even at the centre of the town. This arrangement, seen by anyone going along the main street, isolates the church and makes it more important, as we have already said, while seen from the church it lengthens the small space of the square in front of it and sets back the volume of the town hall, itself made less dense by the very deep portico.

The brick paving with its strips of stone seems to give shape to the network of perspective, as in Brunelleschi's buildings, and the well standing by the façade of the Palazzo Piccolomini is put in as a 'key to the measurements of the whole beautifully proportioned complex'[43] (Fig. 145).

The perspective organization of the square weakens and is lost in the surrounding fabric, which retains all its medieval character. The particular compromise between tradition and the modern style attained in the monumental buildings – where the geometrical layout was modern, the masonry structure traditional and the details drew upon both Gothic and classical models – could be partly reproduced in the more modest buildings; the layout became less rigid and more closely linked to the irregularity of the plots, the details became simpler, lessening the contrast between the stylistic models from which they were derived, while the uniformity of the masonry structures brought the various buildings conclusively together in the continuity of the urban organism.

The continuity of this gradation depended on the sense of moderation with which the main monuments were planned, avoiding excessive contrasts of scale; the hierarchy between important buildings and ordinary ones was thus to be established mainly by the

different emphasis of the factors of geometrical regularity, which in the first case became preponderant over topographical limitations, and were sacrificed to these limitations in the second. It is a subtle distinction, which transfers the relationships of prestige and power to a strictly intellectual sphere.

Here one may recognize the mark of the personality of Pius II, and the city can really be said, without any rhetorical approximation, to be the concrete image of his cultural ideal; love of form and human participation come together in a mood of literary serenity, as in the prose of the *Commentari*, and produce a balance to some degree detached from time and strangely untouched by the struggles of the century.

In the history of architecture this does in fact remain an isolated episode, which was to appear remote and irrelevant a very short time afterwards.

Urbino

Of the town-planning undertakings of the second half of the fifteenth century, the transformation of Urbino by Federigo da Montefeltro was perhaps the most coherent and successful, because for the first time instruments and phases of execution were proportionate to the programmes carried out. Federigo remained in power for an exceptionally long period – from 1444 to 1482 – and realized his intentions through a series of successive approaches, using a large number of artists, Italian and foreign; thus a group of skilled workers, unique in Italy, was formed in Urbino, and the result of their work went beyond the personal contribution of individuals and vitally influenced the course of future events.

Federigo came to power in 1444, after the plot that brought about the death of his half-brother Oddantonio. It is thought that the painting of the *Flagellation* (Fig. 147) was painted by Piero della Francesca (c. 1415–92) for the Montefeltro family in memory of the

146 *Architectural detail from Pienza showing the Piccolomini coat of arms*

147   *The* Flagellation *by Piero della Francesca. Ducal palace, Urbino*

killing of the prince, therefore in the years immediately afterwards (between 1444 and 1451); if this is so, the painting executed by the barely thirty-year-old master so completely outstrips previous achievement in the field of painting as to justify both the wonder of contemporaries and the considered judgment of modern criticism, which considers Piero's début as the main internal cause of the new movement in artistic interests from the second half of the century.

The young painter from Sansepolcro – trained in Florence in the 1430s – appears fully acquainted with the recent developments in figurative culture, but sufficiently foreign to city polemics to assimilate the experience he had gained during his apprenticeship in an independent way: the perspec-

tive of Brunelleschi and Alberti, Masaccio's realism, Fra Angelico's and Filippo Lippi's use of colour and light, the minute realism of the Flemish painters.

Each cultural acquisition was assessed with the straightforward seriousness typical of his temperament and country origin; the result of their scrutiny (which Longhi has defined with the famous formula 'perspective synthesis of form and colour'[44]) was established with no apparent effort and set successive experiments in Italian and European painting moving conclusively, indeed it made the primacy of painting over other forms of artistic endeavour technically a current reality, from the second half of the fifteenth century onwards.

In the extraordinary painting in Urbino

the system of visible forms is intentionally reviewed: the figures in the scene in the foreground and those in the middleground (linked by a complex narrative, mimic and symbolic relationship), establish the depth of the perspective field, spacious and measurable, whose construction has so often been analysed down to its most subtle implications.[45] This field is peopled with painted architecture, painted sculpture, painted geometrical and naturalistic decorations, naked and clothed figures, trees and clouds; all portrayable material – human limbs, fabrics of various kinds, stone, marble, brick, plastered walls, ironwork, metal nails, gilding – is reproduced and compared. Similarly the artist is marshalling a series of representational conventions of differing origins: the doubling of the scene, obtained by means of the architectural framing of the more distant scene, the elimination of a row of columns, replaced by *pendentifs*, so as to allow a better view of this scene, the simultaneous presence of modern, ancient and exotic costumes. Painting takes possession of everything and puts order into the spectacle of the world.

As far as Urbino was concerned, it is known that Piero della Francesca worked for the Montefeltro court on several occasions during his career: in 1465 he painted the twin portraits of Federigo (Fig. 148) and his wife Battista Sforza, about 1474 he painted the Brera altarpiece and the *Madonna di Senigallia*. The documents show that he was also in Urbino in 1460 and his other sojourns were all in places not far from the city. We cannot state exactly the extent of his influence on Urbino circles, but it was certainly continuous, and however one judges the stylistic comparisons suggested by modern scholars, particularly by Salmi,[46] his presence remains the most probable explanation of the high level of figurative art reached in Federigo's building complexes.

The Montefeltro family owned a palace at the top of the southern hill of Urbino and a *castellare* (ruined castle) 150 metres to the north, on the edge of the Valbona precipice.

Federigo began his palace either in 1447 'in rivalry' with the Tempio Malatestiano in Rimini, according to the chronicle of Clementini,[47] or about 1455, as is believed today;[48] he acquired the land between the old palace and the *castellare*, and began work on a large three-storey building, incorporating into it the masonry work of the two houses. At this stage the architectural layout was simple, almost elementary, and contrasted with the complex decoration of the interiors, the work of second-rate Tuscan or local artists.

At a date somewhere between 1464 and 1468[49] work on the Urbino site changed course; the long uniform building erected in the first ten years was incorporated into a complex organism around a large arcaded courtyard and acquired a function that was to be decisive for the layout of the whole town.

Higher up, i.e. towards the traditional centre of the town, the palace opened up with a new L-shaped façade which abandoned the alignment of the first block and left space for a square where Federigo subsequently had the new cathedral built by Francesco di Giorgio. But lower down there was to be a second façade, altogether exceptional in shape and function; it was here that Federigo's apartment and the more private rooms in the palace were to be housed, looking out over the countryside by means of a series of superimposed loggias; these loggias are framed by the two *torricini* (small towers) which contain the stairs and make direct communication possible with the slope of the valley, where a new exit, external to the town walls, was planned. Furthermore the façade with the *torricini* forms the prospect of the palace and indeed of the whole city from the countryside to the west (Fig. 155), i.e. from the road to Rome; it is rotated at an angle in relation to the main building, in that the north-west *torricino* is moved forwards and has its base about eight metres downhill from the other. This conformation, which seems based on pre-existing foundations, helps both

148   Portrait of Federigo da Montefeltro *by Piero della Francesca. Uffizi, Florence*

frontal position *vis-à-vis* the road to Rome, as has been observed;[50] hence the exaggerated accentuation of the two *torricini*, which rise above the roof of the building and become the dominant motif of the outline of the town, for those looking at it coming from the south or east.

The other blocks face west as well, with a series of terraces and courtyards open to the countryside, flanking the block with the towers. To the right the space contained between this block and the old *castellare* is levelled by impressive substructures and laid out as a hanging garden; the garden is closed in from below by a high wall, broken by false windows which frame the view of the hill opposite. To the left the less steep slope is regularized by two broad terraces; the walls facing south have loggias to catch the sunshine; from the broader of the two terraces – called the cortile del Pasquino – the Montefeltro family chapel was to rise, 'which, with its order, beauty and noble ornament, was to transcend every fine building that had ever been'.[51] Thus the gravitation of the palace, as far as the rest of the town was concerned, was tilted: the side facing Valbona, which was initially considered as a mere back, became the main façade of the new palace, and was conceived of as a long diaphragm between town and countryside, between the limited spaces of streets and squares, and the boundless space of the landscape.

The transformation of the palace produced a transformation of the organism of the town, which reproduced the distributive and symbolic concepts of Federigo's palace with impressive coherence.

The medieval town had grown up mainly on the eastern slope of the two hills, and the main streets converged towards the Lavagine gate, where the road to Rimini began; the most important road led from the gate to the saddle and from there, bifurcating, to the summits of the two hills. In older prints Urbino was always viewed from this side; later, at the upper left-hand corner of the city

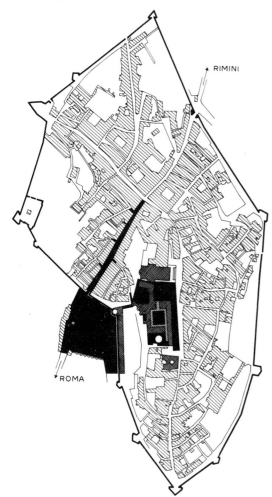

149 *Plan of the city of Urbino. The open spaces laid out by Federigo da Montefeltro are shown in black, the Ducal Palace and cathedral in cross-hatching*

to increase the amount of sun the loggias receive (they thus face south-west, i.e. they receive the sun directly during the warmest hours of the day) and to enable one of the entrances to be placed lower down; here a tower was later built with a ramp that could be used by horses, leading to the stables and the raised square of the Mercatale, built up from the floor of the valley. The rotation of this façade also serves to distinguish it, as an exceptional feature, in relation to the long front of the palace, and places it instead in a

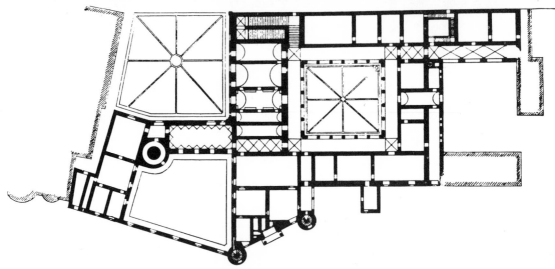

150, 151 *Aerial view and ground plan of the Ducal Palace, Urbino*

panorama, a curious round building with several diminishing storeys appears; this was the theoretical symbol of Federigo's palace – similar to the ideal buildings designed in the treatises of the time by Filarete or Francesco di Giorgio – in that the definitive form of the large building was still unknown (Fig. 158).

But together with the palace, the new district on the Valbona slope grew up, centred along a straight road climbing from the Mercatale to the saddle between the hills, linking up with the road to Lavagine and joining the two entrances to the palace. In this way a street axis was produced which crossed the town along the shortest and easiest route, i.e. by crossing the hollow

152 *View of the Ducal Palace facing the town. Eighteenth-century print*

153, 154 *Courtyard and spiral staircase of a* torricino, *Ducal Palace*

between the two hills. The whole town, like the palace, emerges as a diaphragm between two contrasting routes, the older one towards Rimini and the modern one towards Rome. The palace was set back from the main thoroughfare, to which it is linked at the highest point – by means of the road which runs up from the saddle to the square, and to the ceremonial courtyard – and at the lowest point, by means of the spiral ramp and stairs in the towers. In sixteenth- and seventeenth-century views, in fact, the city was shown from the south, and its silhouette is dominated by the twin spires of the *torricini*. 'The most vivid image of the city has moved round to the southerly arc, where the most significant symbols and most important interest were now concentrated' (Fig. 159).[52]

To carry out so vast and articulate a programme of building and town-planning, grafted on to a medieval organism and on difficult terrain, a subtle reconciliation was needed between the traditional means of intervention – refined over decades so as to be able to resolve every specific difficulty, but foreign to the new demands of building and landscape co-ordination – and the methods of the new architectural culture, based on a unitary feeling for space, but not yet tried out on this scale, in contact with the difficulties of

155   *View of Urbino from the south-west*

156   *Aerial view of Urbino*

157 Architectural prospect *by an unknown author. Ducal Palace, Urbino*

urban transformations. There was therefore a fusion of elements at the root of this experiment, which explains the hesitations and eclecticism of the whole Urbino repertoire, from the architecture to the sculpture and pictorial decorations.

The basic stylistic theme of the palace, and of the scheme of which it is part, is a particular balance between symmetry and asymmetry; the architecture corrects the secondary irregularities of the terrain and older buildings, but registers the main characteristics of the landscape and of the urban organism which grew up on it with extraordinary sensitivity.

Even in the most important and official parts of the buildings, where the need for architectural symmetry would be greatest, the occasional element of asymmetry still persists, referring back to the surrounding elements: for instance on the eastern façade the off-centre position of the door, the unusual relationship between the sides of six and of five arches in the *cour d'honneur*, the position of the windows and chimneypieces in the reception rooms, boldly displaced in relation to the axes of symmetry in order to facilitate the distributive needs and the movement through them. But in other cases an unmistakable desire to rationalize intervenes, altering and, if need be, contradicting the conformation of the landscape: this happened in the raised square of the Mercatale, in the stable built halfway along the slope and in the system of staircase towers along the western façade.

The exquisitely designed decorative elements – orders, arcades, door and window cornices, chimneys, corbels and keystones – are rarely welded into compact systems, and usually stand out in well-spaced splendour on the surfaces of inner and outer walls; for this reason they make possible frequent variations of detail, and introduce numerous isolated perspective suggestions into the building, like pieces of an ideal furnishing in stone; the actual furnishing – furniture, pictures and so on – has almost all been dispersed, and we cannot really imagine their contribution to the general effect.

In the same way the various monumental buildings built at the time of Federigo – the Palma and Luminati palaces on the Valbona road, the convent of S. Chiara, the Passionei palace, the ducal palace itself seen from the east – fit in as salient episodes without interrupting the extended screens of buildings formed by the more modest houses. The frequent fall in the rhythms of perspective isolates the single architectural motifs and heightens their individual perfection.

Even the larger building organisms, particularly Federigo's palace, when seen from a distance do not emerge as single systems, but as an aggregation of minor systems; thus they harmonize perfectly with the rest of the city, because they are not to be compared with the single houses, but with the building masses distributed in the landscape, from which they are distinguished by the concentration and intentional distribution of perspective foci,

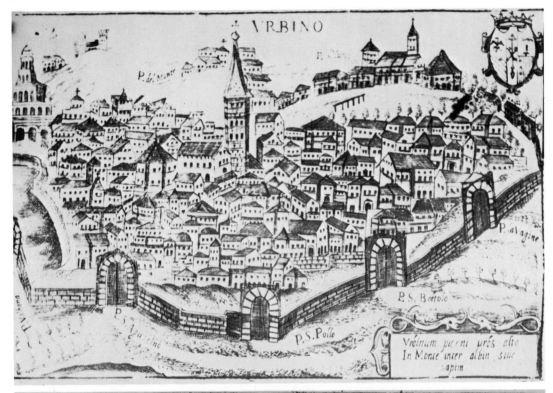

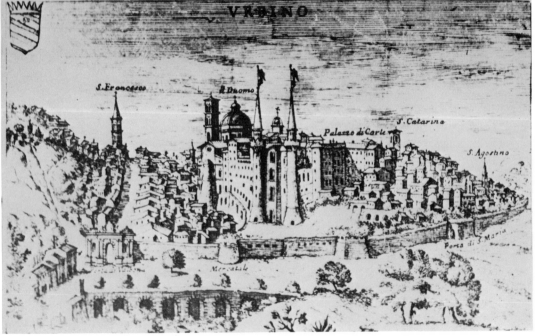

158, 159 *Two prints of Urbino showing the city as seen from the Lavagine and Valbona slopes*

160 *Detail of a ceiling in the Ducal Palace*

161   *A door in the Ducal Palace with inlaid perspective views*

not by a different dimension.

This made possible the special combination between the aristocratic and popular tone which characterizes the whole urban organism. As in Pienza, the hierarchy between the monuments and other buildings is qualitative rather than quantitative, though the quantities involved are greater here and the instruments of gradation far more complex.

The question as to who designed this complex, from 1465 onwards, has still not received a completely satisfactory answer; contemporaries[53] mention the name Luciano Laurana (d. 1479) with high praise; but Vasari omitted this architect from his *Lives*, and attributed the work on the palace at Urbino to Francesco di Giorgio (1439–1502).[54] In the first half of the nineteenth century the letters patent of 1468 were discovered; with this Federigo appointed or confirmed Laurana 'as the Engineer and Capo of the masters engaged upon the said work';[55] Laurana had been in Mantua before 1465 – when Alberti's first design for S. Sebastiano was being executed – and the documents show that he was already active in Urbino in 1467; but he could have directed the work on the palace only until 1472, when he left the city for good.

The works carried out after that date – i.e. the laying out of the secret garden, the loggia opened on to the cortile del Pasquino and the decoration of the eastern façade – are in fact attributed to Francesco di Giorgio (who meanwhile was working in the Marches as Federigo's military architect) on the basis of contemporary evidence and stylistic comparisons with his later work. It has also been noted that the artistic production of the court at Urbino changed character shortly after 1472, possibly in relation to the new political fortunes of Federigo (in 1474 he was appointed Gonfaloniere of the Holy Roman Church and soon afterwards duke by Sixtus IV; he received the Order of the Garter from the king of England and the ermine collar from the king of Naples). His taste became more eclectic; the circle of artists employed on the decoration of the palace broadened to include almost all the major Italian artists of the time, and even specialists in the 'Flemish manner'.

Today Luciano Laurana is generally referred to as the originator of the whole complex structure, and hence as one of the main figures in Italian architecture of the fifteenth century. But this judgment depends solely on the quality of the Urbino palace, and finds no confirmation in his activity before and after his stay in Urbino. In fact there has been a suggestion – unacceptable, but not incompatible with current information – that he worked as a technical executor rather than as a designer.[56] As for Francesco di Giorgio, the Urbino site must be considered rather as the place of his artistic and professional training; the attempt made to confirm Vasari's hypothesis, which regards him as designer of the whole work,[57] has found no following in recent criticism.

Therefore none of the attributions is entirely convincing, and scholars have felt the need to add other explanations: intervention by Alberti has been postulated, since he had dealings with the court of Urbino,[58] Federigo himself has been suggested as planner-supervisor[59] and a decisive importance has been attributed to the presence of Piero della Francesca, with the collection of all traces of his presumed architectural activity.[60]

But these hypotheses could well coexist if one considers the organic character of the complex of Urbino – which concerns not only the palace, but also the whole organism of the town – and if one abandons the idea of identifying a single personality as the author of the work, as one does for paintings, statues and lesser building elements executed in the same way as paintings and statues.

Federigo's undertakings – given the length of his reign, the size of his programme and the very eclecticism of his cultural outlook – set in motion in Urbino a complex cycle of operations which had no parallel in the whole of the fifteenth century. Responsibility for the work appears to have been divided between various skilled workers, and in fact the figure of the designer emerges as fragmented into various figures who contributed in different ways to determining the quality of the final result.

The complex of achievements at Urbino was not only the sole town-planning undertaking conceived and coherently implemented

in the fifteenth century; it also brought to light certain possibilities of the new architectural culture, which remained only potential because of the play of social and political circumstances; it offered glimpses of an alternative to the type of cultural organization which was being consolidated at this time, and revealed – so to speak – the loss of power of the cultural policy elaborated by the previous generation because of the specific difficulties of Italian society in the late fifteenth century.

The more personal productive relationship – in architecture as in the figurative arts – i.e. the reduction of the medieval operative cycle into a direct dialogue between client and artist (from which the actual executors were excluded, unless of course they were the artist himself), should perhaps be interpreted not as a primary requirement of the new ideology, but as the institutional result of the brevity and habitual uncertainty of each single undertaking.

The plan as a personal operation, which settled all the decisions necessary to determine the shape of the work at a single stage, was an approximation feasible precisely within the limits of time and space which became habitual from the fifteenth century onwards; but the need for rationalization inherent in Brunelleschi's approach could have taken concrete form in a more complicated process, as in fact happened on certain exceptional occasions, and only in such circumstances did it become effective on the town-planning scale.

In the case of Urbino the process of planning was certainly strung out over various levels and developed over a time parallel with the execution of the works, even if we are not in a position to reconstruct it with exactitude, precisely because the evidence is falsified by the habit of approximation mentioned above. It could be that Federigo da Montefeltro as co-ordinator, Alberti as theoretical consultant, Laurana and Francesco di Giorgio as technical experts

162   Legend of the Profanation of the Host *by Paolo Uccello. Ducal Palace, Urbino*

and Piero della Francesca as creator of some of the formal models contributed together to determine the characters of the building and town-planning layout; it could also be that the numerous artists involved in the decoration of the palace (Ambrogio Barocci, Baccio Pontelli, Domenico Rosselli, Francesco di Simone, Melozzo da Forlì, Paolo Uccello, Justus of Ghent, Pedro Berruguete, Giovanni Santi, Timoteo Viti, possibly Bramante and Sandro Botticelli) variously affected the work of the former, who were concerned more directly in the building work.

The same intermingling of various responsibilities is found again in the decoration of various individual rooms, for instance Federigo's *studiolo* (Figs 163–8), situated between the *sala delle udienze* and the loggia between the *torricini*, and even in some paintings, for instance the altarpiece of the confraternity of Corpus Domini, commissioned from Paolo Uccello who painted the predella (Fig. 162), then offered to Piero della Francesca and executed in 1474 by

Justus of Ghent, and the Montefeltro altarpiece in the Brera gallery in Milan, in which certain details of Piero's painting may possibly have been repainted by Berruguete.

The lower part of the *studiolo* is panelled with a base of wood inlay, with space for the two doors into the *sala delle udienze* and garderobe, but concealing the door to the loggia; in this way the *studiolo* – though in direct communication with the outside and the panorama – appears as an enclosed space, in contrast with the open expanse of the valley; here the perspective illusion created by the inlay dominates, while from the loggia one sees real space, peopled with real objects.

But even so compact and firmly designed a room is irregular in shape; the basic rectangle is interrupted by a wall at an angle, the upper part of which contains the window which reveals the oblique lie of the continuous loggia; internal and external points of reference subtly balance one another, as in the whole organization of the palace.

The inlay of the dado represents a series of

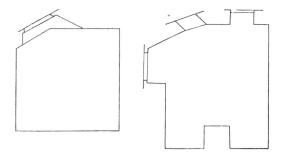

163–165   Studiolo *of Duke Federigo, Ducal Palace*

closed or half-open cupboards, occupied by books and other objects 'as though the prince, after having opened the bookcase and taken out his favourite book, after having taken off cuirass and weapons, laying their various parts here and there, after having prepared to play his musical instruments and opened the scores for the songs of war, had suddenly gone away, leaving his presence in the disorder he himself had created'.[61] It is thought that this panelling required two separate planning operations: a preliminary one of the general perspective organism – and the young Bramante has been mentioned in this context[62] – and a working cartoon of the actual inlay, by Sandro Botticelli or Francesco di Giorgio;[63] the panels were made in Florence in the workshop of Baccio Pontelli and mounted in Urbino;[64] similarly the carved wooden ceiling is probably from the workshop of Giuliano da Maiano,[65] and its border does not exactly tally with that of the room. A painted strip was fitted between the dado and the ceiling, with a double row of portraits of famous men, ancient and modern, painted by Justus of Ghent, Pedro Berruguete and possibly a third painter.[66]

The artists employed by Federigo belong to the second generation of the Renaissance movement; they had assimilated and synthesized the innovations introduced by the masters of the first generation, but they retained sufficient flexibility to adapt to different professional situations, not yet codified by an institutional apparatus which was emerging during these very years. Working together, they produced the exceptional work which epitomized several features of the new culture destined to disappear in the course of future developments. But the effects of this unrepeatable happening remain fundamental for future developments in artistic culture. 'The fact that the most lucid artists of the fifteenth century came together in Urbino made this city the centre of the mathematical disciplines and of the "abstract" art of the Renaissance',[67] even after 1482; the

166   *A section of the wooden panelling in the* studiolo

167 *Detail of the wooden panelling in the* studiolo

168   *Detail of the wooden panelling in the* studiolo

mathematicians Paul von Middelbourg and Luca Pacioli stayed at the court of Urbino, the first as a doctor and the second as Guidobaldo's teacher; Leonardo was present in 1502, when Cesare Borgia conquered the city and transported the famous library to Cesena. Bramante and Raphael left Urbino one after the other to meet again in Rome at the end of their careers.

Contemporaries perceived the exceptional quality of the Urbino palace more clearly than did later observers, irreducible as it was to current models. Baldassare Castiglione's definition is well known, 'a city in the form of a palace',[68] a pithy allusion to the importance of the palace for the whole town; equally evocative was the modest description in verse by Antonio da Mercantello (1480) who

reviewed the courtyard 'with its marble columns and novel shapes', the 'large and well-lit' library, the *studiolo* 'which soars above all others' and all the parts of the palace up to the pinnacles of the *torricini*.

'And your first vision from afar
is the two golden balls perched high on
   their cones.'

The *conclusione* of the poem is another list:[69]

'I hear that there are two hundred and fifty
   rooms
well divided up by subtle brains
six hundred and sixty entrances and
   windows
chambers and halls, loggias with
   courtyards

forty never-smoking chimneys
ante-chambers, delightful little
   sitting-rooms,
well-placed stables and a kitchen
store-rooms for wine, grain and flour.'

Just before Federigo's death, Baccio Pontelli sent Lorenzo the Magnificent a plan of the completed palace, and Federigo Gonzaga in his turn wrote to Matteo di Volterra asking for the designs of the famous building.[70]

Vasari who was writing seventy years afterwards, at the height of the academic period, felt it his duty to substitute the name of the last designer employed by Federigo, i.e. Francesco di Giorgio, for the phrase 'subtle brains'; at that time the palace was admired only retrospectively, in that it was superior to the models of the past ('the entire palace is as fine and well-built as any other that has been erected up to the present')[71] but undoubtedly antiquated in relation to later aristocratic buildings.

Modern criticism is merely perpetuating Vasari's preconception, if it continues to consider the palace as a single work to be attributed to an author. Today when Urbino is being studied anew in its entirety, as one of the most important Italian historic centres to be fitted into a new territorial organization,[72] it is natural, in this context, to reassess the integrated character of Federigo's activity, which may be considered the first town-planning scheme of the Italian Renaissance.

The cycle of the building activities of the Montefeltro family in the territory of the duchy still remains to be examined. The Ducal Palace of Gubbio is a smaller version of the one in Urbino and contains a second *studiolo* decorated with inlay, probably designed by Francesco di Giorgio and executed by the workshop of Baccio Pontelli; the numerous works of fortification, by Laurana and Francesco di Giorgio, are exceptionally beautiful, and in some cases – as in the fortress of Sassocorvaro – have a geometrical rigour

169, 170 *Two panels designed by Francesco di Giorgio, with engines of war. Ducal Palace, Urbino*

not inferior to that of the monuments of Urbino.

In the field of artistic literature, too, the influence of the Urbino experiments is decisive; the most important and technically best-informed treatises of the late fifteenth century came from this circle.

Piero della Francesca wrote a manual on arithmetic, *De abaco*, a manual of perspective, *De perspectiva pingendi*, and the *Libellus de quinque corporibus regularibus*, later transcribed by Pacioli in his *De divina proportione*. Piero's treatise on perspective, composed before 1482 and dedicated to Federigo, laid out the procedures discovered by the artists of the first half of the century in a precise and systematic form, and paved the way for the specialized works of the sixteenth century (those of Pomponio Gaurico, 1504, and Jean Pélerin, 1505). This work soon became famous, and was the authority in Italian artistic circles up to the middle of the sixteenth century; Pacioli tells how Leonardo gave up writing his treatise on perspective when he learned that Piero's was available, and Vasari abundantly praised the writings of his fellow-townsman.

Francesco di Giorgio wrote his *Treatise* on military and civil architecture between 1470 and 1480, also dedicated to Federigo, and, like Alberti, his 'ambition was to create a modern Vitruvius'.[73] He did not have the breadth of civil interests of the great humanist, but included in his text a large number of experiments and ideas of his own or typical of his time, documented with numerous drawings; it thus answered one of the most intense demands of the general culture of the last decades of the fifteenth century, which required a visual illustration for every notion and tended to make scientific research coincide with the systematic representation of the forms of the objects. Leonardo was beginning his research at this same time, as a development of this tendency, and found a large number of suggestions in Francesco di Giorgio's work.

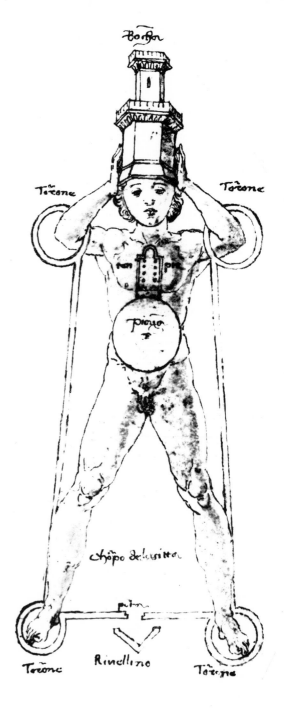

171   *The city and the human body. Drawing from the treatise of Francesco di Giorgio*

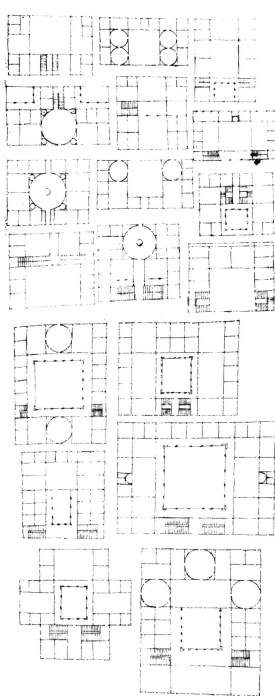

172, 173 *Two pages from the treatise by
Francesco di Giorgio, with a range of plans of villas or
palazzi (Magliabechia MS.)*

CLARVS INSIGNI VEHITVR TRIVMPHO ·
QVEM PAREM SVMMIS DVCIBVS PERHENNIS ·
FAMA VIRTVTVM CELEBRAT DECENTER ·
SCEPTRA TENENTEM

174 Triumphal allegory *by Piero della Francesca, on the back of the portrait of Federigo. Uffizi, Florence*

The lengthy discussion on the layout of cities, contained in the third book, must be regarded as a development of the treatises of Alberti and Filarete, in accordance with the tendency already mentioned. What in Alberti was literary reasoning and in Filarete a symbolic ideogram, here became a survey of many possible forms, always theoretical and independent of concrete experiment. This survey was based on the radial pattern, whose cosmic and super-empirical value has already been noted; it served to give visual form to the variants already described by Alberti, concerning the geographical position of the city: on the plain, on a hill, along a river, etc.

The theoretical scheme with central symmetry was affected by two new facts:

1   The grid plan, which was beginning to be adopted in practice at this time, partly because of the inspiration of the Roman *castramentatio*, described by the Latin authors (the reconstruction of Cortemaggiore took place about 1480). Francesco di Giorgio used the grid plan for the distribution of building lots within the city, but gave a polygonal or circular layout to the walls in this case too (Figs 175, 176).

2   The new techniques of fortification of cities against artillery. Francesco di Giorgio was regarded as one of the greatest specialists in this matter, and the real nub of the treatise (Book V) is devoted to the building of fortresses. The technique of fortification influenced discussions of the form of the city, because one of the requirements of this technique – the polygonal line of the walls, with bastions at the salient corners – coincided with the shape of the perimeters deduced from the theoretical centralized radiating schemes. Thus there began the combination of the two aspects (technical and theoretical) which was to characterize all later treatise-literature for at least two centuries, as we shall see. The inclusion of the defensive factor drew the survey of ground

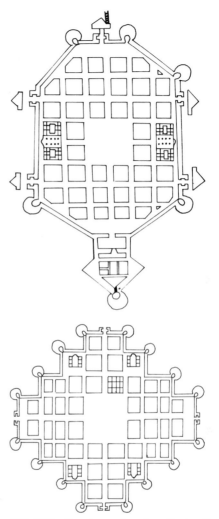

175, 176   *Two town plans from the treatise by Francesco di Giorgio (Magliabechia MS.)*

plans on to a realistic level, but lost the city its character as a general model: it became a fortress, the civic centre became the place where the troops gathered, the street network served to facilitate the comings and goings of the defenders, or to hinder the entrance of the enemy; thus it became possible to plan the ideal city, but it became a specialized settlement, and ceased to function as a cultural myth; the hopes hitherto pinned on this image were directed elsewhere, as we shall see in chapter 4.

Ferrara

In Ferrara the second great town-planning undertaking of the Italian fifteenth century after that of Urbino was realized. Thirty years divided the two operations – the first took place in the 1460s, the second in the 1490s – and they are very different from one another, both because of the difference of the two urban organisms and because of the changes that intervened in the political and cultural circumstances.

As early as the fourteenth century Ferrara was one of the most important cities of the Po plain; here Petrarch stayed and a new university was founded. In 1436 the marquis Lionello d'Este entertained Guarino da Verona, who opened his famous school in the city. 'After a lucky star sent that divine man to Ferrara, there came about a marvellous change in men's minds'; so one reads in his funeral oration, prepared in 1460 by his pupil Ludovico Carbone.[74] Those years did in fact see the dawn of the cultural prestige of the city of the Estensi which was later to become, as Chastel said, 'the capital of modern poetry'[75] and in this sense one of the most important places for the civilization of the Renaissance.

As far as the visual arts were concerned, the short years of the reign of Lionello d'Este, himself poet and connoisseur (1441–50), were rich in important events: in 1441 Jacopo Bellini won the competition with Pisanello for the portrait of the prince; in 1443 Leon Battista Alberti arrived in Ferrara, and may possibly have prepared the designs for the pedestal of the monument to Niccolò III and the campanile of the cathedral (Figs 177–8); about 1449 Mantegna, Piero della Francesca and possibly Roger van der Weyden arrived; Piero's influence is regarded as a decisive factor in the formation of Cosimo Tura and the school of Ferrara.

In 1451 Borso d'Este (1450–71) extended the perimeter of the city to include the delta land of S. Antonio (the so-called '*addizione di Borso*'). Ferrara became more populous,

177 The arco del cavallo, *Ferrara*

and richer; in 1466 Biagio Rossetti (1447–1516) began his building activities and was until 1516 the main architect of Borso and his successors Ercole I (1471–1505) and Alfonso I (1505–34). The palazzi by Rossetti – where popular tradition and learned tradition find a unique balance – provide wall space for splendid pictorial cycles (the frescoes in Rossetti's Palazzo Schifanoia date from 1469 to 1471) and backgrounds for the sumptuous life at court, where Boiardo composed the *Orlando Innamorato* and where from 1486 successive performances of classical and modern dramas took place.

In 1492 Ercole I began work on the *'addizione erculea'* ('Herculean addition'): the new extension of the city, which actually doubled its original area. Biagio Rossetti was the supervisor of the town-planning arrangement, and the architect of the most important buildings in the *terranova*.

The reasons behind this exceptional scheme – the most ambitious hitherto realized in Italy or indeed in Europe – were of a military, economic and ceremonial order. Between 1482 and 1484 Ferrara sustained a war against Venice, and her enemies crossed the Po, directly attacking the city. To the north stood the ducal estate of the Barco, with the castle of Belfiore, captured by the Venetians; the city was defended only by the walls and moat of the Giovecca, too weak to resist the impetus of a modern army; for this reason the people of Ferrara hastily constructed a semi-circular bastion in front of the Estense castle, and resisted until the Peace of Bagnolo. But Ercole I had to cede all the territory north of the Po to Venice, and feared a new invasion more than ever; for this reason he decided to forearm himself by building a new defensive wall to the north of the city, using up-to-date criteria.

The town was going through a period of economic development; the Estensi had encouraged the prosperity of Ferrara in every way, attracting rich exiles from other towns and protecting industrial activity. The

178 *The campanile of Ferrara cathedral*

179 Miracle of St Vincent *by F. del Cossa. Pinacoteca Vaticana, Rome*

revenue of the court depended directly upon the wealth of the city, by means of a fiscal system which was considered the harshest of the time. The population was constantly rising, and even in 1497, when the works of addition were fully under way, there was a serious shortage of houses to rent.[76] This demographic situation explains the extensiveness of the territory included within the new walls. As had been the case when the walls of the big European cities were traced in the thirteenth century, there was a desire to accumulate a stock of building land sufficient to ward off another saturation crisis.

These two themes appear in the comments of the citizens reported in the chronicles of the time: 'It was said that the afore-mentioned duke embarked upon these excavations to increase the body of the city.' 'I . . . understand nothing except that he . . . is doing this to fortify himself against that mob.'[77]

The walls, begun in the summer of 1492, were already completely laid out in 1493, while the final details were completed only in

1510. The occupation of the land for these works of defence met with no resistance, because the private owners realized that their land would gain in value by becoming part of the city. But inside the walls an unusual legal difficulty arose, in that the new streets were traced 'as the duke wanted them to go, across whosoever's property they encountered, to their damage'.[78] In other words a plan of the new street network was decided upon, and the owners of the land occupied regarded themselves as unlucky victims of this unusual imposition. Here, in fact, lay the novelty of Ercole I's intervention, a novelty which set it apart from that of similar earlier operations and reflected the demands of the new architectural culture, applied for the first time on so large a scale.

The plan was prepared in great secret from 1490 to 1491; at the same time the duke concentrated upon 'enlarging his park', i.e. upon enlarging the estate which he already possessed in the new area; this demesne, divided into lots in 1493, made it possible to urbanize much of the zone very fast, and simultaneously.

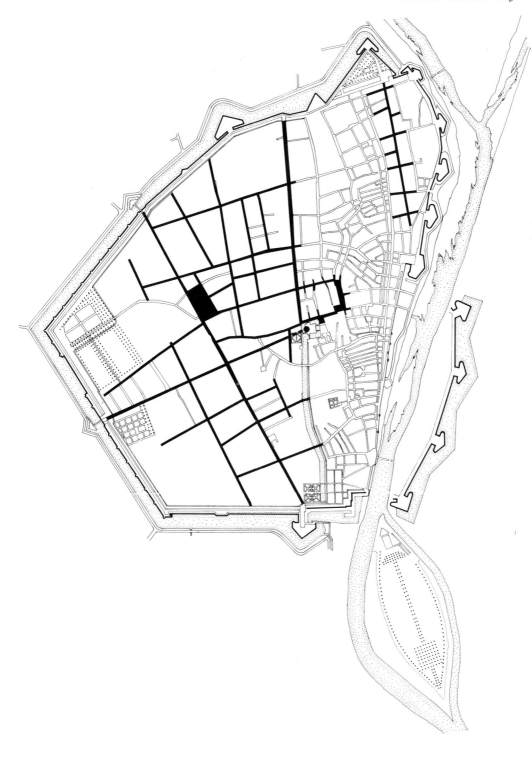

180 *Plan of Ferrara in the sixteenth century. In black the roads of the additions of Borso and Ercole shown in the plan of Pellegrino Prisciani, 1498; to the left: the Belvedere island*

181   *Prospect of Ferrara at the end of the sixteenth century*

It is interesting to consider which elements of the new network were fixed in advance, and which were determined during the course of the work. The ground plan of 1498 by Pellegrino Prisciani shows a series of streets (Fig. 180) which link the already existing buildings in the area of the addition – the castle of Belfiore, the Certosa, the church of S. Maria degli Angeli – streets which presumably were already in existence; among the most important was the avenue running straight between the garden of the Estense castle and the castle of Belfiore, which became one of the main axes of the layout; the other axis – a new road[79] almost perpendicular to the previous ones – crosses the

whole area from south-west to north-east, and intersects the walls linking up with the most important roads of the territory of the Estensi: in one direction towards Modena and Reggio, in the other towards the sea. The 'new square' opened off the second axis and from it ran another straight road which entered one of the main streets of old Ferrara (the present via Bersaglieri del Po) and ended in the market square. Apart from these roads the plan of 1498 marks only one other crossing of the first axis, from the Certosa to the western walls (the present via Aria Nuova). The body of the old walls and moat of the Giovecca still lay between the old and new towns; there were three possible ways

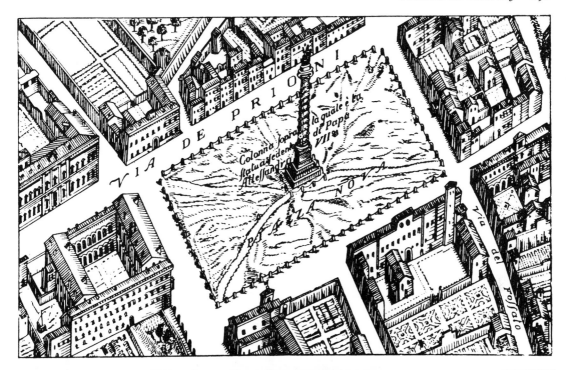

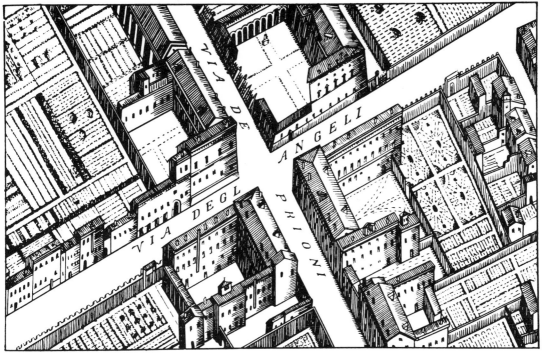

182, 183 *Piazza Nova, Ferrara and the crossroads between via degli Angeli and via dei Prioni, from the view by Andrea Bolzoni, 1747*

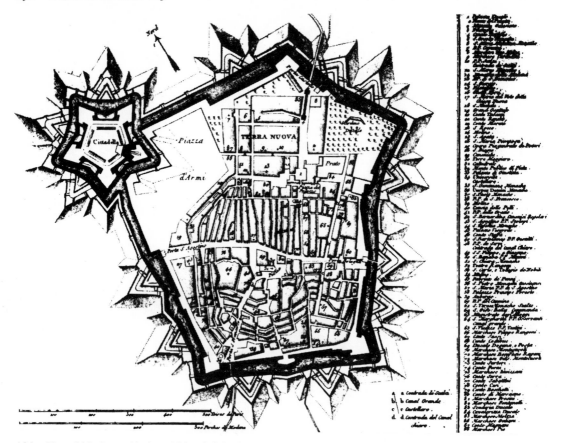

184   *Plan of Modena with the additions of the Estensi of 1546*

through, the one already mentioned and two more at the sides of the Estense castle; but we know that as early as 1496 another was opened up corresponding to via Terra Nuova, and in 1497 free circulation between the two zones of the city was made possible.

We do not know if this plan indicates the state of the works or interventions provided for in the initial plan, or simply the more important elements of a layout that was more complex even then. The street network of the addition was completed slowly in the course of the sixteenth century, and the plan must undoubtedly have been arrived at through successive approximations.

Biagio Rossetti is indicated by all the sources as the designer of the addition; the documents mention his name as supervisor

of the works on the walls (together with the contractor Alessandro Biondo),[80] as designer of twenty or so monumental buildings and as inspector of many other public and private buildings. But not much is known about the cycle of operations set in motion by the works of 1492, and of the role of Rossetti in this cycle, i.e. of the opportunities he may have had to control the strategic decisions of the plan, and not only tactical decisions connected with the form of the single buildings and their adjacent spaces.

One of the most distinctive features of the plan, pointed out by Zevi – the placing of the new square along the secondary axis, some distance from the perspective complex centring round the Estense castle – was required by the function of the castle in the organism of the fifteenth-century city. The residence of the Este family was not a civic centre or a junction of routes, but a citadel surrounded by a controlled zone which interrupted internal communications. The first axis emanated from the controlled zone and continued to function as a ceremonial avenue reserved for the approach to the palace of Sigismondo d'Este and the other ducal buildings situated on this route; only in 1633 was it extended to the corso della Giovecca and integrated into the city's street system. But the square, since it was conceived as a new civic centre, could be linked with the old one only by circumventing the castle zone; hence it had to be shifted to correspond to the centre of gravity of the old city.

The elegance of the solution adopted goes beyond the basic data; we do not know whether it was due to a personal decision of the architect, or whether it emerged from the coming together of a number of skilled contributors, and whether this circumstance was the cause of the flexibility we admire today.

These uncertainties gradually diminish as one moves downwards from general decisions towards decisions of detail, and lastly to the actual laying out of the buildings. There is no doubt whatsoever about the consummate ability of Biagio Rossetti in adapting the buildings to the distribution of the surrounding spaces; a whole series of medieval expedients – the placing of two windows at the corners of each room, which meant that on the outside the windows were grouped in pairs; the arrangement of the arcades around the main square on the continuation of the adjacent roads, as in the *bastides* of southern France; the habit of placing architectural motifs referring to the external setting, and not to the building on which they were placed, on street axes or corners (Fig. 187) – were resumed and translated into modern terms, dominated by the requirements of perspective.

Contemporaries, who had never seen so

extensive a modern urban complex implemented, considered this new scene with astonished admiration; the regular roads and squares imagined by the painter were becoming a concrete reality. The Estensi were eagerly to repeat this same arrangement in their domain of Modena in 1546 (Fig. 184).

A comparison between the layout of Urbino and that of Ferrara is extremely instructive.

The two layouts have in common a free non-conformist attitude in relation to the usual canons of symmetry and perspective regularity, which is the reason for their particular fascination for us. This freedom was certainly the result of the greater complexity of the cycle of operations from which they derived, in comparison with that of the single buildings, i.e. the portion of the urban continuum which corresponded to the typical dimension of operations at that time. But it also revealed the potentialities of the perspective culture which was sacrificed during the fifteenth century as a result of the play of the social circumstances which progressively restricted the space accorded to architectural planning, while architecture tended to emerge as a particular application of a broader visual discipline, now definitively secured for painting.

The layout of Urbino and the 'Herculean addition' are exceptions in a process orientated on the whole in other directions; for this reason they reveal the rejected hypotheses, the possibilities insufficiently explored to become habitual, fascinating for us precisely because of their chronological irrelevance which became, with time, surprisingly modern.

In Ferrara the layout of the buildings along the streets of the 'Herculean addition' repeatedly developed the theme of foreshortened perspective presentation, as in contemporary inlay (Figs 185, 186). Scarcely ever does a monumental building act as backdrop to an axial perspective, and in many cases a frontal view of the building –

185   *Detail of the architectural prospect in the museum of Urbino*

even when it was a monumental one like the Palazzo dei Diamanti – is actually physically impossible: the foreshortened view makes it possible to compare many successive buildings with one another, and exploits the intellectual emotion which derives from the constancy of the vanishing point, i.e. from the perfect convergence of many different forms. Thus the slight distortion of the corners – almost always nearly a right angle, but not exactly – and the slight curve of some successive stretches of road – as in via Ariosto and also in the second of the two main axes – produce expressive feelings of rotation, which find an echo in some oblique perspectives of the later style of Piero. The oblique points of juncture so frequent in Urbino, both in the palace and in the open spaces of the town, but always clearly distinct from the orthogonal ones, are here repeated with

greater subtlety, so as to cast doubt on every apparent constancy of the square.

In other ways Ercole I's layout is very unlike that of Federigo. The thirty-year interval influenced not only the quality of the operation, but also the success of its execution. However one may assess Biagio Rossetti's participation in the operative cycle in Ferrara, this operation was certainly a more personal affair than that in Urbino, so much so that in Ferrara all evidence converges upon a single name, while in Urbino the problem of attributions is still extremely intricate.

Federigo's transformation was primarily a transformation of the core, from which followed a changed pattern for the whole town. Ercole's transformation was above all an extension, which did not affect the old centre of the city and, if anything, set up against it a new secondary centre which was

186 *A view of via degli Angeli with the Palazzo dei Diamanti, Ferrara*

187 *Corner detail of a palazzo in via degli Angeli*

situated in the addition.

In the seventh decade of the fifteenth century there was still the possibility of transforming a medieval town into a modern one; at the end of the century a consciousness of the disparity and detachment between the two cultures and two types of urban landscape crept in; an increasing awareness and decreasing force of decision hindered the simultaneous transformation of centre and outskirts as happened in Urbino and as had happened in the great town-planning operations of the end of the thirteenth century.

In Ferrara, furthermore, a considerably larger urban area was involved; it is true that the technical resources and financial possibilities of the public authorities had increased; but the unity and coherence of the political leadership was declining, and shortly afterwards was lost entirely.

The fact that the addition was begun only in 1492, after more than twenty years of Ercole's reign, largely compromised the completion of the executive process. In 1505 work had already slowed down as a result of the duke's death. The coherence of the initial design firmly secured the completion of the street network in the course of the sixteenth century; but building activity declined and ceased, at the time of the economic crisis which began under Ercole II (1543–59); the population increase anticipated by Ercole I did not take place, and the addition retained a mixed character, urban and rural, which it still has to this day.

The chronological delay also influenced the architectural essence of the addition. The integrated character of the Ferrarese undertaking, like that of Urbino, had as its effect a significant combination of aristocratic and

188   *Via Mortara in the Herculean addition of Ferrara*

popular tones. But here the deep-rooted difference between the two operations emerges: in Urbino the combination of aristocratic and popular – i.e. of intellectual commitment and human participation – took place on a level which at that time was the highest possible, and faithfulness to local motifs coexisted with a striving towards a universal synthesis, broader and more conclusive than any other hitherto attempted. In Ferrara the works of Ercole I bore traces of provincialism, which emerged clearly if they were compared to what was happening at the same time in other Italian centres.

About 1480 there was a tendency towards a grandiose synthetic style, which should transcend the peculiarities of local experiments and make its selection from among the conflicting results hitherto obtained. This tendency – partly influenced in fact by Urbino – was most intense in the big centres – Milan, Venice, Florence and, particularly in the first years of the sixteenth century, in the papal court in Rome.

When work started on Ercole's addition the activities of Bramante and Leonardo da Vinci were already well under way and the young Michelangelo was making his début in the Medici garden. The prestige of the 'third style'[81] was not only soon to eclipse the immense variety of local experiments (this distinction does not necessarily correspond to an objective evaluation of the experiments sacrificed in later development) but, for as long as it made itself felt, it brought a feeling of mistrust to these experiments, which objectively diminished their impact and coherence.

For this reason the rigour of the Urbino venture remained unique in the history of the Renaissance, and found no echo in the experiment in Ferrara, which took place in a situation that was already profoundly different.

Let us examine the technical consequences: in Urbino perspective criteria served to establish a qualitative gradation between main elements and secondary elements of the

189   *Detail of the* Triumph of Venus *by F. del Cossa, Palazzo Schifanoia, Ferrara*

townscape, i.e. to translate the hierarchy of economic and political relationships into exclusively intellectual terms; for this reason there was no system of geometrical rules separable from single building operations. But in Ferrara the need for perspective regularity became the very instrument to control the entire development of the city and to subordinate it to the will of the ruling class: this was how the plan came about, i.e. as a collection of decisions preceding the individual operations, which included the laying out of the walls and some of the roads and main squares. However, control and subordination were not absolute; hence the nuances and subtleties of the actual result.

The plan of Ferrara is more modern, because of the separation of decisions into two distinct groups, which we can begin to call town-planning decisions and architectural decisions. This separation – whose organizational potentialities were largely unknown – now undermined the unity of the operation, and opened up a series of unresolved problems.

For this reason Ferrara lacked any theoretical underpinning, and even any adequate illustration of the actual achievements, which had been so consistent in Urbino. While Rossetti was building the addition, Ariosto was composing the *Orlando Furioso* and Dosso Dossi beginning his career as court painter; but these experiences did not fuse, either directly or indirectly, into a single operational cycle. The ruling class was no longer in a position to synthesize these contributions, and used many independent specialists. Architecture and its final product, i.e. the city, were no longer the comprehensive setting for the advances in culture and civic society, but one of the sectors of a cultural organization that was already moving towards specialization.

Mantua

Mantua, together with Urbino and Ferrara,

was the last of the ideal capitals of the late fifteenth century, whose urban landscape was fixed at this golden period of its history and which remained to bear witness to the prestige of an exceptional political and cultural situation.

The Mantua of the Gonzagas, however, was less altered by Renaissance undertakings than the other cities we have discussed. The form of the city had been fixed around the end of the twelfth century, following the hydraulic works of Alberto Pitentino which defined the lake basins fed by the Mincio, and therefore the situation of the island on which the built-up area stood (Fig. 190). The circle of the walls was built from 1240 to 1242 and completed in 1352. A stone of 1397 says that Francesco I Gonzaga (who reigned from 1388 to 1407) '*perfecit urbem*'; in fact in 1401 he promulgated the statutes for the division of the city into *rioni* and *contrade*, built the church of S. Giorgio, the Zoiosa, the façade of the cathedral, the church of S. Maria delle Grazie and possibly laid down the regulations used in later building transformations.[82]

At this time the organization of the city was already broadly defined, and these general lines were to remain constant until the eighteenth century, when the drying up of one of the lakes transformed the island into a peninsula. The transformations from then onwards concerned the built-up fabric, which was almost entirely replaced, and the monumental buildings, fitted one by one into the urban complex.

The cultural prestige of the city began at the time of Gianfrancesco Gonzaga (1407–44), who had Pisanello working for him and financed the humanistic school of Vittorino da Feltre (from 1423), where many princes of the following generation were educated, including Borso d'Este and Federigo da Montefeltro.

Ludovico III (1444–78) summoned Brunelleschi, Luca Fancelli and Luciano Laurana and had Leon Battista Alberti design a group of buildings fundamental to the history of

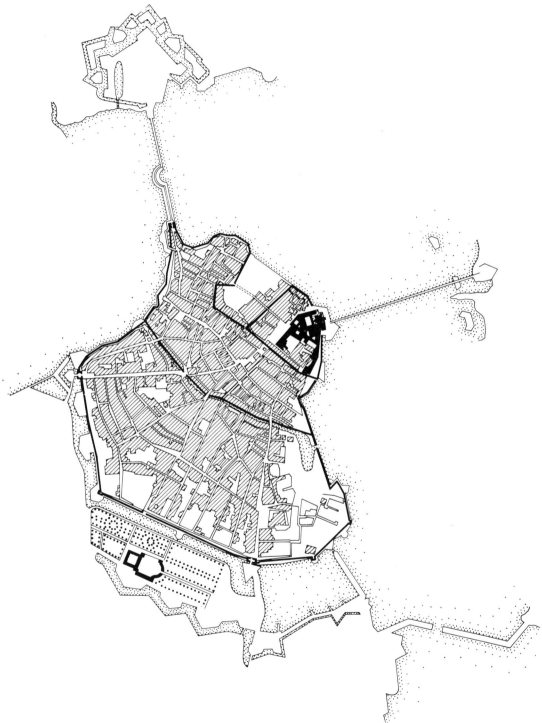

190 *Plan of Mantua. In black the complex of the Ducal Palace (above), the Palazzo del Tè (below) and the circle of walls existing at the end of the fifteenth century*

191 *Prospect of Mantua at the end of the sixteenth century*

Renaissance architecture, which we have already discussed: the church of S. Sebastiano (1460), the church of S. Andrea (1470) and possibly the rotunda of the Annunziata in Florence (c. 1470), financed by the lord of Mantua as a monument in celebration of his family.

The experimental character of Alberti's works explains the difficulties of execution, and the time it took for them to be understood and appreciated; in 1473 Cardinal Francesco Gonzaga described S. Sebastiano in a letter to his father and showed himself perplexed at the novelty of the organism, wondering whether it was church, synagogue or mosque.[83]

Luca Fancelli (1430–95), who was the executor of Alberti's works, himself designed the Ospedale Grande (begun in 1450 and opened in 1472), the renovation of the Palazzo

del Podestà (1461–2), that of Castel S. Giorgio (about 1470), and in 1480 began the building of the *domus nova*.

But the decisive element, in Ludovico's reign, was his summoning in 1457 of Andrea Mantegna (1431–1506), who settled permanently in Mantua three years later.

From Padua Mantegna brought the finest fruits of the 'epigraphic and archaeological'[84] humanism that had grown up in the studio of Squarcione and the learned circles of that city; in Mantua he painted most of his masterpieces, and in particular the *camera picta* in the Ducal Palace; the frescoes on the walls and ceiling cover the entire room, and figured space totally annuls traversable space, achieving a sort of antithesis of Albertian architectural perspective (Fig. 194).

To some degree Mantegna controlled all the artistic undertakings in Mantua, includ-

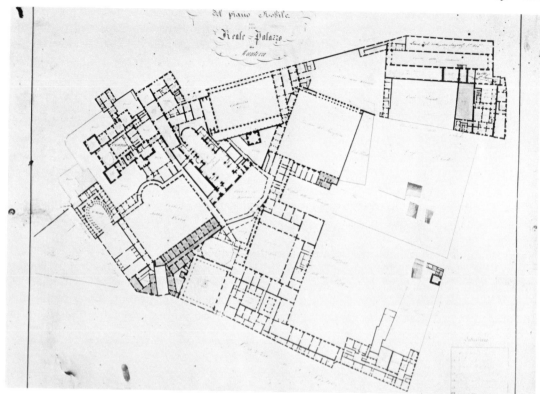

192 *Plan of the Ducal Palace, Mantua*

ing the architectural ones; in 1459 he provided the directions which enabled Fancelli to build the courtyard of the Ducal Palace, and possibly in 1476 he designed his house, with the little cylindrical courtyard set in the cubic structure. The reasons for his pictorial power never having been translated into an original architectural impulse, unlike that of Piero della Francesca in Urbino, still remain to be examined.

The palace of the Gonzagas at Mantua, like that of the Montefeltro family in Urbino, is an aggregate of various blocks, built in successive phases, and it has been suggested that the oldest of them – the one looking on to piazza Sordello – may have served as a model for the first plan of the palace at Urbino.[85] But the relationship of the building with the city is different and almost antithetical. In Urbino the palace is the fulcrum around

which the new general structure of the city was organized, and the schemes of the surrounding terrain – the square to the east, the Mercatale to the west, the Data and staircase towers – act as links and service areas for the whole city. In Mantua the palace is a positive citadel which is its own centre in a corner of the city, without modifying the city's layout.

Mantua thus remains the most typical example of a divided city, where the real headquarters (although not a single element, incompatible in scale with the rest of the built-up area, as was the case in Milan, but formed by successive additions like the other districts) remained a city within the city and, precisely while it was growing, became increasingly independent. The other monumental buildings, too, though impressive like Alberti's S. Andrea or Fancelli's hospital, were fitted into the city as compact and isolated blocks.

In the last years of the century, while the episode of the Herculean addition was beginning in Ferrara, in Mantua the particular geographical situation, already militarily extremely secure, and the stability of the population which remained around 25,000, excluded the need for any expansion. Cultural life was dominated by Isabella d'Este, who arrived in 1490, and the building activities of the court were concerned with putting finishing touches to the existing town organism. In 1483 the title of *superiore delle fabbriche Gonzaghesche* ('chief of the Gonzagas' buildings') was established (granted to Bernardo di Piacenza, then in 1490 to Bernardino Ghisolfo, in 1517 to Gerolamo Arcari and in 1526 to Giulio Romano) and in 1497 the title of *superiore delle vie urbane*, conferred on

Pellegrino Ardizzoni who was one of the builders of S. Sebastiano.[86] In this period the medieval arcades on the central streets were completed, and many of the palazzi and private houses were restored.

At the beginning of the sixteenth century political events produced a halt in building activity. The situation changed in 1524, when Francesco Gonzaga, at the advice of Baldassare Castiglione, sent for Giulio Romano (1492–1546). For over twenty years the artist supervised the renovation of the city and realized a series of monumental buildings: the Palazzo del Tè from 1525 to 1526 (Figs 196–8), the restoration of the castle for the wedding of 1531, the new law court and slaughterhouse, the new cathedral from 1545 onwards. At this time the population of Mantua reached its peak of 30,000 inhabitants (it was reduced to 25,000 after the plague of

193 *Aerial view of the Ducal Palace*   **194** *(right) Fresco of the Gonzaga family by Mantegna, Ducal Palace*

195   *Riding school of the Ducal Palace by Giulio Romano*

196   *Garden front of the Palazzo del Tè, Mantua*

197   *The Doric order with the falling triglyph in the courtyard of the Palazzo del Tè*

198 *Portico of Palazzo del Tè*

199, 200 *Detail of complete Ionic column and section of Ionic column, house of the architect G. B. Bertani in Mantua*

1530) and the ensemble of the 'Gonzagas' buildings' acquired the character of a positive town-planning operation. As well as the public buildings Giulio Romano built a certain number of private houses and laid out streets, fortifications and bridges: a complex of works which largely established the face of modern Mantua and consolidated the fame it already enjoyed throughout Europe.

The work of Giulio Romano in Mantua made use, in a city of medium size, of the recent experience of the 'third style'; his immediate model was the work of Raphael in Rome, and was worked out with the same modes of procedure. The artist had the task of co-ordinating artistic activity in the city and he had the official status to do this – a practice which was to become common in the courts of the sixteenth and seventeenth centuries; he intervened in person to execute

201   *Detail of section of Ionic column, house of G. B. Bertani*

or complete works of painting of special importance, but generally made use of assistants, and in architectural planning his personal contribution was undistinguishable from that of anyone else; his position in the productive cycle was that of director – a situation made necessary by the crisis in patronage and pronounced specialization of the individual collaborators.

Giulio Romano's team included a large number of specialists: Rinaldo Mantovano, Benedetto Pagni, G. B. Bertani, G. B. Scultori, Niccolò da Milano, Teodoro Ghisi, Francesco Segala and some more important figures like Francesco Primaticcio, Giovanni da Udine, Polidoro da Caravaggio; in some cases other extremely famous artists were involved, for instance Titian who in 1536 painted the portraits of the emperors for the *gabinetto dei Cesari* of duke Federigo.

If one excludes Rome, the group of artists who came together in Mantua in the first half of the sixteenth century was the most important in Italy, and could be compared to the Urbino group of fifty years earlier. But no Gonzaga was in a position to play the part of Federigo da Montefeltro; so the co-ordination of the various activities passed from the politicians to the artists themselves, and this episode acquired a super-structural character, which was clearly visible on the terrain of town-planning. Giulio Romano's group was capable of decorating the organism of the city, not of transforming it.

The city culture concerned with civic themes, which had produced the new structures of Urbino and Ferrara, had completed its course: the new town-planning problems of the sixteenth century required other operative instruments, as we shall see.

202 The construction of a palazzo. *School of Piero di Cosimo. Ringling museum, Sarasota*

The large centres at the end of the fifteenth century

At the end of the fifteenth century economic growth increased the importance of the great cities, and these became the centres of attraction of the most important experiments; the characteristic situation of the years between 1450 and 1475, when some small centres made cultural contributions as important as those of the large centres, was not tenable in the new conditions of economic and political life.

In Italy the main cities – the capitals of the five states which kept the political balance after the Peace of Lodi – were Rome, Milan, Florence, Venice and Naples. Rome and Milan, where rebuilding began as early as the middle of the fifteenth century, have already been examined; still to be described are the other three, where it was in relation to the new culture that the extremely disparate legacies of the past became comparable for the first time.

Florence

Among the large cities Florence had a special position as the original centre of the new figurative culture, and the home of a series of artistic activities still unequalled in Italy and Europe. The Florentine workshops retained undisputed sway in many traditional processes – carving and inlay in wood, gold and silverware, leatherwork, sculpture in metal, the weaving of precious fabrics in wool and silk – and in some more recent techniques, for instance engraving. The activity of the wood workshops was important for architecture, because they were equipped to produce the models of the buildings.[87] From these workshops came the most important Florentine architects of this time who were active in many parts of Italy: Giuliano da Sangallo (c. 1443–1516), the brothers Giuliano and Benedetto da Maiano (1442–97) and Baccio Pontelli, and in this way Florence partly maintained her old primacy in the field of architecture.

The period which runs from the end of the wars of Cosimo (1454) to the death of Lorenzo the Magnificent (1492) coincided with an increase in the city's economic prosperity. The chronicles of Benedetto Dei, written in 1472, list with pride the churches and palaces where many generations had accumulated a vast patrimony of ornaments and works of art; together with 270 workshops belonging to the wool guild and 83 to

203 *Dante outside Florence, illustration to the Strozzi codex. Laurentian Library, Florence*

the silk guild, there were 96 workshops for the artistic working of wood and 54 for stone.[88]

Building production was intense, but ever less able to renew Florence's town-planning order. Medici conservatism weighed on the physical organization of the city, which was regarded as fixed once and for all: all that remained was the commitment to decorating and celebrating this organism.

The uncertainties of Florentine artistic culture also hindered a coherent solution of the building problems which remained in the second half of the century. Almost all the works of Brunelleschi, left incomplete by the master in 1446, were completed much later with more or less serious alterations, and often amid heated argument. Between 1481 and 1486 the argument already described, about the façade of S. Spirito, took place as

well as the one about the position of the doors. In 1490 there was a competition for the façade of S. Maria del Fiore, but no decision was reached.

It has been noted that neither the Brunelleschian models nor the Albertian ones, though supported by a minority of intellectuals, were accepted as habitual types in current production. As far as the nobleman's palazzo was concerned – this was the most frequent building theme of the period – the traditionalist model elaborated by Michelozzo prevailed, and about the end of the fifteenth century there was a real return to Michelozzo's repertoire (Fig. 205) when the problem of safeguarding the specific character of her tradition arose in Florence, in connection with the spread, now general, of the new architectural methodology.

The most significant building undertak-

204   View of Florence, *copy of the* della catena *view, c. 1490*

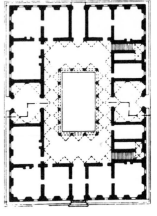

205, 206   *Palazzo Strozzi, Florence*

ings of the Medici are connected with their *ville suburbane*. In 1459 Michelozzo completed the rebuilding of the villa of Careggi, acquired by Cosimo, where the Platonic Academy was established in 1462. In 1479 Lorenzo acquired the property at Poggio a Caiano, and after a sort of competition designated Giuliano da Sangallo as architect of his new abode; the villa is a square block, surrounded by an arcaded base on a con-

tinuous terrace; the nucleus of the building consists of a vast room covered with a semi-circular vault, and the façade is broken by a portico in the ancient style (Fig. 207). The subtle relations between building and garden reflect the new feeling for landscape, of which there is so much evidence in literature and poetry.

But Florentine civilization, at the time of Lorenzo the Magnificent, was characterized by a continuous interaction between the various specializations, and the key of the overall balance belonged to literature rather than to the visual arts. The separation of humanist reflection from civic responsibilities, made inevitable by social and political changes, shifted writers' commitment towards speculation and pure invention; the prestige of the literary group that flourished around Lorenzo did not derive so much from the quality as from the autonomy of the new literature, which became extremely widespread in this form, and which made its mark on even the remotest circles and places.

The theoretical nucleus of this literature was the Neoplatonist movement. Georgius Gemistus Pletho came to Florence for the council of 1430, and was the protagonist in a famous polemic with George of Trebizond about the superiority of Plato over Aristotle, the starting-point taken by Bessarion to develop the thesis of the fundamental agreement of the two ancient thinkers between themselves and with the Christian religion.

Pletho made a great impression on Cosimo de' Medici, who directed the son of his doctor – the young Marsilio Ficino – to study the works of Plato. In 1456, on the advice of Cristoforo Landino, Ficino composed the *Institutiones platonicae*, and successively completed the Latin translations and the commentaries on Greek texts: in 1463 the hermetic books (printed in 1471), in 1470 the complete works of Plato (printed in 1484), in 1484 the complete works of Plotinus (printed in 1492).

From 1462 onwards Cosimo housed at Careggi the Platonic Academy, the meeting-place of Ficino, Poliziano, Diacceto, Landino, Varchi and Pico della Mirandola. In 1482 the *summa* of Ficino's thought, the *Theologia platonica*, appeared, and in 1495 – when he was already considered one of the most illustrious figures of the time – the collection of the *Epistolae*.

As far as art and artists are concerned,

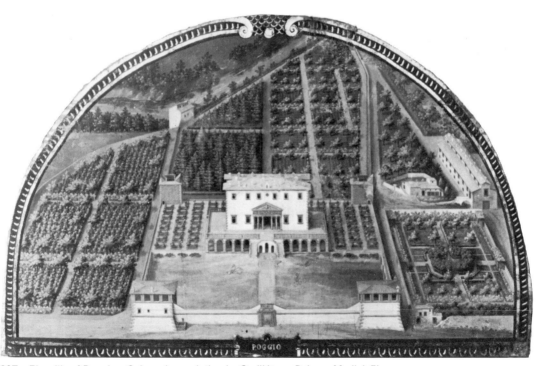

207 *The villa of Poggio a Caiano, in a painting by G. d'Utens. Palazzo Medici, Florence*

research into this field has been diligently carried out by André Chastel,[89] who has described the numerous links between figurative culture and literary culture.

Neoplatonic inspiration produced a continuous change in definitions of the notions of truth, goodness and beauty, feeling and reason, theory and practice; the result of these oscillations was the expansion of the aesthetic sphere, which invaded and affected many other aspects of cultural life.

In the practice of individual arts, and above all that of architecture, Neoplatonism emphasized and supplied a theoretical basis for the existing tendency towards selection from an already known repertoire; it pointed to the ideal type behind every concrete solution, a type of which only a more or less faithful imitation could be provided. At the same time Neoplatonism weakened awareness of the theoretical differences between the various arts, and reference to a higher creative activity, which preceded actual single manifestations, became habitual.

In this way the emancipation of artists from their old condition as artisans was speeded up. Poliziano granted his friendship to Pollaiuolo; Botticelli painted the allegories thought up by the scholars of Careggi; some studios, for instance those of Botticelli and Baccio d'Agnolo, were also literary clubs.

However, after having lost the social integration typical of the old organization, the artists were not in a position to maintain stable links with the Medici court, as many men of letters did. The uncertainty and discomfort of their position now began to emerge: the first signs of psychological strain emerge – Botticelli's negligence, Ghirlandaio's frenetic hard work – and the first figure of the decidedly unbalanced artist appears, that of Piero di Cosimo.

Lorenzo's patronage was completely different in kind from that of the princes of the previous generation. The ambiguity of his political position is not enough to explain the uncertainties of his Florentine enterprises, which reflect the disquiet of his temperament. In recompense he had undisputed authority in the eyes of other Italian and foreign courts in matters of art, and willingly sent Florentine artists abroad to consolidate the prestige of his native city. In the last decade of his life Lorenzo placed Giuliano da Maiano and Luca Fancelli under the patronage of the king of Naples, allowed Leonardo to leave for Milan and Verrocchio for Venice.

In Florence Lorenzo encouraged the extolling of the city's artistic glories. Landino summarized the history of Florentine art in the proem to the 1481 edition of the *Commedia*; in 1488 Filippino Lippi began the monument to his father Filippo in Spoleto cathedral, and in 1490 Benedetto da Maiano designed the monument to Giotto in S. Maria del Fiore; Poliziano composed the epitaphs of the two artists and the famous inscription in the choir of S. Maria Novella, which explicitly celebrates the happiness of the new times.[90] Probably at this time Antonio Manetti was writing the life of Brunelleschi and the story of the *grasso legnaiolo*, to extol not only the work but also the person of the great architect. The Florentine artistic tradition began to be regarded as an accomplished fact and was about to become an academic myth.

Venice

For a long time Venice remained remote from the events of the new artistic culture, and was the only large city where even after the second half of the century a real resistance to the spread of Tuscan models existed, despite the numerous Florentine artists working in Venice – Ghiberti in 1424, Paolo Uccello between 1425 and 1431, Michelozzo between 1433 and 1434, Alberti in 1437, Andrea del Castagno in 1442 – and in Padua – Filippo Lippi in 1434, Donatello from 1443 and Uccello in 1445.

The completion of the Ducal Palace looking on to the piazzetta, begun in 1424,

208   *Ceiling of the chapel of the Cardinal of Portugal in S. Miniato al Monte, Florence*

209   *Sixteenth-century view of Venice and the lagoon*

continued throughout the whole of the fifteenth century, faithfully reproducing the fourteenth-century part of the building overlooking the Molo; this fidelity was maintained in the following century as well when the palace was rebuilt after the fire of 1577 still in conformity with the original style. The other great buildings of the republic and the patrician families demonstrated the continuity of a building tradition which proudly ignored what was happening on the mainland, and admitted only the introduction of single decorative elements in the modern style, for instance the gate of the Arsenal.

At the end of the century, the main innovations concerned painting and the art of printing.

From the time when in 1440 Antonio Vivarini, Giovanni d'Alemagna, Niccolò Pizzolo and Andrea Mantegna worked together on the frescoes of the Eremitani in Padua, there began an intense exchange of experience and influence in an area that covered Venice, Mantua, Ferrara and which, through the Ferrarese, included the contributions of Piero and the international mood of Urbino.

In 1475 Antonello da Messina arrived in Venice. He had assimilated the new technique of Flemish painting in southern Italy, and had been through Rome where he became acquainted with the works of Piero. The meeting between Antonello and Giovanni Bellini is considered crucial for the course of Venetian painting. After the deaths of the masters of the older generation (Squarcione in 1468, Jacopo Bellini in 1470), Giambellino acquired the authority of a leader, and paved the way for the début of Carpaccio about 1488 and Giorgione, Lorenzo Lotto and Titian in the early years of the sixteenth century.

The turning-point in Venetian painting, together with the most vital experiments of other regions and the changes in pictorial technique – the use of canvas and oil paints – lies at the root of all modern painting, from

Et poftala nella fua, ftrengerla fentiua tra calda neue, & in fra coagulo lacteo. Et parue ad me imo cuſi era de attingere & attrectare pur altro che coſa di códitione humana. La onde poſcia che cuſi facto hebbi, ireſtai tuto agitato & concuſſo, & fuſpicoſo, non itédando le coſe inuiſitate ad gli mortali. Ne ancora che dindi ne doueſſe ſequire, cum plebeo habito pannoſo, & cú iſciochi & uulgari coſtumi, difforme allei iſtimantime inepto & diſſimile di tale cóſortio, & illicito eſſere mortali & terrogenio tale delitie fruire. Per laq̃le cagióe arroſſciata la facia, tutto diuerecúda admiratióe reimpleto, al quáto della mia imitate códolédomi, ſectario ſuo me expoſi.

Vltimaméte pur nó cum integro & tutto riuocato animo icominciai de riducere gli pauidi & pturbati ſpiriti, Suadédomi meritaméte beatiſſimo exito eſſere appreſſo tale belliſſimo & diuo obiecto, & in cuſi facto loco. Laſpecto præſtabile della quale ualida uirtute harebbe hauuto di trahere & di tranſmigrare le perdute alme fora delle æterne flamme, & deridure gli corpi icópacti negli monuméti al ſuo cóiuncto, Et bacho harebbe neglecto la iclyta temulétia di Gaurano, Fauſiano, & Falerno, & Puci,

211, 212   *Piazza S. Marco, Venice, as seen by Carpaccio and as it is today*

213 *The* Miracle of the Cross *by Carpaccio, showing the old Rialto bridge. Accademia, Venice*

the sixteenth century onwards. Painting *senza far disegno* (without drawing) shifted the traditional balance between the visual arts and reinforced the aspiration of painting to present itself as a total and simultaneous vision of reality, which the other arts considered only partially.

Meanwhile Venetian painting of the late fifteenth century – particularly in the huge

teleri by Gentile Bellini and Carpaccio (Figs 211, 213, 214) – offers a haunting image of Venice at the height of her prosperity; it reveals the complex society of the lagoon city as a unified whole, and sets down in a lasting form some features of this society which were to remain the same during successive transformations. Here, too, as in Urbino, Ferrara and Mantua, though later and not so directly,

214   Interior of a Venetian church *by Carpaccio. Accademia, Venice*

painting exercised a formative function on the city; not only did it reproduce its landscape, but it selected the features which were to be developed in building activities.

In 1469 Giovanni da Spira founded the first Venetian printing works; in the thirty years that followed almost two hundred printing houses appeared, and Venice became the most important centre of the new book industry. In 1490 Aldus Manutius opened the press near S. Agostino; his shop was also one of the meeting-places of the new Venetian humanistic circle, led by Ermolao Barbaro and Bernardo Bembo. The masterpiece of the art of Renaissance typography, Colonna's *Hypnerotomachia Poliphili*, was published in Venice in 1499 (Fig. 210).

The development of the book industry encouraged cultural exchanges with the whole of Europe, and further influenced the opening of Venetian artistic circles to international culture; here, in 1495 and 1505, Albrecht Dürer encountered the new Italian culture for the first time.

The last decades of the fifteenth century and the first of the sixteenth, in Venice as elsewhere, saw a resumption of building activity, whose protagonists were masters from the mainland: the Lombards, Antonio (d. about 1506), Pietro (c. 1435–1515) and Tullio (d. 1532); Lorenzo Bregno (d. 1523); Mauro Coducci (c. 1440–1504). This activity was intense for almost a century and ultimately produced a profound change in the city organism, which goes largely beyond the chronological limits of this chapter. The continuity of this process is absolutely exceptional in Italy and in Europe, being linked to the social, political and financial stability of the republic. The contribution of

215   *S. Maria dei Miracoli, Venice, by P. Lombardo*

216   *The clock tower, Venice, by M. Coducci*

perspective culture was assimilated gradually and with particular caution; thus in Venice the breaks in dimension so frequent in the other main Italian cities were avoided, and the organization of the city changed gradually without losing its traditional balance.

Le Corbusier wrote:[91]

'I am well aware that after the magnificent functioning machine had been fully established "artists" came to Venice. But everything had already been organized, rooted in the place, made by the collaboration of everyone.'

Naples

Alfonso I of Aragon, who conquered the kingdom of Naples in 1442, belonged with Lionello d'Este and Sigismondo Malatesta to the first generation of humanist princes who backed the undertakings described in this chapter. Naples had suffered a great deal from the war between Anjou and Aragon; the new prince pledged himself earnestly to reconstructing and beautifying the city, possibly upon the advice of Alberti who was also his guest. But the premature ending of his reign in 1458 and the mediocre figure of his successor Ferrante (1458–94) prevented this programme from being implemented. The only feature of Alfonso's plans that was carried out was the reconstruction of Castel Nuovo, with the adjoining gardens (perhaps a restoration of the fourteenth-century gardens of Robert the Wise) and the street of the Incoronata which links it to the traditional centre. The castle was designed in Catalan Gothic forms, while the triumphal arch fitted in between the two entrance towers gave it an air of outer modernity; artists from all parts of Italy came to work on this alone: Francesco Laurana, Pietro di Martino, Domenico Gaggini, Isaia da Pisa, Paolo Romano and Andrea dell'Aquila (Fig. 217).

During the last twenty years of the century the activities of Ferrante's brilliant son,

217 *The arch of Alfonso of Aragon at Castel Nuovo, Naples*

LA CITTA DE NAPOLI GENTILE.

MARE MEDITERRANEO

218   *Plan of Naples in 1585*

Alfonso duke of Calabria (later Alfonso II from 1494 to 1495), were of considerable importance; he held his personal court at Castel Capuano. From 1478 to 1479 he led the war in Tuscany against Florence on behalf of Sixtus IV, and soon afterwards Lorenzo the Magnificent visited Naples; in 1465 he married Ippolita Sforza, daughter of Francesco; in this way the court of Naples remained linked to Florence and Milan, and some of the most celebrated Tuscan and northern artists were summoned here by Alfonso: Giuliano da Maiano in 1485, Giuliano da Sangallo in 1488, Fra Giocondo in 1489, Francesco di Giorgio in 1491 and Guido Mazzoni in 1492.

In 1485 Giuliano da Maiano designed the new walls to extend the city eastwards, in 1487 the *ville suburbane* of Poggioreale and la Duchesca, and about 1490 the della Bolla

aqueduct. Giuliano da Sangallo arrived with the plan for a gigantic palace to be built on the open space near Castel Nuovo, where the *tribunali* or public offices were all to be sited. In 1494 Francesco di Giorgio designed the new western walls, completed in 1501, and in 1495 began work on the reconstruction of Castel Nuovo and Castel S. Elmo, in accordance with the new techniques for fortification against artillery that he himself had worked upon theoretically.

The memories of classical antiquity, which for Naples were linked with the relics and literary fame of the city and its surroundings, haunted these last undertakings of the Aragonese dynasty. The theoretical mind which inspired the works of Alfonso II was that of Pontano, who had arrived in Naples at the court of Alfonso I in 1448 and who died in Naples in 1503, when Ferdinand the

Catholic took over the kingdom of Aragon. In his poem *Lepidina* (1496) the account of the mythical origin of the city was used allegorically to celebrate the works built by Alfonso II, the villa of Poggioreale and the Acqua della Bolla. As in antiquity, villas were once again built around Naples: apart from the two Aragonese ones, there was Pontano's at Antignano and Sannazzaro's fabled one at Mergellina.

Pietro Summonte, in a letter to Marcantonio Michiel of 1524, has left a description of the city plan which Alfonso II hoped to implement:

'In our times our king and ruler Alfonso II of blessed memory was so devoted to building and so desirous of performing great deeds that, if ill fortune had not so soon removed him from his court, he would certainly have embellished this city supremely. Erat illi in animo fluvium e longinquo per magnos aquaeductos in urbem ducere; and, when the great walls of the city were completed (as they very largely were) he intended to extend all the main thoroughfares of the city in straight lines, from wall to wall, after having removed porticoes, corners, irregular humps, and thus to extend across the breadth, also in straight lines, all lanes from one end of the city to the other, so that, not only because of the straightness of the streets and lanes, but also because of the natural slope of the site from north to south, and quite apart from the beauty of such regularity, this city would have been the cleanest and neatest of all Europe, and at every slightest rainfall would have been made brighter than a piaster of burnished silver.'

This programme is comparable to the Herculean addition in Ferrara, planned at the same period of time. Here, however, the grid system of straight roads was the continuation of the old one, Greek or Roman, still perceptible in the historic centre of Naples, and

the plan of the new city coincided with that of the old one as it is described in Vitruvius' treatise (Hamberg has pointed out that, of all the old layouts preserved in Italy or elsewhere, the layout of Naples is the only one perfectly answering Vitruvius' description, except for its orientation; and he has attempted to relate the Aragonese plan to two plans by Fra Giocondo in the Uffizi, where Naples' well-known urban shape, with the three main roads and numerous cross streets – the 'thoroughfares' and 'lanes' of Summonte's letter – was superimposed upon Vitruvius' compass-card.)[92]

If Alfonso II had not been deposed by Charles VIII in 1495, perhaps the proud attempt to establish a great modern city on the very site of an ancient one, of joining architecture and archaeology, would have been realized in Naples before it was in Rome.

The Aragonese humanistic plan was to be partially realized by the Spanish viceroys in the sixteenth century, but in quite another spirit. One residue of the original design was possibly the continuation of the lowest main road over the hill of S. Martino, explicable only in terms of a desire to maintain a straight geometrical line, as De Seta observes.[93]

At the beginning of the sixteenth century the common feature of the situation in Italian cities – with the possible exception of Venice – was the disproportion between programme and implementation. In fact economic resources were distributed so as not to favour investments in real estate; these could not come together to form important changes in city organisms, because of the lack of continuity in political leadership and the persistence of the town-planning structures realized in the recent past.

Artistic culture was encouraged by the same causes to detach itself from the problems of civic organization, because the involvement of artists in a particular place became equally uncertain, and because research

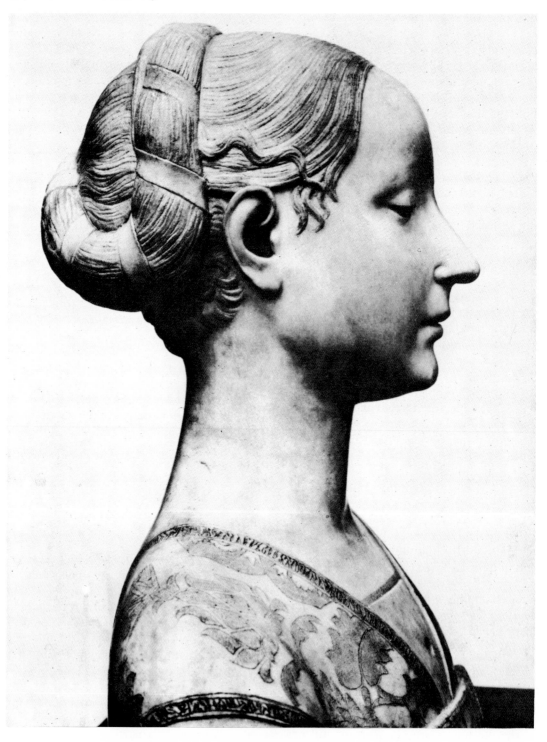

219   *Bust of Ippolita Sforza by Francesco Laurana, 1488–9*

assumed a tendency towards the universal which brought about a lack of the interest in detail inseparable from any town-planning undertaking and which if anything favoured the movement towards a retrospective celebration of city traditions already established.

We have already observed that an attempt was under way to select modes of planning which had already been experimented with; Neoplatonist philosophy supplied this tendency with a theoretical basis, and the selection, as might have been supposed, favoured organisms least adaptable to the limitations of the urban scene.

One of these organisms was the centrally planned temple, occasionally experimented with by Brunelleschi (in the Rotonda degli Angeli, Fig. 220) and by Alberti (in S. Sebastiano in Mantua) but studied and proposed insistently during the latter part of the fifteenth century. The identical perspective views implicit in this model are normally unrealizable in an already built-up setting; hence the tendency to go out into the open country, where the temple could figure as the nucleus of an ideal city, incompatible with the existing city and similar to that represented by painters (Figs 221–8). From about the 1490s onwards there is a long series of examples: S. Maria delle Carceri in Prato (1485), S. Maria della Croce in Crema (1493), S. Maria della Consolazione in Todi (1508), S. Biagio in Montepulciano (1518), the Madonna di Campagna in Piacenza (1522), then the works of Bramante and the many buildings deriving from them.

Another organism of this kind was the isolated villa with a rigorous bilateral symmetry – Poggio a Caiano in 1480, the papal villa of Belvedere in 1489, later the Farnesina of 1505 – or with a central symmetry, like the villa of Poggioreale in Naples of 1487. The taste for a view of the countryside seen from afar – as in Pienza and Urbino – was followed by the attempt to place a single building in the countryside; the stretch of land near the building began to be organized in relation to

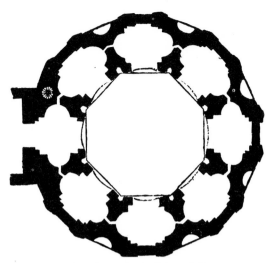

220   *Plan of the Rotonda degli Angeli, Florence*

the architecture and to its axes; this was the dawn of the 'Italian garden', which became one of the most important motifs during the following century.

The 'nomadism' of the Italian artists of this time is simply the inevitable consequence of the research in which they were engaged, and of their detachment from the problems of the specific environment in which they worked. At the end of the fifteenth century artistic culture had already almost entirely completed the course that Garin considered typical of all humanistic culture: 'It had all begun with a vigorous political and moral commitment, and it ended with detached contemplation and devotion to the organic growth of autonomous theory.'[94]

This situation produced a multiplicity of contacts, which complicated the development of experiments and makes any historical reasoning based on the internal criticism of the results difficult. Chance, as Chastel notes,[95] intervened continually to interrupt probable connections and to establish improbable ones. During their wanderings, artists carried around with them a cultural explosive charge which was capable of producing important changes everywhere. Their

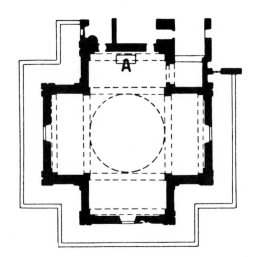

221–223   *S. Maria delle Carceri, Prato*

224, 225 *Details of the* Nativity *by Francesco di Giorgio. S. Domenico, Siena*

226 *Aerial view of S. Biagio, Montepulciano*

field of activity was now not only Italy but the whole of Europe. Aristotele Fioravanti was called to England in 1467 and to Russia in 1475; in 1492 Lorenzo the Magnificent introduced Andrea Sansovino to the king of Portugal; in 1496 Cardinal della Rovere sent Giuliano da Sangallo to the king of France at Lyon.

But at this point an exposition of artistic developments in Italy according to places becomes artificial, and we must give an uninterrupted account of the great cultural adventure of the early years of the sixteenth century which from Vasari onwards has been recognized as the most outstanding event of the Renaissance cycle.

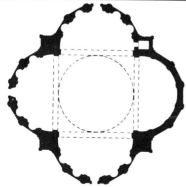

227, 228 *View and plan of the church of the
Consolazione, Todi*

229   *Profile study by Leonardo da Vinci. Uffizi, Florence*

three

Beginning and end of the 'third style'

In the preface to the third part of the *Lives* Giorgio Vasari attempts to arrange historically the experiments carried out by the great masters of the past generation, at the moment when they could be grasped as a concluded cycle, and while his generation was taking stock of the radical changes brought about by this vital episode.

Giotto and the artists of the first phase had 'discovered the principles' of modern art; the artists of the second period, from Jacopo della Quercia to Luca Signorelli,[1]

'made substantial additions to the arts of . . . architecture, painting and sculpture, improving on those of the first part in rule, order, proportion, design and style. If they were not altogether perfect, they came so near the truth, that the third category, of whom we are now to speak, profited by the light they shed, and attained the summit of perfection.'

The five fields of progress, achieved by the artists of the second period, are described as follows:[2]

'Rule in architecture is the measurement of antiques, following the plans of ancient buildings in making modern ones. Order is the differentiation of one kind from another so that every body shall have its characteristic parts, and that the Doric, Ionic, Corinthian and Tuscan shall no longer be mingled indiscriminately. Proportion in sculpture, as in architecture, is the making of the bodies upright, the members being properly arranged, and the same in drawing. Design is the imitation of the most beautiful things of nature in all figures whether painted or chiselled, and this requires a hand and genius to transfer everything which the eye sees, exactly and correctly whether it be in drawings, on paper panel, or other surfaces both in relief and in sculpture. Style is improved by frequently copying the most beautiful things, and by combining the finest members, whether hands, heads, bodies and legs, to produce a perfect figure, which, being introduced in every work and every figure, form what is known as a fine style. . . .

But although the artists of the second period made great additions to the arts in all these particulars, yet they did not attain to the final stages of perfection, for they lacked a freedom which, while outside the rules, was guided by them, and which was not incompatible with order and correctness. This demanded a prolific invention and the beauty of the smallest details. In proportion they lacked good judgment which, without measuring the figures, invests them with a grace beyond measure in the dimensions chosen. They did not attain to the zenith of design, because, although they made their arms round and their legs straight, they were not skilled in the muscles, and lacked that grateful and sweet ease which is partly seen and partly felt in matters of flesh and living things, but they were crude and stunted, their eyes being difficult and their style hard. Moreover, they did not possess that lightness of touch in making all their figures slender and graceful. . . . Their draperies lacked beauty, their fancies variety, their colouring charm, their building diversity and their landscapes distance and variety.'

Some, for instance Verrocchio and Pollaiuolo, approached this perfection, but the imperfection of their work was made obvious by comparison with the ancient statues 'dug out of the ground'; these 'in their softness and in their hardness' were taken from 'the best living examples, with actions which do not distort them, but give them motion and display the utmost grace. This removed a certain dryness and crudeness caused by overmuch study . . .',[3] typical of the painters from Piero della Francesca to Luca Signorelli. Their works in fact lacked 'vigour . . . and they lacked a soft blending of colour, first observable in the Bolognese Francia and Pietro Perugino. The people, when they beheld the new and living beauty, ran madly to see it, thinking that it would never be possible to improve upon it.'[4]

'But the works of Leonardo da Vinci clearly proved how much they erred, for he began the *third style*, which I call the modern, notable for boldness of design, the subtlest imitation of nature in trifling details, good rule, better order, correct proportion, perfect design and divine grace, prolific and diving to the depths of art, endowing his figures with motion and breath. Somewhat later followed Giorgio da Castel Franco, who gave tone to his pictures and endowed his things with tremendous life by means of the well-managed depths of the shadows. No less skilful in imparting to his works force, relief, sweetness and grace was Bartolommeo of S. Marco; but the most graceful of all was Raphael of Urbino, who, studying the labours of both the ancient and the modern masters, selected the best from each, and out of his garner enriched the art of painting with that absolute perfection which the figures of Apelles and Zeuxis anciently possessed and even more, if I may say so. Nature herself was vanquished by his colours, and his invention was facile and appropriate, as anyone may judge who has seen his works, which are like writings, showing us the sites and the buildings, and the ways and habits of native and foreign peoples just as he desired.'

Vasari then names Andrea del Sarto, Correggio, Giulio Romano and others of the younger generation.[5]

'But the man who bears the palm of all ages, transcending and eclipsing all the rest, is the divine Michelangelo Buonarroti, who is supreme not in one art only but in all three at once. He surpasses not only all those who have, as it were, surpassed Nature, but the most famous ancients also, who undoubtedly surpassed her. He has proceeded from conquest to conquest, never finding a difficulty which he cannot easily overcome by the force of his divine genius, by his industry, design, art, judgment, and grace.'

This famous passage strikes us still because of Vasari's effort to express a reality intensely experienced by him, but eluding his definition. The five aspects of progress, in the passage from the first to the second age, are clear and precise; of these two, 'rule' and 'order' concern architecture, and are the recapitulation of the progress introduced by Brunelleschi, of whom he talks more fully in the introduction to the second part and in the life of the master. But the comparison between the second and third age all takes place on the terrain of the figurative arts, and the aspects of progress become more difficult to explain. The success of the masters of the second age according to each of the criteria of judgment – rule, order, proportion, design and style – is not complete because it is attained through 'study' and 'diligence'. For this reason their manner is somewhat 'crude' and lacks a final element, which the author attempts to define in many ways: 'freedom . . . guided by rules', 'order with more ornament', 'beauty of the smallest details', 'lightness', 'polish' and 'grace', 'resolute boldness', 'graceful and sweet ease'; 'that finish and assurance which they lacked they could not readily attain by study, which has a tendency to render the style dry'.[6]

Twice a curious literary comparison occurs, in connection with Raphael, whose 'stories' (works) are like 'writings', and about Polidoro and Maturino: people will wonder 'how they have been able to produce these stupendous works, not by speech, which is easy, but with the brush . . .'.[7] This is praise that runs counter to the assessment of Ghiberti – who a hundred years earlier considered sculpture and painting as 'brief and open' as opposed to rhetoric, and criticized 'those who . . . are conquered by letters alone', because they have the 'shadow, but not the substance'[8] – and to the apologia for painting written by Leonardo fifty years before.[9]

Here there recur all the themes of the Neoplatonist culture that spread during the first half of the sixteenth century: art as an instrument to penetrate into the reality of things, which must therefore grasp not only forms but also essential movement; the conviction that an ultimate perfection must exist for every activity, and a culminating point where the subject of the activity becomes one with its object; the search for an inmost value

which is to be found in the typical, not in the individual; the preference for evoking this essential reality with the word, and the tendency to relate all forms of representation to the condition of the word.

These formulae received from the Ficinian tradition were utilized to describe not a theoretical ideal or hypothetical sight, but an actual experience, which had set the feelings of a generation into motion and which was now fading into the past; therefore it could be described and discussed like every other human experience.

Architecture was involved in this development in that the traditional parallelism of the three major arts, painting, sculpture and architecture, still obtained. From our point of view, it was involved only partially, i.e. in the aspects that belonged to the traditional schema. The new development took place in the sphere of high culture, and directly modified only production of a monumental nature. But it did alter the balance between monumental production and standard production, and changed the way of considering the whole group of the arts. An account must therefore be given of it for its own sake, along with an attempt at isolating the specific role of architecture within the course of artistic development as a whole.

Leonardo da Vinci was enrolled in the guild of painters in 1472, the year Laurana moved away from Urbino leaving the palace incomplete, and began his independent activity about 1475, the year of Antonello's journey to Venice; Michelangelo died in 1564, when Palladio had already designed and realized most of his works. Therefore the work of the great masters whom Vasari regards as instigators of the 'third style', occupies almost a century of history; none the less we cannot take this series of experiments to fix a historical period, nor can they be compared to previous and subsequent periods as an intermediate episode. The 'second style', i.e. the culture of the second half of the fifteenth century (whose coherence

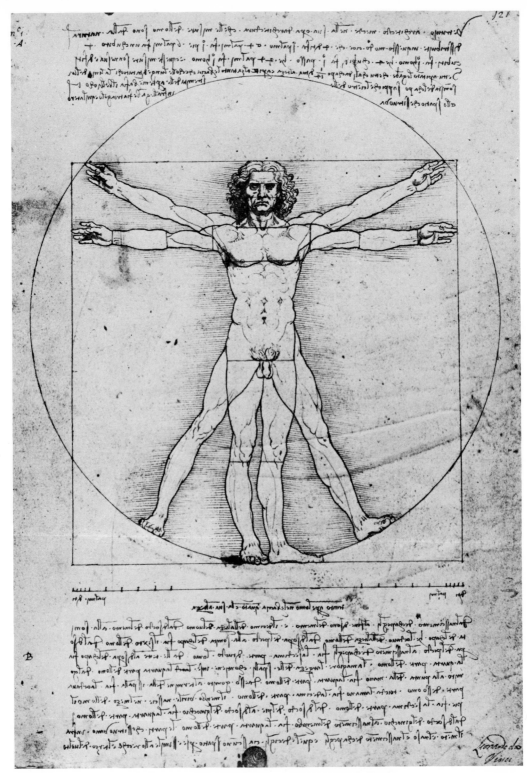

230 *Study of the proportions of the human body by Leonardo. Accademia, Venice*

is recognized by modern criticism on a basis of criteria different from those of Vasari) extended into the sixteenth century, and was fused with the culture known as Mannerist; Giuliano da Sangallo died in 1516, two years after Bramante, and Signorelli, who was almost the same age as Leonardo, died four years after him, in 1523, when Giulio Romano and Jacopo Sansovino had already begun their careers. Every attempt to localize the borderline between the two cultures at one precise moment, and therefore to attribute a chronological foundation to the ideal classicism of the masters, however brief or momentary, seems doomed to failure.

Yet a watershed does exist between the two cultures, dependent in fact on their different relationship with the work of the masters; at first the 'perfect style' was a future ideal, then it became a past ideal. The Neoplatonist culture of the late fifteenth century tended to judge every real experience with the measure of absolute perfection, which it was possible to approach to a degree still unknown. For the following generation this ideal touchstone took on the physiognomy of a human experience; the opportunity of approaching absolute perfection had occurred and had borne its fruits, which were already vanishing into the past.

Hence the differences in tone which mark this transition much more than any specific innovation: one need only compare the uncertainties and reserve of artists like Botticelli and Giuliano da Sangallo, in the last years of their careers, with the certainty of the young men born at the turn of the century, like Pierino del Vaga, who returned to Florence in 1523, after his apprenticeship with Raphael, felt himself in possession of the *bella maniera* and capable of rising above the achievements of Masaccio.

Therefore the story of the masters can be described as a series of human experiments closely connected with the important events of those years but independent of and parallel to many different experiments, only

partly linked by relations of approval and opposition.

In 1475, the year Michelangelo was born, Leonardo da Vinci (1452–1519) was twenty-three, and about to leave the studio of Andrea del Verrocchio, after having received a strict education there and from the Pollaiuolo brothers. For another six years Leonardo was working in Florence, under the rule of Lorenzo the Magnificent, and executed a first series of paintings (the two *Annunciations*, the *Madonna del Garofano*, the Dreyfus *Madonna*, the *Portrait of Ginevra de' Benci*, as well as the unfinished *St Jerome* and the *Adoration of the Magi*) where the instruments of Florentine figurative culture were synthesized and examined in depth, specifically to test their limits; in the *Portrait of Ginevra de' Benci*, the masterpiece of this first phase, the extreme precision of the drawing produced a subtle interchange between the figurative values – graphic, chromatic, chiaroscuro – the expressive values and symbolic superstructures, which made the image somehow unstable though clearly defined at every level, anticipating a new cycle of experiments.

In 1481 Leonardo was called to the court of the Sforza family, and moved to Milan where he stayed for twenty years. In the famous letter to the duke he enumerated his abilities in ten points; the first nine concerned civil and military engineering, the last his artistic skills – architecture, painting and sculpture – which were considered the synthesis of all the other skills.[10]

In Milan the main commission was the equestrian statue of Francesco Sforza; Leonardo approached the problem in a very absolute way, studying the anatomy of the horse, the systems of casting, analysing the possible variants of the respective positions of horse and rider, and finally completed the model in clay which was exhibited in 1493.

At the court of the Sforza family he found a complex and stimulating cultural environment where, at the end of the century, some of the greatest Italian specialists were to be found: Bramante from about 1480, Francesco di Giorgio from 1487, Luca Pacioli from 1496, all from the court of the Montefeltro family at Urbino; Giuliano da Sangallo in 1492, sent by Lorenzo the Magnificent; the musician Franchino Gaffurio, who had worked in Naples with Tinctoris and Spataro, lived in Milan from 1484 to 1522 and composed his theoretical works there;[11] and Italian and German specialists were employed on the completion of the cathedral.

With them Leonardo built up a series of relationships that have not yet been fully documented: he designed the illustrations for the treatise *De divina proportione* published by Pacioli in Venice in 1508; he certainly had frequent dealings with Gaffurio (who may be the musician depicted in the portrait in the Ambrosiana); with Francesco di Giorgio and Bramante, he acted as adviser on the main Sforza buildings – the cathedrals of Milan and Pavia – and dealt in his own way (in the form of theoretical meditations) with the architectural problems that Bramante tackled empirically: the survey of domed buildings and the renewal of the buildings of Milan. But these architectural and mathematical studies are only a part of a wide-ranging programme of exploration of the forms and structures of the visible world, which extended from geometrical figures to natural objects: vapours, waters, minerals, then plants, animals, man and his inventions. The synthesis of all these pieces of research took place in painting, the only activity to which Leonardo devoted himself with constant interest and which he did not tire of praising as the beginning and end of all the sciences:[12]

'But the divine science of painting considers the works, human as well as divine, which are encompassed by surfaces, that is, the lines that are the outlines of bodies, and with these she commands the sculptor to achieve the perfection of his statues. By means of her basic principle, that is, drawing, she teaches the architect to make

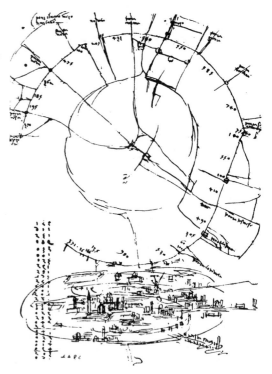

231   *Plan and view of Milan by Leonardo (from the Atlantic codex)*
232, 233   *Topographical drawing of the valley of the Arno northwards from Florence and a drawing of mountains by Leonardo. Royal Library, Windsor*

his edifice so that it will be agreeable to the eye, and teaches the composers of variously shaped vases as well as goldsmiths, weavers and embroiderers. She has discovered the characters by which different languages are expressed, has given numerals to the arithmetician, has taught us how to represent the figures of geometry, she teaches masters of perspective, astronomy, machinists and engineers.'

Leonardo's early departure from the Florentine circle and his continual polemic against 'letters' have fed the image of the solitary genius, cut off from the culture of his time and hostile to the invading Ficinian idealism. This antithesis between Leonardo and the Neoplatonist circle would be less persuasive if, together with documentation on the culture of the literary circles, we also

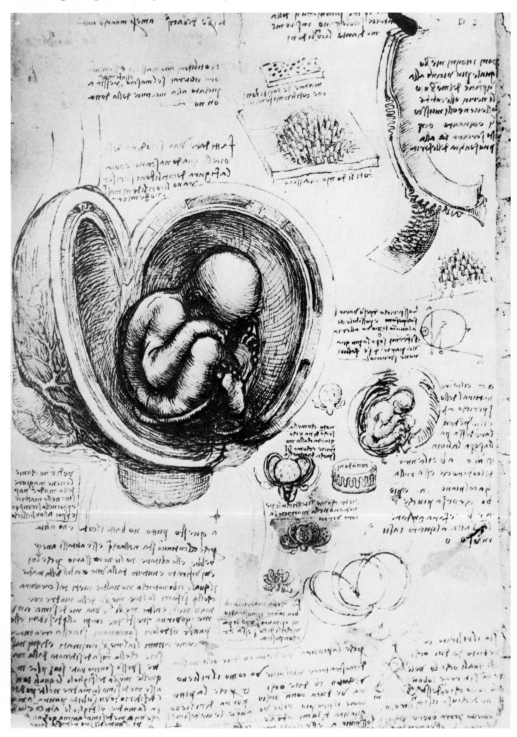

234   *A drawing from Leonardo's anatomy notebooks*

possessed equally broad documentation on the culture of the studios and professional circles where Leonardo had his youthful apprenticeship.[13]

Like Ficino, Leonardo saw the series of natural objects, of living beings, of man and his products as a continuous whole, animated throughout by vital movements and at the same time able to be analysed with the exactitude typical of mathematical processes. His choice of the means for research – drawing rather than words – was different and this choice gave rise to a completely alternative system, because the research, in both cases, began and ended in the total representation of the universe within the semantic system adopted.

In this way the common recourse to mathematics becomes clear: neither Leonardo nor the Neoplatonists used mathematics in the modern scientific sense, i.e. as an instrument to proceed from experiment to the underlying conceptual structures; Ficino used it as a logical model, Leonardo as a formal model to describe or represent the results of an experiment already given in discursive or figurative form. 'By mathematics he understands all order and law accessible to the eye'[14] says Jaspers, and 'for him, to know is to reproduce.'[15] Hence his lack of interest in overspecialized developments, not susceptible of synthesis with the necessary immediacy, and hence a somewhat hasty assessment of the mathematical methodologies already utilized in the field of art; in his *Treatise on Painting* Leonardo worked out his view on perspective, but his treatment was less advanced than that of Piero, as Wittkower has shown.[16]

Leonardo's research included both art and science or, rather, it left out of consideration the later distinction between the two. In his work the idea of a new knowledge of the world obtained through visual verification, guided by the mind and made effective by the work of the hand, became a systematic programme.

To each of the fields with which he was concerned – and of which we are accustomed to thinking as distinct, because in later scientific culture they developed as independent specialities – Leonardo brought a new spirit of observation, and obtained results almost always more precise than the traditional ones. He is regarded as the initiator of the objective and systematic description of natural forms; not, therefore, of mineralogy, geology, botany, zoology and modern medicine, which suppose a structural interest alien to his culture, but of that descriptive component which, incorporated into future development, was to become scientific illustration.

His contribution was particularly decisive in anatomy. Leonardo eliminated all improper transpositions of concepts and literary preconceptions; for instance, he cast aside the traditional representation of the *homunculus* represented as an adult even before birth, and he drew the foetus in the opened uterus with absolute precision (Fig. 234). But his interest began and ended with the ascertaining of the actual form; he drew the heart, with its divisions and valves, and did not suspect the circulation of the blood, which justifies that structure. His specific interest was deflected as the visual terrain was freed from speculation and became more general; from studies of anatomy he continually returned to the thought of the living man ('O speculator concerning this machine of ours, let it not distress you that you impart knowledge of it through another's death, but rejoice that our Creator has ordained the intelligence of such excellence of perfection . . . and thou, man, who by these my labours dost look upon the marvellous works of nature, . . . reflect that it is an infinitely atrocious act to take away the life of man'[17]). Thus Leonardo's anatomy led him not into physiology but into the survey of the positions of the limbs and the study of mimic expressions and found its resolution in painting, where the play of all bodily movements could be synthesized in the subtle

235   *Project by Leonardo for bombardment over a wide area, with a series of cannons sunk in the ground. Royal Library, Windsor*

expression of a face and the point of connection with the world of thought was to be found. This complete humanization of anatomical research, achieved by starting from objective observation, was Leonardo's original contribution, which made its mark on contemporaries and had incalculable consequences, as Chastel has shown; in the following generation, his studies gave rise both to Vesalius' books of anatomical plates of 1538 and 1543, and to the sculptures of Justus (1531) and Bontemps (1548) for the tombs of the kings of France at St-Denis, with the dramatic confrontation of the naked corpses and the effigies of the living sovereigns in ceremonial attire.

Leonardo devoted a great deal of his time to mechanics, and in the letter already mentioned he gives the duke of Milan a complete list of the types of machine he was able to construct, though without ever quoting any work he had actually realized. His notebooks contain an exhaustive review of the machinery known in his time, or realizable on the basis of the mechanical equipment available; real inventions were few – the flying machine, the machine for polishing mirrors, some weaving machines – and they belonged to the sphere of mechanical application, not to that of principle; he did not attempt a systematic ordering of his theoretical reflections in this field or in any other, and accepted that, at the court of the Sforza family, his talent should be used almost exclusively in the production of the ducal festivities and spectacles. From the viewpoint of modern technical research he lacked interest in sustained enquiry, the capacity for abstraction and connection

·137·

236 *Storm in the mountains by Leonardo. Royal Library, Windsor*

between experiment and evaluation; it was easy, at first, to overvalue his abilities – considering the breadth of his fields of study – and then to repudiate them almost entirely, noting the conventional character of his technical repertoire and also the inexactitude of his graphic representations, compared with those of other specialists of the time, for instance Francesco di Giorgio. But Leonardo's research did not aim at this kind of result. For him machines were not a world of independent objects, with laws of development to be studied, but artificial extensions of man's capacities for movement and work, similar to the limbs of the body and reducible to the same vital principles, as the limbs, in their turn, are reducible to mechanisms which are moved directly by the 'soul'.

The real objective of the research lay in comparing and giving a single interpretation of the biological universe and the mechanical universe; the range of mechanical objects measures the gap between the 'works of nature' and the 'infinite number of things which nature never created',[18] hence the field of action of the eye, which Leonardo considers the universal instrument for this sort of investigation:[19]

'It is the master of astronomy, it makes cosmography; it advises and corrects all human arts, it carries men to different parts of the world, it is the prince of mathematics, its sciences are most certain, it has measured the heights and the dimensions of the stars, it has found the elements and their locations. It has predicted future events through the course of the stars, it has created architecture, and perspective, and divine painting.'

Here, too, the qualitative leap of Leonardo's research – fruitless in technology, but rich in consequences in the general balance of culture – lay in the common link it offered to various categories of research, and made itself felt in painting, the culmination of the list just quoted, where the mysterious union of the natural and human universe could be represented and made real.

The same argument applies equally for other fields: into each of them Leonardo introduced the modern prerequisite of precision, verifiability, evidence, universality and progress; but precision, verifiability and evidence began and ended in the visual level, while universality and progress remained a programme of individual, and not collective, research. He was already a scientist but he would not limit himself to a single field; his research did not branch out through the channels of specialization, but continually returned through these channels towards a centre, and found its conclusion in unparalleled mastery in painting.

The leap realized by Leonardo in painting was one of the decisive events in the history of Renaissance culture, and its effects were felt for many years, from Vasari to the nineteenth century.[20] In Milan, too, he painted little, and scarcely ever as a result of accepting a commission: he painted the *Virgin of the Rocks* about 1485, two or three portraits of uncertain attribution, and between 1495 and 1498 the *Last Supper* in S. Maria delle Grazie. When they appeared, the paintings of 1485, now in the Louvre, and the fresco of 1495 produced a sensation which we today can reconstruct only indirectly, by considering the privileged position of painting in the cultural system of the late fifteenth century, and the complexity of interests concentrated in this field.

The *Virgin of the Rocks* (Fig. 237) is characterized by the sensational landscape which gives the painting its name, and celebrates the meeting between the story of man – or rather the story of Christ, where the human lot crosses with the divine plan of the Redemption – and the motionless natural setting, witness of remotest prehistoric changes.

The story of the Redemption is in the realm of future prophecy because the two protagonists, Jesus and St John, are still

237 *The* Virgin of the Rocks *by Leonardo. Louvre, Paris*

children and it is symbolized by the extremely subtle interplay of the four figures: the children, participants but unaware, the angel, aware but not participant, and the Virgin, both participant and aware; her ambivalent expression of acceptance and refusal synthesizes the attitudes of the other figures, and carries the episode into an inward sphere. The natural story, on the other hand, is set in an immemorial past, as can be seen from the strangeness of the rocky landscape, covered with a fleeting vegetation of grass and small bushes.

The technical apparatus used to conjure up this vision is extremely complex: the leaves and part of the drapery are graphically outlined with incredible minuteness, while in the figures and distant objects the graphic contours are progressively veiled by repeated and almost imperceptible expanses of uniform colour: the effect – the so-called *sfumato* – makes the density of the air in which the figures are placed visible and almost measurable, and communicates to their outlines a margin of vibration that the painter can also adjust psychologically, revealing the degrees of potential movement. The image thus acquires an astonishing degree of finish, which removes every trace of the process of execution and brings to visual perception a series of vital faculties hitherto inaccessible to pictorial language: hence Vasari's discussion of Leonardo, who 'really gave his figures movement and breath'. The contrasting stylistic tendencies of the masters of the late fifteenth century (Perugino and Signorelli, Desiderio da Settignano and the Pollaiuolo brothers) were suddenly synthesized and left behind.

Leonardo retained the graphic and atonal approach of the Florentine tradition; from this point of view his manner carried to its limit a pictorial tendency already developed, in part, by the painters of the previous generation, and critically threatened, a few years afterwards, by the tonal tendency of the new Venetian painting. Technically, how-

ever, the influence of his style was necessarily limited. But Leonardo's line of argument reversed the exclusive tendencies of the contemporary schools, reaffirmed the cultural seriousness and responsibility of the pictorial experience and afforded glimpses of a full, integrated style, capable of harmonizing many components; in this sense his line of argument had a decisive influence and established the basic premise for the other painters of the 'third style', and especially Raphael.

The complexity of the intellectual references, far from disturbing the clarity of the visual representation, actually increases it and they form the substance of the pictorial construction: painting deals with 'the motion of bodies and the rapidity of their actions'[21] and 'the mind working through bodily motion';[22] in this way painting can make the perception of movements and their intellectual meanings simultaneous, revealing their harmony, in so far as 'harmony is not engendered except in the moments when the proportion of things is seen and heard'.[23]

In the *Last Supper* in S. Maria delle Grazie (Fig. 239) the simultaneous representation of a multiplicity of movements and meanings is developed to an absolute maximum. The traditional iconography of the Last Supper, laid down by the painters of the fourteenth and fifteenth centuries, is maintained in the frontal presentation of the picture with the guests lined along one side only and in the rigid perspective relationship between table and setting accentuated, in this case, by the skilful complementary relationship between the illusory space of the painting and the real one of the refectory in which it is set (Fig. 238). But this iconography is shaken by a dense pattern of actions and reactions, animating the characters and distinguishing them, based on the passage in the Gospel according to St Matthew, where Christ announces the betrayal by one of the apostles.

The scale of the figures and that of the

238 *The refectory of the convent of S. Maria delle Grazie, Milan*

239 *The* Last Supper *by Leonardo. Convent of S. Maria delle Grazie, Milan*

architectural background are intentionally unrelated – as Heydenreich notes,[24] here we have the first use of the superdimension of the figures which was to become one of the characteristic instruments of the 'third style' – to give maximum prominence to the interplay of human expressions. The figure of Christ, almost frontal and set on the axis of the composition, is the motive centre of the movements and emotions of the other figures, as in Michelangelo's *Last Judgment*; but here the motion proceeds from the stillness, and there is only the faintest initial suggestion of motion in the central figure, while the psychological concentration is at its height here. From this centre the mimic action spreads in waves, emphasized by the light and dark expanses of the architectural background, which widens out towards the sides because of the perspective foreshortening.

As is known, Leonardo covered the wall with a special preparation so as to be able to apply oil colours; the traditional technique of the fresco must have struck him as unsuited to the subtlety of the effects he wanted. This preparation proved unstable, and the painting was already described as decaying about twenty years after it was painted. Thus the actual fascination of the work ('held in the greatest veneration by the Milanese'[25]) was increased soon afterwards by the legendary fascination of the masterpiece too perfect to last, confirming the already widespread myth of Leonardo as a hermetic and mysterious genius.

Behind this myth lies Leonardo's exceptional human condition which was directly linked to the nature of his artistic commitment.

Leonardo's social behaviour was similar to that of the technocrats who had already been moving through the princely courts for some time, and who competed with one another in publicizing their skills while concealing their stock of knowledge and methods; Leonardo utilized this same practice to safeguard the coherence of his 'patient research' in an ever more unstable and agitated world, and earned prestige hitherto unknown by means of the extremely high quality of his paintings where the complexity of his endeavours emerged in a unified way. He was the first artist who, living in contact with the ruling class, managed to introduce equality into his relationship with them and to achieve an economic position that befitted this equality; in Milan he lived in a house furnished like that of the lords of the time, with horses, carriages and servants.

The price of such an intellectual commitment, in everyday life, was not eccentricity or a tendency towards the mysterious, but rather continuous concentration and severe control of his own desires and of external pressures.

Leonardo's behaviour might seem 'capricious and fickle'[26] according to the criteria of a society already moving in the direction of specialization and inclined to grant the artist an increasingly limited role. What we know from the documents concerning the private life of Leonardo by no means confirms the mythical image of the solitary magus; we see a simple, dignified man, sociable though aloof from the quarrels and passions of his time; there is never a word or deed to indicate any indulgence in his personal feelings, but on the contrary an unbounded sympathy for others, which extends even to animals, indeed to every form of life, even down to the potential life of the embryo in the egg ('o how many must be those to whom birth will never be accorded!').[27] The respect for the 'benefit of life'[28] – which is the final objective of his intellectual research – also seems to be his dominant passion.

The nature of his commitment requires – as Le Corbusier says of himself – the 'renunciation of a thousand frivolities of a soft life' – the ability to[29]

'accomplish . . . in the course of the successive twenty-four hour days which are the daily fare of a life . . . the necessary feats which lead to the end of the course: the forming of exact aims, regularity and consistency of effort, exactitude and minuteness of manner, choice of time, steadfast morale . . .'.

On this level, artistic commitment entailed an unprecedented psychological tension and invaded the daily life of the artist to a degree hitherto unknown. The myth of Leonardo may justly be criticized historically speaking, but it reveals a genuine conviction on the part of contemporary witnesses: this type of work demanded a complete commitment of the individual personality and demanded that the artist should underwrite his artistic programme with his human behaviour. The masters of the 'third style' not only survived as characters in later artistic culture, but were forced to behave as such even during the course of their own lives. We shall return to this point later.

And what, then, was the place of architecture in this new cultural perspective?

Leonardo was praised as an 'excellent architect' by Pacioli, by Antonio Billi and by Vasari. But none of them hints at any work built by him, and the documents known so far attest only three actual instances of architectural work: the models supplied between 1487 and 1490 for the dome of Milan cathedral, the opinion given in 1490 on the building of Pavia cathedral, and the unknown architectural works carried out in Milan in 1506 for the French governor. His manuscripts, on the other hand, contain a large number of theoretical studies: plans of cities, sketches of churches and secular buildings and building plans (Fig. 240). These studies date mainly from the Milanese period, and are plainly linked with the actual experiments of the architects active at that time in Lombardy: Amadeo, Dolcebuono, Francesco di Giorgio, Giuliano da Sangallo and particularly Bramante.

It is still uncertain whether these designs document the autonomous thought of Leon-

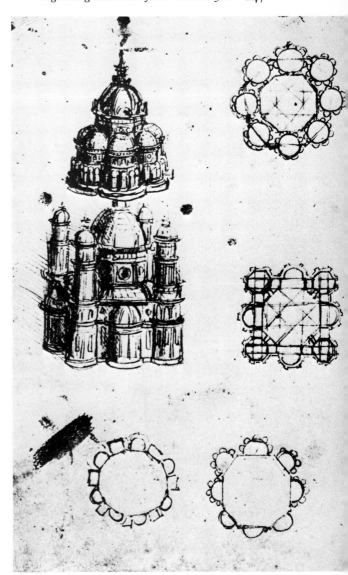

240 *Study of centrally planned churches by Leonardo. Institut de France, col. B*

ardo, transmitted subsequently to the planners of his time, or the influences received from the planners themselves, which Leonardo absorbed and marshalled into his general research. Whatever the influence of Leonardo may have been on other architects, it certainly helped to put architectural research on to a more abstract terrain. In Leonardo's synthesis the particular features of Brunelleschi's and Alberti's architectural culture became perfected: the capacity to distribute decisions over various stages and scales, the distinction between fixed terms and variable terms in the planning equation, the adherence to a repertoire of technical solutions already tried out in relation to this mode of planning procedure.

Leonardo analysed the elements of the traditional repertoire, explored endlessly their possible variations, did not pause when faced with specific difficulties and had no time to involve himself for long with a single problem. In this way he helped to launch the repertoire fixed in the last decades of the fifteenth century without introducing a new methodological principle to direct possible developments; he strongly recalled attention to the human and uncertain value of architectural planning and he weakened faith in the institutional distinctions behind the unity and operative effectiveness of architectural classicism.

His research instigated a critical revision of architecture in the sphere of high culture – thus breaking the links with popular culture or making them more difficult – and tended to reduce architectural problems to general artistic problems. Furthermore his talent for illustration created a new interest in perspective views of monuments and contributed to the rise of collections of drawings by Serlio, du Cerceau, etc. destined both for architects and laymen in the following century.

The idea of an organic unity between all the categories of visible forms, from which the primacy of painting derived, reintroduced, in a particularly thought-provoking way, the priority of formal invention over 'compartition' (i.e. the priority of the procedure common to all the arts over that belonging to architecture); furthermore the preference given to simultaneous representation over successive representation diminished the reference to history in architecture, too, and emphasized that of environment. The 'diachronic' structure of historical reasoning, from which Brunelleschi's brand of classicism proceeds, is particularly obscured by a simultaneous interest in all systems of forms, within classicism and outside it; hence the hints of exoticism to be found in the work of Leonardo,[30] the understanding of the Gothic (which approaches deliberate eclecticism in the studies for the dome of Milan cathedral) and the taste for seeing or imagining distant countries. In contemplating history from a distant viewpoint – prehistoric or otherwise obscure – Leonardo was the first important artist, after Brunelleschi, to succeed in considering classicism from the outside, and thus he implicitly paved the way towards its crisis.

Of the architects working at the court of the Sforza family, Donato Bramante (1444–1514) was the best qualified to perceive the novelty of Leonardo's research, though he in his turn reversed its procedure, i.e. he aimed to transfer the same wealth of references to a specialized activity, architecture.

We know that he was born in Fermignano, near Urbino; but the first documents of his activity date from 1477, when he worked on the decoration of the Palazzo del Podestà at Bergamo. At that time his skills were being exercised in an area midway between painting and architecture and depended on the knowledge of both perspective and a vast repertoire of architectural decoration. In this context his training in Urbino is clear enough; modern scholars have therefore suggested that Bramante had had his apprenticeship at the court of the Montefeltro family, and have attributed to him the decoration of certain parts of the Ducal Palace carried out after the departure of Laurana: the cappella del Perdono and Federigo's *studiolo*.

The fact that artistic circles in Urbino were so closely knit makes it impossible to confirm these attributions in the absence of documentary proof. It is certain that about 1480,

i.e. soon after his arrival in Lombardy, Bramante enjoyed considerable prestige; in 1481 he provided the drawing which was engraved as a perspective model for painters by Prevedari and between 1479 and 1483 he designed the enlargement of the church of S. Maria presso S. Satiro (Figs 241–4). In this case, too, the architectural effect depended largely upon the resources of perspective decoration: the front part of the cruciform building conceived by Bramante was built, the back part is only a representation, with a false choir moulded in stucco on the end wall. The main building was completed by the octagonal sacristy and cappella della Croce, a Byzantine organism on an inscribed cross which Bramante decorated on the outside with a fanciful covering of classical ornaments.

A decorative undertaking of this kind, extended to the scale of a building, retained, indeed further complicated, the system of iconographical and symbolic references which, in Urbino, we have already seen to be

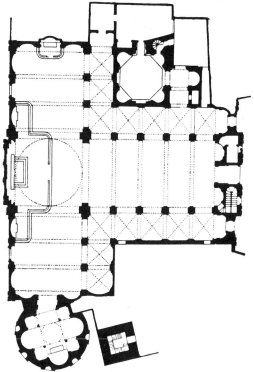

241–243 *Interior, exterior and plan of S. Maria presso S. Satiro, Milan, by Bramante*

inseparable from this repertoire. Bramante, interpreting the universalist requirements of contemporary culture in his own way, immersed himself in historical and literary studies, indeed, knowing Latin, he was in a position to make use of a number of sources inaccessible to Leonardo (who had to depend upon the translations and summaries known in his time); on the other hand, the systematic clarification of all data into a single representational system and the search for a rigorous synthesis, like the visual one towards which Leonardo was aiming, did not seem to interest him. The synthesis to which he aspired was empirical in character, makeshift, and abhorred neither the composite nor more daring experiments. Bramante tried to bring together the greatest number of cultural experiments in the sphere of architecture and to experiment with the repertoire of available forms to discover the limits of their use.

The commissions he received from Cardinal Ascanio Sforza – advice on Pavia cathedral in 1488, the plan for the extension of the abbey of S. Ambrogio in 1492 and later the apse end of S. Maria delle Grazie and the façade of Abbiategrasso cathedral (1497) – enabled Bramante to enlarge his field of experiment (Figs 245–9).

It is not known to what degree Pavia cathedral corresponds to Bramante's plan; the initial phase of the work was suspended in 1492, and the wooden model was completed only after Bramante's death. It was the first large religious building designed to rival the cathedrals of the fourteenth century and was based on a typical plan of the time (a three-aisled cross, its arms converging on an octagonal dome – the same ground plan as S. Petronio in Bologna). The translation of this ground plan into Renaissance terms entailed above all a reordering of the measurements of the elevation, which had to be made to correspond to the cornices of the architectural orders; but it was here that his successors undoubtedly altered Bramante's original concept.

This foray into the field of medieval practice – still operative in Lombardy and probably utilized by Amadeo and Rocchi who were consulted about the design of Pavia cathedral before Bramante – entailed the static and mathematical methodology typical of that tradition, the only one available for advance calculation of vaulted structures covering broad spans.

Bramante must certainly have felt the need to synthesize these ideas with Brunelleschi's and Alberti's theory of proportion. But if fifty years earlier it had been a question of contrasting the new methodology – based on the modular repetition and rationalization of measurements – with the old, based on the use of prearranged geometrical shapes, corresponding to irrational ratios, now the aspiration towards a universal synthesis of knowledge and the spread of Neoplatonist culture created the conditions for an extremely fruitful comparison (this was the moment when Pico della Mirandola was planning the universal congress of scholars to be held in Rome in 1487). The consequences of this comparison were only partially utilizable in actual experiments until the great opportunity of the new St Peter's. Possibly at this time Bramante acquired the empirical knowledge necessary to the designing of large buildings; together with Giuliano da Sangallo, he was considered an undisputed specialist in such problems at the end of the century.

It is significant that his works in Milan – the cloisters of S. Ambrogio, the façade of Abbiategrasso, the apse of S. Maria delle Grazie, like the complex of S. Satiro and the works in Vigevano – should be works of rebuilding or of completion of medieval organisms. In S. Maria delle Grazie Bramante used Brunelleschi's model for the sacristy of S. Lorenzo – the succession of two domed square spaces, one large and one small –

244   *The cupola of S. Maria presso S. Satiro*

245, 246 *Aerial photograph and plan of Pavia cathedral*

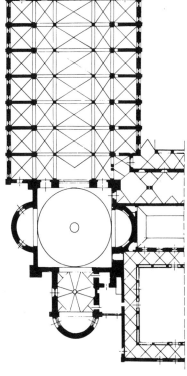

247, 248 *S. Maria delle Grazie, Milan, with the chancel by Bramante*

249 *Detail of Bramante's façade of S. Maria Nascente, Abbiategrasso*

already widely used throughout Lombardy by Michelozzo and Amadeo, for the apse end of the church begun by Guiniforte Solari. In relation to the nave and aisles the larger square has the same function as the octagon in Pavia cathedral, i.e. it determines – here with the proportions of the architectural motif which recurs along the sides and introduces the lesser square; in Pavia with the position of the verticals – the respective widths of nave and aisles, i.e. it brings a variable ratio back to a fixed one; in its turn the dome, which crowns the square or octagon, eases the passage from a differentiated motif to the perfect or undifferentiated form of the circle.

In S. Maria delle Grazie Bramante added the three apses to the Brunelleschian model, and also articulated the traditional decoration, in brickwork and painting, in close relation to the structure of the organism. The circular space, included between the two spaces, is filled with a series of tangential circles which make evident the distance between the two ground plans. The vicissitudes of execution have partly altered the plan and complicate any coherent analysis of the details. The delays and contretemps inseparable from building execution prevented Bramante from exercising satisfactory control over his works, as Leonardo could over his paintings; hence the random and sometimes disappointing character of Bramante's research, always engaged in a feverish race against time.

Even Bramante's economic position at the Milanese court reveals the disadvantage of his vocation; his salary, of sixty scudi a year, was far from the princely sums which Leonardo could ask for and obtain. The friendship of certain cultured people, such as Gaspare Visconti, did not make up for his lowly position.

In professional building circles, on the other hand, Bramante found a satisfactory place and left a lasting influence behind him: Cristoforo Solari, Giovanni Battagio, Gian Giacomo Dolcebuono and Bartolomeo Suardi known as Bramantino reproduced models of his domed organisms in many churches in Lombardy; his pupil Cesare Cesariano published the first illustrated translation of Vitruvius in Como in 1521. The uniform level of civic life and the organization of skilled building workers made possible in Lombardy something that was never possible around Latium, i.e. a widespread diffusion throughout the province of Bramante's repertoire, which continued throughout the whole of the sixteenth century.

The fall of the Sforza government in 1499 brought about the dispersal of the artists employed at the court. Pacioli settled in Venice where he published his books, Leonardo went to Mantua and to Venice – this was the period of Giorgione's sensational emergence – and the following year went back to Florence; Bramante was called to Rome and found himself involved in the feverish building activity in preparation for Holy Year.

The results of the first years of work, under the pontificate of Alexander VI, are only partly known for certain; the only certain work is the convent of S. Maria della Pace, begun in 1500 for Cardinal Carafa (Figs 250–1).

In Rome there was no possibility of collaborating with workers who specialized in architectural decoration; here the workmen were in a position not to design but only to execute – with a technical precision greatly inferior to that of the Lombards – the decorative elements defined in terms of building planning. Bramante used the opportunity to attempt 'total planning', i.e. to subject both the main structures and the details of the organism to a single rigorous process of elaboration.

The convent of S. Maria della Pace – as Bruschi has shown[31] – is divided up on the basis of a modular network with square meshes; the courtyard is set in this network, and its elements – the square space, and the bays of the arcade, also square – are multiples or submultiples of the basic module. The

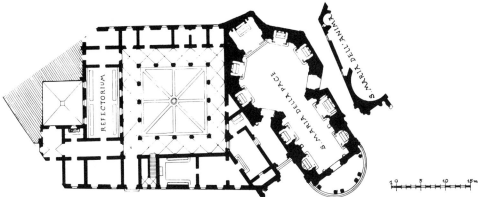

ANNO · SALVTIS · CRISTIANE · MDIIII · IDEO · OPT · MAX · ET · DIVE · MARIE · VIRGINI · GLORIOSE · DEIPARE

REFECTORIVM

S. MARIA DELLA PACE

S. MARIA DELL'ANIMA

250, 251 *Cloister of S. Maria della Pace, Rome, by Bramante and general plan of the complex*

passage from the tracings of the main elements to those of the minor is effected through successive divisions into two; for this reason the submultiples are always even in number: the arcade has four bays on each side, the bays of the arcade on the upper floor, too, are subdivided into two. This procedure – which made it necessary to place the entrance on the continuation of one of the arcades – is reminiscent of Brunelleschi's composition in S. Spirito and may perhaps have been influenced by the discussion about the division of the façade which took place between 1481 and 1486.

The arrangement of the decorative elements, though apparently unpretentious, is in fact extremely complex and ambitious; Bramante set himself to use all four ancient architectural orders, even though the building had only two floors. On the ground floor, where the ceilings are vaulted and the arcade arched, he used the Ionic order to frame the arches – i.e. in the most prominent position, as being the most appropriate to Mary, the patron saint of the building – but distorted the impost cornices of the arches, so as to make them similar to Doric pilasters, and he repeats this motif inside the arcade. On the upper floor, where the ceilings are flat, the arcade is architraved and the supports are formed of composite pilasters or Corinthian columns which alternately support the same entablature.

The coherence of so complex a system is obtained by introducing certain significant elements of licence: one single group of mouldings which appears alternately as capital and cornice, columns or pilasters of different orders beneath the same cornice; nothing exceptional, if one compares it to the far more striking anomalies accepted in the fifteenth-century decorative repertoire, particularly in northern Italy. But the singularities found in the compositions of Amadeo or Coducci derive from a decorative syntax which ignores the limiting value of the canonic rules, and uses the single parts –

columns, cornices, etc. – as elements of a free and often arbitrary combination.

Bramante, on the other hand, was engaged precisely in the demonstration of the new universal value of rules; but he did not restrict himself to using them in the usual conditions, indeed he intentionally sought out the variants of these conditions and, of these, those nearest to the limits of the use of the rules, i.e. he seemed to want to ascertain by experiment the area of validity of the classical repertoire of composition. This research intentionally aimed at the contradictions which in fact marked the existence of the limits of the style.

Bramante's licence was never arbitrary, but necessarily deduced from the approach to the organism; the coherence of the process which picked out the contradictions is much more important than the quality of the solutions adopted; sometimes Bramante would conclude his argument with a trick (in the lower order of the courtyard of the Pace), sometimes he would stop at the mere statement of the difficulty, and leave it in view (in the upper order of the courtyard of the Pace) and sometimes he positively gave up indicating a solution, i.e. he left the work incomplete and incompletable (the staircase of the Belvedere, the courtyard of S. Pietro in Montorio).

The first mode of procedure revealed a magnificent range of stylistic treatment which demonstrated the 'contrived' genius of Bramante so much admired by his contemporaries and was to become the main starting-point for the hybrid Mannerist experiments (Bramante himself, however, did not delight in ambiguity of solutions for their own sake, though this very ambiguity was to become one of the main points of interest for later culture). The second mode of procedure was the most typical of Bramante, and was the clue to his specific intellectual attitude, though it was actually somewhat outdated in the artistic mood of the time and was in fact dropped in the course of successive developments. The third procedure gives rise to the problem of 'unfinished' Bramante, no less difficult and interesting than the similar problem concerning Michelangelo; certainly the major part of Bramante's works remained unfinished because of the conflict between the rate of execution and that of the professional activities of the planner, or the erratic progress of the clients' building programmes, which lengthened the period of execution of some works out of all proportion; but Bramante, in approaching his organisms, sacrificed ease of realization more willingly than stylistic coherence. Separation between ideas and concrete facts, both because of social circumstances and because of the tendencies of Neoplatonist culture, seems to have been a habitual condition of experiment (not only in the artistic field), and one of the ways of accepting this condition was the conscious acceptance of the dearth of concrete facts, to express the very distance of the ideal from the reality. At this point two divergent cultural programmes were possible: if the synthesis of simultaneous experiments were the more important, this could take place only at a certain distance from actual involvement, and lead to the grading of activities according to their greater or lesser independence of material limitations; this was the position of Leonardo, which produced the thesis of the primacy of painting. If, on the other hand, the analysis of successive experiments were the more important, this had to be made in actual commitments, in contact with limitations and real circumstances: this was the position of Bramante, and led him to concentrate his interest in the field of architecture and to pass from one experiment to another, leaving the conclusion of his research open every time.

Thus Bramante – starting from the experience of his contemporaries Giuliano da Sangallo and Francesco di Giorgio – fits into the line of the post-Albertian research into the grading and arranging of the models that made up the heritage of architectural classicism. Bramante, however, pushed this research far beyond the point where his contemporaries had aimed to arrive, and transformed the process of discrimination within classicism into a process of questioning of classicism. Thus he gave rise to a hope for a complete realization of the classical ideal, and at the same time demonstrated the contradictory character of this ideal. Hence the extreme tension of his experiences, the goal of fifteenth-century endeavour and point of departure for subsequent activity.

The Tempietto of S. Pietro in Montorio, built for the Spanish royal family in 1503 or perhaps a little earlier, is virtually the manifesto of the new classicism, apparently simple but in fact rich in numerous ideas.

It is a sort of shrine, on the scale of a building, in a small courtyard on the spot where St Peter was believed to have been crucified, and it covers the entrance to an underground room which contains the hole left by the cross in the ground. From the image of the shaft of the cross Bramante moved, with a simple and persuasive metaphor, to the vertical axis which commands the composition of the Tempietto. The cylindrical body contains a second shrine, accessible only at certain times, surrounded by a colonnade of sixteen columns, on which the drum of the dome rises (Figs 252–5).

The counterpoint between the colonnade and the masonry cylinder determines the character of the organism, which was in fact intended to be contemplated from the outside. The two concentric structures correspond to two different levels of perspective, in that the radial symmetry gives rise to a necessary difference of scale between them. Interpreting the deeply-felt symbolic themes and the conditions of visibility of the small building, Bramante took as the main perspective level that of the external colonnade, and deliberately accentuated the discrepancy in dimension between the two levels, attributing to the colonnade the smallest scale compatible with human measurements and hence with actual accessibility.[32] The level behind – that

252 *Tempietto of S. Pietro in Montorio, Rome, by Bramante*
253 *Design for the Tempietto of S. Pietro in Montorio. Uffizi, Florence*

DELLE ANTICHITA

Nella paſſata carta ho detto di dimoſtrare quel tempietto di Bramante piu diffuſamente, ilquale non è molto grande : ma fu ſolamente fatto per commemoratione di ſan Pietro Apoſtolo,
perche nel proprio luogo ſi dice che'l detto Apoſtolo fu crocifiſſo.   Il detto tempio è miſurato
col piede Romano antico ; il qual piede è ſedici digiti, & ogni digito è quattro minuti : laqual mi-
ſura ſi trouerà nel palmo, col quale è miſurato il Pantheon, & è a carte 50. il diametro di queſto
tempio è piedi uenticinque, & minuti uentidue.   La larghezza del portico intorno al tempio è
piedi ſette.   La groſſezza delle colonne è piede uno, & minuti uenticinque. La larghezza della porta è piedi tre, & mezo.   Quei quadretti con quei tondi dentro che ſono intorno al portico, dinotano i lacunari ſopra le colonne.   La groſſezza del muro è da piedi cinque.   Il rima-
nente delle miſure ſi potrà comprendere per le prime.

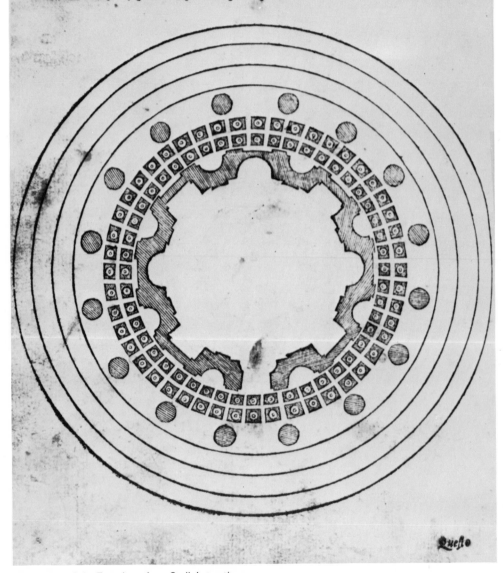

Queſto

254 *Plan of the Tempietto from Serlio's treatise*

255 *View of the courtyard of S. Pietro in Montorio with Bramante's Tempietto*

of the masonry body, punctuated with pilasters which are the projection of the external columns – is thus necessarily below this limit, and is presented as an unreal structure, represented rather than built; in fact the elements which are necessarily linked to the human scale – doors, windows and niches – entirely fill the over-narrow intercolumniations[33] or actually go beyond

them, superimposing themselves upon the pilasters with a paradoxical effect of interference. The architecture of the drum, too, which is seen above, set back behind the balustrade, emerging into the air, is contracted and simplified, as in the 'attic storeys' of the ancient triumphal monuments.

This effect of a falling short of the usual architectural scale is further accentuated by the fact that there is no long-distance view of the Tempietto; it is seen suddenly, as soon as one enters the door to the courtyard, at so short a distance that binocular vision is able to estimate the measurements of all the elements exactly.

The clarity of the compositional arrangement is such that it pushes the details themselves into second place. The Doric order is an almost exact reproduction of that of the theatre of Marcellus; the granite shafts of the twelve columns were probably salvaged from an old building, and almost certainly belonged to a different order, Ionic or Corinthian: Bramante added new bases and new marble capitals, and incorporated them into an architecture of travertine and plaster (though this latter covering was perhaps introduced during a later restoration). There exists a marked difference of executive precision between the parts in marble and those in travertine – they were possibly realized by two groups of workers; the cornice triglyphs are not exactly on an axis with the capitals, the ceiling of the colonnade does not consistently correspond to the triglyphs. In fact the rule on which the decorative arrangement depends is strictly projective in nature, incomprehensible at the technical level for the Roman craftsmen of this period: the form of the outer cornice of the colonnade with the metopes and triglyphs is repeated in the inner cornice and in the cornice of the masonry body, contracting the ground plan measurements only and keeping those in elevation constant. Similarly the pilasters are the precise projection of the columns; for this reason their diameter is slightly smaller,[34] though their tapering does not reproduce the complex outline of the granite shafts and was achieved with the simplified Albertian rule. The decorations of the external metopes refer to the martyrdom of the apostle and are arranged in deliberate sequence, starting from the main axes of the building.[35]

The Tempietto of S. Pietro in Montorio marks the arrival of small-scale research

which was one of the poles of Bramante's investigation into the limits of the use of the classical repertoire. As in Milan he had been working on the small organism of the S. Satiro shrine simultaneously with the huge organism of Pavia cathedral, so in Rome he went from work on the smallest scale – on S. Pietro in Montorio – to work on the greatest, St Peter's itself.

The experiment in the Tempietto of contrasting a group of elements on a very small scale with a group of elements below this scale was, moreover, the logical development of the juxtaposition between real space and space represented in perspective which he had attempted at S. Maria presso S. Satiro.

The attribution of a scale comparable with the human one marks the transition from morphological invention to constructional invention and from the abstract space of perspective representation to the measurable space of architecture. In studying the effects of a leap in scale which crosses the threshold admissible in relation to human stature, Bramante was experimentally testing – and threatening – the thesis of the priority of the proportional and projective characters in relation to those of measurement, and grasped, within architectural experiment itself, the point of transition from representation to construction and hence the relation between the figurative arts and architecture.

This concern or, indeed, this experimental obstinacy is clearly revealed in the plan shown in Serlio's treatise for the circular courtyard which was to have surrounded the Tempietto (Fig. 256). Despite the fact that the colonnade of the courtyard has a diameter double that of the colonnade of the Tempietto, there are still sixteen columns, i.e. the planned colonnade is a further projection of the existing one, and introduces a third perspective level, characterized by a jump in scale greater in the opposite direction than that which we have examined. This new level

ggia con quattro capelette ne gliangoli . La parte D,e cortile . La parte E, e nno templetto, ilquale fece fare il prefato *Bramante* . Le mifure del quale in piu diffufa forma nelle feguenti carte fi dimoftreranno . Delle mifure di quefta pianta non dico co- fa alcuna, ma folamente io l'ho fatta per l'inuentione, della quale l' *Architetto* fi potrà feruire .

Nella

256   *Bramante's plan for the cloister of S. Pietro in Montorio (from Serlio's treatise)*

demonstrates Bramante's experimental aim, but is actually almost impossible to specify in elevation. If in fact – as happened in the transition between the colonnade of the Tempietto and the inner cylinder – the height of the order was to remain constant (even if the difference in level of the steps were made use of), the intercolumniations would widen beyond any permissible limit, from both a constructional and a visual point of view; but if the height of the order were to be increased, the Tempietto would be crushed inside a gigantic shell, blurring all interplay of internal relations of measurement.

The plan reproduced by Serlio must therefore be considered as the working out of a theoretical hypothesis not only unrealized but perhaps unrealizable, situated outside the experimental sphere within which Bramante tried to remain while exploring its boundaries.

This extraordinary building made it possible once again for architectural research to fit in with that already pursued by painters and architects. The premise to be verified – for Bramante as for Leonardo and the young Michelangelo – was still the correspondence between representation and reality, i.e. the crucial value of perspective as the universal instrument of transition from the real to the represented. The unvarying element in this transition was the relationship between measurements perceived simultaneously: 'symmetry' in the original etymological sense. Simultaneous perception of relative values – which Frey in 1929[36] considered the specific basis of the Renaissance mentality in contradistinction to the successive perception of absolute values in the Middle Ages – is certainly the common technical key to many contemporary experiences at the end of the fifteenth century and the beginning of the sixteenth. In considering this picture as a whole, one inevitably comes to see the historicity of Bramante's research, so specifically engaged, in another sense, in the field of architectural practice.

The relativity of spatial dimensions was discussed as a philosophical hypothesis by Nicholas of Cusa before the middle of the fifteenth century; this same notion, translated into geometrical terms and embellished with various esoteric meanings, was circulating at the end of the century in artistic and literary circles; this was 'proportion' which Pacioli celebrated as 'mother and queen of the arts'.[37] Perspective, derived from late medieval mathematical culture and stated by the artists of the *avant-garde*, Brunelleschi, Alberti and Piero della Francesca, to be the basis for the new figurative research, was no longer interesting as a methodological novelty but as a recognized instrument with all its technical consequences to be developed; thus perspective theory was elaborated on its own account by specialists – Gaurico and Pélerin – and in its turn influenced the mathematical research of the following century. Meanwhile the painters born after 1430 – Antonello, Giovanni Bellini, Mantegna, Melozzo, the Pollaiuolo brothers and Verrocchio – explored all the possible conditions of use of the new rules already codified (horizontal or vertical foreshortening, the oblique view, and so on). Leonardo generalized this research and came up against the limits of the graphic representation of space, thus threatening the geometrical structure of the image at the very moment when he was affirming the universal role of pictorial 'science'. This contradiction, which descries the ideological and moral significance of artistic portrayal beyond the technical formulae, gave the impetus to manifestations of the 'third style', as we have described.

Like the figurative arts, polyphonic music is based on the comparison of the intervals of sound, which can be made to correspond to spatial concepts by considering the length of the strings or reeds which produce the musical sounds, as had been known since the time of Pythagoras. In this way it supplied the research of painters and architects with an inspiring term of comparison, but it has a different history. In fact fifteenth-century polyphony was the product of a continuous development, which began with the *ars nova* of the thirteenth century; the works of the Flemish contrapuntalists were admired as results of an already fully developed technique of combination, efficacious as proof of an intellectual harmony which was sought after as the common objective of the arts (see, for instance, the text of Giannozzo Manetti[38] where he describes the impression left by Dufay's motet, *Nuper rosarum flores*, performed in Florence cathedral in 1436 for the inauguration of Brunelleschi's dome); the different conditions of the two techniques – that of music, already confirmed by tradition, those of art and literature still experimental and polemical – allow only for a generic comparison such as the one between music and painting that recurs in texts in the second half of the fifteenth century, from Alberti to Ficino.

Towards the end of the fifteenth century things changed because music embarked upon a series of new pieces of research which had definite similarities with those of the artists: the attempts of the new generation Flemings to push the complexities of polyphonic construction to their limits (Ockeghem wrote a *Deo gratias* for thirty-six parts); the extension of the musical scale (Guido d'Arezzo had considered twenty-one intervals, but Ramis reached three octaves in 1482,[39] Gaffurio four octaves in 1518,[40] Vanneo five octaves in 1535[41]); the organization in depth of musical space, set forth by Aron in 1516.[42] At the same time the theoretical interpretation of counterpoint was also changing: in 1477 Tinctoris was still repeating the medieval definition: 'a regulated and rational harmony, obtained by setting one part against another',[43] while in 1518 Gaffurio proposed this new one: 'Harmony or modulation is like a body, which has in it various parts adapted to the melody arranged among voices distant from one at commensurable intervals. And this by singers is called counterpoint',[44] repeated

almost word for word by Zarlino in 1558[45] and which tended fully to emphasize the common structure of musical space and figurative space. The common principle was Leonardo's 'harmony' which is 'not engendered except in the moments when the proportion of things is seen and heard'.[46] Leonardo – a friend and perhaps collaborator of Gaffurio in Milan – makes the comparison explicit, using almost the same words as Gaffurio ('music is . . . the sum total of many parts'[47]) and constructing two rigorously parallel definitions of painting and music:[48]

'Music is to be termed the sister of painting, for it is subject to the sense of hearing, a sense second to the eye. It composes harmony with the conjunction of proportioned parts sounded at the same time. It is obliged to be born and to die in one or a number of harmonic rhythms, rhythms that surround the proportion of its parts, and create a harmony which is not composed otherwise than is the line which surrounds the forms from which human beauty is derived.'

In the Milanese group and in the Roman group to which Bramante belonged, the observation of the identity of structure between the two activities, and the similarity of the researches currently being undertaken – particularly those to test the limits of application of the rules of proportion – may have produced precious and technically detailed exchanges of experience, of which no specific study has yet been made.

But this momentary meeting was merely a point of transition; the desire to force the application of the same principle, in different fields, produced a different series of difficulties and caused music, like the figurative arts, to proceed towards a number of different developments, which in fact weakened the universal validity of the basic principle. This was the point where Bramante's research fitted in, and experimentally developed the specific consequences of the principle of perspective in the field of architecture. Thus, while he tried to reduce architecture entirely to representation, he was compromising the absolute character of the representational process and rediscovering the very specific nature of architectural research.

After Brunelleschi no architect so lucidly criticized the structural basis of architectural classicism, and no one after him – neither Michelangelo nor the masters of the baroque – pursued this activity with the same depth. On this level Bramante worked alone, and the problems he opened up were only partially solved by his contemporaries or successors.

The Tempietto of S. Pietro in Montorio, built just before or at the beginning of the pontificate of Julius II, was a sensational start to the new period of Roman art, to which the other artists of the 'third style' were to make their contributions a few years later. But for a short time – in fact during the first years of the new century – Florence was once again the centre of the most advanced experiments and the meeting place of artistic trends in Italy.

Political events were closely intertwined with cultural events. The prudent separation of the two fields, which Lorenzo had maintained until 1492 and which was a feature of his personal power, lessened once more when Florence was caught up in the political upheavals following the expedition of Charles VIII, and seems to have been forgotten during Savonarola's political and religious experiment from 1494 to 1498. The cultural and moral decisions upheld by the *piagnoni* and *arrabbiati* became political decisions, programmes for the government of the city. Those whom Savonarola's preaching influenced included, among others, the elderly Botticelli and the young sculptor Michelangelo Buonarroti (1475–1564), who had grown up in the protected and specialized milieu of the Medici garden of S. Marco.

Michelangelo, too, from 1495 onwards, began his wanderings outside his home town:

in Venice, Bologna and at greater length in Rome, from 1496 to 1501; here Michelangelo, like Bramante, worked for various private clients, remote from the court of Alexander VI, and achieved early fame with the *Bacchus* acquired by Jacopo Galli and with the *Pietà* for Cardinal de Lagraulas. His technical mastery was already complete, and the numerous influences synthesized in these works – from ancient statuary and late Gothic sculpture to Ercole de Roberti, Pollaiuolo, Verrocchio and Leonardo – while they pose a real headache for modern criticism, revealed his remarkable capacity for assimilation and the desire to rise above the vicious debate of contemporary tendencies, to aim towards a broader synthesis, like Leonardo in painting and Bramante in architecture.

After Savonarola's execution and the uncertainties of the following years, lived out under the threat of the factions within and of Cesare Borgia from without, the Florentine Signoria was reinforced and reorganized during the years of the government of the gonfaloniere Pier Soderini from 1502 to 1512; this was the moment when the Florentine intellectuals – starting with Machiavelli, who worked in the Chancellery from 1498 to 1512 – were again called upon to make their contribution to the public life of the city.

In this period Florence was the meeting-place of Michelangelo (from 1501 to 1505), Leonardo (from 1500 to 1506, except for the six months he spent in the service of Cesare Borgia, from 1502 to 1503) and Raphael (from 1504 to 1508). The political culture of Soderini, the traditional organization of artistic work and the city's inclination to debate favoured a real and committed confrontation between the three masters which was to have vital consequences.

The confrontation took place on the terrain of the figurative arts and did not extend, for the moment, to architecture. The thesis of the primacy of the figurative arts – painting or sculpture – accepted by the masters, here corresponded exactly to the leanings of the clients, who were interested primarily in commissions of this kind – the statues to be placed in the piazza della Signoria, the apostles commissioned from Michelangelo in 1503 for the pillars of the dome, the frescoes in the Sala del Consiglio commissioned in 1504 from Leonardo and Michelangelo – and took no initiatives of equal prestige in the field of architecture.

Leonardo was at the height of his glory and the rulers of the city considered him not only a superb painter, but also a scientist capable of solving the most daunting technical problems, as Brunelleschi had done a hundred years earlier; Soderini and his colleagues commissioned him to work on the canalization of the Arno and seemed disposed to follow him in his most daring projects; at this period Leonardo suggested raising the baptistery, 'putting steps under it without it falling down',[49] and possibly began his studies for human flight.

From 1500 he was working on the *Madonna and Child with St Anne*. This painting was probably begun independently of any commission: the Servite friars, who wanted a work of his for the main altar of the church of the Annunziata, gave him hospitality in their house with his train, though Leonardo showed no eagerness to complete the work; when the cartoon was ready, a public presentation was organized and 'men and women, young and old, flocked to see it for two days, as if it had been a festival, and they marvelled exceedingly'[50] but Leonardo abandoned the undertaking and only after an unspecified period did he produce the definitive painting from a second cartoon. He took it with him on his travels and it then remained at the court of François I (Fig. 257).

Unlike the *Virgin of the Rocks*, the figures are not in contact with the landscape background but isolated by means of a jump in scale which gives maximum prominence to the internal composition of the group. The perfect harmony of the pyramid-shaped ensemble springs from the balance of opposing tensions: the movement of the Child hugging the lamb, the answering movement of the Madonna who leans forward to restrain him, the scarcely indicated gesture of St Anne to balance or oppose this action. Following the same progression the movement is quietened and becomes inward, revealed in the faces, which mirror one another, reflecting an increasingly pronounced smile. Pietro di Nuvolaria, who saw the cartoon in 1501, saw in it an allegorical meaning: St Anne is the Church, which did not allow Mary to prevent Christ's sacrifice.[51] But the intentional uncertainty of the scene and the multiplicity of meanings typical of Leonardo's painting further complicate this admittedly convincing reference, and upset the conventional relationship between figure and allegory. The painted form is not the diminished illustration of a truth expressed more completely in words, but the direct representation of reality, where the indirect representations offered by reasoning meet and are synthesized. This semantic approach puts many possible symbolic meanings forward: the three ages of man (rather the four ages if one includes the embryo painted on the ground, almost under St Anne's foot)[52] or the cycle of human destiny, compared with the cycles of the plant world – from the fronds on the tree to the dry leaves on the ground – and of the inanimate elements, which have produced, by erosion, the mountains of the background.

In the *Mona Lisa* (Fig. 258) – possibly painted between 1503 and 1506 – there is the same immeasurable detachment between figure and background, but the play of action and reaction in the pyramid-shaped group of the other painting is here compressed into a single figure and almost annulled; almost, because the figure placidly posing is stirred by very slight impulses, revealed by the position of the hands and animation of the features. The delicacies of the *sfumato* enable the painter to limit these effects to the minimum perceptible level, thus allowing the

257 *The* Madonna and Child with St Anne *by Leonardo. Louvre, Paris*

258 *The* Mona Lisa *by Leonardo. Louvre, Paris*

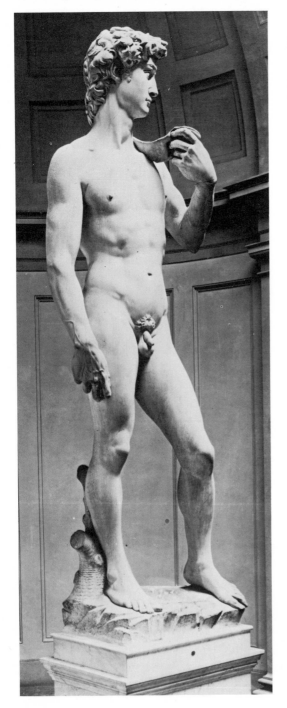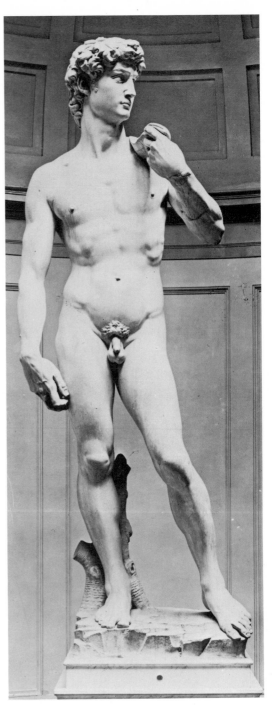

259–262 *Michelangelo's* David *from four different viewpoints. Accademia, Florence*

greatest breadth of possible specific interpretation; this play, as Chastel notes, 'prompts the innumerable literary comments that have accompanied this insidious masterpiece, and immediately renders them pointless'.[53]

These works, which in a certain way touch the frontiers of Leonardo's pictorial research, appeared in a milieu extraordinarily sensitive to figurative values, and made a profound impression on his contemporaries, not excluding the hostile Michelangelo. The *Mona Lisa* and the *Madonna and Child with St Anne*, together with the lost *Leda*, established the prototype of the portrait and the classical composition of an ensemble; they certainly led the other masters to prove themselves at that level, with the specific means of their experience.

In the same period Michelangelo provided one of the most impressive proofs of his genius with his *David* (Figs 259–62) completed between 1501 and 1504, from a block of marble left unfinished by Agostino di Duccio.

If painting, according to Leonardo, 'really places the objects before the eye . . .' and not, like poetry, 'before the imagination in words',[54] sculpture for Michelangelo was the means for an even closer approach to reality, because it made it possible to isolate the chosen object and to represent its real body of volume, in relation to which any pictorial representation must be considered as indirect and derivative.

This isolation was regarded by Leonardo as a diminution, in that the object of representation should be the whole world, which includes and conditions man; but Michelangelo considered it a gain, because a privileged object does exist: the human body, which summarizes all the rest of the world, as the Neoplatonists explained, indeed which contains a reflection of the supernatural order, being formed in God's image.[55]

The immediate response aroused by the *David* – today as at the moment of its presentation to the public in January 1504 – derives

from the extremely striking way in which the figure is placed in the air, before the spectator; though carved from too flat a block, prepared for a frontal view – or perhaps because of Michelangelo's commitment to freeing himself from the limitations of this condition – the statue rejects any kind of two-dimensional setting, hence any graphic relation with architecture: set in piazza della Signoria, in front of the coarse facing of Arnolfo's palazzo, this subtle form carries the pressure of the great empty space wonderfully, because of the charge of movement which distinguishes it from its surroundings (Fig. 263).

Examining the reasons for so fascinating a presence, one's amazement can only increase; in fact these reasons are to be sought precisely in the partial imbalance, which challenges the stability of the plastic form: the slight disproportion between the limbs, with their allusion to the adolescent's state of growth, i.e. they introduce comparison with the mature form, not yet attained, and meanwhile complicate the optical perception of the volume, suggesting different assessments of scale and distance; the muscular tensions that combine towards the equilibrium of the figure, hence the varied plastic treatment of the limbs with muscles showing 'more or less distinctly, according to the greater or lesser strain imposed upon them',[56] attributable neither to a situation of movement nor to one of rest. The figure stands doubtfully, as if to sound out its position in space. The ambivalence of the figurative features is echoed by that of the iconographical references: the statue has the attributes of both David and Hercules, honoured as patrons of Florence, but also considered as the abstract symbols of the republican virtues, strength and courage in defence of the state.

Like Bramante working on the architectural order, Michelangelo obtained the greatest effect from the object represented – the human figure – precisely when he was questioning its objective foundation. From this moment onwards Michelangelo was

263 *Michelangelo's* David *in piazza della Signoria, Florence*

264   *The* Holy Family *by Michelangelo. Uffizi, Florence*

threatening the precise, analytical and detached sculpture of Verrocchio or the Pollaiuolo brothers; form, accentuated in an exceptional way, was already imperceptibly broken down by the very factors of accentuation, and referred to an intellectual reality situated beyond the sensible level. In this his contemporaries saw a telling representation of the Neoplatonist thesis, of a spiritual and transparent universe hidden in the material one.

Involved in work which stood at the limits of artistic possibility and confronting almost exclusively one object – the human figure – the artist's temperament was revealed in his painted and sculpted work with a personal tone which was without precedent in the history of classicism, ancient or modern. It was on this terrain, i.e. the relationship between artistic involvement and human involvement, that Michelangelo's constitutional disagreement with Leonardo, and later with Bramante, emerged.

Things proceeded 'as though the two opposing geniuses carefully supervised one another, in the years they found themselves together in Florence';[57] while Leonardo was painting the *Madonna and Child with St Anne*, Michelangelo was working on the Bruges *Madonna*, the two tondi of the Madonna, Child and St John for Bartolomeo Pitti and Taddeo Taddei – where he developed Leonardo's theme of the compact composition and reflected balance, but polemically adopted a new geometrical figure as a frame and, by varying the degrees of finish of the different parts, used sculptural means to replace the atmospheric effects of *sfumato* – and painted the *Holy Family* for Angelo Doni, also in a round frame which, with its extremely studied pattern of figures, metallic colours, nudes in the background instead of a landscape and biblical symbolism in the place of cosmic, is virtually a polemical antithesis to Leonardo's painting (Fig. 264).

Leonardo, in his turn, in painting the *Leda*, realized with the means of painting a large

statuesque figure, '*serpentinata*' as in the canon of the later Michelangelo, but linked to the figure of the swan and landscape background, i.e. involved in the play of natural forces.

In 1504 the rulers of the city made use of the conflict between the two artists by inviting them to paint frescoes for two walls of the Sala del Consiglio in the Palazzo Vecchio.

The commission to decorate the great hall, which was to house the Consiglio Maggiore conceived by Savonarola, was originally given to Leonardo, possibly through the agency of Machiavelli who had known him in Urbino two years earlier. But Leonardo postponed things as usual and Soderini decided to divide the work between him and Michelangelo, turning the commission into a kind of competition.

The two painters were left free to choose their subjects from among the battles of the city's history; Leonardo chose the battle of Anghiari (Fig. 267) and broadened the meaning of the historical episode, depicting a conflict in which men, animals and also the forces of nature unleashed over the stormy landscape all took part. The unifying theme is the representation of violence, an 'abominable thing' because it destroys the 'marvellous works of nature'.[58] Michelangelo, on the other hand, chose a minor episode from the war with Pisa, where the Florentine soldiers who were bathing in the Arno are warned to prepare themselves for battle; in this way he could limit himself to the representation of a group of naked figures, caught by the announcement in various attitudes or already drawn in the direction of the new action. The artist was concerned not with movement but with the transition from repose to movement, and this enabled him to co-ordinate the composition analysing the various phases of the process and the varying degrees of intensity, as later on in the *Last Judgment* (Figs 265, 266).

The masters prepared cartoons of the two frescoes, and Leonardo even began work on

265, 266 *Two drawings by Michelangelo for the cartoon of the* Battle of Cascina

267 *Copy by Rubens of Leonardo's cartoon for the* Battle of Anghiari. *Louvre, Paris*

the execution, but wanted to experiment with a new system for drying the colours which made them run on the plaster; then both of them, employed elsewhere, abandoned the enterprise. For a long time the cartoons exhibited in the palazzo were copied and commented upon, contributing to the fame of the rivalry between the two painters.

The writers of the time also reported the arguments between the two artists and their mutual accusations, in connection with the skill shown in the exercise of the various arts and their excellence in their favoured art, painting or sculpture.

But the incompatibility between the two artists could not be explained by reasoning; what Leonardo could not accept was the manifest passion of Michelangelo, revealed in his works and polemical thrusts, and what Michelangelo rejected was the intellectual reserve of his adversary who remained silent even in the face of his attacks.[59]

Leonardo and Bramante, born almost a generation earlier and brought up, in two different backgrounds, with a basis of direct experience of Albertian classicism, balanced and reasonable, were involved in a hazardous investigation of the previous cultural synthesis, but remained patient experimenters who kept their differences to themselves and were interested only in the success of their work; their doubts concerned individual results, not the field of activity chosen once and for all, i.e. painting or architecture. But there emerged in Michelangelo a sort of impatience which prevented him from concentrating exclusively on his work; the Neoplatonic background which he had absorbed even before he had settled his professional position had inspired him with a desire to push every concrete experiment to its limit and indeed to transcend such experiments; and his vocation for sculpture was neither exclusive nor constant, as Clements has shown.[60]

His state of mind thus became a hindrance which could never be either dominated or completely developed; Michelangelo was not sufficiently involved in his work to keep it a private matter, which 'must not be known' in Le Corbusier's phrase, but nor was he sufficiently detached to reveal it with the rigorous sincerity of the moralists. Hence his need to confess, but also to stylize, all his actual experiences and his lasting interest in poetry, which offered him the possibility of explaining his thoughts in an explicit fashion and at the same time of veiling them with the artifice of Petrarchan language or of *'rimar chiuso'* (obscure rhyme), learned from his literary friends. At the limit of this phenomenon stood religious commitment, which from a certain moment onwards became a real alternative to artistic commitment. Our concern is to stress not only the presence but also the nature of this commitment which was such that it could act as an alternative to the artistic one. A contrast between Leonardo as irreligious and Michelangelo as religious is unacceptable; the documents do not authorize either of these two definitions which derive from a romantic simplification of the facts. In so far as Leonardo studied the spectacle of the world and recognized the need to reduce it to a precise science, mathematics, far from the 'clamour' of traditional disputes, he discovered the impossibility of grafting a sense of religion directly on to human knowledge, metaphysical on to physical, and – whatever the nature of his personal convictions, attested merely by a few allusions and his will of April 1519 – he anticipated the religious position of Galileo and Pascal. Michelangelo, on the other hand, by means of the Neoplatonic notion of participation or the metaphor of reflection, continually confused physical perfection with metaphysical, the human ideal with the divine; for this reason he lived from within and transferred to the field of art the crisis of traditional religious feeling, triggered off precisely by the thought of the infinite disproportion between merit and grace, faith and works.

The conflict between the two great masters was observed and charted by contemporaries, already eager to cast them as two symmetrical figures in the emergent structure of academic culture, and therefore inclined to emphasize their outward and imitable differences.

But from 1504 the young Raffaello Sanzio (1483–1520) was in Florence; he moved between the two great rivals with a new and rapt spirit of attention; in a short space of time, from 1504 to 1508, he clarified his position which contemporaries regarded as the *quid medium* between those of Leonardo and Michelangelo: a third position, independent from but not opposed to the other two and in a way tending to reconcile the exclusive tendencies of the older masters.

Raphael's short career – which ended twelve years later in Rome – gave substance to, or at least remained the most plausible approximation of, the ideal of perfection cultivated by the previous generation who had been educated in the mood of Neoplatonism. Even during his lifetime, and much more so after his premature death, an extraordinary legend was superimposed upon the real figure: one of his paintings, travelling to Palermo, was brought to safety through something approaching a miracle; his death occurred on Good Friday and after his death a crack appeared in the Vatican palace;[61] Vasari found it particularly difficult to explain the reasons for his greatness and regarded him as a 'mortal God'; in the epitaph on his tomb Bembo compares him with nature:

*'Ille hic est Raphael, timuit quo sospite vinci
Rerum magna parsens, et moriente mori.'*

Required to clarify this judgment, Vasari had recourse to the history of his contacts, first with Perugino, then with Leonardo and Michelangelo; the theory of imitation accepted by Vasari made it possible for him to deduce that Raphael immediately went beyond the style of Perugino; but this theory was no longer of any use when he came to describe his relations with Leonardo and Michelangelo. Vasari tells how the young painter

'seeing the works of Leonardo, who had no equal . . . in rendering his figures graceful . . . was filled with wonder and amazement . . . and gradually and painfully abandoning the manner of Pietro, he sought as far as possible to imitate Leonardo. But in spite of all his diligence and study he could never surpass Leonardo and though some consider him superior in sweetness, and in a certain natural facility, yet he never excelled that wonderful groundwork of ideas and that grandeur of art. . . .'

Similarly Raphael found it difficult to learn 'the beauty of nudes, and the method of difficult foreshortening of the cartoon of Michelangelo Buonarroti for the Sala del Consiglio at Florence'; but he did not manage to surpass him 'at what he had turned his hand to', so he broadened his interest to other topics: landscapes, portraits 'which seem alive' and many other subjects. Later,[62]

'knowing that Fra Bartolommeo of S. Marco had a very good method of painting, solid design and pleasant colouring . . . Raphael borrowed from him what he thought would be of service, namely a medium style in design and colouring, combining it with particulars selected from the best things of other masters. He thus formed a single style out of many, which was always considered his own, and was, and will always be, most highly esteemed by artists . . . and if Raphael had stopped here, without seeking to aggrandize and vary his style, to show he understood nudes as well as Michelangelo, he would not have partly obscured the good name he had earned. . . .'

This passage, added to the second edition of 1568, is the most problematical of all Vasari's criticism, as Venturi recognized.[63] But modern critics have met with no lesser difficulties in defining the development of

Raphael's painting and the nature of his relations with other masters.

The most important influence came from Leonardo; the skilful and balanced composition of the figures in the landscape, the delicacy of the transition from light to shade, the atmospheric mistiness of the colours. Raphael elaborated these in the series of Madonnas with Child or other figures: the *Conestabile Madonna*, the *Terranova Madonna*, the *Granduca Madonna* (Fig. 270), *Madonna of the Meadow* (Fig. 268), *Madonna of the Goldfinch* (Fig. 269), the *Belle Jardinière* (Fig. 271), the *Holy Family with the Lamb*, the *Colonna Madonna*, the *Canigiani Holy Family*, the two *Cowper Madonnas* and the *Tempi Madonna*.

The variety of the compositional models and indeed the number of paintings show that Raphael, in each of them, aimed much lower than Leonardo: not to seize the character of wholeness of the visible universe, but to isolate one of the episodes of universal life; while the sequence of these works and the prodigious capacity to renew a warm, spontaneous approach reveal a boundless interest in the whole range of human experience (Figs 268–71). This grasp of the particular achieves its most extraordinary results in the portraits: those of the Doni couple, the pregnant lady and so-called *Muta di Urbino* (Fig. 272): here, too, Leonardo served as a model, and particularly the *Mona Lisa*, but the intellectual tension that obscured the individuality of the person represented by Leonardo disappears here. Raphael catches the truth of the subject and at the same time sets aside any episodic and anecdotal feature with incomparable assurance; he isolates the essential aspects of the model, and reconstructs its personality – if one can put it like this – in the immutable world of

268 *The* Madonna of the Meadow *by Raphael. Kunsthistorisches Museum, Vienna*

269 *The* Madonna of the Goldfinch *by Raphael. Uffizi, Florence*

painting. The supreme composure of these figures has no equal in the whole of Renaissance art; hence their unfading authority, which removes them from the world of art and makes them, henceforth, landmarks of cultural life and behaviour.

Painted towards the end of his stay in Florence, the Borghese *Deposition* documents the assimilation of the style of Michelangelo; the composition is determined by the fall of a weight – Christ's body, supported by and contrasting with the gestures of the bearers – which generates a dynamic balance clearly derived from Michelangelo's models. Here Raphael's compositional ability met one of its most difficult challenges but the outcome is not entirely a happy one and reveals the profound incompatibility between the aims of the two masters.

In fact the dynamic tension of Michelangelo's compositions is inseparable from his emotional intentions, which Raphael had to eliminate to allow the spontaneity of this representation to persist. Michelangelo's influence, here and above all in the last Roman works, thus becomes a cumbersome technical virtuosity, criticized as early as Vasari.

Raphael's originality cannot be explained without pointing out the discreet but decisive shift that took place in the cultural position of painting.

The aim of assimilating the contributions of others was indeed at the basis of his work; his great virtue was to approach the experiments of older masters – incompatible and impracticable as theoretical hypotheses – by taking them as human experiments, i.e. from the historically most correct and most fruitful

270 *The* Granduca Madonna *by Raphael. Pitti, Florence*

271 La Belle Jardinière *by Raphael. Louvre, Paris*

272 Portrait of an unknown lady *by Raphael. Ducal Palace, Urbino*

angle. Their contribution to progress, fated to be distorted in the intellectual field, could be put to good use in the moral one and painting, enriched by their commitment, could be used to bring the civil behaviour of men into agreement, i.e. to channel it into a common heritage of models of behaviour, transmissible through the channels of a now fully developed social hierarchy.

Vasari, acute as always, even despite his theories, grasped the special virtue of Raphael's painting, when he wrote that 'nature created Raphael to excel in art and manners also . . .'; while in fact 'most artists have hitherto displayed something of folly and savagery . . . which made them eccentric and fanciful . . . in Raphael the rarest gifts were combined with such grace, diligence, beauty, modesty and good character that they would have sufficed to cover the ugliest vice . . .'.[64]

The character that Vasari attributed to Raphael as a person is also the essential virtue of his work; the circuit set up between art and manners broke through the intellectual impasse typical of the experiences of Leonardo and Michelangelo, i.e. the contradiction between the universality of the programme and the isolation of the individual experiment, and is certainly to be considered as the most important of the internal contributions which were to make the new Roman cultural synthesis possible.

By now all the components of the 'third style' have been adequately stated; the main events have still to be described, i.e. the summoning to Rome of Michelangelo and Raphael – Leonardo remained apart and appeared at the Roman court only later, without abandoning his personal policy – and the meeting of the two younger masters with Bramante.

The arrival in Rome also meant an engagement with architecture which had proved impossible in Florence.

In Rome, the election of Julius II to the papal throne, in 1503, brought about a new situation. The new Pope, nephew of Sixtus IV, was eager to continue the political-cultural programme established by Nicholas V and momentarily pushed aside by the family ambitions of the Borgias. The conflict between France and Spain allowed the Holy See to carry out its political manoeuvrings on a European level; the links between the ecclesiastical hierarchy and the new Italian and German banking capitalism, made possible the accumulation of great riches, with which to finance both military operations and works of art (the alternation of these two forms of expenditure was to determine the fate of many works of art, as Michelangelo was to have cause to lament).[65]

Furthermore the spread of Neoplatonic culture gave a new tone to the traditional programme of Nicholas V and Sixtus IV: not only did it encourage and theoretically justify the annexation of pagan culture for the new prestige of the Christian papacy, but it also authorized a near and not always disinterested identification of religious prestige with worldly glory, and enabled artists to exalt religion, power and wealth jointly, when necessary; the reconciliation between these values which had already taken place on the social plane could be confirmed, or at least not contested, on the cultural plane.

In addition the expectation of great changes which was widespread during the last years of the fifteenth century in all strata of society was successfully channelled, with remarkable spontaneity, towards the imperial programme of the Holy See.

In 1481 Cristoforo Landino noted the astrologers' expectation of the conjunction of Jupiter and Saturn in Scorpio which was to take place on 25 November 1484 and linked it to Dante's prophecy of the Veltro;[66] in 1484 Paul of Middelburg published the *Prognostica ad viginta annos duratura*, and claimed that the effects of the celestial event would show themselves in about twenty years. Pico della Mirandola – who planned the great meeting of philosophers in Rome for 1487 – and Ficino – who wrote an enthusiastic letter in

273 Portrait of Julius II *by Raphael. Pitti, Florence*

1492 to Paul of Middelburg, presenting the Neoplatonist movement of Careggi as a prelude to a universal rebirth[67] – both saw this regeneration in the intellectual sphere, while Savonarola, in the dramatic Florentine experiment of 1494–8, transferred this aspiration to the political and moral sphere and did not hesitate to enter into conflict with the Pope.

After his execution Savonarola was violently attacked by his ex-follower Verino[68] and by Ficino;[69] the frescoes by Signorelli at Orvieto, painted from 1499 to 1502, may perhaps have been a product of the reaction against the *piagnoni*, and revert to the themes of the end of the world and the four last things, developing the comparison – already put forward by Ficino – of Savonarola with Antichrist.[70]

But independently of these extreme manifestations, most intellectuals – whether favourable or opposed to the government of Fra Girolamo – rejected the intransigent aspect of his polemic with unanimity; Paolo Orlandi wrote a little poem where he presents Savonarola, Ficino and Pico reconciled in a celestial castle;[71] Raphael, painting the frescoes for the apartments of Julius II, felt able to include his portrait among the theologians in the Disputation.

The gravitation of the cultural ideal towards both religious and social conformism was irresistible; in 1498 Fra Nanni di Viterbo – who published his interpretation of the Apocalypse in 1480 and in 1492 dictated to Pinturicchio the programme for the decoration of the Borgia apartments – had circulated a false chronicle of Fabius Pictor, *De aureo saeculo et origine urbis Romae*, which revived interest in the Roman tradition; Francesco Albertini, who in 1506 published the *Opusculum de mirabilibus novae urbis Romae*, dedicated to Julius II, coupled the description of the ancient marvels with that of the modern ones produced by the new Pope; Aegidius of Viterbo – who about 1490 had praised Ficino as 'sent by divine providence' to establish 'the kingdoms of Saturn'[72] – in the inaugural speech at the Lateran council of 1512 presented the new destiny of the Church as the fulfilling of the predictions of the prophets and the Apocalypse.

The masters of architecture, painting and sculpture were drawn into this mood of faith, with all its contradictions; their personal reactions ranged from the sociability of Raphael to the hermetic isolation of Leonardo, or the recurrent crises of Michelangelo, caught between the need to fit in and the need to escape; but it is not enough to consider this episode as a superstructural manifestation of a limited and largely transient political arrangement. The artists were to some degree at the centre of this social system, for which they provided not only a formal covering of prestige, but also, largely, the actual contents.

Michelangelo, claiming that the cult of the arts must coincide with the cult of peace, expressed the deepest need of the régime inaugurated by Julius II in conventional form: the political and military ambitions were in fact the result of near-sighted calculation, which was to prove untenable even at the time of Clement VII, but the proposal to renew the forms of Christian art – by realizing a definite synthesis between the classical and modern traditions, and offering to the changing hierarchical society a series of universally imitable cultural models – started off a wide-ranging operation and supplied, on the worldly level, the only correlative proportionate to the religious programme of the Church.

This programme mobilized the best cultural energies of the time and explained the significance of Roman 'realism' into which Florentine 'idealism' was resolved. In the sphere of art the elements of modern civilization – reference to history and reference to nature, the continuity of experiments and the selecting of the elements that were unvarying in the course of successive experiments – could become commensurable and fuse into a single image; the only element irreducible to this synthesis – despite the involvement of clients and artists – was in fact the religious element, i.e. the expectation of a supernatural order, which was seen to be all the more strikingly different from the natural order as this latter became more clearly defined. In so far as it appears, the religious urge weakens and annuls the balance of the artistic ideal; this was the dramatic alternative experienced by Michelangelo, and less sensationally by other artists of the same period; one need mention only Bartolomeo della Porta – who became a monk under the influence of Savonarola and began to paint again only about 1505 – or, in Germany, the painters who reacted in various ways to the Lutheran reform, from Dürer – who in 1526 stopped work on an altarpiece with the Madonna and painted the four apostles which were to be offered as a gift to his native city of Nuremberg – to Matthias Grünewald, who stopped painting after 1520, took part in the peasants' revolt and earned his living with mechanical works until his death in 1528.

The programme of Julius II, which aimed at the regeneration of Christian art, was resolutely carried out by the masters of the 'third style' but, for this very reason, lost its qualifying adjective, and produced rather the end of Christian art, in the historical sense, typical of medieval tradition; the Roman synthesis became a civil synthesis, and remained as a fixed point in the history of society until the threshold of the industrial age, i.e. for as long as art had the function of producing the models of behaviour of the ruling class, to be transmitted hierarchically to the rest of the body of society.

The splendid artistic cycle of the 'third style' was not an isolated experience, shielded from the civil and religious contradictions of the age of Charles V, Luther and Erasmus, but produced in the field of art certain complementary changes of position, closely connected to those opposites: the frescoes of the Stanze Vaticane and the Sistine chapel uphold for the last time a system of worldly and religious meanings which were no longer to be able to coexist in the same way and, through this very same attempt at representation, were to be submitted to a crucial scrutiny. Henceforward painting assumed a clearly defined system of human and social values; the meditations on the ultimate fate of man and on spiritual values, which were pressing at the periphery of the social sphere, were carried out elsewhere, in the sermons and writings of Luther, St Ignatius and Calvin.

But let us look at the order of events: soon after the election of Julius II, Giuliano da Sangallo arrived in Rome, hoping for a large part in the artistic programme of the new Pope; at that time work was being done by Bramante, as architect, and the Umbrian or Sienese painters employed by Alexander VI in the Vatican apartments: Perugino, Pinturicchio and Sodoma.

Compared with these artists, Giuliano represented Florentine culture – which was more ambitious and richer in intellectual connections; in fact, as on other occasions, he assumed the part not of protagonist, but of high-level adviser, and precipitated events by persuading the Pope, in the spring of 1505, to call from Florence two masters of sculpture: Andrea Sansovino and Michelangelo. While the former was to begin work on the tombs in the apse of S. Maria del Popolo, the latter received the commission for the mausoleum of Julius II to be placed in St Peter's (Figs 274–7).

Michelangelo committed himself completely to the new project, and designed a free-standing tomb of three decreasing tiers, peopled by forty statues greater than life size: on the lower part, prisoners and groups of the Virtues struggling with the Vices; in the intermediate zone the great seated statues of Moses and St Paul, i.e. the active and the contemplative life; on the top, the Pope's coffin supported by angels. The three zones symbolized the sphere of earthly conflicts,

274, 275   Slaves *for the tomb of Julius II by Michelangelo. Louvre, Paris*

276, 277 *The tomb of Julius II as it is today in S. Pietro in Vincoli, Rome and reconstruction by de Tolnay of Michelangelo's first design*

that of spiritual perfection and that of celestial triumph.

The precedents for this organism are to be found in fifteenth-century tombs and altars which continued the medieval tradition of association between architecture and sculpture but which in the new architectural context, regulated by the canons of perspective, had necessarily to be isolated structures, where the logic of this association was developed in accordance with its laws so as to determine an autonomous spatial system; the last important example was the monument to Sixtus IV, realized by Antonio Pollaiuolo and supervised, after Sixtus' death, by the future Julius II, his nephew.

In these organisms, and in Michelangelo's plan, compositional unity made possible the juxtaposition of figures of varying scales, according to the hierarchy suggested in the iconography; the internal relationship of the

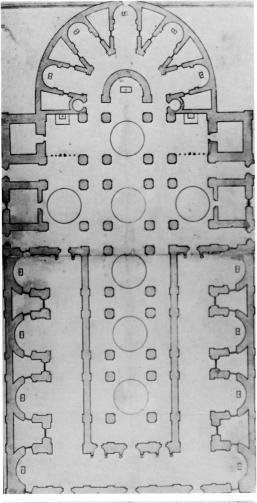

plastic elements became much more important than their external relationship with the scale of man, and held together the image in the figurative rather than the architectural sphere.

The crucial problem, even in the case of a free-standing structure like this, became its precise placing within an architectural space: Michelangelo suggested putting it into the choir begun by Rossellino[73] and Sangallo suggested putting it in a new chapel, which would 'render the work more perfect';[74] at this point discussion became even more complicated and produced a far more serious architectural problem. The new chapel suggested by Sangallo would naturally have to have a central plan, i.e. to reproduce, as it were in reverse, the plan of the mausoleum, regulated by a vertical axis; but the basilica itself – antiquated and in need of restoration, as had been known for some time – was regarded as the tomb of the apostle Peter; hence the proposal, fully consistent with the political and religious programme of Julius II, to combine the two tombs in a single place, and build above them a huge domed organism, which would become the monumental nucleus of the new St Peter's. This suggestion may have come from Giuliano da Sangallo or from the Pope, but probably not from Michelangelo, as has been suggested;[75] in fact it entailed transferring the problem from the figurative to the architectural level and reversing the compositional logic followed in the plan of the mausoleum which was clearly unsuited to the scale of the new building; furthermore it reduced the mausoleum to an inessential detail, and indeed the Pope finally put off its execution, concentrating finances on the building work.

There were now three parts to co-ordinate: the centrally-planned church, with Michelangelo's mausoleum (its position was fixed by that of the tomb of St Peter) and the two

278, 279 *Two plans for the new St Peter's: the first by Fra Giocondo, the second, based on Bramante, by Giuliano da Sangallo. Uffizi, Florence*

structures existing some way away from that position, i.e. Rossellino's unfinished choir and the body (with nave and four aisles) of the Constantinian church. Thus in the summer of 1505 – while Michelangelo was in Carrara selecting the marble – a heated discussion began: Giuliano da Sangallo, Bramante (already employed on the reorganization of the Vatican palace) and Fra Giocondo (specially summoned from Paris, because of his famed technical expertise) presented a series of plans, whose order is still very far

from clear.[76] All that is clear is that in the October of that year Julius II cut short all discussion by choosing Bramante as architect of the new church, and by fixing the laying of the foundation stone for 18 April 1506.

Bramante's plan is documented in various drawings,[77] as well as in the coin by Caradosso minted for the ceremony of 1506; it is not even certain if the plan envisaged a centrally-planned building standing on its own or one linked to a longitudinal body. In any case, the new architectural element – the domed

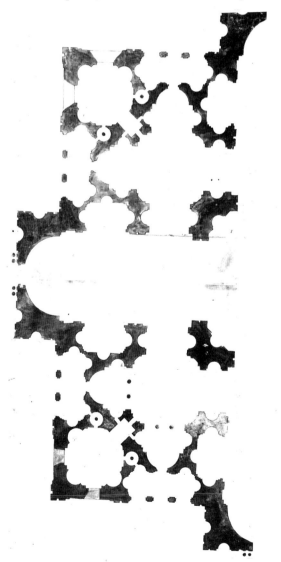

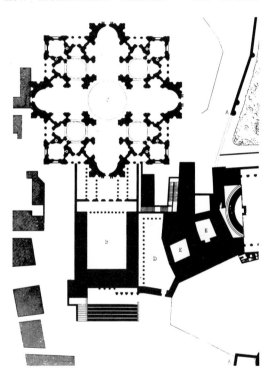

280, 281 *Drawing by Bramante for the plan of St Peter's. Uffizi no. 1; Bramante's plan for St Peter's set amid surrounding buildings (from Letarouilly)*

282   *Drawing by a member of Altdorfer's circle, showing the elevation of the new St Peter's (from Förster)*

organism centred on the tomb – had become absolutely preponderant over all others and had a characteristic articulation which was to remain as a constant motif in subsequent developments (Figs 280–2).

This articulation was based on the geometrical pattern of the 'inscribed cross', already constantly used as a model in Byzantine architecture from the ninth century onwards and known to Bramante through the examples of northern Italy (the chapel of S. Satiro in Milan, which he himself had restored, is a diminutive example of this type; it was characteristic of Bramante's mind to have transferred this model from the tiny scale of S. Satiro to the huge scale of St Peter's).

The Byzantine model relates to the organ-

283 *View from the dome of the interior of St Peter's*
284 *The scale of St Peter's in the new city. Drawing attributed to Fra Giocondo*

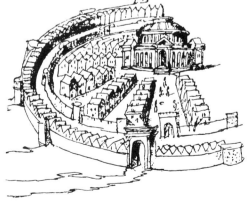

ism of St Peter's as the Gothic model of the longitudinal church with nave and two aisles relates to the Brunelleschian organisms of S. Lorenzo and S. Spirito. In both cases the Renaissance architect isolated the hierarchy of levels typical of the original pattern and regularized it with the use of the architectural orders. Furthermore, in this case, the transfer from small scale to large produced a new pattern of the central supports, which could no longer be considered merely as points, as in the traditional examples, but acquired a dimension comparable to that of the spaces, and therefore modified the general geometrical scheme.

The form of the central pillars was the structural key to the organism, and must be regarded as 'Bramante's real invention'[78] as has been noted; it was so clear and convincing that it was adopted for almost all the domes designed from that time onwards. Their plan is a square modified, on the inside, by a bevel, which made it possible to space the uprights of the supporting arches as required and which, *vis-à-vis* the organism, both increased the diameter of the central dome in relation to the span of the main arms roofed with barrel-vaulting; and set the side domes at a distance from the main arms, i.e. allowed for the placing, around these, of four lesser cruciform systems which constitute a smaller version of the main system.

In this way an extremely significant hierarchy was established in the building: the central dome is given slightly more emphasis in relation to the main cross and acts as a culmination for the whole building; the presence of the lesser cruciform systems establishes a comparison between the two different building scales (as has been noted in previous works) and provides an intermediate transition between the gigantic scale of the dome and the normal one of the surrounding buildings. This hierarchy is entirely regulated by the two pairs of architectural orders which form the supports of the two systems, linked to one another in that the larger order of the small system coincides with the smaller order of the large system.

It is interesting to note that the shape of the dome – as it is reproduced in Serlio's treatise – is similar to that of the Tempietto of S. Pietro in Montorio, and also that the details of the finial, depicted in two illustrations in the treatise, are exactly the same, although the dimensions are extremely different (Figs

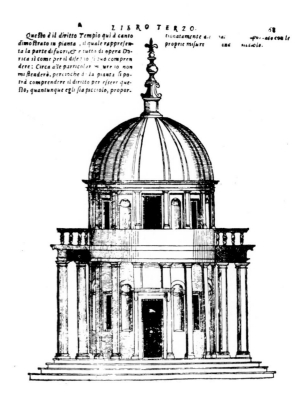

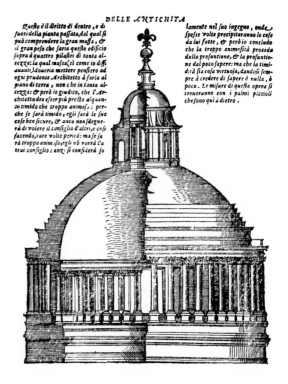

DELLE ANTICHITA

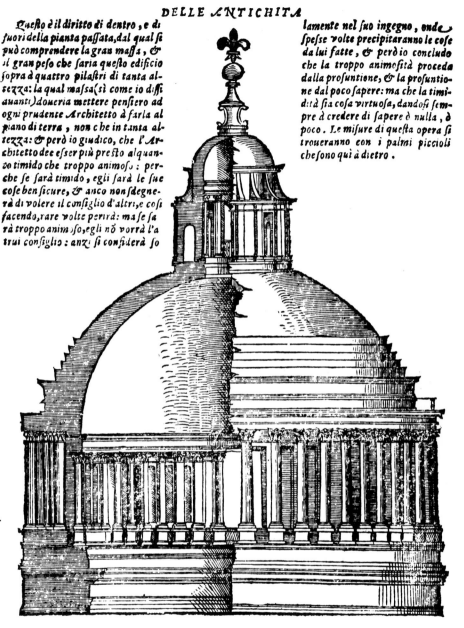

Queſto è il diritto di dentro , e di fuori della pianta paſſata,dal qual ſi può comprendere la gran maſſa , & il gran peſo che ſaria queſto edificio ſopra à quattro pilaſtri di tanta alteʒʒa: la qual maſſa(sì come io diſſi auanti)doueria mettere penſiero ad ogni prudente Architetto à farla al piano di terra , non che in tanta alteʒʒa: & però io giudico, che l'Architetto dee eſſer più preſto alquanto timido che troppo animoſo : perche ſe ſarà timido , egli ſarà le ſue coſe ben ſicure, & anco non ſdegnerà di volere il conſiglio d'altri,e coſi facendo,rare volte perirà: ma ſe ſarà troppo animoſo,egli nõ vorrà l'atrui conſiglio : anʒi ſi confiderà ſo

lamente nel ſuo ingegno, onde ſpeſſe volte precipitaranno le coſe da lui fatte , & però io concludo che la troppo animoſità proceda dalla profuntione, & la profuntione dal poco ſapere: ma che la timidità ſia coſa virtuoſa, dandoſi ſempre à credere di ſapere ò nulla , ò poco . Le miſure di queſta opera ſi troueranno con i palmi piccioli che ſono qui à dietro .

285, 286 *The two pages from Serlio's treatise reproducing the Tempietto of S. Pietro in Montorio and the dome of St Peter's*
287, 288 *The two pages of Serlio's treatise reproduced in the real size ratio of the two buildings*

289   *The three orders of the ceilings in St Peter's*

285–8). The dome was not thought of as an intrinsically larger structure, but as an enlarged structure; hence the need to keep the perspective gradation between dome and surrounding elements unchanged, to set off the effect of expansion on which Bramante was counting. Today this effect has been destroyed from the outside but subsists partially inside because a visual comparison is still possible between the width of the lesser ceilings with barrel-vaulting (though Michelangelo eliminated their cruciform organization), the breadth of the main ceilings with barrel-vaulting and the breadth of the space beneath the dome; these three spaces still form a striking progression and give an idea of the original organism (Fig. 289).

The further specifications contained in the variants worked on by Bramante himself and later planners up to 1546, did not affect this fundamental organism; furthermore Bramante was concerned to fix the organism's points of juncture early on, beginning work with the central piers, the linking arches and a part of the perimetral structure. The details, as in the Tempietto, took second place; in 1508 the architect ordered the stonemasons to reproduce the capitals of the Pantheon, enlarged in the ratio of 12:5.

By fixing the compositional concept of the new St Peter's with extreme clarity, and working in such a way that this concept, because of the logic of its connections, should remain stable throughout the period of its execution, i.e. be able to absorb variants during the course of the work, Bramante established a concrete goal, where the selective research of post-Albertian architectural culture was concentrated.

The reference to Roman models (expressed

in the famous phrase 'the dome of the Pantheon set on the ceiling of the temple of Peace') was only one of the elements to be synthesized, and mainly concerned the details: the organism starts partly from Brunelleschi's experience in S. Spirito and Alberti's in S. Andrea in Mantua, as far as concerns the mechanism of the two orders of ceilings which are set upon or framed by the two architectural orders, and partly from the early Christian tradition (possibly considered as the heritage of the original forms of Christian architecture) as far as the geometrical layout is concerned. Thus Bramante 'was attempting a synthesis of all the essential principles. He aimed at combining the prestige of history, of modern beauty and of a universal symbolism: in fact, to crown the endeavours of a generation.'[79]

Bramante's involvement with the work on St Peter's slowed down the execution of works already under way in the Vatican palace; however he completed the wing of S. Damaso – a first fragment of the magnificent new façade, which was to unify the appearance of the complex looking towards the city – and part of the courtyard of the Belvedere (Figs 290–2) which links the medieval nucleus to the villa of Innocent VIII. Here, too, Bramante was working on a monumental scale never attempted hitherto; the three-storeyed terraced courtyard introduced a prospect of about 300 metres into the organism of the palace, and the lateral blocks accompany the elevational profile of the enormous space all along its length, in that the three superimposed orders correspond to the successive differences in level; the use of the orders as instruments for the regulation of measurement was extended to the scale of the landscape. In this case successive variants have almost completely destroyed the organism conceived by Bramante, but it is still possible to catch the unified character of the layout intended for the whole Vatican complex, church and palace. Both are carefully commensurate with the restrictions of the

actual situation, but at the same time are interpreted as ideal types, obtained from a synthesis of all previous research.

The work of Bramante in the Vatican, particularly that on the new St Peter's, immediately had an extraordinary influence; the discussion of types of ground plan produced a large number of plans in many Italian studios and played a decisive role in the later developments of architectural design, as has been noted.[80] Meanwhile a group of young artists was forming around Bramante – Baldassare Peruzzi (1481–1536, already known for the building of the *villa suburbana* of Agostino Chigi in 1505), Antonio da Sangallo the Younger (1483–1546), Jacopo Sansovino (1486–1570) and from 1508 Raphael, the same age as Antonio – who learned the lesson of the master of Urbino, forty years their senior, in practical terms on the newly inaugurated Vatican building site. In this way a school of architecture was formed which produced not only a new direction in taste, but a heritage of rationally transmissible and verifiable ideas.

Interest concentrated on *dispositio* could procure a balance between *inventio* and *elocutio*; architecture, i.e. the art of spatial distribution, could once again become the dominant and regulating activity in the system of the arts.

This impressive cycle of works greatly diminished the importance, for the purposes of the papal programme, of the mausoleum planned by Michelangelo, where the same ideal contents were expressed in an elliptical form, Florentine in cast and already outdated in terms of the Roman milieu.

What Julius II and his staff of advisers required from the figurative arts was a widespread celebration of the cultural heritage implied in this programme; hence the well-known conflicts with Michelangelo, the suspension of work on the mausoleum (decided on the eve of the war in Romagna, when new financial commitments forced a choice between the numerous projected

290, 291   *Courtyard of the Belvedere in drawings by G. A. Dosio, 1562, and Cartaro, 1574*

292   *Tournament in the courtyard of the Belvedere in the carnival of 1565. Bibliothèque Nationale, Paris*

VERO DISSEGNO DELI STVPENDI EDEFITII GIARDINI BOSCHI FONTANE
ET COSE MARAVEGLIOSE DI BELVEDERE IN ROMA

Disegno del Torneamento fatto il luoc di Carnovale in Roma nel Theatro Vaticano, per Ant. Lafreri forma 1565.

293 *Axial view of via Giulia, Rome*

enterprises), then Michelangelo's return to Rome, in the spring of 1508, and the summoning of Raphael in the autumn of the same year. The two artists were commissioned, almost simultaneously, to execute two complementary pictorial cycles, suited to the character of Bramante's architectural works: the ceiling of the Sistine chapel, and the Stanza della Segnatura.[81]

The ceiling of the Sistine chapel illustrates nine episodes from Genesis, from the Creation to the Drunkenness of Noah, i.e. the mysterious prologue of human history, where the reasons for the whole series of successive events appear: God and sin, the impulse of the Creator and the weakness of the created being (Figs 294, 295).

To organize this representation, Michelangelo projected on to the ceiling of the fifteenth-century chapel the architectural-sculptural system devised for the tomb of Julius II. This system served as a cornice for the actual stories painted in the central panels, but its unusual treatment strongly affects the general composition, and makes this an amazing and unique work, where the artist attempts, in his own way, to fuse the three major arts. Furthermore, only some of the figures which people the architectural cornice are painted statues; the prophets, sibyls and nude youths (*ignudi*) are presented as polychrome figures, similar to those of the panels, and the lower figures, placed in the pendentives and lunettes, have their own perspective backgrounds.

The figures of the cornice, organized in various superimposed zones, introduce another succession of contents, subtler and seen in terms of Neoplatonist symbolism: the figures of the lower strip are Christ's ancestors, imprisoned in sin, and the figures of the intermediate strip are the prophets and sibyls, who announce the kingdom of grace; but the two series also symbolize the passage of the soul from the region of the material passions to that of purifying emotion and lastly to that of spiritual liberation, corresponding to the zone of the nude youths; their liberation enables them to contemplate the truth of biblical history.

The rejection of perspective unity and the marked differences in scale between the various images isolate the single figures or groups of figures, giving them an extraordinary prominence. The polychromy, based on the pairs of complementary colours typical of the Florentine tradition – red and green, orange and blue, violet and yellow – is closely linked to the relief, and serves further to modulate the effects of volume, emphasizing or diminishing them as the case may be; but in certain cases – particularly in the stories of the Creation and in the surrounding figures, which were painted last – the tonal neutrality obtained with the balance of the contrasting fields of colour is broken by the spread of some extremely extensive ones, yellow or violet, varied by light washes of the opposite colour; colour then becomes an alternative means, which invariably weakens the plastic values. This weakening of relief is at its most marked in the figure of Jonah which is placed on the axis of the end wall and is dominated by the iridescent mass of the whale.

As is well known, Michelangelo painted the episodes in the opposite order to the chronological one, and always on his own; examined in this order the fresco documents his progressive confidence in his executive technique, and also, according to one of the interpretations,[82] reflects the spiritual and 'anagogical' meaning of the main narrative, which moves from sin to innocence and the first divine action; as one approaches the divine reality, Michelangelo lessens the plastic solidity of the representation not only with stylistic means, but with a sort of reticence, in striking contrast with his aggressive temperament. This work, with its wealth of formal invention, already reveals the undermining of form, considerably in advance of later experiments.

The frescoes of the Stanza della Segnatura, on the other hand, present a summary of the world of learning of the time, divided into four sectors: theology, philosophy, poetry and ethics, which are personified in the allegories painted in the lunettes (the first of the four cardinal virtues, Justice, appears for ethics). Three of the four walls are covered with single themes: the *Disputation of the Holy Sacrament*, the *School of Athens* and *Parnassus*, while the fourth, which contains the window, is occupied by two historical scenes and two allegories of the other three cardinal virtues, prudence, temperance and fortitude (Figs 296–9).

On the three main walls Raphael accepted the classical principle of the single perspective view, and composed a crowd of figures against an appropriate background: cosmic, architectural or landscape. While respecting a complex symbolic programme, Raphael was always able to replace abstract allegories with real people, and often delighted in superimposing two different identifications, one ancient and one contemporary; in the *School of Athens* Plato resembles Leonardo, Heraclitus resembles Michelangelo; in the *Parnassus* the god Apollo is playing a modern instrument, and in the group there are several ancients – Homer, Virgil, Ovid, Catullus, Propertius, Sappho and Ennius – and some moderns – Dante, Petrarch, Boccacio, Ariosto, Tebaldeo and Sannazzaro. The manifold aspirations of the Roman aristocracy, and primarily the need to reconcile classicism and modernity – which covered the need to reinforce the ruling function, now within the reach of this class – found a clear and inspiring outline in these frescoes. In Rome Raphael came into contact with ancient models, and thoroughly involved himself in analysing them; indeed – together with his contemporaries Peruzzi and Antonio da Sangallo the Younger and later with his assistants – he organized an immense work of historical regimentation, which remains fundamental for sixteenth-century culture. But this was only one element of his research; by a fairly thorough study of the stratification of

300

294, 295 *Ceiling of Michelangelo's Sistine chapel, Rome, and a detail of the* Last Judgment

296 *The* School of Athens *by Raphael, fresco in the Stanza della Segnatura, Vatican Palace, Rome*
297 *Detail from the* School of Athens
Opposite
298 *(above) The* Disputation of the Blessed Sacrament, *Stanza della Segnatura*
299 *(below)* Parnassus, *Stanza-della Segnatura*

traditional forms, he uncovered a common root, and hence a direct piece of evidence for that classicism, permanent in time, to which modern culture was turning; this point of balance could not be drawn directly from ancient models, but had to be reconstructed, with imperceptible processes of grafting and adjustment, starting from an experience of the whole historical tradition. The success of this operation, in the field of painting, authorized confidence in a synthesis of all cultural data, which if possessed by a class might bring with it permanence and justification for the ruling position acquired with money or arms or religious authority.

The two pictorial cycles of the Sistine and Segnatura summarize the religious and worldly demands of the court of Julius II; they are difficult works, indecipherable without a learned commentary, and were painted with the advice of theologians, philosophers and men of letters. They set out to translate into visual terms a system of intellectual and moral meanings, drawn from the whole arc of tradition; like Bramante's architecture, they aim at a very broad synthesis, partly unattainable and destined to disappointment.

But this moment of exceptional tension lasted only a few years: in 1513 Julius II died and in 1514 Bramante. The election of Cardinal Medici, Leo X, produced a shake-up in the Roman cultural scene which became more varied and less demanding. Economic prosperity and the political and religious truce, after the Peace of Noyon and concordat of Bologna, favoured cultural enterprises: the Pope's links with Florence (where Medici rule had been restored in 1512) brought many people from there to Rome, and at the same time opened a new field of action to the artists of the Roman court. The most important artists and literary men settled in Rome: Pietro Bembo, Jacopo Sadoleto, Leonardo da Vinci, Baldassarre Castiglione and Bernardo Bibbiena.

The seriousness of the intellectual synthesis attempted in the previous decade was soon disparaged by criticism of a new tone, as shown by the success of the *Praise of Folly*, published in 1511; the new cultural ideal – now clearly set within the sphere of manners and social relations – was put forward in the *Courtier* (written between 1508 and 1514). The language problem – i.e. the problem of communication, the basis of civil relations – was at the centre of literary debate. The papal secretariat was held by the Ciceronians Bembo and Sadoleto; Bembo laid down the subjects of Raphael's frescoes in the Stanza della Segnatura, and pointed to the experience of the artists who were studying antiquity as an example for the work of men of letters.[83] Raphael was now at the centre of artistic life in Rome. In the last years of the reign of Julius II he was painting the frescoes for the Stanza di Eliodoro: the subjects no longer belonged to the sphere of theory, but to ecclesiastical history – *Heliodorus driven from the Temple*, the *Mass of Bolsena*, the *Freeing of St Peter*, the *Meeting of Leo I with Attila*; Julius II and his train are present at the first two episodes, portrayed with surprising objectivity. A minor event, composed and captured by the painter, entered history, indeed it occupied the forefront of the representation, generating a singular narrative ambiguity. Some of the spectators are already in the fresco, and this is presented to the spectators as an idealized mirror, where contemporaries could converse with figures from the past; Leo X appears in the role of Leo I (Fig. 302) but is wearing modern costume, while the barbarians are wearing the historical costumes of the ancients.

In this second cycle of frescoes Raphael used an extremely wide range of pictorial instruments, and began to introduce the tonal selection of colours which had been perfected by the Venetians in the previous decade.

Contacts between the Roman milieu and the Venetian were frequent and regular from now on; Lorenzo Lotto was in Rome in 1509, and possibly till 1512; Sebastiano del Piombo,

300 Portrait of Leo X *by Raphael. Pitti, Florence*

after contact with Giorgione and the young Titian, painted the frescoes of the Farnesina in Rome in 1511. In 1513 Titian rejected a proposal from Bembo to settle in Rome as court painter. Raphael assimilated the new contributions with his usual intelligence; and indeed this was the moment when he detached himself, with remarkable inventive power, from previous models; after the *Madonna of Foligno* (1511–12) he painted the *Sistine Madonna* and the *Madonna of the Chair* (c. 1514); after the portrait of the Cardinal in the Prado (1513), that of Baldassarre Castiglione (1516) and Leo X between two Cardinals (Fig. 300).

His complete mastery of all processes of draughtsmanship and colour now enabled Raphael to grade his effects with amazing certainty; the last Madonnas still emerged as human people in the full reality of perspective space, but suspended, imperceptibly detached from the world of the spectators; the protagonists of contemporary history and culture pose, in the portraits, fully aware of their importance and revealing the poise proper to their social role through small signs – for instance the complex play of reflection between the three figures, in the portrait of Leo X – that the eye of the painter registers with unfailing certainty. The harmonious form fixed by the painter on the canvas expresses the most genuine, least transient aspect of their historical existence.

For a long time, and through endless reproductions, these images were to continue to exert an unparalleled fascination; they were to be accepted as a yardstick of beauty and propriety even after innumerable changes, which have entirely erased the historical situation in which they were conceived.

301 *Detail of the Vatican loggias decorated by Raphael's pupils*
302 *Leo X in the role of Leo I in the fresco of the Expulsion of Attila by Raphael*
303 *One of the tapestries in the Vatican based on cartoons by Raphael*

304   *The* Madonna of the Chair *by Raphael. Pitti, Florence*

At this time Raphael was harried by an ever-growing number of commitments; he was preparing the cartoons for the hangings in the Sistine chapel (1514–17), staging theatrical performances (in 1519 he staged Ariosto's *Suppositi* for Cardinal Cibo) and had increasingly to hand over to assistants – Giulio Romano, Giovanni da Udine, Pierino del Vaga, Francesco Penni, Polidoro da Caravaggio, Pellegrino Aretusi, Vincenzo da S. Gimignano – the execution of the larger works: the frescoes in the loggias of the Farnesina, in the Stanza dell'Incendio in the Borgo, in the Vatican loggias, and also some canvases such as the *Transfiguration* (begun in 1517); from 1510 he held the post of writer of apostolic 'briefs' and his extremely clear cursive hand (which a modern student of palaeography[84] regards as closely linked to the marks used in painting, as in Chinese art) became the usual model for the official documents of the Papal Chancery; it was from this that Marcantonio Raimondi[85] and Giacomo Mazzocchi[86] derived the characters of the Roman copperplate cursive, used universally until the end of the eighteenth century. Raimondi, who was in Rome from 1509,

prepared the engraved reproductions of Raphael's paintings which caused them to be so widely known.

From 1510 Raphael concerned himself with architectural problems, in the wake of Bramante; his first work was probably the church of S. Eligio, still linked to the Tuscan models and later completed by Peruzzi. A little later, about 1512, Raphael began his collaboration with Agostino Chigi; the most important result of this long relationship was the Chigi chapel in S. Maria del Popolo (Figs 305–7), begun between 1512 and 1514. Here, following a typical Bramantesque procedure, he adapted the model of the dome of St Peter's to a very small space: the drum rests on the typical bevelled pillars, and under the three blind arches a slight moving back of the walls alludes to the arms of a potentially cross-shaped organism: in fact, the cornice continues across these walls but the projections of the moulding are compressed into a sort of bas-relief, i.e. they introduce into real space a reference to depicted space. The side tombs also represent the well-known elementary form of the pyramid on a square base in partial relief, and the drum of the dome, projecting in relation to the vertical of the encircling cornice,[87] suggests an illusory extension of the terminal structures.

Skilfully inverting the Tuscan rule, according to which the material of the architectural orders was usually darker, here pillars and cornices are covered in white marble, while all other surfaces are filled in with red and brown marble, paintings or mosaics; the dome was covered in mosaics in blue and gold by the Venetian Luigi da Pace in 1516. Raphael also provided the designs for the statues in the corner niches, one of which was by Lorenzetto; the others were executed later by Bernini.

The iconographical themes of the chapel mix sacred and profane images, including the signs of the zodiac represented on the ceiling referring to the horoscope of Agostino Chigi, as in the paintings of the Farnesina. All

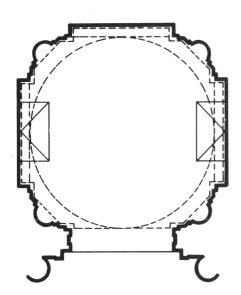

305–307 *The Chigi chapel by Raphael in S. Maria del Popolo, Rome. View from the chapel into the church, detail of the tomb of Sigismondo Chigi and plan*

aspects of this decoration were designed and supervised by Raphael, though none was actually executed by him; he was now in a position to express his talent as director of a collective work, precisely the opposite of Michelangelo, who in 1512 had completed the decoration of the Sistine chapel all by his own hand.

This distribution of energies – no less complex than that realized in Urbino a generation before, but precisely characterized by the presence of an authoritative co-ordinator perfectly conscious of his role – made it possible to perfect and sophisticate form to a degree hitherto never attempted. The team led by Raphael moved along the lines of Bramante's research and diverted research towards a different goal: it aimed not at an intellectual clarification but at a social distinction; the sum of calculated effects and the extremely high level of all the contributions set a work like this apart, in an exclusive sphere, quite distinct from that typical of local fifteenth-century traditions; the new artistic culture broke the links with the old popular culture and took upon itself the task, from its own position of prestige, of orientating afresh the various levels of current production.

In 1514, at Bramante's death, Raphael was appointed director of the works at St Peter's, together with Fra Giocondo (who died in 1515) and Giuliano da Sangallo (who went back to Florence in 1516); thus in 1516 Raphael, only a little over thirty years old, had sole responsibility for the great site, together with Antonio da Sangallo the Younger – at half the salary – who became his most able partner in works of architecture. The building of St Peter's progressed slowly, because of economic difficulties and also because of Leo X's lack of involvement; Raphael developed some of the theoretical hypotheses proposed by Bramante, including that of the longitudinal emphasis documented by Serlio's design, and remained totally faithful to the character of Bramante's

organism. Meanwhile he was receiving other demanding commissions: in 1515 he was appointed *praefectus marmorum et lapidum*, i.e. he had to supervise the finding of the inscriptions that the purist *litterati* of the apostolic secretariat considered the most precious evidence of ancient culture; in 1517 he became superintendent of antiquities, and began work on the great plan of ancient Rome, to which he refers in the famous letter to Leo X;[88] in 1518 he was appointed master of roads (together with Antonio da Sangallo the Younger) and worked on the scheme for piazza del Popolo, with the two converging streets of the Corso and via Ripetta.

Meanwhile, about 1516 – still in conjunction with Antonio – he was designing the Medici villa on the slopes of Monte Mario, later known as Villa Madama (Fig. 308) and introduced Bramante's repertoire into the Tuscan theme of the villa with garden, paving the way for the splendid series of Roman villas of the sixteenth century; the possibility of attributing to Raphael other works, such as Palazzo Vidoni or Palazzo Pandolfini in Florence, is controversial, both because of the unity of the architectural repertoire used by Bramante's pupils, and because of the habit of working with collaborators. At this time, Peruzzi, Giuliano and Antonio da Sangallo were at their peak as well as Raphael:

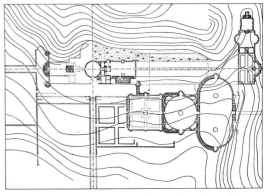

308 *Plan of Villa Madama, Rome, from Geymüller*

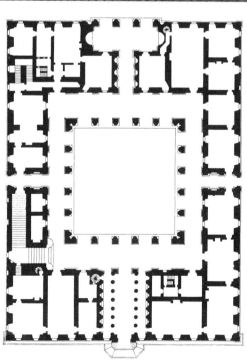

309–311 *Palazzo Farnese, Rome. Façade looking onto the square, architectural motif of the entrance passage and plan*

in 1513 Giuliano designed the papal palace for piazza Navona and Antonio began building Palazzo Farnese (Figs 309–11) and in 1515 Peruzzi produced the model for Carpi cathedral, developing Bramante's motif of the inscribed cross.

In 1520 Raphael died suddenly; we have already noted the exceptional impression this event had on his contemporaries; it raised his fame to the sphere of myth and has made a balanced judgment of his last works difficult. Both in architecture and in painting Raphael's last works were the product of collective activity, which must be regarded as the most singular result of his artistic and human talent: this mode of operating was not only a practical expedient to cope with the enormous quantity of orders, but also a confirmation of the objectivity and transmissibility of his style; the first results, naturally, were not perfect and cannot bear comparison with the splendid paintings by his own hand, but one must consider that this experiment was abandoned virtually at birth; the altarpiece of the Transfiguration, the frescoes of the last two Stanze and the layout of Villa Madama are not the calculated conclusion of a tale of fiction, but fragments of a developing experiment, accidentally isolated by the chance of circumstances; this experiment, if pursued for just a little longer, would have brought about incalculable changes in the course of Roman classicism – changes of which we can only have an inkling. We need note merely that it is in complete contrast with the individualistic tendency that the most important intellectuals of the time, from Machiavelli to Michelangelo, were pursuing in various sectors of culture.

Even one generation later the mood of this experiment was already incomprehensible for Vasari who expands his discussion on Raphael to two discussions, one on his art and one on his human behaviour; none the less these two judgments by Vasari are still the most evocative of the mood of this brief period:

'Such was the greatness of this man that he kept draughtsmen in all Italy, at Pozzuolo, and as far as Greece, to procure everything of value to assist his art.'[89]

'It is said that he would leave his own work to oblige any painter who had known him, and even those who did not. He always kept a great number employed, assisting and teaching them with as much affection as if they had been his own sons.'[90]

And here is the final eulogy:[91]

'It is, indeed, due to him that the arts, colouring and invention have all been brought to such perfection that further progress can hardly be expected, and it is unlikely that anyone will ever surpass him. Besides these services rendered to art, as a friend he was courteous alike to the upper, the middle and the lower classes. One of his numerous qualities fills me with amazement: that Heaven endowed him with a power of showing a disposition quite contrary to that of most painters. For the artists who worked with Raphael, not only the poor ones, but those who aspired to be great – and there are many such in our profession – lived united and in harmony, all their evil humours disappearing when they saw him, and every vile and base thought deserting their mind. Such a thing was never seen at any other time.'

Chance had it that Raphael's death coincided with a series of other events, which in a short time altered the institutional and social basis of his activities: Charles V's election to the imperial throne in 1519, the Bull *Exsurge Domine* with Luther's excommunication in 1520, Leo X's death in 1521. Thus events not only compressed his work into a very short space of time (Raphael's stay in Rome lasted in all twelve years) but after a few years they radically transformed even its circumstances and helped to present it as a favoured and compact episode which was shortly followed by a group of decisive events.

But these changes did affect and disturb the work of Michelangelo who, at the time of Leo X, could be regarded as operating on the fringe of Roman artistic circles.

From 1513 to 1516 he was once more at grips with the monument to Julius II: he prepared a new plan, made another contract with the Pope's heirs and took the house near Trajan's Forum where he worked for three years on the first statues: the *Moses* and the two slaves now in the Louvre. The monument became a frontal composition, though still pyramid-shaped, and the statues acquired more importance in relation to the architectural base. As has been noted, Michelangelo made use of his experience, with the ceiling of the Sistine chapel, of organizing a complex system of images different in scale and in plastic distinctness.

The statues are naturally linked to the frontality of the whole, but contrast with it in their strongly twisting movements; the representation of movement is further complicated by its attempt to catch the moment of transition between repose and action, or between dynamic tension and relaxation. In the *Moses*, too, which was finished with absolute precision, the relief of the limbs is stressed in certain parts and minimized in others, with a flowing modelling which softens and, as it were, colours the effect of the volume. These figures in fact remained unfinished fragments, and we are not in a position to assess the further effects deriving from their relationship with the architectural setting.

The 1513 contract had fixed the term of completion at seven years; but in the conditions of the years 1510–20 this plan was too long and was inevitably disrupted by later events. In fact 1516 saw the beginning of the conflict between the Della Rovere and Leo X; Michelangelo made a new contract, for the execution of a smaller project, and exerted himself to obtain other commissions from the Pope. Leo X's two great architectural enterprises were to be the completion of the Medici

church of S. Lorenzo in Florence, and the building of the church of S. Giovanni dei Fiorentini in Rome: for the first there was a competition in 1515 (won, after some uncertainty, by Michelangelo, who received the commission in 1518) and for the second in 1518 (won by Jacopo Sansovino).

The plan for the façade of S. Lorenzo is regarded as Michelangelo's first important architectural work, and he devoted himself to it with exceptional enthusiasm; in 1518 he moved to Florence where he had the blocks for the statues of Julius II's tomb sent him as well, but spent many months in the quarries of Carrara, choosing the marbles for the new work.

The great façade was still an autonomous plastic system, similar to that planned for the various versions of the tomb and represented on the Sistine ceiling, but enlarged here to the scale of a building; the architectural support – possibly based on designs by Giuliano da Sangallo – was intentionally unarticulated, to stress the population of statues and reliefs which here, too, obey a complex iconographic and symbolic programme. The façade thus became an object distinct from the church, a sort of enormous retable set in the open air and possessing a figurative coherence of its own which would have dominated the surrounding buildings and spaces.

This commission, too, was cancelled in 1520; in recompense Michelangelo received the commission to design the Medici tombs and their setting in the new sacristy of S. Lorenzo which was symmetrical to Brunelleschi's. In 1521 Leo X died and the heirs of Julius II pressed Michelangelo for the tomb of their kinsman, but in 1523 another Medici, Clement VII, was back on the papal throne and he engaged the artist in further work in S. Lorenzo: the design for the Medici library (from 1524) and the ciborium for the church (1525).

The new sacristy of S. Lorenzo had been partly built following the model of Brunel-

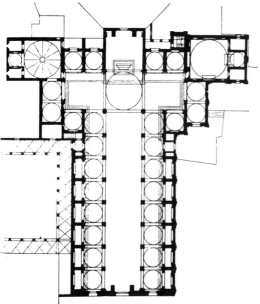

312–314   *S. Lorenzo, Florence. Plan of the church and two sacristies (that of Michelangelo to the right) and two interior views of Michelangelo's sacristy*

leschi's (Figs 312–14), and possibly the architectural order in *pietra serena* was already there. Michelangelo thought of bringing together the tombs in a monument in the centre of the space, in contrast with the architectural shell; then he identified the tombs with the shell and treated the whole internal surface as it were as a monument in reverse: he thus intended to introduce the spectator into a plastic composition similar to previous ones, but turned in upon itself, capable of defining an isolated space and of producing an exceptional concentration of figurative and symbolic effects within this space.

The significance of the chapel thus becomes extremely ambiguous. It is a religious shrine but also a profane one; the representation of the Medici figures is elevated to a representation of human destiny which goes from the ephemeral values of earthly life to the eternal ones of heavenly life; the recurrent theme throughout the composition is that of death, conceived as the transition from one life to the next and treated, with a last reference to the repertoire of Neoplatonism, as a sort of final recapitulation. At the same time the chapel celebrates the synthesis of the arts and summarizes Michelangelo's personal repertoire in a similarly retrospective way, as though he had wanted to leave at least one example of the complete and definitive work designed in vain elsewhere.

To support this figurative and conceptual construction the architectural organism was first stripped of the original spatial articulation: the complexity of the chapel was purely two-dimensional, and required a simplification of the three-dimensional layout, which is immediately evident when one compares it with Brunelleschi's sacristy; there the mechanism of the plastic elements fixes all the articulations of the masonry organism and only them; in Michelangelo's the organism is reduced to a prism with four identical faces, and the plastic elements distributed over the sides are systematically liberated from the

articulations: in fact the presence of the smaller space is reduced to a secondary episode, through the repetition of the arch on the other walls and the slight setting back of the inscribed wall panels; furthermore the corner at the entrance to this space does not correspond to the pilaster, but to an abutment in *pietra serena* brought up alongside the pilaster; in this way Michelangelo preserved the order as seen from the frontal position, and could superimpose a second order of pilasters on top of the first, without interfering with the extradoses and setting back the final dome; he thus prevented any comparison between the dome and the arrangements of the supporting element and destroyed the similarity between the main domed space and the smaller one.

The wall-space included between the elements in *pietra serena* is occupied in the lower part by a secondary architectural composition in white marble, which acts as a setting for the sculptures; the upper part was to have had paintings, accentuating the gradation between the two orders.

The statues mark the points of maximum plastic accumulation, and are linked to the architecture with studied balance; none the less the four recumbent figures do exceed their supports with a leap in scale which was probably decided upon from the very start; they thus stand out as autonomous images and the violence of their effect threatens the precarious finish of the general composition: we shall return to this later.

The Medici library, fitted in along one side of the cloister of S. Lorenzo, is organized as a succession of enclosed spaces; the anteroom (Fig. 315), the reading-room and the rare books room (never built) at the end of the reading-room; each of these spaces is characterized by autonomous wall decoration like that of the sacristy: in this case the distortion of the canonic elements – columns, pilasters, cornices, surrounds of doors and windows – is much more pronounced, so much so that it almost compromises their recognizability;

315   *Entrance to the Medici library, Florence, by Michelangelo*

Michelangelo thus obtains a very close fusion of these elements with the other details of decoration (floors, ceilings and furniture; the statues planned for the ante-room were never executed). Hence the importance of the work as a source of the Mannerist repertoire in the second half of the century.

Michelangelo worked on the sacristy and library until 1527, when the sack of Rome brought about the expulsion of the Medici from Florence and the restoration of the republic.

In the spring of 1529 the artist put himself at the service of the city, was elected a member of the *nove della milizia* (Nine of the Militia) and governor general of the fortifications; none the less his relations with the city government are uncertain: in August 1529 he was sent to Ferrara to study the fortified walls and came into contact with Alfonso d'Este; a month afterwards he fled from Florence to Ferrara, then to Venice, and was declared a rebel; but in November he went back to the besieged city and took part in its defence until its fall in August 1530.

When the Medici returned he hid in the tower of S. Niccolò; then Pope Clement VII asked him to resume the work on S. Lorenzo; Michelangelo worked on the tomb sculptures until 1534 when he left the chapel and library unfinished and settled permanently in Rome.

The interpretation of these events is anything but easy. Up to a certain point Michelangelo made a distinction between his work as an artist and his civic responsibilities: he may have continued to work on the Medici tombs even during the conflict, and soon afterwards he carved an *Apollo* for Baccio Valori, captain of the army of occupation; his patriotic commitment was sincere, but it conflicted with his concern for his personal fate and he moved uncertainly between these two impulses. Every attempt to find an immediate reflection of his political decisions in his artistic production has proved vain, with respect to both their symbolic intentions (the interpretation of *Night* in relation to the

'ruin and dishonour' of Florence is expressed in an epigram composed fifteen years later),[92] and their expressive features. (The drawings for the fortifications of Florence picked upon by Gotti and de Tolnay are the result of a chance foray into the field of military engineering; Michelangelo used his imagination to complicate and transfigure the forms of the works of defence, just as in the Medici library he re-elaborated the orders; but here his activity became an arbitrary game, and he exercised himself within the limits of a constant two-dimensional abstraction. In this episode, as in some of the contemporary sculptures – the *Apollo* and the *Christ* of the Minerva – stylistic involvement comes near to formalism.)

The inconsistency of any political and patriotic interpretation of the works of this period has been demonstrated by de Tolnay;[93] but to come closer to an understanding of this aspect one must set aside from the start the modern concept of ideology, i.e. of a commitment which puts civil and religious considerations on the same level, and consider instead the sharp distinction between the two orders of values, as was typical of the spiritual mood of the time.

The family, social and patriotic commitments of the artist were all placed on a common plane of human values; Michelangelo cultivated these commitments in a completely normal way, and did not relate them to artistic commitments, except very occasionally. On this level de Tolnay's judgment is valid: 'his works of art did not directly mirror his daily life, and he never tried to adapt his manner of living to his artistic ideals; . . . he remained the Florentine artist-artisan, leading a sober bourgeois existence'.[94]

But his religious commitment was continually confronted with his artistic commitment; all art was conceived, Neoplatonically, as an apprenticeship to the ascent from human values to divine ones. Michelangelo not only believed that 'excellent and divine painting . . . is that which most resembles and best imitates some work of the immortal God',[95] and establishes a scale of topics according to their relative closeness to divine reality (at the head of which was the human figure, made in God's image), but also compared the procedure of the artist to that of God the creator:[96]

'When my rude hammer to the stubborn stone
gives human shape, now this, now that, at
  will,
following his hand who wields and guides it
  still,
it moves upon another's feet alone;
but that which dwells in heaven, the world
  doth fill
with beauty by pure motion of its own;
and since tools fashion tools where else
  were none,
its life makes all that lives with living skill.
Now, for that every stroke excels the more
the higher at the forge it doth ascend,
her soul that fashioned mine hath sought
  the skies:
wherefore unfinished I must meet my end,
if God, the great artificer, denies
that aid which was unique on earth before.'

But this comparison became ever less persuasive, as the artist absorbed the concept of the infinite distance between God and the world, which was one of the basic themes of the religious crisis of the first half of the sixteenth century. The acceleration of external events influenced this train of thought, in that it dispelled the memory of the Florentine and Roman circles at the turn of the century, in which the synthesis between the two orders of values had been most strongly formulated.

Thus, while the classical ideal established in the early part of the sixteenth century was losing its religious connotations and moving firmly into the sphere of civic values, Michelangelo was losing his faith in artistic commitment, and finally considered religious commitment as a positive alternative:[97]

'Painting nor sculpture now can lull to rest
my soul that turns to His great love on high,
whose arms to clasp us on the cross were
  spread.'

His declarations can be taken literally: from a certain point onwards he leapt from art to religion and the outcome of his crisis was hidden in the depths of his conscience.

In fact the impasse of this situation depends on the Neoplatonic notion of art as an absolute commitment; every open conflict between this commitment and worldly, social or political duties could be resolved with compromise, but conflict with the demands of religion could lead only to total deadlock: artistic commitment had to be abandoned (as happened for painting and sculpture) or reduced to an act of obedience (as happened with some paintings and much architecture).

This development took place gradually and at least two phases should be distinguished: the first lasted from the fall of Florence (1530) to the death of Vittoria Colonna (1547) and was characterized by hesitation between religious and Neoplatonic themes; the second included most of the architectural works from 1546 onwards, and coincided with the break with the original Neoplatonic ideal.

Sculpture remained the most intimate and least conventional field of expression. In the Medici chapel, on the unfinished tomb of Lorenzo the Magnificent and his brother Giuliano, stands the isolated statue of the Madonna feeding her Child (Fig. 316) which bears no relationship to the architecture of the walls; the splendid figure, with her impassive and slightly distorted face as in the mythological drawings of Picasso, communicated the artist's feeling of bewilderment when faced with the stone that was to be cut away and reduced to a definite shape, and is sufficient to make us feel the artificiality of the framework of polished decoration in the surrounding chapel.

Michelangelo's return to Rome coincided with a new cycle of feverish activity. In 1532 his great passion for Tommaso Cavalieri

316 *The* Madonna *of the Medici tombs. S. Lorenzo, Florence*

burst upon him and inspired in him a series of mythological drawings and a new interest in corporeal beauty; in 1532 the new Pope Paul III placed his complete trust in Michelangelo and commissioned him to conclude the decoration of the Sistine chapel, painting frescoes for the two end walls; in 1536 or 1538 Michelangelo met Vittoria Colonna and began to frequent her circle which included Ochino, Pole, Giulia Gonzaga, Contarini and Valdès.

The fresco of the *Last Judgment* (Fig. 317) was conceived in 1535 and carried out between 1536 and 1541. Its great novelty was the abandoning of any architectural framework: the naked figures are hurled into empty space, devoid of qualifying background and only partly analogous to the perspective space of the great traditional frescoes from Signorelli to Raphael. Any suggestion of depth is lacking, or remains secondary, and the figures crowd into the foreground; the overall composition is not regulated by any hierarchy of position within the continuity of perspective, but by a series of breaks in this continuity, which sets off a chain of dynamic impulses among these figures or groups of figures. The figure of Christ, isolated from the others by a slight jump in scale, is thrown off balance by the violent position of the arms, which are performing two contrary gestures; following the rotation which results from this movement, all the other figures move around Christ, pulled along by this same irresistible force. The general movement is complicated by the secondary movements of the figures, 'absolutely infinite' as Vasari writes, not so much in number as in variety of attitude, which suggests the representation of all humanity. Here Michelangelo used many of the plastic inventions he had studied for previous works; but their very character of secondary movements, overwhelmed by the general rotation, removes much of their intentional vigour from the movements of the figures. Gestures fade into air, passionate movements painfully bend

leaden limbs. The effortful accumulation of many figures in some parts of the fresco contrasts strongly with other empty parts, brightly coloured by the uniform and unreal blue of the sky; this was one of the theoretical precepts that Michelangelo recommended to Francisco de Hollanda in the same period,[98] though it is used in this case with baffling liberality. The composition comes to resemble a collage, and suggests the idea of an infinite assemblage, perceptible only as a series of successive excerpts. Even the signs of the process of execution, by small juxtaposed areas, typical of fresco technique, were intentionally left visible.

This work coincided with the period in which Paul III was backing the most decisive effort at the reform of the Catholic Church and meeting with the Protestants; it was begun while Pole and Contarini were preparing the *Consilium de emendenda ecclesia*, and was completed at the time of the Ratisbon meeting; Michelangelo's great epic representation certainly registers the cultural mood of the first years of Paul's pontificate, i.e. the momentary prevalence of a religious tendency linked to the humanist, Neoplatonic and Erasmian tradition. Primarily this mood made such a commission possible, and may have inspired Michelangelo to this celebration of a religious mystery through the exclusive representation of the human body; none the less his agreement with the aims of the group that commissioned the work was not as untroubled as at the time of the frescoes of the ceiling. Now the autobiographical component had a decisive influence on his mode of portrayal and a new distrust of the importance of the visible world was superimposed upon the representation of its end; thus, while he was recapitulating his repertoire of nudes in their infinite attitudes, Michelangelo dwelled upon the various degrees of decomposition of the human form, down to the corpses and grotesque demons of the base of the fresco (Figs 317–19).

In the *Last Judgment* Michelangelo took

317 *The* Last Judgment *by Michelangelo. Sistine chapel, Rome*

318   *A detail from the* Last Judgment

319   *A detail from the* Last Judgment

the exhaustive treatment of his range of pictorial themes as the object of the representation and, in a sense, ruined his final opportunities. When in 1542 Paul III asked him to paint the frescoes for the Pauline chapel, Michelangelo painted the *Fall of St Paul* between 1542 and 1545, and the *Crucifixion of St Peter* between 1546 and 1550, not only with great physical effort – as he confided to Vasari[99] – but with a new spirit of indifference and submission; the best-disposed stylistic analysis cannot explain away the weakness of these paintings, where the artist's mastery is used with singular reluctance; Michelangelo was now acting out of obedience.

Between 1542 and 1545, in the same spirit, he completed the tomb of Julius II, settling his debt with the Pope's heirs; in the centre of the monument he placed the *Moses*, completed in 1516, and had the other sculptures made by his assistants.

At this point Michelangelo entered into architectural activity in Rome, inheriting the legacy of Bramante's school.

After the sack of Rome many artists left the city: Sansovino and Sanmicheli settled in the Veneto, Peruzzi in Siena, Giulio Romano in Mantua in 1524; Antonio da Sangallo the Younger – now working alone, but supported by an efficient collective organization – continued to direct the building of the great and unfinished works (Palazzo Farnese, the Vatican palaces and the church of St Peter's), was immensely active as a military engineer and was awarded a large number of commissions, achieving an eminent professional position; between 1540 and 1546 he built two palazzetti on the via Giulia for himself and his household, and after 1537 built a whole town in Alto Lazio for Paul III: Castro, where he simultaneously designed both fortifications and a unified complex of public buildings.

Peruzzi collaborated with Antonio da Sangallo on St Peter's from 1531 to 1536, and also built the Palazzo Massimo, the splendid goal of his personal journey; in this building, and in others only planned, he developed the hypothesis of an architecture based on the use of the free column, which was to have no following in the immediate future but was extremely influential in the long term.

After Peruzzi's death in 1536 Antonio da Sangallo clarified his final plan for St Peter's and had built the great wooden model which is now in the Museo Petriano. Antonio had already provided a first model in 1521, known through various designs in the Uffizi[100] and conceived as a logical regularization of the variants proposed between 1514 and 1521 by Peruzzi, Raphael, Fra Giocondo, Giuliano da Sangallo and Antonio himself on the basis of Bramante's organism. We have already tried to describe the basic features of this organism, and to explain the development of the relevant debate until the moment when – between the proposal of Antonio and that of Michelangelo – it reached a critical point and actually cast doubt once again upon the basic organism.

Bramante's plan comprised a basic cruciform system and four minor ones; the architectural effect both internally and externally was based on the gradation between the two structural orders, similar but different in scale.

In the initial plan (Uffizi drawing no. 1 (Fig. 280) and Caradosso's coin) the apses of the main system emerge on the perimeter of the building, and thus tie the solution to the Greek cross, in that the addition of a block with longitudinal naves would have produced an insoluble anomaly of juncture.

In the second plan (Uffizi drawing no. 20) (Fig. 322) the main variant is the introduction of the ambulatories, which made it possible to have a series of structures dependent on the lesser systems running along the whole perimeter; whether or not this plan anticipated the introduction of a longitudinal block, the above-mentioned variant made this introduction actually possible, in that the aisles could run into the minor systems, and

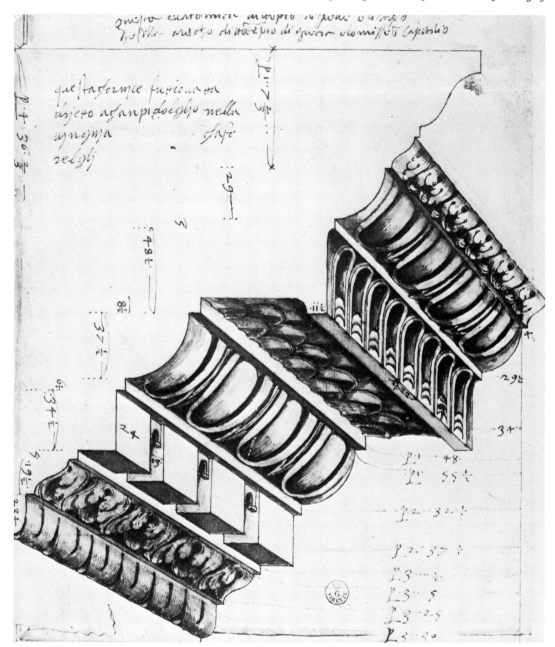

320 *Measured drawing of an ancient cornice by Antonio da Sangallo the Younger, Uffizi, Florence*

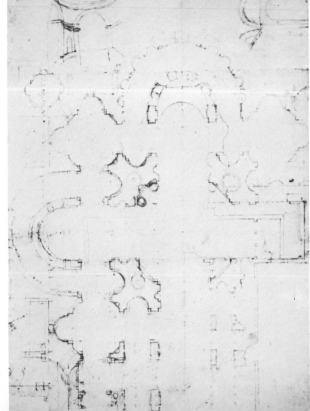

321, 322 *Designs by Peruzzi and Bramante (no. 20) for St Peter's. Uffizi, Florence*

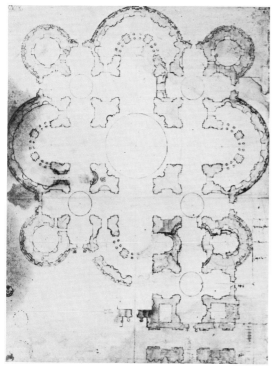

323, 324 *Designs by Antonio da Sangallo for St Peter's. Uffizi nos 37, 39*

could appear to be the continuation of the series of low structures running round the building; the gradation between the main system and the lesser ones was thus established, from the outside, in terms of the elevation.

Raphael and his colleagues worked on this second plan from 1514 to 1520, and Antonio da Sangallo with Peruzzi from 1520 to 1527; the 1521 model was one of the proposed solutions, uninspired in its details (the dome with the wide drum, decorated with blind arches) but perfectly logical (Figs 325, 326).

In the model of 1538 (Figs 327, 328) Antonio introduced two important modifications:

1 He took the organism of the church back to the Greek cross, and in the place of the longitudinal block he incorporated an atrium with the *loggia delle benedizioni*, linked to the church by an open colonnade and flanked by two campanili.
2 He raised the ambulatories, so as to obtain a wall of equal height all around the organism, with three superimposed orders.

The second modification is the more important. Antonio did not actually eliminate Bramante's hierarchy between the two systems, but projected it on to a surface, in that the first order of the outer wall corresponded to the major order of the small system (or to

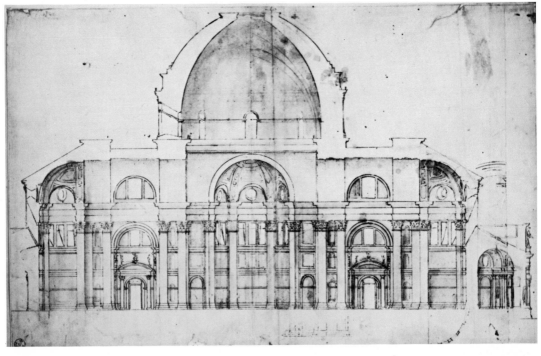

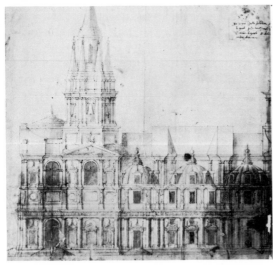

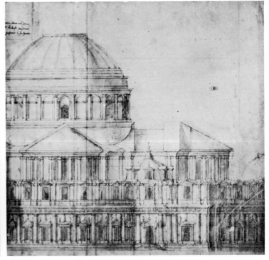

325, 326 *Design of 1521 for St Peter's by Antonio da Sangallo. Uffizi nos 66, 259*

327, 328 *Design of 1538 for St Peter's by Antonio da Sangallo. The model is in the Museo Petriano, Rome*

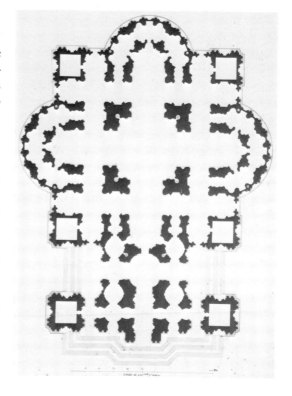

the minor order of the large system); the second order, suitably contracted, corresponded to the difference in level between this and the main order of the larger system (or to the spread of the ceilings of the small system) and the third order to the spread of the ceilings of the main system. In order to dominate this organism, the central dome is considerably heightened and the drum is broken up into two orders of arches, the first light-giving and the others blind, while the side domes are hidden under the slope of the roofs.

The system of the three wall orders made an impeccable solution possible in the juncture with the frontal projection; the campanili, too, with their diminishing tiers, act as continuations of the lower plastic system.

This plan, which was far from well chosen, is an extreme development of Bramante's organism; it retains his logic of grouping and leaves the internal organism intact (indeed Sangallo considered this as established once and for all), but brought with it new demands for visual co-ordination, different in kind from those of the initial theme, and made interior and exterior largely independent of one another. Bramante's open-mindedness and courage in experiment were forgotten by now, while correctness, propriety and monumentality were much more important than before. The great building was now thought of as a compact volume, and the intended effect of the exterior was no longer one of gradation between the two spatial systems of different scales, but the articulation between the body of the church and the projection of the loggia; indeed the designer concealed the inner organization of the church to underline this articulation, and covered the organism with a façade entirely deduced, basically, from the measurements of the lesser systems, so much so that the spaces in the main system never receive their light directly from the outside at all, but only through the ambulatories – which in the third order are mainly loggias – or from special openings in the ceiling.

Michelangelo criticized this plan for the 'numerous projections and angles' which were reminiscent of the 'German manner' rather than the 'good antique or modern manner';[101] and when after the death of Sangallo (1546) the Pope invited him to direct the building, in the winter of 1546 and 1547 he prepared a new model for the whole church, which was faithfully adhered to from then on; later, in a letter of 1555, he praised Bramante, 'as skilled in architecture as anyone, from the ancients down to the present day' and added:[102]

'It was he who laid down the first plan of St Peter's, not full of confusion, but clear, simple, luminous and detached in such a way that it in no wise impinged upon the Palace. It was held to be a beautiful design and manifestly still is, so that anyone who

has departed from Bramante's arrangement, as Sangallo has done, has departed from the true course.'

Michelangelo therefore presented his solution as a return to Bramante's; but what he did was exactly the opposite. In fact the 'projections and angles' used by Sangallo were precisely the means of retaining the correspondence between external and internal architecture; Michelangelo abolished the 'projections', but retained Sangallo's need for a continuous wall, which would surround the whole organism at the same height, and sacrificed the completeness of the organism itself to this need; in fact he did away with not only the semi-circular ambulatories, but also the external arms of the minor cruciform systems, and retained only the pairs of internal arms, which form a great square ambulatory around the central domed space. The wall, built round this ambulatory and the apses of the main arms, was thus not only more compact in its scheme but was also partially independent of the internal spaces, because the re-entrant angles between the ambulatory and the apses are softened by bevels of 30°, to emphasize the impression of continuity; furthermore its make-up is completely unrelated to the internal architecture: a single giant order, topped by an attic, runs around the church, framing a series of windows or niches, which do not correspond to the sequence of the internal spaces either in plan or elevation (Figs 329, 330).

The contraction of the perimeter diminished the previously estimated expense, and Michelangelo also used this argument to criticize Sangallo's plan; proceeding along these lines, he did away with the whole projection with the loggia and campanili, and left the organism isolated as a Greek cross (but retained the old façade with the medieval loggia, and did not begin the execution of the new one, thus handing down the problem unsolved to the next generation); furthermore, by drawing the perimeter wall closer

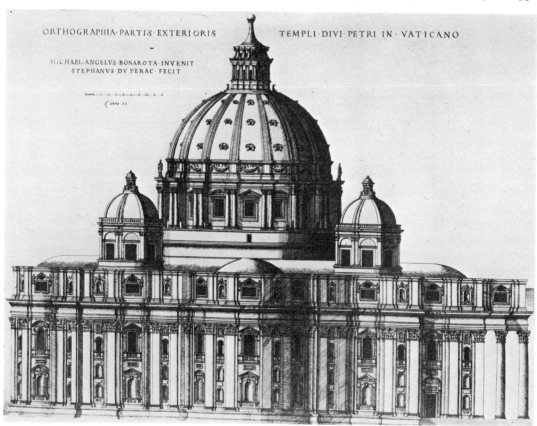

ORTHOGRAPHIA·PARTIS·EXTERIORIS   TEMPLI·DIVI·PETRI·IN·VATICANO

MICHAEL·ANGELVS·BONAROTA·INVENIT
STEPHANVS·DV·PERAC·FECIT

329, 330 *Michelangelo's design for St Peter's: elevation engraved by du Perac, plan from Letarouilly*

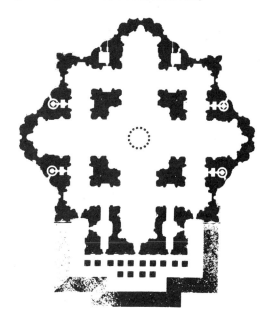

to the nucleus of the building, he improved the visibility of the dome and once more considered a hemispherical or nearly hemispherical shape, set on a single order of supporting elements.

With the dome planned in this fashion, comparison with Brunelleschi's masterpiece, and hence with the structural system already recognized and accepted by Brunelleschi, became inevitable.[103]

Here, too, the choice of detail was decisive, and produced a result completely different from the earlier one. In fact, in the Florentine dome the marble ribs represent the angles of the geometric volume, which is an octagonal domical vault; only where this ceases, above the point where the ribs come together, does the lantern translate the geometrical scheme into a plastic theme. In St Peter's, as has been noted, the organism of the dome develops the motif of Brunelleschi's lantern,[104] but is based on a system of protruding ribs (formed of the buttresses of the drum and attic, the ribs and seven radials of the lantern) independent of the undifferentiated base beneath. Their number (sixteen, rather than eight) makes it difficult to reconstruct optically the total spatial network, and makes it almost impossible to perceive the rotundity of the intermediate fields, except from very close to. In fact the purpose of these elements, like the orders of the new sacristy of S. Lorenzo, is to represent the three-dimensional organism frontally, translating its rotundity into a gradation of chiaroscuro; for this reason the elements are the same colour as the intermediate fields, from which they are distinguished solely because of the effect of the shadows, which vary according to the curvature (Figs 331, 332).

This solution was highly praised by contemporaries because it corresponded to the aspirations of the time (simplification of volume, lessening of expense, translating of artistic interest from spatial organization to the treatment of the wall or the details: dome and façade) and it soon acquired a quite disproportionate prestige – which began with Vasari's tendentious account, positively defamatory for the 'Sangallo faction' – or else was censured for generic reasons which were historically out of place (lack of functionality, classical formalism). It has still to be criticized objectively and set once more in its real historical place.

The solution marked the real turning-point in the history of the building of St Peter's; all later vicissitudes – including Maderno's extension – were consequences of the decision made by Michelangelo in a few months. Bramante's organism, maimed at its most delicate point (i.e. the similarity between the two spatial systems), was put into an independent masonry casing; what remained of the lesser systems, including the domes, was hidden deep below the level of the

perimeter wall, so that the artist, to bring the volumes of the minor domes to flank the main dome, had to design four empty kiosks above the circular holes giving light to the real domes below (two of these were to be built by Vignola after Michelangelo's death) (Fig. 334).

Instead of spatial organization, henceforward there was to be talk of views, of relation between dome and façade, of the advantages and disadvantages of the façade set further forward or further back, of the curvature of the dome to be heightened or not to be heightened. In fact Michelangelo himself, who returned to the Greek cross, eliminated the possibility of evaluating the basic symmetry of the internal layout, made the choice of the Greek cross or Latin cross depend upon a visual evaluation variable according to the changes in taste, and marked

331 *Model of Michelangelo's dome. Museo Petriano, Rome*

332 *The dome of St Peter's*

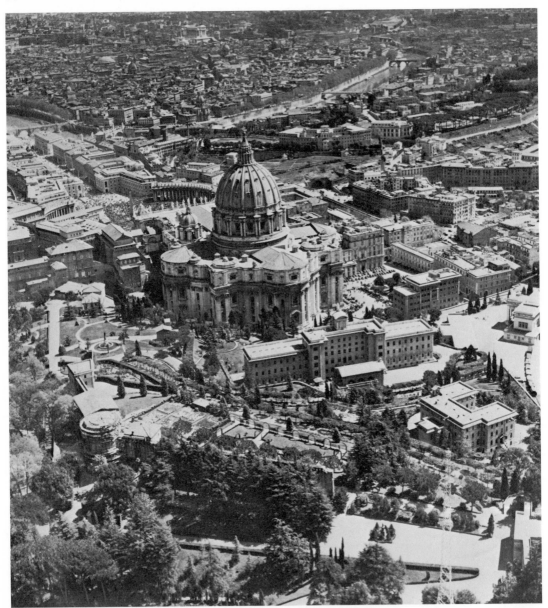

333   *The dome of St Peter's amid surrounding buildings of Rome*

(as in almost all his architectural or figurative works) a preferential axis, where this evaluation was localized; this was the origin of the problem of the axial relations between church and city, successfully resolved by Bernini with the laying out of the square, and later invoked, unhappily, for the laying out of the district which precedes the square, still starting from Michelangelo's concept; the planners of via della Conciliazione, too, claimed to wish to restore this view which was reduced to a lifeless backcloth.

334 *One of the smaller domes of St Peter's*

335   *Michelangelo's St Peter's, as represented in a fresco in the Vatican Library*
336   *The façade of St Peter's seen frontally*

The nature of this approach depended upon the very nature of Michelangelo's plan; the seventy-year-old artist intervened to conclude the age-old problem and acted just as he had done in the execution of the monument for Julius II: he sacrificed the complexity of the problem, failed to consider the character of the organism and superimposed upon it a curt, formal piece of stage scenery.

There is no reason not to take his declarations literally: the initial hesitations, 'saying, to escape such a burden, that architecture was not his art',[105] the outburst to Paul III: 'Holy Father, you see what a profit I have; for if these labours do not benefit my soul, I am losing my time and trouble';[106] the letter to Vasari of 1557:[107]

'I call God to witness that it was against my will that I was forced by Pope Paul III, ten years ago, to take up the building of St. Peter's. If the work had been carried on until now as it was then I should be near the end and should like to return to Florence, but it has been much delayed for lack of money, and to abandon it now that we have come to the most difficult part would be harmful, and I should lose the fruit of the labours of the last ten years which I have endured for the love of God.'

Michelangelo worked out of duty, obsessed by the idea of completion; this attitude found a parallel in the programme of Paul III for the reform of the Church, and later – but with greater reserves – in the programme of the Counter-Reformation: hence his position of permanent adviser on all Roman architectural undertakings from 1546 onwards, and his final attainment of a sheltered position without external stress.

While he was working on St Peter's, Michelangelo was also designing a large number of other works: the piazza of the Campidoglio, the completion of Palazzo Farnese, the gates of the Aurelian walls, the church of the Gesù for Ignatius Loyola, the church of S. Maria degli Angeli in the *tepidarium* of the baths of Diocletian. The most important was the layout of the Campidoglio, which the artist approached with particular conviction because his friend Tommaso Cavalieri was his collaborator and which was, as it were, the secular counterpart of St Peter's in the programme of Paul III, the secular pole of the new Rome (Figs 337, 338, 340).

Here, too, Michelangelo did not have to create an organism, but had to put the finishing touches to an already existing place: the acropolis of the old city had already changed its orientation and the palace of the Senate backed on to the Tabularium and looked towards the city, determining the axis of the composition. Michelangelo created a

337 *The Campidoglio, Rome, and its access from surrounding streets*

338   *The Campidoglio*

trapezoid square in front of the palace, building two symmetrical façades along the sides (heedless of the fact that only one could actually have a building behind it, while the other was a screen hiding the side of the church of the Aracoeli); in this way he produced a terrace suspended over the roofs of the city and cut off from the surrounding buildings, which could be decorated with a collection of ancient statues. Here the celebratory and simplifying procedure, adopted for St Peter's, was more appropriate to the theme, because the aim was to evoke a past organism and vanished meaning; the buildings had no other purpose than to act as an emotional and retrospective stage set.

The other Roman works are fragments of a broader scenic scheme. Rome was thought of as a monument to itself; the image of the ancient city was no longer studied and reconstructed, as at the time of Raphael, to act as a term of comparison for the new city to be built, but tended to be identified, rhetorically, with the present city, depopulated and impoverished after the sack and the outbreak of plague. Michelangelo registered this tendency and interpreted it faithfully, developing architectural motifs in a decorative way; his real interests, and those of many people involved in that difficult moment of history, lay elsewhere, and no longer found an echo in architectural forms. Today we tend to see not only this approach but also the personal contribution of the artist, i.e. the haughty and gloomy tone of these reconstructions; but contemporaries, and even more so the following generation, were struck rather by the total transference of architectural experience into the commemorative sphere and by the singular mixture of the aristocratic and the sentimental; *dispositio* was reduced to *elocutio*, as was admitted at the time, with satisfaction or with regret, by the literary theorists Sperone Speroni (in 1542) and Francesco Patrizi (in 1562). Hence the enormous impact of these works, both in the late sixteenth century – when the conflict between indi-

vidual feeling and collective rules was experienced with the greatest intensity – and in the seventeenth century, when the two demands were reconciled and when architecture was practised as a calculation of emotive effects.

The argument is only partly different for Michelangelo's last works of sculpture; it is different, because here every compromise with the external mood, indeed any kind of relationship with other people, disappears. Michelangelo was working for himself, without commissions, and returned several times to the same theme: the Pietà. About 1550 he began the group destined for his tomb, and about 1552, another group, the so-called *Rondanini Pietà* (Fig. 341); the first was left incomplete in 1555, the second was modified in 1555 and again in 1564, a few months before his death.

The first *Pietà* was a pyramid-shaped group which started from a symmetrical pattern – the body of Jesus supported under the arms by Mary and Mary Magdalene, and from behind by Joseph of Arimathaea – but he complicated this with the double bending of the falling body and the contrasting gestures of the other figures. The other group is based on the simpler contrast between the body and the Madonna who supports it.

The *Rondanini Pietà* has come down to us as a montage of elements produced in the three phases of execution; their juxtaposition produced a sort of impressive 'flashback' and shows us the sequence of activities 'by taking away', which manage almost to destroy the block of marble; in the last version the body of Christ merges with that of Mary, and the obliterated faces are masks insensible to mimic movements, i.e. to the expression of positive feelings (Fig. 341).

Traditional aestheticism has exercised itself on these works, and has accumulated a quantity of arbitrary comments, invalidated from the start, by the artist's reticence. Form is stretched to the maximum by an experience which, essentially, lies outside the field of art; in this sense the sculptures reveal a

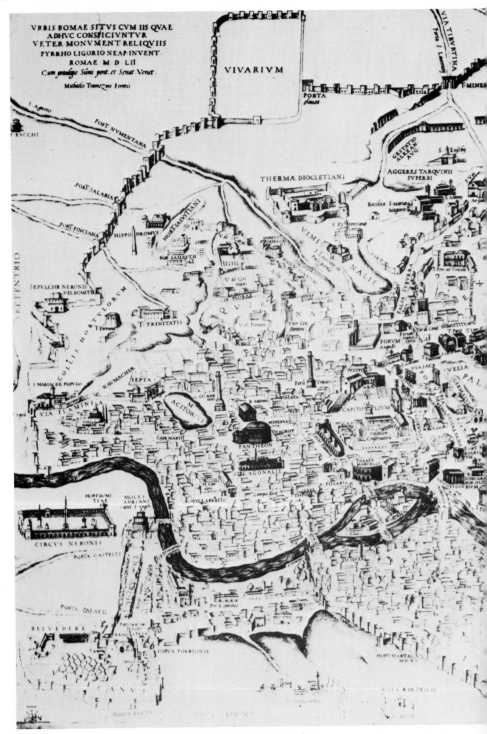

339 *View of Rome drawn by Pirro Ligorio in 1551; in the centre the Capitoline Square*

340   *The Campidoglio, as shown in a fresco in the Vatican Library*

human condition similar to the one mentioned in connection with architecture. The motives are different: here a jealously personal experience, in the architecture the spirit of obedience to a series of collective demands, both irreducible to aesthetic analysis.

In 1552 – while he was beginning the *Rondanini Pietà* – Michelangelo wrote:[108]

'If for your name some image I conceive,
Merciless death soon comes along with it,
and its appearance wins both art and mind'

and again:

'My art and death do not go well together.'

A few years later St John of the Cross described the state of renunciation with common words applicable to all men:[109]

'Alone, without face, form, or features,
Foothold, or prop, you would advance
To love that thing, beyond all creatures,
Which may be won by happy chance.'

The great adventure of the 'third style' thus ended, after the middle of the century, outside the boundaries of art. The exceptional tension set up in the field of artistic culture moved to other fields, and artists found themselves faced with other tasks, more modest and more precise.

The cultural synthesis elaborated in the first twenty years of the century could no longer be presented as an attempt to resolve current conflicts. The reform of the Church – i.e. of the world, because at that time 'to reform the Church meant to reform the world'[110] – could no longer be the object of generic representation, because it was already the subject of immediate and dramatic decisions; the technical organization of the world could no longer be unified and guided by the power of art, because in every sector of technical experience an autonomous heritage of methods had grown up, and soon these methods were to find their centre of gravity in scientific research, outside the precincts of traditional culture.

What then remained, in this ambitious proposal?

There remained two classes of consequences which concerned the general artistic tradition and the Roman tradition.

In the general tradition there remained the memory of an exemplary experiment, which became an inevitable point of reference for the new institutional ordering of artistic work. Bramante, Raphael and Michelangelo not only provided some stylistic models to architects, painters and sculptors, but they justified the prestige and social function of architects, painters and sculptors; they were the 'geniuses' who revealed the range of the possibilities of art.

Their excellence did not depend on a single stylistic system, and was not measurable with any single yardstick. Castiglione wrote:[111]

'In painting, the most excellent are Leonardo da Vinci, Mantegna, Raphael, Michelangelo and Giorgio da Castelfranco; all the same, they are all very dissimilar one from the other, so that none of them seems to lack anything in their own style, because each can be seen to be utterly perfect in his own manner.'

Chastel suggests that Neoplatonist culture not only supplied the guidelines of this enthusiasm, but suggested to the artists a range of ideal types, consciously to be assumed:[112]

'Leonardo, Michelangelo and Raphael all reacted to "modern" culture. Depending on their origins, their training, their temperament and even their age, each of them retained and developed one aspect rather than another; each in his own way realized one of the faces of the ideal artist, of the "genius" invoked by the ideology of the time, to recognize himself in it. The form that the fame each of them assumed can only be the reflection of his personality, the outward and spectacular aspect of the direction he has chosen. If each of the "giants" has so clearly defined a face, it is

341 *Michelangelo's* Rondanini Pietà. *Museo del Castello, Milan*

because he has cultivated within himself and consciously taken on the form of that particular principle of the life of the spirit which his "glory" affirms. With Leonardo, Raphael and Michelangelo we are confronted with personalities who have realized the idea of the artist in so powerful a form, who have secured it so firm a value, that the significance of their figures goes beyond the specific sphere of art. They therefore supply a justification to sixteenth century aestheticism which preferred to relate the principles of culture to artists rather than to scholars or philosophers. In the last analysis each of these masters may have done nothing more than to incarnate, in accordance with his preference, the whole mass of problems connected with a certain essential attitude: Raphael that of Eros, Leonardo that of Hermes and Michelangelo that of Saturn. In this way it will become easier to understand why the aesthetics, iconology and artistic history of the Renaissance always, ultimately, come to crystallize around these three dominant figures and around the themes of Neoplatonism; and at the same time one will have a clearer understanding of the transition from the myth of human *renovatio* to that of the accomplished fact, and that changed attitude, typical of the age of the academies, which led to scanning the immediate past for the signs of a now concluded "age of gold".'

This interesting hypothesis could be literally true, or only likely; in any case the process of stereotyping the masters took place as a result of their own fame, and inevitably blurred some of their individual characteristics; at the same time it replaced the ideal models invented by the previous generation with a series of actual people, who had lived at a precise moment in history.

The ideal of perfection which inspired artistic endeavour from the early fifteenth century onwards was now localized in a specific area of the past; in this way it acquired a completely new social stability, and lost the uncontrollable acceleration which characterized the first hundred years of the Renaissance.

As far as architecture is concerned, discussion must be restricted even further. The 'third style' developed to its extreme consequences the thesis of the primacy of the figurative arts over architecture. Only the courage of Bramante succeeded in introducing architectural research into this movement and, at a certain point, imposing it as a dominant field of endeavour (but only for a short time, from about 1505 to 1514). Bramante's research was too hazardous and difficult to become a general experiment, and the figure 'Bramante' could not be reduced to an ideal type, as happened with Raphael, Leonardo and Michelangelo; thus the admiration of contemporaries and of posterity remained, in point of fact, generic and conventional, like that accorded, seventy years earlier, to Brunelleschi.

Under Leo X, Raphael's talent developed and ended prematurely; it concerned architecture only marginally, and offered a glimpse – interrupted almost at birth – of the possibility of group work; if this experiment had lasted, it might possibly have affected architecture and have changed the course of future events. But here, too, the brevity of the time span (from about 1512 to 1520), incompatible with the nature of architectural problems, prevented the attainment of telling results. Finally Michelangelo came on to the scene, overthrew the programme of an architecture dominated by intellectual calculation and disfigured even the most important monument of this programme, the new St Peter's. In architecture, therefore, the final balance of the 'third style' was largely negative; what remained was the memory of an extraordinary but unrepeatable intellectual courage, partly incomprehensible, certainly unsuited to the vastness and variety of the new tasks in building and town-planning.

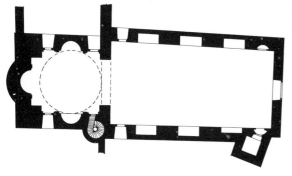

342, 343 *The church of Capranica Prenestina with the 1520 apse*

Thus Bramante's tradition soon came to a dead end and architectural research was obliged to take a new starting-point in accordance with other tendencies that we shall discuss in the next chapter.

In Roman circles this experiment naturally left a lasting mark; from this moment onwards Rome became the capital of artistic and European culture, the genuine source of international classicism, and the organization to administer this cultural heritage was also born.

In 1542 Claudio Tolomei instigated the setting up of the Accademia delle Virtù, devoted to Vitruvian studies; in 1582 Gregory XIII set up the Accademia di S. Luca, in 1593 Federico Zuccaro founded the Accademia del Disegno, along the lines of the Florentine one founded in 1562. A list of 1550[113] recalls a hundred or so Roman archaeological collections, including the most important one of the Farnese begun by Paul III. The treatise by Sebastiano Serlio (1475–1554)[114] collected together a part of the material worked upon

344-346 *Details from the 'sacred wood' of Villa Orsini, Bomarzo : the giant overthrowing an adversary, the entrance to a grotto in the shape of a mask and the domed tempietto*

347 *Moulding on a cornice from the ruined Villa Orsini, Pitigliano*

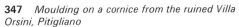

in Rome in the first decades of the century, and was immediately vastly successful in the main countries of Europe.

Despite this no local artistic tradition was formed in Rome comparable, from the viewpoint of richness and exemplary value, with that of Florence and Venice; side by side with monumental production for the papal court (partly dependent upon that of Florence) there was a lesser or positively rustic tradition, where the influences of the 'third style' died away in an archaic and timeless setting. Already at the time of Leo X the elements of Bramante's architecture were to be reduced and impoverished in the church of Capranica Prenestina which bears the date 1520 (Figs 342, 343) and in the nymphaeum of Villa

348 *View of the Villa Orsini, Pitigliano*

Colonna at Gennazzano. Later not only the canonic elements, but also the striving after contrast in scale typical of Bramante and his successors were utilized paradoxically and equivocally in the Villa Orsini at Bomarzo[115] (Figs 344–6); the learned forms of the classical repertoire proved they could be combined both with exotic contributions and with the original ones of the remotest past, e.g. medieval or Etruscan. In the Villa Orsini at Pitigliano[116] the process of debasement of the classical forms reached an absolute limit: orders and moulding were confused with a succession of elementary masses and spaces, which depended upon the extremely ancient technique of tunnelling into the tufaceous rock (Figs 347, 348).

Jacopo Barozzi da Vignola (1507–73), who succeeded Michelangelo in directing the building of St Peter's, was the protagonist of this winding up of the inheritance of the 'third style'. With his wide-ranging activities both in Rome, in the monumental public works, and in the smaller cities and even in the smallest centres in Latium, he acted as a link between the mood of the capital and that of the province; furthermore in 1562 he published his extremely successful treatise, where the great legacy of the 'third style' was reduced to the schematic listing of the constant elements: the five orders of architecture. His most important work was the church of the Gesù in Rome which was adopted by the Society of Jesus as the uni-

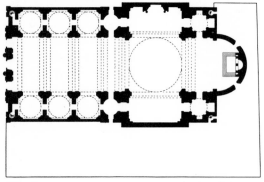

349–351   *The Gesù, Rome by Vignola; façade by Giacomo della Porta*

form building type for its churches throughout the Catholic world. In 1554 Michelangelo had offered Ignatius Loyola a design which was possibly utilized by Vignola when he planned the organism of his church in 1568: a barrel-vaulted hall buttressed by transversal masonry partitions with chapels between them; at the level of the presbytery this space became the front arm of a small cruciform system, contained within the width of the chapels and crowned by the dome (Figs 349–51).

This organism could be derived from late Gothic churches, from the structures of Roman baths and from Alberti's S. Andrea; but it was also the schematic realization of a more or less inevitable structural system, if the aim was to realize a large space with unbroken masonry structures. For this reason – apart from the ecclesiastical value of the building type – it turned out to be suitable for reproduction in all places and all cultural conditions, in cities and small towns, for every class of client – Jesuits or not – and for every class of executor.

The renewed tendency towards the stereotype explains the vast success of Vignola's model from about 1570 to 1650. After the incident of the 'third style' architectural culture resumed the work of the selection of building types for the new city, in the new spirit of the Counter-Reformation. We shall discuss this further in the next chapter; meanwhile it is to be noted that, in the short term, stylistic features were exhausted in the infinite repetitions of this type, and that technical features became preponderant; at most, the dome remained to introduce a reference to date into an organism that was elementary and without history, particularly in the more modest examples. Thus the pursuit of the standard type hastened the winding up of the court repertoire of the 'third style'.

The field where the new generation of architects working in Rome obtained the most notable results was that of the laying out

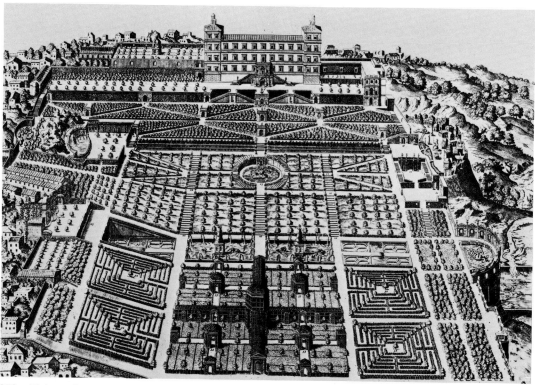

352 *Eighteenth-century engraving of the Villa d'Este, Tivoli*

of gardens. Starting from the models of the Belvedere by Bramante (designed in 1505) and the Villa Madama (designed in 1516) Giovanni Lippi designed the gardens of the Villa Medici (1544); Pirro Ligorio (c. 1500–83) designed the Villa d'Este at Tivoli (1550) (Fig. 352) and the *casina* for Pius IV in the Vatican (1558); Vignola, together with Ammannati and Vasari, designed the Villa Giulia (1551), then the Villa Farnese at Caprarola (1559) (Figs 353–6), the Villa Lante at Bagnaia (1578) (Fig. 357) and the Villa Aldobrandini at Frascati (1598) (Fig. 358). These schemes selected a limited portion of the natural environment, to be subjected to the rules of architectural symmetry, and in the following century, together with the Roman schemes – and the Tuscan ones of the same period which we shall discuss in chapter 4 – they were taken as an example by the whole of Europe, as the usual models for the architectural garden *all'italiana*.

But in the examples we have mentioned from Rome and Latium the need to impose an intellectual rule on nature was counterbalanced by the opposite need to incorporate these artificial schemes into the original landscape setting. Hidden, uneven spots were chosen, and often the architectural portion was a slender strip, like the upper garden of Caprarola, surrounded on all sides by the masses of the woods. In the most successful of these works, the Villa Lante at Bagnaia, there is a continuous gradation between the upper part, virtually incorporated into the side of the hill, and the lower part, rigidly designed and almost devoid of vegetation. At the extreme, the informal landscapes of Bomarzo and Pitigliano became possible, where the natural setting definitely predominated over the artificial modifications.

The fusion, figuratively highly successful,

353–355   *Aerial view of the Villa Farnese, Caprarola, and details of the upper garden*

356 *Detail from the upper garden of Villa Farnese, Caprarola*

357 *Aerial view of Villa Lante, Bagnaia*

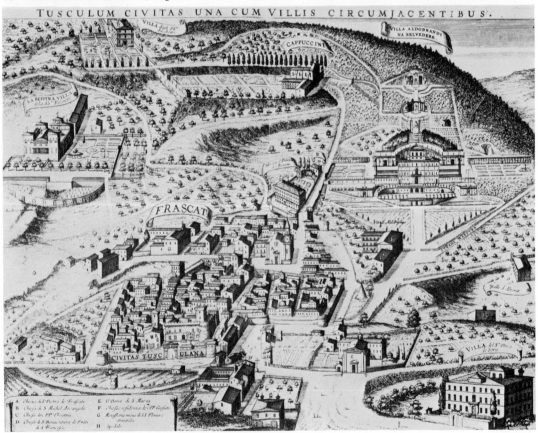

358 *Seventeenth-century print of Frascati and its villas*

359 *Detail of the monumental entrance to Zagarolo from Rome*

between aristocratic models, popular building types and natural environment produced no transformation in the urban or rural scene comparable to what happened in the Tuscan countryside around the towns, or in the Venetian plain; the aristocratic forms soon lost their orderly logic, and were absorbed into a timeless, unchanging scene. Neither palaces nor castles nor the marvellous gardens imparted a new character to, or suggested a new possibility of development for, the land where generations of peasants and shepherds were still performing the same labours and repeating the same patterns of life.

The repertoire of the 'third style' was evolved for a restricted class of people whose aim was to emphasize their hierarchical detachment from the lower classes and it was used as an instrument of social discrimination contrary to popular tradition and hence unrelated to the legacy of popular culture. It was used to introduce the Roman ruling class into the scene of international culture, but prevented the formation of a solid provincial culture that could have involved all social classes, even if hierarchically. Only a few miles from the site of St Peter's, the fervour of Roman cultural life left no trace and did not affect the life of the common people.

360   *An assembly of European rulers: print of 1501 with the apocryphal signature of Dürer.*
Bibliothèque Nationale, Paris

four

Urban changes in the sixteenth century

At the end of the fifteenth century the great European monarchies firmly asserted their power against the feudal political hierarchies.

In 1469 and 1474 the treaties between Ferdinand of Aragon and Isabella of Castile brought about the political unity of Spain; in 1483 Louis XI left to his successor Charles VIII – who was married to Anne of Brittany, heiress of the last independent feudal duchy – a united and pacified country; in 1485 the election of Henry VII put an end to England's dynastic wars; in 1486 the emperor Frederick III had his son Maximilian nominated king of the Romans; Maximilian succeeded him in 1497 and founded the European power of the house of Hapsburg with a shrewd policy of alliances.

The national monarchies fought over the possession of territories where the persistence of city powers had prevented the process of national unification, and where the wealth and civilization of the European world were still concentrated.

The successors of Louis XI – Charles VIII from 1494 to 1495, Louis XII in 1499 and in 1501, and François I in 1515 – came down into Italy, to vindicate the Angevin claim on the kingdom of Naples and imperial investiture for the duchy of Milan; the political balance set up in 1453 was upset, and the

alternative of alliances with France or Spain began for the Italian states in 1509; Venice, which was in a position to face foreign powers as an equal, was subjected to the attack of a European coalition in 1509, just at the most delicate moment of her struggle with the Portuguese for the possession of the trade routes to the East.

Maximilian married Maria, heiress of the Low Countries and feudal possessions still belonging to the house of Burgundy after the defeats of Charles the Rash. Maximilian took action to affirm the authority of the Hapsburgs and to eliminate municipal authority, and achieved his aim in 1492, after the surrender of Ghent: some years earlier, in 1488, he transferred the commercial privileges of foreign nations and the headquarters of the wool trade from Bruges – which was part of the Hanseatic League – to the free city of Antwerp; in 1490 Bruges obtained the restoration of its privileges, but the decline of the city and its outer harbour, buried by the sands of the Zwyn, was now definitive; in 1499 the *feitor* of the king of Portugal was established at Antwerp and spices brought from the East arrived here regularly coming round Africa by the long sea route. The commercial power of the Hansa received another blow in 1494, when Novgorod, terminus of the eastern caravan routes, fell into the hands of Ivan the Terrible.

Meanwhile geographical discoveries opened up new economic, political and cultural horizons to the peoples of Europe.

After the taking of Ceuta in 1415 the Portuguese began the exploration of the African coast and islands of the Atlantic; they settled in the islands of Cape Verde, Madeira and the Azores, and the Castilians settled in the Canaries, where they tried out their system of colonization for the first time. In 1479 Castile and Portugal shared out the zones of influence, the Portuguese keeping the southern part for themselves, for they were confident that here they would find the sea route to the Indian Ocean; in fact in 1487 Bartolomeo Diaz rounded the Cape of Good Hope, and opened up the new route to the Indies.

But the idea of the unity of terrestrial space – theoretically acquired some time ago – was already able to inspire other even bolder ventures. A letter written in 1474 by Paolo Toscanelli to a Portuguese canon, and a copy of the *Imago mundi* by Pierre d'Ailly, printed in Louvain in 1483, seem to have given Christopher Columbus the idea of setting off westwards to cross the Atlantic Ocean and reach the other shore, which was thought to correspond to the countries of the Far East.

In 1492 a map of the world by the geographer Martin Behain of Nuremberg showed the great ocean between Europe and Asia, open to the exploits of the navigators; but Christopher Columbus – who in 1491 received authorization from the Catholic kings at the camp of Santa Fé de Granada – had already set out from Palos, and disembarked in October on an unknown shore.

The information brought by Columbus to Europe caused further discussion about the zones of influence assigned to Spain and Portugal; the line of demarcation now had to be established according to the longitude, and was fixed in 1494, with the Treaty of Tordesillas, at 270 leagues to the west of the Azores.

In their respective zones, Spain and Portugal started to develop their colonial empires.

In 1497 Vasco da Gama set out from Lisbon with four ships, arrived in India and came back with the first cargo of spices; in 1500 Alvarez Cabral led a second expedition, which touched in at the coast of Brazil on its journey out; in 1520 Vasco da Gama led a whole fleet eastwards, armed with artillery, and started hostilities against the Arab ships which were carrying their cargoes of spices through the Red Sea and Persian Gulf, and from here over the land routes of Egypt and Syria, to the ports of the Mediterranean controlled by the Venetians.

In 1503 Alfonso d'Albuquerque arrived in India, at first as aide to the viceroy Francisco de Almeida and then himself as viceroy from 1512; Albuquerque built the first fortified Portuguese base in Cochin, seized the Arab trading stations of Socotra (1506) and Ormuz (1507) and destroyed the Arab fleet in battle in 1509.

At that time the Venetians were working on the ambitious plan for cutting through the Suez isthmus, to send a naval fleet to the east, but soon afterwards they had to contend with the league of Cambrai, and to use the accumulated capital to defend their positions on the mainland.

In 1510 Albuquerque founded the base of Goa, in 1511 he conquered the trade centre of Malacca, and secured command of the straits towards the Sunda islands; in 1513 he arrived in Canton, where he established the first relations with the Chinese Empire. Before his death, in 1515, he outlined a definitive plan to eliminate the competition of Egypt and the Arab world: he would bring, from the Azores, workers accustomed to digging work in the sugar industry, to dig a tunnel through the chain of Arabian mountains and to channel the Nile into the Red Sea; meanwhile he would organize a *coup de main* to steal the Prophet's body from Mecca, so that it could then be offered in exchange for the Holy Places in Palestine.

The programmes of the Spaniards in the new lands discovered by Columbus were differently orientated from the very start. Columbus' second expedition, which left in 1493, included seventeen ships without armaments or goods for barter, but carried 1,200 persons of different social categories to begin the colonization of the islands.

The organization of these dominions, at an enormous distance from the mother country, posed completely new problems. The first colonists settled in Hispaniola, where in 1496 they founded the town of Santo Domingo. In 1503 the Catholic kings created the Casa de Contratación in Seville, a centre for trade operations with the New World, and in 1511 the Council of Castile appointed the first committee, which in 1524 became the Council of the Indies. In Burgos in 1512 Ferdinand of Aragon laid down the laws for the new territories, and in 1515 Las Casas started the polemic on the criteria of colonization, which continued throughout the century.

Meanwhile Vasco Nuñez de Balboa conquered the isthmus of Darien, and gazed for the first time, in 1513, on the Pacific Ocean; Diego Velasquez occupied the island of Cuba in 1514, and in 1519 sent his lieutenant Hernando Cortés into the Mexican mainland. The new king, Charles V, reaped the benefits of the most important overseas ventures: between 1519 and 1522 Cortés was conquering the Mexican empire of the Aztecs, and in the same years Magellan made the first journey round the world; through the Pacific Ocean the Spaniards arrived in the East and fought the Portuguese for the possession of the spice islands. With the treaty of Saragossa of 1529 a new demarcation line was fixed 17° east of the Moluccas. Meanwhile the Spaniards continued with the conquest of the American continent: in 1528, starting from Mexico, an unsuccessful expedition explored the plains of north America; also in 1528 began the race for the discovery of the country of Eldorado, where Spanish captains

fought with the German agents of the Welsers; in 1532 Pizarro set out to conquer the empire of the Incas.

The new administrative organization instigated by the Council of the Indies gradually supplanted the authority of the *conquistadores*. In 1535 Charles V nominated the first viceroy of Mexico, and in 1542 that of Peru; he also promulgated a new body of laws; in 1551 he authorized the founding of two universities, in Mexico and in Lima.

These colonial enterprises forged a new link between the European governments and the great capitalists who financed them; capital interests became increasingly disengaged from national and local ones, thus speeding up the transformation of the old economic geography.

The ports on the Atlantic and North Sea became important as bases of the ocean routes, but their development depended on their relations with the hinterland. The presence of the Portuguese in Asia made a new ocean trade of oriental produce possible in competition with the traditional trade passing through the Mediterranean and controlled by the coastal cities of Italy; to this was added shortly afterwards the trade between Spain and the American colonies; but the products accumulated at Lisbon and Seville had to be transported to Antwerp to be sold on the European market, confirming the importance of Flanders as a commercial gateway to Europe. The cities of south Germany such as Augsburg and Nuremberg, situated halfway along the series of roads between Antwerp and Venice and near the mining centres of Bavaria, the Tyrol and Hungary, developed into economic centres of the greatest importance at this time; from here the Fuggers, Welsers and Höchstetters – like the Medici, Strozzi and Grimaldi of Florence and Genoa – controlled their financial empires which reached to the American frontiers and spice islands, and conditioned the politics of the kings.

As in the economy, the presence of the

Asian and American 'frontier' had a continual effect upon cultural life. The great spaces opened up by the explorers were places of economic and intellectual risk; they stimulated commercial calculation, philosophical speculation and the imagination.

The geographical discoveries had an immediate echo in the scientific and literary world, arousing a mixture of reasoning and fantasy. In 1493 there appeared the *Lettere dell'isola che ha trovato nuovamente il re di Spagna,* by Giuliano Dati; in 1500 the *De situ terrarum* by Antonio Ferrari related the newly discovered lands to the Platonic myth of Atlantis; in 1501 Amerigo Vespucci dedicated the epistle *Mundus novus* with its description of his voyages to Lorenzo, son of Piero de' Medici; in 1504 an extract of *De orbe novo* by Pietro Martire was printed in Venice, and it was published in full in 1530. In 1507 the work of Fracanzano da Montalboddo on the *Paesi nuovamente ritrovati* appeared in Vicenza; of this work five other Italian editions, six French and two German ones came out in quick succession, and in the same year Martin Waldseemüller published the account by Vespucci as an appendix to his *Cosmographiae introductio,* suggesting the name America for the new continent.

These works and the maps that went with them – such as Columbus' one of 1498 which was copied in 1513 by the Turkish cartographer Piri Reis – point out and vastly magnify the strangeness of the things found in the New World: monsters or mythical animals, such as the sirens encountered by Columbus, peoples living in a state of nature, without clothes and sometimes without heads: possibly the *gens beatissima* of which Pierre d'Ailly had talked a century before.

The explorations and conquests involved people of all kinds: unlettered adventurers like Pizarro, or ones with cultural ambitions like Cortés, monks educated at the school of Cardinal Cisneros, noblemen like Antonio de Mendoza, the first governor of Mexico, businessmen like Ehinger, Sailer and Federmann, the agents of the Welsers in Venezuela, philanthropists like Las Casas and saints like Francis Xavier. They sometimes found themselves exposed to extreme conditions of danger and conflict with the new environment, but also remained in contact with the mother country; they took the instruments of European culture to the New World, and brought to Europe an awareness of the ventures and changes experienced in the vast spaces of the distant continents.

Alvaro Nuñez Cabeza de Vaca, who led the unfortunate expedition to the plains of North America in 1528, told how for seven years he and two companions lived naked among the Indians, 'and since they were not used to it, they changed their skin twice a year, like snakes';[1] when in 1534 they returned to Mexico, they found it hard to reaccustom themselves to wearing clothes; five other members of the expedition, cut off from the rest, ate one another 'until there was only one left who, being alone, remained uneaten'.[2] But Villegaignon, the former fellow-disciple of Calvin who in 1555 organized an expedition into the bay of Rio de Janeiro, founded a fort where he remained with his companions for five years, not only observing all the forms of civilized life, but engaging in endless theological discussions while hunger, disease and hostile natives were making their position all but unbearable. Calvin sent ten Genevans, together with Jean Léry who was to write the account of the adventure, to prevent Villegaignon from straying from Protestant orthodoxy, and subsequently the settlers sent an emissary to Geneva, to ask Calvin to resolve certain controversial points. Villegaignon was on the verge of madness, the theologians – as happened in Europe – sent their adversaries to their deaths until in 1560 the fort was conquered by the Portuguese.[3]

During the conquest of Mexico Alvaro organized an ascent of Popacatepetl, the spontaneous nature of which made it a remarkable anticipation of the mountaineering feats of the late eighteenth century. In

1529 the court of Charles V at Toledo saw the meeting of Hernando Cortés, already covered with glory, and the unknown Francisco Pizarro, who obtained a decree of authorization for the conquest of Peru; the decree, like the laws so far promulgated, recommended just government and no violence against the natives. In 1535 Hernando Pizarro appeared before Charles V at Catalayud, and brought him news of the effected conquest; two years later in Peru the bloody succession of rebellions and vendettas began in which all the *conquistador* captains met their deaths, with the exception of Hernando Pizarro, locked up for life in a Spanish gaol. Meanwhile at the other end of the world, Francis Xavier left in 1541 for Asia, and began his work as an unarmed preacher, until his death in 1552 off the coasts of China, witnessed only by an Asian companion.

While the geographical frontiers of the Old World were vanishing, in Europe the frontiers of the political, religious and intellectual *status quo* were also fading. The balance between the nation states was broken in 1519 by the election of Charles V as emperor, and the ambitious programme of the young sovereign, heir of the Hapsburgs and Catholic kings, opened up a new series of conflicts. After the battle of Pavia the Italian political system collapsed; in 1527 the imperial army occupied and sacked Rome, in 1530 it overcame the resistance in Florence and wiped out the city institutions which had been in force since 1293.

Meanwhile in 1517 – one year before the critical edition of the New Testament with Erasmus' commentary in Basle and the publication of More's *Utopia* in Louvain – Luther presented his ninety-nine theses on indulgences at Wittenberg; in 1521 he was excommunicated by the Pope and outlawed by the emperor; in 1530 the Protestant schism became fact at the Diet of Augsburg; in 1534 the English schism occurred, in 1537 Calvin began preaching in Geneva. Erasmus died in 1536 without formally adhering to

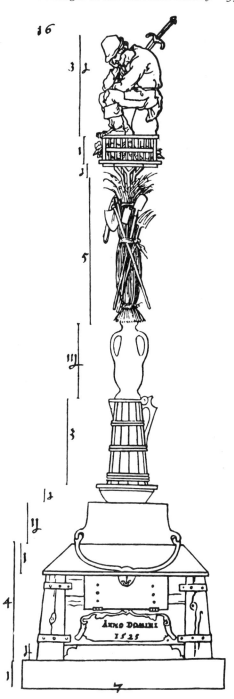

361 *Design by Dürer for a monument celebrating the repression of the peasants' revolt, 1525*

362   Portrait of Erasmus *by Hans Holbein the Younger*

363   Portrait of Luther *by Lucas Cranach*

either church; in the same year Paul III appointed the commission which in 1537 published the report *De emendenda ecclesia*, and prepared for a colloquy with the Protestants; the colloquy failed in 1541, at the Diet of Ratisbon, and the Roman church worked out the norms of individual and collective religion on its own account; in 1540 the Society of Jesus was set up, in 1545 the Council of Trent opened, and in 1548 the *editio princeps* of the spiritual exercises of Ignatius Loyola was published in Rome.

Before 1540 the whole first generation of the artists and writers who had dominated European cultural life disappeared: Raphael in 1520, Pomponazzi in 1524, Machiavelli in 1527, Dürer in 1528, Castiglione in 1529, Ariosto in 1533, Correggio in 1534, More in 1535, Erasmus and Lefèvre in 1536, Guicciardini in 1540; Luther, old and sick, lived on until 1546, in a world already greatly changed since the times of Wittenberg and Augsburg. But in the following decade the globe

designed by Mercator (1541), the *De revolutionibus orbium coelestium* by Copernicus (1543), the *De humani corporis fabrica* by Vesalius (1543), the *Cosmographia universalis* by Münster (1544), the *Ars magna* by Cardano (1545), the *De contagione et contagiosis morbis* by Girolamo Fracastoro (1546) and the *De re metallica* by Agricola (published posthumously in 1556) breathed new life into scientific and technical research.

This group of events, which marked the beginning of the modern age, offered new opportunities for ventures into town-planning, and abruptly modified the working conditions of architects and artists. As we shall see, the methodology of architecture emerges as one of the most stable elements of the sixteenth-century cultural system, and was pressured into change by the scope and breadth of its new applications, rather than by internal debate, which took place in scholarly circles.

The peripheral applications – and in

particular those taking place in the American colonies – appear more important and more instructive than those taking place in the ancient centres of European civilization. In Europe the persistence of the medieval schemes and scant effectiveness of the new ventures – due to the fragmentary nature of the political directives and the detachment of the artists from civil responsibilities – almost always limited the coherence of their urban realizations; in Asia and Africa the difficulties of maintaining stable settlements on terra firma restricted the scope of the new schemes from the start; but in the empty spaces of the American continent the spirit of initiative and steady legal continuity of the Spanish administration made possible a vast programme of urbanization and the invention of a new urban model, founded on the premises of perspective culture.

The poor quality of the colonial achievements, in comparison with the European ones, simply emphasizes the deficiencies and limitations of the latter, in comparison with the freedom and range of the schemes overseas.

In 1552, while Michelangelo, virtually unemployed, was moving from the façade of S. Lorenzo to the Medici tombs, the *xumétrico* Alonso Garcia Bravo, at the order of Cortés, designed and executed a new city on the ruins of the Aztec capital, which in 1552 according to Gomara had 100,000 houses. This parallel is sufficient to underline the disastrous distribution of energies produced by the circumstances of cultural, social and economic development at the beginning of the century.

The lack of co-ordination of ability and opportunity, between ideas and concrete experiment, was already irremediable a hundred years after Brunelleschi's revolution, and could only be diminished, not completely made good, in the future.

'Mannerism', i.e. the system of the culturally more distinguished experiments between about 1520 and 1630, becomes comprehensible only within the framework of this tension between centre and periphery, which already existed early in the century, while the episode of the 'third style' was under way. While Bramante, Raphael, Leonardo, Michelangelo, Giorgione and Titian were pushing the stylistic research begun in the fifteenth century to its extremes, a host of more modest artists and technical experts were at work to apply the models already defined literally, but on a vast scale, consciously or unconsciously selecting those that could be transmitted from those that could not.

As was the case in politics, the best energies were distributed far away from the most important commitments: hence the simultaneous crisis of élite experiments – progressively cut off from the changes under way – and mass experiments, which made only a minimal use of the models elaborated by the independent researchers.

The centres of political power

In France the structure of the settlements created and consolidated in the Middle Ages was preserved for the whole of the fifteenth century without important changes. Paris was the largest European city and remained one of the most important economic and cultural centres of Christianity; its development was due to the city's activities and institutions – the parliament, the university – not to the presence of the royal court, which in any case resided in the châteaux and small towns of the valley of the Loire. In the provinces the balance between town and country was based on an already highly developed agricultural economy, and land settlement could be regarded as having been stable for at least a century.

The political and administrative unification of the kingdom, achieved by Louis XI, was slow to produce effects in the field of town-planning and architecture; building activity, set solidly within the framework of

364 Portrait of François I. *Musée Condé, Chantilly*

the traditional guild pattern, depended on the organizations of the *maîtres maçons*, who combined the functions of designers, contractors and executors, and co-ordinated the activities of the *maîtres charpentiers, serruriers* and *couvreurs*. For the most important buildings they sometimes provided the *plan*, i.e. the ground plan, and the *pourtraict*, i.e. a depiction in elevation, but these operations were regarded as distinct from the execution and supervision of the works.

The collective organization of the master builders was strengthened by the links of kinship; there were positive dynasties, which operated for long periods – the families of Biart, Chambiges, Métezeau, Androuet du Cerceau, de Brosse, Lemercier, Mansart, de Cotte – from which the most important architects of the centuries to come were to emerge.

Religious architecture in particular remained linked to the Gothic models throughout the sixteenth century, and was barely touched, as far as its repertoire of ornaments was concerned, by the new Renaissance culture.

Contacts between France and Italy were fairly frequent in the fifteenth century, but only in the sphere of the figurative arts; Jean Fouquet worked in Rome for Eugene IV (1443–7) and he met Fra Angelico; Francesco Laurana worked in France from 1461 to 1466, and from 1475 onwards, as sculptor and medallist; Niccolò Spinello was at the court of Charles the Rash in 1468, then settled in Lyon where he died in 1499; Louis XI acquired a painting by Gentile Bellini in Venice, and in 1463 the abbot Guillaume Fillestre commissioned his tomb from the Florentine workshop of Andrea della Robbia. The French humanists travelled in Italy (G. Fichet in 1469 and J. Lefèvre d'Etaples in 1490 and 1499); and scholars from all over the world frequented the Sorbonne, as did Pico della Mirandola in 1487 and Erasmus in 1500.

From the end of the fifteenth century onwards the court became the main instrument of these cultural exchanges. After his Italian campaign Charles VIII took back with him in 1495 a large group of *ouvriers*, including the humanist Giovanni Lascaris, the sculptor Guido Mazzoni, the architects Fra Giocondo and Domenico da Cortona, the garden designer Pacello da Mercogliano, together with goldsmiths, cabinet-makers, tailors, embroiderers, velvet-cutters, a distiller of perfumes, a breeder of chickens and an organ-maker.

Fra Giocondo stayed in France from 1495 to 1505, working mainly as a hydraulic engineer, while Domenico da Cortona (1470–1549) and Pacello da Mercogliano (d. 1534) settled permanently at the French court and exerted an important influence on the French scene; Domenico taught the construction of wooden models of buildings and of apparatus for entertainments, where the images of the new architectural repertoire appeared for the first time; Pacello laid out the gardens of the royal residences at Amboise and Blois, and of Georges d'Amboise's château at Gaillon, initiating the series of French landscape schemes.

François I stressed the importance and complexity of life at court, and surrounded himself with Italians, beginning with his grand equerry G. A. Maraviglia; to his court came Luigi Alamanni, Matteo Bandello, Bernardo Tasso, Giovanni Rucellai and some of the most important Italian artists of the time: Leonardo in 1516, Andrea del Sarto and Girolamo della Robbia in 1518, G. B. Rosso in 1530, Francesco Primaticcio in 1532, Benvenuto Cellini in 1537, Vignola and Sebastiano Serlio in 1541.

Their presence brought about a vast movement of ideas, and hastened the maturing of the first generation of French designers involved in the new culture, which we shall discuss further. None the less until the middle of the century the artistic activities of the court consisted largely of the building of new residences, to house the sovereign and his train.

In 1493 Charles VIII showed the Florentine ambassador an ambitious project for the reconstruction of the château of Amboise; work began on it after his journey to Italy, and was broken off in 1498 at his death; Louis XII enlarged the château at Blois from 1499 to 1502; François I continued the work at

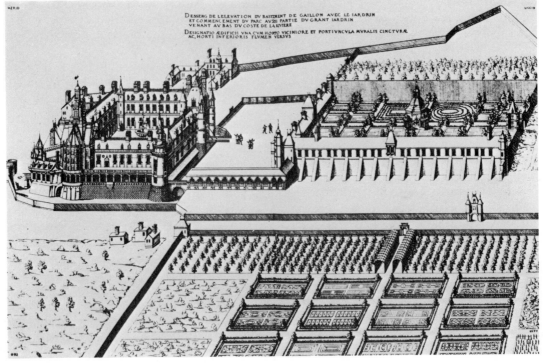

365 *Château of Gaillon (from du Cerceau)*

Blois, building a new open block with loggias looking towards the town (from 1515), and created a series of new residences, where the novel concepts of symmetry and regularity could be fully demonstrated: Chambord from 1519, the château de Madrid in the Bois de Boulogne from 1528, the château of St-Ange at Challuau from 1540, the château de la Muette at St-Germain-en-Laye from 1542; furthermore he enlarged the old royal châteaux of Fontainebleau (from 1527) and St-Germain (from 1532), where he was concerned with the regularization of their ground plans, and began the transformation of the Louvre, demolishing the old medieval *donjon* in 1528.

The example of the kings was followed by other patrons such as Georges d'Amboise, archbishop of Rouen, who had the château of Gaillon built in 1498 (Fig. 365), and by the families of the great financiers: Briçonnet,

Beaune, Robertet (who built the château of Bury from 1511), and Bohier who from 1515 built the château of Chenonceau, which spans the Cher on the piers of an old mill (Fig. 366).

It is interesting to see that all these works were due, as far as the actual building was concerned, to French *maîtres maçons* such as Pierre de Chambiges who worked on the royal sites after 1540; the Italian artists – Pacello da Mercogliano, Domenico da Cortona, Girolamo della Robbia, Francesco Primaticcio – were employed on decorative details and secondary schemes.

Hence a certain lack of engagement between structure as a whole and detail, which long remained typical of French court production; one exception, however, was the château of Chambord, one of the most remarkable of the buildings of François I which was born of a most complex and

366 *Aerial view of the château of Chenonceau*

singular set of circumstances (Figs 370–6).

The château stands in the middle of the royal forest of Chambord. The ground plan was not new, and was similar to that of the medieval château of Vincennes: a rectangle with corner towers, where one of the long sides is broken by the central *donjon*; this scheme was developed with rigorous symmetry, and based upon a precise geometrical outline: the overall rectangle is broken down into six squares, and the *donjon* occupies one of these, broken up in its turn by a cross-shaped central structure which isolates four square apartments at the four corners. The details are subordinated to the general effect; the design of the windows varies from floor to floor, to give an idea of gradation, but the spacing is repeated exactly at equal distances from the axis. The asymmetry reappears in the roof, peopled with chimneys and lanterns – built after 1530 – which use the Renaissance

decorative repertoire with inspired freedom. The axis of the building also commands the surrounding layout, and runs right into the forest, announcing the presence of the château from a great distance.

The master builders who worked at Chambord and are named in the documents – François de Pontbriand, then Jacques Sourdeau and Pierre Trinqueau – were certainly not the designers of this organism. Sourdeau did not know how to read or write, and could not even keep the books of the works. They must therefore have used a plan or model, which still existed at the time of Félibien[4] and which has been attributed to Domenico da Cortona, Girolamo della Robbia or Leonardo, who was designing the village of Romorantin at that time for the queen mother. None the less in the château of Chambord there is not so much an imitation of Italian models – much more obvious

367, 368 *The François I wing, Fontainebleau*

369 *Detail of Primaticcio's decorations in François I's gallery, Fontainebleau*

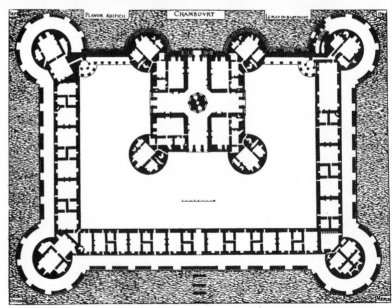

370–373 *The château of Chambord: aerial view, plan (from du Cerceau), the park as it is today and an axial view of the château from the park*

374–376   *Details of the château of Chambord*

in the later château de Madrid, Challuau and La Muette – as the anticipation of certain features of the architecture of the *grand siècle*: the extension of the perspective layout to the scale of landscape, the whole of the volume enlivened by the variety and subtlety of the details. Possibly the participation of Leonardo or the influence of his presence may explain so striking a glimpse into the future, which has no parallel anywhere in the first half of the century.

From the 1540s onwards a series of important changes occurred not only in the economic and social situation but also in the building sector.

Now, between the end of foreign wars and the beginning of the religious struggle, France was at a most prosperous moment of her history: Paris was once again the political and cultural centre of the country, from 1528 when François I returned to settle in the Louvre, and had as many as 300,000 or 400,000 inhabitants, a number which was to be halved by the end of the century; the court, according to Cellini, employed 18,000 persons and 12,000 horses.[5] The first effects of the monetary inflation produced by American silver caused the value of landed property to increase and therefore encouraged building and speculation; the king broadened the field of his building enterprises, which

377 *1530 map of Paris (known as 'the map with three figures')*

extended from the division into plots of the Hôtel St-Paul, in old Paris (1543), to the building of the new planned towns such as Le Havre (1541) and Vitry-le-François (1545); the great lords of the realm and the *haute bourgeoisie* intensified their building programmes according to their possibilities.

At the same time the first generation of French Renaissance architects was coming to maturity, men of the generation of Rabelais and sharers of his enthusiasm for the new culture, which was obliterating the habits of the past: Jean Goujon (c. 1510–c. 1565), Jacques Androuet du Cerceau (c. 1510–c. 1586), Philibert de l'Orme (c. 1515–70), Jean Bullant (c. 1510–78), Pierre Lescot (c. 1510–78).

This generation demanded primarily a precise rational organization of the new repertoire. G. Tory and Jean Martin spread the work of the Italian treatise-writers,[6] and Serlio finished writing his treatises in France, from 1541 to 1554.[7] Goujon designed the plates for the translation of Vitruvius' treatise published by Martin in 1547; from 1549 to 1576 du Cerceau prepared a series of illustrated handbooks, which made up a positive encyclopedia of the known classical buildings and modern ones built up to his time;[8] in 1561 de l'Orme published the *Nouvelles Inventions pour bien bastir*, subsequently rewritten in the *Premier Tome d'architecture* (1567–8) and Bullant published his treatise on the five orders in 1564.[9]

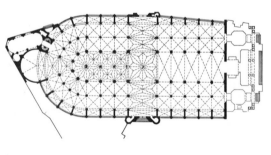

378–380   *St-Eustace, Paris (1532–89): detail of a doorway, exterior view and plan*

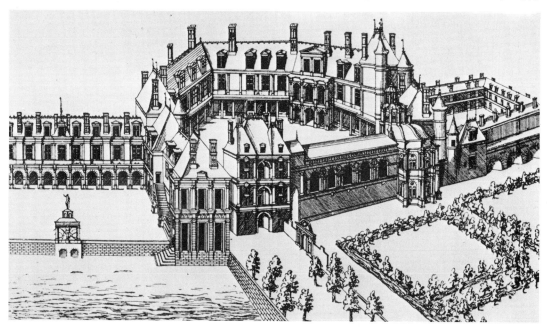

381 *The château of Fontainebleau (from du Cerceau)*

De l'Orme, the most perceptive of all, tried to synthesize both the legacy of the French master builders and the data of the new culture; he had a thorough knowledge of the monuments of antiquity and of Italy, where he had travelled between 1533 and 1536, but did not hesitate lucidly to criticize his models, with a systematic commitment reminiscent of that of Alberti (Figs 382–5).

This group of artists brought about the transition from the old professional condition of the *maîtres maçons* to that of the architect. They were no longer tied to the guilds, and were selected by clients for their individual prowess; furthermore they were involved in all aspects of architecture: they were not merely advisers or decorators – like the Italian artists summoned to court – but they had full responsibility for the building ventures on which they worked.

This change of position was felt above all in court building programmes. The king used *maîtres maçons* as designers and contractors, and appointed a superintendent who had under him supervisors and paymasters, all

382 *Imaginary building drawn by de l'Orme*

LIVRE VIII. DE L'ARCHITECTVRE

Iaçoit que toute la maifon cy-deuant métionnée, ne foit encores accompagnée d'vn corps d'hoftel que i'auois deliberé faire par le deuant fur la rue de la Cerifaye pres les Celeftins à Paris, fi eft-ce que ie ne lairray de vous mettre la face dudit corps de logis, que i'auois enuie d'y faire baftir, & l'euffe faict long temps a, fi Dieu m'euft prefté mon treffouuerain prince & bon maiftre le feu Roy Henry, de qui Dieu ait l'ame. Ie vous prefenteray donc la face dudit corps d'hoftel, à fin que vous cognoiffiez mieux la difpofition & ordre des portes & feneftres, comme auffi des enrichiffements qu'on leur peult donner, fans y faire grand ourage ne grand ordre de colomnes, auec leurs ornements. Eftant

Situation & bien d'vn logis propre à l'auteur.

fur

DE PHILIBERT DE L'ORME.   255

fur ces propos, volontiers ie môftrerois tout d'vne venue les mefures & departiments du dedans des logis comme ils doiuent eftre, mais ie me detournerois de ma deliberatiô, qui ne tend icy à autre fin, finon de vous monftrer, apres les portes, la conftitution & ordonnance des feneftres & lucarnes: ainfi que ie feray, Dieu aydant, & referueray la refte pour le fecond Tome de noftre Architeẽ, auquel ie vous donneray non feulement ce logis que i'ay faict faire pour moy à Paris, mais encores plufieurs autres de diuerfes fortes, foient pour les grãds, ou pour les petits, auec leurs plans & ce qui fera requis pour les cognoiftre.

Promeffe de l'auteur touchant le fecõd Tome de fon Architecture

383–385 *Drawings by de l'Orme from the* Architecture *and* Nouvelles Inventions pour bien bastir: *the architect's own house in Paris and the allegory of the bad architect*

belonging to the administration. Some Italian artists had received the title of royal architect, for instance Serlio in 1541 for Fontainebleau, but without any precise function. But in 1546 Lescot was appointed superintendent of the building work at the Louvre; in 1548 de l'Orme received the title of inspector of royal building at Fontainebleau, Villers-Cotteret, Yerres and the Bois de Boulogne, and in 1550 the title of superintendent of all royal buildings; in 1559 Primaticcio received the same title from Catherine de' Medici, and the royal example was followed by the great families like the Montmorency who employed Primaticcio and Bullant.

Thus architects replaced the old super-intendents, while the organizations of the master builders acted as contractors and helped to group the various categories of workmen.

The results of this new division of labour were limited at first; throughout the second half of the century the wars of religion and economic difficulties prevented any real development of building programmes, either by the court or by private individuals. Some organizational procedures, however, were established, and these were to be fully exploited during the following century.

In the other great power, which was fighting with France for European domination – Spain – a very different situation was to be found. The political unification of the country had been achieved only in 1469, through the marriage of Isabella and Ferdinand, and the Catholic kings completed the conquest of their national territory, taking the last Arab capital, Granada, in 1492.

The state of permanent war and scant economic development prevented any important building activity throughout the fifteenth century; but military requirements made it possible for the central power to co-ordinate building ventures closely; during the last campaign against the Moors, the Catholic kings founded two new cities: Puerto Real on the bay of Cadiz (1483) and Santa Fé (1492), the fortified camp at the gates of Granada which became a permanent settlement (Fig. 386). These town organisms were originally conceived as both strategic bases and centres of settlement; the plans echoed those of the medieval *bastides* founded here and in southern France, in similar circumstances: Puente de la Reina (1121), Sangüesa (1122), Castellon de la Plana (1251), Villareal (1272 (Fig. 387)), Briviesca (1314).

This experimentation in town-planning was interrupted during the economic depression of the fourteenth century and the beginning of the fifteenth; but theoretical interest in these problems continued in Spain for at least a century.

Between 1382 and 1586 the Franciscan Eximenics composed an encyclopedia, *El crestia*, in which one chapter is entitled *Quina forma deu haver ciutat bella e be edificada*;[10] the city must be square, with sides of a thousand feet, and divided into four districts by two straight roads; in each district there was to be a square, and in the centre the main square, with the cathedral and bishop's palace.

The humanist Rodrigo Sanchez de Are-valo, ambassador to various European courts, wrote the *Suma de la politica* from 1454 to 1455, at the time of Alberti's treatise, and explained '*como deben ser fundadas e edificadas las ciudades e villas*' (how towns and cities should be founded and built).[11]

Thus the medieval tradition and the theoretical propositions of the new culture came together in the undertaking of the Catholic kings; we must remember these experiments, and the orderly spirit that pervaded them, when we discuss the cities founded in the New World.

At the beginning of the sixteenth century, and particularly with the advent of Charles V, building activity increased. The new king, brought up in the Low Countries, alive to the rational programmes of the most advanced European culture, found a country that was still medieval, with small, isolated towns and almost devoid of communications. He, too, like the French kings, did not choose a capital, but moved from Toledo to Granada, Valladolid, Burgos. Everywhere he was eager to build palaces, churches, schools, hospitals, town halls, exchanges, to regularize roads and squares and above all to create an efficient network of means of communication.

These activities stood out clearly in the fabric of Spanish cities, which generally retained their tortuous and disjointed Moslem plans. Sixteenth-century intellectuals were disconcerted by and alien to such cities, which retained their structures tenaciously,

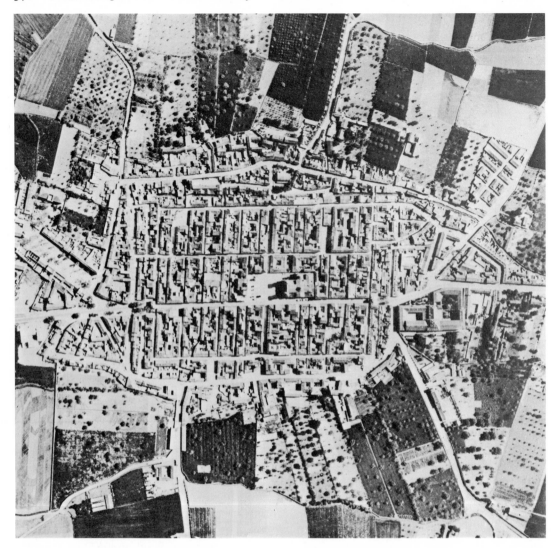

386, 387   *Aerial view of Santa Fé de Granada (from Reps) and plan of Villareal (from Gutkind)*

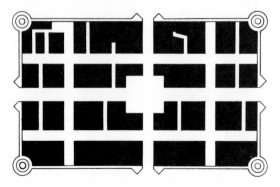

closely linked as they were with the people's habits. 'The Moors are accustomed to living in great privacy and seclusion', noted the Venetian ambassador Andrea Navagero in 1525;[12] 'all the architecture is within the body of the houses, with no care for the exterior', observed Alonso Morgado, who wrote the *Historia de Sevilla* in 1587.[13] The new building activities broke up this environment with their orthogonal layouts and the importance they attributed to external volume. In Granada Charles V settled in the Alhambra, and in 1527 had a new palace built within the

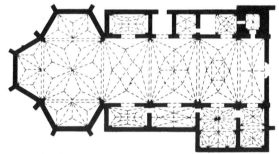 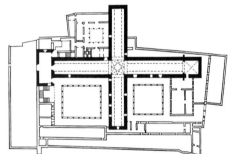

388–391 *Toledo: view painted by El Greco; plans of S. Juan de los Reyes (1479) and of the hospital of Santa Cruz (1504) and a panorama of 1574 by Braun*

Alcázar, in pedantically Renaissance forms (though he avoided tampering with the medieval palace, and had the royal baths restored for his use) (Figs 392–4; in Cordova a new cruciform chapel was fitted into the mosque, towering above the horizontal stretches of the Arab roofs with its bulk (Figs 395–7).

Elsewhere the new activities were better integrated into the original setting; this was the case with the university city of Alcalá de Henares, where Cardinal Cisneros built the university (1496–1508) and founded seven religious houses, which fitted smoothly into the city fabric and created a series of squares with appropriate setbacks. The city bore the mark of the prelate's cultural commitment: he effected the reform of the monastic schools, from which the élite of the Spanish clergy emerged, open to the humanitarian ideas of Erasmus and active in the first phase of American colonization.

In these buildings the stylistic repertoire was only a tenuous covering, independent of the character of the organisms and linked rather to religious or political considerations.

The Fleming Juan Guas brought the Renaissance decorative repertoire to Spain about 1450, combining it with the late Gothic and Arabic. Around the end of the century Lorenzo Vasquez, who may have travelled in Italy, designed the first architecture inspired by the Italian, such as the Medinaceli palace in Cogolludo in 1492.

At the beginning of the sixteenth century these contributions combined in a special decorative synthesis, which has been called the Plateresque, and is considered characteristic of Spanish architecture of the first half of the century; in reality until 1540 four types of decorative finish co-existed: Plateresque, traditional late Gothic, classical and Arabic (which made use of *mudejar* labour and was known as the Cisneros style).

In 1530 Diego de Riaño presented the designs of rooms in three different styles to the chapter of Seville cathedral: Gothic, Plateresque and classical. The progressive ideas which were in fashion at the court of Charles V at this time were interpreted by Diego de Siloe (1495–1563), who in 1528 designed the new cathedral of Granada: a late Gothic organism with nave and two pairs of aisles, leading into a rotunda with a double ambulatory; the rotunda was a version of the usual Spanish *chevet*, possibly influenced by knowledge of Alberti's design for the Tempio Malatestiano and the Annunziata, and by the humanistic symbolism of the religious spirit of Erasmus (Fig. 398); at the centre was the altar with the eucharistic sacrament which was now to dominate the city freed from Moslem dominion. None the less Siloe's Renaissance plan worried Charles V, who suspended work on it in 1529 and summoned Siloe to Toledo to justify himself: indeed side by side with the cathedral there is the Gothic chapel with the tombs of Ferdinand and Isabella, and the stylistic innovation produced a political reaction.

In the middle of the sixteenth century, when the prince Philip (born in 1527) began to direct building activity, classicism became the official style for public works, both in Spain and in the Spanish dominions.

When he became king, Philip II fixed the capital at Madrid in 1561, but chose to have his residence in the heart of the Guadarrama, where he commissioned Juan Bautista de Toledo to build the Escorial; here, a single block of buildings accommodated a monastery, a palace for the court, a church and the mausoleum of Charles V (Figs 399–403).

Toledo had been staying in Italy, where he had been director of the viceroy's buildings in Naples and had known the chief Roman architects; he returned to Spain in 1559 at the king's request, and in 1562 began the building of the royal residence; before his death, in 1567, he established the general plan of the building and executed the whole southern façade and one of the courtyards, determining the bleak and geometrical character of the external architecture.

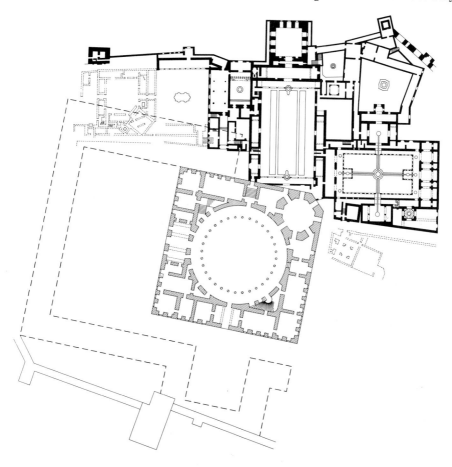

392–394 *The palace of Charles V incorporated into the Alhambra, Granada (no. 11 in the plan)*

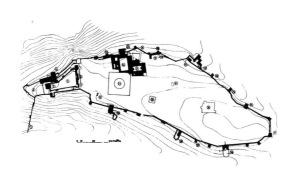

395 *The Mosque at Cordova with the sixteenth- century church introduced into the centre*

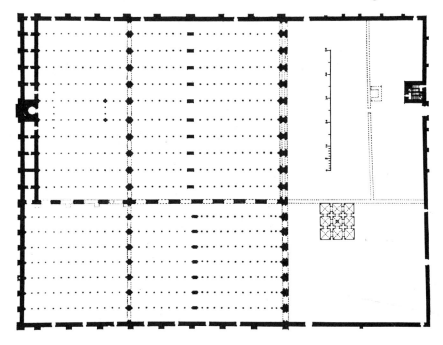

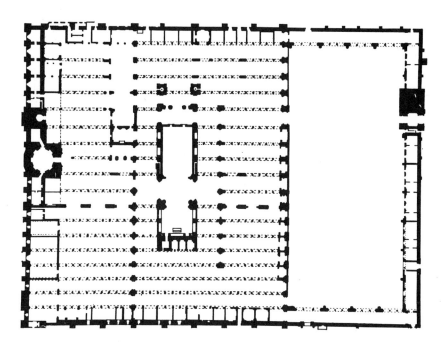

396, 397 *Original plan and present-day plan of the Mosque at Cordova*

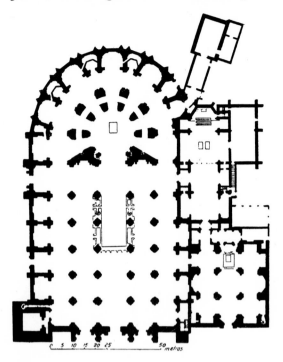

398   *Plan of Granada cathedral*

Juan de Herrera (1530–97) began his career in 1563 at the Escorial, as Toledo's assistant; he had been with Philip II in Italy and Flanders, and with Charles V at Yuste. He became director of works at the Escorial in 1572, replacing the Italian G. Castello; he improved the organization on the site and built the infirmary and central church. For this Philip II, not satisfied with Toledo's plan, announced a sort of competition among the best Italian architects, including Alessi, Tibaldi and Palladio, but then turned to Herrera, who chose a central plan with an inscribed cross, derived from St Peter's and possibly more immediately from S. Maria di Carignano in Genoa, built by Alessi about the same time.

This skilfully proportioned building unified the great mass of the palace, and was as advanced as anything in European architecture of the time, not excluding the Italian.

Relations have been shown to exist between Herrera and Palladio, from whom Herrera received a number of points of inspiration and also the idea for several technical expedients. Like his contemporaries de l'Orme and Lescot in France, he was the first Spaniard fully to embody the new professional condition of the Renaissance architect; he combined an undoubted technical competence with a cultured and indeed positively erudite background, which earned him a reputation for being 'obscure and metaphysical'.[14] In his later works he established the canonic types of Spanish public buildings, long to be repeated: the *villa suburbana* of Aranjuez (1567), the Seville Casa Lonja (1582) (Fig. 437), Valladolid cathedral (1585); here he created a church with nave and two aisles that was symmetrical in both directions, i.e. broken by a transept and dome halfway along its length, and with a rectangular ending.

Similarly the Escorial was the prototype of monastic building which became a typical form of addition to Spanish cities from the late sixteenth century onwards; both the king and other dignitaries – for instance the duke of Lerma at the beginning of the seventeenth century – built many in the cities and countryside alike, adding a characteristic element to the Spanish countryside.

At this time the first large-scale schemes in accordance with the classical canons were carried out, and in particular the *plazas mayores*: the first was that of Valladolid, rebuilt in 1561 after a fire; there followed those of Toledo (1590) and Madrid (1617). But these schemes must be considered in relation to the American ones which preceded the Spanish and were possibly the real models for what was done in the mother country after the middle of the century.

America afforded boundless opportunities for Spanish building and town-planning to produce its most important results from the beginning of the sixteenth century, and we shall shortly discuss this more fully.

399, 400 *General view of the Escorial and plan of the monastery*

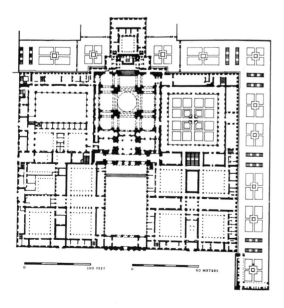

Events in the two great powers, France and Spain, were repeated in smaller measure in the other countries of Europe. The courts were the first to feel the impact of Italian Renaissance culture, which was on the way to becoming the international culture as far as the courts were concerned.

In Portugal at the beginning of the century the national style, used for all court undertakings, was a national variant of late Gothic, which was called the Manueline style. Italian contributions became prevalent only in the middle of the century, in the works of Diego de Torralva (1500–66) and later of the Italian Filippo Terzi (1520–97), of the same generation as Herrera; but they were balanced by Flemish contributions, which derived from

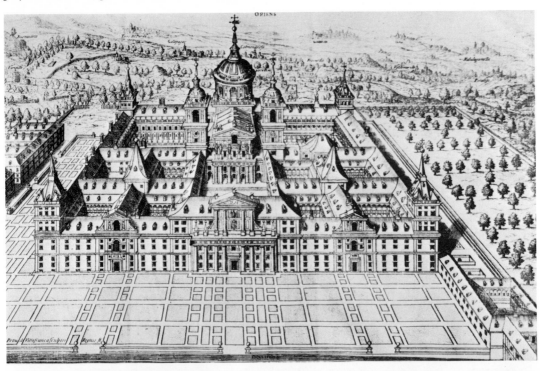

401–403 *Sixteenth-century print of the Escorial, a detail of the interior and the façade of the monastery*

404–407 *Two views of the courtyard of Heidelberg castle in the sixteenth century (engravings from Kraus), the city and the castle (engravings from Merian)*

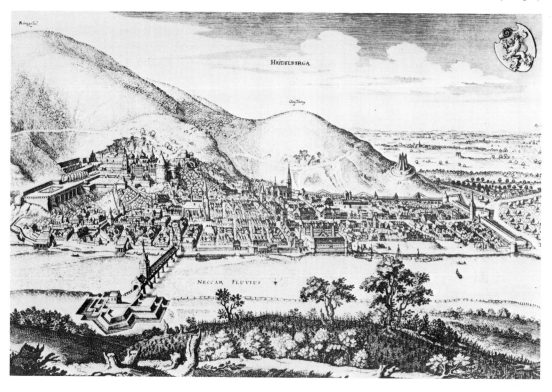

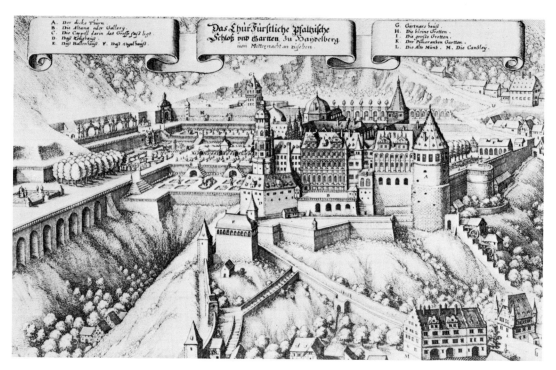

408 *A plate from W. Dietterlin's* Architectura, *1598*

409 *Illustration from W. Jamnitzer's* Perspectiva corporum regularium, *1568; the themes of Italian figurative culture are developed beyond all traditional measure*

Atlantic trade and were important mainly in the north of the country.

In England court architecture long remained faithful to the Perpendicular; some of the most important works in this style such as St George's chapel at Windsor (completed in 1516) and the oldest part of Hampton Court (completed by Henry VIII in 1536) were contemporaneous with the buildings of Bramante and Peruzzi. Later, after the schism, Italian influence was equally limited for nationalistic reasons.

Italian artists worked in Germany, Poland, Hungary and even Russia and, after the middle of the sixteenth century, a limited group of artists grew up in these countries initiated in the classical repertoire. Many of them felt the need to catalogue this repertoire, which in the middle of the sixteenth century seemed no less exotic than the oriental; such catalogues were written by Coeck in 1550,[15]

Floris from 1548 to 1557,[16] de Vries from 1560 onwards[17] and Dietterlin in 1598 (Fig. 408).[18]

No mediation yet seemed possible between classicism and local traditions, apart from a clever admixture of decorative ingredients which sometimes produced positive eclecticism.

The delicate balance between court and popular values, partially achieved in some urban schemes in the second half of the fifteenth century – as in Urbino, Ferrara and Mantua – was completely lost abroad. The classical repertoire became an emblem of power, all the more effective in so far as it was remote from the popular one. Thus the different styles coexisted for a long time, in some cases until the baroque age and threshold of the industrial revolution.

Meanwhile economic and organizational development offered new subjects for build-

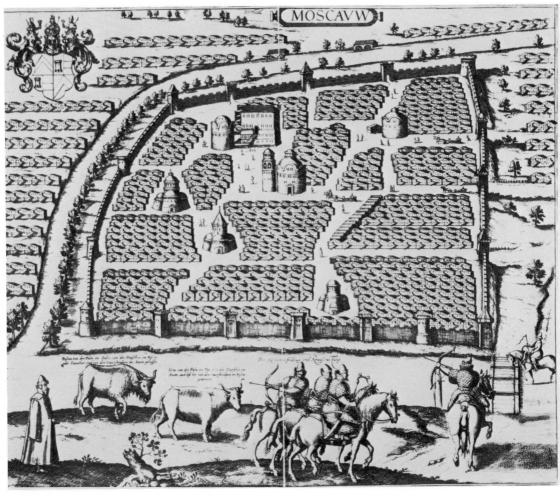

410 *View of Moscow (from Jansonius)*

ing, which could be tackled only with the means of the new artistic culture. This was the case with the new towns founded for strategic reasons, with the ports and canals, or with the landscaped schemes which completed royal or noble residences. Here the new methods of planning produced their most notable and eloquent results, though independent even here of the stylistic details.

This lack of contact persisted until the late seventeenth century, as we shall see in chapter 7.

The centres of economic power

The power of kings and courts was balanced by that of bankers and traders, which was concentrated in a few cities, cornerstones of the new economic geography.

The development of these cities produced a series of building and town-planning ventures different from those examined hitherto. The courts adopted the classical repertoire as a token of power, but had to resolve the conflict with the national traditions of which they felt themselves to be custodians and which they utilized as marks of independence.

Economic power did not know this kind of conflict. Large-scale capitalists operated in every part of the world, uncurbed by local limitations, and remained largely indifferent – at least in the first half of the century – to the demands of ostentation. Some capitalists like the Fuggers adopted the forms of classicism as symbols of social advancement – for instance in their private dwellings and tombs – but always with moderation, and in a solidly conservative context. Economic power used these instruments of the new figurative culture in so far as they were of use in resolving the problems imposed by progress in production: infrastructures (roads and ports), utilitarian buildings (warehouses, stores and exchanges), new urban districts or indeed new towns; therefore, practically, it selected from artistic culture the aspects connected with scientific and technical progress, combining them with those traditional processes that could be utilized with profit.

Thus the building and town-planning schemes fostered by economic power – in Augsburg, Antwerp, Lisbon, Lyon, Seville, Genoa and in other commercial centres of the Old World – depended upon two factors: medieval methods of intervention, adjusted and rationalized on the basis of new planning models.

In these schemes – as in some of the more important works promoted by political power – the synthesis of the two factors was effective, though it did not actually manage to produce a uniform and imitable praxis.

The centres of economic power, in the Europe of the sixteenth century, were those listed at the beginning of this chapter: Augsburg, situated at the junction of the trade routes between Italy and Flanders with the Piedmontese routes leading to the mining centres of the Tyrol and Silesia, and which became the headquarters of the most important German capitalist enterprises; Antwerp, where traffic from the Atlantic was unloaded on to the European market; the Spanish and Portuguese cities, starting-points for the routes to America and the Indies, i.e. Lisbon and Seville; the French cities near the Channel, especially Rouen, with the new outer harbour of Le Havre at the mouth of the Seine; Lyon, where the trade and industries of southern France were concentrated; Genoa and Messina, the two main Italian ports involved in the economy of the Spanish empire. Side by side with these the traditional centres of medieval economic life – Paris, Ghent, Lubeck, Venice, Florence – retained their importance and we shall say more about them later on; but their building structure remained largely as it had been in the previous centuries.

Augsburg

As early as the fifteenth century Augsburg was one of the richest cities in Germany; Aeneas Silvius Piccolomini in his *Commentarii* praised the comfort of the houses and elegance of the women.[19] At the end of the fifteenth century Augsburg was the most important commercial and industrial centre of southern Germany: it sold goods to Venice for a million ducats, had 6,000 weavers and a large number of printing works. In 1497 it had 17,000 inhabitants, and in 1526 a little over 21,000, but within this interval the wealth of the inhabitants – indicated by the tax revenue – had increased roughly tenfold. The painters' guild included Hans Holbein the Elder and Hans Burgkmair, the painter of the Fuggers and the emperor Maximilian; among the humanists were Clemens Sender and Conrad Peutinger, the Welsers' son-in-law.

In the first decades of the sixteenth century Jacob Fugger, the omnipotent banker of Charles V and Leo X, exercised a supremacy in Augsburg similar to that of the Medici in Florence: in 1509 he financed the building of the family chapel in the church of St Anne, with the tombs which were the first classical

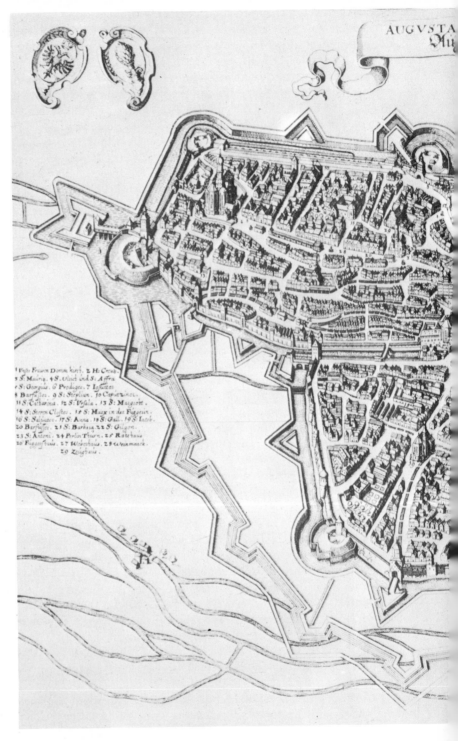

411   *View of Augsburg, 1643 (from Merian)*

ELICORUM.

LECH FLVVIVS.

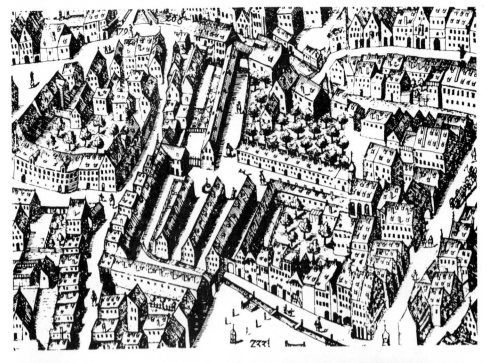

412, 413   *The Fuggerei, Augsburg, in an engraving of 1626 and today*

414 *The main crossroads in the Fuggerei*

compositions to be executed in Germany, though they were housed under a late Gothic rib-vault. In 1511 on the Weinmarkt – the business street of the old city – he began to build the new Fugger palace, severe and traditional in appearance, with frescoes on the outside by Burgkmair (to a scheme dictated by Peutinger) and furnished with unusual comfort. A contemporary man of letters commented: 'Inside and out it is all decorated with pictures, and though everything is of the greatest value one rarely notes a sense of excessive show, but on the contrary a pleasing taste and moderation in display.'[20]

He had a house and garden built near the walls of the city, which the same writer considered preferable to that of the king of France at Blois;[21] 'here there are fountains', observed another contemporary, 'from which water is taken up to the rooms by means of a system of gears'.[22] Far from Augsburg, the banker even entered into competition with the emperor, building the castle of the Weissenhorn in 1513 and acquiring from Maximilian the castles of Schmiechen and Kirchberg; these he had impressively restored, and since the sovereign retained the right of redemption, Fugger claimed that in such an eventuality he should be reimbursed for the expenses; naturally Maximilian and his successors, always short of money, were never in a position to exercise their feudal right and the castles remained the definitive property of their new owner.

415   *The Weinmarkt, Augsburg, from the Perlach tower; in the background, on the right, the Fugger palace*

In 1514 Jacob Fugger instigated the last extension to the medieval city – in the suburb of St James; here, between 1519 and 1523, he built the Fuggerei (Figs 412–14), a district of 106 terraced houses, surrounded by a wall and provided with various amenities: a fountain, a school, a church (built in 1581). This complex was similar to the Dutch *béguinages*, but was built for workers' families and appeared as a model district integrated into the city.

The foundation deed of 1521 says:[23]

'These houses must be given freely in praise and honour of God to those pious workers and artisans, burghers and inhabitants of the city of Augsburg, who are in need and who are the most deserving. Each community of tenants must pay annually, for maintenance, one Rhenish florin as a guarantee that each shall put in order anything he may have broken. Furthermore each individual, young or old, as he is able, must say a Pater noster, an Ave Maria and a Credo every day for the founders and their ancestors and descendants.'

The spirit of this venture still seems medieval; the Fuggers registered an account in the name of St Ulrich, patron of the city, and from this they withdrew the capital for the building of the district. On the stone over the main entrance we read that the Fuggers

'in consideration of the fact that they were born for the common good and that they owe their very great fortunes above all to the Most High and Clement Lord to whom they must indeed be rendered, out of piety and individual liberality, serving as an example, they have given, donated and dedicated this foundation to their poor but worthy fellow citizens.'

None the less the Fuggerei is rightly considered the first example of subsidized building in Europe. The development of the great capitalists brought about the formation of a vast urban proletariat; the number of

416 *Detail of the fountain of Augustus, Augsburg*

people owning no property increased from 40 to 54 per cent in the first quarter of the sixteenth century. The logic which was to lead the industrialists of the nineteenth century to create their workers' districts was clearly anticipated here; in fact economic development assigned certain public responsibilities to the entrepreneur, and these could be satisfied, to some small extent, in accordance with the forms of private liberality.

417   *The fountain of Hercules, Augsburg, in Merian's engraving*

Bildnús des Zierlich vnnd Schönen Brunnens, auff
dem Perlach in Augspurg.

I.
IMP. CÆ. S
DIVI. F
AVGVSTO
PARENTI
COLONIA
AVGVSTA
VINDEL .

II.
POSITA
ANNO. A. CHRNATO
MD. XCIII.
IMP. CÆ. S. RVDOL,
PHO. P. F AVG.

III.
ANNO.
A. COL.
DED.
MDCV.
IOANVEL
SERVS .
IIVIR.
PROBA.
VIT.

FONS AMPLISSIMVS REIPVBLICÆ AVGVSTANÆ.
ANTE IPSAM CVRIAM POSITVS .

418 *The fountain of Augustus, Augsburg, in Merian's engraving*

419 *The fountain of Hercules, Augsburg, today*

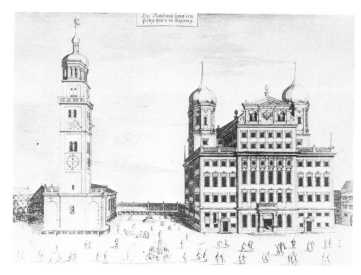

420 *The Rathaus and Perlach tower, Augsburg (engraving by Merian)*

The plan of the Fuggerei is simple and schematic, with roads intersecting at right-angles; the irregularities derive from the random course of the boundaries of the property. This very orderliness was something new, noted by contemporaries, and it has been suggested that the initial idea came from Dürer, who stayed in Augsburg in 1518.

Thomas Krebs, the superintendent of the work on the Fuggerei, also built workers' houses for Jacob Fugger in Georgethal and other mining centres run by the Augsburg house.

Jacob died in 1525, and the prosperity of the Fuggers, Welsers, Höchstetters and Augsburg capitalists generally declined in the middle of the century, especially after the first bankruptcy of Philip II in 1557. But the city remained one of the richest centres in Germany, had 50,000 inhabitants, and during the first years of the seventeenth century, at the threshold of the Hundred Years' War, was beautified by a series of public works which defined its appearance once and for all.

Between 1593 and 1599 the Flemish artists Hubert Gerhard and Adrien de Vries, a pupil of Giambologna, built the three fountains of the emperor Augustus, Hercules and Mercury, imitated from Italian models (Figs 416–19). Soon afterwards Elias Holl (1573–1646) began his career, and the municipal authorities commissioned him to carry out a vast programme of public works: the arsenal (1602), the school of St Anne (1613), the top part of the Perlach tower (1614), the new town hall (1615), the hospital of the Holy Spirit (1626) and the new town walls and monumental gates (Figs 415, 420).

Holl simplified and clarified the complicated repertoire of Renaissance architecture that had spread throughout Germany in the late sixteenth century; though times had changed, these works remained collective creations, carefully considered and not over-personalized. The spirit of the new century emerged rather in the emphasis of some ceremonial aspects, for instances, the Goldene Saal of the town hall which protrudes from the volume of the building and interrupts the uniform spacing of the windows with a more elaborate motif.

In 1632 the city was besieged and conquered by Gustavus Adolphus, in 1637 it was retaken by the imperialists: war interrupted building development and after the Peace of Westphalia Augsburg became once again a peaceful provincial town, with its wealth of monuments and memories.

421   Death the Strangler, *by Hans Burgkmair*

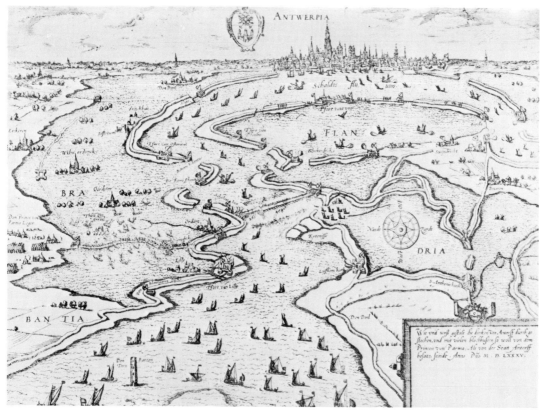

422   *The estuary, Antwerp, in a sixteenth-century print*

Antwerp

In 1488, as we have said, Maximilian transferred the commercial privileges of Bruges to Antwerp. A few years afterwards, in 1496, there were 6,000 houses in Antwerp and 68,000 inhabitants; the city was contained within the walls of 1410, and was rectangular in shape, with one side along the estuary of the Scheldt.

The next census, in 1516, enumerated 8,785 houses and 87,000 inhabitants; at this point there began the building activity which within fifty years transformed the city into the most modern trading port in Europe.

In 1515 Dominicus de Wagemaker built the Exchange; in 1521 the top part of the cathedral tower was begun; it was completed in 1530 and dominated the two expanses of city and harbour; in 1531 the same architect

built a much more important building for the Exchange, with an arcaded courtyard (Fig. 423). Meanwhile the city was growing beyond the 1410 limits; in 1540 Charles V brought an Italian expert to Antwerp, Donato Pellizuoli from Bergamo, to build a new circle of fortifications; he also designed the monumental gates, including that of St Joris, on the road to Malines, opened by the emperor in 1545. But the building up of the new land included in this perimeter went ahead slowly, and Charles V's sister, Mary of Hungary, governor of the Low Countries, turned to Gilbert van Schoonebeke (1495–1560), a remarkable planner and entrepreneur who had grown up in the mood of the economic boom. In 1548 Mary suggested to the administration that they should sell the crown lands and acquire the land involved within

423–425   *The Antwerp Stock Exchange in a sixteenth-century print; the Grote Markt and a view of the city with the new district on the right (from F. Guicciardini, 1567)*

the area of expansion, to sell it off subsequently to the builders. Van Schoonebeke prepared two plans, one with all the necessary land, the other with only crown property, plus three hundred *verges* to be acquired in any case. Mary put the plans to the administration, then drew up a contract with van Schoonebeke, who was to divide the land into lots and sell the municipal sites in person, paying out a fixed sum of 300,000 florins (Fig. 425).

We know these circumstances from the letters patent of Charles V of 1549, which ratify the pledge taken.[24] Van Schoonebeke carried the operation ahead with success; the land for the zone of expansion was divided into plots according to a geometrical plan, which was dependent upon the three canals running off the estuary of the river; here were

built not only houses but commercial premises, such as the twenty-four breweries built by the same entrepreneur along a single road, and provided with water by means of a hoisting apparatus (the Waterhuis) which is still one of the curiosities of Antwerp.

Van Schoonebeke also worked in the old city and its surroundings; at the border between the medieval nucleus and the extension of 1540, he organized a public weighbridge system; near the eastern edge, on a still unoccupied piece of land, he opened up a square for the corn market, which became the centre of a small district on a grid plan; near the river he opened up the Friday market square, regularizing here too adjacent roads and blocks of buildings. In 1546, along the road to Malines, he acquired a piece of land where he built a district of noblemen's

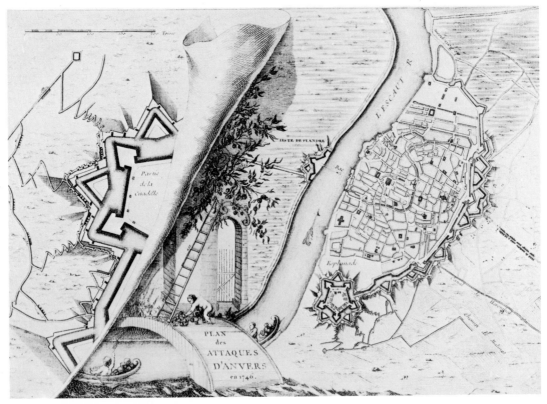

426 *Plan of Antwerp in 1746*

houses along a tree-lined avenue (Fig. 426); in the contract the various owners were obliged to plant rows of trees twenty steps apart, to preserve the green nature of the area.

For these ventures – which established a new relation between public works and piecemeal development, and anticipated almost all the activities typical of the bourgeois cities of the nineteenth century – van Schoonebeke was given the title of *Meliorator van de stad Antwerpen*, and worked in complete accord with the city's authorities. The forces of political and administrative power were not in a position to realize such sweeping ventures as the extension of Amsterdam without committing themselves to the new mechanisms of private enterprise.

Furthermore van Schoonebeke did nothing more than extend to the field of building the speculative systems which had created the economic prosperity of Antwerp, and which had therefore created the needs which his schemes answered. This approach emerges in the rigorous and almost mechanical character of his plans; the sixteenth-century extension was the fifth in the history of the city, and was distinguished not by any desire to put other aesthetically more up-to-date models beside traditional ones, but by the new systematic spirit which rationalized and standardized the old procedures of intervention. Thus the novelty is more evident in maps than in the appearance of the urban environment, contrary to what happened in many schemes originated by the various courts, where the whole characterization lay in the details, while the organisms were based upon models from the past.

Soon after the middle of the sixteenth century Antwerp achieved the peak of its prosperity. The Venetian ambassador Marino Cavalli, in 1551, wrote in his report:[25]

'Antwerp does so many deals in exchanges and every kind of trade, that in truth I am amazed at the sight, thinking that it may outstrip this city [Venice]. In all places money flows to such an extent, and the sale of all things is so brisk, that there is no man, however low and idle he may be, who is not rich considering his degree, and who cannot make contracts in the markets of Antwerp.'

In 1572 George Braun wrote:[26]

'This city, in virtue of its illustrious, valiant and numerous inhabitants and its noble citizens, surpasses all other cities in the world in wealth, magnificence, power, splendour and fine houses. . . . This city of Antwerp possesses all things, whether needful for life or conducive to pleasure, a circumstance at which all foreign merchants wonder exceedingly.'

The census of 1568 registered 104,981 inhabitants, i.e. the highest figure reached until the nineteenth century; at this point, as normally happened in the sixteenth century, reasons of prestige were superimposed upon functional ones, and produced a marked change in the style of the more important buildings.

The headquarters of the weavers' guild, built in 1541 on the Grote Markt, was still a reproduction of analogous medieval organisms, with adaptations of the classical ornaments; but the town hall built by Cornelis Floris (1514–75) from 1561 to 1566 is a palace correctly divided up by superimposed orders and dominated by a central motif of columns and arches which was the rigorous canonic translation of the Flemish *beffroi* (Figs 428–9).

In 1562 the council of the Hanseatic league fixed its headquarters in Antwerp, and in 1564 commissioned a large building from Floris which is similar to the earlier one but is more unified because the central motif is less emphatic (Fig. 427). This building, placed in the centre of van Schoonebeke's expansion, was the town's great novelty when Braun and Hogenberg's book of plates, *Civitates orbis terrarum*, was published in 1572 and was described as follows:[27]

'This house, or more properly palace, is an adornment to the whole of the new city. It occupies a fortunate position in that the water flows past it on either side in two arms, so that even large ships can sail almost up to the building and load or unload their goods in comfort. Inside is an open courtyard, and there are fine rooms within, adorned with noble paintings and precious tapestries. The merchants also have their separate counting houses and offices. In addition, the building possesses a magnificent tower constructed of hard hewn stone, at whose summit [is] a winged eagle which is readily turned by a wind and shows which way the wind is blowing.'

The third building project in the second half of the sixteenth century was the building of the citadel in 1567, at the southern extremity of the city; but this was a consequence of the war which was beginning between Philip II and the rebellious cities of the Dutch provinces and was ultimately to interrupt the city's development.

Antwerp tried repeatedly to free itself from Spanish occupation, was sacked in 1566 and again, more seriously, in 1576; finally it was subdued by Alessandro Farnese, and saw the triumphal entry of the sovereigns Isabella and Albert in 1599. But the Dutch who remained independent in the north were able to block the mouths of the Scheldt and were in the process of equipping the port of Amsterdam which inherited Antwerp's prosperity.

A plan of 1580 for a further extension of the city eastwards has been preserved;[28] but in the census of 1589 the inhabitants had dwindled to 55,000; however, Antwerp still continued to be a cultural centre of the first

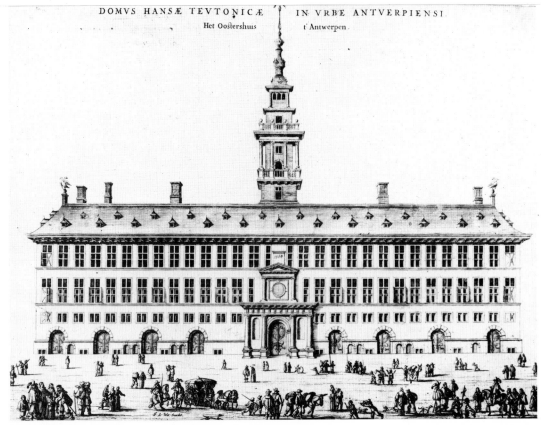

DOMVS HANSÆ TEVTONICÆ   IN VRBE ANTVERPIENSI.
Het Ooſtershuis   t'Antwerpen.

427   *A building of the 'new town' of Antwerp: the Hansa headquarters*
428, 429   *Antwerp town hall, burnt by the Spaniards in 1576*

order, made famous by the paintings of Rubens and the printing of Jean Moretus, the successor of Christopher Plantin.

The monuments of the sixteenth century acted in the seventeenth century as backdrops for courtly celebrations; one of these, for the entry of the prince Ferdinand, governor of the Low Countries in 1635, was staged by Rubens, who designed a series of triumphal arches and *tableaux vivants* as lively as his paintings. Among so many conventional subjects, one did reflect the concerns of the time, and brought an unusual realistic note into the baroque triumphal apparatus: the 'scene of commerce abandoning the city of Antwerp'. Elaborately surrounded by tritons and sea gods, a weeping young woman shows to the august visitor the god Mercury, who is about to fly away, while the Scheldt sleeps at his feet.[29] In 1648 the Peace of Westphalia prohibited sea-going ships from using the Scheldt and eliminated the causes that had produced the growth of the city in the sixteenth century once and for all.

ANTWERPIA.

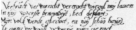

430   *View of Antwerp in 1600 by H. Grimmer and H. van Balen*

431   *The Deposition by Rubens, 1612, in Antwerp cathedral*

The centres of ocean-going trade in the Iberian peninsula : Lisbon, Seville and Cadiz

Lisbon has been the capital of the Portuguese kingdom since the twelfth century and occupies a splendid natural position on the Tagus estuary; here the country's economic functions were increasingly concentrated, and they caused the organism of the city to grow continuously, though it retained a fixed proportion between its river frontage and its depth, about two to one.

The perimeter of the medieval nucleus was defined by the walls of king Ferdinand, built in 1373–5, almost contemporaneously with the walls of Charles V in Paris. The centres of town life were some distance from the river, on the intermediate hills and valleys: the palace of the Alcaçova, built at the end of the thirteenth century on the highest peak, the Gothic cathedral at its feet, and the square of the Rossio, around which stood the All Saints' hospital, the Dominican convent and the palace of the Ambassadors, subsequently the Inquisition.

The streets were narrow and irregular, with the exception of two created by the civic administration: the rua nova dos Ferros in the fourteenth century and the rua nova d'el Rey of the fifteenth. The city guilds dominated city life, and resisted any interference from the court, which often sat elsewhere, at Evora and Sintra.

The growth of Lisbon was speeded up in the fifteenth and sixteenth centuries, *pari passu* with the expansion of maritime trade; the 60,000 inhabitants of the beginning of the fifteenth century became 80,000 at the beginning of the sixteenth and about 100,000 by the middle of the century. At this time the city was not only expanding beyond the 1375 limits, but acquired a new functional organization, closely connected with the activity of the port.

In the first years of the sixteenth century Emanuel I had a new royal palace built on the bank of the Tagus near the naval shipyards, the Paço de Ribeira; it was a low, plain

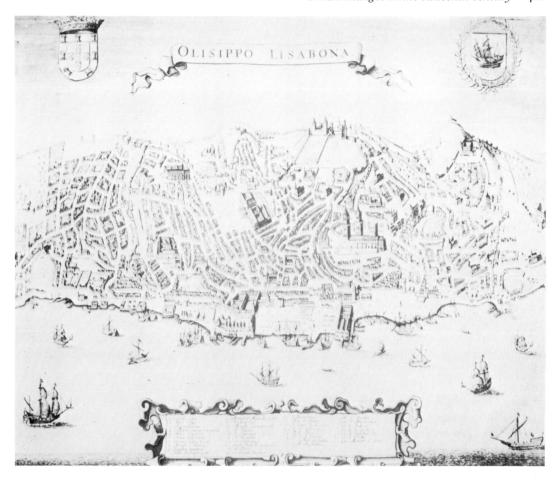

432, 433 *Lisbon in the late sixteenth century, from Jansonius' collection of plates*

structure, linked to the warehouses of the Casa de la Mina and the Casa de India. Near the palace was a large esplanade parallel to the estuary, the Terreiro do Paço, which became the square for court entertainments, parades and ceremonies. Meanwhile the Jeronymite house (1502) and the tower of Belem (1515) were being built, the first important buildings in the new Manueline style; below the royal palace, also along the river, court dignitaries built other palaces and noble residences, with loggias looking on to the water.

These buildings, though large, retained a traditional, utilitarian character, and a few decades later appeared antiquated in relation to the requirements of Renaissance artistic culture; in 1571 Francisco de Hollanda wrote a dissertation on the lack of monuments in the Portuguese capital[30] and the Venetian ambassadors sent in 1580 to receive Philip II, when he became king of Portugal, noted that 'all the houses, even the largest, are built with little regularity'.[31]

Meanwhile Lisbon was spreading: in 1498, after the decree expelling the Jews, the three Jewish districts, like the Arab ones, were annexed to the city; in those years two gentlemen of the court acquired the properties of a rich Jewish astrologer to the west of the city, and in 1513 began to divide it into plots, giving birth to a new densely populated district, the Bairro Alto.

The division into plots was carried out in two different stages: the first on the sloping land nearer the river, where sailors, port workers and small traders settled, then on the high land behind it, where rich burghers and some nobles settled. The Jesuits became attracted by the new district, settled on its margins in 1553 and in 1555 began to build a new church in the modern style, which was to become famous.

Towards the end of the century this district took on the name of Bairro Alto de S. Roque; it was considered 'a town that was sufficient unto itself' with buildings 'in the Roman style' and according to 'modern plans'.[32]

This extension of Lisbon can be compared to the extension of Antwerp, almost contemporary with it; here the name of the planner is not known, but the plan has the same characteristics: a grid of orthogonal roads, which produced regular sites perspectively aligned, while adapting itself to the lie of the land and accepting its restrictions. There was no dominant architectural feature conceived in advance, and the plan aimed at ensuring the best conditions for the architecture to be designed on the sites. The alignment of this architecture and the choice of a suitable road width were enough to establish the minimum conditions of visual control of public spaces, as in many ideal views of the time. The realization of these conditions was something new; indeed the roads of Bairro Alto were considered 'beautiful' and 'if not the most frequented, the most praised'.[33]

Only in 1580, after the annexation to Spain, did real court architecture, modelled on the classical examples, come to Lisbon. In fact Philip II employed Filippo Terzi, a Bolognese military engineer who settled in Portugal from 1577, and had him build the Torrao de Tercio, a new quadrangular pavilion at the end of the Paço de Ribeira, to balance the long stark Manueline block with its vertical emphasis and the richness of its façades.

National decline, and the scourges that struck Lisbon in the sixteenth century – the earthquakes of 1531 and 1551 and the plague of 1569 – did not prevent the city from continuing to grow; there were 113,000 inhabitants in 1620, 165,000 in 1639 and about 200,000 at the beginning of the eighteenth century. The disproportion between the capital and the country, which concentrated all its vital functions in a small city, set up a sort of vicious circle and produced a continuous growth of the city itself; but any town-planning originality was exhausted, and further development was always

434   *A seventeenth-century view of Seville*

built on the structure of the sixteenth century.

The case of Seville was different, for here the Spanish kingdom's international trade was concentrated. Already flourishing under the Arabs and conquered by the Christians in 1248, Seville was the most important city of Andalusia, set on the only navigable river, the Guadalquivir, and surrounded by well-cultivated countryside.

Even after the conquest Seville preserved the Moslem building pattern and retained her Moslem skilled workers who continued to serve the new rulers; the Alcázar was enlarged by Pedro I (1346–66) still in the original style, and the mosque was turned into a Christian church. Later it was replaced by the cathedral, completed in 1506 in the late Gothic style.

Because of its position and its already considerable growth, Seville was chosen in 1503 as seat of the Casa de Contratación, the public body controlling all trade with the American colonies. The Casa, created by the Catholic kings to supervise relations with the colonies in the interests of the court, was dominated in practice by Seville trading concerns which secured the monopoly of ocean-going trade; its duties were very wide-ranging, and led to the setting up of various specialized services, a hydrographic office, a clearing house for payments between Spain and the colonies, a naval school (whose first director, from 1509 to 1512, was Amerigo Vespucci); here the most important nautical map of the sixteenth century was kept, the *Padròn Real,* continually updated as new discoveries were made.

435   *A view of the most ancient quarter of Seville from the cathedral tower. One can see clearly the traces of the Arab city with the houses arranged round courtyards*

436, 437 *The town hall of Seville by D. de Riaño and the Casa Lonja by Herrera*

From 1501 navigation to the West Indies was regulated by detailed laws; all departures had to take place from Seville, or the outer harbour Sanlúcar, and in special cases from Cadiz; the state fixed the dates of departure every year. Ships had to sail in convoys escorted by armed vessels; the return could be made only from three authorized ports: Vera Cruz for Mexico, Porto Belo (after crossing the Panama isthmus) for Peru, Cartagena for New Granada (Venezuela and Colombia) and with the same modes of procedure.

This trade, and the textile industries which in the sixteenth century were producing as much as in the Arab period, earned Seville an economic supremacy which lasted until the seventeenth century. At the same time Seville was becoming one of the most up-to-date cultural centres; in 1502 the university was founded; from 1517 one of the best-known Spanish artists, Diego de Riaño, was employed as foreman of the cathedral; in 1527 he built the new town hall, which was one of the most notable examples of the combination between the Italian style and medieval building tradition (Fig. 436). The organism is a sequence of rooms that differ in form and function, covered by a symmetrical outer wall that is made up according to the elements of Bramante's style. The Florentine sculptor Pietro Torrigiani settled in the city and died there in 1522.

For much of the sixteenth century, however, the city's architectural pattern remained the one laid down in the Middle Ages, and is not comparable with that of Lisbon or Antwerp; the merchants' meetings were still held in the cathedral, and it was only in 1582 that Herrera designed the Casa Lonja, modelled on the Exchange in Amsterdam: a quadrangular block of rooms on two floors, surrounding an arcaded courtyard; here the architectural solution of the façades, measured and skilful, reveals the inner organism and emphasizes its regularity (Fig. 437).

Linked to the prosperity of Seville was that of Cadiz which had already been an important city port at the time of the Romans but declined in the Middle Ages and was repopulated only after 1262. The street system, which is still contained within the circle of the seventeenth-century walls, though based on the Roman grid, was created in the fifteenth and sixteenth centuries, with the spirit of regularity typical of the trading cities of the time we have already discussed.

438 *View of Rouen (from* Chroniques de Normandie*)*

French centres : Rouen, Le Havre and Lyon

We have already mentioned Georges d'Amboise, archbishop of Rouen from 1495, as being one of the most notable patrons of the time of Louis XII; Rouen was then one of the richest French trading cities, being halfway between the mouth of the Seine and the river port of Paris, and was inhabited by a wealthy and enterprising bourgeoisie.

The archbishop financed the reconstruction of the bishop's palace and contributed to other works of public interest, particularly to the city's new water supply system, which fed the famous fountains.

Soon after his appointment, he decided that the palace built a generation earlier by the Cardinal d'Estouteville was inadequate to his needs, and had a series of enlargements carried out which involved a good part of the centre of Rouen; there was also an Italian garden, with a marble fountain brought from Italy (1495–1507); he employed the *maîtres maçons* Pierre de l'Orme and Pierre Fàin, and a series of sculptors who mingled the classical ornaments admired by the archbishop on his travels with those of Flamboyant Gothic; he was also involved in the work on the cathedral, urgently requested in 1502 by the chapter which was unable to continue with work on the façade, and assisted with the building of the porch, designed by the *maître d'oeuvre* in charge, Roullant Leroux.

But the most important works, partly financed by the archbishop, were those of the aqueduct and urban water supply, documented in the *Livre des fontaines* by Jacques Le Lieur, of 1526;[34] the end points of the network took the form of monumental fountains, which combined traditional motifs with others from the Italian Renaissance.

In the fifteenth century the traders of Rouen used the outer harbour at the mouth of the Seine, which had fallen into disrepair; in 1515 an assembly of notables decided to present a petition to François I to build another outer harbour 'to keep the ships and vessels that sail the high seas in safety'.[35] In 1516 the king sent admiral Bonnivet to choose the most favourable spot, and in 1517 he granted him 'full power and authority to build the said fortified harbour at the place of Grâce in the said village of Caux'.[36] This was the origin of Le Havre, destined to become France's most important port for northern seas.

Building was supervised by Guyon le Roy, captain of the nearby town of Honfleur, and various masters from Rouen were involved in it, including Roullant Leroux, master builder of the cathedral.

Guyon le Roy decided to build a new city
beside the port, and obtained from the
inhabitants of the nearest village twenty-four
acres of land on which he traced an elementary series of plots: the grid was irregular,
possibly because of the presence of already
existing alignments; the main roads converged on the *quais* of the harbour, and the
main square was just an empty space near the
town defending the entrance to the harbour;
but the streets were straight and very wide
(12–15 metres) (Fig. 439).

Soon afterwards Guyon le Roy entered
into litigation with the Seigneur de Graville,
who claimed the ownership of the land, and
in 1524 lost the case before the Parlement of
Rouen, so that he was obliged to return the
various plots and the income already received
from them. Meanwhile the venture none the
less continued to develop even in the absence
of any precise plan; about 1530, a regularly
shaped market square was formed at the back
of the first settlement.

But the sentence of 1524 had reserved the
king the right of compulsory purchase. Thus
in 1541 – when the increasing importance of
Le Havre made further planning activity
necessary – François I reacquired the ownership of the land and commissioned the Italian
engineer Girolamo Bellarmato 'to build the
said city and port, and to adorn them both
with fortifications and buildings, great streets
and well-built houses, in accordance with a
design approved by us following the advice
of people most expert in these matters'.[37] In
reality Bellarmato worked on both the general
plans and the plans for the main buildings,
and laid down a series of restrictions to ensure
the efficiency and regularity of the new urban
organism.

Bellarmato's design included the previous
division into plots, regularizing its layout and
doubling the surface area; the city now had
the shape of a square, crossed diagonally by
the widest of the streets begun by Guyon le
Roy and surrounded by the new fortifications.
Beside this nucleus, beyond one of the arms

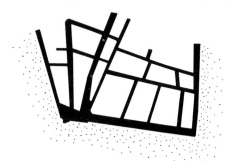

439 *Plan of the original settlement of Le Havre in
1524 (from Lavedan)*

440, 441 *Seventeenth-century view of Le Havre by
the abbé Hautier and an old photograph of the rue
St-François*

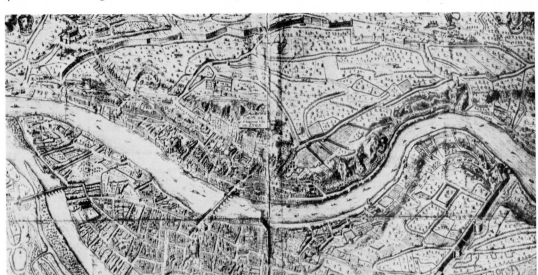

442　*Plan of Lyon in the first half of the sixteenth century*

of the harbour, Bellarmato built the district of St-François, on a regular grid plan; the central street, though only 5 metres wide, was treated as an axis of perspective, leading up to the church of St-François (Figs 440, 441).

Thus the organism of Le Havre, as it appeared after the beginning of the sixteenth century, combined both the criteria of utilitarian town-planning, common to the enterprises examined in this section, and those of court-inspired town-planning, which we discussed in the previous one.

On this scale the two methodologies proved to be largely reconcilable, though the very detailed rules of academic culture – which were translated into the restrictions imposed by Bellarmato – proved to be artificial, and were made partly unworkable by the process of growth.

Lyon's prosperity began in 1462, when the Champagne fairs were transferred there. Later it became the capital of the French printing industry and silk industry, encouraged by the exemptions granted it by François I in 1536.

The city was growing rapidly, and occupied a large part of the peninsula at the confluence of the Rhône and Saône. The new districts, such as that of St-Nizier, were collections of plots, which followed the grid plan rule as far as possible, but had to take into account numerous topographical limitations which complicated and distorted the outline of the plots.

These groups of plots did not obey an overall plan, as happened at Antwerp and Lisbon, and there was therefore no hierarchy between the public spaces; streets were uniform and narrow, just sufficient to create

443 *View of the present-day centre of Lyon, showing the expanse of the place Bellecoeur*

the maximum number of plots on which very tall houses were built.

In the second half of the century the first public square, needed for the city markets, appeared. In 1566 and 1567 the cemeteries near the churches of the Jacobins and Cordeliers were done away with, to form the two squares bearing their names; these are irregular spaces around which the existing blocks of buildings were retained.

From 1562 to 1563 Lyon was occupied by the Maréchal des Adrets, who laid out the southern tip of the peninsula with strategic considerations in mind, opening up a *place d'armes* – place Bellecoeur – and tracing the roads that link it to the city and bridge over the Rhône, rebuilt in 1560; the great parade ground served the city for many other uses, and was repeatedly transformed in the seventeenth and eighteenth centuries. This scheme followed the rules of perspective culture, now linked to military engineering, and fitted a regular episode into the urban fabric of Lyon, which was to be the starting-point for later baroque schemes (Fig. 443).

The course of events in Rouen and Lyon, though different, does reveal certain circumstances peculiar to French town-planning culture; the new concepts of regularity and symmetry, typical of the official culture which had grown up around the court, still found no echo in bourgeois culture which was still linked firmly to the medieval tradition. Furthermore official culture was sufficiently well-equipped and articulate to intervene successfully even in the outskirts, and planned interventions in Paris had a definite value throughout France, as was to be increasingly clear in the centuries to come.

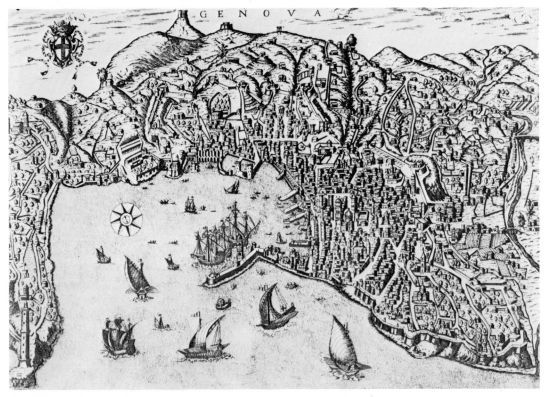

444   *Plan of Genoa in the sixteenth century*

Genoa and Messina

In 1528, after the Sack of Rome, the Genoese government went over to the side of Charles V and agreed to become a stable part of the Spanish political system, though retaining its internal autonomy and dispensing with the admission of an imperial garrison. This was the beginning of a period of prosperity which lasted until the end of the century; the Genoese fleet guaranteed communication between the two parts of Charles V's European dominions, made impossible overland by continual wars with France; Genoese bankers partly replaced German and Florentine ones, advancing the sums derived from American gold and silver to the Catholic king; the republic encouraged export industries, particularly that of silk.

This industrial development produced a remarkable change in the town-planning and buildings of the city. Genoa, though at this time the main banking power in Italy, was not comparable in layout with the oldest and best endowed centres such as Venice and Florence; but it was the only important Italian centre where the building pattern was largely determined by sixteenth-century activities and bore the mark of the new capitalist mentality, like Antwerp and the other cities examined in this section.

The population, which amounted to 51,000 in 1531, rose to 70,000 in 1570. In the restricted area of the traditional centre the density was further increased by the division into plots of the few open spaces and further building up of houses; but the office of the Padri del Comune, which had been in existence since 1399, did have it in its power to implement a reorganization of the public spaces. Between 1530 and 1540 the squares

445 *Plan of Genoa in the seventeenth century;* the strada nuova *is towards the top right*

of Fossatello, Banchi and Soziglia were enlarged, and the new squares of Ferraria and Ponticello created. Meanwhile in 1537 Andrea Doria had a new circle of walls built, larger than the medieval one of 1115; the new areas added to the city were immediately rationally exploited and indeed the most important undertakings were distributed along these walls, around the edges of the medieval nucleus: Andrea Doria's *villa suburbana*, begun in the 1530s at the western extremity of the port, which was worked on by Pierino del Vaga – the most authoritative pupil of Raphael after Giulio Romano had settled in Mantua, who may have been responsible for the layout and terraces running down to the sea, derived from Raphael's Villa Madama – and, later on, Silvio Cosimi, and G. A. Montorsoli; Andrea Doria's palace near the Porta dell'Acquasola,

begun in 1542; the *strada nuova* opened between 1550 and 1558 amid a former district of gardens on the hill to the north-east of the city, to give access to the new houses of the commercial aristocracy;[38] the church of S. Maria di Carignano, designed in 1552 by Galeazzo Alessi for the Saoli family, on one of the hills included within the new walls to the south-east, a stone's throw from the ruins of the Palazzo Fieschi destroyed by the Dorias after the plot of 1547.

Of the architects working towards the middle of the century, one of the most striking for his ability to handle the more up-to-date stylistic repertoires and for his continuity of involvement, was Galeazzo Alessi from Perugia (c. 1512–72) who had designed a *strada nuova* in his native Perugia as early as 1547, and who had been in Genoa since 1548, as architect of the cathedral. In the second

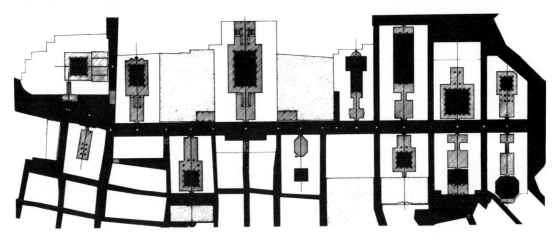

446, 447 *Eighteenth-century view of the* strada nuova *in Genoa and plan showing the entrance halls of the palazzi (from Vagnetti)*

edition of his *Lives*, which came out in 1568, Vasari added this piece of information:[39]

'[Galeazzo Alessi] made the Via Nuova at Genoa, with the numerous modern palaces designed by him, so that many declare it to be the most magnificent street in Italy, and the richest in palaces. The nobles are under a great debt to Galeazzo, who has designed and carried out a work with buildings which render their city incomparably grander than before.'

The documents indicate Bernardo Cantone as responsible for the division into plots (from 1546 he worked for the municipality and was one of Alessi's assistants at S. Maria di Carignano); but in this achievement – as in others of the fifteenth and sixteenth centuries closely linked to the needs of the community – we can glimpse a complex operative cycle where architectural planning was the result of the coming together of a variety of different skills.

The road was thirty palms (7·50 metres) wide and inaccessible to vehicles because it was originally blocked at one end by the garden of the Brignole and at the other by a series of steps. The idea of the straight road, so well-suited to a foreshortened view of independent but rigorously aligned architecture, was here developed in the most consistent way, eliminating every broadening out and every superfluous addition; the central axis, which is dominant from the very end of the street, is subsequently counterbalanced by the orthogonal axis of the courtyards, which extend in a series of terraces to the green backdrop of the gardens, visible through the grilles which stand across the main entrances (Figs 446–8).

The size of the sites was possibly unified in the plans, because the first three pairs of palazzi have the same width, and are separated by narrow streets for tradesmen, also constant in width; but later Niccolò Grimaldi – known as the 'monarch' because of his enormous wealth – built two palazzi on the area destined

for three, one of which (Palazzo Tursi) was extremely large. Later the building became irregular, and towards the other end of the road was completed only in the late seventeenth century.

Alessi built some of the palazzi – Cataldi (1557), Cambiaso (1565), Parodi (1567) – and laid down the distributive type which was to be repeated later by his pupils and successors; for these same families he created a series of *ville suburbane* – Cambiaso (1548), Pallavicino (1560) (Figs 453–4), Scassi 1560) – compact in volume and exquisitely judged in their internal distribution. These and other villas built on the two sides of the coast, at Sampierdarena and Albano, were aligned in rows running down over the hills overlooking the sea, like the palazzi along the *strada nuova*, and formed a not dissimilar district, unified because of the constancy of the distributive types but relieved by the variety of plastic detail (Fig. 452).

The models established by Alessi about the middle of the sixteenth century remained constants in Genoese building practice for at least a century, and had a considerable influence outside as well. From 1606 to 1619, on the pattern of the *strada nuova*, via Balbi was built, at the extreme western end of the city. At the same time Rubens, who was travelling in Italy, gathered together the measured drawings of Genoese villas and palazzi, and published them in Antwerp in 1622, offering them as an example to the wealthy European bourgeoisie. In the dedication 'to the kind reader', he caught most perceptively the difference between these achievements and those of the courts, which were being codified in the European capitals according to completely different criteria:[40]

'We see that in these parts the mode of architecture which is called barbarian, and Gothic, is gradually falling out of use, and that some extremely fine minds are introducing the true symmetry of that which conforms to the rules of the ancient

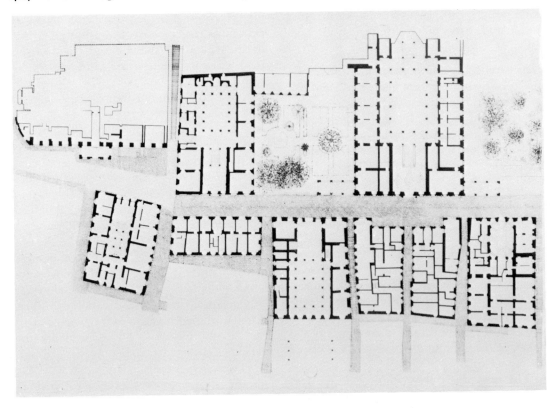

448   *Ground floor plans of the palazzi on the* strada nuova *(from Vagnetti)*

449–451   *Façades of Palazzo Pallavicino (from Rubens), Palazzo Grimaldi and Palazzo Doria-Tursi, Genoa*

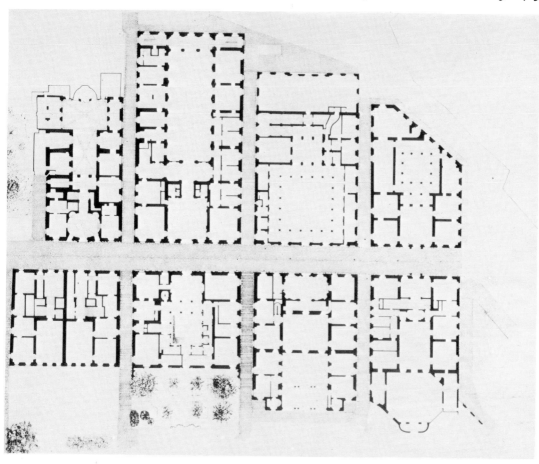

452 *Seventeenth-century view of Sampierdarena, showing the nobles' houses*

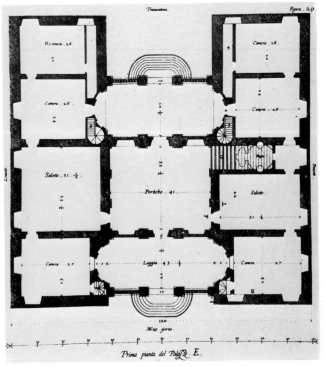

453 *Plan of the Villa Pallavicino* 'delle peschiere' (*from Rubens*)

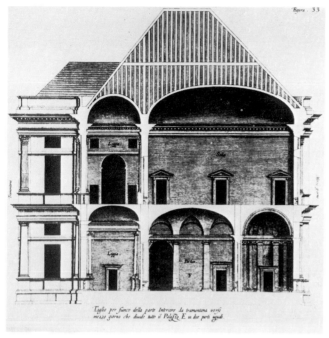

454   *Section of the Villa Pallavicino (from Rubens)*

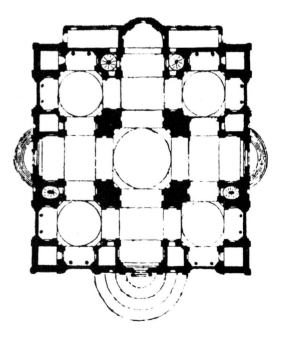

455, 456   *View of one of the three identical façades of S. Maria di Carignano, Genoa, and plan*

457   *Plan of Messina in 1567, before the* palazzata *was begun*

458   *The* palazzata *of Messina in an engraving made before the earthquake of 1783*

Greeks and Romans . . . it appears in the famous Churches recently built by the venerable Society of Jesus, in the cities of Brussels and Antwerp. Which, for the dignity of the divine office, must be the first to change for the better; not that this means that private buildings must be neglected, because it is in their number that the body of a city consists. . . . It therefore seemed to me a worthy undertaking . . . to produce the drawings I gathered together during my wanderings in Italy, of some Palazzi of the superb city of Genoa. Because as this Republic is typified by its Gentlemen, so their own buildings are beautiful and convenient in terms rather of families, however numerous, than of the Court of an absolute Prince. As is seen for instance in the Palazzo de Pitti in Florence, and the Farnesiano in Rome, the Cancelleria, Caprarola, and many others throughout Italy, as also in the well-known building of the Queen Mother in St. Germain in Paris. All of which are greater, in size and expense, than the possibilities of private Gentlemen would allow. But I wish to serve the common use, to be of help to the many rather than to the few.'

The fame of the *strada nuova* did not diminish in the baroque age; in a French guide of 1781, this road was judged 'the most magnificent in Genoa, and perhaps in Europe'. But at that very time the district was changing character; the author adds that in this year 1779, for the convenience of carriages, means of communication had been begun between via Nova and via Balbi, which would be carried out at the expense of private individuals, by means of voluntary contributions.[41]

This extremely flattering judgment by writers of the past can be upheld even today; the Genoese *strada nuova* is perhaps the most successful of the sixteenth-century achievements of commercial power; road and palazzi are fused together into a single work

of architecture. The success of this work is dependent only partly upon the talents of the artists, and much more upon the coherence of the operative cycle, i.e. upon the balance of the relations between administrators, clients, artists and technical experts.

The other important port at the service of the Spanish empire in southern Italy was Messina. This city was part of the viceroy's kingdom, but enjoyed a certain autonomy; here, too, as in Genoa, this combination of circumstances produced a long period of prosperity and a transformation of the built-up organism, which took place between about 1550 and 1630, *pari passu* with the works in Naples, Palermo and the other southern cities, but in a different way: it was less dependent upon the bureaucratic rule of the Spanish governors and more dependent upon the initiatives of rich local entrepreneurs.

From 1537 a new circle of walls, bastioned along their inland stretch, was built, and took in not only the medieval castle – destined for the viceroy – but also a park and a 'modern' district, on the grid system, the *terra nuova*. Towards the sea the medieval walls between city and port were still in existence; but in 1555, at the end of the long, natural quay, Montorsoli built the Forte del Salvatore, whose artillery made the old sea-based defences superfluous. Indeed in 1557 this same Montorsoli built the fountain of Neptune in front of the Porta della Dogana, i.e. he laid the basis for the idea of making the city face on to the harbour. At the end of the century Giacomo del Duca built a triumphal arch behind the fountain, and near this the imposing Palazzo Senatorio, which brought in its train a vast programme of building; the mercantile nobility gradually demolished the whole curve of the walls, and replaced them with a line of architecturally uniform palazzi, which repeated the motifs of the original curve, on a smaller scale. In this way the impressive screen of buildings acquired the character of a single organism, the *palazzata*

459 *The* Conquest of the West Indies *by Jan Mostaert. Frans Hals Museum, Haarlem*

or *teatro a mare*, as exemplary for the future as the Genoese *strada nuova* and the model for numerous baroque compositions looking on to an open space (Fig. 458).

The colonial cities

The European schemes examined so far – promoted by the political or economic powers – only partly modified the urban or rural landscape of the old continent. All the examples quoted are in some measure exceptions, linked to special circumstances, and were not to determine a common rule; Renaissance culture did not manage to produce a new type of city, and managed only – speaking generally – to modify the cities created in the Middle Ages.

The colonial schemes, and the American ones in particular, were a different matter; here the Europeans could work in an empty space, and had to achieve an immense colonization programme within a few decades. This sense of freedom and novelty was the salient characteristic of sixteenth-century achievements beyond the ocean, and the protagonists were well aware of it. On the doorpost of the palace of the archbishop of Mexico this phrase from the Apocalypse appeared: '*Dixit qui sedebat in Throno : ecce nova facio omnia.*'[42]

It would be a mistake to consider these American experiments as marginal episodes in the history of the architecture of the sixteenth century; they were not only quantitatively the most remarkable schemes realized in the sixteenth century, but were also in some ways the most significant, because their characters depended more upon the cultural concepts developed at this time, and less upon the resistance put up by the environment.

In 1494 Alexander VI fixed the demarcation line between the two colonizing powers, Spain and Portugal; this line is relevant to our study, also, to distinguish two types of settlement, differing one from the other both in origin and in later development.

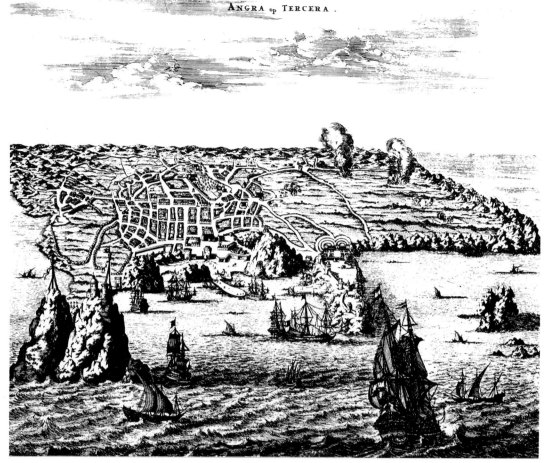

460 *The city of Angra in the Azores, as shown in the plan by Jacob van Meurs, Amsterdam, 1763*

The Portuguese hemisphere

The Portuguese, benefiting from eighty years of exploration of the sea route to the Indies, retained the eastern hemisphere. Their main aim – realized in 1498 by Vasco da Gama – was to gain access to the spice-producing countries. Thus the criteria of the colonizing activities were laid down: they entered into contact with local peoples technically least equipped in both navigation and firearms, but too numerous, organized and aggressive to be easily overwhelmed; they were so interested in the immediate gains of trade – on which the budget of the royal house was entirely dependent – that wherever possible

they preferred agreement with the local powers; they were too few for large-scale occupation and colonization of the unoccupied territories they came upon their route eastwards: in Africa, Brazil, in the Atlantic islands and those of the Indian Ocean.

Thus for a long time the encounter between the Portuguese and overseas peoples remained a trial of strength and a commercial arrangement but was culturally not very important. Conquest of the territories did not matter – in India it was impossible after the failure of the occupation of Calcutta, and in Africa or America it did not extend beyond the coastline – but what did matter was control of the ocean trading-space, with a chain of interlinked naval bases. These outposts, isolated in an enormous hostile or unknown space, did not on the whole manage to develop to the dimension of real towns, and did not become occasions for inventing new types of urban organism; the settlers aimed rather at reproducing, in every corner of the world, a model typical of medieval Portuguese towns (such as Lisbon and Oporto) – a built-up area on one or more steep hills, and a trading-post at sea level – which we find repeated at Angra in the Azores (Fig. 460) (founded in the second half of the fifteenth century), at Macao in China (founded in 1533), at São Paulo de Luanda in West Africa (founded in 1576).

The heart of the Portuguese empire was the *estado de India*, i.e. the system of possessions on the west coast of the Indian peninsula. Goa, the capital, was conquered by Albuquerque in 1510, when it was already one of the most important maritime cities of India. The city, with a small area of surrounding territory, functioned as an indigenous state, on the edges of the Hindu empire of Vijayanagar, and the Portuguese viceroy, thus placed, could negotiate with the Asian sovereigns in accordance with the traditional forms; but it was also the main base of the Portuguese military fleet in Asia, the inevitable terminus for all trade with Lisbon, and after 1542 the organizational centre for the Jesuit missions in the area of the Indian Ocean, from Africa to China.

This state managed to survive and to retain its link with Europe despite the enormous distance and scarcity of means. It was a year's journey from Lisbon to Goa; every year a fleet of six or seven ships left the Portuguese capital, with 10,000 tons of merchandise and 3,000 men, of whom less than 2,000 arrived safe and sound in India. In the *estado* there were no more than 6,000 or 7,000 fighting Portuguese. The life of this colony was thus based on an adjustment, precarious but durable, between Europeans and Indians,

signs of which were also to be found in the architectural form of the city.

In the decades after the conquest Goa struck visitors with its extraordinarily mixed character, its combination of exotic and European. The Portuguese kept up local constitutions and customs, registered in the *foral* of 1526; but they also tried obstinately to reproduce the civic forms of their mother country. From the beginning Goa had the same municipal status as Lisbon, in 1520 it was given the first hostel for the poor, in 1538 its first bishop. The viceroy kept a magnificent court to impress his Asian contacts, and here Portuguese merchants lavishly ate up the profits of their trade; all this nourished a sumptuous and dissipated existence, and Camoens called Goa the 'Babylon of the Orient'.

The urban layout remained the enclosed and inconvenient one of the native centre, barely altered by the Portuguese and strangely similar to that of Lisbon with narrow sloping streets, as the European travellers of the following century observed with disapproval. But Christian churches grew up side by side with Hindu temples: the cathedral founded by Albuquerque in 1511 and rebuilt in 1623, the Franciscan convent of 1517. Between 1538 and 1540 the most important Portuguese painter of the time, Garcia Fernandes, was working in the cathedral; at the same time traffic arriving at Goa from both east and west made possible the most singular exchanges of cultural influence: the Chinese porcelain commissioned by Portugal from 1521 onwards arrived here and was the source of the eastern allusions found in Portuguese painting throughout the first half of the sixteenth century. The heterogeneous scene in this city was described with amazement by Francis Xavier, when he arrived at Goa in 1542.

The arrival of Francis Xavier, and in the same year that of the new viceroy Alfonso de Souza, marks a turning point in Portuguese colonial policy. John III tried to introduce

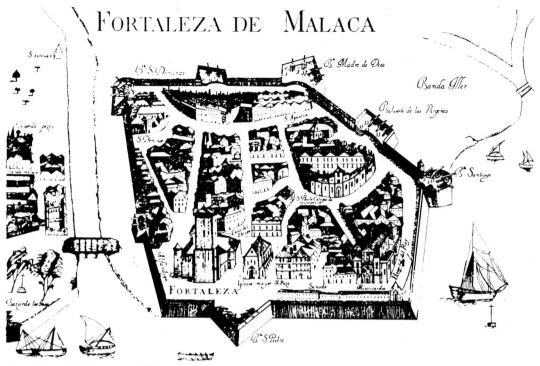

461   *View of the fortress of Malacca*

more rigid bureaucratic order into the colonies, and the Jesuits began a vast new programme of diffusion of the Christian faith. In 1540 the order to demolish the pagan temples arrived; in 1557 the bishop of Goa became the primate of the Orient, with jurisdiction extended progressively over the whole of the Indian Ocean; in 1560 the Inquisition was introduced. In 1570 the king renounced monopoly of the spice trade; trade with Europe diminished, but the *estado de India* became the main emporium for inter-Asian trade, and reached its peak of prosperity, while the activities of the Jesuits brought it a new international character (apart from Francis Xavier from Navarre, one might mention the Italians Padre Vagliano and Padre Ricci). In the second half of the sixteenth century the most important monuments were built, the churches of St Catherine (1551) and of Bom Jesús (1594), and the eastern capital, 'Goa dourada', reached its greatest splendour (Fig. 462).

At this time the Portuguese were also extending their possessions; from 1587 to 1594 they were carrying out the conquest of Ceylon (with 1,000 men). In the territories scattered along the western coast of India the fortresses of Daman (Fig. 463) and Beçaim, built according to the 'modern' criteria of European military engineering (the grid plan and polygonal bastioned walls) and the cities of Chaul, Cangranor and São Tomé, also approximately regulated according to a geometrical plan, indicate at least an intention of urbanizing the Indian possessions coherently; but this programme was interrupted at the end of the century by the competition of the Dutch.

The *estado de India* is one of the most singular successes of European colonization, if one considers the effort necessary to main-

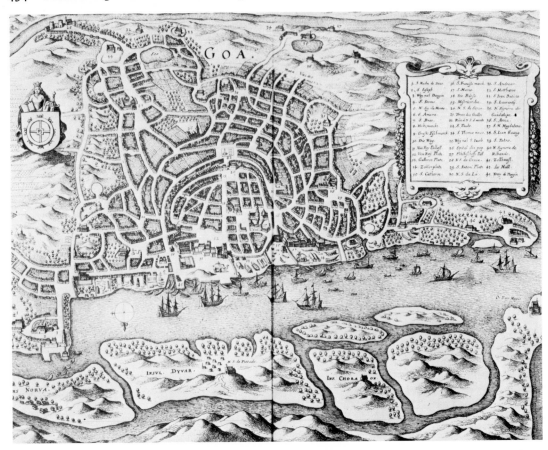

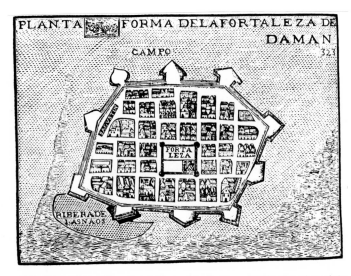

462, 463　*Plan of Goa (from Merian's collection, 1649) and plan of the fortress of Daman, 1674*

tain an outpost of western society and culture at the other end of the earth and with such small forces. But if we consider it from the point of view of Asia, i.e. in the political and cultural framework of sixteenth-century India, it appears as a negligible episode and was able to survive, basically, because it was so out of proportion with the empires and great human concentrations that surrounded it. In the immediate hinterland the city of Vijayanagar flourished, capital of a vast empire; the modest monuments of Goa could not even be compared with those of the Indian city, such as the shrine of Vitthala begun in 1513, celebrated by Arab, Portuguese and Italian travellers before being destroyed in 1565 (the Portuguese Domingo Paes gives a fabulous description of it; the pillars seemed to him 'romanesque' and 'so well executed that one might have thought they were made in Italy'). In the north the Mogul empire was being formed, and the great Akbar, who died in 1605, encouraged the building of Agra and Delhi. A real comparison between the two civilizations could not yet be made; it was postponed until the moment when the Europeans had the technical means to confront the Asian states with advantage.

On the eastern coasts of the South American continent comparison is likewise excluded, for quite different reasons. Here the Portuguese came upon immense, almost deserted territories, with a scant and primitive population which had no goods to offer and could not absorb European products, and which furthermore was devoid of the mineral resources found by the Spaniards further to the west. In the first thirty years the Portuguese founded only a series of coastal trading posts, and shipped away the most profitable natural products, including the reddish wood, *brasil*, which was to give its name to the whole region. In 1532 the Portuguese began to think of extending their exploitation inland; the extremely long Brazilian coast was divided into *capitanias*, allotted to agents who were answerable to the crown; the territory of each one of them extended inland between the two parallels corresponding to the extreme points of the stretch of coast, to meet the meridian of Tordesillas which marked the theoretical border of the Spanish zone. In 1549 John III sent Tomé de Souza to America with an expedition of soldiers and settlers – including six Jesuits led by Manuel de Nobrega – and set up a general government; thus began the organized colonization of the territory, similar to that already embarked upon by the Spaniards, and based on the employment of natives – or negroes imported from Africa, who had more resistance to hardship – as subordinate workers; but this almost exclusively agricultural settlement, drawn out over an immense territory, faced with an indigenous culture that was so humble and mild, settled into elementary static forms, once again unpropitious to any organized experiments in new urban settlements. The new cities founded in the second half of the middle of the century – Bahia in 1549, seat of the general government; São Paulo in 1554; Rio de Janeiro in 1565; Natal in 1599 – were places of concentration of political and economic power, all situated along the coast where exchanges between the distant mother-country and its new rural hinterland took place, chosen where there was a landing place near a hill, i.e. where it appeared possible to reproduce the medieval model already utilized in Asia and Africa. Only in the seventeenth and eighteenth centuries, when these centres had to expand into the adjacent non-hilly zones, was the by now widespread model of the grid plan used.

Thus the Portuguese experience, though begun earlier and with ambitious economic and military aims, produced modest results in the civil and cultural sphere, and also in the sphere of architecture. The first phase, strictly faithful to the commercial interests of the 'spice kings', excluded from the start any broad programme of colonization of overseas territories; the second phase, when the need

464   *The first settlement at Rio di Janeiro in 1624*

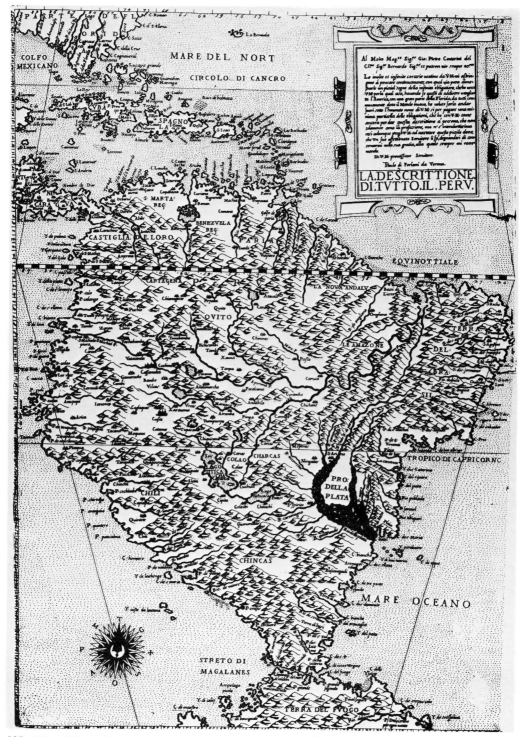

465 *Map of South America, from the second half of the sixteenth century. Vatican Library*

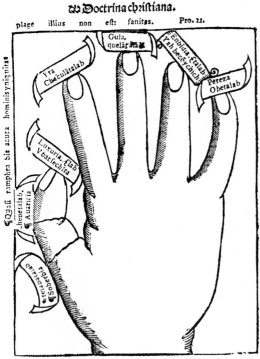

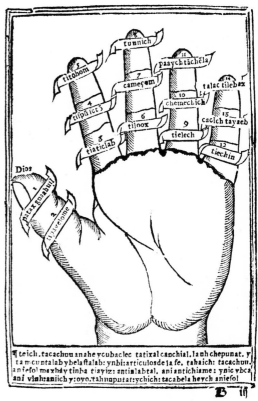

466, 467 *Two pages from the* Doctrina cristiana en le lengua guasteca, *1571; the seven deadly sins and fourteen articles of faith, to be remembered on the fingers*

to order and consolidate the vast *de facto* empire acquired earlier, was developing in the already normative climate of the Counter Reformation and increasing bureaucratic rigidity of the late sixteenth century, and settled into permanent forms before having been able to experiment with and compare different approaches to the European presence in the exotic environment.

The Spanish hemisphere

The Spanish experience was different and more crucial. Columbus set out on behalf of the king of Spain attracted by that same mirage of the Indies, the land of spices; but as soon as it became clear that a New World had been discovered, Spain was able to embark on colonization, which continued on a larger scale that already begun in the Canary Islands; Columbus' second expedition carried 1,200 settlers with equipment, seeds, domestic animals and religious accoutrements for the encounter with the natives.

Later the division of Tordesillas proved to be unexpectedly favourable to the Spaniards, who came upon the more populated, more civilized territories in the New World, and those richest in mineral resources; settlement thus became a vital task, as much a military and economic undertaking as a cultural, spiritual and religious adventure. The initial and creative phase of conquest took place in the first half of the sixteenth century under the cosmopolitan government of Charles V, and engaged some of the finest energies in

Europe, from Spain, the Empire, Flanders and Italy, while ideas of Renaissance culture were still circulating freely and had not yet found clear-cut institutional bounds. This inventive phase did not last more than thirty or forty years and can be regarded as concluded when Philip II succeeded Charles V; but it was vital for the destiny of the new society; three centuries of bureaucratic rule were not to be enough to damp it down completely, indeed it lingers on in the dramatic situation of the present day. The stake played then – lost in the political field but partially gained in the area of social relations – was in fact a lasting arrangement between the two cultures, which proved capable of surviving colonial exploitation: the foundation of a mixed society, Christian even after the historical relationship between European missionaries and the natives was ended.

From the European side, the intellectual contributions employed in this confrontation concerned not only soldiers and entrepreneurs, but also men of culture, belonging to the élite of secular and religious European society; they travelled continually, plying between Europe and America, and brought with them not only precious merchandise but also books, documents and relics of all kinds of both civilizations.

The first Franciscan missionaries sent by Charles V to Cortés in 1523 were three Flemings chosen by Adrian VI, including Peter of Ghent, one of the organizers of the Mexican church, and the following year the famous 'twelve', led by Martin of Valencia, who had studied in the universities of Salamanca and Alcalá and some also at the Sorbonne; in 1526 and 1528 the Dominicans of Domingo de Batanzos arrived, 'the radical churchmanship of Cisneros'.[43]

Juan de Zumarraga, the first bishop of Mexico (from 1528), was a Franciscan who admired Erasmus, the author of the first manuals for preaching to the natives;[44] Antonio de Mendoza, the first viceroy (from

1529), was a gentleman from one of the most important noble families in Spain, with an excellent classical education; the first vice-chancellor of the university of Mexico, set up in 1553, was Francisco Cervantes de Salazar, from the university of Salamanca, who tended to judge American affairs through classical models, and quoted Vitruvius[45] when for the first time he saw Mexico rebuilt by the Spaniards. Cortés himself, with his ambitions, has been judged a 'product of the Renaissance of Salamanca'.[46] In the second half of the sixteenth century the university of Mexico had a library of 10,000 volumes, and in 1573 the friar Alonso de la Vera Cruz brought back to Spain sixty crates of books, including a book of *cosas romanas* (possibly a treatise on architecture) which Cervantes had borrowed.[47]

The judge Vasco de Quiroga who arrived in Mexico in 1531, at the age of sixty, sold all his goods to build two self-supporting Indian settlements – Santa Fé de Mexico and Santa Fé de la Laguna – organized as positive ideal cities, following the rules of More's *Utopia* (a copy of which figures among the books of his friend Zumarraga); each took in 30,000 Indians who lived, worked and studied communally. Ten years afterwards Quiroga was appointed bishop and organized the building of the cathedral of Pátzcuaro, one of the most extraordinary buildings of the New World, which we shall discuss later on.

Quiroga was an exceptional man, but his work did not stand alone. Antonio de Mendoza, his successor Luis de Valesco, fray Motolinia[48] and the priest Las Casas energetically defended the Indians against the abuses of the Spaniards, and made good, at least in part, the exploitation of the indigenous peoples organized by the *encomenderos*; Las Casas was one of the inspirers of the *nuevas leyes* of Charles V of 1542. The same contradiction can be seen in the scientific field; while the *conquistadores* were destroying the indigenous civilization, and all evidence of it, scholars were collecting together the remaining documents, and discussing the relations between the two peoples even at the most elevated academic level, as at Salamanca in 1539, during the lectures of Francisco de Vitoria;[49] in the university of Mexico, together with the Spanish language, the Aztec and Otomi languages were taught (but it was precisely the very humanitarian commitment and religious zeal of the most cultured Europeans that produced the greatest violence *vis-à-vis* the natives, and broke up their history and moral autonomy by penetrating into the sphere of private relations).

This cultural apparatus, though far from negligible, was involved in a series of transformations unprecedented in extent and speed. In America the relation between theory and practice was reversed; instead of the conflict between a wide range of ideal programmes and a scarcity of implementation, there was a lack of proportion between forces, schemes and rate of progress, and the enormity of the operations to be carried out. In the middle of the sixteenth century Mexico had 10,000,000 inhabitants, more than Spain which had 7,000,000; from 1524 to 1530 the 'twelve' of Martin de Valencia personally baptized more than 1,000,000 of them. The Archivio de Indias at Seville possesses the plans of over a hundred cities founded in the colonies[50] in the first fifty years (and they are only the most important); they include Mexico, which by the mid-century was the largest city in Charles V's dominions.

There were very few workers available, and the ruling élite had to make an exceptional effort to translate ideal criteria into simple rules, suited to application on a large scale. To do this it was necessary to seek a new point of contact between specialist culture and popular culture, which were in fact tending to diverge so noticeably in Europe. The undoubted impoverishment of the cultural contents sometimes became a significant piece of discrimination, which isolated the aspects that were to be most vital and fruitful in the future.

Another circumstance, which acted as a touchstone *vis-à-vis* European culture, was the absolute difference in kind between the civilization of the *conquistadores* and that of the natives, 'so different from one another that our first explorers could not believe that they were inhabited by members of the same species'.[51]

This heated discussion of the relation between the two cultures and its cultural consequences – which began in 1510, with the inquests organized on Hispaniola,[52] continued with the accounts of the *conquistadores*, in the academic dissertations of Vitoria, Sepulveda,[53] Las Casas,[54] in the papal Bull of 1537 (which condemned as heretical the opinion that the Indians were incapable of receiving the evangelical message) and in the Spanish laws of 1512, 1542 and 1573 – only partly diminished the inhuman exploitation of the natives, and did not prevent the violent destruction of the forms of traditional life. But it also became a discussion of the foundations of European life, and in some cases a dramatic examination of conscience; in studying the natives the Europeans were studying themselves, and their cultural models – including architecture – could not but emerge changed.

While the doctor Zorita, towards the middle of the century, questioned the Indians on their unease, and received replies of this kind: 'Neither do you understand us nor do we understand you nor what you want. You took away our good order and way of governing ourselves, and we do not understand what you have put in its place; hence everything is very confused, and without order or harmony',[55] a very similar uncertainty was appearing in the applications of the models of European life, apparently rigid and intransigent. The condition of the *conquistadores* and that of the natives, which were exactly opposed in the political, legal and economic sphere, were revealed as partly identical in the cultural sphere; for both groups the declaration of another native,

468–471 *Santo Domingo cathedral (1512–41) and an early sixteenth-century house: examples of the styles imported from Europe*

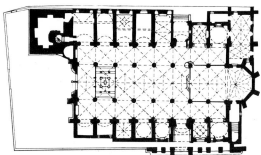

noted in 1562 by fray Mendieta, was valid: 'and now too much liberty is harming us'.[56] The common unease possibly explains the numerous indigenous features which re-appeared in civil experiments and particularly in architecture, as we shall see.

The heterogeneity of the two cultural systems did not seem to hamper these exchanges because the exceptional circumstances of the encounter between the two cultures caused reciprocal influences to take place, in certain cases, at the deepest human level, surmounting every obstacle of habit and tradition.

The traces of this dialogue – occasional and informal yet rich in consequences – are obvious on the European side, and crop up in various sectors of social life; they are more difficult to find on the native side, but equally real, if a person like Vasco de Quiroga, four hundred years later, is still considered present by the Indians of the Pátzcuaro region with the name *Tata Vasco*.

472   *View of Santo Domingo in* 1671

URBS DOMINGO IN HISPANIOLA

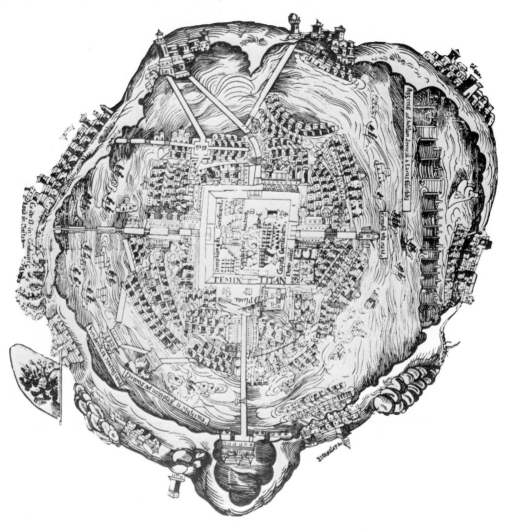

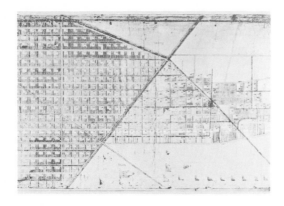

473   *Illustration to the Latin translation of the second letter of Cortés to Charles V, published in Nuremberg in 1524. This is the only copy of the drawing of Tenochtitlán, made by Cortés and enclosed with the letter*

474   *Eighteenth-century copy of the plan of Mexico City on maguey paper (Mexican National Museum)*

475 *Plan of Tenochtitlán, published with the account by the anonymous* conquistador

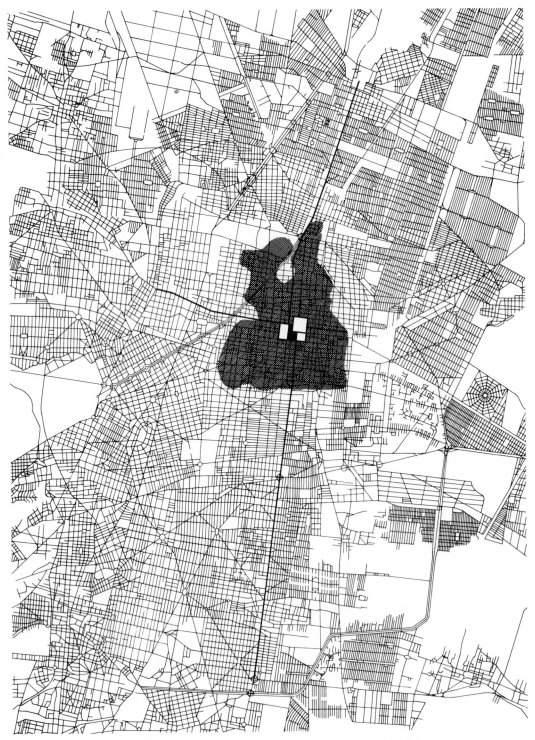

476 *The outline of the native city traced on the street system of present-day Mexico City*

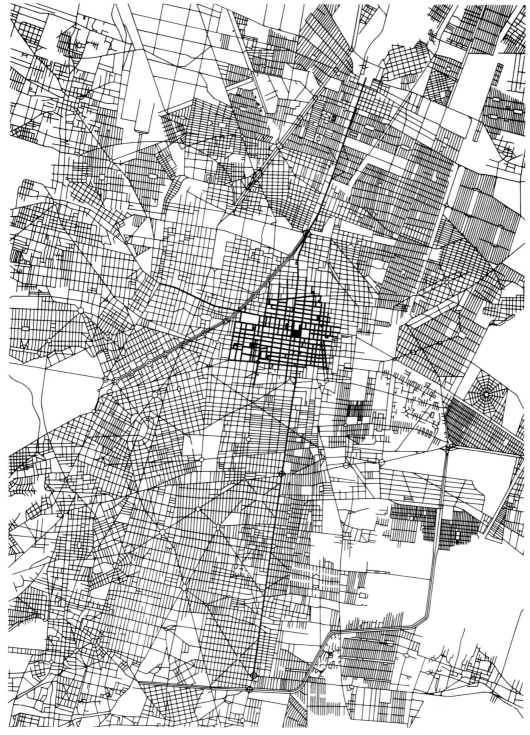

477 *The outline of the Spanish city traced on the street system of present-day Mexico City*

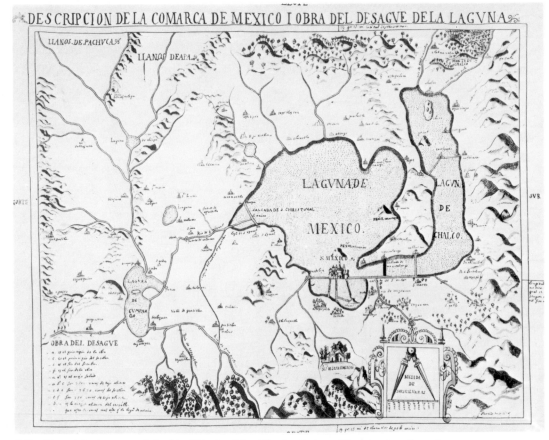

DESCRIPCION DE LA COMARCA DE MEXICO I OBRA DEL DESAGVE DE LA LAGVNA

478 *Plan of the lagoon and district of Mexico City at the beginning of the seventeenth century*

The first cities founded by the Spanish and Portuguese settlers in the Atlantic islands, and later in the Antilles, were mere outposts, whose layout was still largely random. The exception was Santo Domingo, founded in 1496 according to a plan reminiscent of that of Santa Fé de Granada (both probably derive from the conventional form of the fortified camp).

Between 1510 and 1520 the founding of cities became a frequent operation and plans, based on an elementary grid plan with a square mesh, were closely adapted to the terrain; they were in fact harbour towns, located at distinctive points on the coastline: San Miguel de Balboa in 1513, Santiago de Cuba in 1514, Havana in 1517 and Panama in 1519.

In 1519 Cortés landed on the coast of Mexico and founded the city of Villa Rica de Vera Cruz, according to a detailed plan prepared by his faithful *xumétrico* Alonso Garcia Bravo; this traced 'the church, square, naval shipyard and all things necessary for it to become a city'.[57]

Three years later Cortés stormed the capital of the Aztec empire, Tenochtitlán, and on its ruins had the same Garcia Bravo build the new Spanish capital, Mexico; he kept Charles V continually informed of his undertakings, sent him a drawing of the plan of the Aztec city, and in 1524 – when 30,000 Indians had returned to the capital – assured the emperor that 'within five years it will be the noblest and most populated city in the world, and one of the best built'[58] (Fig. 473).

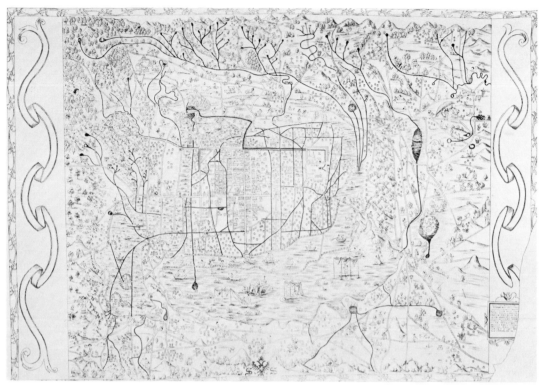

479, 480   *Plan of Mexico City attributed to Alonso de Santa Cruz, cosmographer to Charles V, 1555 and view of Mexico City in 1628 (in the centre the Zócalo with the cathedral)*

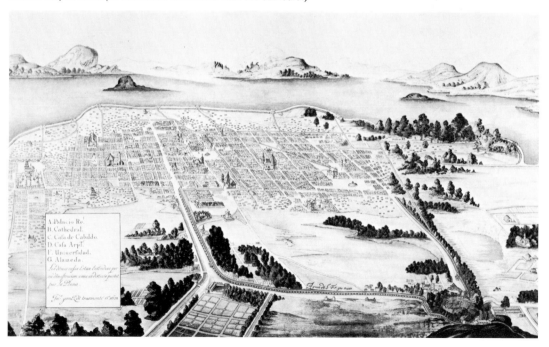

In 1530 Mexico was ready to receive the *Audiencia*, who wrote in his report: 'We know no city that has so many good houses, and all are on a *traza* save a very few.'[59]

Motolinia, in 1537, considered the town 'well-planned and even better built, with good large strong houses and very handsome streets. It is well supplied with all the necessities, both native and Spanish.'[60] The viceroy Mendoza saw his capital triple in the period of his mandate (1535–50) and in 1552 Gomara estimated – exaggeratedly – that there were 'about 100,000 houses'.[61] At the end of the century Mexico still amazed European visitors: Ponce praised 'the fine roads, broad and long, which all seem based on the same model, they are so regular and uniform';[62] Samuel de Champlain wrote: 'I had not supposed [it] to be so superbly composed, of splendid churches, palaces and fine houses, and the streets extremely well laid out.'[63] Ojea believed that it had 'the best plan one could wish in the world'[64] and a chronicler of the eighteenth century compared it to the square city of the Apocalypse.[65]

The organism of this city – praised by contemporaries because it realized the ideal of regularity lacking in European cities on a large scale – none the less derived from a singular fusion of pre-existing Aztec features and the new town-planning criteria of the *conquistadores*.

We have no exact representation of the original Tenochtitlán; but there is no doubt that some main elements – the sacred area in the centre of the city, with the temples and palaces of Montezuma, and the causeways running out through the lagoon towards the cardinal points – were drawn according to a geometrical scheme; around these elements the city was an aggregate of 'pockets' with houses and kitchen gardens accessible only by way of the lagoon and canals; the population, at the time of the conquest, is estimated at about 62,000 inhabitants.

Aztec culture implied a notable capacity for the overall representation, and hence for the planning, of the physical environment; there existed native plans of Tenochtitlán, which were seen by Pedro Martin, and copied by Juan de Ribera, Cortés' amanuensis:[66]

'Among the maps of these territories, we have examined one which is thirty feet wide or a little less, woven of white cotton, where the lagoon and provinces friendly and adverse to Montezuma are described at length. . . . Apart from the large map, we saw a slightly smaller one, which aroused no less interest. It included the city of Mexico, with its temples, bridges and lagoons, painted by hand by the natives.'

The Europeans, whose enterprises were dependent at every step upon just such systems of spatial representation, were stimulated by these analogous aspects of native culture. The unbridgeable gap on the other hand lay in the fundamental concept of the city, which for the Americans was a service centre for a largely scattered population and consisted of temples, roads and public buildings, while for the Europeans it was a favoured or indeed exclusive system of settlement, as in Spain, and therefore made up mainly of houses.

This difference affected architecture, and its significance in relation to the natural landscape. The pyramid-shaped temples stood out alone against the backdrop of nature, the common setting for both life and work, as signs of the human presence, and instruments of a possible compromise with all-powerful natural forces (Fig. 481). But public and private buildings, according to European ideas, had significance because gathered together into a city they formed a human landscape, man-made and compact, in contradistinction to that of the country-side.

Mexico, and the other cities built by the Spaniards all over America, were therefore dependent first of all on a plan of redistribution of settlements, which was considered vital for all economic, political and religious

481 *The Pyramid of the Sun at Teotihuacán*

change; the official term used for this operation was *poblar*, to populate.

The first council of the Mexican church, in 1555, requested that the Indians 'should be persuaded – or compelled by Royal authority, if necessary, but without the least possible vexation – to congregate in convenient locations and in reasonable towns where they may live in a polite and Christian manner.'[67]

Padre Juan de San Miguel, who was working in Mexico immediately after the conquest, 'to carry to its full effect the great zeal he felt to convert the Indians, persuaded them to leave the wild and mountainous regions where they lived, and to transfer themselves lower down where the terrain was less hilly, more fertile and fresh. Here he founded orderly cities, and thus made their inhabitants worthy of being called men, while

they were not so where they had been living before, scattered far from one another.'[68]

Bearing in mind this absolute ideological contrast, it is possible to interpret correctly the way Garcia Bravo's mind was working when he designed the new plan for the Mexican capital. He accepted the principal lines of the Aztec city, sited the *plaza mayor* in the sacred area and the new buildings of religious and political importance – the cathedral, Cortés' palace – in the place of the temples and palace of Montezuma. But he put these elements at the service of a plan for a residential settlement, equalizing public and private buildings within the street grid, as well as plots whose future was already settled and plots whose purpose was still unfixed.

It is permissible to think that the great experiment of Mexico City influenced the

482, 483 *Aerial view and plan of Oaxaca*

plans of the other cities founded in large
numbers from the 1520s onwards on Mexican
territory and in the other regions of Latin
America. The same Garcia Bravo drew up
the plan of Oaxaca (Figs 482–3) and the
second Vera Cruz;[69] we know the names of
various other planners: Juan Alanis (plan for
Santiago de Queretaro, 1534), Alonso Martin
Perez (plan of Puebla de los Angeles 1531),
Juan Ponce (plan of Valladolid, now Morelia,
1541).

The frequency of these undertakings gave
rise to the need for a common rule: the blocks
were square (or, more rarely, rectangular) and
the central square was obtained by doing
away with one of these blocks. In 1525 Cortés
gave a series of instructions which implied a
positively standardized model:[70]

'After felling the trees you must begin to
clear the site and then, following the plan I
have made, you must make out the public
places just as they are shown: the plaza,

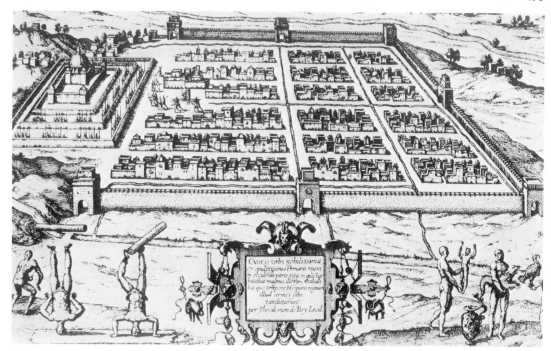

484 *Fantastic view of the city of Cuzco by Teodoro de Bry*

church, town hall and jail, market and slaughterhouse, hospital. . . . Then you will indicate to each citizen his particular lot, as shown on the plan, and do the same for those who come later. You will make sure that the streets are very straight, and accordingly will find people who know how to lay them out.'

In 1530 Pizarro, who aspired to repeat the deeds of Cortés, founded the city of San Miguel in Peru, 'in accordance with the rule, with the central square'[71] and later, on the same model, Quito and San Francisco de Quito (1532), the new Cuzco (1533) and Lima (1535).

In Peru, too, the *conquistadores* found a highly evolved urban civilization, which used geometrical layouts to organize its settlements: Cuzco, the Inca capital, was spontaneously represented by European draughtsmen according to the now widespread grid plan (Fig. 484); some cities excavated re-

485 *Plan of the city of Pikillaqta in Peru (from Kubler)*

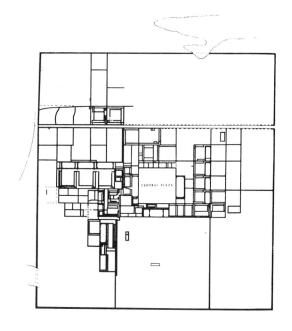

486 *Inca walling at Cuzco*

cently, such as Viracochapampa and Pikillaqta (Fig. 485) were based on a rigid orthogonal grid, and were probably built during the Spanish conquest or a little before.

At Cuzco and in other places the building methods of the natives and *conquistadores* were fused over the course of time and made any precise distinction between the two phases difficult. But town-planning development comparable to the Mexican began only after the arrival of the viceroy Toledo in 1570. The population gradually concentrated in the new cities, such as Lima, which grew and acquired a complex organization, with a main square and other secondary ones.

At the same period Spanish colonization was spreading further into South America, and later to the Philippines; the same town-planning model was utilized in all climates and all circumstances, in Cartagena in 1533,

487 *Inca walling and Spanish walling in a street in Cuzco*

Guayaquil and Buenos Aires in 1535, Bogotà in 1538, Santiago in 1541, Concepciòn in 1550, Caracas in 1567 and Manila in 1571.

The central authority seems to have been involved only indirectly in this tremendous effort of town-planning invention and experiment.

In 1501 king Ferdinand gave Oviedo only vague instructions:[72]

'As it is necessary in the island of Hispaniola to make settlements and from here it is not possible to give precise instructions, investigate the possible sites, and in conformity with the quality of the land and sites as well as with the present population outside present settlements establish settlements in the numbers and in the places that seem proper to you.'

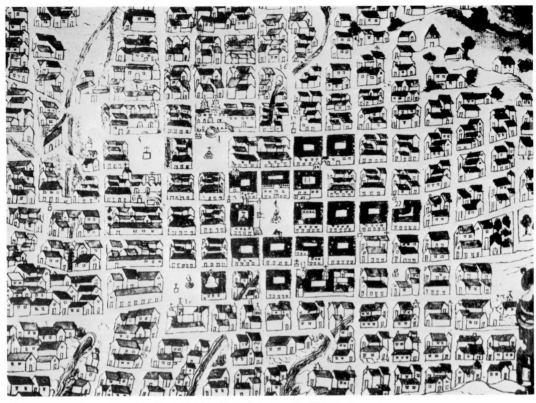

488   *Detail from the plan of Quito, 1734 (Archivio de Indias, Seville)*

In 1513, the instructions to Pedrarias Davila affirmed the need to proceed according to a rule only in general terms:[73]

'One of the most important things to observe is that . . . the places chosen for settlement . . . be healthy and not swampy . . . if inland, on a river if possible . . . good air and water, close to arable land . . . seeking the best site in these terms for the town, then divide the plots for houses, these to be according to the status of the persons, and from the beginning it should be according to a definite arrangement; for the manner of setting up the *solares* will determine the pattern of the town, both in the position of the plaza and the church and in the pattern of the streets, for towns being newly formed may be established according to plan without difficulty. . . . If not started with form, they will never attain it.'

Only much later, when the cycle of these experiments was largely completed, did Philip II promulgate the law of 3 June 1573: a real town-planning law with detailed regulations which were to remain unchanged in the following two centuries.

The text of this law was partly a compendium of theoretical notions established in the culture of the time, and partly the summary of an already well-established experience: it therefore described a model arrived at through a process of convergence on practical grounds (two Argentinian cities already built – Mendoza in 1561 and San Juan de la Frontera in 1562 – were virtually identical[74] to the rulings of 1573):[75]

'On arriving at the locality where the new settlement is to be founded (which according to our will and ordinance must be one which is vacant and can be occupied

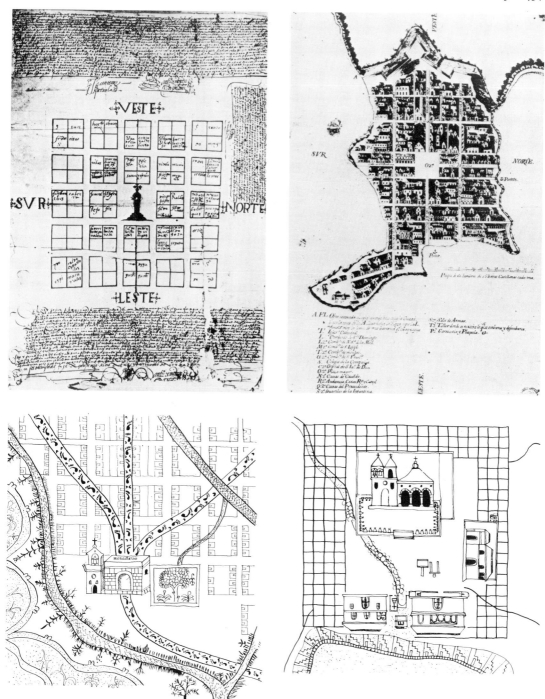

489–492 *Plans of Mendoza, 1562, and of Panama, 1673, in the Archivio de Indias, Seville and native plans of Tejupan, 1579, and Tenango del Valle, 1582. The representation of the highways (shown by footprints) interferes with the representation of the urban grid plan (from McAndrew)*

without doing harm to the Indians and natives or with their free consent) the plan of the place, with its squares, streets and building lots is to be outlined by means of measuring by cord and ruler, beginning with the main square from which streets are to run to the gates and principal roads and leaving sufficient open space so that even if the town grows it can always spread in a symmetrical manner. . . . The main plaza should be in the centre of the town and of an oblong shape, its length being equal to at least one and a half times its width, as this proportion is the best for festivals in which horses are used and any other celebrations which have to be held. . . . The size of the plaza shall be in proportion to the number of residents, heed being given to the fact that the towns of Indians, being new are bound to grow and it is intended that they shall do so. Therefore the plaza is to be planned with reference to the positive growth of the town. It shall not be smaller than two hundred feet wide and three hundred feet long nor larger than eight hundred feet long and three hundred feet wide. A well proportioned medium size plaza is one six hundred feet long and four hundred feet wide.

From the centre of the plaza the four principal streets are to diverge, one from the middle of each of its sides, and two streets are to meet at each of its corners. The four corners are to face the four points of the compass, because thus the streets diverging from the plaza will not be directly exposed to the four principal winds, which could cause much inconvenience. The whole plaza and the four streets diverging from it shall have arcades, for these are a great convenience to those who have to resort thither for trade. . . .

The eight streets which run into the plaza at its four corners are to do so freely without being obstructed by the arcades of the plaza. These arcades are to end at the corners in such a way that the sidewalks of

the streets can easily join those of the plaza. In cold climates the streets shall be wide; in hot climates narrow, however, for purposes of defense and where horses are kept the streets had better be wide. . . .

In inland towns the church is not to be on the plaza but at a distance from it in a situation where it can be seen from all sides. It can thus be made more beautiful and it will inspire more respect. It would be built on high ground so that in order to reach its entrance people will have to ascend a flight of steps. . . . The hospital of the poor who are ill with non-contagious diseases shall be built facing the north and so planned that it will enjoy a southern exposure. . . . No building lots surrounding the main plaza are to be given to private individuals for these are to be reserved for the church, Royal and Town House, also shops and dwellings for the merchants, which are to be the first housed. . . . The remaining lots shall be distributed by lottery to those of the settlers who are entitled to build around the main plaza. Those left over are to be held for us to grant to settlers who may come later or to dispose of at our pleasure.

The building lots and the structures erected thereon are to be so situated that in the living rooms one can enjoy air from the south and from the north, which are the best. All town houses are to be so planned that they can serve as a defence or fortress against those who might attempt to create disturbances or occupy the towns. . . . Settlers are to endeavour too, as far as possible, to make all structures uniform, for the sake of the beauty of the town. . . .

A common shall be assigned to each town, of adequate size so that even though it should grow greatly there would always be sufficient space for its inhabitants to find recreation and for cattle to pasture without encroaching upon private property.'

Both the settlements already built and the

text of the law of 1573 posed the problem of the relations between European and American experiments. How far was what happened in the New World an application of European models, and how far was it an original affair?

The plans of the American cities have been compared to Roman ones, to the medieval *bastides*, to the Renaissance grid towns such as Cortemaggiore (1480), Ferrara (1492), Gattinara (1526), Guastalla (1539), Vitry-le-François (1545), Sabbioneta (1560), Valletta (1566). But all these comparisons are unconvincing.

There is no difficulty in stating that the Spaniards of the sixteenth century were acquainted with the remains of Roman cities on orthogonal grid plans that had survived in the Iberian peninsula – Tarragona, Merida, Braga – and even the more distant and better known ones, Nîmes, Turin, Zara; that they knew the grid-plan cities founded in Spain from the twelfth to fourteenth centuries – Sanguesa, Villareal, Briviesca – and even more certainly the more recent ones such as Alicante and Gandia (the home town of one of the first missionaries, fray Alonso de Borja); that they would have known of the French *bastides* situated on the main communication routes, such as Montpazier, Villeneuve-sur-Lot, Ste-Foy-la-Grande, and that they knew the famous Italian examples by hearsay.

But this knowledge did not influence practical experiments. The period of settlement on the land had been over in Spain, as in the rest of Europe, for almost two centuries, and the few new cities founded at the end of the fifteenth century such as Cortemaggiore, Santa Fé de Granada and Puerto Real, seem to depend not so much on ancient or modern tradition as on the military practice of the *castramentatio*, diffused both in treatises on war and ancient texts like Polybius and Vegetius (Figs 496–7). This practice – also described in Machiavelli's *Arte della guerra* which appeared in 1521 – has been considered one of the possible

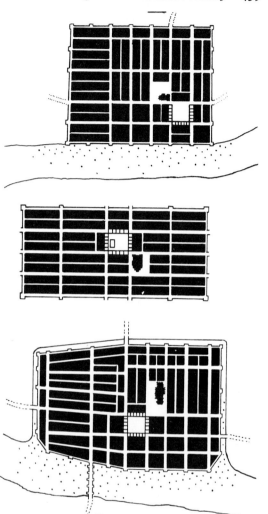

493–495 *Plans of Villeneuve-sur-Lot, Montpazier and Ste-Foy-la-Grande*

immediate sources of the Mexican experiments, in the first decades after the conquest;[76] what remains to be explained is the transition between sectorial practice, closely linked to military necessities, and these uses of it, which covered all the needs of a civil society, from one end of the continent to the other. Lastly, the new cities of the Renaissance, in Italy and France, were almost all later than the first American cities, and were so many isolated occasions, not the results of a regular praxis.

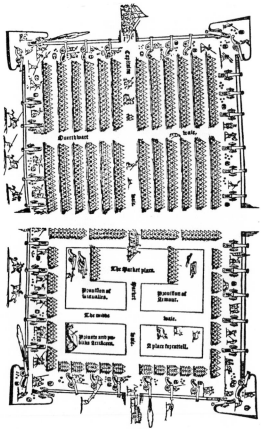

496 *Plan of an encampment for 24,000 men and 2,000 horses, from Machiavelli,* Arte della guerra, *1521*

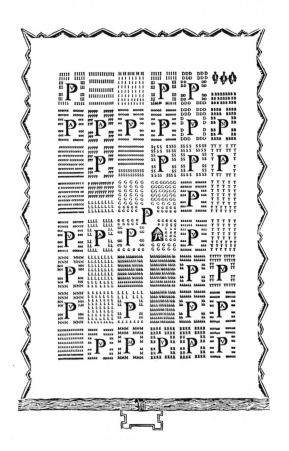

497 *Plan of an encampment, from Cesare D'Evoli,* Delle ordinannza e battaglie, 1586

The opposite opinion, which minimizes cultural precedents and considers the grid system as an elementary device, invented anew by the American colonizers on a basis of purely technical criteria, is equally unpersuasive. The geometric culture of the Renaissance, before being a repertory of aristocratic solutions, was a mental habit now linked to the functioning of industry, trade, exploration and business. Both productive techniques and the visual habits which had acquired the significance of a contemplative pause in everyday life, were based on the premise of regularity, i.e. on the spatial conception gradually elaborated in the two previous centuries.

At the beginning of the sixteenth century, this conception was the common property of all European nations and all social classes. Its results in the field of town-planning were few and sporadic in Europe, because of the importance of the already existing urban apparatus, inherited from the Middle Ages, but enormous in America, where settlements had to be organized *ex novo* in a way totally different from the traditional one (and furthermore the indigenous tradition offered additional stimulus, with the geometrical rigour of its layouts, even on the scale of the landscape). Therefore the grid system adopted in America, if it did not derive from a still living operative tradition, certainly derived

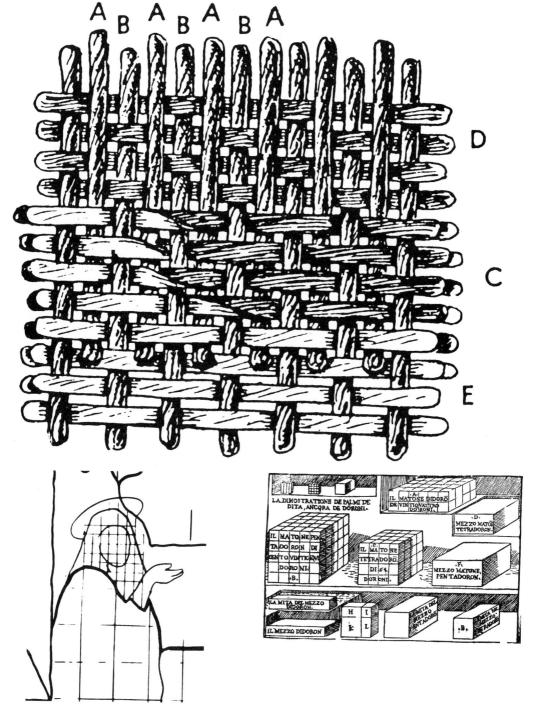

498–500 *The right-angled network in European technical and figurative culture: weaving patterns in use at the beginning of the seventeenth century; detail of the* sinopia *of the* Trinity *of Masaccio, 1424; brick measurements from the 1536 edition of Vitruvius (Caporali)*

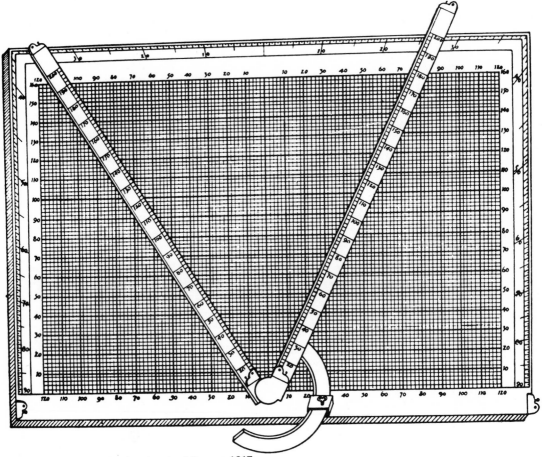

501 *Measurements for the triangle of Bramer, 1617*

from a cultural ideal, which was only partially and occasionally applied in Europe in the field of town-planning, but appeared in all the 'modern' schemes and was usually present, in general opinion, as an index of modernity.

At the time of the founding of Santo Domingo, Oviedo considered the grid plan '*de nuestro tiempo*', while the bishop Alessandro Geraldini, an Italian humanist, believed it to be derived from classical antiquity.[77] Both judgments are justified, in the cultural situation typical of the beginning of the sixteenth century.

Having established the cultural homogeneity between Europe and the colonies, one can approach the comparison between the two orders of experiments correctly. The new American cities could be compared not so much with the new European cities – almost always artificial and superstructural products of political power – but with the schemes furthered by economic power such as the new districts in Augsburg and Nuremberg, the extension of Antwerp and the Bairro Alto of Lisbon. Even without discussing possible reciprocal influences it is easy to recognize at the basis of all these enterprises, varying as they did according to the circumstances, the same bold and expeditious, though methodical, mentality, receptive to erudite, theoretical and even Utopian suggestion.

Precisely because of the characteristics of

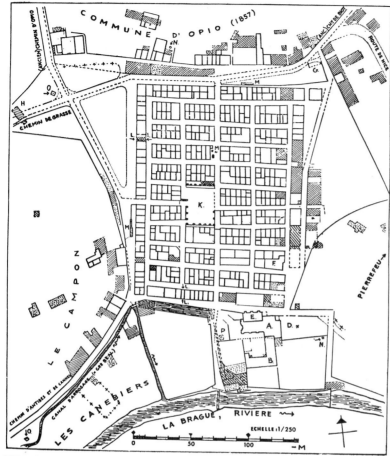

502 *Plan of Valbonne (from Kubler)*

this mentality, freed from traditional hier-archical precedence, relationships between individual European and American experi-ments must be regarded as possible, in both directions, from Europe to America, and from America to Europe, and must be regarded as probable only when, beyond formal analogy, one can point to the actual channel linking the two.

In accordance with this criterion, the cases to be considered are these:

1 The towns built by the abbé Grimaldi on the coast of Provence to repopulate the region and particularly Valbonne (Fig. 502) founded in 1519, about ten kilometres east of Grasse.[78] The Genoese family of Grimaldi had close

relations with Spain, and the abbé, whose headquarters were on the Îles d'Hyères, was certainly in contact with Spanish monastic cultural circles.

2 The small town of Gattinara (Figs 503–5), laid out in 1242 according to a grid plan (like other Piedmontese towns of the same period: Cherasco, Frossasco, Borgomanero) des-troyed by the French in 1525, and rebuilt soon afterwards – whether retracing or correcting the original plan it is not known – by Mercurino Arborio da Gattinara, chan-cellor of Charles V. He was one of the central figures of the Spanish court until his death in 1530; an extremely cultured man, he had considerable influence on imperial policy

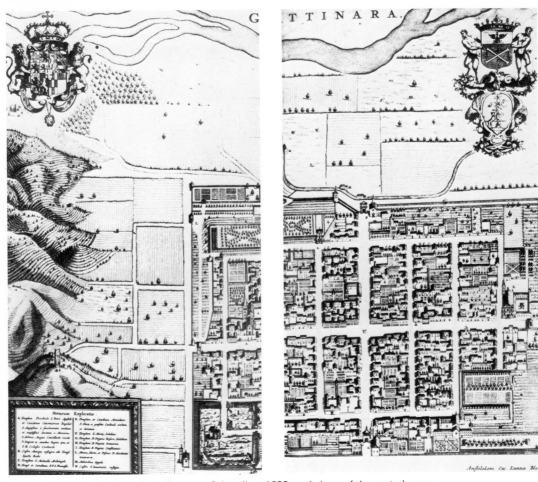

503–505 *Plan of Gattinara from* Theatrum Sabaudiae, *1682, and views of the central square*

both in Spain and in America and, as both diplomat and soldier, consistently upheld the humanitarian and reformist ideals typical of his generation, which was that of Cisneros, Adrian of Utrecht and Erasmus.

Both at Valbonne and Gattinara the general plan was a rectangle divided into a cross by two main streets, formed of two series of oblong blocks, perpendicular to the main dimension. These two towns – together with Cortemaggiore (1480), Puerto Real (1483), Santa Fé de Granada (1492) – gave evidence of the standard type of European town-planning culture at the end of the fifteenth and beginning of the sixteenth centuries. Gattinara certainly retraced the medieval layout, particularly in the shape of the square which is an expansion of the central crossroads, formed by the narrowing of the longitudinal street, at both its ends, by arcades; the regularization of this layout was possibly influenced by Valbonne, but could also be a momentary echo of the great town-planning ventures that were taking place overseas, certainly well-known to Mercurino.

3   The order of the Hospital of St John of Jerusalem, which until 1522 had its centre in Rhodes (where there existed one of the most important Hippodamian layouts of all antiquity), then was driven out by the Turks and in 1530 obtained a new headquarters from Charles V on the island of Malta; here in 1566 the Grand Master La Vallette founded the city which bears his name. Also, some building models typical of this order (the fortified monasteries, and the corner ciboria in the churches of San Juan del Duero and of Paros, from which the Mexican *posas* were derived) have been suggested as possible sources of those of the New World.[79] Influence of the order of the Knights of Rhodes is possible, but only hypothetical; as far as Valletta is concerned (Fig. 628), it is known that in 1566 American experiments were widely known and discussed, at least in Spain, as may be deduced from the laws in

1573, and the order had close relations with Spain, which provided two of its seven divisions; the plan of Valletta either derived from the American ones or arose independently from similar cultural premises.

From the middle of the sixteenth century onwards influences coming from America to Europe became increasingly probable, and almost certain as far as the central squares of the Spanish towns built or rebuilt on a regular plan during the last decades of the century were concerned. With the passing of time, however, the difference between the urban organisms of the New World and similar ones founded in Europe increased (Vitry, Valletta and Sabbioneta and later Livorno, Nancy and Charleville); these, originally conceived for special military or political requirements, remained fixed once and for all in the shape and size of the initial design; while American cities were organisms in continual growth, whose further developments it was impossible initially to foresee. Furthermore European cities were normally fortified, and the fortifications formed a ring which settled their perimeter definitively; while the American cities, at least throughout the sixteenth century, were almost entirely lacking in fortifications and any pre-established perimeter; the grid system could expand indefinitely, prolonging the straight roads in the direction desired. Later, in the seventeenth century, some cities near the coast (Panama, Vera Cruz, Lima, Manila, etc.) were also surrounded with walls; but it is interesting to see that the dynamism of growth continued to produce new suburbs beyond the ring of fortifications, as happened in the Middle Ages (Fig. 506).

Another factor to be noted is the increasing influence of academic culture, in America as in Europe, from the reign of Philip II onwards. It was now that the classical and Italian treatises were widely diffused throughout Spain, in accordance with the Counter-Reformationary mood imposed by the new king; Serlio was translated into Spanish in

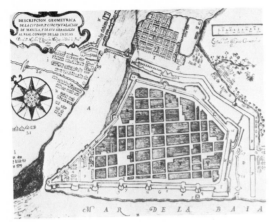

506 *Plan of Manila, 1671, in the Archivio de Indias, Seville*

1563, Vitruvius in 1565, Alberti in 1582 and these texts also circulated in Mexico and Lima, both in public libraries and in book-shops. In 1589 the Mexican guild of carpenters and masons required masters to take an ex-amination in the drawing of the five orders.

Many passages of the law of 1573 derive from theoretical sources: St Thomas Aquinas' *De regimine principum*, Eximenics' *Crestia*, the treatises of Vitruvius and Alberti; for instance those on the winds and choice of site, which are rhetorical and heedless of the American geographical reality; Stanislawsky has worked out a detailed parallel between Vitruvius' text and that of the law.[80] In reality these academic references merely helped to consolidate and rigidify a body of experience already gained, though far from unreceptive to such contributions.

But the crucial proof of the originality of the American experience can be found by proceeding from the town-planning scale to the building scale.

From the 1520s onwards most of the medium-sized and small Mexican towns were founded by religious orders, Francis-cans, Dominicans and Augustinians, and were intended for the Indians, to protect them from the overbearing behaviour of the Europeans; in 1550 the Spaniards were forbidden to live in them.

The grid plan, regularly adopted in such towns, not only included an open space of some size – the central square – but also another equally important enclosed space adjacent to the first: the *atrio*, which stood in front of the buildings of the church and monastery, and was used as a meeting place to hear Mass on special holidays (the church was used only for everyday services).

This enclosure was enlivened by terraces, and flights of steps, and equipped with a series of architectural elements: the *capilla de indios* (an open chapel which, like theatre scenery, protected and framed the altar where the Mass was said), the *posas* (small chapels used as stopping-places during pro-cessions) and crosses on great stone pedestals.

Thus the new cities, instead of having a series of positive volumes at their centre, as happened in European cities, had a large empty space, articulated in a complex way and often terraced on various levels, especi-ally where the ground was sloping. This meant that the city ceased to seem an enclosed place, and it opened up the sweeping perspectives typical of indigenous architec-ture right in the monumental heart of the city.

Furthermore even today the sensation of contrast between non-Christian schemes and Christian ones is one of the most inspiring experiences for anyone visiting the territories of the Spanish colonies. The scale of the pagan shrines is cosmic, intentionally alien to the measurements of man; even the elements capable of introducing a reference to these measurements, such as the staircases, have steps almost inaccessible to human stature. Their alignments were regulated along the trajectories of the stars, and run independently of the features of the places in which they are set. On the other hand the Christian schemes, even if impressive, did respect the human scale in every element, and were quick to absorb every irregularity caused by the accidents of the terrain, or the ups and downs of construction; grandiosity was reserved for empty spaces, which in some

507, 508 Atrio *and church of Izamal, Yucatán, 1553–61*

cases surpassed any European comparison: for instance the Zócalo in Mexico City is a regular area measuring 300 by 250 metres, but the surrounding buildings, both in the sixteenth century and the centuries that followed, were low and welcoming, making no attempt to emulate the measurements of the empty space (Fig. 532).

The space formed of the square and *atrio* was the real architectural core of the Mexican cities, in relation to which the actual buildings – houses, church, convent, *capilla* and *posas* – amounted to decorative accessories; the church was reduced as always to a single long narrow nave, like the more modest late Gothic parish churches, and rarely stood out as a higher volume; but the façade, that is the smooth wall filling in the front end of the nave, was moulded and decorated as an autonomous architectural motif, in that it helped to characterize the space of the *atrio*.

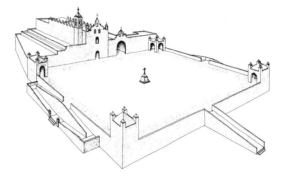

There is no need to stress the originality of this model, after the analysis made of it by McAndrew; one need only say that he considers it 'the most dramatic American architectural innovation before the skyscraper'.[81]

The architectural focus of the whole complex was the *capilla de indios*, which took on a great variety of shapes and utilized

various models: the late Gothic apses, the tabernacles used in Europe inside churches, and even the hypostyle halls of the Moslem mosques as in San José de los Naturales and at Cholula (Figs 512–16). These motifs, taken out of doors and used as backcloths for an open space, acquired an unexpected chiaroscuro, and in their turn demanded to be incorporated into an architectural proscenium, suitably shaped above to resolve the transition skywards.

The stylistic ornaments became secondary accessories, i.e. accessories of accessories; they were taken from the Gothic, Plateresque or Renaissance repertoires, or from the indigenous tradition, with disconcerting blitheness; some motifs were taken wholesale from treatises, such as the staircase of San Francisco at Quito (Fig. 520), the porch of

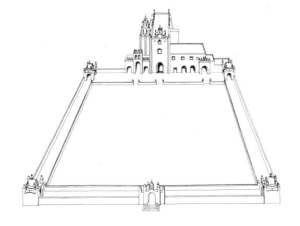

509, 510 *Detail of a fresco and general view of the* atrio *and church, Atlatlauhcán*

511 *One of the* posas *of the* atrio *of Atlatlauhcán*

512, 513   *Aerial views of the city of Cholula and its central complex*

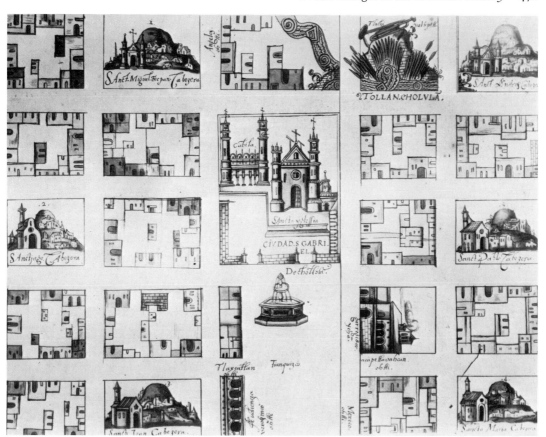

514–516 *Details of a 1581 plan of Cholula; plan of the central complex, showing* atrio, church *and* capilla de indios; *interior view of the* capilla de indios

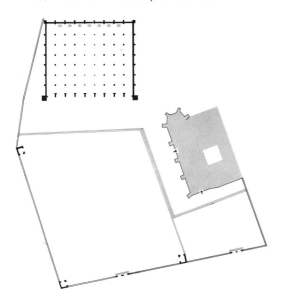

517, 518 *The atrio of Tepotzotlán and battlemented enclosure of the atrio of Tula, c. 1550; the battlements are used to mark the limits of the open space*

519   *Façade of the church of Acolmán, 1558*

the church of Tecali and the décor of the roof of the *capilla* at Actopán (Fig. 522), reproduced from the illustrations to Serlio's treatise.

Thus the novelty of the functional programme – i.e. the need, in the centre of the city, for a space where all the citizens could gather together – gave birth to an original building typology, for which only negligible precedents existed, in Spain or elsewhere.

But from this same programme, in special circumstances, even more singular architectural solutions were deduced. At Cuilapán about 1555 the Dominicans built a large church with nave and two aisles, where the side walls were pierced by a series of arches, and the organism became a sort of open portico (Figs 523–4). At Pátzcuaro the bishop Quiroga, whom we have already mentioned, ended his extraordinary career by

building, between 1540 and 1565, a cathedral which was to hold 30,000 people (Fig. 525); the plan made provision for five blocks, converging towards the altar, of which only one was completed amid innumerable difficulties; the initial idea seems to have come from the bishop himself, and was possibly inspired by the cathedral of Granada with its rounded end, designed by Siloe when Quiroga was leaving for America.

Quiroga's cathedral was the translation into architecture of his cultural and humanistic programme, which was termed Utopian because of the European sources upon which it depended (Erasmus and Thomas More); in Europe More's *Utopia* was regarded as a piece of philosophical speculation, while in America it could become a guide to concrete undertakings.[82]

The architectural schemes in the big cities

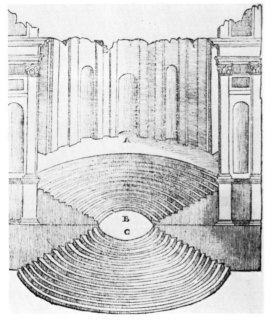

520–522   *The outside staircase of San Francisco at Quito, c. 1580, derived from Serlio; the* capilla de indios *at Actopán, c. 1550, with Serlian decorations*

523, 524   *The church of Cuilapán, c. 1555, with its outside walls pierced by a succession of arches. The natural light removes the distinction between interior and exterior*

ESTAS·SON·LAS·AR
MAS·QVE·DIO·EL·REI·

E STA CIVDAD DE
MECHVACÁN

525 *Plan of the church at Pátzcuaro, carved on the pedestal of the cross, 1553 (from McAndrew)*

– Mexico, Lima, Cuzco – were more conventional and closer to European models; the cathedral of Santo Domingo, founded in 1512, reproduced the pattern of the great Spanish Gothic cathedrals, but introduced into it a series of extremely significant geometrical simplifications (the plan was the result of a combination of squares) (Fig. 470); the cathedral of Mexico City, begun in 1563, and of Puebla, begun in 1565, followed a

scheme analogous to that of the cathedral of Valladolid, designed by Herrera in 1585, i.e. they anticipated or promptly reproduced the most modern model known at the time.

The Spanish architect Francisco Becerra travelled from Mexico to Peru, and designed religious buildings, including the Dominican and Franciscan houses at Quito (1581), the cathedrals of Lima (1582) and Cuzco (1589). Some clients had the designs sent directly from Rome, as was done by the Jesuits for their church at Quito.

Considered in its entirety, the architecture of the American colonies bears out neither the thesis of *hispanidad* as the prevailing feature of the new society, nor the thesis of vestiges of feudalism, which prolonged the life of the forms of settlement typical of medieval Europe on the American continent.

Architecture was not necessarily the mirror of the whole of social life, but it was a sector where the spirit of novelty and invention prevailed over the traditional conformism, and imparted this spirit, in so far as it was qualified to do so, into everyday life. Architectural experiments, particularly on a town-planning scale, were influenced not so much by similar European experiments and deeply-rooted habits, as by the patrimony of ideas and aspirations, which could not become reality in Europe; they were an integral part of what has been described as 'the most extraordinary adventure in the history of Europe',[83] and despite the wastage caused by an abnormal distribution of energies, they helped to lessen the weight of the past and they paved the way for the future.

The town-planning pattern created in America in the first decades of the sixteenth century and strengthened by the law of 1573 was the only model for a new city produced by Renaissance culture and regulated in all its executive consequences;[84] this model continued to function for four centuries both in America and elsewhere and, after being generalized within the framework of neoclassical culture, was to serve as the

526, 527   *Aerial views of Malinalco and Tlaxcala*

528   *The Zócalo and the cathedral of Puebla*

basis for the greatest territorial transformation of the modern era: the colonization and urbanization of the USA.

Alternative developments in Italian architectural culture

The crisis of the 'third style' – i.e. of a comprehensive synthesis, including all aspects of modern artistic culture – and the unexpected broadening of the field of experiment, of which we have talked in previous sections, altered the nature of architectural debate even in its traditional centres, i.e. in the great Italian cities.

The most important aspect was the lack of a common aim recognized as valid for all branches of activity; artists and critics gradually accustomed themselves to considering the simultaneous presence of differ-

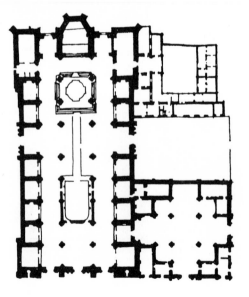

529   *Plan of the cathedral of Mexico City*

530–532 *The urban environment of the colonial city: Mexico City. The façade of the cathedral onto the Zócalo; one of the adjoining streets; aerial view of the centre; one can see the Zócalo with the cathedral on the left and the town hall facing towards one*

ent cultural ideals – between which one had to choose – and different criteria of judgment.

Vasari, too, who elaborated the most important single historical interpretation of the modern movement, in the edition of the *Lives* of 1550, rigidly upheld the hierarchy of values which culminated with the art of Michelangelo (and he talked of Michelangelo only in the superlative, attributing to him every perfection); but in the edition of 1568 he toned down this approach, introduced several reservations about his idol, and recognized the originality of other experiments: those of Raphael, Correggio and the Venetian painters.[85]

Discussion of certain recurrent problems (such as the comparison between the arts and that between the artistic schools of the various cities) took on a new character. The comparison between painting and sculpture became, after the well-known declarations of Leonardo and Michelangelo, a commonplace of sixteenth-century literature; it was developed in Castiglione's *Courtier* (1527), in Cardano's *De subtilitate* (1550), and at considerable length in Varchi's address of 1546 to the Florentine Academy, for the author had carried out an enquiry among the main Florentine artists of the time; opinions naturally continued to differ, but the arguments were partly new: painting and sculpture were judged preferable in proportion to their difficulty (Pontormo, Francesco da Sangallo) or because of their universality or ease of communication (Vasari); Michelangelo, now an old man, questioned by Vasari and Varchi, ironically refused to decide.[86] The other discussion on the superiority of Florentine or Venetian artists was still of topical interest; but the Florentine claim to dictate a universal norm through drawing was made increasingly difficult by the successes of Venetian painting; the scale of values typical of Venetian painting, hence the importance of colour in relation to drawing, was defended by the Tuscan Pietro Aretino, Paolo Pino[87] and Lodovico Dolce.[88]

In Pino there was also mention of the eclectic solution of the conflict (perfection lies in the drawing of Michelangelo and the colour of Titian). Though hampered by inadequate language, criticism was becoming accustomed to observing differences, as essential values of artistic culture.

But it is pointless for our purposes to follow the details of this debate, which concerns the figurative arts almost exclusively, and is heavily conditioned by literary rhetoric.

Architecture appears only incidentally in these discussions, and the problems of architecture were virtually ignored as belonging to another order of ideas and being incapable of expression in these terms. In architecture, too, the main problem that arose in the sixteenth century was the problem of differences; universality, which was the ideal of the 'third style', retained a positive meaning if translated into a suitable multiplicity of models, befitting the variety and scale of the new requirements. But to do this the most important difficulties were those of the distribution of energies, the division of labour and the point of application of the single individual contributions. Sixteenth-century Italian culture was completely unfitted to talk of these things, and continued to conceive architectural planning as a single operation similar to painting and sculpture. Solutions to these difficulties were thus reached gradually, in the practical sphere, outside and in a sense despite the schema of official culture.

In this context it is interesting once again to contrast the Florentine and Venetian scenes, where two completely different organizational hypotheses were being worked out.

This contrast was only partly linked to the preceding one, widespread in literary and figurative culture, or rather it included the figurative contrast as a particular case, because it revealed two classifications of productive activities and showed that Venetian painters occupied a different place in their circle from that of Florentine painters in theirs, so that the direct stylistic comparison concealed a structural comparison that was more complicated and richer in implications.

The Florentine hypothesis

The siege of 1530 and the collapse of the republican institutions left Florence in a profoundly agitated state which lasted for several years.

Soon after the fall of the city Michelangelo was working, as we have said, on the statues for the Medici chapel in S. Lorenzo, and in 1534 he finally left for Rome.

Although the constitution of 1532 attributed sovereign powers to him, Alexander I continued to live in the palazzo in via Larga, and did not alter the layout of the city; he restricted himself to having the Fortezza da Basso built, to put himself in safety from internal disturbances. At this time most Florentine and Tuscan artists were working elsewhere (Sansovino in Venice, Cellini, Rosso and Primaticcio in France, Ammannati in Venice and then in Rome with Vasari).

The re-establishment of the Florentine cultural apparatus began after 1537, when Cosimo I took power; in 1541 he took under his protection the Accademia degli Umidi, founded in 1540 by Giovanni Mazzuoli for the study of the Italian language, and turned it into the Accademia Fiorentina, with a complex programme for the reappraisal of the local artistic and literary heritage; in 1545 he laid out the botanical gardens or Giardino dei Semplici, and summoned Andrea Cesalpino to run it; in 1549 he established the posts of supervisors of rivers, bridges and roads. Meanwhile some of the main Tuscan artists were returning to Florence: in 1545 Cellini came back from France, in 1551 Vasari returned from Rome, having published the first edition of his *Lives*, with tremendous success, the previous year; he became Cosimo's artistic adviser and an effective mediator between the world of artists and that of writers. At his suggestion Cosimo called

Giambologna to Florence in 1553, Ammannati in 1555, and in 1562 founded the Accademia del Disegno, where architects, painters and sculptors lived together according to the same rules as the men of letters.

Cosimo made use of these artists to realize a vast programme of public works; at first he employed Giovan Battista del Tasso (d. 1555) who built the loggia of the Mercato Nuovo (from 1547 to 1551) and was responsible for the alterations to the Palazzo Vecchio (from 1549 to 1566) and, for works of fortification, Giovan Battista Bellucci (1506–54) who began building the new fortified town of Portoferraio in 1548. After the middle of the century he employed Giorgio Vasari (1511–74) and Bartolomeo Ammannati (1511–92), who had returned from Rome and were able to give the Medicean works a new courtly character; it was on their sites that Bernardo Buontalenti (1536–1608), the best-trained and most talented of the Florentine designers of the second half of the sixteenth century, began his career.

Cosimo established his official residence in Palazzo Vecchio, where from 1555 Vasari reorganized the internal decoration and fixed the purposes – functional and symbolic – of the various rooms created by the history of the Signoria; meanwhile Cosimo acquired the unfinished Palazzo Pitti through his wife Eleanora of Toledo, and gradually transformed it into a new grand-ducal palace (Ammannati enlarged Brunelleschi's building from 1558 to 1570; in 1565 Vasari built the suspended corridor which joins Palazzo Pitti to Palazzo Vecchio; Tribolo, Ammannati and then Buontalenti laid out the Boboli gardens on the slopes behind); in the area between the piazza della Signoria and the Arno he demolished one of the oldest quarters of the city and in 1560 commissioned Vasari to design a building for the offices attached to Palazzo Vecchio; the building was continued after 1574 by Buontalenti, who laid out the terrace on the loggia dei Lanzi as a hanging garden, and created the famous gallery for the

533   *The* Siege of Florence, *fresco by G. Vasari in the Palazzo Vecchio*

exhibition of *objets d'art*, which became the first nucleus of the Uffizi.

Cosimo and his successors put the finishing touches to the official centre of the city, i.e. piazza della Signoria (the loggia was brilliantly transformed into a museum of sculpture where Cellini's *Perseus* – cast in 1553 – and several groups by Giambologna dating from 1583 and 1599 stand out among various classical statues; in 1577 Ammannati built the fountain at the corner of the palace, and in 1594 Giambologna placed the statue of Cosimo I at the centre of the minor arm); they extended the Medici family centre of S. Lorenzo (in 1540 Bandinelli placed the monument to Giovanni delle Bande Nere, father of Cosimo, in the piazza; from 1554 to 1557 Vasari completed Michelangelo's works, the new sacristy and Medici library, with scrupulous devotion; in 1566 it was decided

to build a third sacristy, for the tombs of the grand dukes, which was to be built by Matteo Nigetti from 1604); and provisions were made to complete the city's traditional buildings and meeting places: Ammannati rebuilt the ponte S. Trinità from 1566 to 1569 (Fig. 538) possibly making use of an idea of Michelangelo's; with a large number of assistants Vasari, from 1572, and Federico Zuccaro, from 1574, frescoed the interior of Brunelleschi's dome.

These same artists designed the most important undertakings in the territory of the grand duchy; in 1562 Vasari designed the piazza dei Cavalieri in Pisa, and in 1573 the loggias of piazza Grande in Arezzo; Buontalenti laid out the new Appennine town of Terra del Sole (in 1564) and the extension of Livorno (in 1576) (Figs 546–7).

The series of Medici villas built and rebuilt

534 *View, in mosaic and gold by B. Gafurri, of the piazza della Signoria with the statue of Cosimo I. Museum of Silver, Palazzo Pitti, Florence*

during this period deserves separate discussion. The first specialist in the architectural laying-out of gardens was Niccolò Pericoli known as il Tribolo (1500–50), who in 1540 designed the gardens for the Villa di Castello, and in 1550 produced the initial plan for the Boboli gardens. His activity should be seen in the context of that of Giovanni Lippi, Pirro Ligorio and Vignola who were in Rome developing Bramante's idea of the axial garden with a series of terraces and from 1540 to 1560 built the Villa Medici, the Villa d'Este at Tivoli, the Villa Giulia, the *casina* of Pius IV in the Vatican and the Villa Farnese at Caprarola.

This tradition was carried on with increasing sophistication by Ammannati, Giambologna and Buontalenti, who built the villa at Pratolino from 1569 (Fig. 548) and from 1576 the Villa della Petraia; in 1576 Buontal-enti built the grotto where Michelangelo's four unfinished prisoners were placed (Fig. 549).

It is impossible to attempt to characterize these works within a small space so a mere list must suffice. The basic concern of Florentine culture was precisely the study of differences. Michelangelo introduced a degree of personal commitment, unknown in the generation to which he belonged, not only into painting and sculture, but also into architecture; his example affected artists of the following generation, even where they did not share his ideal motivation, and led them to explore their field of action, large or small, in the same way. Each of them built up his personal style, and at the same time sought a specific, unrepeatable solution for each individual piece of work.

The artists' work was facilitated by their

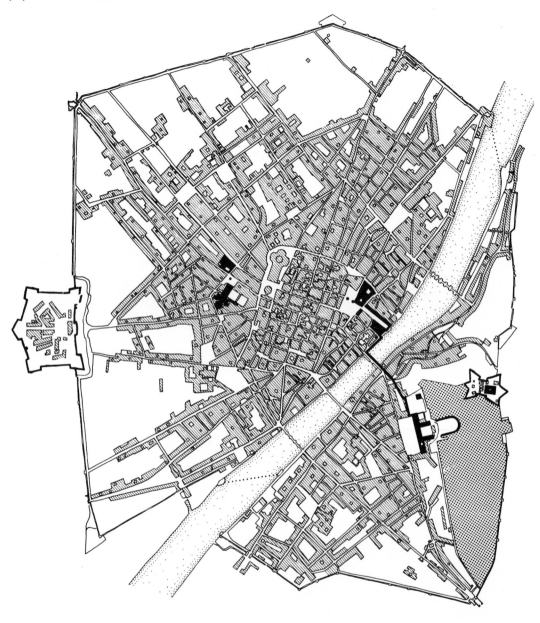

535 *Plan of Florence with the Medici transformations shown in black. From the right: Fort Belvedere, Boboli gardens, Palazzo Pitti, the corridor, the Uffizi, Palazzo Vecchio, the enlarged Palazzo Medici, S. Lorenzo with the cappella dei Principi, Fortezza da Basso*

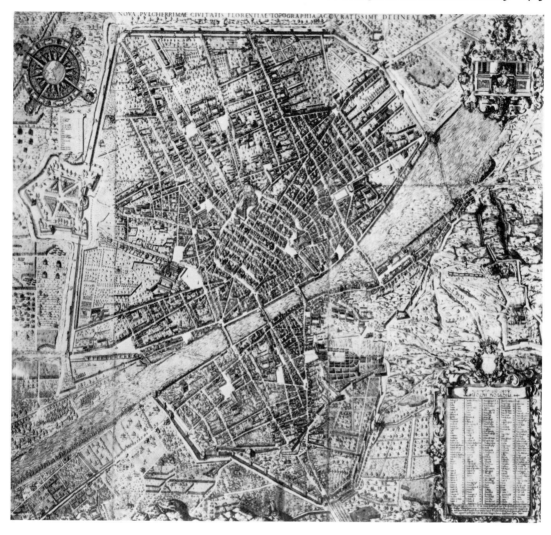

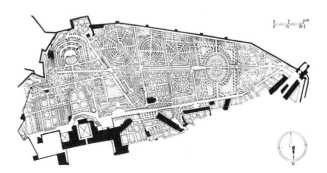

536, 537 *Plan of Florence published by S. Bonsignori, 1584; plan of Palazzo Pitti and the Boboli gardens*

538 *Ponte S. Trinità, Florence*
539 *Buontalenti's project for the façade of S. Maria del Fiore, Florence*

540, 541   *The two façades of Palazzo Pitti – towards the city and towards the Boboli gardens*

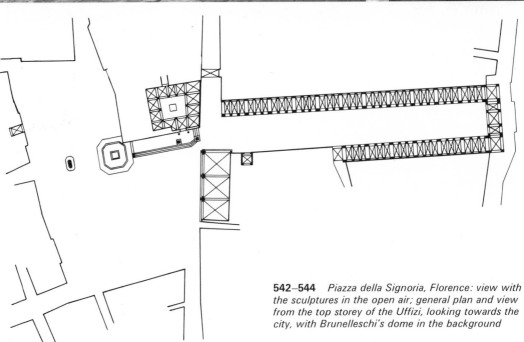

542–544   *Piazza della Signoria, Florence: view with the sculptures in the open air; general plan and view from the top storey of the Uffizi, looking towards the city, with Brunelleschi's dome in the background*

545   *Aerial view of Florence with the Piazza della Signoria and the Uffizi. In the background, on the hills beyond the Arno, Fortezza di Belvedere*

546, 547 *Views of Livorno: inlaid table in Museum of Silver, Florence and fresco in Palazzo Vecchio*

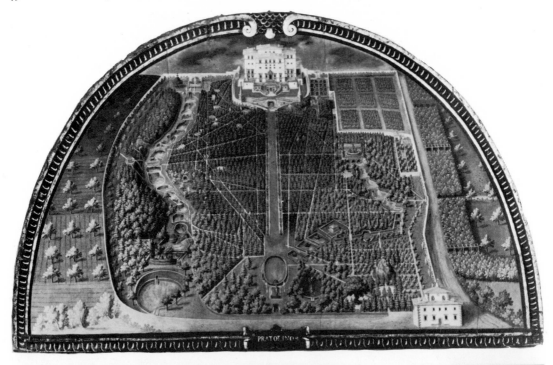

548 *The villa at Pratolino as shown in a painting by G. d'Utens. Palazzo Medici, Florence*
549 *Buontalenti's grotto in the Boboli gardens, Florence, with the Michelangelo slaves*

550 *Table of* pietra dura. *Museum of Silver, Florence*

first-class knowledge of technical and cultural matters; some were experienced writers, such as Vasari, or skilled in mathematics or mechanics, like Buontalenti; in other cases they were helped and advised by all manner of specialists – e.g. men of letters like Vincenzo Borghini and Cosimo Bartoli and professional and amateur men of science like Cesalpino, Vernio and duke Francesco I himself – or else they used teamwork to complement each other's skills; gardeners and hydraulic engineers, architects and sculptors worked together with unparalleled understanding, particularly in the laying-out of gardens. Frequently the amateur element was a key factor of the artists' training, and almost always prevented them from becoming specialized in any one single sector. There were some pure painters, like Bronzino, who registered the faces and places of grand-ducal

551   Eleonora of Toledo with her son Ferdinand *by Bronzino. Uffizi, Florence*

society with impassive exactitude (Fig. 551), but no important pure architect. Vasari was both architect and painter, Ammannati and Buontalenti were architects and sculptors; they had direct experience of perfecting and decorating buildings and could count on highly qualified workmen, particularly for the working of stone. Technical skills and customary precision were typical of Tuscan culture, in the decades which preceded Galileo's appearance on the scene and he was already famous in 1586, after his report to the Florentine Academy on the hydrostatic balance, while Buontalenti was working on the Petraia and the musicians of the Florentine Camerata were meeting in the house of Count Bardi.

All these circumstances helped to enrich and refine artistic research into both the general and the specific; but this research had only two possible outlets: scrupulous and detached personal experiment – as was the case with some painters such as Pontormo and Bronzino – or the intelligent and tractable fitting into a ready-made situation.

In architecture the best works of this period were closely dependent upon a natural setting or urban landscape, interpreted with the resources of a highly refined sensibility: the villas (considerably altered), the Uffizi, the complex of Palazzo Pitti.

In the Uffizi Vasari felt the need to subdivide the extremely long and uniform façade with a complex recurrent motif, i.e. to move away from the natural typology of buildings for offices, already established in Venice by the Procuratie of Coducci and Sansovino. But this motif allowed him to come up with a masterly solution for the linking of the free ends with the bulk of Palazzo Vecchio and the loggia dei Lanzi, and to differentiate the deep chiaroscuro of the side porticoes from the luminosity of the end arches which reveal the width of the river panorama lying beyond the end of the building, right from the entrance into the long narrow space. At the same time, the new porticoed square acted as a perspective telescope pointing towards the Signoria and brought together, as a single scene, a foreshortened view of Palazzo Vecchio – with the statues by Bandinelli, Michelangelo and Donatello – the fountain by Ammannati and the dome of the cathedral (Fig. 544).

At Palazzo Pitti Ammannati's layout started from the bare block of Brunelleschi's palace, which set the harsher tone of the whole composition; starting from this the other elements were ranged judiciously so that they linked up on the one hand with the man-made landscape of the piazza, on the other with the woody masses of the Boboli gardens.

The outline of the ponte S. Trinità, too, was a sophisticated variant on that of the ponte Vecchio, and its fluidity helped to reduce to a minimum its occupation of the open river space; lastly Ammannati's proposal to open one end of the presbytery of S. Lorenzo, so that it could communicate with the cappella dei Principi, revealed a sharp understanding of the still unresolved imbalance in the organism of Brunelleschi's church.

But because of this very respect for the environment, the grand-ducal schemes, as a whole, did not substantially change the organism of Florence which had been fixed since republican times; the environmental continuity and subtlety typical of Florentine schemes were not, however, found to the same extent in provincial ones, as has been frequently noted.

Indeed the architectural virtues of the Florentine works could be neither repeated nor generalized; thus artistic production in the grand duchy, considered as a whole, did not have its own system of internal rules, and their place was necessarily taken by external ones: by the precepts of academic culture – already evident in the painting of Vasari; by religious moralism – which in 1582 led the old Ammannati to write the famous letter to the Accademia del Disegno, in which he repudiated the freedom of his previous works;[89] and lastly by *fiorentinismo*, i.e. the codifying into

552, 553   *Crystal cup with gold base and handle and an engraved crystal dish. Museum of Silver, Florence*

convention of the city's artistic heritage (cf. the 'return to Michelozzo' in some works by Buontalenti, for instance Villa Artiminio or the Belvedere fort).

When these external rules became preponderant, the architect's margin of freedom was reduced to a laboured variation of details; in this field, too, the consummate experience of designers and the virtuosity of executors produced admirable results: the 'inventions' of the inexhaustible Buontalenti – the broken segmental pediment of the Porta delle Suppliche at the Uffizi (Fig. 555), the winged windows of the Palazzo Non Finito, the staircase of S. Stefano derived from the metamorphosis of a shell (Fig. 554) – or certain garden ornaments like the statue of the Apennines at Pratolino (Giambologna), the grottoes of Castello (Tribolo) and Boboli (Buontalenti) where the point of transition between work of art and work of nature is probed with insuperable subtlety. But in this way the artists of the late sixteenth century finally reversed the method started by Brunelleschi, by re-establishing the pattern of ruinous waste of energies in revolt against which Brunelleschi's reform had started.

Thus while the generation that ran from Vasari to Buontalenti built up the myth of sacred Florentine history in the shadow of grand-ducal power, and did away with the conflicts of the past in order to accredit the thesis of a continuity of convention (in politics from the commune to the grand duchy, in literature from Dante to the Accademia della Crusca, in art from fourteenth-century precursors and the great innovators of the early fifteenth century to the golden age of Lorenzo de' Medici, which foreshadowed and justified the academic culture protected by Cosimo I) it did in effect dispose of the impressive legacy accumulated during the previous centuries within a few decades.

Indeed the artistic fervour of the last decades of the sixteenth century died out suddenly in the following one, and Florence

554 *Buontalenti's staircase, built for S. Trinità and now in S. Stefano, Florence*

ceased to supply world culture with any further innovatory experiments in this field.

The literary counterpart of this last artistic flowering could not be a treatise, but a collection of biographies: Vasari's *Lives*, the last living image of a cultural tradition already exhausted. Treatises were still written: Vasari himself composed an elaborate theoretical introduction, with the help of Borghini, for the 1568 edition, on the three arts of drawing, and frequently used the categories of academic aesthetics – invention, draughtsmanship and colour – in his judgments. Yet the liveliness of his monographic portraits derives from the conviction that a supreme and arbitrary quality does exist, that cannot be attained through 'study' and 'the rule', but through a lucky spontaneity, a sublimation of native temperament. For the greatest artists, such as Leonardo, Raphael and Michelangelo, Vasari talks of 'celestial influences', of a gift of nature and the grace of God; but it is

555 *The Porta delle Suppliche by Buontalenti, Uffizi*

already clear that perfection in art does not coincide absolutely with perfection in reason and rational endeavour. This conviction did not become a thesis and did not find a suitable terminology to enable it to be adequately argued; it emerged in the aptness of the judgments on individuals and the general vision of the work, which was striking (particularly after the 1568 additions) for the number and variety of the facts and characters reported in it.

The final declaration, 'to artists', is one of the most revealing pages of the work, where Vasari recapitulates the difficulties and hardships suffered in order to 'discover the truth', i.e. to go beyond the generic and reach the specific:[90]

'If therefore I have seemed unduly longwinded and prolix in places, it is because I was particularly anxious to make myself clear without any possible ambiguity. Repetitions are due to two causes, the nature of the subject and the interruption of my task for days and even months, by journeys or heavy work, painting designs and buildings, while I freely admit that it seems impossible to avoid errors entirely. If some think that I have given excessive praise to certain ancients or moderns, . . . my answer is that I have only praised the ancients after making every allowance for place, time and circumstance. . . . But one cannot always hold the goldsmiths' balance and those accustomed to the art of writing, especially where comparisons are concerned, which are by nature odious, or forming a judgment, will hold me blameless. I know too well the toil, trouble and expense which this has cost me for many years past, and I have encountered so many difficulties that frequently I have despaired. But for the assistance of many true friends, to whom I shall feel indebted, I should never have had the courage to persevere with the collection of notes and materials upon various matters upon which I was in doubt. This

help was so efficient that I was able to ascertain the truth and publish it, bringing to life the memory of rare and pioneer spirits which was all but lost to sight, for the benefit of those who come after us. I have received no little assistance from the writings of Lorenzo Ghiberti, Domenico Grillandai and Raffaello of Urbino. Although I have confidence in them, I have always checked their remarks by inspecting the works, since long practice teaches careful painters to recognize the various styles of artists, just as a good secretary recognizes the handwriting of his colleagues, and as everyone does that of his friends and relations.'

Thus Vasari's book, poised between the cult of the rule and a feeling for the exception, reproduces in the field of literature the same contradiction in which artistic production of his time was locked. It is a splendid monument to the age now drawing to a close, not a programme or stimulus for the future.

The Venetian hypothesis

In Venice the same impulses towards change and the same uncertainties we mentioned in connection with Florence were felt, but their effects were somewhat different.

In the case of architecture, one must bear in mind not only the well-known political and economic events which distinguished the Venetian scene from that of the rest of Italy but also three special circumstances:

1   The rigid standards that restricted building production in the capital city and the activities of the central power in the mainland territories.
2   The particular tone of Venetian literary classicism which influenced all fields of culture.
3   Comparison with the sensational developments in Venetian painting, from Giorgione onwards.

We have already emphasized the continuity of Venetian building production in the fifteenth century. The ruling class accepted the new repertoire of forms as it accepted the new commitments derived from its changed economic, social and diplomatic circumstances; but the basic mechanisms of the state, and the mechanisms on which the functioning of the urban organism was based, were protected from these changes, because they depended upon certain elementary organizational and physical relations. For both, Le Corbusier's observation was valid: 'This is an exacting function, and neither pomp nor academicism can be admitted.'[91] The organization of the possessions on the mainland, too, helped to defend the vital interests of the republic, engaged as an equal with the great European powers: hence the importance of military works and the uniformity of typology in civil works. The close relation between public and private activities derived from the fact that the Venetian aristocracy continued to be concerned collectively in the management of political power, while Cosimo and the other Italian princes ruled on their own.

To illustrate the character of Venetian classicism, one may allude simply to the polemic between Pietro Bembo and Gian Francesco Pico between 1512 and 1513.[92]

Pico defended the thesis of the Florentine Platonic academy: perfect style is obtained by imitating a number of authors, not a single author, because the model should be sought beyond individual experiences, 'in nature itself, and particularly in the mind, whence it descends directly into words and letters'; therefore 'not in a page of a single writer, but in all, or in very many writers, because the virtues of the efficient causes are various and scattered throughout the whole realm of living beings'.[93] The ability to choose the virtues to be imitated presupposed the possession of an innate idea, a 'personal instinct of the soul' by which 'we judge both our things and those of others'.[94]

This thesis, also propounded by Alberti for the figurative arts, and currently accepted in Florentine and Roman circles as a basis for the imitation of ancient models, left the Ciceronian Bembo unsatisfied; he criticized:[95]

'the desire to reproduce and contain – within a single form and species of writing – the forms and species, with all their parts and members, various and often extremely different one from the other, typical of various writers. It would be as though you might think possible, in building a single house, literally to reproduce many models different in conception and execution.'

The polemic concerned literary style and the arguments brought forward by the two authors were taken, largely, from classical literature. But the tone of the two arguments shows that imitation was understood in two completely different ways: for Pico it was an approximate parallel, with personal instinct as mediator and useful as a guide to the core of an idea; for Bembo it was a 'literal reproduction', i.e. a rigorous and concrete discipline:[96]

'Imitation embraces the whole form of the writing imitated, and tries to possess itself of every single part; it involves the whole structure and substance of the style. Anyone wishing to deserve the name of imitator, and to be regarded by me as worthy of that name, must reproduce the entirety of the style of his model.'

In 1513 Bembo was appointed secretary to Leo X and until 1521 was one of the main cultural authorities in Roman art circles; his thesis acted as an invitation to rigour, and was one of the two poles between which the experiments of the great artists present at the papal court fluctuated, and particularly that of Raphael: the pole of precision, contrasting with the pole of universality. But his thought fits far more naturally into the tradition of Venetian humanism, purist and Aristotelian,

556 *The* Pesaro Madonna *by Titian. S. Maria dei Frari, Venice*

which goes from Ermolao Barbaro to the scholars of the circle of Aldus Manutius and which, in philosophy, produced the bold speculation of Pietro Pomponazzi. In this circle his influence was enormous; as Elwert wrote, 'all roads lead to Bembo'[97] and not only in literature, as we shall see. As far as architecture was concerned, his demand for precision not only directed the selection of the formal repertoire, but led to the dropping of the over-simple comparison with the figurative arts and to the scrutiny of specific problems of planning buildings and town-planning: the distribution of decisions in the cycle of operations, the function of rules and models.

In this context Bembo's position aroused only momentary interest among exponents of Roman classicism, but it did correspond to the permanent features of Venetian architectural classicism, particularly those of the third decade of the sixteenth century, when Bembo returned to settle in Padua, then in Venice as the official historian and director of the Biblioteca Marciana.

After the death of Mauro Coducci in 1504 and that of Pietro Lombardo in 1515 and the end of the period of the decorative fusion between classical and traditional repertoires, the problem of classicism, with its methodological implications, was tackled with an earnestness unknown in the rest of Italy; above all it was transferred on to a professional level where the problems of Florentine and Roman culture had necessarily to be faced.

Only on this level does comparison with the experience of the painters become intelligible. On several occasions modern critics have tried to make direct comparisons between the styles of Venetian painters and architects (e.g. Sansovino and Titian, Palladio and Veronese). These comparisons, even if they are partly acceptable, remain subordinate to the nature of the painter's commitment, which is a specialized one, inseparable from the specific results achieved. The persuasive power of the painting of Giorgione, Titian and Bassano (and not only the excellence attained in their best works, but their transmissibility and the opening they made for the future) were dependent upon the investigation of a field of specific values, not transferable and inseparable from the exercise of painting: the 'chromatic alchemy' of which Lomazzo talks; this research balanced or excluded the intellectualist tutelage inherent in Renaissance culture, hence the pre-arranged hierarchy of formal values (expressed in the concept of Florentine *disegno*) and the tendential interchange between word and image which from Alberti onwards introduces a characteristic ambiguity into figurative experiment. The criticism of Pino and Dolce, too, as Lionello Venturi notes, 'had the virtue of allowing itself to be led docilely by the painting contemporary with it'.[98]

For this reason the example of the painters led Venetian architects not to attempt to transfer their experiences into architecture, but to tackle the problems of architecture with the same specifically professional mentality. The tendency to amateurism – the statistical consequence of Renaissance intellectualism – in the Veneto affected the clients rather than the artists and had the effect of giving a new equilibrium to the artist-client relationship which had become so precarious after the experiments of the 'third style'.

The first episode in the new architectural classicism was the meeting between Giovanni Maria Falconetto (1468–1535) and Alvise Cornaro.

Falconetto, a native of Verona, a professional painter with a passion for ancient architecture, served his apprenticeship travelling round and drawing ancient monuments; in Rome he came into contact with the circle of Raphael and Peruzzi, then went back to Verona and, about 1520, to Padua, where he became acquainted with Pietro Bembo. Bembo introduced him to the nobleman Alvise Cornaro, an amateur architect and author of a treatise recommending the reconciliation of the rigorous use of the ancient orders with the comfort demanded by modern life.[99]

A warm friendship grew up between the Venetian patrician and the humble artist, already over fifty years old;[100] they travelled together to Rome, then Cornaro offered him the opportunity of working as an architect, commissioning him to build the loggia (Fig. 557) and music room in his palazzo in Padua, the façade of his villa at Este, and to rebuild the other villa at Luvignano. In Padua Falconetto became master builder of the church of S. Antonio; between 1528 and 1530 he designed two gates for the city, still rigorously applying the ancient orders and using the simplest variants of Bramante's or Peruzzi's repertoire. Vasari has painted a vivid portrait of this artist, 'a brave and fearless man', who 'had a lofty spirit and desired nothing better than the opportunity of carrying into practice things of like grandeur to the antiquities he had copied'; he was 'of amiable and pleasant conversation, so that Cornaro declared that his sayings would fill a book'. Vasari recounts how, during a discussion in Verona on the measurements of an ancient cornice, 'at last he said "I will soon clear up this question!" and off he went to Rome'.[101] As far as his work was concerned:[102]

'He was the first . . . to bring the true method of building and good architecture to Verona, Venice and the neighbourhood, where no one had previously been able to make a cornice or capital or to understand the true proportions of the columns, or the orders, as is shown by the buildings.'

Falconetto's literal and discrete classicism was immediately obscured by the vicissitudes of architectural culture in Venice, set in motion by the numerous writers and artists who moved there after the Sack of Rome: Aretino, Jacopo Sansovino, Sanmicheli, Ammannati (and the Flemish master of the Villaert chapel, who is regarded as the initiator of Venetian musical culture) in 1527, Michelangelo for some months in 1529 and

557   *The Cornaro loggia, Padua, by Falconetto*

Serlio in 1531 (he published his treatise there in 1537). Jacopo Sansovino (1486–1570) and Michele Sanmicheli (1484–1570) brought with them direct knowledge of Roman experiments, complicated already by Mannerist stirrings at the time of Clement VII. But both worked with specific official responsibilities – Sanmicheli as military architect of the republic, Sansovino from 1529 as *proto* of St Mark's, i.e. director of city buildings – and the clash of their habitual repertoire with the restricting pattern of the kinds of buildings with which they were concerned, is extremely significant.

Sansovino's works in the centre of the city were exceptionally influential, and long remained the inevitable touchstone for Venetian monumental building.

In Palazzo Corner (and later in Sanmicheli's Palazzo Grimani of 1557) the composition of the façade looking on to the canal was fixed in relation to the traditional distributive plan, with the *salone* running through the middle and the apartments at either side. In the Scuola della Misericordia of 1537 specific functional requirements dictated the size of the great inner spaces, with their wooden beamed ceilings, and the spacing of the outer walls which make up a foursquare shell.

But Sansovino's great work was the completion of piazza S. Marco; he concluded the

558, 559 *Early seventeenth-century plan of Venice (from Merian) and the district around St Mark's, from the campanile of S. Giorgio*

560 *Aerial view of the piazza and piazzetta of St Mark's*

work on the Procuratie Vecchie, then between 1536 and 1537 designed the Library, the Mint, the loggia beneath the campanile and the church of S. Geminiano, and thus defined the architectural décor of the two arcaded piazze, giving the medieval buildings – the Ducal Palace, the basilica, the campanile – the value of backdrop to a grandiose complex of monuments. The composition of single buildings was naturally subordinated to the demands of the continuity of the general setting, and while some – the church and the loggia – acted as secondary perspective foci for the composition, others – the Library and the Mint – served as rhythmic backcloths devoid of axial references, in that the ratios between height and length were irreducible to the traditional requirements, as in the Procuratie Vecchie (Figs 559–63).

To adapt themselves to these limitations Sansovino and Sanmicheli were forced to loosen and simplify the canonic models of association between the architectural elements, or to isolate a single system of association – for instance the arch framed between half-columns – and use it as a recurrent motif, unconnected with the proportions of the whole.

These extremely striking buildings were based on a clear distinction between façades and internal organisms, and on the very subtle proportioning of the secondary plastic elements; respect for these two rules made it possible subsequently for the buildings to weather unscathed the rough handling and additions typical of Venetian building practice; the top part of the Mint, the continuation of the motif of the Library into the Procuratie Nuove, with the addition of another storey, and finally into the Procuratie Nuovissime, with the addition of the neoclassical attic and the organic articulation of the ground level portico.

In other cases – and particularly in the churches, where there was ultimately no restricting distributive rule – the uncertainties of Sansovino's style emerged with some

force. In S. Francesco della Vigna the original plan with nave and two aisles was reduced to the nave alone, and the doge Andrea Gritti consulted the humanist Francesco Giorgi about the proportions of the building; he suggested a series of ratios based on musical harmonies;[103] a commission which included Titian and Serlio gave its opinion on this matter.

The case of S. Francesco della Vigna demonstrates that Venetian culture of the 1530s did possess, in an abstract state, the elements later synthesized in the work of Palladio. These erudite skirmishes, in fact, became possible in so far as the problem was to mediate between three independent and still inflexible cultural data: discussions on distributive types, discussions on mathematical ratios and the stylistic repertoire of elements or associations of elements.

The great architect able to unify this system of variables by working on the last of them, thereby reducing all the problems to strictly architectural terms, was Andrea di Pietro della Gondola (1508–80) who at the time of Sansovino's triumphal beginnings in Venice was still an unknown stonecutter: only after 1540, through the good offices of Trissino, did he receive the universally known nickname of Palladio.

Giangiorgio Trissino, man of letters, poet, and amateur architect, built his villa at Cricoli between 1535 and 1538, near Vicenza, possibly based on a personal design of his own. It was here that the young workman came to the writer's attention and was introduced by him to classical studies and taken on a journey to Rome in 1541; soon afterwards Palladio began his career as a designer of villas and palazzi in the district around Vicenza, and in 1546 he received his first important commission: the reconstruction of the city basilica which had partly collapsed in 1496.

For this undertaking Serlio had been consulted in 1530, Sansovino in 1536, Sanmicheli in 1541 and Giulio Romano in 1542. It is

561 *The Library, Venice, from the loggia of St Mark's*

known that Giulio Romano had advised against the incorporation of classical elements into the Gothic organism; Palladio – who in many ways brilliantly contradicted Giulio Romano and the artists trained in Rome in the first half of the sixteenth century – chose the opposite solution, which is clear and almost mechanical; he enclosed the medieval building in a modern shell rhythmically independent of it, as Alberti had done in Rimini a hundred years before (Figs 565–6).

This decision entailed only two further stages: the choice of the recurrent motif, which was repeated all round calmly ignoring connections with the surrounding buildings, and the choice of the treatment of the corners, conditioned by the fact that the width of the arcade was not equal to the rhythm of the main motif.

The recurrent motif was taken from Bramante's repertoire and corresponds to the 'Serliana' which figures in Serlio's fourth

562 *The meeting of the orders of the Mint and the Library*
563 *Aerial view of the St Mark's complex*
564 *The commercial centre of the Rialto, seen from the steps on the bridge*

book. But this combination of two orders, which in post-Bramantesque and Sansovinian practice served to divide up the plastic facing of a wall, here becomes a bare proportional frame, establishing the ratio between the main measurements of the building: those of the two actual floors and those of the imposts of the two orders of arches. This serried play of spatial ratios is immediately legible even from a distance, and the delicately pierced wall in gleaming white *pietra d'Istria*, suspended between the two voids of the porticoes and surrounding piazze, takes on the meaning which is typical in Palladian architecture, of a two-dimensional diaphragm of an organism that extends in depth; for this reason he did not approve of the presence of plastic ornament except in clearly subordinate positions, like the statues on the rooftop which prolong the axes of the main columns, the reliefs of the metopes and the human heads on the keystones of the arches; on the other hand, the arrangement of the airy façade is underlined by the clear-cut outline of the openings and particularly of the circular openings cut straight out of the wall without any intervening moulding; so that, despite the strong relief of the two orders, the reference of the whole plastic composition to the Albertian wall remains clear, establishing the plane of reference for all the projections (Fig. 567).

After 1549 Palladio was appointed *proto* of the basilica and was commissioned to design numerous palazzi and villas for the nobility of Vicenza, including two extraordinary masterpieces: Palazzo Chiericati and the Villa Rotonda, on the outskirts of the city. In the case of both villas it is doubtful whether they were designed in the middle of the century or later on.

In a field as well worked as the nobleman's palazzo, the architect was concerned primarily to breathe new life into the 'compartition' of the organism, independently of any traditional typology; to do this, he inverted current procedure with extraordinary confidence, i.e. he limited the field of variation of the standardized plastic elements – orders, rustication, door and window surrounds – and strengthened their function as parameters of the spatial relationships, but opened up an unlimited series of distributive variations, and transferred the research into various combinations that the Florentines and heirs of the 'third style' were pursuing on details, to the composition as a whole.

The organism of Palazzo Chiericati is perhaps the most surprising of these variations: within the canonic frame of the two superimposed orders alternate solid windowed walls, porticoes and loggias; the corner junctures of the distributive structure are resolved not with exceptional elements, but with exceptional arrangements of the standardized elements themselves, such as the columns staggered at 45° and partly sunk into the wall, which produce the setback of the two lateral blocks, or the partitions with arches which partially close in the porticoes and loggias to the sides (Figs 569–71).

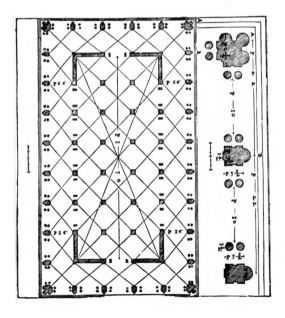

565, 566 *Plan of the basilica at Vicenza from Palladio's treatise, and the basilica in the surrounding townscape*

567   *The order of the basilica at Vicenza*

The Villa Rotonda (Figs 572–7) is virtually the manifesto of this new compositional freedom. The square block of the house, with the domed central *salone* and four identical façades, naturally makes one think of Sangallo's and Bramante's central compositions of the early sixteenth century. But one should bear in mind the following facts.

1   This is a villa, not a church; the central symmetry was used independently of religious symbolism and was transferred into the secular world, where it did not determine a type to be repeated, but exemplified one of the possible distributive options with no restrictive meaning attributed to it.

2   The external symmetry is not completely realized inside, where one of the axes – corresponding to the entrance from the city – gives access to the main rooms, and the other to the minor ones.

3   The identical appearance of the four façades – as in Le Corbusier's Villa Savoye – is only the starting-point for a series of subtle variations; the four porticoes are differentiated not only by the appearance of the rooms inside, but also by the directions they face (in fact the four points in the compass) and by the various views of the landscape. What is lost is the usual axial sequence between villa and garden; the axes of the villa are two, and they vanish right at the bottom of the stairways going down from the porticoes; these become four aerial observation points, to admire the detachment between the architectural orders in the foreground – illuminated in so many different ways – and the background of endless landscape (Figs 576–7).

All this weakens the Platonic character of the architectural invention, hence the typical and repeatable aspects of the image; a Platonic and idealizing classicism is replaced by an empirical version, which could be called Aristotelian, if one bore in mind the Paduan tradition from Bembo to Daniele Barbaro. The correlative of this empiricism was an extraordinary freedom, all the more

568   *Two columns from the lower order of the basilica*

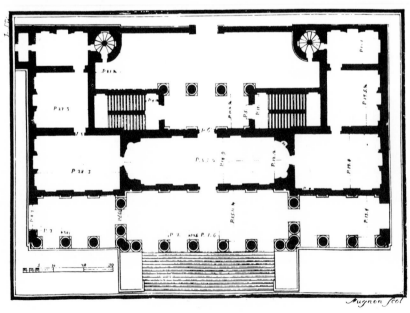

569–571 *Palazzo Chiericati, Vicenza: façade, plan (from Bertotti-Scamozzi) and view along the portico*

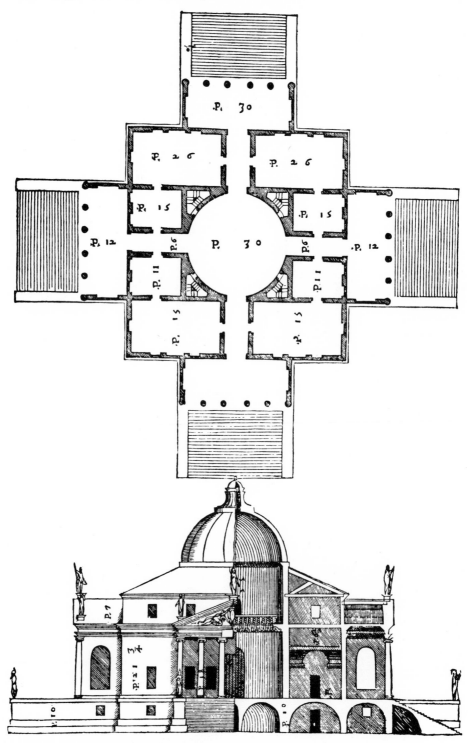

572 *The Villa Rotonda, Vicenza (from* Four Books)

real for the limits of its field being so precise.

In the Villa Rotonda the use of the architectural orders was limited to the porticoes, but all the elements of the building, even the functional and unadorned, were drawn with impeccable rigour into the composition as a whole; in particular, the slope of the pediments reproduces that of the roof, and the sloping planes of the roof are linked closely to the positioning of the cornices of the stringcourses; those of the projections fix the difference in level between the cornice of the *piano nobile* and that of the attic, while those of the main body establish the further difference in level up to the impost cornice of the cupola.

Though professionally so busy, during this period Palladio was engaged equally in the theoretical and practical fields. From 1547 to 1554 he made four further journeys to Rome, first for some modest commissions, then purely to study ancient monuments; here he saw the last architectural works of Michelangelo, took the measured drawings of the imperial monuments which were destined for a future treatise (among them were those of the baths published in 1732 by Lord Burlington), and in 1554 he published the short guide to the antiquities of Rome which immediately became very widely circulated in Italy and abroad. His precise geometrical drawings and his graphic system of completely separating the diagrammatic representation of the organisms – in plan and elevation – from the precise representation of sections and details, was an immediate success, and made the collections of approximative drawings published previously completely antiquated. His knowledge of ancient monuments put him in a position to collaborate with Daniele Barbaro in the publication of Vitruvius' treatise in 1556. Here his experience as a former stonecutter was combined with the rigorous and seasoned tradition of Venetian humanism.

After 1555 Palladio remained in his home town and was employed on numerous works in the cities of the terra firma – including Palazzo Antonini in Udine, the Palazzi Valmarana, Barbarano and Porto-Breganze in Vicenza, a long series of villas on the plain and in the foothills of the Alps – and after 1560 also in Venice, where in 1570 he succeeded Sansovino as *proto* of St Mark's. Here he built the convents of S. Giorgio Maggiore and the Carità, the façade of S. Francesco della Vigna, the churches of S. Giorgio, the Redentore, the Zitelle and S. Lucia. After the flooding of 1559, he rebuilt a series of bridges for the republic, and was called as consultant to various north Italian cities. His last great villa was that for the Barbaro family at Maser, where he died in 1580.

Among the Vicenza palazzi of the last period Palazzo Valmarana stands out. It adopted the gigantic Michelangelesque order for its façade on to the street, to frame the minor divisions of the various floors, and the result is a complex interplay of projections between the superimposed elements, resolved in *stiacciato* (extremely low relief) because of the lack of space available on the narrow street (Fig. 578).

The series of villas shows a spectacular variety of distributive schemes; unlike the Rotonda, a villa intended for relaxation built very near the city, most of the others were also agricultural concerns, and included a series of secondary buildings, usually in the form of wings flanking the main house. This mode of distribution excluded central symmetry and made bilateral symmetry inevitable; but Palladio, despite the large number of similar plans, did not work on a recurring model and invented many organisms, all 'varied and different' in accordance with Brunelleschi's programme: without a portico; with a portico under a pediment; or a continuous one; or linked in a C-shape to that of the wings; with one or two storeys; with an inner courtyard arcaded on one, two, three or four sides; with the main building aligned with the secondary ones, or isolated

573, 574   *The Rotonda from Monte Berio and from the garden entrance*

575 *View of the Rotonda from the south*

576, 577 *Two views of the portico on the east of the Palladian Rotonda, taken at the same time, looking in opposite directions*

578 *Palazzo Valmarana, Vicenza*

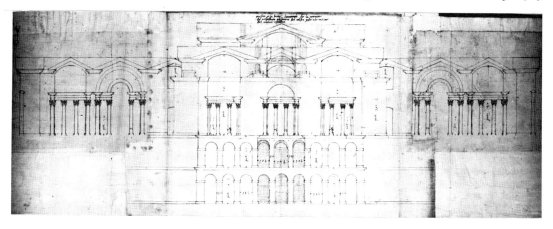

579 *Palladio's drawing of the Baths of Titus at Rome*
580 *The uncompleted Palazzo Porto, Vicenza*

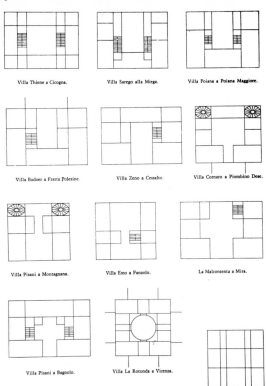

Villa Thiene a Cicogna.

Villa Sarego alla Miega.

Villa Poiana a Poiana Maggiore.

Villa Badoer a Fratta Polesine.

Villa Zeno a Cessalto.

Villa Cornaro a Piombino Dese.

Villa Pisani a Montagnana.

Villa Emo a Fanzolo.

La Malcontenta a Mira.

Villa Pisani a Bagnolo.

Villa La Rotonda a Vicenza.

Schema geometrico
delle piante
delle ville palladiane.

or protruding as a projection; with rectilinear enclosing buildings or semi-circular ones, in front or behind, or both as in Maser.

The presence of farm buildings required a gradation of the decorative details from the most important – the architectural orders – to the most modest, which were scarcely differentiated from the bare constructional elements. Thus Palladio was led to pursue another Brunelleschian line of research: the classification and standardization of other elements, different from the orders and deduced from everyday building practice, but suited to co-ordination with these and susceptible to the same laws of proportion; hence a link between aristocratic and everyday architecture, i.e. a broadening of the social basis of architectural classicism. Palladio was one of the designers who pursued this research furthest in the sixteenth century (Fig. 587) virtually exposing its constructional limits (which derived from the con-

581, 582 *Ground plans of eleven Palladian villas (from Wittkower) and plan of Villa Trissino, Meledo (from Bertotti-Scamozzi)*

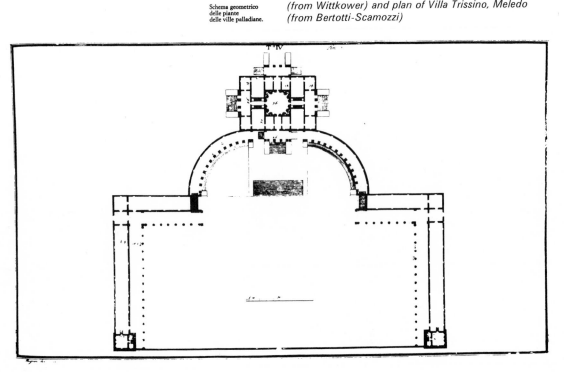

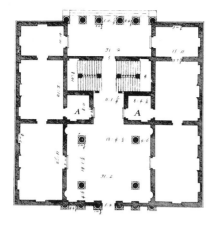

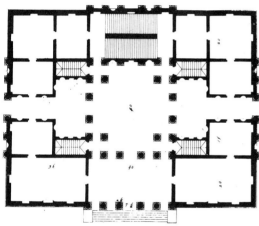

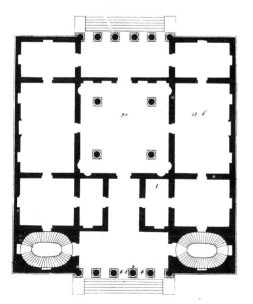

ventional character of the classical repertoire, reinforced during over a century of use); he found the inspiration for this research not only in the use of rustication already codified in Serlio's treatise but also in the study of ancient Roman buildings, such as the baths, whose ruined state had deprived them of their magnificent decorative refinements, and which emerged as masonry masses cut into by holes of various types (rectangular, arched and the so-called thermal windows with their tripartite arches).

In some cases the use of the canonic orders was restricted to the portico – as in the Malcontenta – or was entirely absent, and the main building itself was decorated simply with a calculated assortment of openings, as in the villa at Poiana Maggiore (Fig. 586).

The group of Venetian works reveals an exceptional commitment, and made a crucial contribution to the Venetian landscape.

In the convents of the Carità and S. Giorgio Maggiore Palladio continued with the distributional researches pursued in the mainland palazzi and villas, making use of theoretical references to the Vitruvian 'Roman house'. The façade of S. Francesco della Vigna is independent of Sansovino's organism, and here – following the isolated example

583–585 *Plans of Villa Torneri, Schio, Palazzo della Torre, Verona and Palazzo Garzodore, Vicenza (from Bertotti-Scamozzi)*
586 *Villa Poiana, Poiana Maggiore*

587   *Rear façade of the Malcontenta, Mira*

588–590 *Side view, interior and plan of S. Giorgio Maggiore, Venice*

of Peruzzi at Carpi – Palladio takes up the motif of the fitting together of two architectural orders, which measure the height of the aisles and the nave respectively. But in S. Giorgio and the Redentore church and façade are intimately linked; in both, the composition of the internal organism and that of the façade are dominated by two interconnected orders, while the relationships between them – which reveal the inner spatial layout – are different.

In S. Giorgio (Figs 588–90) the internal major order supports the ceiling of the central cross, the minor one supports the ceilings of all the secondary spaces and closes in as it passes around the presbytery, creating the columned screen, beyond which is the monks' choir, independent in plan and elevation of the alignments of the church. The two orders on the façade and the two

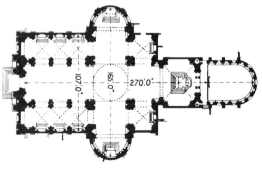

superimposed pediments fix the position of
slopes of the roofs covering the two systems
of ceilings respectively; for this reason the
general height of the minor order on the
façade is equivalent to the height of the
secondary ceilings – which here corresponds
to the height of the columns of the main
internal order – and the height of the main
order on the façade extends to the top of the
ceiling of the nave (a rule observed elsewhere
by Palladio, when the external order has to
contain a vaulted space).

In the Redentore (Figs 591–5), on the
other hand, the organism has no aisles but a
single nave, which runs into a three-apsed
presbytery, and the supports of this space are
defined exclusively by the major order, which
runs round the end and creates the colonnade
that separates choir from church in an even
more magnificent manner. The minor order
supports only the ceilings of the chapels
around the nave, and its cornice – suitably
reduced – runs only as a stringcourse along
the rest of the perimeter; furthermore the
disproportion between the ceiling of the nave
and that of the chapels, both in plan and in
elevation, made it advisable to introduce
external buttresses. All these elements are
projected on to the façade, where the minor
order, as usual, supported the pediment
corresponding to the ceiling of the chapels
(and its height is equivalent to the highest
point of their barrel-vaulting); the main
order on the other hand, free from any direct
connection with the internal measurements,
has the function of separating this roof from
all the structure above. In fact the columns
extend to the top of the side pediments, and
the top of the central pediment fixes the
height of the impost cornice of the hipped
roof of the nave, beneath which the buttress
cornices end, inclined at a very slightly more
pronounced angle.

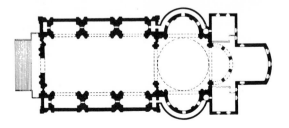

591–595 *Façade, interior, plan, rear façade and
detail of the bases of two columns on the façade, the
Redentore, Venice*

The composition of the Redentore, both compact and articulate, is one of the conclusive products of Palladian research. The stone façade – often criticized for its complexity, if taken independently – functions as a perspective section of the three-dimensional organism which extends behind it, and establishes the geometrical ratios between all the measurements. In this case the system of the architectural orders is not continued on the other faces – if one excepts the repetition in plaster of the minor order on the back of the chapels, possibly added by the later builders and incongruous with the windows – and the organism is revealed only by the play of the plastered volumes which join the plain blocks of the monastery and outbuildings. Here, from the façade to the apses, Palladio ran the whole gamut of his architectural repertoire, from the courtly to the popular, and established a persuasive continuity between the two extremes.

The convent of the Zitelle is a small organism, and the church is extremely simple, proportioned with insuperable elegance. But the placing of the church, between the two symmetrical wings of the building, and the way the façade soars above the internal structures, emphasize the presence

596, 597   *Axial view of the façade of S. Giorgio and the basin of St Mark's in a painting by Canaletto*

598 *Axial view of the façade of the Redentore*

of this architecture on the great stretch of lagoon on to which S. Giorgio and the Redentore also look.

The vastness of this sheet of water by which they stand justifies the role of the three Palladian façades and makes it convincing. Venice's urban décor was now almost completed, and Palladio was asked to work on the outskirts, in less important districts. In his attempts to give his buildings a monumental character, and by utilizing the old Venetian distinction between façade and organisms to this end, Palladio integrated these districts into the body of the city; at the same time he qualified the stretch of water between Venice and the islands to the south as a space intrinsic to the city, though possessed of a new dimension incommensurable with the traditional one (Figs 596–8, 601).

The Renaissance buildings hitherto realized in Venice, including those by Sansovino, had served to qualify or regularize the internal spaces of the medieval nucleus. All the main monuments, with the exception of the Ducal Palace, looked on to these spaces; even the composition of piazza S. Marco was an episode enclosed within a built-up area, separated from the lagoon space by the propylaeum of the two columns. But the Palladian façades were reflected in the lagoon and their powerful axial structure made itself felt over many hundreds of yards, like those of the villas in the countryside around Vicenza. Concern with this distant view is also quite clear in the façade of S. Giorgio, whose axis passes exactly through the punta della Dogana (Fig. 596). Thus Palladio's activities fixed the urban scenery of the basin of St Mark's, enriched subsequently by the buildings of S. Maria della Pietà and S. Maria della Salute. (But even in the heart of the city he had no doubts about the conclusive significance of his architecture: hence the two proposals for the Rialto bridge – about

599, 600 *Palladio's Rialto bridge in the setting of the Grand Canal, as shown in a painting by Canaletto and the Rialto bridge completed by Antonio da Ponte in 1592*

601 *St Mark's basin. Around the water's edge: S. Giorgio and the church of the Zitelle by Palladio, the Salute by Longhena; the Redentore is to the right, outside the photograph*

1570 (Figs 599–600) – and for the façade of the Ducal Palace looking on to the piazzetta, damaged by the fire of 1577.)

In 1570 his treatise on architecture came out, and in it most of these works were described and drawn; the *Four Books* deal with the elements of architecture (orders and materials), of houses (palazzi and villas), of cities and churches ('temples'), and therefore suggest a kind of encyclopedia of classical architecture, simpler and less pretentious than Alberti's and much more stimulating, because examples were drawn from both ancient buildings and those of the author.

In the proem Palladio tells how, guided by his natural inclinations, he began his study of architecture, took Vitruvius as his guide, and:[104]

'sought out for all such ruins of ancient edifices . . . and having found them much more amusing and worthy of note than I had at first imagined, I began to measure their various members with the utmost accuracy and application . . . to find what the whole must have been, and to give the design of them.

Whereupon perceiving how much this

602 *The title page of Palladio's* Four Books of Architecture, *1570*

common use of building was different from the observations I had made upon the said edifices, and from what I had read in Vitruvius, Leon Battista Alberti and other excellent writers who have been since Vitruvius, and from those also which by me have lately been practised with the utmost satisfaction and applause of those who have made use of my works; it seemed to me a thing worthy of a man, who ought not to be born for himself only, but also for the utility of others, to publish the designs of those edifices (in collecting which I have employed so much time and exposed myself to so many dangers) and concisely to set down whatever in them appeared to me more worthy of consideration; and moreover, those rules which I have observed, and now observe, in building; that they who shall read these my books, may be able to make use of whatever will be good therein, and supply those things in which . . . I shall have failed. . . .'

In this way the treatise, unlike Alberti's, consists essentially of drawings, with brief captioned comments; the drawings are of both ancient works and buildings by Palladio, and are put together to form a single unified corpus. For instance, in the book on private houses, 'as we have but very few examples from the antients, of which we can make use, I shall insert the plans and elevations of many fabricks I have erected, for different Gentlemen. . . .'[105]

This singular combination, which incorporates Palladian examples into the ancient tradition, explains the enormous success of the *Four Books*. Tradition was given a new lease of life through modern examples, and, as in the books of Le Corbusier, the technical apparatus was reinforced by reference to works built; the treatise became a manifesto, i.e. a way of presenting a theoretically and practically tested architectural proposal.

The impressive corpus of Palladian works, available for inspection both in reality and in the pages of the treatise, was to exercise an enormous influence throughout the next two centuries: Palladio broke away from the stylistic complications of recent Italian tradition, dependent upon an antiquated distribution of energies, and hence linked to the limited circulation of the respective regional circles, and started up a European dialogue, which was to be taken up at the beginning of the seventeenth century in the main countries of Europe. We shall examine the vicissitudes of the new Palladian tradition, and its successive elaborations when the time comes. We must now discuss the initial causes of this 'revival of classicism' which was to prove so fertile for the future.

The historicity of Palladio's work, i.e. the logicality of its introduction into the situation of the Venetian republic, at this time the only Italian state that was important on a European level, has already been pointed out.

In what has been called 'the Indian summer of the Italian economy',[106] Venice was still the richest city in Italy and put up a long and steadfast resistance against the causes of the ultimate inevitable decline: the transfer of trade to the Atlantic, pressure from the Turks, momentarily alleviated by the victory of Lepanto in 1571, and the monetary crisis common to all European capitalism. The state assumed more precise financial responsibilities, setting up the Banco della piazza di Rialto in 1587; export industries were developing, particularly that of wool; the economic situation encouraged investment in real estate, including agrarian and building investments; Venice became the greatest market of European consumer goods and enjoyed what Braudel defined as 'a wave not of prosperity but of well-being'.[107] The Venetian ruling class was accustomed to combining public interests with private ones, to cultivating regular relations with the rest of the world, and included a group of men used to taking the cultural and religious commitments of their youthful background seriously; this was the atmosphere in which

603 Portraits of colleagues *by Tintoretto. Accademia, Venice*

the future doge Leonardo Donà (1606–12) grew up; where later Paolo Sarpi and Galileo were welcomed, and where the polemic with the Holy See arose at the time of the interdict, in 1606. Vicenza, too, where Palladio found most of his opportunities for work, was 'a city of no very large circumference, but full of most noble intellects and abounding sufficiently with riches'[108] and in the *Four Books* Palladio enumerated the cultural virtues of his clients with pride.

Palladio's architecture was just the answer to the needs of this class; rationality and distributive rigour, apart from being stylistic requirements, were economic ones, in that Palladio's buildings, rather than being prestige monuments, were items subject to precise economic calculation. At the same time the elimination of superfluous ornament and the endeavour to take classical forms scrupulously back to their original ancient sources corresponded to the desire for authenticity which was typical of the cultural circle referred to and which was later to find its ideal expression in the austerity of Sarpi.

If such was the structure of the demand, the Palladian proposal was all the more apposite in that it was rigidly specialized. Palladio was the first important architect of the Renaissance to concern himself solely with architecture; his apprenticeship did not start from the figurative arts, but from the manual exercise of building, and enabled him to avoid, at least in part, the Renaissance clash between plan and execution. Furthermore, after Brunelleschi and Leonardo, he was the first Italian architect to have made a lasting contribution to the progress of building technique (particularly in the field of structural work in wood and in bridge building) (Figs 604, 605); his technical competence was undisputed, and was one of the reasons for his professional success, particularly if compared with the inexperience of, say, Sansovino.

It should be noted that Palladio's professional specialization resulted in poverty, despite the great number of commissions he received; only in the last ten years of his life did his salary as *proto* of St Mark's procure him a certain degree of comfort. His vocation, of which he seems to have been quite aware and which was confirmed by the praise of his most cultured collaborators such as Daniele Barbaro,[109] became a difficult moral discipline, and forced him to considerable sacrifices; in 1563, at the height of his success, he had to write a begging letter to have his eldest son accepted at a boarding school in Padua for poor children.

His apprenticeship as a worker and his modest professional figure should not make one forget his cultural education, which enabled him to absorb the lesson of Paduan and Venetian humanism, and also to collaborate with men of letters. The text of the treatise, though partly imitated from those of Vitruvius and Alberti, demonstrates the certainty of his reasoning; but in Barbaro's

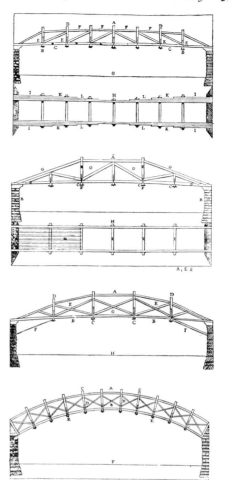

604, 605 *Bridge structures by Palladio and view of the seventeenth-century bridge at Bassano*

comments, too, it is possible to trace – behind the screen of specialized humanistic prose – precise references to Palladio's artistic programme, which show the breadth of the cultural hinterland from which his choices derived.

One might take as an example the substitution of the Aristotelian terminology ('matter', 'form', 'agent', 'means', 'end') for the Platonic and Ficinian one; the famous Platonic word, 'idea', naturally could not be neglected, but its content was notably down-graded and made concrete; the architect 'forms in his thoughts three Ideas and figures of the work: one is the Plan . . . the other is the Elevation . . . the third . . . is the section known as Schiography'.[110] Or one might consider the insistence on civil and social motives, already hinted at by Alberti:[111]

'The power to gather rough men together for their common benefit is a marvellous thing, to bring them to worship and discipline, safe and peaceful in cities and fortresses; then, with greater violence to nature, to carve rocks, force mountains, fill valleys, dry out marshes, build ships, drain rivers, equip harbours, build bridges. . . .'

Discussion of harmonious proportions certainly derived from contact with the literary world; it was a theme that Palladio made his own in the treatise and used regularly, according to his own statements, in the design of plans and elevations.[112]

He did not limit himself, as did Brunelleschi, to the use of a modular network, hence a scale of whole numbers, but he distinguished possible sequences of numbers according to criteria similar to those of musical theory, as Wittkower has shown, i.e. he accepted, and systematically used, one of the canons of early sixteenth-century Neoplatonist culture, codified by the philosophers (from Ficino to Giorgi), the mathematicians (Pacioli), musical theorists (Gafurio, Fogliano) and theoreticians of art (Alberti, Leonardo, Dürer, Gaurico, Serlio and de l'Orme).

In Palladio's time Venetian musical theorists, in particular Zarlino,[113] were able to classify the notions handed down from antiquity with scientific rigour, and to broaden the traditional harmonic repertoire (Fig. 606) by laying down the premises for the work of the great musicians from Andrea Gabrieli onwards. Students of architecture such as Barbaro, with the instruments of Aristotelian culture, were able to develop discussion on the proportions of buildings in the same way, referring them back to the universal laws of harmony. Theoretical speculation therefore offered a series of models sufficiently extensive to be accepted by composers and designers not as a limitation, but as an intellectual framework, capable of producing an enormous variety of solutions, through the numerous combinations that could be obtained from these same elements. For both, there was still 'a rich means of harmonic variety . . . in the various consonances, and in the various ways of combining them'.[114]

Palladio made use of the whole range of ratios suggested by theory, and often in a single building he kept strictly to the same progression, for instance the sequence of two diapenti used in the Villa Godi at Lonedo.[115] However, beyond the extremes of the scale, he admitted exceptions, i.e. he used ratios which 'fall under no rule',[116] and retained a margin of professional independence *vis-à-vis* the commonplaces of theory.

Now that we have said something about the system of cultural and social relations within which Palladio's experience was set, we must bear in mind that this – like every other vital architectural experience – was not limited to reflecting the demands of his environment, but took its place in the environment as an active component, and partly modified its balance.

Palladio's ideal themes were no different from those of Alvise Cornaro and Falconetto; it was his procedure that was different, because he did not restrict himself to simpli-

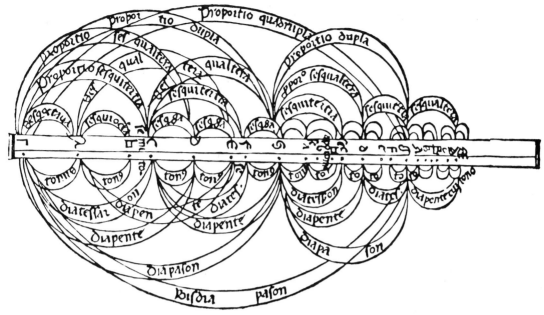

606 *An illustration from Zarlino's* Institutioni harmoniche, *1558*

fying and rationalizing the current stylistic repertoire, but transformed it by selecting, from the world of classical and Bramantesque tradition, the syntactical and grammatical variants least restricting to the aims of general composition; he therefore put aside most of the associative models already experimented with and invented a richer, indeed virtually unlimited, range of new distributive solutions.

In this way he instantly lightened the pressure of compositional habits on the functions of city life; he demonstrated that it was possible to invent a solution appropriate to the new and manifold functions of modern society, and indeed to stimulate, with architectural inventiveness, the process of clarification and differentiation of civil functions: a good example is the theatre, which took form as an autonomous building type just when new original forms of theatrical entertainment were being elaborated. The reference to ancient building types – theatres, colosseums, baths, basilicas and so on – served as a guide line for experiment with the new range of building types needed for the

modern city, as was to be the case later with Ledoux and Durand.

These developments were made possible by a series of historically-based innovations, which formed the dynamic nucleus of the Palladian revolution, and which can be seen in the context of the grammatical, phonetic and typographical research of his master Trissino. An exhaustive documentary study of Palladio's architecture is still to be done, and would probably provide the key to a correct interpretation of his feverish sense of novelty, as well as his overwhelming success, a generation later.

This study was begun by the neoclassical critics with a polemical note, to denounce the decisions of the master in relation to the systematic and stylistic demands of the culture of the Enlightenment. More recent critics have utilized these criticisms to demonstrate Palladio's inventive freedom, and indeed his anti-classical bias, but have added little that is really precise to the observations of Bertotti-Scamozzi and Milizia. Useful contributions have come from books dealing with general matters, such as the Wittkower work quoted, or the book by Forssmann on the use of the architectural orders;[117] but a specialized and complete study is not yet available.

In its absence one can proceed only with examples, and at least two episodes characteristic of Palladian research can be cited: on a grammatical level, the clarification of the relationships between column and pilaster, and on a syntactical level the study of the equivalents in height between the various orders, used in different parts of a building.

The relation between column and pilaster is one of the most problematic points in the Bramantesque and post-Bramantesque repertoire; the pilaster was considered analogous to the column, had the same profile, was coupled with the column to support a single entablature, but was not usually tapered, because it was really part of the wall and its width corresponded to the diameter of the column at its base; but since the projections of the entablature were measured on the diameter of the column at its top, which did not correspond to the width of the pilaster, the coupling produced some characteristic complications, at the expense of the entablature and supports. These difficulties are found in the architecture of Sansovino: for instance in the Library at Venice the presence of corner half-columns, among the pilasters of the portico, produced dentils between the adjacent abaci with nothing corresponding to them on the upper entablature, and the presence of the corner pilasters, among the half-columns of the façade, aiming to respect the alignment of the bases and cornices, produced a flattening of the outline of the pilaster. Difficulties of this kind could be used positively by designers, like Sansovino in the second of the two cases quoted,[118] but had to be resolved case by case, and reduced the number of possible spatial combinations; Palladio, on the other hand, was concerned to remove these restrictions, to secure the freedom to couple columns and pilasters in any way whatsoever, and generally tapered pilasters as well; the pilaster thus became the rigorous projection of the column on one plane, and made possible any general composition, independently of the shape of the details.

The problem of making the orders of the various parts of the building tally has already been referred to in connection with the Venetian churches; one might also bear in mind the typical drawings – like that of Palazzo Valmarana – where Palladio juxtaposes views of the façade and courtyard to pick out the points of coincidence of the measurements of height (Fig. 607). By means of such research the elements of the traditional language became disarticulated and available for new elaboration suited to the needs of the new times: old words to express new thoughts, as Garin observed in connection with Jacopo Zabarella and the Paduan scientists who, at this time, were discussing the problems of the new science in Aristotelian terminology.[119]

Palladio's was the first architectural answer proportionate to the great urban and territorial changes described so far. He explored to the limit the combinations possible in the classical style, and the ambivalence of some of his solutions, poised between classicism and anti-classicism, reveal not so much his personal interpretation as the intrinsic limits of the style codified during the previous two centuries. The extremely personal organization of the work and the conventional character of the reference to antiquity now began to conflict with the needs of the times; the Palladian formula, which harmonized this conflict as far as possible, was the authority for later developments, though it left a series of residual insoluble contradictions destined to accumulate over the years.

The decline of the ideal city

The experiments described so far produced the disintegration of the humanistic concept of the ideal city.

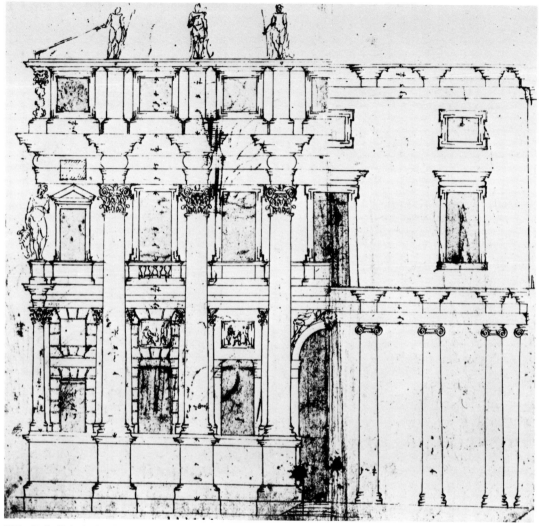

607 *Palladio's design for Palazzo Valmarana, showing the respective levels of the façade and the courtyard*

Born as an image and normative criterion of past experiment in the planning of towns, partly translated into reality by the Montefeltro, Este and Gonzaga families in the second half of the fifteenth century, transferred into the ideal sphere of Neoplatonist culture at the turn of the century, by the beginning of the sixteenth century it was already losing all direct contact with concrete experience. However, it continued to attract to itself a very wide range of ideas and aspirations, and acted indirectly upon reality, as a stimulus for the reconciliation and harmonizing of the dawning conflicts of the early sixteenth century.

While it broke off connection with reality, Neoplatonist idealization did broaden the cultural content of the old model of civic perfection. The municipal ideal of the Italian fifteenth century became the universal ideal of Europe in the sixteenth and acquired a sharply political content, i.e. it was a useful way of judging – with irony, optimism or bitterness – the contradictions of contemporary society. Plato's *Republic* was still the original model for these discussions, but highly topical concerns were introduced as well.

In 1516 More's *Utopia* was published in Louvain. It should be remembered that in the same year Ariosto published the *Orlando Furioso*, Michelangelo sculpted his *Moses*, Raphael painted the Stanza di Borgo and Castiglione was finishing the *Courtier*. More's book is virtually a reply to his friend Erasmus, who had dedicated *The Praise of Folly* to him in 1511, and who in 1516 was still writing the *Institutio principis christiani* dedicated to the future Charles V, in opposition to Machiavelli's *Prince* composed three years earlier; this was the moment of the most intense hopes of political and religious regeneration: from 1512 to 1517 the Lateran Council was meeting in Rome, in 1513 Paolo Giustiniani and Pietro Querini put out the *Libellus ad Leonem X* from the retreat of Camaldoli, in 1517 Francesco de Meleto published his *Quadrivium temporum prophetarum* and Luther nailed up his theses at Wittenberg.

Thomas More's serene prose reflected the happiness of this privileged moment in cultural history and registered the tension of the ideological debate which later was to involve him personally and lead him to the block. We cannot here examine the collectivist political programme contained in the book, but it is relevant to consider its repercussions in the town-planning field as worthy of note since the influence of the work was great.

The description of the physical appearance of the island of Utopia and its cities is referred to in the beginning of the second book:[120]

'The island of Utopia extends in the centre (where it is broadest) for two hundred metres and is not much narrower for the greater part of the island, but towards both ends it begins gradually to taper. These ends form a circle five hundred metres in circumference and so make the island like a new moon, the horns of which are divided by straits about eleven miles across. . . . The island once was not surrounded by sea. But Utopus, who as conqueror gave the island its name . . . ordered the excavation of fifteen miles on the side where the land was connected with the continent and caused the sea to flow round the land. . . . The island contains fifty four city states all spacious and magnificent, identical in language, traditions, customs and laws. They are similar also in layout and everywhere, as far as the nature of the ground permits, similar even in appearance. None of them is separated by less than twenty four miles from the nearest, but none is so isolated that a person cannot go from it to another in a day's journey on foot. Amaurotum (the capital) is situated on the gentle slope of a hill, and is almost foursquare in outline. Its breadth is about two miles starting just below the crest of the hill and running down to the river Anydrus; its length along the river is somewhat more than its breadth . . . they have also another river, not very large, but very gentle and pleasant, which rises out of the same hill whereon the city is built and runs down through its middle into the river Anydrus. The head and source of this river (just outside the city) has been connected with it by outworks, . . . from this point the water is distributed by conduits made of baked clay into the various parts of the lower town.

This city is surrounded by a high and broad wall. . . . A moat, dry but deep and wide . . . surrounds the fortifications on three sides; on the fourth the river itself takes the place of moat.

The streets are well laid-out both for traffic and for protection from the winds. The buildings, which are far from mean, are set together in a long row, continuous through the block and faced by a corresponding one. The house fronts of the

608 *Frontispiece to More's* Utopia, *Louvain, 1516*

respective blocks are divided by an arc twenty feet broad. On the rear of the houses, through the whole length of the block, lies a broad garden enclosed on all sides by the back of the blocks. . . . There is nothing which their founder seems to have cared so much for as these gardens.'

This text – where echoes of the reports of the first geographical discoveries are so evident – carefully describes the natural setting, with its irregularities, and uses the same criterion to describe the man-made scene which is considered an intrinsic part of the landscape sharing its organic characteristics, as in Alberti's treatise. More does not seem concerned to give the ideal city a precise geometrical pattern and the description could be adapted either to a medieval city or to a planned city of the Renaissance. He was aware, however, of the distinction between the plan and its implementation as a series of buildings:[121]

'In fact, they report that the whole plan of the city had been sketched at the very beginning by Utopus himself. He left to posterity, however, to add the adornment and other improvements . . . at first the houses were low, mere cabins and huts . . . but now all the houses are of handsome appearance with three stories. The exposed faces of the walls are made of stone or cement or brick, rubble being used as filling for the empty space between the walls. The roofs are flat and covered with a kind of cement which is cheap but so well-mixed that it is impervious to fire and superior to lead in defying the damage caused by storms.'

We therefore see that the intensity of the political pressures became a matter of relative indifference in the alternative possibilities of town-planning; the politician provided the standard types and left the expert with the task of applying the geometrical models available at any determined moment. This was the same combination of circumstances which produced the first American cities and which determined their characteristics, both positive and negative.

The body of political and town-planning directions was subject to the pessimism and irony implied by the book's very title, and made explicit in the final pages: 'there are very many features in the Utopian commonwealth which it is easier for me to wish for in our countries than to have any hope of seeing realized'.[122] This mistrust was something new, and it began to split the unity of the humanistic ideal and foreshadowed its imminent disintegration.

Discussion of an imaginary and rational republic, starting from More's *Utopia*, was frequent until about the middle of the sixteenth century, though it sank to an increasingly modest ideological level.

In 1526 Antonio da Guevara published the *Libro llamado Relox de los principes* and recounted the visit of Alexander the Great to the Garamantes who enjoyed the benefits of peace and egalitarian communism in an idyllic setting; this work was widely read and was paraphrased in Italy by Mambrino Roseo.[123]

Anton Francesco Doni, who published the first Italian translation of More's book in 1548, completed the dialogue *Il mondo pazzo e savio* in the same year; here he described a collective republic like the previous ones, but much more rigidly organized.[124] Doni's 'folly' – to continue to use the Erasmian antithesis – was of a less elevated type than More's, indeed it was bizarre and facetious and in certain ways not dissimilar to that of Aretino, with whom he engaged in bitter polemic in Venice, their common refuge.

The town-planning organization of Doni's ideal city was extremely restrictive: every road was to house two 'guilds', one on each side, and employees were to exchange services in such a way as to achieve a perfect balance. The centre of the city was to be dominated by the 'temple', where the citizens would gather under the direction of the priests, of whom there would be a hundred, and who would supervise one street each.

In 1552 Francesco Patrizi published *La città felice*, where he recommended an oligarchic republic similar to that of Venice, and described a detailed town-planning arrangement, benefiting from the functional directions given by the treatise-writers on architecture: the city was to be divided into districts of moderate size, each with its own community centre (*stanze pubbliche*).

These works were inspired by an uncompromising rationalism (applied to the advantage of all or that of an educated minority) and in some ways anticipated the enlightened thought of the eighteenth century. But in the middle of the sixteenth century they were already something of a rarity.

From 1552 to 1553, when the books of Doni and Patrizi came out, the ideals of reconciliation and tolerance preached by Pole, Contarini, Rabelais and Melanchthon were also definitely failing: Calvin sent Michael Servetus to the stake, the Paris Faculty of Theology censured the works of Rabelais, in England the reign of Bloody Mary was beginning. In 1556 Paul IV had the naked figures in Michelangelo's *Last Judgment* covered; the old Aretino, converted to the moralism of the Counter-Reformation, died with the title of knight of St Peter and in the Pope's good graces.

Political theory left the sphere of pure reason, and took note of the realities of the new state organisms: in 1556 Vitoria's *Relectiones* were published, in 1576 Jean Bodin's *République*; at the end of the century the two opposing conceptions of the Spanish and Dutch state were theorized about by Mariana,[125] Suarez[126] and Althusius.[127] Beyond the Atlantic the creative phase of the American town-planning experience was ending, and the bureaucratic one beginning.

During this period the Utopian tradition lost contact with current political debate and disintegrated into its various component parts.

The ideological component was once more incorporated into pure philosophical discussion and assumed the character of irrelevant protest or of a prophecy realizable only in a distant future. Thus the last Renaissance Utopias were born: Campanella's *La città del sole* – written in prison in 1602 and published in 1623 – and Bacon's *New Atlantis*, written in 1624 and published for the first time in 1638. In these discussions architecture, as a system of historically motivated choices, no longer has any place; details of a formal kind (for instance the concentric structure of the '*città del sole*'[128]) have only a symbolic value.

The technical and organizational component, on the other hand, is one of the main features of the discussions born of the spirit of the Counter-Reformation, such as the *Repubblica immaginaria* by Ludovico Agostini (1534–90).[129] Religious inspiration – which at this time corresponded to powerful and concrete institutional pressure – replaced political ideology and limited the scope of rationalist research, which was restricted to the field of administration, public welfare, hygiene. Architecture had an important place in these discussions.

The first requisite of Agostini's 'imaginary republic' was 'health', which included dietary, medical, economic and town-planning precepts. The roads were to be traced according to a grid plan, were to be provided with sewers and washed every eight or ten days with running water. The distance between the roads was to depend on the shape of the plots; in fact:[130]

'In the dividing up of the city the roads shall run in rows in such a way that between one and the next a space shall be produced proportionate to the courtyards and gardens of each house; and anyone wanting a house bigger than the others shall do this lengthways and not with the width of his site; and if he wishes to exceed the terms of the others he shall be able to make a house extend from one road to the other, and have two façades on to the two roads.'

All houses were to be built at public expense and inhabited by the common people on the lower storeys and by the nobility on the upper; possible extensions would have to occupy the space of the garden but not add to the frontage looking on to the road. The rich might build palazzi at their own expense, but could not exceed a 'legal limit' of height, and had to obtain plans from the 'architect of the city'[131] who, 'by serving public and private interests alike, would sincerely carry out the affair by producing a suitably proportioned structure'.[132]

These discussions were not mere theoretical speculations, but found definite correspondence in practice, and were part of the great effort of technical and administrative organization, which was the corollary of the hardening of political and religious conflicts; but the pressure of practical tasks gradually outdated general treatises such as these, and produced a specialized literature where Utopian suggestions were lost once and for all.

The geographical, economic and social circumstances upon which the development of cities depended were discussed in the political works of Ludovico Guicciardini[133] and Giovanni Botero.[134] There was already an enormous range of information available about the cities of the whole world; in 1556 the first plates of Antoine Lafréry were published, in 1567 the *Descrizione di tutti i Paesi Bassi* by Ludovico Guicciardini, in 1570 the *Theatrum orbis terrarum* by Ortelius and in 1572 publication began of the collection of plates by Braun and Hogenberg, the *Civitates orbis terrarum*; Francesco Sansovino published the *Ritratto delle più nobili e famose città d'Italia* in 1576, and in 1581 the great description of Venice.

In the field of treatises on architecture the last encyclopedic treatise of the Albertian type – if one excepts the voluminous folio by Scamozzi[135] – was the one published by Pietro Cataneo in 1554,[136] which includes theoretical arguments, technical and stylistic precepts, and embraces the whole field of building, from civil to military.

After the middle of the century architectural treatises were limited to the field of civil constructions (and sometimes only to the rules of the architectural orders, like that of Vignola);[137] meanwhile treatises on surveying,[138] mechanics,[139] hydraulics,[140] rural architecture[141] and even on aseismic buildings[142] were being published and were among the best-sellers of the time, taking their place as of right beside the scientific manuals of Agricola, Vesalius and Fracastoro; but the most numerous series was that of treatises on military architecture, which followed up the traditional texts of Valturio[143] and Dürer,[144] outdated by progress in artillery and techniques of fortifications; among these – to quote only the most important – were the manuals of G. Lanteri,[145] G. Maggi and G. Castriotto,[146] G. Alghisi,[147] C. Theti,[148] A. Lupicini,[149] D. Speckle,[150] B. Lorini,[151] G. B. Bellucci,[152] M. Savorgnan,[153] F. De Marchi[154] (Figs 612–17) and J. Perret.[155]

Traditional discussion of the city, too, broke up into two parts: reflections on the site, climate and characteristics of the buildings remained in the books on civil architecture, while precepts on general layout were dealt with mainly in the books on military architecture; surveys of orthogonal or star-shaped schemes – born of the cosmic symbolism which inspired the treatise-writers of the late fifteenth century (Filarete, Francesco di Giorgio and later Fra Giocondo) and kept alive by the editors of the illustrated editions of Vitruvius (Fra Giocondo in 1511, Cesariano in 1521, Caporali in 1536, Martin in 1547, Rivius in 1548, Barbaro and Palladio in 1556, who had to interpret the author's obscure text on the orientation of roads) – fitted the needs of military technique, which required a central space for the gathering of troops and a preferably polygonal perimeter with obtuse angles.

Perhaps it is no coincidence that the two

609 *The search for water, after Vitruvius. Rusconi,* Della architettura, *Book VIII*

architecturally most important discussions on the city, still dependent on the inter-disciplinary tradition of the High Renaissance – those by Ammannati[156] and Giorgio Vasari the Younger[157] (Fig. 611) – remained un-published; there was no longer a market for studies of this kind.

The graphic variations thought up by these theoreticians – partly motivated by functional arguments, partly by the taste for combina-tion which is typical of this period – gradually exhausted the old symbolic meanings, and multiplied possible models *ad infinitum*; a really scientific ordering of this material, independent of all indulgence in form, was to be achieved only in the seventeenth century.

This expansion of military treatise-writing was justified by the fact that the new towns founded in the late sixteenth century were mostly fortified frontier towns.

In general the new European towns could be classified as follows, according to their main functions:

1 fortified towns,
2 residential towns, to house minorities expelled during religious wars, and
3 new capitals of small states.

1 Fortified towns, as we have said, were the most numerous. After the Peace of Crépy-en-Laonnais, the Bolognese engineer Girolamo Marini designed two new fortified towns for François I in 1545 – Vitry-le-François and Villefranche-sur-Meuse – in the place of two towns destroyed by the imperial armies.

In both cases a new position was chosen and a regular plan traced; in Vitry it was a grid plan composed of sixteen square blocks, with a large square in the centre obtained by doing away with the four central blocks – and

610 *Thirty plans of Italian cities published by G. Orlandi,1607*

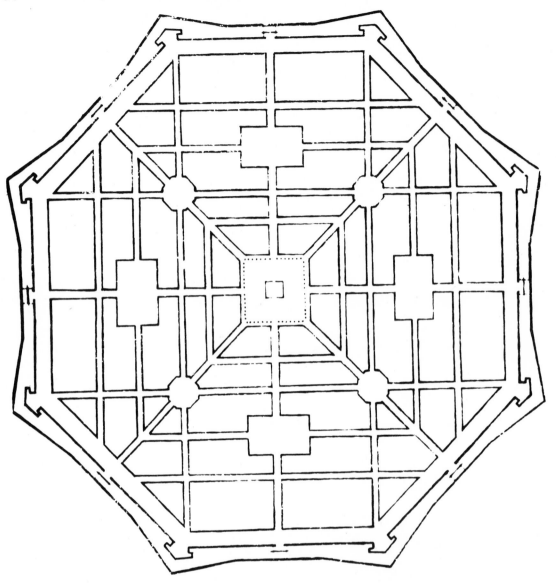

611   *The ideal city designed by G. Vasari the Younger*

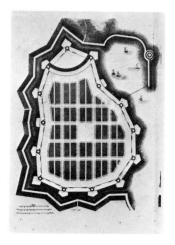
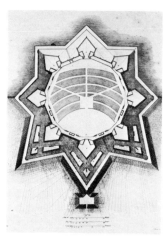
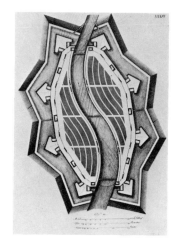

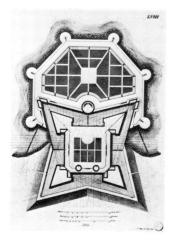

612–617 *Six examples of fortified cities, from the treatise of F. De Marchi, 1599*

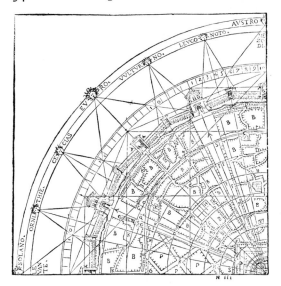

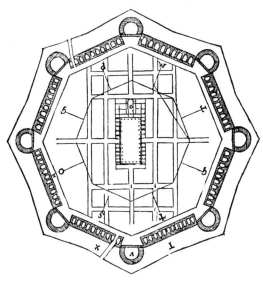

618, 619 *Interpretations of Vitruvius' city in designs by Caporali, 1536, and Barbaro, 1556*

enclosed by a square perimetral wall. The blocks had been divided into plots by dividing the square into two with a secondary road, running in various directions and segmenting the rectangular blocks into so many parts (Figs 620–2).

This arrangement derived from the schemes of an economic character already examined (see pp. 390–430), and was analo-

gous to that of the new American cities, but was here adapted to military needs: the main square was used for parades, so that a second square for markets had to be created in one of the adjacent blocks.

Villefranche was a much smaller town, whose military role predominated absolutely over others; here, too, the perimeter was square, and the internal area was divided up by eight roads – arranged according to the axes and diagonals – which came together into a rectangular square.

The fortified town of Marienbourg, opposite Villefranche, was built by the imperial forces in 1546; the designer is not known, but it followed the same plan almost exactly.

In 1552 Marienbourg was taken by the French, and Charles V ordered the building of two other fortresses, Charlemont and Philippeville; the latter was planned in 1555 by the Flemish engineer Sebastian van Noyen, who chose a pentagonal plan, with a radiating series of ten roads which converge, somewhat laboriously, on to a rectangular square. The same plan was adopted for the fortified town of Rocroi (Figs 623–5).

In Italy, too, the strengthening of the political frontiers, after the middle of the century, required the building of new fortified strongholds, but the increased density of the inhabited centres almost always implied the more or less complete reorganization of some of the existing cities. The most important of the new fortified towns in val Padana, at this time, was Guastalla, planned in 1549 for the Farnese family by Domenico Giunti; the network of internal streets retraces the irregular course of those of the earlier town, while the ring of fortifications describes an almost regular pentagon.

The Tuscan fortified towns planned by Cosimo de' Medici reveal an extraordinary scientific and cultural commitment that still bears the mark of the Utopian ambitions of the first half of the century, as well as a flexibility in adapting to actual situations: the very qualities which we noted in the main

620–622 *Aerial view of Vitry-le-François, plan of the city (from Lavedan) and view of the central square*

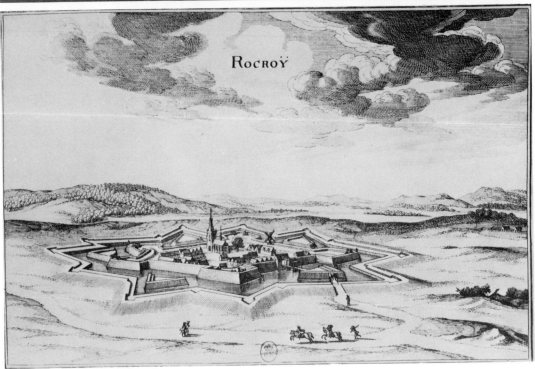

623 *Aerial view of Rocroi*
624 *The fortress of Rocroi in the seventeenth century*
625 *The central square of Rocroi*

works of this period. At least three of them are original urban organisms, regulated right down to the architectural forms: the first is the maritime fortress of Portoferraio, built by G. B. Bellucci between 1548 and 1559, on the site of a modest village, and renamed Cosmopoli; the layout was roughly orthogonal, but distorted in accordance with the lie of the land, and had two squares in the centre: that of the Gran Guardia (main guard), narrow and elongated, near the port, and the larger piazza d'Armi (parade ground) further up in the town. Then came the two towns planned by Buontalenti: the small fortress of Terra del Sole in the Apennines (1564) and the great harbour of Livorno (1576) (Fig. 627). The latter included the previous medieval town, and fulfilled a variety of needs: military, commercial and even those of prestige, so much so that

Lavedan classifies it together with the new capitals of the same period, Nancy and Charleville.[158]

The internal orthogonal patterns favourable to the architectural layout of the blocks and squares, were disengaged from the perimeter of the fortifications, which tended – in the larger towns – to become polygonal, to increase the number and efficacy of the bastioned salients. This rule also made it possible to accommodate the new fortified cities brilliantly around the medieval ones, as in the case of Grosseto (1574–93).

The same approach is found in many other fortified towns designed by Italian experts in all parts of the world: Daman in Portuguese India (1558, by G. B. Cairato), Valletta in Malta (1566, by Francesco Laparelli, with the assistance of Bartolomeo Genga and Baldassarre Lancia) and Zamosc in Poland

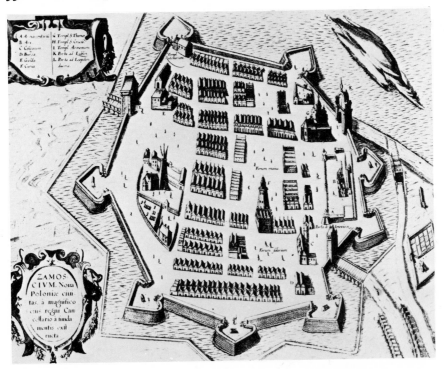

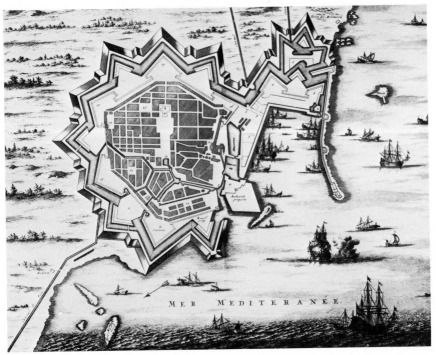

626 *The fortress of Zamosc, Poland (from Jansonius)*
627 *Plan of Livorno (from Mortier)*

628, 629   *Fresco of Valletta in the Gallery of Maps in the Vatican and aerial view of Palmanova*

630 *Aerial view of Coerworden*

(1578, by Bernardo Morandi) (Fig. 626).

At the end of the century the influence of the military theorists, from Maggi and Castriotto onwards, gave rise to the need to combine the course of the walls more closely with the inner streets, making these, too, subject to a polygonal design.

Two of the most important fortified towns built in the last decade of the sixteenth century rigorously reproduced the recommendations of the treatise-writers: Palmanova, built in 1593 by the Venetians, and Coerworden, built in 1597 by the Dutch (Figs 629–30).

Palmanova is a nine-sided polygon, with eighteen radial roads, six of which converge on the central square; each group of three roads enclosed a district, with a smaller square. The extremely elegant plan was probably by Savorgnan, while the monumental architecture was by Scamozzi.

The arrangement of Coerworden is simpler: a perimeter with seven sides and a central space, also seven-sided, where fourteen roads converge; the symmetry of the scheme is broken by the citadel incorporated into one of the perimetral vertices.

2 The cities built for the religious minorities were usually small fortified towns. Some of them – Pfalzburg built in 1560 by the count of Veldenz, Bourg Fidèle built in 1566 by the count of Porcien, and later Lixheim, founded in 1608 by the Elector Palatine, Frederick IV, were fortresses very similar to those already listed; there was also the extension of Hanau (1597) (Fig. 631) and two more important new towns, Freudenstadt founded in 1599 by Frederick I of Württenberg and Henrichemont built by Sully between 1608 and 1610 for Henri IV, are distinguished by the importance accorded to their residential role, and by their links with the tradition of the ideal humanist city.

Freudenstadt was built in the Black Forest to house the Protestant refugees from France

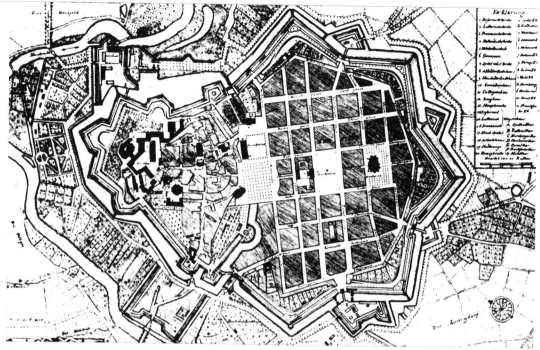

631 *Plan of Hanau in 1790*

(or, according to other authors, the workers from the nearby mines); the plan was drawn up by Heinrich Schickhardt (1558–1634), architect to Frederick IV, and was similar both to that for Dürer's ideal city of 1527 (Fig. 635) and to that of Christianopolis published by Andreae in 1619 (Fig. 632). These two connections have been discussed; it has been suggested that Schickhardt wished to translate Dürer's model into reality a century later, or else that when travelling in Alsace he met Andreae before 1599;[159] in its turn Dürer's plan, according to Palm's hypothesis,[160] may derive from descriptions and drawings of Tenochtitlán, such as that published in Nuremberg in 1524 (this play of stimuli – though only hypothetical – from the plateau of Mexico to the valley of the Rhine, once again demonstrates the complexity and breadth of the sixteenth-century architectural debate).

Schickhardt described the process of planning as follows:[161]

'I inspected the site for the first time when it was still covered by forest, and had the soil investigated to a great depth and in many places. But since not much good was found I humbly submitted that it would not be advisable to build a town on this site. However, I designed a plan for a large town and a castle because it was the gracious wish of his Highness. . . . I arranged for every house to have a courtyard and a small garden, and the castle was to be situated at the corner of the town. But his Highness decided that every house should directly adjoin a street and wanted the castle to be placed in the centre of the market square. And therefore I made a new plan, each side of which was 1418 feet in length and the market square seven hundred and eighty. The castle was to be erected in the middle of the market square. On this layout the town was built, but the castle has not yet been executed.'

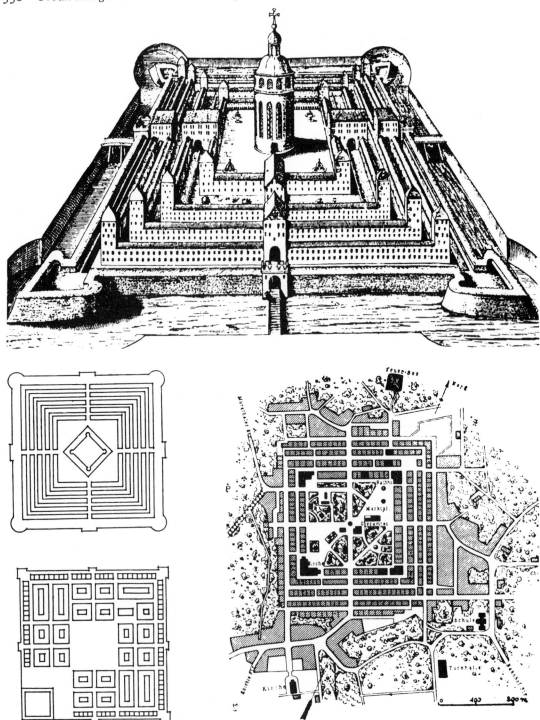

632–634 *The Christianopolis of Andreae, 1619; two plans of Freudenstadt by Schickhardt and the city as it is (from Lavedan and Morini)*

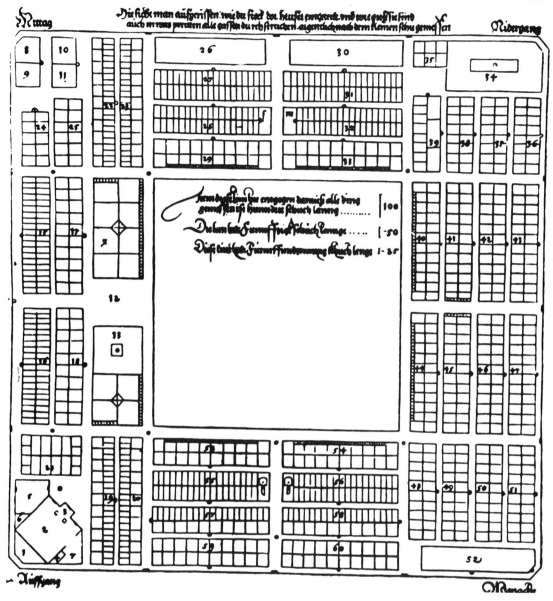

635 *Dürer's ideal city, 1527*

Of the organism described by Schickhardt, three or four rows of terrace houses remain, distributed around the enormous central esplanade. The church – which in the first plan was situated in a special square, on the site of a missing block – in the definitive plan was incorporated into the first row of houses, and was formed of two naves meeting at a right angle, one for men and one for women.

Henrichemont (Fig. 636) was both a residential town and a fortified town. Its plan is much less obvious because work on it was interrupted after two years; none the less it is possible to recognize a square grid plan, with two diagonal streets, which link a central square and four other smaller ones. This arrangement makes Henrichemont similar to the fortified towns previously described.

3   In talking of the new capitals, we must once again consider the relations between political power and architecture, already discussed in the first part of this chapter (see pp. 361–90). But in the latter part of the sixteenth century political power had new requirements and altered its mode of behaviour particularly in the field that concerns us.

A feature we have frequently met hitherto has been the detachment of court life from that of the great cities: the rulers lived in castles, or moved their place of residence from one town to another, and did not actually manage to modify the organism of the city very profoundly with their building ventures. Indeed, it was precisely in court-inspired schemes that conflict between traditional praxis and the new architectural culture emerged at its clearest, weakening the coherence of the results.

But at the end of the century the introduction of the new ruling class into the city was an accomplished fact, and political power was now firmly assuming responsibility for the running and transformation of the urban organism. Furthermore, the new class of administrators and lesser technical experts,

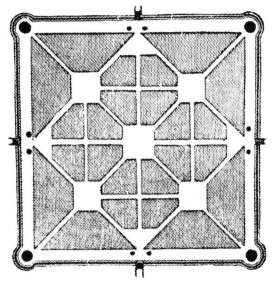

636   *Plan of the city of Henrichemont (from Lavedan)*

637   *Galleria degli Antichi, Sabbioneta*

638 *Plan of Sabbioneta (from Puerari)*
1 Ducal Palace 2 Church of the Incoronata 3 Porta Vittoria 4 Teatro Olimpico 6 Palazzo Giardino
8 Galleria 10 Remains of Gonzaga Castle 11 Church of S. Maria Assunta 12 Baptistery
13 Church of S. Rocco 19 Porta Imperiale

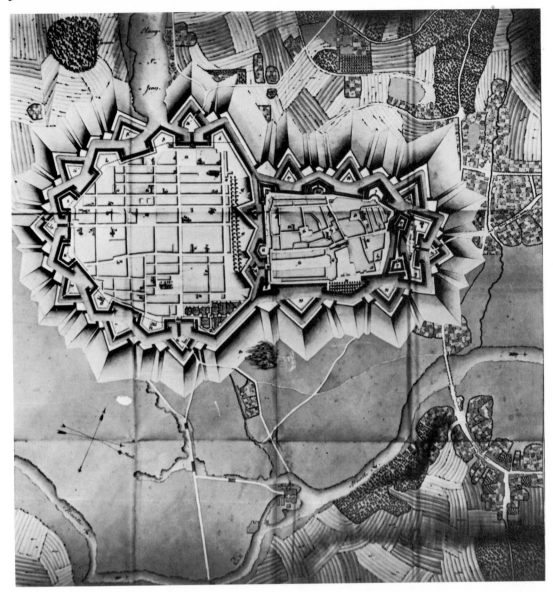

on which the functioning of the state machine depended, was in a position to utilize the criteria of regularity and symmetry typical of architectural classicism with the confidence we found earlier among the class of entrepreneurs and business men.

In this passage from the entrepreneurial to the bureaucratic sphere, the models of classicism were further impoverished. The repertoire of solutions and patterns examined so far was taken up by the holders of political power, for prestige purposes, but lost its links with technical requirements and underwent a process of abstraction, i.e. became transformed into a repertoire of conventional forms. For this reason the court-based transformations of the late sixteenth century – particularly in the countries affected by the Counter-Reformation – have a schematic and artificial character, in comparison with the

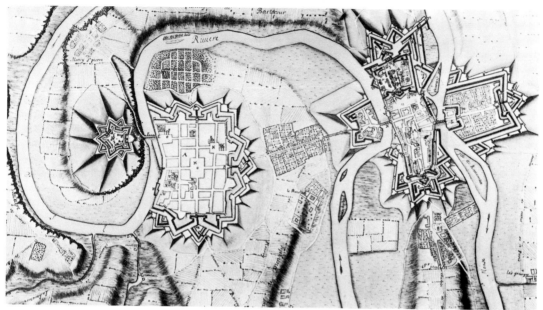

639 *Seventeenth-century plan of Nancy*
640, 641 *Seventeenth-century plan of Charleville and diagram showing traces of the original plan that exist in the modern street system between Charleville and Mézières*

founding of the vice-regal capitals of the Spanish dominions in Italy).

About 1560 Vespasiano Gonzaga began to extend and rebuild his feudal palace at Sabbioneta. The plan of the town (Fig. 638), with the grid plan street network – including the palace and Ducal Gate – were built between 1560 and 1562; in the same year Vespasiano established the *studio di humanità*, then the mint and the hospital for the poor. From 1568 to 1578 Vespasiano was in Spain in the service of Philip II, as governor and military engineer; then he returned home and organized the building of further monuments: the Imperial Gate in 1579, the church of S. Maria Assunta, the Galleria degli Antichi in 1583 (Fig. 637), the church of the Incoronata in 1586 and the *teatro all'antica* by Scamozzi in 1588.

In Sabbioneta – as in Ferrara and the monumental cities of the early Renaissance – the orthogonal layout of the roads and blocks was simply a prerequisite for the regular

spontaneity of earlier ones and to the calculated sophistication of later ones.

To complete this survey we shall consider first the *ex novo* creation of some small capitals (Sabbioneta, Nancy and Charleville); in this context we shall discuss the schemes partially carried out in the large cities selected as capitals at this time (Madrid) or transformed according to the new bureaucratic methods of government (Rome and the

642, 643   *Views of the central square of Charleville as it is today*

pattern of the palazzi and churches, and the city was important above all as a complex of monuments, supervised individually, at different times, by the prince, a patron of architecture and an amateur architect. But the prestige of architecture was no longer great enough to justify such a procedure, and the town remained the belated product of a town-planning culture by now outmoded.

On the other hand, the extension of Nancy, begun by Charles III of Lorraine in 1588, had the character of a closely planned and authoritarian operation.

Nancy included a fortified medieval nucleus, and three suburbs, one to the north and two to the south; Charles III's plan provided for the complete demolition of the first and

the rearranging of the other two, to form a new fortified city adjoining the old one. The layout of the new city was designed by the military engineer Gerolamo Citoni and included a network of new roads on a grid plan, amid which the main, winding road of one of the old districts meandered; this could not be demolished because of the value of the buildings already existing along it (Fig. 639).

Charles III made every effort to avoid land speculation, and in 1591 appointed a commission to draw up a register of all building land, prohibiting any further increase in prices. The buildings of the new city were executed mainly by the religious orders, and in 1605 the prince had the perimeter of the walls extended to make room for a new

cathedral; thus ultimately the new part absorbed almost all the functions of the old centre.

Charleville, unlike the two previous towns, was founded by Charles of Gonzaga-Nevers on an unoccupied site, near Mézières. Here, too, the street network followed a grid plan, but the city fabric was organized in relation to the monumental squares – a main square and five lesser ones – which give a courtly character to the whole organism of the town (Figs 640–1).

The plan was drawn up between 1608 and 1620, by the ducal architect Clément Métezeau; its limited dimensions and skilful incorporation into the countryside make Charleville the best of the town-planning

644   *Aerial view of the* plaza mayor, *Madrid*

undertakings hitherto described; but because of the uniformity of the architectural design (the buildings around the squares were all to have identical façades, and a *voyer*, according to the ruling of 1533, was appointed to 'give the alignments . . . following the official plan')[162] it anticipated the characteristic eighteenth-century court-inspired schemes.

To what extent were these methods applicable in the large capitals that were already in existence?

Madrid, which in 1561 was chosen by Philip II as capital of his kingdom, had, according to the census of 1563, only 2,500 houses (about 30,000 inhabitants); in 1567 it had 60,000 inhabitants and in 1621 about 130,000, plus a floating population of about 20,000, i.e. almost as many as Lisbon.

This development took place in a disorderly fashion, along the streets which ran out of the original village, and many of the houses were of one storey only, to escape the *Regalia de Aposento*, which imposed the housing of royal functionaries on upper floors. The two planned elements stand out clearly amid this random fabric: the monumental Segovia bridge built in 1584 to a plan by Herrera, and the calle Mayor, the only artificial straight street, lined with the houses of the noble families. In the first decades of the seventeenth century a pupil of Herrera, Francisco de Mora, and his nephew Juan Gomez de Mora, were to design the first regular squares in Spanish cities, including that of Madrid in 1617 (Fig. 644).

In the Italian possessions the scheme for Naples implemented by the governor Oledo (1532–53) preceded the large-scale works in Spain; this was still influenced by the Utopian plan of Alfonso II, as we noted in chapter 2, and was frozen into impoverished and bureaucratic forms, particularly in the Spanish district beyond the uncompromisingly straight via Toledo. But the rebuilding

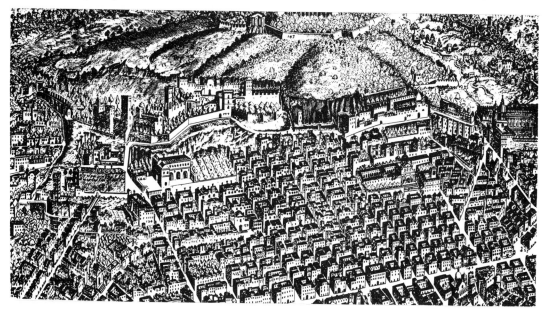

645, 646 *Via Toledo, Palermo, straightened by the Spanish and the military quarter of Naples, organized on a grid plan and adjoining via Toledo*

of Palermo with the regularizing of the Cassero (1564–81) and the opening of via Maqueda (1597) belong to a category of public works now standardized and confused; the crossroads with four blunted corners decorated symmetrically was laid out in 1611 (Figs 645–6).

Via Toledo in Naples, the two straight roads in Palermo and the calle Mayor in Madrid follow the same perspective model as the *strada nuova* in Genoa, but have a quite different character; in Genoa – and in general in the schemes promoted by economic power – the street was realized for the benefit of the surrounding buildings, and its line ensured the correct placing of these buildings; but in the schemes promoted by Spanish bureaucracy the road was conceived in the abstract as the vehicle for an axial view, or as a passage for traffic, having absolutely no proportional relationship with the surrounding buildings which were put up amid various difficulties, and some time later. (The exceptions, in the Spanish world, were Messina and Milan, where a class of landowners, ecclesiastical bodies, *latifundisti* and merchants invested their wealth in town houses, and here large-scale schemes, including regular ones like the *palazzata* in Messina that has already been mentioned, were produced by the combination of buildings; Messina also retained partial autonomy until the revolt of 1674.)

Similar in its approach, though more ambitious and consistent, was the scheme for Rome, implemented by Domenico Fontana (1543–1607) at the instigation of Popes Gregory XIII (1572–85) and Sixtus V (1585–90).

It was the logical continuation of the partial schemes promoted by the previous Popes: Sixtus IV (the Borghi and trident of roads at ponte S. Angelo), Alexander VI (via Alessandrina), Julius II (via Giulia and via della Lungara), Leo X (via Ripetta) and Paul III (trident of piazza del Popolo, via Condotti, via dei Baullari); even at this time

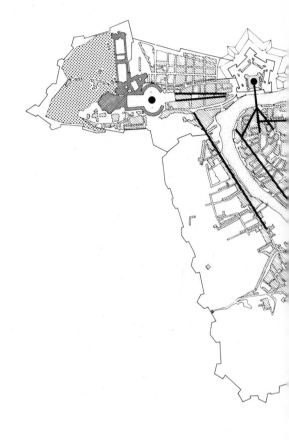

647   *Map of the Roman streets still functioning and the streets created by the Popes of the fifteenth and sixteenth centuries*

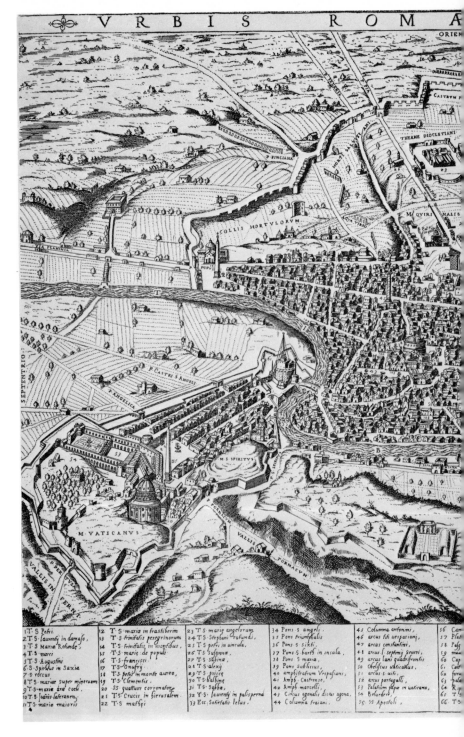

648 *Plan of Rome after the works of Sixtus V, in 1602*

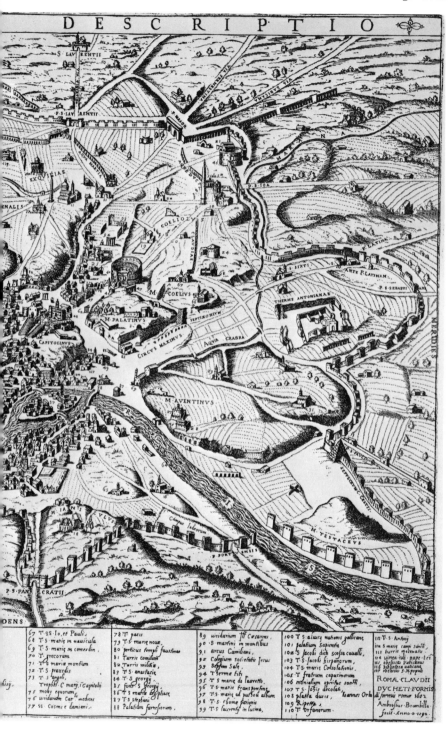

67 T̄ ss̄ Io̅ et Pauli,	78 T̄ pacis	89 uiridarium ff̄ Cæsaris,	100 T̄ s̄ aluiꝛ nationis gallicanꝛ,	111 P̄ s̄ Antonij
68 T̄ s̄ mariꝛ in nauicula,	79 T̄ s̄ mariꝛ noue,	90 s̄ martini in montibus,	101 palatium Sapientiꝛ	112 s̄ mariꝛ campi s̄nctȳ,
69 T̄ s̄ mariꝛ in comensdin	80 porticus templ faustinꝛ	91 arcus Camilani,	102 s̄ Iacobi dictꝛ scossa caualli,	113 turris nicꝛ¯natꝛ
70 T̄ grecorum	81 Turris comitum	92 Colegium societatis Iesus	103 T̄ s̄ Iacobi hispanorum,	114 uinea illꝰ pape̅ terꝛ
71 T̄ s̄ mariꝛ montium	82 Turris militiꝛ,	93 Septem Sala	104 T̄ s̄ mariꝛ Consolationis,	115 obeliscus Vaticanus
72 T̄ s̄ prꝛxedis	83 T̄ s̄ anastasiꝛ,	94 T̄ hermꝛ titi	105 T̄ fratrum capucinorum,	116 biblioteca uaticana,
73 T̄ s̄ angeli,	84 T̄ s̄ georgij,	95 T̄ s̄ mariꝛ de lauretto,	106 monialium spiritus sanctȳ,	117 obeliscus S̄ M̄ maggioꝛ
Tuopletī C̄ mariꝛ i̅ Capitolij	85 fons̄ s̄ georgij	96 T̄ s̄ mariꝛ transtiberim,	107 T̄ s̄ Iohis decolatꝛ	
74 mons̄ equorum	86 T̄ s̄ mariꝛ egiptiacꝛ	97 T̄ s̄ mariꝛ ad puteū album	108 platꝛa ducis,	ROMÆ CLAVDII
75 uiridarium Car̄ medices	87 T̄ s̄ stephani	98 T̄ s̄ thomꝛ pictorū	Ioannes Orlꝛ	DVCHETI FORMIS
76 s̄ uiridarium Car̄ medices		98 T̄ s̄ thomꝛ pictorū	109 Ripetta ;	di formis romꝛ 1602
77 ss̄ Cosmꝛ e damiani,	88 Palatium farnesiorum ,	99 T̄ s̄ lauentij in lucina,	110 T̄ orfanorum,	Ambrosius Brambilla
				fecit Anno D 1590

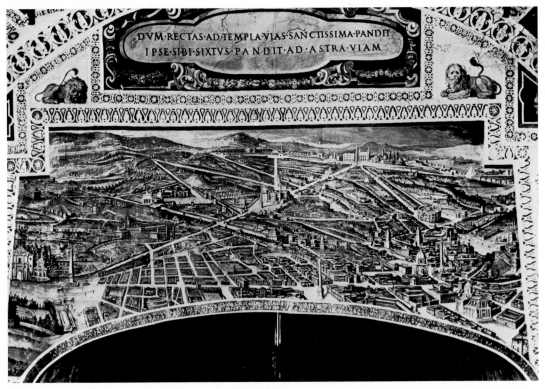

DVM·RECTAS·AD·TEMPLA·VIAS·SANCTISSIMA·PANDIT
IPSE·SIBI·SIXTVS·PANDIT·AD·ASTRA·VIAM

649 *Sixtus V's plan of Rome, in a fresco in the Vatican Library*

town-planning activities appear co-ordinated in a general programme, the work of Giovanni Manetti, while the monumental building operations – St Peter's, the Campidoglio and Palazzo Farnese – go back to Michelangelo; the new roads linked up with the straight roads of antiquity (via Lata, via Flaminia, via Nomentana and via dei Coronari) and provided the medieval city with a 'modern', though partial and interrupted, street system.

Gregory XIII (the Pope who established the Roman Academy in 1577 and brought about the reform of the calendar in 1582) built via Gregoriana, began the building of via Merulana, but above all – with the Bull *Quae publice utilia* of 1574 – laid down the building standards that were deferred to throughout the seventeenth century: the modes of procedure for the widening of

roads, for the straightening of winding streets, the elimination of the passages between one house and another and the obligation to maintain the continuity of street frontage by hiding vacant areas with high surrounding walls.

Sixtus V, continuing the work of his predecessor, promoted a large number of works during his brief pontificate: he completed the building of the dome of St Peter's (1588–90), laid out the monumental nuclei of S. Maria Maggiore and S. Giovanni, and extended the new road system over the hills to the east of the city, opening up a series of straight roads with the two basilicas or the obelisks taken from the ruins of the imperial city as perspective foci, but which ran through the open country for the most part. At the same time he had the ancient aqueducts

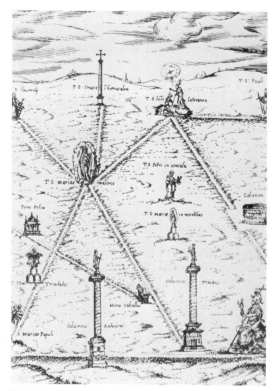

650–653 *Sixtus V's road plan, after Francesco Bordino, 1588; piazza Colonna and piazza S. Giovanni in Laterano in two frescoes in the Vatican Library; the fountain of Acqua Felice*

repaired, built a new one running to the fountain of Acqua Felice, on one of the highest points of the eastern side, and tried to improve the economic life of the city by encouraging the organization of industry (the Colosseum was to have become a great woollen-spinning mill); thus he laid the foundations for the repopulation of this part of the city and, like the patrons in the new cities previously described, he granted a series of privileges to anyone wanting to build along the new roads (Bull of 12 September 1587); it has been calculated that at the end of his pontificate the population of Rome had risen to 100,000. None the less the disproportion between the architectural layout and the civil content of the scheme remained enormous, because the new building increased the prosperity and crowding of the older city, on the plain near the Tiber, and only partly changed the rural character of the hilly eastern part.

We should not overestimate this plan, so much talked of from Giedion's book[163] onwards; contemporaries were struck by the sheer size of the works, and by the changes introduced into a countryside that had remained unchanged for many centuries. Domenico Fontana describes them in these words:[164]

'As our Lord wished to facilitate the way for those who, moved by devotion . . . would visit the most holy places in Rome . . . he has in many places opened up broad and straight roads so that, on foot, horse or coach, one can start out from any part of Rome you wish, and go almost directly to the most famous places of devotion. . . . At truly incredible expense, and as befits the soul of so great a Prince, he has drawn the said roads from one end of the city to the other, heedless of mountains and valleys that lay in his way; but flattening the former, and filling in the latter, he has reduced them to gentle plains and pleasant sites, revealing at several points the lowest parts of the city with various and different perspectives, so that the holy places still restore our bodily senses with their beauty.'

The little known poem by Francesco Bordino,[165] which talks '*de viis quas Sixtus P.M. ab Equilino Monte in sideris formam aperuit*',[166] insists on the symbolic meaning of the works. But the functionalist or prestige aims, apart from not being actually realized, were devoid from the start of any fitting empirical foundation. The abstract spaces created by Sixtus V and Fontana were to be progressively humanized and enriched by baroque artists, though without completely losing their characteristic vastness which struck Giacomo Leopardi: 'The immense buildings, and these equally interminable roads, are so many spaces thrown between

men, instead of being spaces which contain men.'[167]

Confirmation of the sketchiness and bureaucratic insensitivity of Sixtus V and Fontana was given by the new Vatican library, which cuts the courtyard of the Belvedere in two (Fig. 654). The great vista conceived by Bramante, one of the most important spaces of the Renaissance, was destroyed for ever and was replaced by two courtyards of traditional proportions, just as in any other Counter-Reformation building.

In 1590, the year of the death of Sixtus V, Tommaso Campanella's trial began. The young monk, having grown up in the remote background of Spanish Calabria, and so ready to perceive, belatedly, the regenerating themes of humanistic rationalism, found himself thrown into the midst of the philosophical and religious debate of the time, and when he returned home he imagined not only an ideal 'Christian Monarchy', but in 1599 took part in the plot to bring it into being, on a peak in Aspromonte.

After the failure of this attempt a long period of imprisonment began for Campanella, as well as a round of accusations, confessions and lies, which were the human consequences of his cultural idealism and the realism of institutions, and concern things quite other than architecture. In 1602 he put down his meditations on the ideal city in his book – *La città del sole* – whose imminent realization seemed to be foretold by the stars. But the great planetary conjunctions of 1603 passed without effect; Campanella took his Utopia with him from prison to prison, and then, as an old man, into exile with him to Paris. Here in 1636 he presented Richelieu with the '*Civitas Solis per me delineata ac per te aedificanda*',[168] in 1637 he published the text of 1602 in a definitive edition, and in 1638 dedicated it to the newborn son of Louis XIII, who was to be the sun king:[169]

'*Admirandam urbem, Solis de nomine dictam,*
me signasse tibi, puer, alto ex corde resigno. . . .'

In the mythical city conceived by Campanella there were all the mechanical devices that modern science was already producing, or whose creation seemed possible: new systems of cultivation, telescopes, apparatus to hear sound a long distance away, vehicles driven by the wind, boats without oars or sails and aeroplanes. In the *New Atlantis*, too, imagined by Francis Bacon in 1624, many new scientific devices were used 'to extend the limit of human power towards every possible aim'; the hope of building a better city was entrusted to science and was no longer the concern of the present but that of the far-off future.

654 *The Vatican, with the Belvedere courtyard blocked by the body of the Library, and the obelisk put up in front of the basilica of St Peter's (from the plan by F. di Paoli, 1623)*

Notes

Introduction

1 G. Scott, *The Architecture of Humanism*, Constable, London, 1924.
2 R. Wittkower, *Architectural Principles in the Age of Humanism*, Tiranti, London, 1962.
3 W. Morris, 'The prospects of architecture in civilization', lecture given at the London Institution on 10 March 1881, reprinted in *On Art and Socialism*, Lehmann, London, 1947, p. 245.
4 D. Cantimori, *La periodizzazione dell'età del Rinascimento* (1955), reprinted in *Studi di storia*, Turin, 1959, p. 340.
5 E. Garin, introduction to the Italian translation of Denys Hay, *The Italian Renaissance in its Historical Background* (Cambridge University Press, 1961), Florence, 1966.
6 P. Hazard, *The European Mind*, Hollis, London, 1953.
7 L. Venturi, *Storia della critica d'arte* (1936), Turin, 1964, p. 125.

1 The inventors of the new architecture

1 Cf. M. Jammer, *Concepts of Space*, Harvard University Press, Cambridge, Mass., 1954, chapter III.
2 *Vita di Filippo di ser Brunellesco*, attributed to Antonio Manetti: English translation, *Life of Brunelleschi*, ed. H. Saalman, Pennsylvania State University Press, 1970, p. 50.
3 Ibid., p. 38.
4 Cf. R. Davidsohn, *Storia di Firenze* (Italian translation, Florence, 1965), vol. VI, chapters I and II.
5 Ibid., p. 24.
6 Written in the last years of the fourteenth and first years of the fifteenth centuries.
7 F. Antal, *Florentine Painting and its Social Background*, London, Kegan Paul, 1947, p. 374.
8 E. Garin, *Science and Civil Life in the Italian Renaissance*, Doubleday, New York, 1969, p. ix.

9 The phrase was used by a correspondent of Giovanni Tortelli, quoted in E. Garin, *Italian Humanism*, Blackwell, Oxford, 1966, p. 55.
10 L. Ghiberti, *Commentari*, ed. O. Morisani, Naples, 1947, I, 1, p. 2.
11 G. C. Argan, *Filippo Brunelleschi*, Milan, 1955, p. 154.
12 L. Venturi, *Storia della critica d'arte* (1936), Turin, 1964, p. 95.
13 Ibid., p. 96.
14 E. Garin, *Medioevo e rinascimento* (1954), Bari, 1961, p. 153.
15 H. Baron, *The Crisis of the Early Italian Renaissance*, Princeton University Press, 1955.
16 Cf. A. Chastel, *Art et humanisme à Florence*, Paris, 1961, p. 184.
17 G. Vasari, *Lives of the Artists*, Dent, London, 1963 (Everyman Library), vol. I, p. 272.
18 Cf. Antal, op. cit., p. 58.
19 Quoted in E. Garin, *L'educazione umanistica in Italia*, Bari, 1964, p. 43.
20 Vasari, *Lives*, ed. cit., vol. I, p. 272.
21 Ibid., p. 297.
22 As written in the directions of 3 July 1420, par. 1.
23 Ibid., par. 2.
24 Argan, op. cit., p. 57.
25 P. Sanpaolesi, *La cupola del Brunelleschi*, Florence, 1966.
26 Cf. P. Sanpaolesi, *La cupola di S. Maria del Fiore*, Rome, 1941; *Brunelleschi*, Milan, 1962, pp. 53 ff.
27 Vasari, *Lives*, ed. cit., vol. I, p. 286.
28 *Life of Brunelleschi*, ed. cit., p. 94.
29 Ibid., p. 92.
30 Ibid., p. 92.
31 Vasari, *Lives*, ed. cit., vol. I, p. 290.
32 Directions of 3 July 1420, par. 9.
33 L. B. Alberti, *De pictura*: English translation, *On Painting*, by J. R. Spencer, Routledge & Kegan Paul, London, 1956, p. 40.
34 *Life of Brunelleschi*, ed. cit., p. 34.

35 Ibid., pp. 50–4.
36 Ibid., p. 52.
37 Vasari, *Lives*, ed. cit., vol. I, p. 275.
38 Ibid.
39 Garin, *Medioevo e rinascimento*, p. 103.
40 Ibid., p. 106.
41 H. Saalman, 'Filippo Brunelleschi, capital studies', *Art Bulletin*, xl, 1958; M. Gosebruch, 'Florentinische Kapitelle von Brunelleschi bis zum Tempio Malatestiano, *Römisches Jahrbuch für Kunstgeschichte*, vii, 1958; E. Luporini, *Brunelleschi, forma e ragione*, Milan, 1964, pp. 170 ff.
42 C. Brandi, *Eliante o dell'architettura*, Turin, 1956, pp. 149–50.
43 *Life of Brunelleschi*, ed. cit., p. 42.
44 Ibid., p. 42.
45 Alberti, *On Painting*, ed. cit., p. 56.
46 Piero della Francesca, *De perspectiva pingendi*, ed. by G. Nicco Fasola, Florence, 1942, pp. 68 ff.
47 Leonardo, *Treatise on Painting*, ed. A. P. McMahon, Princeton University Press, 1956.
48 F. de Sanctis, quoted in Garin, *Medioevo e rinascimento*, p. 120.
49 Antonio Billi, quoted in Luporini, op. cit., p. 83.
50 On a fairly small scale, the use of the *braccio* as module (58·6 cm) was necessitated by its coincidence with the traditional dimensions of the brick; on a larger scale, the use of figures which, expressed in *braccia*, correspond to round figures, becomes significant.
51 *Life of Brunelleschi*, ed. cit., p. 106.
52 Ibid., p. 116.
53 Ibid., p. 108.
54 Ibid.
55 Ibid., p. 106.
56 Vasari, *Lives*, ed. cit., vol. I, p. 293. As a result, the ratio between support and entablature is different in the two cases; for the pilasters, which are also repeated around the transept, it is 7:1.
57 G. Laschi, P. Roselli, P. A. Rossi, 'Indagini sulla cappella dei Pazzi', *Commentari*, no. 1, 1962, p. 24.
58 Ibid., p. 32.
59 *Life of Brunelleschi*, ed. cit., p. 126. The following reflections on the church of S. Spirito are the result of a direct study of the building, made by L. Benevolo, S. Chieffi, G. Mezzetti in 'Indagine sul S. Spirito di Brunelleschi', *Quaderni dell'istituto di storia dell'architettura*, Rome, December 1968.
60 In the book by Antonio Billi we read: 'Here too they did not obey his orders, for the pilasters have been made too high, and the capitals of the columns, and the part above them' (*Arch. stor. it.*, 5th series, vol. VII, 1891, p. 316).
61 H. Folnesics, *Brunelleschi*, Vienna, 1915.
62 R. Wittkower, *Architectural Principles in the Age of Humanism*, Tiranti, London, 1962, p. 117.
63 Vasari, *Lives*, ed. cit., vol. I, p. 299.
64 Sanpaolesi, *Brunelleschi*, p. 78.
65 Cf. the documents transcribed by Luporini, op. cit., p. 237.
66 Chastel, op. cit., p. 129.
67 *Life of Brunelleschi*, ed. cit., p. 98.
68 Brandi, op. cit., p. 152.
69 Vasari, *Lives*, ed. cit., vol. I, pp. 300–1.
70 Sanpaolesi, *La cupola di S. Maria del Fiore*.
71 Argan, op. cit., p. 40.
72 Sanpaolesi, *Brunelleschi*, pp. 51–2.
73 Argan, op. cit., pp. 111–12.
74 *Metaphisicorum*, tract. I, chap. XI (mid-thirteenth century). '*Opinamus artifices artis rationem habentes, sapientiores esse quam expertos. . . . Unde architectores . . . significamus nobiliores esse circa quodlibet genus artificiatorum; et hos significamus ipso nomine principalitatis magis scire et artifices tales esse sapientiores. Causa autem hujus significationis est, quio architectores sciunt factorum sive artificiatorum causas : quia aliter non haberent rationem certam : hi ergo magis sciunt quam hi qui dicuntur manu artifices, sive usuales*' (quoted in R. Assunto, *La critica d'arte nel pensiero medioevale*, Milan, 1961, pp. 187–8).
75 Boccaccio, *Decameron*, day VI, story V (1349–53).
77 Filippo Villani, *De Cimabue, Maso, Stephano et Taddheo pictoribus* (about 1390).
77 Cennino Cennini, *Il libro dell'arte* (end of fourteenth century).
78 Cristoforo Landino, *Disputationes camaldulenses*, I (about 1475).
79 Translated in Garin, *L'educazione umanistica in Italia*, p. 88.
80 P. P. Vergerio, quoted in E. Garin, *Storia della filosofia italiana*, Turin, 1966, p. 188.
81 Alberti, in *De pictura*, observes: '*Sed hoc in primis honore a majoribus honestata est, ut cum caeteri ferme omnes artifices fabri nuncuparent solus in fabrorum numero pictor non esset habitus*' (Book II, introduction).
82 E. Panofsky, *Idea, a Concept in Art Theory*, Columbia University Press, 1968, pp. 47 ff.
83 Alberti, *De re aedificatoria*, Book VI, chapter II.
84 Alberti, *On Painting*, ed. cit., p. 64.
85 P. Francastel, *Peinture et société : naissance et destruction d'un espace plastique de la Renaissance au cubisme*, Lyon, 1951, chapter I.
86 C. Lévi-Strauss, *The Savage Mind*, Weidenfeld & Nicolson, London, 1966, p. 23.
87 'It is a frequent practice of nature when she produces a person of great excellence in any profession to raise up another to rival him at the same time and in a neighbouring place, so that they may help one another by their emulation and talents. . . . That this is true is shown by Florence having produced in the same age Filippo, Donato, Lorenzo, Paolo Uccello and Masaccio, each one pre-eminent in his kind, who not only rid themselves of the rude and rough style in vogue until then, but by their beautiful works incited and inflamed the minds of their successors to such an extent that these employments have been brought to their present state of grandeur and perfection. For the good style of painting we are chiefly indebted to Masaccio' (Vasari, *Lives*, ed. cit., vol. I, p. 263).

88 A. Chastel, *The Golden Age of the Renaissance, Italy 1460–1500*, Thames & Hudson, London, 1965, p. 179.
89 B. Baldi, *Descrizione del palazzo ducale di Urbino* (10.6.1587), ed. 1859, p. 550.
90 Chastel, *The Golden Age*, pp. 181–2.
91 Vasari, *Lives*, ed. cit., vol. III, p. 68.
92 Ibid., p. 74.
93 The treatise on painting was finished in Latin on 26 September 1436, and in the vernacular on 17 July 1436; the *De statua* is of uncertain date, but generally placed just before the *De pictura*, which it mentions as planned for the future.
94 *De statua*, translated by John Evelyn, in R. Fréart, *A Parallel of the Antient Architecture with the Modern*, London, 1664, reprinted 1970, p. 145.
95 Ibid., p. 149.
96 Ibid., p. 152.
97 *The Sonnets of Michelangelo*, trans. J. A. Symonds, Vision Press, London, 1950, p. 47: 'The best of artists hath no thought to show which the rough stone in its superfluous shell doth not include; to break the marble spell is all the hand that serves the brain can do.'
98 Chastel, *Art et humanisme*, p. 98.
99 *On Painting*, ed. cit., p. 43.
100 For instance in *Momus*, book III.
101 *On Painting*, ed. cit., p. 44.
102 Ibid., p. 45.
103 Ibid.
104 Ibid., pp. 46 ff.
105 Ibid., p. 51.
106 Ibid., pp. 54–5: 'It would be well to add to the above statements the opinion of philosophers who affirm that if the sky, the stars, the sea, mountains and all bodies should become – should God so wish – reduced by half, nothing would appear to be diminished in any part to us.'
107 Ibid., p. 63.
108 Ibid., p. 56.
109 Ibid., p. 68.
110 Ibid., p. 65.
111 Ibid., p. 67.
112 At this time he was writing the *Ludi mathematici*, the *De lunularum quadratura*, and the *De punctis et lineis apud pictores*.
113 The treatise, composed a few years earlier, was circulating in manuscript from 1452 onwards, and was printed in 1485. From the sixteenth century onwards it was known mainly in the vernacular translation by Cosimo Bartoli (Venice, 1565).
114 Quoted in P. Portoghesi, *Il tempio malatestiano*, Florence, 1965.
115 M. Dezzi Bardeschi, 'Nuove ricerche sul S. Sepolcro nella cappella Rucellai a Firenze', *Marmo*, 2, 1963, p. 135.
116 Alberti, *Ten Books on Architecture*, trans. G. Leoni, ed. J. Rykwert, reprinted Tiranti, London, 1955, p. 17.
117 A. Bruschi, 'Osservazioni sulla teoria architettonica rinascimentale nella formulazione albertiana', *Quaderni dell'istituto di storia dell'architettura*,

31–48, 1961, p. 124.
118 Dezzi Bardeschi, op. cit., p. 157.
119 V. Zoubov, 'Quelques aspects de la théorie des proportions esthétiques de L. B. Alberti', *Bibliothèque d'humanisme et de renaissance*, xxii, p. 54.
120 Alberti, *Ten Books*, ed. cit., p. ix.
121 Ibid., p. xi.
122 Ibid., p. ix.
123 Ibid., p. 1.
124 Ibid., p. 2.
125 Ibid., p. 112.
126 Ibid.
127 Ibid., p. 113.
128 Ibid., p. 194.
129 Ibid., p. 196.
130 Ibid., p. 207.
131 Cf. Antal, op. cit., part III, chapter IV.
132 Alberti, *Ten Books*, ed. cit., p. 111.
133 Quoted in E. Garin, 'Thought of L. B. Alberti', *Encyclopedia of World Art*, McGraw-Hill, New York, 1959–68, vol. 1, column 208.
134 Alberti, *Ten Books*, ed. cit., p. 138.
135 Ibid., p. 139.
136 Ibid.
137 H. von Geymüller, *Die ursprünglichen Entwürfe für S. Peter in Rom*, Vienna, 1875, p. 7.
138 Vasari, *Lives*, ed. cit., vol. I, p. 349.
139 After having given the rules for the proportions of the chapels, Alberti adds: 'Divide the breadth of the temple into four parts, and give two of these parts to the breadth of the chapel', p. 139.
140 During those same years Ficino and Pico were developing the Albertian distinction between *disegni* and *muramenti* in a Platonic sense, emphasizing the esoteric interpretation of musical ratios, and praising the philosophical tone of the Albertian treatise, as against the empiricism of Vitruvius; see M. Ficino, *Commento al Convito*, 1469 and *Commento al Timeo*, 1486, with the appreciation of Alberti; Pico della Mirandola, *Commento sopra una canzone de amore*, 1484, quoted in Chastel, *Art et humanisme*, p. 131.
141 Wittkower, op. cit., pp. 47 ff.

2 Towards the ideal city

1 L. B. Alberti, *On Painting*, trans. J. R. Spencer, Routledge & Kegan Paul, London, 1956, pp. 39 ff.
2 A. Chastel, 'Un épisode de la symbolique urbaine au XV siècle: Florence et Rome, Cités de Dieu', in *Urbanisme et architecture, études écrites et publiées en l'honneur de Pierre Lavedan*, Paris, 1954, p. 75.
3 L. B. Alberti, *Ten Books on Architecture*, trans. G. Leoni, ed. J. Rykwert, reprinted Tiranti, London, 1955, p. 2.
4 Ibid., p. 14.
5 Ibid., p. 70.
6 Ibid., p. 74.
7 Ibid., p. 75.
8 Ibid.
9 Ibid.
10 Ibid., p. 172.

11 Ibid., pp. 172–5.

12 Ibid., p. 170.

13 Ibid., pp. 71–2.

14 Quoted in A. Chastel, *Italian Art*, Faber, London, 1963, p. 182.

15 The expression is used by G. Manetti, in the life of Nicholas V; cf. E. Battisti, 'Roma apocalittica e re Salomone' in *Rinascimento e barocco*, Turin, 1960, p. 81.

16 Published in Muratori, *Rerum italicarum scriptores*, III, II.

17 T. Magnuson, *Studies in Roman Quattrocento Architecture*, Stockholm, 1953; T. Magnuson, 'The project of Nicholas V for rebuilding the Borgo Leonino in Rome', *Art Bulletin*, June 1954; cf. Battisti, op. cit.

18 Ibid., p. 77.

19 Ibid., pp. 81 ff.

20 Transcribed in Magnuson, *Studies in Roman Quattrocento Architecture*.

21 L. Quaroni, 'Una città eterna, quattro lezioni da ventisette secoli', *Urbanistica*, 27, 1959, pp. 66–7.

22 A. Chastel, *The Golden Age of the Renaissance, Italy 1460–1500*, Thames & Hudson, London, 1965, p. 101.

23 F. Albertini, in the *Opusculum* dedicated to Julius II in 1510:
'Sixtus IV began the reconstruction of Rome. First of all he destroyed the dark porticoes, widened the streets and squares of Rome and paved them with brick, and rebuilt many churches that were tottering from their foundations. His successors tried to imitate him, until his Holiness, within a short time, surpassed Sixtus himself and all the others.'
(R. Valentini and G. Zucchetti, 'Codice topografico della città di Roma', in *Fonti per la storia d'Italia*, vol. IV, Rome, 1953, p. 499).

24 G. Voigt, *Die Wiederbelebung des klassischen Altertums*, Berlin, 1893, quoted in Denys Hay, *The Italian Renaissance in its Historical Background*, Cambridge University Press, 1961.

25 Chastel, *The Golden Age*, p. 316.

26 Filarete criticizes the 'ill-ordered' design of the previous Venetian architect, and reproduces his own plan in the treatise (Magliabechia MS., 169, v et seq.).

27 Bibl. Naz., E.B. 15, fifteenth century. The passage quoted is transcribed in M. Lazzaroni and A. Muñoz, *Filarete*, Rome, 1908, p. 240.

28 Filarete, *Treatise on Architecture*, ed. J. R. Spencer, Yale University Press, New Haven and London, 1965, p. 5.

29 Ibid., p. 12.

30 Ibid., p. 21.

31 Ibid., p. 22.

32 Quoted in G. B. Mannucci, *Pienza, arte e storia*, Rome, 1937, p. 28.

33 *Commentari*, book IX. Both the medieval discussion of the metaphysics of light (Scotus Erigena, Suger, Dante) and the anti-Gothic polemic in favour of the lightness and brightness of the new architectural spaces, come together in this statement. It has been noted that the last theoretician of the Platonic metaphysics of light, the Carthusian Dionysius of Ryckel, a friend of Casanus who accompanied him on the apostolic journey of 1450–2 to Germany and the Low Countries, was living at the time of Pius II. The pope could have known him directly or through Cusanus, and later Dionysius supported the papal initiative for a crusade at the court of Philip the Good. Cf. E. Carli, *Pienza, la città di Pio II*, Rome, 1966, p. 37.

34 Cf. L. Heydenreich, 'Pio II als Bauherr von Pienza', *Zeitschrift für Kunstgeschichte*, VI, 1937.

35 Alberti, *Ten Books*, book VII.

36 Ibid., ed. cit., p. 150.

37 Ibid., p. 136.

38 Ibid.

39 Quoted in Mannucci, op. cit., p. 31; but the author points out soon afterwards that the Bull was abrogated by Gregory XIII in 1583.

40 Alberti, *Ten Books*, ed. cit., p. 75.

41 *Commentari*, quoted by Carli, op. cit., p. 44.

42 Ibid.

43 Ibid., p. 46; the observation is taken up by G. Giovannoni, *Saggi sull'architettura del Rinascimento*, 1935.

44 R. Longhi, *Piero della Francesca*, Rome, 1927.

45 R. Wittkower in *Journal of the Warburg and Courtauld Institutes*, 17, 1952.

46 M. Salmi, *Piero della Francesca e il palazzo ducale di Urbino*, Florence, 1945.

47 *Racconto istorico della fondazione di Rimini e delle origini e vite de' Malatesti*, Rimini, 1627, II, p. 354; cf. P. Rotondi, *Il palazzo ducale di Urbino*, Urbino, 1951 (a version of which has appeared in English as *The Ducal Palace of Urbino*, Tiranti, London, 1969), p. 82.

48 Ibid., pp. 153–4.

49 The following dates may be deduced from the older writers:
1463–4 (Ba. Baldi, *Vita e fatti di Federico da Montefeltro*, ed. Bologna, 1826, III, p. 45).
1466 (Porcellio de' Pandoni, *Feltria*, c. 1475).
1468 (Filippo de Lignamine, *Continuatio Chronici Ricobaldini*, 1474, in *Rerum italicarum scriptores*, IX, col. 274); Rotondi (op. cit., pp. 109–25) dates the beginning of the works around 1466.

50 Ibid., p. 29.

51 As described in the *Cronaca* of Giovanni Santi, quoted in Rotondi, op. cit., p. 446.

52 G. de Carlo, *Urbino. La storia di una città e il piano della sua evoluzione urbanistica*, Padua, 1966, p. 76.

53 Giovanni Santi, *Cronaca*, cf. Rotondi, op. cit., p. 443.

54 G. Vasari, *Lives of the Artists*, Dent, London, 1963 (Everyman Library), vol. II, p. 26.

55 The famous document discovered in 1836 by Gaye and published many times from then onwards, also contains an evocative statement of intent, which

illustrates the cultural attitude of Federigo and his circle:

'We shall judge particularly worthy of honour and commendation those who are blessed with talent and virtue et max, with those virtues which were always prized by the ancients and moderns such as that of Architecture rooted in the art of arithmetic and geometry, which are among the seven liberal arts, and the principal ones, because they are in primo gradu certitudinis, and it is an art of great learning and great ingenuity, very much esteemed and appreciated by us, we who can be said to have searched everywhere, and particularly in Tuscany, which is the fount of architects, and who have found no man seeming really to understand the subject, and who was really skilled in this craft. . . .' (Cf. Rotondi, op. cit., p. 109.)

56 R. Papini, *Francesco di Giorgio*, Florence, 1946.
57 Ibid.
58 A. Chastel, *Art et humanisme à Florence*, Paris, 1961, p. 361.
59 The myth of Federigo as architect, started by his dependants (Vespasiano da Bisticci and Giovanni Santi) is discussed by Rotondi, op. cit., pp. 54 ff.; the same author refers (p. 63) to the possible influence of Battista Sforza, at the time when she was with her husband (1460–72).
60 Salmi, op. cit.
61 Rotondi, op. cit., pp. 337–8.
62 Ibid., p. 353.
63 Ibid., pp. 348 ff.; Chastel, *Art et humanisme*, p. 365.
64 Ibid.
65 Ibid.
66 Ibid.
67 Ibid., p. 362.
68 Castiglione, *The Courtier*, book I.
69 Quoted in Rotondi, op. cit., pp. 440–2.
70 Ibid., pp. 292, 446–7.
71 Vasari, *Lives*, ed. cit., vol. II, p. 26.
72 De Carlo, op. cit.
73 J. Schlosser-Magnino, *La letteratura artistica* (1924), Italian translation, Florence, 1935, p. 121.
74 Quoted in E. Garin, *L'educazione umanistica in Italia*, Bari, 1964, p. 192.
75 Chastel, *The Golden Age*, p. 177.
76 Diario ferrarese, quoted in J. Burckhardt, *The Civilization of the Renaissance in Italy*, Phaidon, London, 1928, p. 47.
77 Hondadio de Vitali, *Cronaca*, quoted in B. Zevi, *Biagio Rossetti*, Turin, 1960, p. 186.
78 Caleffini, *Cronica*, quoted in Zevi, op. cit., p. 189.
79 This road – the present corso Porta Po and corso Porta Mare – is represented in the 1498 plan with a markedly curved line; in execution its line is almost straight, with slight deviations possibly deriving from adaptations to pre-existing ground plan restrictions.
80 Zevi, op. cit., p. 192.
81 This is Vasari's phrase, in the introduction to the third part of the *Lives* (ed. cit., vol. II, p. 153).
82 This is the supposition made by G. Paccagnini, *Mantova, le arti*, vol. I, *Il medioevo*, Mantua, 1960;

the source for the town-planning situation of Mantua until the fifteenth century is S. Davari, *Notizie storiche e topografiche della città di Mantova nei secoli XIII, XIV, XV*, Mantua, 1903.
83 Quoted in A. Chastel, *Studios and Styles of the Renaissance*, Thames & Hudson, London, 1966, p. 81. This is another proof that the classical forms were still regarded as exotic fifty years after Brunelleschi's crucial work.
84 Chastel, *The Golden Age*, pp. 41 ff.
85 Rotondi, op. cit., pp. 57–8.
86 Paccagnini, op. cit.
87 Chastel, *The Golden Age*, pp. 66 ff.
88 Ibid., p. 67.
89 A. Chastel, *Marsile Ficin et l'art*, Geneva-Lille, 1954.
90 '*AN MCCCCLXXXX, quo pulcherrima civitas opibus victoriis artibus aedificiisque nobilis copia salubritate pace perfruebatur*'; cf. Chastel, *Art et humanisme*, p. 16.
91 Le Corbusier, *When the Cathedrals were White*, Reynal & Hitchcock, New York, 1947, p. 7.
92 G. Hamberg, 'Vitruvius, Fra Giocondo and the city plan of Naples', *Acta Archaeologica*, 1965, p. 105. The drawings are numbered 4142r and 4142v.
93 C. de Seta, *Cartografia della città di Napoli*, Naples, 1969, vol. I, p. 108.
94 E. Garin, *Science and Civil Life in the Italian Renaissance*, Doubleday, New York, 1969, p. viii.
95 Chastel, *Studios and Styles*, p. xii.

3 Beginning and end of the 'third style'

1 G. Vasari, *Lives of the Artists*, Dent, London, 1963 (Everyman Library), vol. II, p. 151.
2 Ibid.
3 Ibid., p. 153.
4 Ibid., p. 154.
5 Ibid.
6 Ibid., p. 152.
7 Ibid., p. 154.
8 L. Ghiberti, *Commentari*, ed. O. Marisani, Naples, 1947, I, 1, p. 2.
9 'Painting itself includes all the forms of nature, but you, poet, have nothing but their names, which are not universal, as are their forms. If you have the effects of the manifestations, we painters have manifestations of the effects.' Leonardo da Vinci, *Treatise on Painting*, ed. A. P. McMahon, Princeton University Press, 1956, p. 19.
10 *The Notebooks of Leonardo da Vinci*, ed. E. MacCurdy, Cape, London, 1956, vol. II, p. 496.
11 *Practica musicae*, 1490 and *De harmonia musicorum instrumentorum*, 1518.
12 *The Notebooks of Leonardo da Vinci*, ed. cit., p. 30.
13 A list of names in the Codice Atlantico may indicate the Florentines with whom Leonardo was in contact: the astronomer Carlo Marmocchi, the notary Benedetto da Cieperello, the mathematicians Benedetto dell'Abbaco and Paolo Toscanelli, the humanist Giovanni Argiropulo, one 'Calvo de li

Alberti', the artists Domenico da Michelino and
Francesco Averlino (Cod. Atl. 12 v. a). Another
leaf bears a list of books, possibly those forming the
personal library of Leonardo in Milan: among the
authors are Paolo dell'Abbaco, Pliny, Valturio,
Livy, Elio Donato, Pulci, Platina, Isidore of Seville,
Ovid, Filelfo, Bracciolini, Diogenes Laertius, Cecco
d'Ascoli, Albertus Magnus, Ficino and Petrarch
(Cod. Atl. 210 r.a).

14 K. Jaspers, *Leonardo, Descartes, Max Weber*,
Routledge & Kegan Paul, London, 1964, p. 6.
15 Ibid., p. 14.
16 R. Wittkower, 'Brunelleschi and "proportion in
perspective"', *Journal of the Warburg and
Courtauld Institutes*, 16, 1953, pp. 285–7.
17 *Quaderni di anatomia*, II, 5v. in *Notebooks*, ed. cit.,
p. 161. For a historical assessment of Leonardo's
studies on anatomy, see A. Chastel, 'Le baroque et
la mort' in *Retorica e barocco*, Proceedings of the
Third Congress of Humanistic Studies, Rome,
1955, p. 40.
18 *Treatise on Painting*, ed. cit., p. 23.
19 Ibid.
20 The gulf recognized by Vasari between Leonardo
and the *quattrocentisti* (*Lives*, ed. cit., vol. II, p.
153) remained as a historiographical canon for a
long time. Delacroix wrote:
'One cannot fail to marvel at the immense progress
that Leonardo caused his art to make. Almost a
contemporary of Ghirlandaio, a fellow-student of
Lorenzo di Credi and Perugino . . . he broke
sharply with the traditional painting of the
Quattrocento; without errors, without weaknesses,
without exaggerations and virtually at one jump, he
arrived at a judicious and skilful naturalism.'
(*Revue de Paris*, 1830.)
21 *Treatise on Painting*, ed. cit., p. 5.
22 Ibid., p. 19.
23 Ibid., p. 16.
24 L. Heydenreich on Leonardo in *Encyclopedia of
World Art*, McGraw-Hill, New York, 1959–68,
vol. IX, col. 214.
25 Vasari, *Lives*, ed. cit., vol. II, p. 161.
26 Ibid., p. 157.
27 Cod. Atl. 370 r.a.
28 Ibid., 91 v.a.
29 Le Corbusier, *The Complete Architectural Works,
1952–7*, Thames & Hudson, London, 1966, vol. VI,
pp. 8–9.
30 A. Chastel, *Art et humanisme à Florence*, Paris,
1961, p. 505.
31 A. Bruschi, *Note bramantesche*, Rome, 1966, pp.
15 ff.
32 In book III Serlio writes that the Tempietto is
measured with 'the old Roman foote, to which
foote is sixteen fingers, and every finger is four
minutes' (about 28 cm); the width of the
ambulatory, still according to Serlio, is seven feet
(about 1·96 m) and the interaxis of the columns is
five and a half feet (about 1·55 m).
33 The intercolumniation between the pilasters is two
feet twelve fingers (78 cm); the net span of the

door is three feet and a half according to Serlio (in
reality, 90 cm).
34 The columns are about 40 cm (a foot and twenty
five minutes, according to Serlio); the pilasters,
about 38 cm.
35 Bruschi, op. cit., pp. 41 ff.
36 D. Frey, *Gotik und Renaissance als Grundlagen der
modernen Weltanschauung*, Augsburg, 1929.
37 *De divina proportione*, 1496.
38 See E. M. Lowinsky, 'The concept of physical and
musical space in the Renaissance', *Papers of the
American Musicological Society*, 1941 (ed. 1946),
pp. 82–3.
39 B. Ramis, *Musica practica*, 1482.
40 F. Gaffurio, *De harmonia musicorum
instrumentorum*, 1518.
41 S. Vanneo, *Recanetum de musica aurea*, 1533.
42 P. Aron, *Toscanello in musica*, 1523.
43 J. Tinctoris, *Liber de arte contrapuncti*, 1477.
44 F. Gaffurio, *Angelicum ac divinum opus musicae*,
1518.
45 G. Zarlino, *Istituzioni harmoniche*, 1558.
46 *Treatise on Painting*, ed. cit., p. 16.
47 Ibid., p. 31.
48 Ibid.
49 Vasari, *Lives*, ed. cit., vol. II, p. 157.
50 Ibid., p. 164.
51 Letter of 3 April 1501 to Isabella d'Este; L.
Beltrami, *Documenti e notizie riguardanti la vita e le
opere di Leonardo da Vinci*, Milan, 1919, p. 65.
52 R. S. Stites, 'More on Freud's Leonardo', *College
Art Journal*, 1948–9, I, p. 40; see Chastel, *Art et
humanisme*, p. 440.
53 Ibid., p. 435.
54 *Treatise on Painting*, ed. cit., p. 13.
55 'Nor God hath designed to show himself elsewhere
more clearly than in human forms sublime;
which, since they image him, alone I love.'
The Sonnets of Michelangelo, trans. J. A. Symonds,
Vision Press, London, 1950, p. 134.
56 *Treatise on Painting*, ed. cit., p. 124.
57 Chastel, *Art et humanisme*, p. 501.
58 *Fogli di anatomia* A 2 r.
59 A passage from the Cod. Atl. (119 v.a.) may help to
explain the point of difference between Leonardo
and Michelangelo:
'These rules will cause you to know the true from
the false; and this means that men aim at possible
things, with greater moderation, and that you will
not veil yourself in ignorance, which would mean
that, if you did not succeed in what you set out to
do, you would become desperate and melancholy.'
60 R. J. Clements, *Michelangelo's Theory of Art*,
Routledge & Kegan Paul, London, 1963,
chapter V.
61 Chastel, *Art et humanisme*, p. 499.
62 Vasari, *Lives*, ed. cit., vol. II, p. 245.
63 L. Venturi, *Storia della critica d'arte* (1936),
Turin, 1964, p. 119.
64 Vasari, *Lives*, ed. cit., vol. II, p. 221.
65 F. de Hollanda, *Dialogos em Roma*, 1548, Dialogue
III; see Clements, op. cit., p. 120.

66 C. Landino, *Dante*, Venice, 1596, fol. 7 v.
67 A. Chastel, *Marsile Ficin et l'art*, Geneva-Lille, 1954, p. 61.
68 Chastel, *Art et humanisme à Florence*, p. 400.
69 *Apologia pro multis Florentinis ab Antichristo Hieronymo ferrariense . . . deceptis* (1499).
70 A. Chastel, 'L'Apocalypse en 1500: la fresque de l'Antéchrist de la chapelle Saint-Brice à Orvieto', *Humanisme et Renaissance*, 1952, p. 124.
71 Quoted in E. Garin, *Ritratti di umanisti*, Florence, 1967, p. 183.
72 P. O. Kristeller, *Supplementum ficinianum*, Florence, 1937, II, p. 314.
73 A. Condivi, *Life of Michelangelo*, ed. C. Holroyd, Duckworth, London, 1903, section XXVII.
74 Vasari, *Lives*, ed. cit., vol. II, p. 217.
75 C. de Tolnay, under 'Michelangelo' in *Encyclopedia of World Art*, McGraw-Hill, New York, 1959–68, vol. IX, col. 880.
76 O. H. Förster (*Bramante*, Vienna, 1956) discusses the traditional order, and suggests a new one, accepted with many reserves by other scholars; see also G. Giovannoni, *Antonio da Sangallo il Giovane*, Rome, 1959.
77 Uffizi, nos. 1, 8 and 20.
78 R. Bonelli, *Da Bramante a Michelangelo*, Venice, 1960, p. 36.
79 Chastel, *Art et humanisme*, p. 461.
80 Ibid., p. 457.
81 *Speculum historiae* and *Speculum doctrinae*, according to the interpretation of Chastel in ibid., p. 470.
82 De Tolnay, op. cit., vol. IX, col. 886.
83 'All the time numerous artists from near and far flock to the city, and studiously attempt, within the cramped space of their paper or their tablets, to reproduce the form of the beautiful old marble figures, and sometimes the copper ones, and the baths, and theatres, and other different buildings.' (P. Bembo, quoted in H. Gmelin, 'Das Prinzip der Imitatio in den romanischen Literaturen der Renaissance', *Romanischen Forschungen Organ*, xlvi, 1 and 2, p. 209).
84 B. Wolpe, quoted in A. Petrucci, 'Raffaello calligrafo', *Il Messaggero*, 10 October 1969.
85 In the engravings taken from the frescoes of the Farnesina with the story of Psyche.
86 In the book by A. Fulvio, *Illustrium imagines*, published in 1517 and dedicated to Pope Leo X.
87 Bonelli, op. cit., p. 54.
88 Förster (op. cit., pp. 284 ff.) attributes this writing to Bramante; it was however certainly rewritten (or composed) by Castiglione on behalf of Raphael.
89 Vasari, *Lives*, ed. cit., vol. II, p. 240.
90 Ibid., p. 248.
91 Ibid.
92 *Sonnets of Michelangelo*, ed. cit., p. 186.
93 C. de Tolnay, *The Medici Chapel*, Princeton University Press, 1948, p. 110.
94 De Tolnay, under 'Michelangelo', in *Encyclopedia of World Art*, vol. IX, col. 861.
95 F. de Hollanda, *Dialogos em Roma*, in Clements, op. cit., p. 76.
96 *Sonnets of Michelangelo*, ed. cit., p. 150.
97 Ibid., p. 158.
98 Cf. Clements, op. cit., p. 170.
99 Ibid., p. 359.
100 Uffizi, nos 66, 67 and 259.
101 Vasari, *Lives*, ed. cit., vol. IV, p. 146.
102 *The Letters of Michelangelo*, tr. E. H. Ramsden, Peter Owen, London, 1963, II, p. 69.
103 R. di Stefano (*La cupola di S. Pietro*, Naples, 1963) has studied the differences between the load-bearing system of Brunelleschi's dome – where the internal ribs serve only to strengthen a continuous masonry structure – and that of Michelangelo's, where the outer ribs correspond to so many independent internal partitions, and carry the intermediate sections. But the different static function has not led to a different choice of outline; the two variants concern mainly the execution, and operate in a single structural concept.
104 C. Brandi, *Struttura e architettura*, Turin, 1967, p. 181.
105 Vasari, *Lives*, ed. cit., vol. IV, p. 145.
106 Ibid., p. 153.
107 Ibid., p. 156.
108 *Complete Poems of Michelangelo*, trs. and ed. J. Tusiani, Owen, London, 1961, p. 151.
109 *Poems of St. John of the Cross*, trs. Roy Campbell, Penguin, Harmondsworth, 1960, p. 103.
110 E. Bizer in *Cambridge Modern History*, Cambridge University Press, 1958, vol. II, p. 161.
111 B. Castiglione, *The Courtier*, I, xxxviii, 43.
112 Chastel, *Art et humanisme*, pp. 488–9. The three psychological types based on Eros, Hermes and Saturn are discussed in Ficino's *De vita triplici*.
113 F. H. Taylor, *The Taste of Angels*, Hamish Hamilton, London, 1949.
114 Published from 1537 to 1557.
115 *Quaderni dell' Istituto dell' Architettura*, 7, Rome, 1954. A. Bruschi, 'Nuovi dati documentari sulle opere orsiniani di Bomarzo', ibid., 55–60, 1963, pp. 13 ff.
116 P. Portoghesi, 'Nota sulla villa Orsini di Pitigliano', in *Quaderni . . .*, 7–9, 1954, p. 74.

4 Urban changes in the sixteenth century

1 Quoted in J. B. Teràn, *La nascita dell' America spagnola*, Italian trans., Bari, 1931, p. 23.
2 Ibid.
3 C. Lévi-Strauss, *A World on the Wane* (Hutchinson, London, 1961, pp. 87–8) tells this extraordinary tale in his account of his first journey to America.
4 *Mémoires pour servir à l'histoire des maisons royales*, published in 1824, p. 28; cf. L. Hautecoeur, *Histoire de l'architecture classique en France*, I, 1, 1963, p. 194.
5 Ibid., p. 229.

6 In 1512, in Paris, Tory published the second edition of Alberti's Latin text, after the first Florentine one of 1485; Martin translated into French the *Orlando Furioso*, 1544, the poetry of Bembo, 1545, the *Sogno di Polifilo*, 1546, the treatise of Vitruvius, 1547, and that of Alberti, 1553.

7 The first two books were translated by Martin in 1545, with engravings by the author.

8 *Premier Livre d'architecture contenant les plans et desseings de cinquante bastiments*, 1559; *Second Livre*, 1561; *Troisième Livre*, 1572; *Livre de perspective*, 1576; *Plus Excellens Bastiments de France*, 1576–9; *Livre des édifices antiques romains*, 1583.

9 *Reigle générale d'architecture des cinq manières de colonnes, . . . au profit de tous ouvriers besognans au compas et à l'esquerre*, Paris, 1564.

10 Cf. L. Torres Balbas, L. Cervera, F. Chueca, P. Bidagor, *Resumen historico del urbanismo en España*, Madrid, 1954, p. 89.

11 Ibid., p. 90.

12 A. Navagero, *Viaggio in Spagna*, 1524–6, in ibid., p. 116.

13 Alonso Morgado, *Historia de Sevilla*, 1587, book I, chapter 9.

14 J. M. Guallart, quoted in G. Kubler and M. Soria, *Art and Architecture in Spain and Portugal and their American Dominions from 1500 to 1800*, Penguin, Harmondsworth, 1959, p. 15.

15 Coeck and Graphaeus, *Raccolta delle decorazioni allestite a Anversa nel 1549 per l'ingresso di Carlo V*; in 1539 Coeck translated the first two books of Serlio into Flemish, and later, the others.

16 C. Floris, *Veelderly veranderingle van grotissen en compartinenten*, Antwerp, 1548, 1554, 1556, 1557.

17 J. V. de Vries, *Scenographiae sive perspectivae*, Antwerp, 1560; the three volumes on the five architectural orders, Antwerp, 1566–78; *Architectura oder Bauung der Antiques*, Antwerp, 1581; *Variae architecturae formae*, Antwerp, 1601.

18 W. Dietterlin, *Architectura*, Nuremberg, 1598.

19 W. Winker, *Fugger il ricco*, Italian trans., Turin, 1943, p. 56.

20 Ibid., p. 237.

21 Antonio de Beatis; cf. ibid.

22 Beatus Rhenanus; cf. ibid.

23 Ibid., p. 245.

24 Published by M. L. Galesloot, *Les Agrandissements de la ville d'Anvers en 1549*, Commission Royale d'Histoire, Brussels, 1881; cf. also F. Prims, *Antwerpen door de eeuwen heen*, Antwerp, 1951.

25 Quoted in G. Luzzatto, *Storia economica dell'età moderna e contemporanea*, Padua, 1932, vol. I, p. 145.

26 This is the caption in *Civitates orbis terrarum*; cf. R. Oehme, *Old European Cities*, Thames & Hudson, London, 1965, p. 28.

27 Ibid.

28 Map engraved by Petrus Verbst II, Antwerp, 1662, published by F. L. Ganshof, *Catalogus mapparum geographicarum ad historiam pertinentium*, Warsaw, 1933; the plan was by A. Adrianssen and concerned only the outer walls, with no reference to the internal street layout.

29 L. van Puyvelde, 'La décoration d'une ville par Rubens' in *Urbanisme et architecture: études écrites et publiées en l'honneur de Pierre Lavedan*, Paris, 1954, p. 305.

30 'De fabrica que falece à ciudade de Lisboa', published in R. Acynski, *Les Arts en Portugal*, Paris, 1846.

31 Report by Tron and Lippomani, quoted in J. A. Franca, *Une Ville de lumières, la Lisbonne de Pombal*, Paris, 1965, pp. 24–5.

32 B. Telles, *Cronica de Companhia de Jesus*, 1645, in ibid., p. 27.

33 Ibid.

34 Published by V. Sanson, Rouen, 1911; cf. A. Cerné, *Les Anciennes Sources et fontaines de Rouen*, Rouen, 1930.

35 Quoted in P. Lavedan, *Histoire de l'urbanisme*, Paris, 1959, vol. II, p. 93.

36 Ibid.

37 Ibid., p. 96.

38 Cf. M. Labò, '"Strada nuova" – più che una strada, un quartiere' in *Scritti di storia dell'arte in onore di Lionello Venturi*, Rome, 1956, p. 403; E. Poleggi, *Strada nova. Una lottizzazione del cinquecento a Genova*, Genoa, 1968.

39 G. Vasari, *Lives of the Artists*, Dent, London, 1963 (Everyman Library), vol. IV, p. 243.

40 *Palazzi moderni di Genova raccolti e disegnati da Pietro Paolo Rubens*, Antwerp, 1652.

41 *Description des beautés de Gênes*, Genoa, 1781, p. 83.

42 Quoted in P. Rojas, *Historia general del arte Mexicano, epoca colonial*, Mexico and Buenos Aires, 1963, p. 5.

43 J. H. Parry, *The Age of Reconnaissance*, Weidenfeld & Nicolson, London, 1963. p. 232.

44 *Doctrina breve*, 1544, published in facsimile by Z. Englehardt and S. H. Horgan, New York, 1928; *Doctrina Cristiana*.

45 F. Cervantes de Salazar, *Dialogues*, 1554, published by C. E. Castaneda, Austin, 1953; cf. J. McAndrew, *The Open Air Churches of Sixteenth-century Mexico*, Oxford University Press, 1965, p. 107.

46 Parry, op. cit., p. 31.

47 Cervantes de Salazar, op. cit., p. 42; McAndrew, op. cit., p. 107.

48 This was the nickname of fray Toribio de Bonavente, and meant 'poor' in the Nahuatl language; McAndrew, op. cit., p. 39.

49 *Reflectiones de Indias*, published in J. B. Scott, *The Spanish Origin of International Law*, Oxford University Press, 1924.

50 Published in F. Chueca Goitia and L. Torres Balbas, *Planos de ciudades iberoamericanas y filipinas existentes en el archivio de Indias*, Madrid, 1951.

51 Lévi-Strauss, op. cit., p. 78.

52 Ibid., p. 79.

53 J. G. Sepulveda, *Democrater alter*, Madrid, 1570.

54 B. de las Casas, *Erudita et elegans explicatio . . .*, Frankfurt, 1571; cf. Parry, op. cit., chapter 19.

55 Quoted in McAndrew, op. cit., p. 17.

56 Ibid.

57 B. Diaz del Castello, *Historia verdadera de la conquista de la Nueva España*, vol. I, chapter 48.

58 Quoted in McAndrew, op. cit., p. 111; but towards 1540 Motolinia regarded this undertaking as 'the seventh plague' suffered by the Indian population; *Memoriales*, ed. L. Garcia Pimentel, Mexico, 1903, p. 24.

59 Ibid., p. 112.

60 Ibid., p. 139.

61 F. Lopez de Gomara, *Historia general de las Indias*, English trans., New York, 1940, vol. II, pp. 352–3.

62 A. Ponce, *Relacion breve y verdadera . . .*, published Madrid, 1873, vol. I, p. 174.

63 S. de Champlain, *Opere*, English trans., Toronto, 1922, vol. I, p. 41; he visited Mexico in 1599.

64 H. Ojea, *Libro tercero de la historia religiosa de la provincia de Mexico*, circa 1608, published Mexico, 1897, p. 6.

65 J. J. de la Cruz y Moya, *Historia de la santa y apostolica provincia de Santiago de Predicadores de Mexico . . .*, 1756–7, published Mexico, 1954, vol. I, p. 83. These views are brought together in McAndrew, op. cit., pp. 113–14.

66 Quoted in M. Toussaint, F. Gomez de Orozco, J. Fernandez, *Planos de la ciudad de Mexico, siglos XVI y XVII*, published Mexico, 1938, p. 20.

67 Quoted in McAndrew, op. cit., p. 91.

68 I. F. de Espinosa, *Cronica de la Provincia franciscana de los apostoles San Pedro y San Pablo de Michoacàn*, circa 1571, published Mexico, 1945, pp. 142–3.

69 M. Toussaint, *Información de meritos y servicios de Alonso Garcia Bravo*, published Mexico, 1956.

70 Quoted in McAndrew, op. cit., p. 93.

71 Quoted in Lavedan, op. cit., vol. II, p. 470.

72 Quoted in D. Stanislawski, 'Early Spanish town planning in the New World', *Geographical Review*, January 1947, p. 95.

73 Ibid., p. 97.

74 J. W. Reps, *The Making of Urban America*, Princeton University Press, 1965, p. 29.

75 Archivio Nacional, MS. 3017; text published in *Hispanic American Historical Review*, 1922, p. 249.

76 T. C. Bannister, quoted in Reps, op. cit., p. 32; this discussion is summed up in McAndrew (op. cit., pp. 104–10) and in G. Kubler, 'Mexican urbanism in the sixteenth century', *Art Bulletin*, 1942, p. 160.

77 E. W. Palm, 'El arte del nuevo mundo después de la conquista espagnola', *Boletin del Centro de Investigaciones Historicas y Esteticas*, 4, Caracas.

78 Prof. Kubler is working on a study on this subject.

79 McAndrew, op. cit., pp. 300–1.

80 Stanislawski, op. cit., pp. 102–4.

81 McAndrew, op. cit., p. vii.

82 Ibid., p. 623.

83 R. Romano and A. Tenenti, *Alle origini del mondo moderno*, Milan, 1967, p. 195.

84 Kubler (op. cit., p. 170) points out that a copy of Filarete's treatise, made between 1470 and 1490, for the house of Aragon, was present in a Hieronymite monastery near Valencia in 1513, and possibly in the possession of the missionaries sent to America; this connection cannot be proved, but it is an apt illustration of the situation of American activity *vis-à-vis* the European culture of the early sixteenth century.

85 L. Venturi, *Storia della critica d'arte* (1936), Turin, 1964, p. 118.

86 J. Schlosser-Magnino, *La letteratura artistica* (1924), Italian trans., Florence, 1935, pp. 198–201.

87 P. Pino, *Dialogo di pittura*, Venice, 1548.

88 L. Dolce, *Dialogo della pittura intitolato l'Aretino*, Venice, 1557.

89 B. Ammannati, *Lettera scritta agli Accademici del Disegno l'anno 1582 . . .* reprinted by Baldinucci, Florence, 1687.

90 Vasari, *Lives*, ed. cit., vol. IV, p. 290.

91 Le Corbusier, *The Radiant City*, Faber, London, 1967, p. 269.

92 Texts published by G. Santangelo, *Le epistole 'de imitatione' by Giovanfrancesco Pico della Mirandola e di Pietro Bembo*, Florence, 1964; cf. E. Battisti, *Rinascimento e barocco*, Turin, 1960, pp. 177 ff.

93 Ibid., p. 179.

94 Ibid., pp. 182, 183.

95 Ibid., p. 185.

96 Ibid., p. 187.

97 W. T. Elwert, 'Pietro Bembo e la vita letteraria', in *La civiltà veneziana del Rinascimento*, Florence, 1958, p. 137.

98 Venturi, op. cit., p. 114.

99 G. Fiocco, 'Alvise Cornaro e i suoi trattati sull' architettura', *Atti dell' Accademia Nazionale dei Lincei*, 1952, p. 195.

100 According to Vasari, Alvise Cornaro had arranged 'that he should be laid in his tomb, which was also to contain the comic poet Ruzzante, another great friend who lived and died in his house' (*Lives*, ed. cit., vol. III, p. 47).

101 Ibid., p. 46.

102 Ibid., p. 47.

103 Published in R. Wittkower, *Architectural Principles in the Age of Humanism*, Tiranti, London, 1962, p. 102.

104 Palladio, *Four Books of Architecture*, London, 1738, reprinted by Dover, New York, 1965, unpaginated author's preface.

105 Ibid.

106 G. Gozzi, quoted in E. Garin, *Science and Civil Life in the Italian Renaissance*, Doubleday, New York, 1969, p. 79.

107 F. Braudel, 'La vita economica di Venezia nel secolo XVI', in *La civiltà veneziana del Rinascimento*, p. 99.

108 *Four Books*, preface.

109 'Andrea Palladio, architect from Vicenza, who has with incredible profit, more so than any one else I have ever known . . . acquired a knowledge of true architecture not only by grasping the beautiful and

subtle reasons that underlie it, but also by putting them into practice' (*I dieci libri dell'architettura di M. Vitruvio tradotti e commentati da Monsignor Barbaro*, Venice, 1556, Book I, p. 40).

110 Ibid., p. 19.

111 Ibid., p. 15; cf. M. Tafuri, *L'architettura del manierismo nel cinquecento europeo*, Rome, 1966, pp. 200 ff.

112 Cf. Wittkower, op. cit., pp. 107 ff.

113 Zarlino, *Instituzioni harmoniche*, Venice, 1558.

114 M. Shirlaw, quoted in Wittkower, op. cit., p. 136.

115 Ibid., p. 129.

116 Ibid., p. 140.

117 E. Forssmann, *Dorisch, Jonisch, Korintisch, Studien über den Gebrauch der Säulenordungen in der Architektur des 16–18 Jahrhunderts*, Uppsala, 1961.

118 The reduction of the protrusions of the pilaster lessens the chiaroscuro on the corner, and makes up, with a fairly marked pause, for the uniform repetition of the motif of the arcades.

119 E. Garin, *La cultura del Rinascimento*, Bari, 1967, p. 140.

120 Thomas More, *Complete Works*, Yale University Press, New Haven and London, 1965, vol. IV (*Utopia*), pp. 111 ff.

121 Ibid., p. 121.

122 Ibid., p. 122.

123 *Instituzione del principe cristiano*, Rome, 1543.

124 A. F. Doni, *I mondi*, Venice, 1552–3.

125 J. Mariana, *De rege et regis institutione*, Toledo, 1599.

126 F. Suarez, *De legibus*, 1612.

127 J. Althusius, *Politica methodice digesta*, Herbora, 1603.

128 'In the wide countryside a hill rises, on which most of the city stands; but its perimeter extends well beyond the base of the hill. . . . The city is divided into seven large districts, named after the seven planets, and one goes from one to the other by four roads and four gates, looking on to the four corners of the world.'
(L. Bortone, *L'Utopia, un'antologia degli scritti di Moro, Campanella, Bacone*, Turin, 1958, p. 94.)

129 This is the fourth part of the dialogue *L'infinito*, published by L. Firpo, Turin, 1957; see also L. Firpo, *Lo stato ideale della controriforma*, Bari, 1957, pp. 272 ff.

130 Quoted in E. Battisti, *L'Antirinascimento*, Milan, 1962, p. 322.

131 Ibid.

132 The ideological pendant to the *Repubblica immaginaria* of Agostini is the *Forma d'una Repubblica Catholica* published in 1581 and possibly written in England by the Italian heretic Francesco Pucci. Here the ideal city is a future objective, which can be prepared for by a minority of Christians living in the present day city, and organized as a secret society. This programme naturally excluded any visible manifestation in the field of architecture and town planning.

133 *Dei governi dei regni e delle repubbliche così antiche come moderne*, Venice, 1561.

134 *Cause della grandezza e magnificenza delle città*, Venice, 1589; in the same year the *Ragion di stato* came out.

135 *Dell' idea dell' architettura universale*, Venice, 1615.

136 *I quattro primi libri di Pietro Cataneo senese*, Venice, 1544 and 1567.

137 *Regole delle cinque ordini d'architettura*, Rome, 1562.

138 V. Leigh, *The Surveying of Lands, Tenements and Hereditements*, 1557.

139 J. Besson, *Theatrum instrumentorum*, Lyon, 1578. A. Ramelli, *Le diverse et artificiose macchine*, Paris, 1588.

140 S. Stevin, *Statica e idraulica*, 1586.

141 C. Estienne, *L'agriculture et la maison rustique*, Paris, 1564.

142 I. A. Buoni, *Del terremoto*, 1572.

143 R. Valturio, *De re militari*, 1472.

144 A. Dürer, *Unterrichtung zur Befestigung der Städte, Schlösser und Flecken*, Nuremberg, 1527.

145 G. Lanteri, *Modi di disegnare le piante e le fortezze delle città*, Venice, 1557.

146 G. Maggi and G. Castriotto, *Della fortificazione delle città*, Venice, 1564.

147 G. Alghisi, *Delle fortificazioni libri tre*, Venice, 1570.

148 C. Theti, *Discorsi delle fortificazioni*, Venice, 1575.

149 A. Lupicini, *Della architettura militare*, Florence, 1582.

150 D. Speckle, *Architectura von Vestungen*, 1589.

151 B. Lorini, *Fortificazioni di B. Lorini*, Venice, 1596.

152 G. B. Bellucci, *Nuove invenzioni di fabbricar fortezze di varie forme*, Venice, 1598. Bellucci demands a rigorous separation of fields of activity between architects and military engineers: 'It would be good that architects concern themselves with palazzi, churches, funeral monuments, cornices, entablatures, bases, columns, foliage, shields, masques and trophies, because fortresses need good swords, good parapets . . . and good men' (p. 53).

153 M. Savorgnan, *Trattato di architettura terrestre e marittima*, Venice, 1599.

154 F. De Marchi, *Dell'architettura militare*, Brescia, 1599.

155 J. Perret, *Des fortifications et artifices d'architecture et perspective*, Paris, 1604.

156 Contained in a pamphlet in the Gabinetto di Disegni e Stampe at the Uffizi, nos 3382 A–3463, acquired and bound by Vincenzo Viviani; cf. Tafuri, op. cit., pp. 235 ff.

157 *Libro di diverse piante che possino occorrere nel fabbricare una città* (Uffizi, nos 4529–94), published by T. Zarebska, Warsaw, 1962; cf. Tafuri, op. cit., pp. 238 ff.

158 Lavedan, op. cit., vol. II, p. 106.

159 Ibid., p. 103.

160 E. W. Palm, in *Journal de la Société des Américanistes*, 1951, pp. 59 ff.; cf. Battisti, *L'Antirinascimento*, p. 478.

161 Quoted in E. A. Gutkind, *Urban Development in Central Europe*, Collier-Macmillan, London, 1964, p. 309.

162 Lavedan, op. cit., p. 117.

163 S. Giedion, *Space, Time and Architecture*, Oxford University Press, 1941, p. 75.

164 Quoted in L. Pastor, *Die Stadt Rom zu Ende der Renaissance*, Freiburg, 1916, p. 102.

165 *De rebus preclare gestis a Sixto V*, Rome, 1588.

166 Ibid., quoted in Giedion, op. cit., p. 93.

167 Letter from Giacomo Leopardi to his sister Paolina, 1822.

168 T. Campanella, *Lettere*, ed. Bari, 1927, p. 374.

169 T. Campanella, *Poesie*, no. 164, vv. 121–2; quoted in Firpo, op. cit., p. 327.

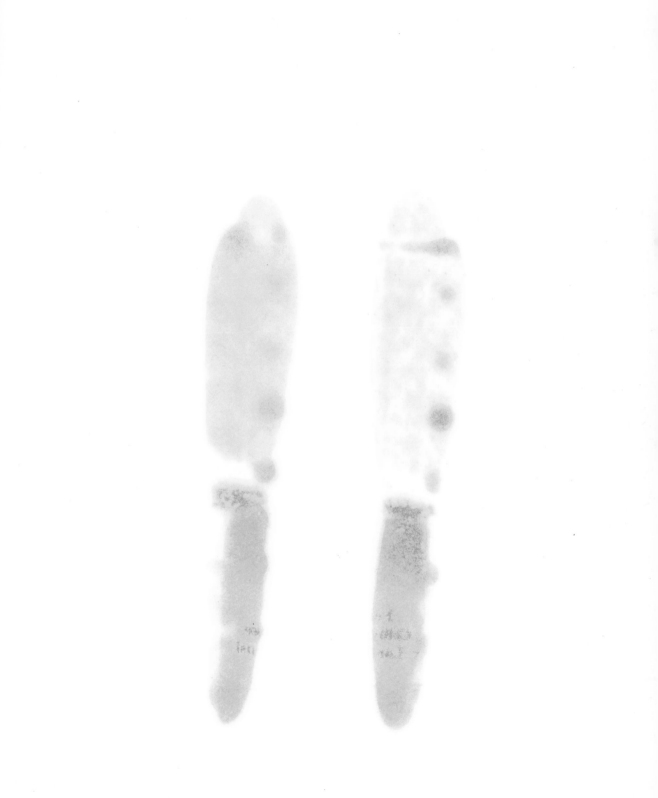

DATE DUE	
MAY 07 2002	
MAR 05 2013	
GAYLORD	PRINTED IN U.S.A.